AMERICA'S #1 CAMPUS-BASED TESTPREP

ACT® • PLAN® • EXPLORE®* Victory

Student Text

Volume 2

ACT® • PLAN® • EXPLORE® • SAT • PSAT • GRE® • GMAT® • LSAT® • MCAT® • TOEFL® • GED® • PRAXIS® • PSAE™ • WorkKeys® • Stanford • ITBS • State Tests • CollegePrep™ • Learning Styles • Guidance Services • Professional Development • Motivation & Admissions Workshops • Data Services • Formative Assessments

Our Mission: Progress Through Partnership
Cambridge Educational Services partners with educators who share the significant mission of educational advancement for all students. By partnering together, we can best achieve our common goals: to build skills, raise test scores, enhance curriculum, and support instruction. A leading innovator in education for twenty years, Cambridge is the nation's premier provider of school-based test preparation and supplemental curriculum services.

If you have purchased Cambridge ACT Software:

Cambridge Publishing, Inc.
www.CambridgeEd.com

 First edition 1994
Tenth edition 2010

Printed in the United States of America
13 12 11 10 2 3 4 5

ISBN-13: 978-1-58894-098-8

TABLE OF CONTENTS

HOW TO USE THIS BOOK

This book is organized into four parts:

- **Test Mechanics, Concepts, and Strategies.** Items resemble those on the real tests, which your instructor will use to teach tested concepts and applicable strategies.
- **Practice Test Reinforcement.** Four full-length ACT practice tests allow you to practice your skills in a testing format.
- **Post-Assessment.** A diagnostic post-assessment helps you to see how far you've come.
- **Personal Action Plan.** Recommended courses of action help you to continue your study after the course, as well as to prepare your college applications.

The following introduction will briefly explain how to use each part of this volume.

Test Mechanics, Concepts, and Strategies

Test Mechanics, Concepts, and Strategies make up the heart of this course. This part of volume 2 contains items that look like those found on the real ACT, PLAN, and EXPLORE tests. When compared with items on the real tests, the items in this part of the book have similar content, represent the same difficulty levels, and can be solved by using the same problem-solving skills and alternative test-taking strategies.

There are five chapters in Test Mechanics, Concepts, and Strategies, each chapter representing a core component of the exams:

- English
- Mathematics
- Reading
- Science
- Writing

Each of the above chapters begins with a Course Concept Outline, which acts as a syllabus, listing the concepts that are tested for each item type. The items in each chapter are organized to correspond with the respective outline. For each concept in the outline, there is a group of items. The group contains a greater number of items if the item type appears with great frequency on the real test, and it contains a lesser number of items if the item type appears with less frequency. Although the concepts are not grouped in this way on the real ACT, PLAN, or EXPLORE test, we organize the lessons in this manner so that the concepts are emphasized and reinforced. After you learn the concepts, you will be able to practice applying this conceptual knowledge on the practice tests.

Practice Test Reinforcement

In the Practice Test Reinforcement portion of volume 2, there are four full-length ACT practice tests. In these tests, the items not only mimic the real test in content and difficulty level, but they are also arranged in an order and with a frequency that simulates the real test.

The first test is arranged as a Self-Guided Practice Test. You will see the test problems alongside the correct answers and explanations. This format allows you to work through a test with some guidance before tackling a practice test that functions like the real exam. After you complete the Self-Guided Practice Test, you will complete three additional practice tests with time restrictions. You may complete these items in class or your instructor may assign them as homework. Either way, adhering to the time restrictions forces you to pace yourself as you would on the real test. If you complete all four of the practice tests, any test anxiety you may have will be greatly reduced. Answers and explanations to Timed Practice Tests I–III are located in Appendix A of this book. Perforated essay response and bubble sheets for Timed Practice Tests I–III are located in Appendix B of this book.

Post-Assessment

In order to know how far you've come since the pre-assessment, you have to take a second official, retired ACT, PLAN, or EXPLORE test. You will take this post-assessment under actual testing conditions. You will then receive a second Student Summary report to help you determine final areas for review.

Step Five contains two "Winning Strategies" sections to help you see how far you've come:

- "Post-Assessment Administration" explains the logistics of taking the post-assessment. Perforated essay response and bubble sheets for the post-assessment are located in Appendix B of this book for programs not utilizing the Cambridge Assessment Service.

- "How to Use the Post-Assessment Report" shows you how to use the Student Summary report you will receive to identify areas of study, as well as particular items in your textbook, upon which to focus as you continue to prepare for the real test.

Personal Action Plan

The last part of volume 2 provides a short guide to help you design a personal action plan for the days or weeks between the end of the course and the real test. At this stage of the course, you will put into action what you learned in earlier "Winning Strategies" sections to make the most of your remaining study time, as well as review the following additional "Winning Strategies" sections that will help you beyond the course:

- "Planning for Further Study" includes advice on how to make the most of an effective and concrete action plan. You will learn how to maximize your remaining course time and prioritize material to be reviewed before you take the actual ACT, PLAN, or EXPLORE test.

- "Application Preparation" teaches you how to highlight your unique qualities to maximize your chances of admission into your first-choice school.

- "Six Ways to Jumpstart Your College Admissions Essays" gives examples of actual college admissions essay questions/responses and shows you how to ace the essay.

Test Mechanics, Concepts, and Strategies

Objectives:

Learn everything you need to know about the five tested core subjects: English, Mathematics, Reading, Science, and Writing.

Identify the test mechanics information you need to know to make a positive impact on your test score.

Review the most commonly-tested concepts on the ACT®, PLAN®, and EXPLORE® tests.

Discover the powerful alternative test-taking strategies that will give you an edge when taking the ACT®, PLAN®, and EXPLORE® tests.

Snapshot of Test Mechanics, Concepts, and Strategies:

This part of the book contains many items that look like those found on the ACT®, PLAN®, and EXPLORE® tests. When compared with items on the real test, these items have the same content, represent similar difficulty levels, and are solved by using the same concepts and alternative test-taking strategies. You will go over these items with your instructor in class.

English

COURSE CONCEPT OUTLINE

What You Absolutely Must Know

I. Test Mechanics (p. 8)

A. Basics (p. 8)

B. Anatomy (Items #1–4, p. 9)

C. Pacing (p. 11)

D. Time Trial (Items #1–8, p. 12)

E. Game Plan (p. 14)

1. Don't Read the Directions
2. Do the Passages in Order
3. Start Each Set of Items by Reading the Passage
4. Read Any Items with Underlined Parts, Looking for Errors
5. Work Backwards from the Answer Choices
6. Don't Look for Spelling or Capitalization Errors
7. Make Educated Guesses
8. Don't Be Afraid to Pick "No Change"

II. Lesson (p. 16)

A. Preliminaries

1. What Is Tested
2. Directions
3. Item Profiles
4. Notational Information
   - a) Underlined Words or Phrases
   - b) Boxed Numbers
   - c) Bracketed Numbers
   - d) Boxed Information

B. Item-Types

1. Grammar and Usage
2. Sentence Structure
3. Punctuation
4. Strategy
5. Organization
6. Style

C. Usage and Mechanics Review

1. Grammar and Usage
   - a) Subject-Verb Agreement (Item #1, p. 16)
     - (1) Material Inserted Between Subject and Verb (Items #2–7, p. 16)

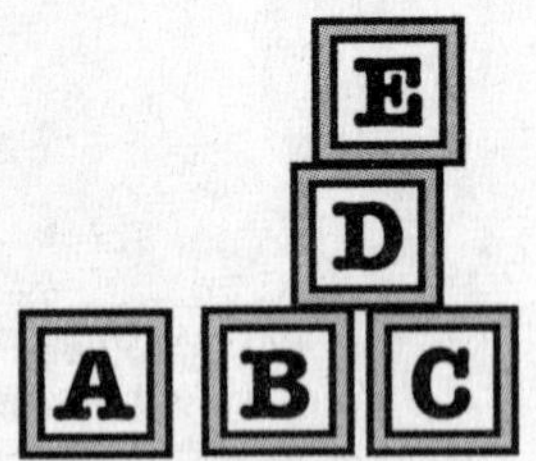

BASICS

It would not be too far wrong to say that the English Test is a test of your understanding of the rules of grammar, and that announcement should be enough to strike dread into the hearts of most students: "You mean like '*i* before *e* except after *c*'?" No, that's a rule of spelling, not grammar, and the English Test does not test spelling. Actually, the English Test doesn't really test your knowledge of the formal rules of grammar either, though it does test your ability to correct sentences using those rules.

You might be asked to correct an error.

Example:

> The recently created wildlife refuge, which includes nearly 30 small ponds for migrating geese and ducks, <u>were</u> made possible by substantial gifts by an anonymous donor to the Wildlife Protection Fund.
>
> A. NO CHANGE
> B. was
> C. have been
> D. being
>
> The correct answer is (B) because the sentence should read "refuge...was," not "refuge...were." But you would not be asked to state the grammatical rule that explains the error or how to correct it: *a verb must agree in both number and person with its subject.*

The items used by the English Test fall into one of two categories: Usage and Mechanics or Rhetorical Skills. The Usage and Mechanics category (UM) includes all of the items that you would normally associate with a writing test, such as choosing proper verb tense and pronoun usage, while the Rhetorical Skills category (RH) includes items that ask about the development of a selection, such as crafting topic sentences and selecting effective transitions. You'll see specific examples of both types in the "Anatomy" section that follows.

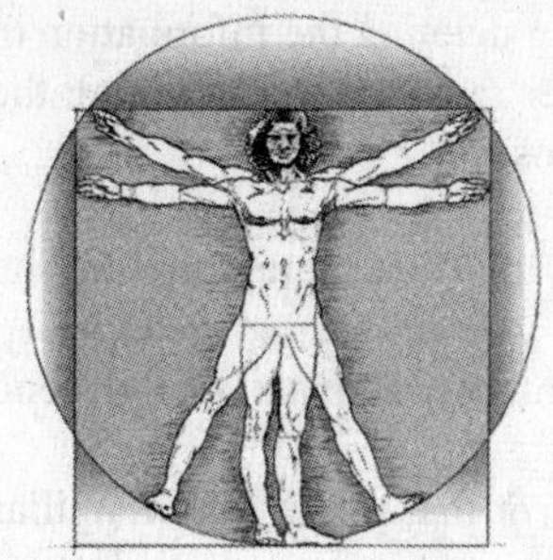

ANATOMY

DIRECTIONS: In the passage below, certain parts of the sentences have been underlined and numbered. In the right-hand column, you will find different ways of writing each underlined part; the original version is indicated by the "NO CHANGE" option. For each item, select the choice that best expresses the intended idea, is most acceptable in standard written English, or is most consistent with the overall tone and style of the passage.

There are also items that ask about a section of the passage or the passage as a whole. These items do not refer to an underlined portion of the passage; these items are preceded by statements that are enclosed in boxes.

Read the passage through once before you begin to answer the accompanying items. Finding the answers to certain items may depend on looking at material that appears several sentences beyond the item. So, be sure that you have read far enough ahead before you select your answer choice.

The directions for the English Test are fairly long, and it would take you a while to read them during the test. You'd be wasting valuable time that could be used to answer questions. By the time you get to the test, you'll know what to do in the English Test, so skip the directions altogether.

Coastal Polynyas in Antarctica

Although you might not think it, the Antarctic waters are rich in nutrients. The lack of ice, combined [1] with shallow coastal waters, provides the top layers of

1. **A.** NO CHANGE
   B. ice combined
   C. ice combined,
   D. ice—combined

1. **(A)** *This item tests punctuation. When you insert an aside or clarifying remark, you need to set off that material from the main part of the sentence, usually with commas—one at the start and one at the end of the material. The original sentence is correctly punctuated.*

the ocean with added sunlight, so polynyas <u>(large open areas of waters surrounded by sea ice)</u> [2] offer ideal conditions for phytoplankton blooms. Because the ice around polynyas is thin in the early spring when the long days begin, they are the first areas to get strong sunlight. The open waters retain more heat, further thinning ice cover and leading to early, intense, and

2. The writer is considering deleting the information in parentheses. If the writer removed this material, the essay would primarily lose:

   F. a transition from the first paragraph to the second paragraph.
   G. further examples of the animals that depend upon krill for food.
   H. a definition of a term that might be unfamiliar to the reader.
   J. additional information about the climate of Antarctica.

2. **(H)** *Why does the writer include the parenthetical material? The writer includes the parenthetical material to define a key term that might otherwise be unfamiliar to the reader.*

short-lived plankton blooms. These blooms feed krill, <u>a tiny, shrimp-like animal</u> [3], which in turn are eaten by Adelie penguins, seals, whales, and other seabirds and animals.

3. **A.** NO CHANGE
   B. tiny, shrimp-like animals
   C. a tiny animal like a shrimp
   D. an animal like a tiny shrimp

3. **(B)** *The original sentence lacks parallelism. In the main part of the sentence, the writer is talking about krill in the plural: "krill...which in turn are eaten." But in the appositive phrase, the writer uses the singular "animal." "Animal" is not parallel to "krill," which is used here as a plural noun.*

<u>Because</u> [4] relatively small in area, coastal polynyas play an important role. In eastern Antarctica, more than 90 percent of all Adelie penguin colonies live next to coastal polynyas. Polynya productivity explains, to a great extent, the increase and decrease in penguin population.

4. **F.** NO CHANGE
   G. Although
   H. Therefore
   J. Furthermore

4. **(G)** *"Because" is a word used to introduce an explanation, so the reader expects the information in the independent clause to be the outcome of the information provided in the dependent ("because") clause. The writer, instead, intends to contrast the two ideas in the sentence: even though polynyas are small in area, they are very important to Adelie penguins.*

PACING

The English Test consists of five passages, each approximately 300 words in length and with 15 corresponding items, for a total of 75 items. The time limit is 45 minutes. So, a fairly simple and easy-to-follow plan is to allocate nine minutes to each of the five passages:

Task	*Allotted Time*	*Remaining Time*
Read first passage	1.5 minutes	43.5 minutes
Answer accompanying items	7.5 minutes*	36 minutes
Read second passage	1.5 minutes	34.5 minutes
Answer accompanying items	7.5 minutes*	27 minutes
Read third passage	1.5 minutes	25.5 minutes
Answer accompanying items	7.5 minutes*	18 minutes
Read fourth passage	1.5 minutes	16.5 minutes
Answer accompanying items	7.5 minutes*	9 minutes
Read fifth passage	1.5 minutes	7.5 minutes
Answer accompanying items	7.5 minutes*	0 minutes

*Approximately 30 seconds per question

This schedule describes what would happen in a perfect world; but, of course, the ACT test does not take place in a perfect world. Some items are going to take longer than others, particularly those that ask about the overall development of the passage. This means that you'll need to spend less time on the simple grammar items, building up a time reserve for those more difficult items that are coming. And the more difficult items are usually placed at the end of a passage because that's where it makes sense to ask, "What is the main idea?" and "How could the passage be improved?" The schedule actually gives you a feedback loop that lets you know whether you need to skip some items. For example, if you are nearing the "36 minutes left in the section" mark and still have two or three items to do on the first passage, then skip any Rhetorical Skills items and go straight away to the next passage. The Rhetorical Skills items take longer, and there will be some simple grammar items waiting to be cherry-picked in the next passage.

TIME TRIAL

8 Items
Time—5 minutes

DIRECTIONS: In the passage below, certain parts of the sentences have been underlined and numbered. In the right-hand column, you will find different ways of writing each underlined part; the original version is indicated by the "NO CHANGE" option. For each item, select the choice that best expresses the intended idea, is most acceptable in standard written English, or is most consistent with the overall tone and style of the passage.

There are also items that ask about a section of the passage or the passage as a whole. These items do not refer to an underlined portion of the passage; these items are preceded by statements that are enclosed in boxes.

Read the passage through once before you begin to answer the accompanying items. Finding the answers to certain items may depend on looking at material that appears several sentences beyond the item. So, be sure that you have read far enough ahead before you select your answer choice.

PASSAGE I

The Orchid Family

The orchids are the most diverse plant family with 20,000 to 30,000 species in over 800 genera. This represents about 10 percent of all flowering plant species. DNA research suggesting (1) that the orchids are among the most ancient flowering plant families, as old as 90,000,000 years. They are still evolving rapidly into new species. For example, many endemic species

1. A. NO CHANGE
   B. suggest
   C. suggests
   D. to suggest

in the genus Telipogon are found in the Andes Mountains in areas that were buried under glaciers as recent as[2] 10,000 years ago. Orchids are found on all continents except Antarctica.

2. F. NO CHANGE
   G. as recently as
   H. so recently as
   J. recently

Like all monocots, including lilies orchids[3] are flowering plants that have only one seed leaf and typically lacks[4] woody tissue. All orchids have a single reproductive structure, called the column, which is forming[5] by the fusion of the male stamens and female style. These structures are separate in the flowers of most other families. Orchids also have a modified third petal called a lip, and produce[6] enormous numbers of very tiny seeds.

3. A. NO CHANGE
   B. lilies orchids,
   C. lilies, orchids,
   D. lilies, orchids

4. F. NO CHANGE
   G. lacking
   H. lack
   J. lacked

5. A. NO CHANGE
   B. forming
   C. are formed
   D. is formed

6. F. NO CHANGE
   G. lip and produce
   H. lip and produce,
   J. lip, and produces

The vast majority of orchid species are native to the tropics, and its[7] numbers increase with proximity to the equator. The most richest[8] diversity of orchid species is found in the lush tropical forests of equatorial South America, Southeast Asia, and New Guinea. New species are constantly being discovered in these areas.

7. A. NO CHANGE
   B. their
   C. one's
   D. your

8. F. NO CHANGE
   G. more richer
   H. richest
   J. richly

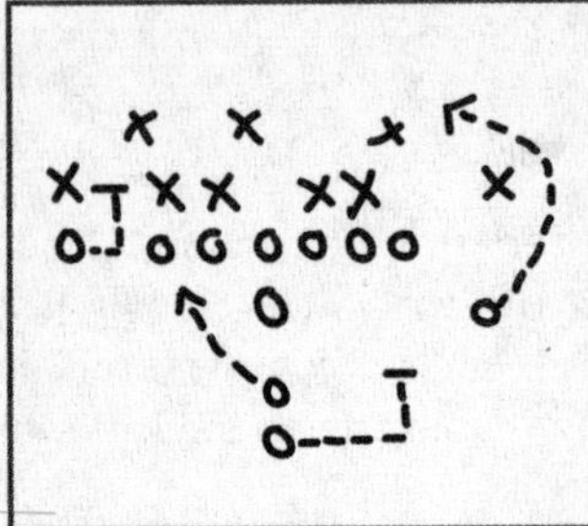

GAME PLAN

Don't Read the Directions

By the time you get to the test, you'll know what to do when you see the English Test just by the way it looks. Do a quick preview and let the appearance of the items on the page be all the direction you need, and then get started immediately.

Do the Passages in Order

Unlike the Reading Test with passages that fall into categories such as Humanities and Natural Science, the passages on the English Test are not really about any particular subject-area. Of course, the passages do have a topic and some items do ask Reading-type questions, but the English items basically test usage, not reading comprehension. In Reading, there is an advantage to predetermining an order for the passages; in English, however, you should just do them in the order presented.

Start Each Set of Items by Reading the Passage

You really need to read the passage before you start answering questions because some items will not make sense without the proper context. Since the passages are about 300 words in length, you can finish a read-through in a little more than a minute. Read primarily for overall development so that you'll understand the logic in the author's presentation, and don't worry overly much about details. Later, you can study the specific parts of the passage in which the various items appear.

Read Any Items with Underlined Parts, Looking for Errors

When an item asks about rewriting an underlined part, begin by reading the sentence, looking for an error. If you can spot an error, then you're more than halfway home. Later in the English Lesson, you'll cover the important principles of writing and grammar that are tested, and there is a list of these principles provided in the English "Course Concept Outline" (p. 5). You can treat this outline as a checklist of important things to look for in English items.

Work Backwards from the Answer Choices

If you are having difficulty locating the right answer, use the answer choices to help you. Compare each answer choice with the original, and explain to yourself what the important difference is between the two of them. This can help you see an error that you may have overlooked. Additionally, you can compare choices to each other, asking yourself, in what way is this choice better or worse than the other one? Again, this technique can help you uncover a hidden error and make the right choice.

Don't Look for Spelling or Capitalization Errors

These topics are not tested, so don't waste your time looking for errors of this sort. Even if you think you've found a spelling mistake (and you're almost certain to be wrong anyway), there is nothing you can do with the information. The correct response is correct because it "follows the requirements of standard written English."

Make Educated Guesses

You should be able to eliminate some answer choices on most items because they introduce new errors that are not found in the original. Or, a choice may fail to correct an error that you know to be in the underlined part of the sentence. You should always guess, even if you are unable to eliminate any answer choices, because there is no penalty for guessing on the ACT test. However, your chances improve if you are able to eliminate even one answer choice.

Don't Be Afraid to Pick "No Change"

Choose (A), "NO CHANGE," if you think that the original is correct as written. Many students automatically refuse to pick "NO CHANGE" because they figure that there must be something wrong with the original—even if they are unable to say what. But this reasoning is faulty. "NO CHANGE," when it is an option, is statistically as likely to be correct as is one of the other three choices.

The items in this section accompany the in-class review of the skills and concepts tested by the ACT English Test. You will work through the items with your instructor in class. Answers are on page 631.

DIRECTIONS: Items #1–114 consist of two types of items: (1) When four separate parts of a sentence are underlined, identify the underlined part that contains an error. Some of these sentences may not contain any errors; in such a case, choose "No change." No sentence contains more than one error, and no sentence contains an error that is not underlined. (2) When a single part of a sentence is underlined or the entire sentence is underlined, identify the re-phrasing that best expresses the meaning of the underlined material. (A) is always NO CHANGE, which indicates that the underlined material is correct as written.

1. The professor were traveling in Europe when she
A B
received notice of her promotion. No change
C D E

2. The professor voted Teacher of the Year by the
F
students were traveling in Europe when she
G H
received notice of her promotion. No change
J K

3. Most teachers, unless they have an appointment
A
to a prestigious university, earns relatively less as
B C
a teacher than they might in business. No change
D E

4. Many nutritionists now believe that a balanced
F G
diet and not large doses of vitamins are the best
H J
guarantee of health. No change
K

5. Television comedies in which there is at least one
A B
really detestable character captures the interest of
C D
viewers. No change
E

6. The opposition to smoking in public places are prompting many state legislatures to consider banning smoking in such locations.

F. NO CHANGE
G. is prompting many state legislatures to consider
H. are prompting many state legislatures considering
J. is prompting many state legislatures considering
K. is prompting many state legislatures' consider

7. Diplomats sent to an unstable region or a genuinely hostile territory usually is assigned an aide or chauffeur who function also as a bodyguard.

A. NO CHANGE
B. are assigned an aide or chauffeur who function
C. are assigned an aide or chauffeur who functions
D. is assigned an aide or chauffeur that function
E. are assigned an aide or chauffeur which functions

8. Though this is the wealthiest country in the world, within a few blocks of the White House, there is scores of homeless people who live on the streets. No change
F: Though; G: few; H: there is; J: who live; K: No change

9. Just a few miles from the factories and skyscrapers stand a medieval castle which looks exactly as it did in the twelfth century. No change
A: Just; B: stand; C: which looks; D: exactly as; E: No change

10. John, his wife, and the rest of his family plans to attend the award dinner to be given by the company for the employees with the most seniority. No change
F: plans; G: to attend; H: to be given; J: most; K: No change

11. Either the governor or one of his close aides prefer not to have the Senator seated at the head table where he would be conspicuous. No change
A: prefer; B: not to have; C: seated at; D: would be; E: No change

12. Surrounded by layers of excelsior, none of the crystal goblets were broken when the workers dropped the crate. No change
F: Surrounded by; G: were broken; H: when; J: dropped; K: No change

13. During her rise to fame, she betrayed many of her friends, and because of it, very few people trust her.

A. NO CHANGE
B. and in spite of it
C. and because of her friends
D. and even though
E. and because of her behavior

14. In New York City, they are brusque and even rude but quick to come to one another's assistance in a time of crisis. No change
F: they; G: but; H: to come to; J: in a time of; K: No change

15. Ten years ago, the United States imported ten times as much French wine as Italian wine, but today Americans are drinking more of it. No change
A: imported; B: as much; C: are drinking; D: it; E: No change

16. Although a police officer used to be a symbol of authority, today they receive little respect from most people. No change
F: used to be; G: they receive; H: little; J: from most; K: No change

17. The Abbot was an effective administrator who attempted to assign each monk a task particularly suited to their talents and training. No change
A: was; B: who attempted to; C: particularly suited; D: their; E: No change

18. After three years of college education, a person should be allowed to apply to graduate school, because by that time you are ready to choose a profession. No change
F: should be allowed to; G: because; H: you are; J: to choose; K: No change

19. If one wishes to apply for a scholarship, you must submit a completed application by March 1. No change
A: If; B: to apply for; C: you; D: completed; E: No change

20. The judges were (F) unable to make a final decision on a single winner, so they (G) divided the first prize between (H) John and he (J). No change (K)

21. Although Peter had been looking (A) forward to (B) the debate for weeks, a sore throat prevented him (C) taking part (D). No change (E)

22. The company's mission statement took into consideration the significant changes that were made in the field of technology.

F. NO CHANGE
G. significantly changes
H. significant changed
J. significantly changed
K. significantly to change

23. When asked about the chance that the defenders might concentrate their forces at the beachhead, the general responded tart that he was fully aware of all the possibilities.

A. NO CHANGE
B. tartly that he was full
C. tart that he was full
D. tart that he fully was
E. tartly that he was fully

24. When the door burst open, Kevin looked up angry from his desk.

F. NO CHANGE
G. was looking up angry
H. looked up angrily
J. looks up angrily
K. looked angry up

25. The director explained that the scene required Edmund to look distraughtly on hearing the news of his sister's death.

A. NO CHANGE
B. looking distraughtly
C. to have looked distraughtly
D. to have looked distraught
E. to look distraught

26. Some psychologists maintain that a child who (F) has seen (G) violence on television is (H) more likely to react violent (J) in situations of stress. No change (K)

27. The recent created (A) commission has done (B) nothing to address the problem except to approve (C) the color of its (D) stationary. No change (E)

28. The track meet begins at 10:00 a.m., so the team needs to depart from the school at a reasonable early hour.

F. NO CHANGE
G. at a reasonably early hour
H. during a reasonable early hour
J. while a reasonably early hour
K. at a reasonably hour that is early

29. Not hardly (A) a sound could be heard (B) in the auditorium when (C) the speaker approached (D) the dais to announce the result of the contest. No change (E)

30. Although she had been hired (F) by the magazine to write (G) book reviews, she knew (H) scarcely nothing (J) about current fiction. No change (K)

31. The reason Harriet fired her secretary is because
A B
he was frequently late and spent too much time
C D
on personal phone calls. No change
E

32. The reason the manager changed catchers was because he hoped that the opposing side would put in a left-handed pitcher.

F. NO CHANGE
G. The reason that catchers were changed by the manager was because
H. The reason the manager changed catchers which
J. The manager changed catchers because
K. The manager changed catchers, the reason being

33. I read in a magazine where scientists believe that
A B
they have discovered a new subatomic particle.
C D
No change
E

34. The company offers a plastic key card
F
so that employees can carry it in their wallet.
G H J
No change
K

35. The great pianist Vladimir Horowitz plays the
A
music of the Romantic Era better than any pianist
B C D
in history. No change
E

36. Like Neil Simon, many of Tennessee Williams' plays reflect a culture familiar to the playwright.

F. NO CHANGE
G. Many of Tennessee Williams' plays, like Neil Simon's,
H. Many of Tennessee Williams' plays, like Neil Simon,
J. Many of Neil Simon and Tennessee Williams' plays
K. As with the plays of Neil Simon, many of Tennessee Williams' plays

37. Educators are now expressing their concern that
A B
American school children prefer watching
C
television to books. No change
D E

38. The novels of Nathaniel Hawthorne contain
F
characters who are every bit as sinister and
G H
frightening as the master of cinematic suspense,
J
Alfred Hitchcock. No change
K

39. After the broken glass and other debris were cleaned up, we realized that the thief had took not only the necklace but a valuable ring as well.

A. NO CHANGE
B. had taken
C. was took
D. was taken
E. were took

40. Everyone was very surprised when Sylvia brought her grandfather to music class and asked him to perform several Spanish songs on the guitar.

F. NO CHANGE
G. because Sylvia bringing
H. while Sylvia brought
J. that Sylvia brang
K. for Sylvia to bring

41. The sheriff called off the search for the escaped convict because he doubted that the convict can successfully cross the river because the current was so swift.

A. NO CHANGE
B. the convict successfully crossed the river because the current was so swift
C. the convict successfully crossed the river being that the current was so swift
D. the convict would have been successful in crossing the river, the current being so swift
E. a successful attempt to cross the river was made by the convict because the current was so swift

42. Elaine is the favorite to win the final event because she had always run well at the 100-meter distance.

F. NO CHANGE
G. has always run
H. have always run
J. always ran
K. will always run

43. My computer crashed several times before I finally figured out that I had loaded a corrupted copy of the program.

A. NO CHANGE
B. had finally figured out that I loaded
C. had finally figured out that I had loaded
D. finally had figured out that I loaded
E. figured out finally that I would load

44. At the current rate of consumption, we have exhausted our supply of firewood before the weather turns warm.

F. NO CHANGE
G. had exhausted
H. exhausted
J. will exhaust
K. will have exhausted

45. The will is going to be read at 3:00 p.m., so the lawyer has asked that all family members are present in the office at that time.

A. NO CHANGE
B. are presently
C. are going to be present
D. be present
E. being present

46. A dangerous situation could arise if the override switch were left open and the water drops below 50 percent of capacity.

F. NO CHANGE
G. dropped
H. allowed to drop
J. allowed dropping
K. allows to drop

47. The teacher began to discuss (A) the homework assignment when (B) he will be (C) interrupted by (D) the sound of the fire alarm. No change (E)

48. The conductor announced (F) that the concert would resume as soon as (G) the soloist replaces (H) the broken string on her (J) violin. No change (K)

49. Many (A) patients begin to show (B) symptoms again after they (C) stopped (D) taking the drug. No change (E)

50. The winter was so severe that (F) several (G) of Hillary's prize rose bushes had sustained (H) serious (J) damage from the frost. No change (K)

51. In contrast of the prevailing opinion, the
A
editorial lays the blame for the strike on the
B C
workers and their representatives. No change
D E

52. Although ballet and modern dance are both
concerned in movement in space to musical
F
accompaniment, the training for ballet is more
G H
rigorous than that for modern dance. No change
J K

53. By midnight the guests still had not been served
A
anything to eat, so they were ravishing.
B C D
No change
E

54. The raise in the number of accidents attributable
F G
to drunk drivers has prompted a call for stiffer
H J
penalties for driving while intoxicated.
No change
K

55. The idea of trying completing the term paper by
A B
Friday caused Ken to cancel his plans for the
C D
weekend. No change
E

56. Psychologists think that many people eat
F
satisfying a need for affection that is not
G H
otherwise fulfilled. No change
J K

57. The armor plating on the new tank protects more vulnerable areas than the armor on the old tank, it costs about three times as much to manufacture and install.

A. NO CHANGE
B. areas than the armor on the old tank, because it costs
C. areas than the armor on the old tank, and it costs
D. areas than the armor on the old tank which costs
E. areas than the armor on the old tank, it costs

58. The filibuster continued late into the night some Senators slept sitting upright in the chairs while others slumped over their desks.

F. NO CHANGE
G. As the filibuster continued late into the night, some
H. Because of the filibuster continuing late into the night, some
J. The filibuster continued late into the night with
K. The filibuster, which continued late into the night, some

59. The weather forecast predicted heavy rain, the baseball game was postponed until the following day.

A. NO CHANGE
B. rain while the
C. rain, so the
D. rain the
E. rain or the

60. The devastation caused by the flood was so complete, it was impossible to tell that the pile of debris had once been a house.

F. NO CHANGE
G. so complete, and it
H. so complete that it
J. so completely, it
K. so that it

61. The audience, dazzled by the sequined costumes and brilliant lights and applauded wildly.

A. NO CHANGE
B. The audience, dazzled by the sequined costumes and brilliant lights, applauded wildly.
C. The audience was dazzled by the sequined costumes and brilliant lights applauding wildly.
D. The audience, applauding wildly and dazzled by the sequined costumes and brilliant lights.
E. Dazzled by the sequined costumes and brilliant lights, the applauding audience.

62. Most of the delegates, who were from smaller villages and rural areas and so opposed any plans to improve conditions in the large cities.

F. NO CHANGE
G. Most of the delegates from smaller villages and rural areas and so opposed any plans to improve conditions in the large cities.
H. The delegates, most of whom were from smaller villages and rural areas and so opposed any plans to improve conditions in the large cities.
J. The delegates who opposed any plans to improve conditions in the large cities and were from smaller villages and rural areas.
K. Most of the delegates, who were from smaller villages and rural areas, opposed any plans to improve conditions in the large cities.

63. Carlos telephoned to say that weather had delayed his plane, but he will not be able to attend the meeting.

A. NO CHANGE
B. plane, so he will
C. plane, but he was
D. plane when he will
E. plane because he could

64. By the fifth inning, Cindy was showing signs of fatigue and walked three consecutive batters, so the coach refused to take her out of the game.

F. NO CHANGE
G. batters, when
H. batters, moreover
J. batters during
K. batters, but

65. Because the wetlands were protected by federal law, the owners were not able to build the shopping center that they had planned.

A. NO CHANGE
B. In fact
C. However
D. Moreover
E. So that

66. Victoria was nominated to the office of club president, or it is doubtful that she would serve even if elected.

F. NO CHANGE
G. president so
H. president, though
J. president, in that
K. president, even

67. The driving snow made the roadway slippery and reduced visibility to no more than a few feet, and fortunately there were no accidents despite the heavy volume of traffic.

A. NO CHANGE
B. but fortunately there were no
C. and fortunately there were some
D. while fortunately there were no
E. so fortunately there were no

68. The land surrounding Las Vegas is characterized by parched red dunes and flats with dry ravines, but it is almost entirely lacking in vegetation.

F. NO CHANGE
G. and they are
H. and it is
J. but they are
K. but are

69. Kari was just about to mail in her deposit for her second-choice school and that was when the letter arrived notifying her of her acceptance at her first choice.

A. NO CHANGE
B. and then the letter that arrived notified her
C. when she received notification by letter
D. and then they told her
E. when she learned

70. Although the American relay team did not qualify for the finals, the anchor runner dropped the baton shortly after the hand-off.

F. NO CHANGE
G. When the American relay team did not qualify for the finals, the
H. The American relay team did not qualify for the finals, and the
J. The American relay team did not qualify for the finals because the
K. Not qualifying for the finals, the American relay team's

71. To abandon their (A) homes, leave behind their families, and traveling (B) across the ocean required (C) great courage on the part of the immigrants who moved (D) to America. No change (E)

72. The review praised (F) the wit, charm, and interpreting (G) of the recitalist but never once (H) mentioned (J) her voice. No change (K)

73. To acknowledge that one (A) has (B) something to learn is (C) taking (D) the first step on the road to true wisdom. No change (E)

74. The students are critical of (F) the dean because he is (G) either unfamiliar or (H) doesn't care about the urgent need for (J) new student housing on campus. No change (K)

75. Baseball has and (A) probably always will be the sport that (B) symbolizes (C) for people in (D) other countries the American way of life. No change (E)

76. Letters were received by the editor of the newspaper that complained of its editorial policy.

F. NO CHANGE
G. Letters were received by the editor of the newspaper having complained of its editorial policy.
H. The editor of the newspaper received letters complaining of the newspaper's editorial policy.
J. Letters were received by the editor in which there were complaints to the editor of the newspaper about its editorial policy.
K. Letters were received by the editor complaining of the newspaper's editorial policy by the editor.

77. Riding in a coach and wearing the crown jewels, the crowd cheered the royal couple.

A. NO CHANGE
B. cheering for the royal couple was done by the crowd
C. the royal couple was cheered by the crowd
D. the royal couple's cheering was done by the crowd
E. the royal couple, who was being cheered by crowd

78. Wrapped in several thicknesses of newspaper, packed carefully in a strong cardboard carton, and bound securely with tape, the worker made sure that the fragile figurines would not be broken.

F. NO CHANGE
G. Wrapped in several thicknesses of newspaper, packed carefully in a strong cardboard carton, and then binding the carton securely with tape, the worker made sure that the fragile figurines would not be broken.
H. The figurines, having been securely wrapped in several thicknesses of newspaper, packed carefully in a strong cardboard carton which was then securely bound with tape, the worker made sure would not be broken.
J. The worker, wrapping the figurines in several thicknesses of newspaper, packing them carefully in a strong cardboard carton, and securely binding the carton with tape, made sure that they would not be broken.
K. To make sure that the figurines would not be broken, the worker wrapped them in several thicknesses of newspaper, packed them carefully in a strong cardboard carton, and securely bound the carton with tape.

79. Mary Lou was awarded the gold medal because she scored more points than any child participating in the field day.

A. NO CHANGE
B. more points than any other child participating
C. most points than any child participating
D. more points than any child who had participated
E. more points as any child participating

80. Appearing in his first American tour, the British singer's album rose to the top of the charts.

F. NO CHANGE
G. While appearing
H. While he was appearing
J. When appearing
K. Upon appearing

81. I think that Dore's illustrations of Dante's *Divine Comedy* are excellent; but my favorite drawing is "Don Quixote in His Library."

A. NO CHANGE
B. are excellent, but my favorite drawing is "Don Quixote in His Library."
C. are excellent and my favorite drawing is "Don Quixote in His Library."
D. are excellent in that my favorite drawing is "Don Quixote in His Library."
E. are excellent even though "Don Quixote in His Library" is my favorite drawing.

82. Practically (F) all nitrates are crystalline and readily (G) soluble, and (H) they are characterized by marked decrepitation when (J) heated on charcoals by a blowpipe. No change (K)

83. The door was (A) ajar, (B) and the house had been (C) ransacked. (D) No change (E)

84. Since many diseases and insects cause serious damage to crops, (F) special national legislation has been passed to provide for the quarantine of imported plants; (G) and under provisions of various acts, (H) inspectors are placed at ports of entry to prevent smugglers from bringing in plants that might be (J) dangerous. No change (K)

85. A full train crew consists of a motorman, a brakeman, a conductor, and two ticket takers.

A. NO CHANGE
B. A full train crew consists of a motorman, a brakeman, a conductor and two ticket takers.
C. A full train crew consists of a motorman, brakeman, conductor, and two ticket takers.
D. A full train crew consists of, a motorman, a brakeman, a conductor, and two ticket takers.
E. A full train crew consists of a motorman a brakeman a conductor and two ticket takers.

86. The procedure requires that you open the outer cover plate, (F) remove the thermostat, (G) replace the broken switch, (H) and then (J) replace the thermostat. No change (K)

87. After (A) Peter finished painting the bird feeder (B) he and (C) Jack hung it (D) from a limb of the oak tree. No change (E)

88. When (F) Pat explained to his mother that ten was the highest mark given (G) on the entrance test (H) she breathed (J) a sigh of relief. No change (K)

89. Tim hopes to score well on the exam because he plans to go to an Ivy League school.

A. NO CHANGE
B. Tim hopes to score well on the exam and he plans to go to an Ivy League school.
C. Tim hopes to score well on the exam, because he plans to go to an Ivy League school.
D. Tim hopes to score well on the exam, and he plans to go to an Ivy League school.
E. Tim hopes to score well on the exam he plans to go to an Ivy League school.

90. In this impoverished region with its arid soil a typical diet may contain only 800 calories per day.

F. NO CHANGE
G. In this impoverished region with its arid soil; a typical diet may contain only 800 calories per day.
H. In this impoverished region, with its arid soil, a typical diet may contain only 800 calories per day.
J. In this impoverished region with its arid soil, a typical diet may contain only 800 calories per day.
K. In this impoverished region with its arid soil: a typical diet may contain only 800 calories per day.

91. Begun (A) in 1981 and completed in 1985 (B) the bridge provided (C) the first link between (D) the island and the mainland. No change (E)

92. To slow the bleeding Van tied a pressure bandage around the lower portion of the leg.

F. NO CHANGE
G. To slow the bleeding—Van tied a pressure bandage around the lower portion of the leg.
H. To slow the bleeding, Van tied a pressure bandage around the lower portion of the leg.
J. To slow the bleeding, Van tied a pressure bandage, around the lower portion of the leg.
K. Van tied a pressure bandage, to slow the bleeding, around the lower portion of the leg.

93. Niagara Falls, (A) which (B) forms part of the border between the United States and Canada, (C) was the site of a saw mill built by the French in 1725. (D) No change (E)

94. Secretary of State Acheson, however, made a reasoned defense of the treaty. No change
(Underlined: Acheson, = F; however, = G; reasoned = H; of = J; No change = K)

95. Until the end of the eighteenth century, the only musicians in Norway, were simple unsophisticated peasants who traveled about the countryside. No change
(Underlined: century, = A; Norway, = B; who = C; about = D; No change = E)

96. Prizes will be awarded in each event, and the participant, who compiles the greatest overall total, will receive a special prize. No change
(Underlined: will be = F; event, = G; participant, who compiles the greatest overall total, = H; will receive = J; No change = K)

97. Since learning of the dangers of caffeine, neither my wife nor I have consumed any beverage, containing caffeine. No change
(Underlined: caffeine, = A; neither = B; nor = C; beverage, = D; No change = E)

98. After months of separation, Gauguin finally joined Van Gogh in Arles in October of 1888, Gauguin left a few weeks later.

F. NO CHANGE
G. in Arles; Gauguin, however, leaving a few weeks later
H. in Arles, while Gauguin left a few weeks later
J. in Arles, it was three weeks later when Gauguin was gone
K. in Arles, in October of 1888, but left a few weeks later

99. By the middle of June, the foliage on the trees and the underbrush was lush and green and so thick that it was impossible to see very far, into the woods. No change
(Underlined: By the middle of June, = A; was = B; that = C; very far, into = D; No change = E)

100. Students who plan to graduate with joint majors must, declare their intention and identify the two areas of study by the end of their junior years.

F. NO CHANGE
G. must declare
H. must, declaring
J. must declaring
K. must declared

101. He grew up on a farm in Nebraska; he is now the captain of a Navy ship.

A. NO CHANGE
B. He grew up on a farm in Nebraska, he is now the captain of a Navy ship.
C. He grew up on a farm in Nebraska he is now the captain of a Navy ship.
D. He grew up on a farm; in Nebraska he is now the captain of a Navy ship.
E. He grew up on a farm in Nebraska but he is now the captain of a Navy ship.

102. The Smithtown players cheered the referee's decision; the Stonybrook players booed it.

F. NO CHANGE
G. The Smithtown players cheered the referee's decision the Stonybrook players booed it.
H. The Smithtown players cheered the referee's decision, the Stonybrook players booed it.
J. The Smithtown players cheered the referee's decision: the Stonybrook players booed it.
K. The Smithtown players cheered the referee's decision, but the Stonybrook players booed it.

103. When John entered the room; everyone stood up. No change
(A: When; B: room;; C: everyone; D: up.; E: No change)

104. Clem announced that the prize would be donated to Harbus House; a well-known charity. No change
(F: announced; G: that; H: would be; J: House;; K: No change)

105. The nineteenth-century composers Wagner and Mahler did more than just write music, they conducted their own works.

A. NO CHANGE
B. music, in that they conducted
C. music; they conducted
D. music, with their conducting of
E. music; as conductors, they did

106. The seemingly tranquil lane has been the scene of many crimes including: two assaults, three robberies, and one murder. No change
(F: seemingly; G: including:; H: assaults,; J: robberies,; K: No change)

107. In addition to test scores, college admissions officers take into consideration many other factors such as: grades, extracurricular activities, and letters of recommendation. No change
(A: scores, college; B: as:; C: grades,; D: activities, and; E: No change)

108. Peter notified Elaine. The guidance counselor, that he had been accepted.

F. NO CHANGE
G. Peter notified Elaine the guidance counselor, that he had been accepted.
H. Peter notified Elaine, the guidance counselor that he had been accepted.
J. Peter notified Elaine, the guidance counselor, that he had been accepted.
K. Peter notified Elaine that the guidance counselor had been accepted.

109. Peanuts—blanched or lightly roasted, add an interesting texture and taste to garden salads.

A. NO CHANGE
B. Peanuts—blanched or lightly roasted—add an interesting texture and taste to garden salads.
C. Peanuts: blanched or lightly roasted, add an interesting texture and taste to garden salads.
D. Peanuts, blanched or lightly roasted—add an interesting texture and taste to garden salads.
E. Peanuts blanched or lightly roasted; add an interesting texture and taste to garden salads.

110. The rug gets its striking colors from the weaver's skilled use of dyes—both natural and synthetic to create shades in subtle variations.

F. NO CHANGE
G. dyes—both natural and synthetic, to create
H. dyes, both natural and synthetic—to create
J. dyes—both natural and synthetic—to create
K. dyes—both natural and—synthetic to create

111. The first chapter of *The Scarlet Letter* is "The Custom House."

A. NO CHANGE
B. The first chapter of *The Scarlet Letter* is "The Custom House".
C. The first chapter of *The Scarlet Letter* is The Custom House.
D. The first chapter of *The Scarlet Letter* is *The Custom House.*
E. The first chapter of "*The Scarlet Letter*" is "The Custom House."

112. According to legend, King Arthurs court consisted of twenty-four knights, each of whom was chosen by Arthur for a special talent or virtue.

F. NO CHANGE
G. King Arthurs' court
H. King Arthur's court
J. King's Arthur court
K. Kings' Arthur court

113. In the turmoil of our modern times, it is important to try to keep in mind the fundamental moral values that structure our society.

A. NO CHANGE
B. modern times'
C. modern time's
D. modern-like times'
E. modern and time

114. While he addresses the barbell, a weightlifters face has an expression of deep concentration which immediately gives way to one of complete exertion during the lift and to total exhaustion as the bar is allowed to fall to the ground.

F. NO CHANGE
G. the weightlifters face
H. the weightlifters faces
J. the weightlifters' face
K. a weightlifter's face

DIRECTIONS: Item #115 requires punctuation of the paragraph.

115. On Monday Mark received a letter of acceptance from State College He immediately called his mother herself a graduate of State College to tell her about his acceptance When he told her he had also been awarded a scholarship she was very excited After hanging up Mark's mother decided to throw a surprise party for Mark She telephoned his brother his sister and several of his friends Because the party was supposed to be a surprise she made them all promise not to say anything to Mark Mark however had a similar idea a party for his mother to celebrate his acceptance at her alma mater He telephoned his brother his sister and several of his parents' friends to invite them to a party at his house on Saturday night and he made them all promise to say nothing to his mother On Saturday night both Mark and his mother were surprised

DIRECTIONS: The following passages are early drafts of essays. Some parts of the passages need to be rewritten. Read each passage and answer the items that follow. Some items are about particular sentences or parts of sentences and ask you to improve sentence structure and word choice. Other items refer to parts of the passage or the entire passage and ask you to consider organization and development. In making your decisions, follow the conventions of standard written English.

Items #116–120 are based on the following essay, which is a response to an assignment to write about an issue that is facing America and what might be done to resolve it.

[1] In my mind, one of the most pressing issues facing America today is healthcare. [2] One aspect of the problem is lack of access to a doctor. [3] Many people just cannot afford to pay for a visit to a doctor. [4] They avoid going to the doctor until they are really sick. [5] If they were treated in the first place, they wouldn't get so sick. [6] This practice not only causes human suffering but is wasteful. [7] Health insurance for surgery is also an issue. [8] Many people do not get adequate health insurance with their jobs and cannot afford to pay for it. [9] The inability to pay for health insurance also creates an unfair distribution of healthcare in America.

[10] An even more important aspect of the healthcare problem in America is the choices that people make for themselves. [11] Take smoking for example. [12] Scientific evidence proves that smoking causes lung cancer and other diseases. [13] Yet, many people continue to smoke, and young people continue to start smoking. [14] There are other health problems such as being overweight and using drugs that may also come from private choices.

[15] Some government assistance is needed for those who cannot afford medical care or health insurance. [16] The most important thing is for people to be concerned with their own health. [17] If we take care of ourselves by eating better, exercising more, and avoiding destructive choices, we will all live longer, healthier, and happier lives.

116. The author considers inserting the following factual statement between sentences 13 and 14:

Nicotine, which is found in tobacco, is one of the most addictive chemicals known to science.

Would this statement add to the development of the paragraph?

A. Yes, because the paragraph identifies smoking as a serious problem.
B. Yes, because the sentence explains why young people start to smoke.
C. No, because scientific evidence is irrelevant to the author's point.
D. No, because the addictive mechanism behind smoking is not relevant.
E. No, because essays should emphasize positive points, not negative ones.

117. Which of the following revisions to Sentence 15 best clarifies the author's position?

F. NO CHANGE
G. Some government assistance is needed for those who cannot afford medical care or health insurance and people need to be concerned with their own health.
H. The most important thing is for people to be concerned with their own health and for them to ask for government assistance.
J. Even though some government assistance is needed for those who cannot afford medical care or health insurance, the most important thing is for people to be concerned with their own health.
K. OMIT Sentence 15

118. In context, which of the following best describes the main purpose of the essay?

A. To expose faulty reasoning
B. To evaluate a theory set forth earlier
C. To provide specific illustrations
D. To propose a solution to a problem
E. To persuade the reader to change an opinion

119. In writing this passage, the author was most probably addressing:

F. a convention of surgeons.
G. a group of concerned citizens.
H. a meeting of insurance executives.
J. a conference of tobacco executives.
K. an assembly of noted scientists.

120. What should be done to Sentence 7 to strengthen the organization of the essay?

A. NO CHANGE
B. Begin a new paragraph
C. Switch Sentence 6 with Sentence 7
D. Switch Sentence 7 with Sentence 8
E. OMIT Sentence 7

Item #121 is based on the following essay, which is a response to an assignment to write about a chore for which you have a responsibility and why you like or dislike doing the chore.

[1]

Each year, my family plants a vegetable garden. Both my parents work, and with this, it is the job of the children to tend the garden.

[2]

Work starts several weeks before the growing season actually begins. We put little pots of soil containing seeds that must sprout before they are planted outdoors on the sun porch. Then, my father prepares the ground with a rototiller. When the danger of frost is past, it is time to plant.

[3]

For the first few weeks, we water the seed beds regularly and pull weeds by hand. Once the plants are established, the leaves of the good plants block the sunlight so weeds can't grow. However, there are other jobs such as staking tomatoes and tending to running vines.

[4]

Then the blossoms appear and are pollinated by bees and other insects. As small vegetables appear, the blossoms drop off. They continue to grow and later in the summer begin to ripen. Up to this point, tending the garden has been a chore, but now it becomes a pleasure. Each afternoon, we pick the ripe ones and wash them so that they are ready for cooking. I suppose that I feel proud that I have helped to feed my family. I have to admit that I enjoy the taste of the freshly picked vegetables.

121. The overall organization of the passage can best be described as:

- **F.** chronological development.
- **G.** explanation of two sides of an issue.
- **H.** generalization of a statement with illustrations.
- **J.** posing a question and then answering it.
- **K.** citing an authority and then drawing a conclusion.

Items #122–127 are based on the following essay, which is a response to an assignment to write about a significant activity or experience from the summer vacation.

[1]

On my vacation to Alaska, I took a trip to Porcupine. In 1905, Porcupine was a thriving town of 2,000 people, retail stores, and a post office. Hardly any of the town remains today, but there is still gold there, and our guide showed us how to pan for gold. It's easy to learn how, and anyone can do it. [122]

[2]

The technique of panning depends on the weight of gold. It's about 20 times heavier than water, so the gold stays at the bottom of a stream and gets caught in the sand in slow flowing water around bends and along the edge of the stream. It can also get stuck in small crevices of rock and even wedged into pieces of wood. [124]

[3]

You need to find where the gold is. There's no sense in panning for gold in a stream where there isn't any, so go to a stream where people have found gold before. Then concentrate on those areas that are most likely to trap the little bits of gold.

[4]

Keep moving the pan until about half the original material has been carried away. Lift the pan out of the water, tilt it toward the side with the riffles (the small ridges), [125] and swirl until the water is gone. Repeat this process until nearly all the material is gone.

[5]

To start panning, put a few handfuls of material into your gold pan. Then submerge the pan in the water of the stream. Hold the pan under the surface and move it in a circular motion so that the lighter material sloshes over the edge. You have to be careful not to be too aggressive or you'll send your gold downstream along with the silt and other debris.

[6]

Use a small stream of water suction pipette (or even a spray bottle with a concentrated setting on the nozzle) to sort the gold from the remaining debris. Pick up the flecks with a tweezers or your fingers and place them in a small glass container such as a test tube or a medicine bottle.

[7]

Panning takes practice, patience, and luck, but even a little bit of gold is a big thrill. [126] You're probably not going to find a lot of gold.

122. Which of the following sentences inserted at [122] would best introduce the remaining paragraphs of the essay?

- **A.** Gold is one of the most valuable substances on earth.
- **B.** Just follow these simple instructions.
- **C.** I try to do a lot of different things on my vacations.
- **D.** Did you even know that there was a gold rush in Alaska?
- **E.** Porcupine, the town, was named for the small quilled animal.

123. Which of the following sequence of paragraphs is most logical?

F. NO CHANGE
G. 6, 4, 5
H. 4, 6, 5
J. 5, 4, 6
K. 5, 6, 4

124. The best placement for the final sentence in Paragraph 2 would be:

A. where it is now.
B. as the first sentence of Paragraph 2.
C. in Paragraph 2, following the sentence ending "…weight of gold."
D. as the first sentence of Paragraph 3.
E. as the last sentence of Paragraph 4.

125. Is the parenthetical note following the word "riffles" in Paragraph 4 appropriate?

F. Yes, because it clarifies a technical term for the reader.
G. Yes, because it presents an idea that is essential to the passage.
H. No, because it distracts the reader from the directions for panning.
J. No, because the author does not cite a source for the definition.
K. No, because technical jargon is out of place in this essay.

126. The best placement for the sentence: "Panning takes practice, patience, and luck, but even a little bit of gold is a big thrill" would be:

A. where it is now.
B. at the end of the passage.
C. at the beginning of Paragraph 2.
D. at the beginning of Paragraph 6.
E. at the beginning of the essay.

127. Suppose the author had been assigned to write a brief essay on an interesting travel destination. Assuming that all of the following statements are true, would this essay successfully fulfill the assignment?

F. Yes, because many gold-seekers came to Porcupine during the nineteenth century.
G. Yes, because panning for gold would be a fun activity on a trip.
H. No, because very little remains today of the town of Porcupine.
J. No, because most people have never before heard of Porcupine.
K. No, because many people prefer silver jewelry to gold jewelry.

DIRECTIONS: Items #128–135 consist of two types of items: (1) When four separate parts of a sentence are underlined, identify the underlined part that contains an error. Some of these sentences may not contain any errors; in such a case, choose "No change." No sentence contains more than one error, and no sentence contains an error that is not underlined. (2) When a single part of a sentence is underlined or the entire sentence is underlined, identify the re-phrasing that best expresses the meaning of the underlined material. (A) is always NO CHANGE, which indicates that the underlined material is correct as written.

128. Angela is hoping to save enough for a trip to Europe, during which the small village where her grandparents were born will be visited.

A. NO CHANGE
B. the small village where her grandparents had been born will be visited
C. she will visit the small village where her grandparents were born
D. there will be a visit to the small village where her grandparents were born
E. a visit to the small village where her grandparents were born will be included

129. Finally and at long last the old dog opened his eyes and noticed the intruder.

F. NO CHANGE
G. Finally
H. So finally
J. Yet at long last
K. Finally and long lastingly

130. The speaker declared that alternative ways of utilizing waterfront land ought to be explored.

A. NO CHANGE
B. alternatives of use for
C. alternative utilizations of
D. alternative ways of utilization of
E. alternate uses of

131. Since only (F) the ruling party is allowed to (G) vote, its (H) members are able to maintain the existing (J) status quo. No change (K)

132. Each year, the geese make (A) their annual (B) migration (C) from Northern Canada to their winter habitats (D) in the United States. No change (E)

133. Although (F) the committee met for over two weeks and issued a 50-page report, its findings (G) were of little (H) importance or (J) consequence. No change (K)

134. Along with an end to featherbedding and no-show jobs, the new head of the Transit Authority has eliminated many other inefficient employment practices.

A. NO CHANGE
B. In addition to eliminating featherbedding and no-show jobs
C. Not only did he end featherbedding and no-shows jobs,
D. Besides featherbedding and no-show jobs coming to an end
E. Together with the ending of featherbedding and no-show jobs

135. Being that (F) the hour was (G) late, we agreed (H) to adjourn the meeting and reconvene (J) at nine o'clock the following morning. No change (K)

DIRECTIONS: Items #136-145 are based on the passage below. In the passage, certain parts of the sentences have been underlined and numbered. In the right-hand column, you will find different ways of writing each underlined part; the original version is indicated by the "NO CHANGE" option. For each item, select the choice that best expresses the intended idea, is most acceptable in standard written English, or is most consistent with the overall tone and style of the passage.

There are also items that ask about a section of the passage or the passage as a whole. These items do not refer to an underlined portion of the passage; these items are preceded by statements that are enclosed in boxes.

Read the passage through once before you begin to answer the accompanying items. Finding the answers to certain items may depend on looking at material that appears several sentences beyond the item. So, be sure that you have read far enough ahead before you select your answer choice.

Appalachia's European Settlers

The first Europeans who adopted Appalachia as home, followed (136) the trails pounded out by those earliest mountain engineers: the (137) buffalo, elk, deer, and other wild game. (Later, they found the great traces forged by the Indian tribes on their trading and fighting forays.) (138) Gradually, these first Europeans hewed out

136. **A.** NO CHANGE
B. home followed
C. home: followed
D. home; followed

137. **F.** NO CHANGE
G. engineers, the
H. engineers the
J. engineers. The

138. **A.** NO CHANGE
B. Great traces forged by the Indian tribes, however, were later found on their trading and fighting forays.
C. (Finding later, great traces forged by the Indian tribes, on their trading and fighting forays.)
D. Later, they found the great traces forged by the Indian tribes on their trading and fighting forays.

passages that <u>become part of</u> [139] America's history, and portions of which may still be discovered along today's interstates and back roads. Their very names <u>connect us to</u> [140] the past in the region: The Great Warrior's Trail, Boone's Trace (which became the Wilderness Road), and the Cumberland Gap.

139. F. NO CHANGE
G. will become a part of
H. became part of
J. became part

140. A. NO CHANGE
B. connecting us to
C. connected us to
D. connect us

<u>Geographic isolation</u> [141] greatly influenced the region's culture. From the beginning, numerous ethnic groups contributed to Appalachian settlement. During the late 1600s and into the next century, Germans from the Rhineland settled in the Great Appalachian <u>Valley. Building</u> [142] fat barns and tight houses on the fertile fields of Pennsylvania, Maryland, Virginia, and North Carolina. They were the "Pennsylvania Dutch."

141. F. NO CHANGE
G. Geographically isolated
H. Isolated geographically
J. Isolated geography

142. A. NO CHANGE
B. Valley, building
C. Valley: building
D. Valley,

<u>The German settlers made important contributions.</u> [143] One of the important contributions made by German settlers to frontier life was the Pennsylvania rifle—also called the Kentucky rifle the Long rifle. A weapon born of necessity and economy, its extended barrel assured greater <u>accuracy and precision</u> [144] than could be achieved with the old muskets, and its smaller bore required less powder and lead for each shot <u>(precious commodities)</u> [145]. Such rifles were highly prized possessions, and their manufacture was one of the central industries of pioneer Appalachia.

143. F. NO CHANGE
G. (The German settlers made important contributions.)
H. "The German settlers made important contributions."
J. OMIT the underlined portion.

144. A. NO CHANGE
B. accuracy as well as precision
C. accuracy plus precision
D. accuracy

145. The most appropriate placement of the underlined phrase in this sentence would be:

F. where it is now.
G. after the word *powder*.
H. after the word *lead*.
J. after the word *each*.

This section contains three English quizzes. Complete each quiz under timed conditions. Answers are on page 632.

Quiz I *(32 items; 20 minutes)*

DIRECTIONS: In the passages below, certain parts of the sentences have been underlined and numbered. In the right-hand column, you will find different ways of writing each underlined part; the original version is indicated by the "NO CHANGE" option. For each item, select the choice that best expresses the intended idea, is most acceptable in standard written English, or is most consistent with the overall tone and style of the passage.

There are also items that ask about a section of the passage or the passage as a whole. These items do not refer to an underlined portion of the passage; these items are preceded by statements that are enclosed in boxes.

Read the passage through once before you begin to answer the accompanying items. Finding the answers to certain items may depend on looking at material that appears several sentences beyond the item. So, be sure that you have read far enough ahead before you select your answer choice.

PASSAGE I

Shakespeare's Mirror of Life

No writer can please many readers and please them for a long time excepting by[1] the accurate representation of human nature. Shakespeare, however,[2] is above all writers, the poet of human nature, the

1. **A.** NO CHANGE
   B. except by
   C. except for
   D. excepting

2. **F.** NO CHANGE
   G. moreover
   H. therefore
   J. furthermore

writer who holds up to his readers a faithful and true [3] mirror of manners and life.

3. **A.** NO CHANGE
   B. faithful
   C. faithfully true
   D. true and real

Shakespeare's characters are not modified by the customs of particular places unknown to the rest of the world, by peculiarities of study or professions known to just a few, or [4] by the latest fashions or

4. **F.** NO CHANGE
   G. about by only a few, and
   H. to just a few, but
   J. to only a few, since

popular opinions. Shakespeare's characters are each [5] genuine representations of common humanity. Hamlet

5. **A.** NO CHANGE
   B. every
   C. all
   D. each one a

and Othello act and speak [6] according to the general passions and principles that affect all of us. In the

6. **F.** NO CHANGE
   G. acting and speaking
   H. acted and spoke
   J. acted and spoken

writings of other poets, whoever they may be, [7] a

7. **A.** NO CHANGE
   B. whoever they may be
   C. whomever they may be,
   D. OMIT the underlined portion.

character is too often an individual; in that of Shakespeare, [8] it is commonly a species.

8. **F.** NO CHANGE
   G. the one of Shakespeare,
   H. those of Shakespeare's,
   J. those of Shakespeare,

Other dramatists can gain attention only by using exaggerated characters. Shakespeare has no heroes; his [9]

9. **A.** NO CHANGE
   B. has no heroes: his
   C. has no heroes his
   D. has no heroes, his

scenes only [10] are occupied by persons who act and

10. The most appropriate placement of the underlined phrase in this sentence would be:

    F. where it is now.
    G. after the word *act*.
    H. before the word *act*.
    J. after the word *occupied*.

speak as the reader thinks he or she <u>would of spoken</u> [11] or acted on the same occasion. This, therefore, is the praise of <u>Shakespeare that</u> [12] his drama is the mirror of life. [13]

11. **A.** NO CHANGE
    B. would have speaked
    C. would have spoken
    D. would speak

12. **F.** NO CHANGE
    G. Shakespeare,
    H. Shakespeare. That
    J. Shakespeare: that

13. Is the final sentence an appropriate ending?

    A. Yes, because it makes a final point about Shakespeare that was not previously mentioned and will leave the reader with something to think about.
    B. Yes, because it is a summary of what was said in the introductory paragraph and will give the reader a sense of closure.
    C. No, because it is irrelevant to the essay and will leave the reader confused.
    D. No, because it is so repetitious that it will make the reader impatient.

Items #14–17 ask about the preceding passage as a whole.

14. What assumption is the essay's author making?

    F. Everyone believes Shakespeare is a good writer.
    G. No one has ever heard of Shakespeare.
    H. An accurate representation of human nature is important for great art.
    J. We could not understand Shakespeare's characters in the twentieth century.

15. Where might you find this essay published?

    A. In a book of literary criticism
    B. In a journal for Renaissance scholars
    C. In a Shakespeare biography
    D. In a sociology textbook

16. Which of the following is NOT a strategy the author uses to make his/her point?

F. Comparison
G. Argument
H. Examples
J. Personal anecdote

17. Which of the following would most strengthen the author's argument that Shakespeare is the poet of human nature?

A. A discussion of Shakespeare's poetry
B. An analysis of the characters Hamlet and Othello
C. Biographical background on Shakespeare
D. A description of Shakespeare's Globe Theater

PASSAGE II

Diary of a Black Hole

[1]

In the course of billions of years, millions of stars may <u>sometimes occasionally</u> [18] be concentrated into a region, or regions, only a few light years across, <u>and in these crowded conditions colliding</u> [19] with one another. Some of these collisions <u>would occur</u> [20] at high speeds, in which case the stars are partially or completely torn apart. Other collisions are gentle

18. F. NO CHANGE
G. sometimes, occasionally
H. occasionally
J. off and on

19. A. NO CHANGE
B. colliding
C. and in these crowded conditions, they collide
D. which causes them to collide

20. F. NO CHANGE
G. will occur
H. to occur
J. occur

bumps, but the stars coalesce. [21] The bigger the star becomes, the more likely [22] it is to be hit again and the faster it grows until it reaches instability, collapses on itself, and forms a black hole. [23]

[2]

When most of the stars and gas in the core of a galaxy has been [24] swallowed up by the black hole, the nucleus of the galaxy settles down to a relative [25] quiet existence. This is probably the state of the nucleus of our own galaxy, but every hundred million years or so it may flare upto [26] a brightness 100 times its present level when a globular cluster or especially large gas cloud of enormous size [27] spirals into the nucleus.

[3]

Once formed, a central "seed" black hole grows mainly through the accretion of gas accumulated in the nucleus; gas [28] obtained from disrupted stars, from supernova explosions, or from stars torn apart by the gravitational field of the black hole. Perhaps an entire

21. **A.** NO CHANGE
    B. bumps, since the stars
    C. bumps, and the stars coalesce
    D. bumps, with the stars coalescing

22. **F.** NO CHANGE
    G. becomes the more
    H. becomes the more,
    J. becomes; the more

23. **A.** NO CHANGE
    B. and a black hole is formed
    C. and when this happens a black hole is formed
    D. and thus a black hole is formed at this very moment

24. **F.** NO CHANGE
    G. have been
    H. will have been
    J. would have been

25. **A.** NO CHANGE
    B. to a relatively
    C. for a relative and
    D. relatively

26. **F.** NO CHANGE
    G. up
    H. up to
    J. OMIT the underlined portion.

27. **A.** NO CHANGE
    B. of great enormity
    C. which is huge
    D. OMIT the underlined portion.

28. **F.** NO CHANGE
    G. nucleus and gas
    H. nucleus. Gas
    J. nucleus gas

galaxy can collide with another <u>galaxy, and the result would be</u>[29] the transfer of large amounts of gas from one galaxy <u>to each other</u>[30].

29. **A.** NO CHANGE
B. galaxy to result in
C. galaxy. Such a collision could result in
D. galaxy with the results that

30. **F.** NO CHANGE
G. to the other
H. an other
J. and another

Items #31–32 ask about the preceding passage as a whole.

31. Which of the following represents the most logical sequence for the paragraphs?

A. 1, 2, 3
B. 1, 3, 2
C. 2, 3, 1
D. 3, 1, 2

32. The author's intended audience is most likely:

F. astronomers.
G. young children.
H. high school students.
J. physicists.

Quiz II *(29 items; 20 minutes)*

DIRECTIONS: In the passages below, certain parts of the sentences have been underlined and numbered. In the right-hand column, you will find different ways of writing each underlined part; the original version is indicated by the "NO CHANGE" option. For each item, select the choice that best expresses the intended idea, is most acceptable in standard written English, or is most consistent with the overall tone and style of the passage.

There are also items that ask about a section of the passage or the passage as a whole. These items do not refer to an underlined portion of the passage; these items are preceded by statements that are enclosed in boxes.

Read the passage through once before you begin to answer the accompanying items. Finding the answers to certain items may depend on looking at material that appears several sentences beyond the item. So, be sure that you have read far enough ahead before you select your answer choice.

PASSAGE I

The Influence of the Southwest on Artists

Georgia O'Keeffe, <u>who's</u> [1] death <u>at age ninety-eight</u> [2] closed one of the most fertile chapters of American <u>creativity and flourished</u> [3] as a maverick in her life and work. <u>Since other</u> [4] painters spent a season or two in the country trying to come to terms with the scenes and settings of the Southwest—O'Keeffe stayed

1. **A.** NO CHANGE
   B. which
   C. that
   D. whose

2. **F.** NO CHANGE
   G. at the old age of ninety-eight
   H. at the age of ninety-eight years
   J. when she was ninety-eight years old

3. **A.** NO CHANGE
   B. creativity, and flourished
   C. creativity—flourished
   D. creativity, flourished

4. **F.** NO CHANGE
   G. Because other
   H. In that other
   J. Other

a lifetime. When the canvases of other <u>artists, working in the region</u>[5] faded from view and <u>then were neglected in the chronicle of American visual history</u>[6], her stylized images made an <u>indelible and permanent</u>[7] impression on countless eyes.

Between 1900 and 1945, the region now called New Mexico both fascinated <u>and also it perplexed</u>[8] two generations of American artists. <u>Despite successes,</u>[9] many of those artists wearied of the industrial world of the east. <u>The vast expanse of the West offered a promise for inspiration.</u>[10] For these artists, life and art, so separate in New York and Paris, seemed <u>inextricably bounded</u>[11] in Southwestern cultures. Painters of every

5. A. NO CHANGE
   B. artists working in the region,
   C. artists working in the region
   D. artists, who worked in the region

6. F. NO CHANGE
   G. got neglected then in the chronicle of American visual history
   H. were also then neglected in the American visual history chronicle
   J. then they were also totally neglected in the chronicle of American visual history

7. A. NO CHANGE
   B. indelible
   C. indelible—and permanent—
   D. indelible but permanent

8. F. NO CHANGE
   G. and perplexed
   H. while perplexing
   J. but perplexed

9. A. NO CHANGE
   B. Despite successes
   C. In spite of their successes
   D. Ensuring successes,

10. F. NO CHANGE
    G. America's West, with its vast expanse, offered an inspiring promise.
    H. America's vast expanse of the West offered a promise for inspiration.
    J. Offering a promise of inspiration to the artists was the vast expanse of the American West.

11. A. NO CHANGE
    B. inextricably bound
    C. inextricable bounding
    D. inextricably bounding

persuasion were convinced [12] that sampling this mysterious phenomenon will strengthen [13] and enrich their own work. Most were touched by what D.H. Lawrence called the "spirit of the place." Besides the scenic beauty bathed in clear golden light. The [14] rich traditions of New Mexico's Indian and Hispanic people who were living there [15] became frequent subjects of the artists who traveled to Taos and Santa Fe.

12. **F.** NO CHANGE
G. could be convinced
H. will be convinced
J. are convincing

13. **A.** NO CHANGE
B. would strengthen
C. strengthens
D. strengthening

14. **F.** NO CHANGE
G. light, the
H. light the
J. light: the

15. **A.** NO CHANGE
B. who lived there
C. living there
D. OMIT the underlined portion.

Items #16–17 ask about the preceding passage as a whole.

16. Is the author's quote of D. H. Lawrence in the last paragraph appropriate?

F. Yes, because the author is talking about how this spirit inspired artists, and the quote strengthens his argument.
G. No, because the author has already made his point about the spirit, and the quote is redundant.
H. No, because the author does not make it clear that Lawrence is an authority on the subject.
J. Yes, because it is always a good idea to end an article with a quotation.

17. How might the author have developed the essay so that it was more interesting?

A. The author could have told an anecdote about D. H. Lawrence.
B. The author could have eliminated all mention of Georgia O'Keeffe.
C. The author could have discussed the settling of New Mexico.
D. The author could have been more specific about the other artists who went to the Southwest.

PASSAGE II

Chippewa Chief Demands Timber Payment

Early in November 1850, the work of a logging detail from Fort Gaines in the Minnesota Territory was errupted by a party of Chippewa warriors who demanded payment for the timber. The loggers refused, so [18] the Indians, acting at the direction of Chief Hole-in-the-Day [19] confiscated the government's oxen. The loggers had established their camp on Chippewa lands without his authorizing it [20]. Therefore [21], in a move designed to force reimbursements for the timber, Hole-

18. F. NO CHANGE
G. The loggers refused—
H. The loggers refused:
J. The loggers refused so

19. A. NO CHANGE
B. that acted at the direction of Chief Hole-in-the-Day,
C. acting at the direction of Chief Hole-in-the-Day,
D. (acting at the direction of Chief Hole-in-the-Day),

20. F. NO CHANGE
G. without his authorization
H. without their authorizing it
J. without his authorization of it

21. A. NO CHANGE
B. Henceforth
C. Since
D. On the contrary

in-the-Day was ordering[22] his braves to seize the oxen.

Captain John Todd, the commanding officer at Fort Gaines, demanded that the cattle had to be returned to them[23]. The chief's reply was firm, and at the same time, it was friendly[24]. In his message to Captain Todd, Hole-in-the-Day explained that he had delayed to seize[25] the cattle until he could meet Todd in council and had sent a messenger to the officer requesting a conference at Crow Wing. When Todd did not come, he acted, additionally[26] he later decided that since the army had not paid for timber cut the previous winter, he intended to keep the oxen until the tribe was reimbursed by[27] all the timber taken for the fort. Hole-in-the-Day concluded by saying, "Do not think hard of me, but I do as others would—the timber is mine." [28]

22. **F.** NO CHANGE
    G. gave orders that
    H. orders
    J. ordered

23. **A.** NO CHANGE
    B. the return of the cattle
    C. the cattle's returning
    D. that they return the cattle

24. **F.** NO CHANGE
    G. but, at the same time, it was friendly
    H. yet friendly
    J. at the same time—friendly

25. **A.** NO CHANGE
    B. delayed to have seized
    C. delayed to seized
    D. delayed seizing

26. **F.** NO CHANGE
    G. acted but additionally
    H. acted. Additionally,
    J. acted additionally,

27. **A.** NO CHANGE
    B. reimbursed for
    C. reimbursed
    D. was reimbursed for

28. Is the author's use of the quote in the final paragraph appropriate?

    F. Yes, because it neatly summarizes the main point of the essay.
    G. No, because the chief's thoughts were irrelevant to the events.
    H. Yes, but the author should have included a quotation from Captain Todd.
    J. No, because quotations have no place in expository writing.

Item #29 asks about the preceding passage as a whole.

29. Which of the following best describes the overall character of the essay?

    A. Description of a scene
    B. Narration of events
    C. Comparison of two theories
    D. Argument for a change

Quiz III *(31 items; 20 minutes)*

DIRECTIONS: In the passages below, certain parts of the sentences have been underlined and numbered. In the right-hand column, you will find different ways of writing each underlined part; the original version is indicated by the "NO CHANGE" option. For each item, select the choice that best expresses the intended idea, is most acceptable in standard written English, or is most consistent with the overall tone and style of the passage.

There are also items that ask about a section of the passage or the passage as a whole. These items do not refer to an underlined portion of the passage; these items are preceded by statements that are enclosed in boxes.

Read the passage through once before you begin to answer the accompanying items. Finding the answers to certain items may depend on looking at material that appears several sentences beyond the item. So, be sure that you have read far enough ahead before you select your answer choice.

PASSAGE I

The Con Game Is No Game

Most people have a certain crime that one believes (1) should be ranked as the worst of all crimes. For some, its' (2) murder; for others, it may be selling drugs to children. I believe, moreover (3), that the worst of all crimes may be the confidence scheme.

The confidence scheme may seem an odd (4) choice for the worst crime since con games are usually

1. **A.** NO CHANGE
   B. that they believe
   C. which one believes
   D. that you believe

2. **F.** NO CHANGE
   G. they are
   H. it's
   J. its

3. **A.** NO CHANGE
   B. however
   C. further
   D. therefore

4. **F.** NO CHANGE
   G. obvious
   H. irrelevant
   J. apt

nonviolent. Although, it is a crime that ranks in heartlessness. Con artists are the most devious, the most harmful, and the most disruptive members of society because they break down the most important bonds of the social order, honesty and trust.

The con games themselves are simplistic almost infantile. They work on account of a con artist can win complete confidence, talk fast enough to keep the victim slightly confused, and dangling enough temptation to suppress any suspicion or skepticism. The primary targets of these criminals will be the elderly and women. (And they prefer to work in large crowds.)

5. **A.** NO CHANGE
   B. nonviolent, though
   C. nonviolent, but
   D. nonviolent, and

6. **F.** NO CHANGE
   G. it breaks
   H. of its breaking
   J. of them breaking

7. **A.** NO CHANGE
   B. order, honesty, and trust
   C. order: honesty and trust
   D. order: honesty, and trust

8. **F.** NO CHANGE
   G. simplistic; almost infantile
   H. simplistic, almost infantile
   J. simplistic, yet almost infantile

9. **A.** NO CHANGE
   B. on account of a con artist's ability to
   C. owing to a con artist's ability to
   D. because a con artist can

10. **F.** NO CHANGE
    G. and dangles
    H. and has dangled
    J. and dangle

11. **A.** NO CHANGE
    B. to be
    C. are
    D. is

12. **F.** NO CHANGE
    G. women, and the con artists prefer to work in large crowds.
    H. women, preferring, of course, to work in large crowds.
    J. women (who prefer to work in large crowds).

Items #13–15 ask about the preceding passage as a whole.

13. Which of the following is most probably the author's opinion rather than a fact?

A. Con artists are the most disruptive members of society.
B. Most con games are nonviolent.
C. Most of the targets are the elderly and women.
D. Most con games are simple.

14. What would be the most logical continuation of the essay?

F. A description of some confidence games
G. An account of the elderly as crime victims in society
H. An account of the author's experience with con artists
J. An explanation of crowd psychology

15. What would strengthen the author's contention that con games rank first in heartlessness?

A. Statistics to show the number of people who were taken in by the con artist
B. A discussion of the way the police handle the problem
C. An example that shows how the con artist breaks down honesty and trust
D. An example to illustrate that con games are nonviolent and simple

PASSAGE II

Elizabeth I's Intellect Ruled Supreme

Elizabeth I had a sensuous and indulgent nature that she inherited from her mother, Anne Boleyn (who was beheaded by Henry VIII)[16]. Splendor and pleasure is[17] the very air she breathed. She loved gaiety, laughter, and wit. Her vanity remained even, to old age. The[18] vanity of a coquette.

The statesmen who she outwitted[19] believed, almost to the end, that Elizabeth I was little more than a frivolous woman who was very vain[20]. However, the Elizabeth whom they saw was far from being[21] all of Elizabeth. The willfulness of Henry and the triviality of Anne played over the surface of a nature so hard like[22] steel—a purely intellectual temperament. Her vanity and caprice carried no weight whatsoever[23] in state affairs. The coquette of the presence chamber

16. F. NO CHANGE
    G. (having been beheaded by Henry VIII)
    H. beheaded by Henry VIII
    J. OMIT the underlined portion.

17. A. NO CHANGE
    B. is,
    C. were
    D. were,

18. F. NO CHANGE
    G. remains, even to old age, the
    H. remains, even to old age the
    J. remained, even to old age, the

19. A. NO CHANGE
    B. that she outwitted
    C. whom she outwitted
    D. who she was outwitting

20. F. NO CHANGE
    G. and she was also very vain
    H. known for her great vanity
    J. OMIT the underlined portion.

21. A. NO CHANGE
    B. to be
    C. having been
    D. OMIT the underlined portion.

22. F. NO CHANGE
    G. as hard as
    H. so hard as
    J. as hard like

23. A. NO CHANGE
    B. no matter what
    C. whatever, at all
    D. whatever, despite everything

had became [24] the coolest and hardest of politicians at the council board.

It was this part that gave her marked superiority over [25] the statesmen of her time. No more nobler a group [26] of ministers ever gathered round the council board than those of Elizabeth, but she was the instrument of none. She listened and she weighed, but her policy, as a whole, was her own. It was the policy of good sense, not genius, she [27] endeavored to keep her throne, to keep England out of war, and she wanted [28] to restore civil and religious order.

24. **F.** NO CHANGE
G. became
H. used to become
J. becomes

25. **A.** NO CHANGE
B. superiority in regard to
C. superiority about
D. superior quality to

26. **F.** NO CHANGE
G. nobler a group,
H. nobler a group
J. more nobler of a group,

27. **A.** NO CHANGE
B. not genius she
C. not genius. She
D. —not genius, she

28. **F.** NO CHANGE
G. wanting
H. and wanting
J. and

Items #29–31 ask about the preceding passage as a whole.

29. What might logically have preceded this essay?

A. Some biographical background on Elizabeth I
B. A discussion of the wives of Henry VIII
C. A discussion of the politics of Tudor England
D. A discussion of the policies of Elizabeth's ministers

30. This essay is most probably taken from a:

F. scholarly work on Renaissance England.
G. biography of Elizabeth I.
H. diary kept by one of Elizabeth's ministers.
J. political science textbook.

31. Which of the following would most strengthen the essay?

A. Knowing who the ministers were and what their policies were
B. Examples of Elizabeth's dual nature
C. A discussion of Henry VIII's policies
D. A discussion of the role of the woman in Tudor England

This section contains additional English items for further practice. Answers are on page 632.

DIRECTIONS: In the passages below, certain parts of the sentences have been underlined and numbered. In the right-hand column, you will find different ways of writing each underlined part; the original version is indicated by the "NO CHANGE" option. For each item, select the choice that best expresses the intended idea, is most acceptable in standard written English, or is most consistent with the overall tone and style of the passage.

There are also items that ask about a section of the passage or the passage as a whole. These items do not refer to an underlined portion of the passage; these items are preceded by statements that are enclosed in boxes.

Read the passage through once before you begin to answer the accompanying items. Finding the answers to certain items may depend on looking at material that appears several sentences beyond the item. So, be sure that you have read far enough ahead before you select your answer choice.

PASSAGE I

Significance of Symbolism in Medieval Art

Art of the Middle Ages is first and foremost a sacred script, the symbols and meanings of which <u>are well settled</u>[1]. A circular halo placed vertically behind the head of a figure signifies <u>sainthood, meanwhile</u>[2] the halo impressed with a cross signifies divinity.

1. **A.** NO CHANGE
   B. is well settled
   C. are settled well
   D. would be settled

2. **F.** NO CHANGE
   G. sainthood, because
   H. sainthood because
   J. sainthood, while

A tower with a window indicates a village, and should an angel be watching from the battlements, that city is thereby identified as Jerusalem.

3. A. NO CHANGE
   B. (Do NOT begin a new paragraph) A tower
   C. Towers
   D. Having a tower

Mathematics is also an important element of this iconography. "The Divine Wisdom," wrote Saint Augustine, "reveals itself everywhere in numbers." A doctrine derived from the Neoplatonists who revived the teachings of Pythagoras. Furthermore, require numbers symmetry. At Chartres, a stained-glass window shows the four prophets Isaac, Ezekiel, Daniel, and Jeremiah carrying on their shoulders the four evangelists Matthew, Mark, Luke, and John.

4. F. NO CHANGE
   G. numbers," which
   H. numbers." This doctrine was
   J. numbers" which

5. A. NO CHANGE
   B. Neoplatonists that
   C. Neoplatonist's that
   D. Neoplatonist's who

Every painting is also an allegory, showing us one thing and inviting us to see another. In this respect, the artist was asked to imitate God, who had hidden a profound meaning behind the literal and who wished nature to be a moral lesson to man. In a painting of the final judgment, the foolish virgins can be seen by us at the left hand of Jesus and the wise on the right, and we understand that this symbolizes those who are lost and

6. F. NO CHANGE
   G. (Do NOT begin a new paragraph) Every painting
   H. However, every painting
   J. (Do NOT begin a new paragraph) However, every painting

7. A. NO CHANGE
   B. Furthermore, the artist was
   C. The artist, however, was
   D. Generally, artists are

8. F. NO CHANGE
   G. meaning which was behind
   H. meaning being behind
   J. meaning behind and in back of

9. A. NO CHANGE
   B. by all of us
   C. by each of us
   D. OMIT the underlined portion.

those that have been saved.
10

Within such a system, even the most mediocre
11
talent was elevated by the genius of centuries, and the
12
first artist of the Renaissance broke with the tradition at great risk. Even when they are great, medieval artists are no more than the equals of the old masters who passively followed the sacred rules. When they are not outstanding, they scarcely avoid banality and
13
insignificance in their religious works.

10. **F.** NO CHANGE
G. those who have been saved
H. those who are saved
J. the saved

11. **A.** NO CHANGE
B. (Do NOT begin a new paragraph) Within such a system,
C. (Do NOT begin a new paragraph) Inside of such a system,
D. (Do NOT begin a new paragraph) To be inside such a system,

12. **F.** NO CHANGE
G. with
H. however
J. since

13. **A.** NO CHANGE
B. always
C. ever
D. OMIT the underlined portion.

Items #14–16 ask about the preceding passage as a whole.

14. The author most likely wrote this essay for which of the following?

F. A scholarly art journal
G. A book tracing the history of mathematics
H. A history of the Catholic Church
J. A book surveying the history of Western art

15. The author relies on which of the following to develop the passage?

    A. Examples
    B. Extensive quotations from other authorities
    C. Statistics
    D. Personal experience

16. The author probably quotes Saint Augustine in order to:

    F. ridicule his position.
    G. emphasize the importance of numbers and symmetry.
    H. prove the importance of Church teaching.
    J. illustrate Augustine's knowledge of art.

PASSAGE II

Pursuit of the Bottomless Pit

A persistent and universal symbol in the mythology of virtually every culture, is [17] that of a bottomless pit or an engulfing whirlpool. It was the maw of the abyss: and those [18] venturing too close were dragged inward toward chaos by an irresistible force. Socrates (a Greek philosopher who committed suicide) [19] talked of a chasm that pierced the world

17. A. NO CHANGE
    B. culture is
    C. culture are
    D. cultures are

18. F. NO CHANGE
    G. abyss, and those
    H. abyss meanwhile those
    J. abyss due to the fact that

19. A. NO CHANGE
    B. (a philosopher from Greece who committed suicide)
    C. (a Greek philosopher who had committed suicide)
    D. OMIT the underlined portion.

straight through from side to side. Ulysses also encountering it, as did a mythical Cherokee who escaped, but not before he was drawn down to the narrowest circle of the maelstrom where he could peer into the netherworld of the dead. Many primitive cultures bury their dead with tools in the belief that the tools will be useful to them in the afterlife.

20. F. NO CHANGE
G. also encountered it,
H. also encountered them,
J. encountered them also,

21. For the sake of the logic and coherence of this paragraph, the underlined sentence should be:
A. left as it is now.
B. placed before the word *Ulysses*.
C. placed at the end of the passage.
D. omitted.

On the other hand, the search for a solution to one of astronomys' most persistent and perplexing riddles, black holes, could be viewed by one as a continuation of the search for the whirlpool that is the maw of the abyss, a depth our telescopes cannot reach and from which nothing will have returned. What is incredible to contemplate, and what sets us apart from

22. F. NO CHANGE
G. The search
H. (Do NOT begin a new paragraph) The search
J. Also, the search

23. A. NO CHANGE
B. astronomy's
C. astronomy
D. astronomys

24. F. NO CHANGE
G. by one astronomer
H. by those
J. OMIT the underlined portion.

25. A. NO CHANGE
B. continuing the search of
C. continuation to the search for
D. continuation for the search for

26. F. NO CHANGE
G. will return
H. returns
J. returning

27. A. NO CHANGE
B. setting us
C. and that sets us
D. and we are set

the ancients, is that we think we have a fair idea <u>not only as to</u> [28] how they are formed, but also how large they are and so forth. A combination of theory and observation <u>have led to</u> [29] the growing suspicion among astrophysicists that the nucleus of virtually every galaxy harbors a massive black hole.

28. **F.** NO CHANGE
G. about
H. not about
J. OMIT the underlined portion.

29. **A.** NO CHANGE
B. has led to
C. has led
D. led

PASSAGE III

Tradition Preservation During Meiji Restoration

Instead of casting aside traditional values during the Meiji Restoration of 1888, those who strove to dismantle feudalism and to modernize the country chose to preserve three traditions as the foundations <u>on which they could build a modern Japan upon.</u> [30]

30. **F.** NO CHANGE
G. on which they could be building a modern Japan upon
H. upon which they could build a modern Japan
J. upon which they someday could probably build a modern Japan

The <u>older</u> [31] tradition and basis of the entire Japanese value system was <u>respect for and even worshipping</u> [32] the Emperor. During the early centuries of Japanese history, the Shinto cult, in which <u>the Imperial family traced its ancestry to the Sun Goddess,</u> [33]

31. **A.** NO CHANGE
B. oldest
C. old
D. OMIT the underlined portion.

32. **F.** NO CHANGE
G. respecting and even worshipping
H. respect for and even worship of
J. respect and even worship

33. **A.** NO CHANGE
B. the Imperial family got its ancestry traced back to the Sun Goddess
C. the Imperial family's ancestry was traced back to the Sun Goddess
D. the Sun Goddess was considered to be the ancestor of the Imperial family

became the people's sustaining faith. Being later subordinated to imported Buddhism and Confucianism, Shintoism was perpetuated in Ise and Izumo, the great shrines of the Imperial family, until the Meiji modernizers established it as a quasi state religion to unify the people and restore the Emperor as the symbol of national unity and the object of loyalty to the Japanese.

34. F. NO CHANGE
G. Later subordinated
H. Later subordinated,
J. Subordinated later,

35. A. NO CHANGE
B. the Japanese had
C. by the Japanese
D. for the Japanese

Another tradition that was enduring was the heirarchical system of social relations based on feudalism.

36. F. NO CHANGE
G. Another tradition
H. (Do NOT begin a new paragraph) Another tradition
J. The other tradition

Confucianism prescribed a pattern by ethical conduct between groups of people within a fixed hierarchy.

37. A. NO CHANGE
B. patterns by
C. a pattern for
D. patterns with

Four of the five Confucian relationships (those between ruler and subject, husband and wife, father and son, and elder brother and younger brother) were vertical since they required loyalty and obedience from the

38. Is the author's use of parentheses appropriate?

F. Yes, because the examples are irrelevant to the passage.
G. Yes, because although the information is relevant, the material is not part of the main development of the passage.
H. No, because the examples are relevant to the meaning of the sentence.
J. No, because the material is essential to the reader's understanding of the passage.

39. A. NO CHANGE
B. was
C. are
D. could be

40. F. NO CHANGE
G. vertical, they
H. vertical, since it
J. vertical, being they

inferior toward the superior and benevolence and protection from the superior to the inferior.[41] Only the fifth relationship, that[42] between friend and friend—was horizontal. A[43] third tradition was respect for learning, another basic idea of Confucius.[44] In traditional Japan, study was the absolute duty of man. It was a religious mandate as well[45] as a social duty and was a means of promoting a harmonious and stable society. The individual's behavior[46] was strictly prescribed by law and custom. Only the Samurai had the right to retaliate with force if they were displeased. But his[47] primary duty was to the lord.

41. A. NO CHANGE
    B. and also benevolence and protection from the superior to the inferior
    C. with the benevolence and protection being from the superior to the inferior
    D. and from the superior to the inferior, the benevolence and protection

42. F. NO CHANGE
    G. relationship that
    H. relationship—that
    J. relationship

43. A. NO CHANGE
    B. Furthermore, a
    C. (Begin a new paragraph) A
    D. (Begin a new paragraph) Also a

44. F. NO CHANGE
    G. Confucius idea
    H. idea of Confucianism
    J. Confucianism idea

45. A. NO CHANGE
    B. mandate as well as being
    C. mandate as well,
    D. mandate,

46. F. NO CHANGE
    G. An individual behavior
    H. Behavior by individual's
    J. The individuals behavior

47. A. NO CHANGE
    B. But their
    C. Being that their
    D. Because their

Item #48 asks about the preceding passage as a whole.

48. The best description of the development of this essay would be:

F. argument and rebuttal.
G. a personal narrative.
H. a three-part exposition.
J. question and answer.

STRATEGY SUMMARY SHEET

GENERAL STRATEGIES:

1. After you have memorized the directions, they can be safely ignored; therefore, do not waste valuable test time by re-reading instructions.

2. Read the entire selection for comprehension of the overall meaning. Look for possible errors. Mentally note how to correct possible errors.

3. Study the answer choices, looking for one that matches your anticipated answer.

4. Compare the answer choices. What makes them different from one another?

5. Do not choose answer choices that introduce new errors or change the meaning of the selection.

6. Use the additional strategies presented below when searching for errors.

STRATEGIES FOR USAGE AND MECHANICS CONTENT AREA:

1. Check for grammatical errors.

   a) Look for obvious subject-verb agreement problems. The test-writers may try to obscure agreement by inserting material between the subject and the verb, inverting the sentence structure so that the verb precedes the subject, or introducing compound subjects.

   b) Check for proper pronoun usage. Remember that all pronouns must have antecedents. The pronoun must clearly refer to the antecedent and must agree in case, number, and person.

   c) Be alert to the proper usage of adjectives and adverbs. Note that adjectives modify nouns, while adverbs modify verbs. Also, adjectives, not adverbs, follow linking verbs. Lastly, watch out for adjectives posing as adverbs. Sometimes, adjectives can be transformed into adverbs by adding "ly," so it is important to identify whether the modifier is an adjective or an adverb.

   d) Watch for double negatives. Even though double negatives are sometimes used colloquially, they are not grammatically correct.

   e) Check for proper noun clause introductions. A noun clause is a group of words that functions as the subject of a sentence and must be introduced with "that." Note that "because" and "why" should not be used to introduce noun clauses.

   f) Watch for illogical comparisons. Comparisons can only be made between similar objects. Be alert to the use of the comparative form of an adjective (for comparing two objects) and the superlative form of an adjective (for comparing three or more objects). Remember that some adjectives and adverbs express the highest degree of quality; therefore, they cannot be improved upon.

   g) Check for improper verb and mood shifts. The same verb tense and mood should be used within a sentence or paragraph unless there is a valid reason for a change. Also, be alert to the improper usage of verb tenses in general. Make sure that the verb tense within a sentence or a paragraph is logical.

h) Make sure that the choice of verb tense in a sentence reflects the sequence and the duration of the events described.

i) Check for diction errors such as wrong prepositions, improper word choice, and gerund-infinitive switching.

2. Check for sentence structure errors.

a) Check to see if the sentence is a run-on.

b) Be aware of comma splice errors in sentences.

c) Check to see if the sentence is a fragment.

d) Make sure the sentence contains logical coordinating conjunctions.

e) Watch for faulty parallelism in a sentence. Note that whenever elements of a sentence perform similar or equal functions, they should have the same form.

f) Be alert for sentence structures in which a thought that is interrupted by intervening material is completed later in the sentence. Check that the interrupted thought is correctly completed. A simple way to check for this type of error is to read the sentence without the intervening material—the sentence should make sense, be grammatically correct, and represent a complete thought.

g) Look for misplaced modifiers. Modifiers should be placed as close as possible to what they modify. Errors in placement of modifiers create ambiguous and illogical constructions.

h) Be alert to misplacements or omissions of certain elements of a sentence. These errors lead to unintended meanings. Make sure the intended meaning of the sentence follows from its logical structure.

3. Check for punctuation errors.

a) Check to see if the comma is used correctly in the sentence. The following list summarizes the most important uses and misuses of commas:

(1) Use a comma before a coordinating conjunction joining two clauses.

(2) Use commas for clarity.

(3) Use commas to separate words in a series.

(4) Use commas to mark the end of an introductory phrase.

(5) Use pairs of commas to set off appositive, parenthetical, and non-restrictive elements.

(6) A comma should not be used to separate a subject from its verb.

(7) Commas should not be used to set off restrictive or necessary clauses or phrases.

(8) A comma should not be used in place of a conjunction.

b) Check for correct semicolon usage. The following list summarizes the appropriate uses of semicolons:

(1) Use a semicolon to separate two complete ideas.

(2) Use a semicolon to separate a series of phrases with commas and a series of numbers.

(3) Use a semicolon to separate independent clauses.

(4) Do not use semicolons to separate dependent clauses.

c) Check for correct end-stop punctuation. Make sure that any material that has a period is a complete sentence.

d) Check for correct usage of dashes. The following are the rules for situations requiring the use of a dash:

(1) Use a dash for emphasis or to set off an explanatory group of words.

(2) Use a dash before a word or group of words that indicates a summation or reversal of what preceded it.

(3) Use a dash to mark a sudden break in thought that leaves a sentence unfinished.

e) Check for correct apostrophe usage. Apostrophes are most commonly used to show possession. They are also used when a noun is used to modify another noun or a gerund.

f) Check to see if a punctuation mark is needed to clarify the selection.

STRATEGIES FOR RHETORICAL SKILLS CONTENT AREA:

1. Check to see if the strategy used by the writer is appropriate.

a) Make sure that all supporting material is appropriate to the selection.

b) Be alert to opening, transitional, and concluding sentences. Check to see if they are effective or if they need improvement.

c) Read the selection for the main ideas and identify the main purpose of the entire passage.

d) Look for diction, purpose, and tone clues that identify the writer's audience.

2. Check for organization errors.

a) Check the sentence-level structure. Sentences should be in logical and appropriate order within the paragraph.

b) Check the paragraph-level structure. Paragraphs should be divided logically and unified around central theme.

c) Check the passage-level structure. Passages should follow an identifiable pattern of development, with paragraphs appearing in a logical order.

3. Check for stylistic problems.

a) Make sure that the sentences are concise and to the point.

(1) Look for awkward sentences or weak passive verbs.

(2) Look for needlessly wordy sentences.

b) Check for ambiguous sentences. Such sentences run two or more ideas together and require further clarification to separate and connect the disparate ideas.

c) Check for idiomatic usage.

NOTES:

Mathematics

COURSE CONCEPT OUTLINE

What You Absolutely Must Know

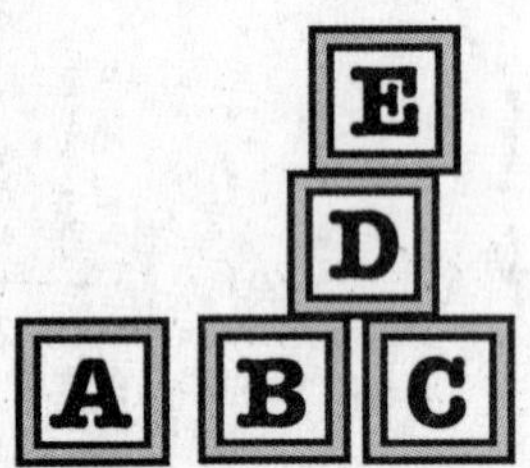

BASICS

The ACT Mathematics Test, according to the test-writers, presupposes a knowledge of pre-algebra and algebra, intermediate algebra and coordinate geometry, and geometry and trigonometry. And the ACT Mathematics Test items are pretty much the same kind of questions you'd see on a regular test—except that they are multiple-choice questions.

In reality, however, you do not have to know all of those topics to do pretty well on the test. Intermediate algebra, coordinate geometry, and trigonometry combined account for less than 40 percent of the test. Here is the breakdown of items by topic on the ACT Mathematics Test:

ACT Mathematics Test Topics
(60 items; 60 minutes)

Content	*Approximate Number*	*Approximate Percent*
Pre-Algebra	14	23%
Elementary Algebra	10	17%
Intermediate Algebra	9	15%
Coordinate Geometry	9	15%
Plane Geometry	14	23%
Trigonometry	4	7%

This means that you could blow off all of the trigonometry items and the hardest half of the coordinate geometry and intermediate algebra items, miss another nine questions, and still get a 24 on the ACT Mathematics Test. And 24 is a pretty good score. For a very respectable score of 21 or so (above the average of everyone in the country who's thinking about college), you need a raw score of about 33, which you can get if you blow off all the trigonometry, intermediate algebra, and coordinate geometry and keep your wrong answers down to five.

This is not a recommended strategy. You want to make sure that you answer any questions you know how to answer. But these little "thought experiments" show that you can do quite well on the math even if you're not exactly a math whiz.

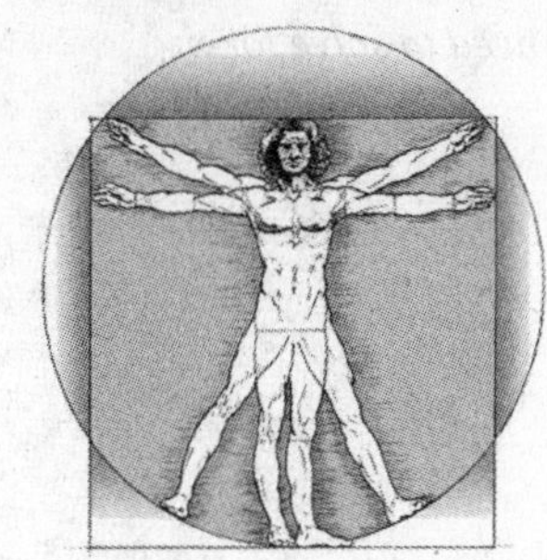

ANATOMY

DIRECTIONS: Solve each item and choose the correct answer choice. Calculator use is permitted; however, some items are best solved without the use of a calculator.

Note: All of the following should be assumed, unless otherwise stated.

1. Illustrative figures are NOT necessarily drawn to scale.
2. The word *average* indicates arithmetic mean.
3. The word *line* indicates a straight line.
4. Geometric figures lie in a plane.

You really do not need the directions at all. Problem-solving is your standard-issue Mathematics item. You can use a calculator, and there will be further discussion of this in class.

Also, figures are not necessarily drawn to scale. However, in practice, the figures are almost always drawn to scale. Again, this issue will be discussed in detail later during the Mathematics Lesson.

1. Paulo bicycled $6\frac{1}{3}$ miles on Wednesday and $8\frac{2}{5}$ miles on Thursday. How many miles did he bicycle during those two days?

A. $14\frac{2}{15}$
B. $14\frac{1}{4}$
C. $14\frac{3}{8}$
D. $14\frac{11}{15}$
E. $14\frac{13}{15}$

1. (D) *This item is solved by addition:*

$$6\frac{1}{3}+8\frac{2}{5}=\frac{19}{3}+\frac{42}{5}$$
$$=\frac{95}{15}+\frac{126}{15}$$
$$=\frac{221}{15}$$
$$=14\frac{11}{15}$$

2. The average weight of 5 packages in a shipment is 8.7 pounds. The weights of 4 of the packages are 6.3 pounds, 7.5 pounds, 8.9 pounds, and 9.6 pounds. What is the weight of the fifth package?

F. 8.5
G. 8.8
H. 9.4
J. 11.2
K. 12.3

2. (J) *This item is a bit more difficult. First, set up an equation:*

$$\frac{6.3+7.5+8.9+9.6+x}{5}=8.7$$

Then, solve for the missing weight:

$$(6.3+7.5+8.9+9.6)+x=(8.7)(5)$$
$$x=43.5-32.3=11.2$$

3. If $3x+4=7x-2$, $x=$?

A. $-\frac{1}{4}$

B. $\frac{1}{2}$

C. $\frac{3}{5}$

D. $\frac{2}{3}$

E. $1\frac{1}{2}$

3. (E) *For this item, you need to solve for x:*

$$\begin{aligned} 3x+4&=7x-2\\ 3x-7x&=-2-4\\ -4x&=-6\\ 4x&=6\\ x&=\frac{6}{4}=\frac{3}{2}=1\frac{1}{2} \end{aligned}$$

4. The ratio of the radii of two circles is $3:4$. What is the ratio of their areas?

F. $7:1$
G. $3:4$
H. $9:16$
J. $3:4\pi$
K. $9:16\pi$

4. (H) *With this item, since the ratio of the radii of the two circles is* $3:4$*, the ratio of their areas is:*

$$\frac{\pi(3)^2}{\pi(4)^2}=\frac{9\pi}{16\pi}=\frac{9}{16}=9:16.$$

There are three other features of Mathematics items to note:

- ***Answer choices are arranged in order.*** For most Mathematics items, answer choices are arranged from largest to smallest or vice versa. However, there are some exceptions. Choices that consist entirely of variables do not follow the rule, and items that ask "which of the following is the biggest?" obviously do not follow the rule. That the answer choices are usually arranged in order makes it easier for you to find your choice in the list. It also sets up an important test-taking strategy of starting with the middle choice when applying the "test-the-test" strategy, which you'll learn about later in the Mathematics Lesson.

- ***Answer choices are well-defined.*** The choices are not created so that you have to do "donkey math." You are not likely to find a problem with answer choices like the following:

  A. \$183.27
  B. \$183.28
  C. \$183.29
  D. \$183.30
  E. \$183.31

  You might find answers like this on an ordinary math test but not on the ACT test. Instead, the choices usually correspond to errors in thinking—not errors in arithmetic. This feature is important because it is the basis for a couple of time-saving strategies that you'll learn shortly.

- ***Items are arranged on a ladder of difficulty.*** Of course, you can't tell this from the four examples provided here, but the ladder is an important feature of the math test. Given that the problems become more difficult as you proceed, you're obviously going to have to make some important decisions about speed and skipping items. You'll get more advice on this later in the Mathematics Lesson.

PACING

The Mathematics Test consists of 60 items. The time limit is 60 minutes. The items are arranged on a ladder of difficulty, so you'll need a pacing plan that helps you move more quickly through the easier items at the beginning of the test and allows you to build up a time reserve for the harder items that are toward the end. The following table summarizes the timing for this approach:

Item Numbers	*Time to Spend per Item*	*Remaining Time*
#1–10	36 seconds	54 minutes
#11–20	42 seconds	47 minutes
#21–30	54 seconds	38 minutes
#31–40	66 seconds	27 minutes
#41–50	72 seconds	15 minutes
#51–60	90 seconds	0 minutes

This table is a schedule for the best of all possible math worlds. It's intended to be a guideline, not a rule. Try to stay on schedule, but be prepared to adjust your timing according to how many items it is realistic to expect that you'll be able to do. Trying to stay on a schedule during the test will help you to avoid the two biggest time-sucks ever created for a timed test.

First, staying on schedule will ensure that you are not plodding through the easy items earlier in the test. At the beginning, with a 60-minute time limit, it will seem to you like you've got all the time in the world. But you don't. From the moment the flag drops, you're behind schedule and playing catch-up. So, keep that sense of urgency about you.

Second, the schedule will serve as a constant reminder that you cannot afford to spend too much time on any one problem. If you make a mistake and spend three minutes on item #22, you'll find that you're falling badly behind schedule. Leave that problem, hoping you'll have time at the end of the test to come back and finish it. But spending three minutes to get +1 when three minutes could get you +5 is a score-killer.

TIME TRIAL

5 Items
Time—5 minutes

DIRECTIONS: Solve each item and choose the correct answer choice. Calculator use is permitted; however, some items are best solved without the use of a calculator.

Note: All of the following should be assumed, unless otherwise stated.

1. Illustrative figures are NOT necessarily drawn to scale.
2. The word *average* indicates arithmetic mean.
3. The word *line* indicates a straight line.
4. Geometric figures lie in a plane.

1. $\frac{1}{10^{25}} - \frac{1}{10^{26}} = ?$

A. $\frac{9}{10^{25}}$

B. $\frac{9}{10^{26}}$

C. $\frac{1}{10^{25}}$

D. $-\frac{9}{10^{25}}$

E. $-\frac{1}{10}$

2. The table below shows readings of water levels for the Red River at various times. If readings of the rise of the water level followed a geometric progression, the water level at 3:00 p.m. was how many inches above normal?

Floor Readings for the Red River				
Time (p.m.)	1:00	2:00	3:00	4:00
Inches above Normal	0.5	1.5	?	13.5

F. 4
G. 4.5
H. 4.75
J. 5
K. 5.25

3. If s, t, and u are different positive integers and $\frac{s}{t}$ and $\frac{t}{u}$ are positive integers, which of the following CANNOT be a positive integer?

A. $\frac{s}{u}$

B. $s \cdot t$

C. $\frac{u}{s}$

D. $(s+t)u$

E. $(s-u)t$

4. In the figure below, $\overline{AD} = \overline{DC}$. What is the value of $\overline{AD} + \overline{DC}$?

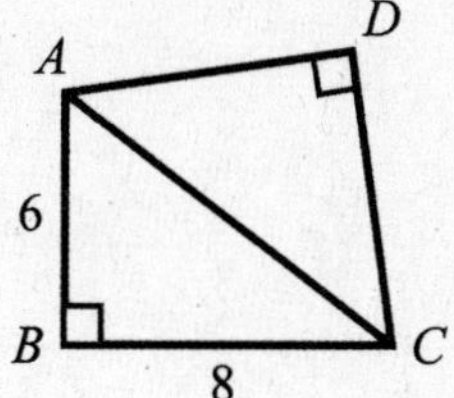

F. $18\sqrt{2}$
G. 18
H. $10\sqrt{2}$
J. 10
K. $6\sqrt{2}$

5. In the figure below, the length of $\overline{AC}$ is 5 units. Which of the following is the best approximation for the number of units in the length of $\overline{BC}$? ($\tan 22° \approx 0.4$)

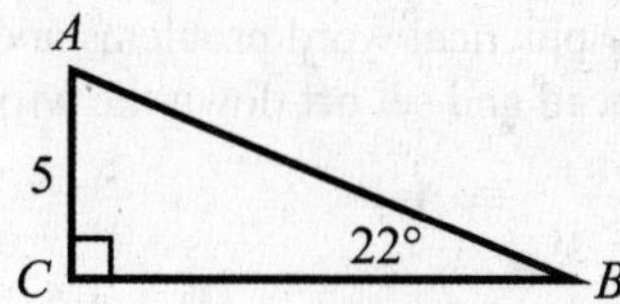

A. 2.0
B. 3.0
C. 7.5
D. 12.5
E. 16

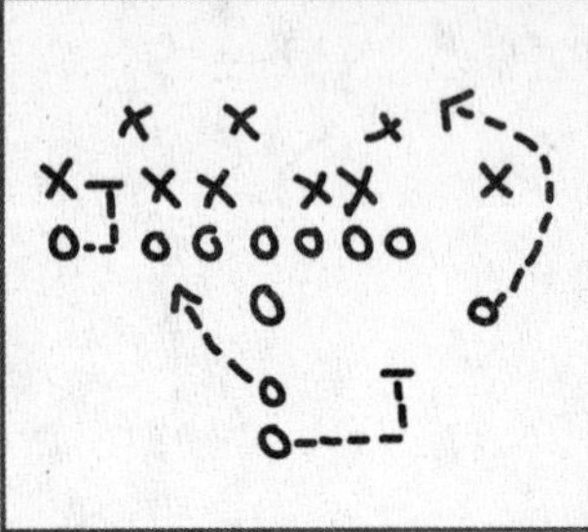

GAME PLAN

Quickly Preview the Test, but Skip the Directions

As you get started, take a few seconds to preview the Mathematics Test. It's 99.99% certain that you're going to find everything in place and just as you expected. But a quick overview will guarantee against any unanticipated changes. Do NOT, however, read the directions. Remind yourself of your pacing plan and then get to work.

Answer the Question That Is Being Asked

Read the Question Carefully

Some problems are fairly simple, but others are more complex, particularly practical word problems and more difficult geometry problems. The more complex the question, the easier it is to misread and set off down the wrong track. If the question is very long, then underline the key part of the question.

Example:

If Mark traveled 20 miles in 3 hours and Lester traveled twice as far in half the time, what was Lester's average speed?

A. $3\frac{1}{3}$ miles per hour
B. $6\frac{2}{3}$ miles per hour
C. 12 miles per hour
D. 26 miles per hour
E. $26\frac{2}{3}$ miles per hour

The stem states that Lester traveled twice as far as Mark in half the time, or 40 miles in 1.5 hours. Therefore, Lester's average speed was $\frac{40 \text{ miles}}{1.5 \text{ hours}} = 26.66\overline{6} = 26\frac{2}{3}$ miles per hour, (E).

Pay Attention to Units

Some items require you to convert units (e.g., feet to inches or hours to minutes). The item stem will tell you what units to use, and if the test-writer senses any possible confusion, the units for the answer choices will be emphasized—underlined or in bold face or capitalized. When you see a word emphasized with any of those signals, circle it and put a star beside it. It is very important.

Example:

A certain copy machine produces 13 copies every 10 seconds. If the machine operates without interruption, how many copies will it produce in an hour?

F. 780
G. 4,200
H. 4,680
J. 4,800
K. 5,160

Create an expression that, after cancellation of like units, gives the number of copies produced in an hour: $\frac{13 \text{ copies}}{10 \text{ seconds}} \bullet \frac{60 \text{ seconds}}{1 \text{ minute}} \bullet \frac{60 \text{ minutes}}{1 \text{ hour}} = 4{,}680 \text{ copies/hour}$. Therefore, the copy machine produces 4,680 copies in an hour, (H).

Pay Attention to Thought-Reversers

A thought-reverser is any word, such as "not," "except," or "but," that turns a question inside out. As shown, below, make sure that you mark the thought-reverser so that it is staring you in the face as you work the problem.

Example:

How many integers in the set of integers from 1 to 144, inclusive, are NOT a square of an integer?

A. 0
B. 2
C. 12
D. 132
E. 144

Since 1 is the square of 1, and 144 is the square of 12, there are a total of 12 integers in the set of integers from 1 to 144, inclusive, that are a square of an integer (1^2, 2^2, 3^2, 4^2, 5^2, 6^2, 7^2, 8^2, 9^2, 10^2, 11^2, 12^2). Therefore, there are a total of $144 - 12 = 132$ integers in the set that are NOT a square of an integer, (D).

Use the Answer Choices

In the Mathematics Lesson, you will learn some very powerful test-taking strategies that use the answers. For now, there are two procedural points to consider.

Eliminate Answer Choices That Cannot be Correct

Sometimes, the array of answers will include choices that, taken at face value, seem to be plausible, but when examined more carefully, must be incorrect.

Example:

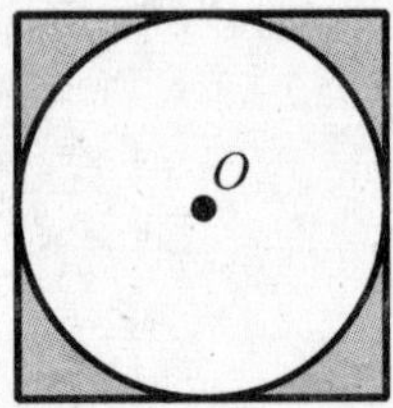

In the figure above, a circle with center O and a radius of 2 is inscribed in a square. What is the area of the shaded portion of the figure?

F. $2-\pi$
G. $4-2\pi$
H. $16-2\pi$
J. $16-4\pi$
K. $16-6\pi$

The shaded area is equal to the area of the square minus the area of the circle. Since the radius of the circle is 2, the side of the square is 4 and its area is $4 \bullet 4 = 16$. The area of the circle is $\pi(2)^2 = 4\pi$. Therefore, the shaded area is $16-4\pi$, (J). Notice that without even solving the item, you can eliminate answer choices. Take a closer look at (F), (G), and (K). Since π is approximately 3.14, (F), (G), and (K) are negative. Area, however, cannot be a negative number, so (F), (G), and (K) must be wrong, and you can eliminate them without doing any other work. Now, if you had to, you can make an educated guess from the remaining choices and the odds of guessing correctly are 50 percent. (Note: Even if you are unable to eliminate answer choices, you still must guess, even if randomly, since the ACT test does not penalize for wrong answers.)

Use the Answer Choices to Check Your Math

While the ACT test does not test "donkey math," some items do require a calculation or two. One of the fundamental rules of math in school is "check your work." On the ACT test, however, this is a real time-suck. Let's say that you do a calculation (with or without your calculator) and the result is \$23.10. If one of the choices is \$23.10, pick it, mark your answer sheet, and move on to the next item. Do NOT check your arithmetic. The possibility that you did the arithmetic, made a mistake, and still got a number like 23.10 is just too remote to consider. On the other hand, if you do not find a choice that matches your calculation, then you'd better check both your set-up of the problem and your arithmetic to find the error. In this way, the answer choices function as a feedback loop on the accuracy of your manipulations.

Don't Go Calculator Crazy

Just because you are allowed to use a calculator on the test does not mean that you should try to solve every problem with your calculator. In fact, for most problems, the calculator is the less efficient method of arriving at a solution. Assume, for example, that you have to do the following arithmetic to get your answer: $\left(\frac{2}{3}\right)\left(\frac{7}{4}\right)\left(\frac{1}{6}\right)$. Since using a calculator would require that you enter decimal equivalents for these fractions, it's going to be easier to do the arithmetic with a pencil than with a calculator: $\left(\frac{2}{3}\right)\left(\frac{7}{4}\right)\left(\frac{1}{6}\right) = \frac{2 \bullet 7 \bullet 1}{3 \bullet 4 \bullet 6} = \frac{14}{72} = \frac{7}{36}$. By all means, use the calculator since it will be a definite advantage, but don't automatically assume that every problem requires its use.

CALCULATOR EXERCISE

This exercise is designed to illustrate when and when not to use your calculator. Make sure that the calculator you bring to the ACT, PLAN, or EXPLORE test is one with which you are thoroughly familiar. (The calculator requirements are the same for the ACT, PLAN, and EXPLORE tests. For more detailed information on calculator usage, including specific models that are prohibited on all three tests, go to http://www.actstudent.org/faq/answers/calculator.html.) Although no item requires the use of a calculator, a calculator may be helpful to answer some items. The calculator may be useful for any item that involves complex arithmetic computations, but it cannot take the place of understanding how to set up a mathematical item. The degree to which you can use your calculator will depend on its features. Answers are on page 633.

DIRECTIONS: Label each of the items that follow according to one of the following categories.

Category 1: A calculator would be very useful (saves valuable test time).
Category 2: A calculator might or might not be useful.
Category 3: A calculator would be counterproductive (wastes valuable test time).

1. What is the average of 8.5, 7.8, and 7.7?

A. 8.3
B. 8.2
C. 8.1
D. 8.0
E. 7.9

2. If $0 < x < 1$, which of the following is the largest?

F. x
G. $2x$
H. x^2
J. x^3
K. $x+1$

3. If 4.5 pounds of chocolate cost $10, how many pounds of chocolate can be purchased for $12?

A. $4\frac{3}{4}$
B. $5\frac{2}{5}$
C. $5\frac{1}{2}$
D. $5\frac{3}{4}$
E. 6

4. What is the value of $\frac{8}{9}-\frac{7}{8}$?

F. $\frac{1}{72}$
G. $\frac{15}{72}$
H. $\frac{1}{7}$
J. $\frac{1}{8}$
K. $\frac{15}{7}$

5. Which of the following fractions is the largest?

A. $\frac{111}{221}$
B. $\frac{75}{151}$
C. $\frac{333}{998}$
D. $\frac{113}{225}$
E. $\frac{101}{301}$

6. Dr. Leo's new office is 2.8 yards by 4 yards. She plans to run a decorative border around the perimeter of the office. How many yards of wallpaper border should she purchase?

F. 8
G. 13.2
H. 13.6
J. 14.2
K. 16.7

7. What is the value of $\frac{2}{3}-\frac{5}{8}$?

A. 1
B. $\frac{15}{16}$
C. $\frac{3}{24}$
D. $\frac{1}{24}$
E. $\frac{1}{100}$

8. If $3x+y=33$ and $x+y=17$, then what is the value of x?

F. 8
G. 12
H. 16
J. 24
K. 33

9. If the perimeter of the rectangle below is 40, what is its area?

15

w

A. 5
B. 15
C. 25
D. 45
E. 75

10. If the price of a book increases from \$10.00 to \$12.50, what is the percent increase in price?

F. 2.5%
G. 12.5%
H. 25%
J. 33%
K. 50%

LESSON

The items in this section accompany the in-class review of the skills and concepts tested by the ACT Mathematics Test. You will work through the items with your instructor in class. Use any available space in this section for scratch work. Answers are on page 633.

DIRECTIONS: Solve each item and choose the correct answer choice. Calculator use is permitted; however, some items are best solved without the use of a calculator.

Note: All of the following should be assumed, unless otherwise stated.

1. Illustrative figures are NOT necessarily drawn to scale.
2. The word *average* indicates arithmetic mean.
3. The word *line* indicates a straight line.
4. Geometric figures lie in a plane.

1. If the price of fertilizer has been decreased from 3 pounds for \$2 to 5 pounds for \$2, how many more pounds of fertilizer can be purchased for \$10 than could have been purchased before?

A. 2
B. 8
C. 10
D. 12
E. 15

2. Five students formed a political club to support a candidate for local office. They project that club membership will double every three weeks. Which of the following can be used to find the number of members that the club projects to have after twelve weeks?

F. $5\left(2^{\frac{2}{3}}\right)$
G. $5\left(2^{\frac{3}{2}}\right)$
H. $5\left(2^{\frac{12}{3}}\right)$
J. $5\left(2^{\frac{3}{12}}\right)$
K. $5+5(2^4)$

3. If $\frac{2x-5}{3}=-4x$, then $x=?$

A. -1
B. $-\frac{5}{14}$
C. 0
D. $\frac{5}{14}$
E. 1

4. A vending machine dispenses k cups of coffee, each at a cost of c cents, every day. During a period d days long, what is the amount of money in dollars taken in by the vending machine from the sale of coffee?

F. $\frac{100kc}{d}$
G. kcd
H. $\frac{dk}{c}$
J. $\frac{kcd}{100}$
K. $\frac{kc}{100d}$

5. If $f(x) = 2x - 3$ and $g(x) = x^2 - 2$, then what does $f(g(2))$ equal?

A. -1
B. 0
C. 1
D. 4
E. 7

6. If $|x + 3| = 5$, then $x = ?$

F. -8 or 2
G. -2 or 8
H. -8
J. -2
K. 2 or 8

7. In the figure below, line m has a slope of 1. What is the y-intercept of the line?

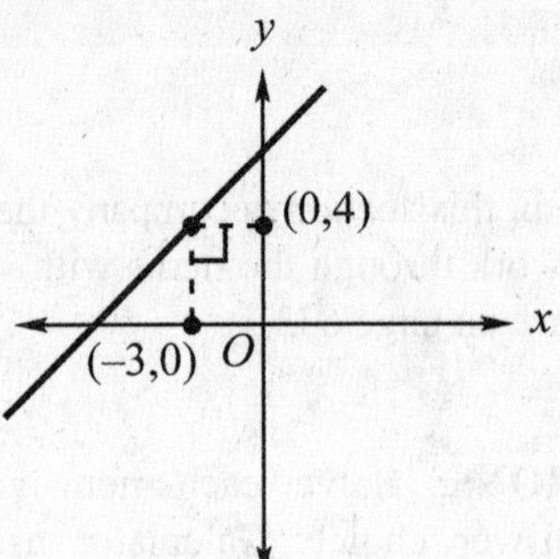

A. –5
B. –3
C. 0
D. 3
E. 7

8. If a circle has a radius of 1, what is its area?

F. $\frac{\pi}{2}$
G. π
H. 2π
J. 4π
K. π^2

9. In the figure below, ΔPQR is inscribed in a circle with center O. What is the area of the circle?

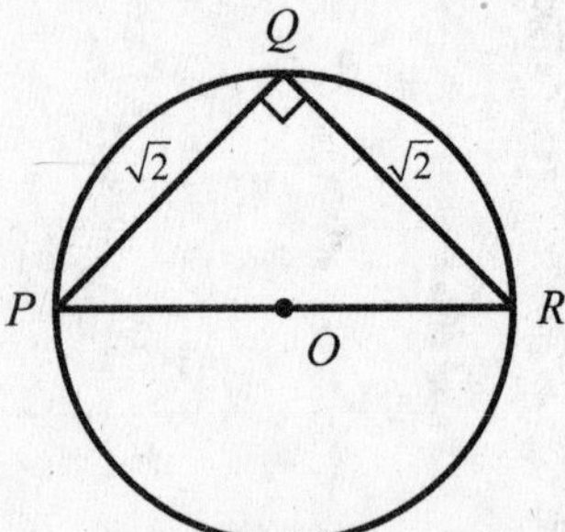

A. $\frac{\pi}{2}$
B. $\frac{\pi}{\sqrt{2}}$
C. π
D. $\pi\sqrt{2}$
E. 2π

10. In the figure below, $\overline{QP}$ is tangent to circle O at point P, and $\overline{QR}$ is tangent to circle O at point R. What is the degree measure of the minor arc PSR?

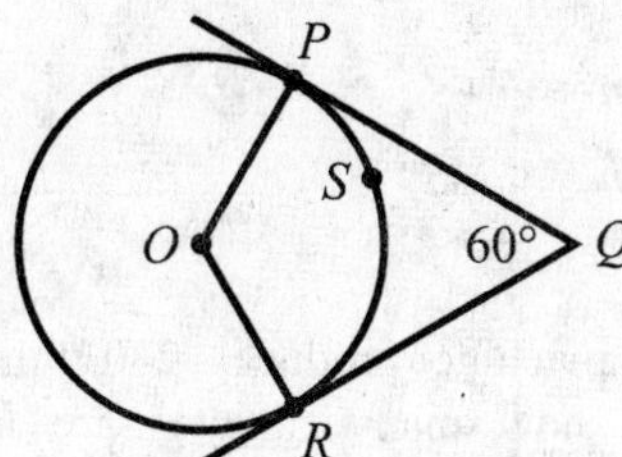

F. 30
G. 60
H. 90
J. 120
K. 180

11. In the figure below, $\sin A = ?$

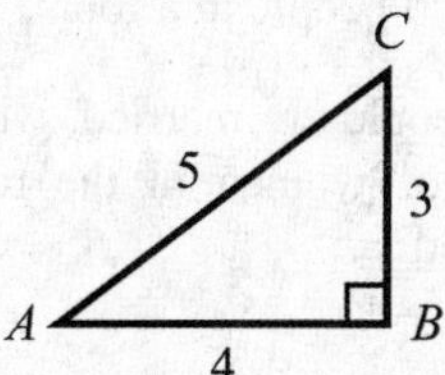

A. $\frac{3}{4}$

B. $\frac{3}{5}$

C. $\frac{4}{5}$

D. $\frac{5}{3}$

E. $\frac{5}{4}$

12. What is the average of 8.5, 7.8, and 7.7?

F. 8.3
G. 8.2
H. 8.1
J. 8.0
K. 7.9

13. In the figure below, $x = ?$

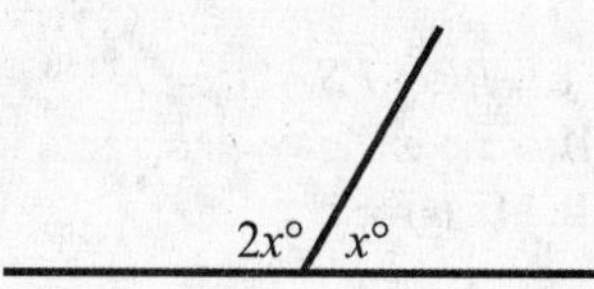

A. 15
B. 30
C. 45
D. 60
E. 120

14. In the figure below, what is the length of $\overline{AB} + \overline{CD}$?

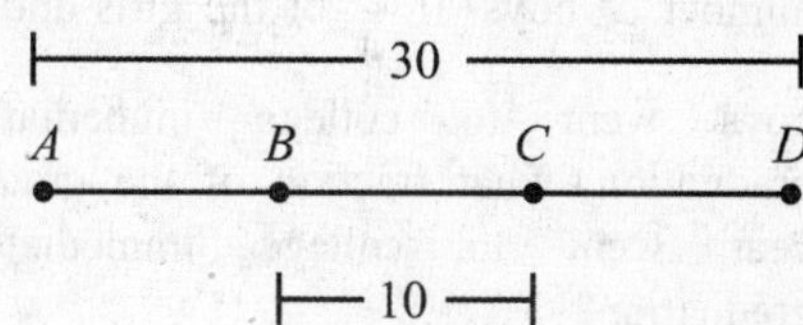

F. 5
G. 10
H. 15
J. 20
K. 40

Items #15–16 refer to the following figure:

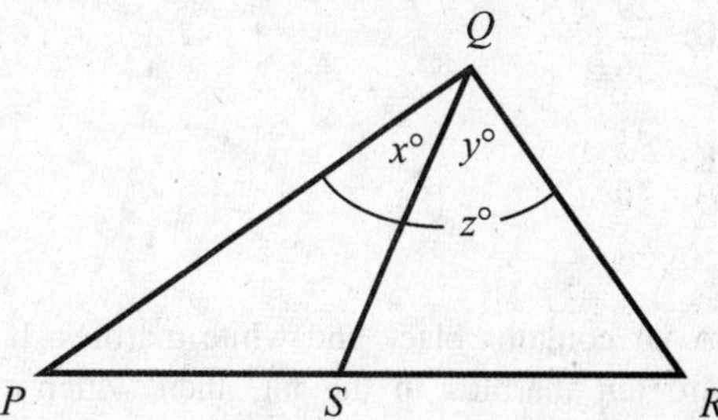

15. Which of the following must be true?

I. $\overline{PS} < \overline{SR}$
II. $z = 90$
III. $x > y$

A. I only
B. I and II only
C. I and III only
D. I, II, and III
E. Neither I, II, nor III

16. Which of the following must be true?

I. $\overline{PR} > \overline{PS}$
II. $z > x$
III. $x + y = z$

F. I only
G. I and II only
H. I and III only
J. I, II, and III
K. Neither I, II, nor III

17. In a certain year, the number of girls who graduated from City High School was twice the number of boys. If $\frac{3}{4}$ of the girls and $\frac{5}{6}$ of the boys went to college immediately after graduation, what fraction of the graduates that year went to college immediately after graduation?

A. $\frac{5}{36}$
B. $\frac{16}{27}$
C. $\frac{7}{9}$
D. $\frac{29}{36}$
E. $\frac{31}{36}$

18. A jar contains black and white marbles. If there are ten marbles in the jar, then which of the following could NOT be the ratio of black to white marbles?

F. 9:1
G. 7:3
H. 1:1
J. 1:4
K. 1:10

19. If n is a negative number, which of the following is the least in value?

A. $-n$
B. $n-n$
C. $n+n$
D. n^2
E. n^4

20. If a machine produces 240 thingamabobs per hour, how many minutes are needed for the machine to produce 30 thingamabobs?

F. 6
G. 7.5
H. 8
J. 12
K. 12.5

21. Of the 120 people in a room, $\frac{3}{5}$ are women. If $\frac{2}{3}$ of the people are married, what is the maximum number of women in the room who could be unmarried?

A. 80
B. 72
C. 48
D. 40
E. 32

22. Three friends are playing a game in which each person simultaneously displays one of three hand signs: a clenched fist, an open palm, or two extended fingers. How many unique combinations of the signs are possible?

F. 3
G. 9
H. 10
J. 12
K. 27

23. If $\frac{1}{3}$ of the number of girls in a school equals $\frac{1}{5}$ of the total number of students, what is the ratio of girls to boys in the school?

A. 5:3
B. 3:2
C. 2:5
D. 1:3
E. 1:5

24. Peter walked from point P to point Q and back again, a total distance of 2 miles. If he averaged 4 miles per hour on the trip from P to Q and 5 miles per hour on the return trip, what was his average walking speed in miles per hour for the entire trip?

F. $2\frac{2}{9}$
G. 4
H. $4\frac{4}{9}$
J. $4\frac{1}{2}$
K. 5

25. After a 20% decrease in price, the cost of an item is D dollars. What was the price of the item before the decrease?

A. 0.75D
B. 0.80D
C. 1.20D
D. 1.25D
E. 1.5D

26. On a certain trip, a motorist drove 10 miles at 30 miles per hour, 10 miles at 40 miles per hour, and 10 miles at 50 miles per hour. What portion of her total driving time was spent driving 50 miles per hour?

F. $1\frac{13}{51}$
G. $\frac{5}{7}$
H. $\frac{5}{12}$
J. $\frac{1}{3}$
K. $\frac{12}{47}$

27. What is the maximum number of non-overlapping sections that can be created when a circle is crossed by three straight lines?

A. 3
B. 4
C. 5
D. 6
E. 7

28. At Glenridge High School, 20% of the students are seniors. If all of the seniors attended the school play, and 60% of all the students attended the play, what percent of the non-seniors attended the play?

F. 20%
G. 40%
H. 50%
J. 60%
K. 100%

29. The water meter at a factory displays the reading below. What is the minimum number of cubic feet of water that the factory must use before four of the five digits on the meter are again the same?

Water Usage in Cubic Feet

A. 10,000
B. 1,000
C. 999
D. 666
E. 9

30. A telephone call from City X to City Y costs \$1.00 for the first three minutes and \$0.25 for each additional minute thereafter. What is the maximum length of time, in minutes, that a caller could talk for \$3.00?

F. 8
G. 10
H. 11
J. 12
K. 13

31. In the figure below, $m+n+o+p+q+r=$?

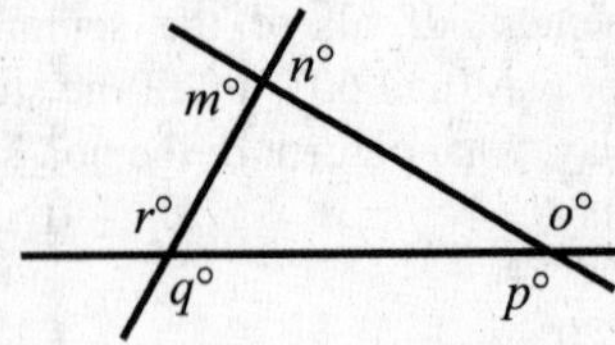

A. 360
B. 540
C. 720
D. 900
E. Cannot be determined from the given information

32. $\frac{8}{9}-\frac{7}{8}=$?

F. $\frac{1}{72}$
G. $\frac{1}{8}$
H. $\frac{1}{7}$
J. $\frac{15}{72}$
K. $\frac{15}{7}$

33. $\sqrt{1-\left(\frac{2}{9}+\frac{1}{36}+\frac{1}{18}\right)}=$?

A. $\frac{1}{5}$
B. $\sqrt{\frac{2}{3}}$
C. $\frac{5}{6}$
D. 1
E. $\sqrt{3}$

34. $\frac{1}{2}\cdot\frac{2}{3}\cdot\frac{3}{4}\cdot\frac{4}{5}\cdot\frac{5}{6}\cdot\frac{6}{7}\cdot\frac{7}{8}=$?

F. $\frac{1}{56}$
G. $\frac{1}{8}$
H. $\frac{28}{37}$
J. $\frac{41}{43}$
K. $\frac{55}{56}$

35. $86(37) - 37(85) = ?$

A. 0
B. 1
C. 37
D. 85
E. 86

36. Which of the following is a prime factorization of 120?

F. (2)(2)(15)
G. (2)(3)(4)(5)
H. (2)(2)(3)(10)
J. (2)(2)(2)(3)(5)
K. (2)(2)(3)(3)(5)

37. $-4.01(3.2) + 0.2(0.4) = ?$

A. −12.752
B. −4.536
C. 0.432
D. 1.251
E. 12.783

38. $\frac{0.2521 \cdot 8.012}{1.014}$ is approximately equal to which of the following?

F. 0.25
G. 0.5
H. 1.0
J. 1.5
K. 2.0

39. Which of the following fractions is the largest?

A. $\frac{111}{221}$
B. $\frac{75}{151}$
C. $\frac{333}{998}$
D. $\frac{113}{225}$
E. $\frac{101}{301}$

40. If $z = \frac{x+y}{x}$, $1 - z = ?$

F. $\frac{1-x+y}{x}$
G. $\frac{x+y-1}{x}$
H. $\frac{1-x-y}{x}$
J. $-\frac{y}{x}$
K. $1-x-y$

41. $0.125 \cdot 0.125 \cdot 64 = ?$

A. 0.625
B. 0.125
C. 0.5
D. 1
E. 8

42. $\frac{0.111 \cdot 0.666}{0.166 \cdot 0.125}$ is approximately equal to which of the following?

F. 6.8
G. 4.3
H. 3.6
J. 1.6
K. 0.9

43. If the senior class has 360 students, of whom $\frac{5}{12}$ are women, and the junior class has 350 students, of whom $\frac{4}{7}$ are women, how many more women are there in the junior class than in the senior class?

A. $(360-350)\left(\frac{4}{7}-\frac{5}{12}\right)$
B. $\frac{(360-350)\left(\frac{4}{7}-\frac{5}{12}\right)}{2}$
C. $\left(\frac{4}{7}\bullet\frac{5}{12}\right)(360-350)$
D. $\left(\frac{4}{7}\bullet 350\right)-\left(\frac{5}{12}\bullet 360\right)$
E. $\left(\frac{5}{12}\bullet 360\right)-\left(\frac{4}{7}\bullet 350\right)$

44. If the price of candy increases from 5 pounds for \$7 to 3 pounds for \$7, how much less candy (in pounds) can be purchased for \$3.50 at the new price than at the old price?

F. $\frac{2}{7}$
G. 1
H. $1\frac{17}{35}$
J. 2
K. $3\frac{34}{35}$

45. If n is any integer, which of the following is always an odd integer?

A. $n-1$
B. $n+1$
C. $n+2$
D. $2n+1$
E. $2n+2$

46. Which of the following expressions represents the product of two consecutive integers?

F. $2n+1$
G. $2n+n$
H. $2n^2$
J. n^2+1
K. n^2+n

47. If n is any integer, which of the following expressions must be even?

I. $2n$
II. $2n+n$
III. $2n\bullet n$

A. I only
B. II only
C. III only
D. I and II only
E. I and III only

48. If n is the first number in a series of three consecutive even numbers, which of the following expressions represents the sum of the three numbers?

F. $n+2$
G. $n+4$
H. $n+6$
J. $3n+6$
K. $6(3n)$

49. If n is an odd number, which of the following expressions represents the third odd number following n?

A. $n+3$
B. $n+4$
C. $n+6$
D. $3n+3$
E. $4n+4$

50. If n is any odd integer, which of the following expressions <u>must</u> also be odd?

I. $n+n$
II. $n+n+n$
III. $n \bullet n \bullet n$

F. I only
G. II only
H. III only
J. II and III only
K. I, II, and III

51. If n is a negative number, which of the following expressions <u>must</u> be positive?

I. $2n$
II. n^2
III. n^5

A. I only
B. II only
C. III only
D. I and II only
E. II and III only

52. If $0 < x < 1$, which of the following expressions is the largest?

F. x
G. $2x$
H. x^2
J. x^3
K. $x+1$

53. If $-1 < x < 0$, which of the following expressions is the largest?

A. -1
B. x
C. $2x$
D. x^3
E. $x-1$

54. If set $S = \{2, 3, 4\}$ and set P is the set of all products of different elements in set S, then set $P = ?$

F. {6, 8, 12}
G. {6, 8, 18}
H. {6, 8, 12, 24}
J. {6, 8, 12, 18, 24}
K. {6, 8, 12, 18, 24, 36}

55. If set X is the set of all integers between 1 and 24, inclusive, that are evenly divisible by 3, and set Y is the set of all integers between 1 and 24, inclusive, that are evenly divisible by 4, what is the set of all elements in both sets X and Y?

A. {12}
B. {3, 4}
C. {12, 24}
D. {4, 12, 24}
E. {3, 4, 12, 24}

56. If x is an element of set X, in which set X is the set of integers evenly divisible by 3 such that $6 < x < 11$, and y is an element of set Y, where set Y is the set of integers evenly divisible by 4 such that $7 < y < 12$, what is the intersection of sets X and Y?

F. {}
G. {8}
H. {9}
J. {12}
K. {8, 12}

57. If set S is the set of all positive odd integers and set T is the set of all positive even integers, then the union of sets S and T (the set of all elements that are in either set or both sets) is the set of:

A. positive integers.
B. integers.
C. even integers.
D. odd integers.
E. real numbers.

58. In a certain school, each of the 72 music students must participate in the marching band, the orchestra, or both. If only music students participate, 48 students total participate in the marching band, and 54 students total participate in the orchestra, how many students participate in both programs?

F. 6
G. 18
H. 24
J. 30
K. 36

59. $|-2|+3-|-4|=?$

A. –5
B. –4
C. –1
D. 1
E. 9

60. $|5|-|-5|+|-3|=?$

F. –8
G. –3
H. 3
J. 8
K. 13

61. $|-3|\bullet|-4|\bullet-5=?$

A. –60
B. –30
C. –7
D. 20
E. 60

62. $(3+i)(4-3i)=?$

F. $12+3i^2$
G. $12-3i^2$
H. $9-5i^2$
J. $9-5i$
K. $15-5i$

63. $\dfrac{1}{2-i}=?$

A. –2
B. –1
C. $\dfrac{2+i}{5}$
D. $\dfrac{2-i}{5}$
E. $\dfrac{2+i}{3}$

64. A jar contains 24 white marbles and 48 black marbles. What percent of the marbles in the jar are black?

F. 10%
G. 25%
H. $33\frac{1}{3}\%$
J. 60%
K. $66\frac{2}{3}\%$

65. A group of 3 friends shared the cost of a tape recorder. If Andy, Barbara, and Donna each paid \$12, \$30, and \$18, respectively, then Donna paid what percent of the cost of the tape recorder?

A. 10%
B. 30%
C. $33\frac{1}{3}\%$
D. 50%
E. $66\frac{2}{3}\%$

66. Twenty students attended Professor Rodriguez's class on Monday and 25 students attended on Tuesday. The number of students who attended on Tuesday was what percent of the number of students who attended on Monday?

F. 5%
G. 20%
H. 25%
J. 80%
K. 125%

67. If the population of a town was 20,000 in 1997 and 16,000 in 2007, what was the percent decline in the town's population?

A. 50%
B. 25%
C. 20%
D. 10%
E. 5%

Items #68–70 refer to the following table:

Capitol City Fires	
Year	*Number of Fires*
2002	100
2003	125
2004	140
2005	150
2006	135

68. The number of fires in 2002 was what percent of the number of fires in 2003?

F. 25%
G. $66\frac{2}{3}\%$
H. 80%
J. 100%
K. 125%

69. The number of fires in 2006 was what percent of the number of fires in 2005?

A. 90%
B. 82%
C. 50%
D. 25%
E. 10%

70. What was the percent decrease in the number of fires from 2005 to 2006?

F. 10%
G. 25%
H. 50%
J. 82%
K. 90%

71. A groom must divide 12 quarts of oats between two horses. If Dobbin is to receive twice as much as Pegasus, how many quarts of oats should the groom give to Dobbin?

A. 4
B. 6
C. 8
D. 9
E. 10

72. If the ratio of John's allowance to Lucy's allowance is $3:2$, and the ratio of Lucy's allowance to Bob's allowance is $3:4$, what is the ratio of John's allowance to Bob's allowance?

F. $1:6$
G. $2:5$
H. $1:2$
J. $3:4$
K. $9:8$

73. If 4.5 pounds of chocolate cost \$10, how many pounds of chocolate can be purchased for \$12?

A. $4\frac{3}{4}$

B. $5\frac{2}{5}$

C. $5\frac{1}{2}$

D. $5\frac{3}{4}$

E. 6

74. At Star Lake Middle School, 45% of the students bought a yearbook. If 540 students bought yearbooks, how many students did <u>not</u> buy a yearbook?

F. 243
G. 540
H. 575
J. 660
K. 957

75. In the equation $y = kx$, k is the constant of variation. If y is equal to 6 when $x = 2.4$, what is the constant of variation?

A. 0.4
B. 2.5
C. 3.4
D. 3.6
E. 14.4

76. A train traveling at a constant speed, *k*, takes 90 minutes to go from point *P* to point *Q*, a distance of 45 miles. What is the value of *k*, in miles per hour?

F. 20
G. 30
H. 45
J. 60
K. 75

77. The cost of picture framing depends on the outer perimeter of the frame. If a 15-inch-by-15-inch picture frame costs \$35 more than a 10-inch-by-10-inch picture frame, what is the cost of framing, in dollars per inch?

A. \$3.50
B. \$2.75
C. \$2.25
D. \$1.75
E. \$1.50

78. Walking at a constant speed of 4 miles per hour, it took Jill exactly 1 hour to walk home from school. If she walked at a constant speed of 5 miles per hour, how many <u>minutes</u> did the trip take?

F. 48
G. 54
H. 56
J. 72
K. 112

79. Ms. Peters drove from her home to the park at an average speed of 30 miles per hour and returned home along the same route at an average speed of 40 miles per hour. If her driving time from home to the park was 20 minutes, how many minutes did it take Ms. Peters to drive from the park to her home?

A. 7.5
B. 12
C. 15
D. 24
E. 30

80. Which of the following is the larger of two numbers the product of which is 600 and the sum of which is five times the difference between the two?

F. 10
G. 15
H. 20
J. 30
K. 50

81. If $\frac{1}{3}$ of a number is 3 more than $\frac{1}{4}$ of the number, then what is the number?

A. 18
B. 24
C. 30
D. 36
E. 48

82. If $\frac{3}{5}$ of a number is 4 more than $\frac{1}{2}$ of the number, then what is the number?

F. 20
G. 28
H. 35
J. 40
K. 56

83. If both 16 and 9 are divided by *n*, the remainder is 2. What is *n*?

A. 3
B. 4
C. 5
D. 6
E. 7

84. The sum of the digits of a three-digit number is 16. If the tens digit of the number is 3 times the units digit, and the units digit is $\frac{1}{4}$ of the hundreds digit, then what is the number?

F. 446
G. 561
H. 682
J. 862
K. 914

85. If the sum of five consecutive integers is 40, what is the smallest of the five integers?

A. 4
B. 5
C. 6
D. 7
E. 8

86. If $a^3 + b = 3 + a^3$, then $b = ?$

F. 3^3
G. $3\sqrt{3}$
H. 3
J. $\sqrt[3]{3}$
K. $-\sqrt{3}$

87. Which of the following expressions is equivalent to $4a + 3b - (-2a - 3b)$?

A. $2a$
B. $12ab$
C. $2a + 6b$
D. $6a + 6b$
E. $8a + 9b$

88. If $x = 2$, what is the value of $x^2 + 2x - 2$?

F. −2
G. 0
H. 2
J. 4
K. 6

89. If $x = 2$, then $\frac{1}{x^2} + \frac{1}{x} - \frac{x}{2} = ?$

A. $-\frac{3}{4}$
B. $-\frac{1}{4}$
C. 0
D. $\frac{1}{4}$
E. $\frac{1}{2}$

90. If $\frac{1}{3}x = 10$, then $\frac{1}{6}x = ?$

F. $\frac{1}{15}$
G. $\frac{2}{3}$
H. 2
J. 5
K. 30

91. If $p = 1$, $q = 2$, and $r = 3$, what is the value of $\frac{(q \cdot r)(r - q)}{(q - p)(p \cdot q)}$?

A. −3
B. −1
C. 0
D. 3
E. 6

92. $\frac{9(x^2y^3)^6}{(3x^6y^9)^2} = ?$

F. 1
G. 3
H. x^2y^3
J. $3x^2y^3$
K. $x^{12}y^{12}$

93. $2\left(4^{-\frac{1}{2}}\right) - 2^0 + 2^{\frac{3}{2}} + 2^{-2} = ?$

A. $-2\sqrt{2} - \frac{1}{4}$
B. $2\sqrt{2} - \frac{1}{4}$
C. $2\sqrt{2}$
D. $2\sqrt{2} + \frac{1}{4}$
E. $2\sqrt{2} + \frac{5}{4}$

94. Which of the following expressions is equivalent to $\frac{x^2 - y^2}{x + y}$?

F. $x^2 - y^2$
G. $x^2 + y^2$
H. $x^2 + y$
J. $x + y^2$
K. $x - y$

95. Which of the following expressions is equivalent to $\frac{x^2 - x - 6}{x + 2}$?

A. $x^2 - \frac{x}{2} - 3$
B. $x^2 - 2$
C. $x - 2$
D. $x - 3$
E. x

96. Which of the following is the factorization of $6x^2 + 4x - 2$?

F. $(6x + 1)(x - 3)$
G. $(6x + 3)(x - 1)$
H. $(3x - 1)(2x - 2)$
J. $(2x + 2)(3x - 1)$
K. $(2x + 4)(3x - 2)$

97. In a certain game, a player picks an integer between 1 and 10, adds 3 to it, multiplies the sum by 2, and subtracts 5. If x is the number picked by a player, which of the following correctly expresses the final result of the game?

A. $x + (3)(2) - 5$
B. $3x + 2 - 5$
C. $2(x + 3 - 5)$
D. $2(x + 3) - 5$
E. $(2)(3)(x) - 5$

98. At 9:00 a.m., when the heat is turned on, the temperature of a room is 55°F. If the room temperature increases by n°F each hour, which of the following can be used to determine the number of hours needed to bring the temperature of the room to 70°F?

F. $(55+70)(n)$
G. $(55-70)(n)$
H. $\frac{(70-55)}{n}$
J. $\frac{n}{(70-55)}$
K. $\frac{n}{(55+70)}$

99. In a geometric sequence of positive numbers, the fourth term is 125 and the sixth term is 3,125. What is the second term of the sequence?

A. 1
B. 5
C. 10
D. 25
E. 50

100. City University projects that a planned expansion will increase the number of enrolled students every year for the next five years by 50%. If 400 students enroll in the first year of the plan, how many students are expected to enroll in the fifth year of the plan?

F. 200
G. 600
H. 675
J. 1,350
K. 2,025

101. Jimmy's uncle deposited $1,000 into a college fund account and promised that at the start of each year, he would deposit an amount equal to 10% of the account balance. If no other deposits or withdrawals were made and no additional interest accrued, what was the account balance after three additional annual deposits were made by Jimmy's uncle?

A. $1,030
B. $1,300
C. $1,331
D. $1,500
E. $1,830

102. A tank with a capacity of 2,400 liters is filled with water. If a valve is opened that drains 25% of the contents of the tank every minute, what is the volume of water (in liters) that remains in the tank after 3 minutes?

F. 1,800
G. 1,350
H. 1,012.5
J. 600
K. 325.75

103. If $(2+3)(1+x)=25$, then $x=?$

A. $\frac{1}{5}$
B. $\frac{1}{4}$
C. 1
D. 4
E. 5

104. If $2x+3>9$, which of the following can be the value of x?

F. –4
G. –3
H. 0
J. 3
K. 4

105. If $\frac{12}{x+1} - 1 = 2$, and $x \neq -1$, then $x = ?$

A. 1
B. 2
C. 3
D. 11
E. 12

106. If $\frac{x}{x+2} = \frac{3}{4}$, and $x \neq -2$, then $x = ?$

F. 6
G. 4
H. 3
J. 2
K. 1

107. If $\frac{x}{x-2} - \frac{x+2}{2(x-2)} = 8$, and $x \neq 2$, which of the following is the complete solution set for *x*?

A. {}
B. {–2}
C. {2}
D. {4}
E. {8}

108. If $\frac{3}{x-2} > \frac{1}{6}$, which of the following defines the possible values for *x*?

F. $x < 20$
G. $x > 0$
H. $x > 2$
J. $0 < x < 20$
K. $2 < x < 20$

109. If $\sqrt{2x+1} - 1 = 4$, then $x = ?$

A. –5
B. –1
C. 1
D. 12
E. 24

110. Which of the following is the complete solution set for $\sqrt{3x-2} - 3 = -4$?

F. {}
G. {–1}
H. {1}
J. {–1, 1}
K. {1, 2}

111. If $\sqrt{2x-5} = 2\sqrt{5-2x}$, then $x = ?$

A. 1
B. 2
C. $\frac{5}{2}$
D. 10
E. 15

112. Which of the following is the complete solution set for $\sqrt{x^2 + 9} = 5$?

F. {–4, 4}
G. {–4}
H. {0}
J. {4}
K. {}

113. If $4^{x+2} = 64$, then $x = ?$

A. 1
B. 2
C. 3
D. 4
E. 5

114. If $8^x = 2^{x+3}$, then $x = ?$

F. 0
G. 1
H. $\frac{2}{3}$
J. 3
K. $\frac{3}{2}$

115. If $3^{2x} = \frac{1}{81}$, then $x = ?$

A. -2
B. $-\frac{3}{2}$
C. $-\frac{2}{3}$
D. $\frac{2}{3}$
E. $\frac{3}{2}$

116. If $5^3 = \left(\sqrt{5}\right)^{-2x}$, then $5^x = ?$

F. $\frac{1}{125}$
G. $\frac{1}{25}$
H. $\frac{1}{5}$
J. 5
K. 25

117. Which of the following is the complete solution set for $\left|\frac{2x+1}{3}\right| = 5$?

A. $\{-8, -7\}$
B. $\{-8, 7\}$
C. $\{-7, 8\}$
D. $\{7\}$
E. $\{8\}$

118. Which of the following is the complete solution set for $|x+6| = 3x$?

F. $\left\{-3, \frac{3}{2}\right\}$
G. $\left\{-\frac{3}{2}, 3\right\}$
H. $\left\{\frac{3}{2}, 3\right\}$
J. $\{3\}$
K. $\{\}$

119. Which of the following is the complete solution set for $|2x-1| > 3$?

A. All real numbers
B. The null set
C. All real numbers less than -1 or greater than 2
D. All real numbers less than -2 or greater than 1
E. All real numbers less than -3

120. If $|3x-6| > 9$, then which of the following must be true?

F. $-3 < x < 2$
G. $-2 < x < 3$
H. $x < -3$ or $x > 2$
J. $x < -1$ or $x > 5$
K. $x < -1$ or $x > 9$

121. Which of the following identifies exactly those values of x that satisfy $|-2x+4| < 4$?

A. $x > -4$
B. $x < 4$
C. $x > 0$
D. $0 < x < 4$
E. $-4 < x < 0$

122. If $f(x) = x^2 + x$, what is the value of $f(-2)$?

F. -8
G. -2
H. 2
J. 8
K. 12

123. If $y = f(x) = \left(\frac{6x^2 - 2^{-x}}{|x|}\right)^{-\frac{1}{2}}$ for all integers and $x = -1$, what is the value of y?

A. 2
B. $\frac{1}{2}$
C. $\frac{1}{4}$
D. $-\frac{1}{2}$
E. -2

124. If $f(x) = x + 3$ and $g(x) = 2x - 5$, what is the value of $f(g(2))$?

F. -2
G. 0
H. 2
J. 4
K. 10

125. If $f(x) = 3x + 2$ and $g(x) = x^2 + x$, what is the value of $g(f(-2))$?

A. 15
B. 12
C. 6
D. 3
E. -2

126. If $f(x) = 2x^2 + x$ and $g(x) = f(f(x))$, what is the value of $g(1)$?

F. 3
G. 18
H. 21
J. 39
K. 55

127. If $f(x) = 3x + 4$ and $g(x) = 2x - 1$, for what value of x does $f(x) = g(x)$?

A. -5
B. -2
C. 0
D. 3
E. 7

128. If $\boxed{x} = x^2 - x$ for all integers, then $\boxed{-2} = ?$

F. -6
G. -2
H. 0
J. 4
K. 6

129. If $\boxed{x} = x^2 - x$ for all integers, then $\boxed{\boxed{3}} = ?$

A. 27
B. 30
C. 58
D. 72
E. 121

130. If $f(x) = 3x - 2$ and $-5 < x < 5$, which of the following defines the range of $f(x)$?

F. $-17 < f(x) < 13$
G. $-13 < f(x) < 17$
H. $-5 < f(x) < 12$
J. $0 < f(x) < 17$
K. $3 < f(x) < 13$

131. If $f(x)=\frac{x+2}{x-1}$, for which of the following values of x is $f(x)$ undefined?

A. -2
B. -1
C. $\frac{1}{2}$
D. 1
E. 2

132. If $f(x)=\frac{2-2x}{x}$, which of the following defines the range of $f(x)$?

F. All real numbers
G. All real numbers except -2
H. All real numbers except 0
J. All real numbers except 2
K. All real numbers greater than 2

133. If $|4x-8|<12$, which of the following defines the possible values of x?

A. $-8<x<-4$
B. $-4<x<8$
C. $-1<x<5$
D. $1<x<5$
E. $4<x<8$

134. The cost of making a call using a phone-card is \$0.15 for dialing and \$0.04 per minute of connection time. Which of the following equations could be used to find the cost, y, of a call x minutes long?

F. $y=x(0.04+0.15)$
G. $y=0.04x+0.15$
H. $y=0.04+0.15x$
J. $y=0.15-0.04x$
K. $y=0.04-0.15x$

135. If $x+y=3$, then $2x+2y=?$

A. $-\frac{2}{3}$
B. $\frac{1}{2}$
C. $\frac{2}{3}$
D. 6
E. Cannot be determined from the given information

136. If $2x+y=8$ and $x-y=1$, then $x=?$

F. -2
G. -1
H. 0
J. 1
K. 3

137. If $7x=2$ and $3y-7x=10$, then $y=?$

A. 2
B. 3
C. 4
D. 5
E. 6

138. If $2x+y=8$ and $x-y=1$, what is the value of $x+y$?

F. -1
G. 1
H. 2
J. 3
K. 5

139. If $4x+5y=12$ and $3x+4y=5$, what is the value of $7(x+y)$?

A. 7
B. 14
C. 49
D. 77
E. 91

140. Which of the equations that follow correctly describes the relationship between the values shown for x and y in the table below?

x	-2	-1	0	1	2
y	$\frac{10}{3}$	$\frac{8}{3}$	2	$\frac{4}{3}$	$\frac{2}{3}$

F. $3x+2y=6$
G. $3x-2y=3$
H. $3x+3y=-6$
J. $6x+4y=7$
K. $2x+3y=6$

141. Which of the following is the solution set for $2x^2-2x=12$?

A. $\{-3, -2\}$
B. $\{-2, 3\}$
C. $\left\{\frac{2}{3}, 3\right\}$
D. $\left\{\frac{3}{2}, 2\right\}$
E. $\{2, 3\}$

142. If $x^2-3x=4$, then which of the following shows all possible values of x?

F. $\{4, 1\}$
G. $\{4, -1\}$
H. $\{-4, 1\}$
J. $\{-4, -1\}$
K. $\{-4, 1, 4\}$

143. If $x^2-y^2=0$ and $x+y=1$, then $x-y=$?

A. -1
B. 0
C. 1
D. 2
E. 4

144. Which of the following is the solution set for $3x^2+3x=6$?

F. $\{1, -2\}$
G. $\{1, 2\}$
H. $\left\{\frac{1}{2}, 1\right\}$
J. $\left\{\frac{1}{2}, \frac{1}{3}\right\}$
K. $\{-1, -2\}$

145. Which of the following is the solution set for $2x^2-3x=2$?

A. $\left\{\frac{1}{2}, 2\right\}$
B. $\left\{-\frac{1}{2}, 2\right\}$
C. $\left\{-\frac{1}{2}, -2\right\}$
D. $\{2, -2\}$
E. $\{2, 4\}$

146. Diana spent $\frac{1}{2}$ of her weekly allowance on a new book and another \$3 on lunch. If she still had $\frac{1}{6}$ of her original allowance left, how much is Diana's allowance?

F. \$24
G. \$18
H. \$15
J. \$12
K. \$9

147. In a certain game, a player had five successful turns in a row, and after each one, the number of points added to his total score was double what was added the preceding turn. If the player scored a total of 465 points, how many points did he score on the first play?

A. 15
B. 31
C. 93
D. 155
E. 270

148. At a certain firm, d gallons of fuel are needed per day for each truck. At this rate, g gallons of fuel will supply t trucks for how many days?

F. $\frac{dt}{g}$
G. $\frac{gt}{d}$
H. dgt
J. $\frac{t}{dg}$
K. $\frac{g}{dt}$

149. Y years ago, Paul was twice as old as Bob. If Bob is now 18 years old, how old is Paul today in terms of Y?

A. $36+Y$
B. $18+Y$
C. $18-Y$
D. $36-Y$
E. $36-2Y$

150. After filling the car's fuel tank, a driver drove from point P to point Q and then to point R. She used $\frac{2}{5}$ of the fuel driving from P to Q. If she used another 7 gallons to drive from Q to R and still had $\frac{1}{4}$ of a tank left, how many gallons does the tank hold?

F. 12
G. 18
H. 20
J. 21
K. 35

151. If pencils cost x cents each, how many pencils can be purchased for y dollars?

A. $\frac{100}{xy}$
B. $\frac{xy}{100}$
C. $\frac{100y}{x}$
D. $\frac{y}{100x}$
E. $100xy$

152. A merchant increased the original price of an item by 10%. If she then reduces the new price by 10%, the final price, in terms of the original price, is equal to which of the following?

F. a decrease of 11%
G. a decrease of 1%
H. no net change
J. an increase of 1%
K. an increase of 11%

153. Harold is twice as old as Jack, who is three years older than Dan. If Harold's age is five times Dan's age, how old (in years) is Jack?

A. 2
B. 4
C. 5
D. 8
E. 10

154. A tank with capacity T gallons is empty. If water flows into the tank from pipe X at the rate of X gallons per minute, and water is pumped out by pipe Y at the rate of Y gallons per minute, and X is greater than Y, in how many minutes will the tank be filled?

F. $\frac{T}{Y-X}$

G. $\frac{T}{X-Y}$

H. $\frac{T-X}{Y}$

J. $\frac{X-Y}{60T}$

K. $\frac{60T}{XY}$

155. Machine X produces w widgets in five minutes. Machine X and Machine Y, working at the same time, produce w widgets in two minutes. How long will it take Machine Y working alone to produce w widgets?

A. 2 minutes, 30 seconds
B. 2 minutes, 40 seconds
C. 3 minutes, 20 seconds
D. 3 minutes, 30 seconds
E. 3 minutes, 40 seconds

156. If a train travels m miles in h hours and 45 minutes, what is its average speed in miles per hour?

F. $\frac{m}{h+\frac{3}{4}}$

G. $\frac{m}{1\frac{3}{4}h}$

H. $m\left(h+\frac{3}{4}\right)$

J. $\frac{m+45}{h}$

K. $\frac{h}{m+45}$

157. On a playground, there are x seesaws. If 50 children are all riding on seesaws, two to a seesaw, and five seesaws are <u>not</u> in use, what is the value of x?

A. 15
B. 20
C. 25
D. 30
E. 35

158. In the figure below, what is the length of $\overline{PQ}$?

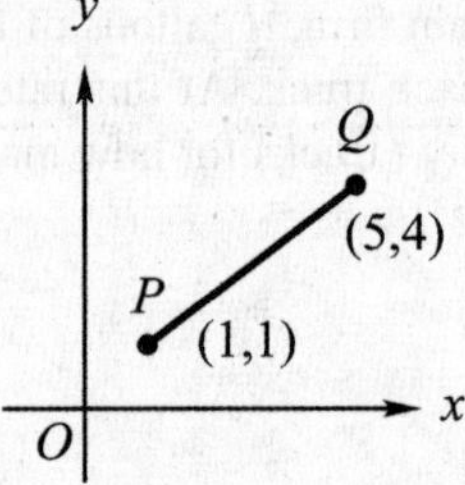

F. $\sqrt{2}$
G. $\sqrt{3}$
H. 3
J. 4
K. 5

159. In the figure below, the line segment joining points (3,3) and (7,3) forms one side of a square. Which of the following CANNOT be the coordinates of another vertex of the square?

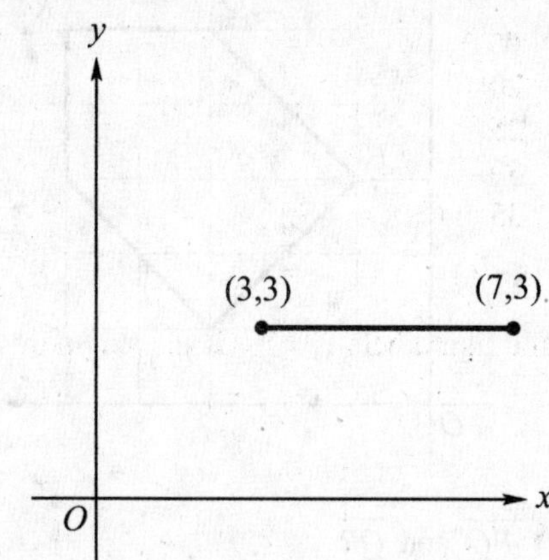

A. (3,–1)
B. (3,7)
C. (7,–3)
D. (7,–1)
E. (7,7)

160. Which of the following is a graph of the line that passes through the points (–5,3), (–1,1), and (3,–1)?

F. J.

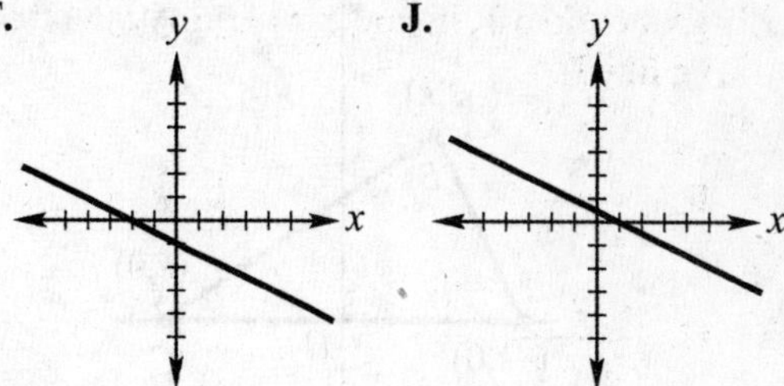

G. K.

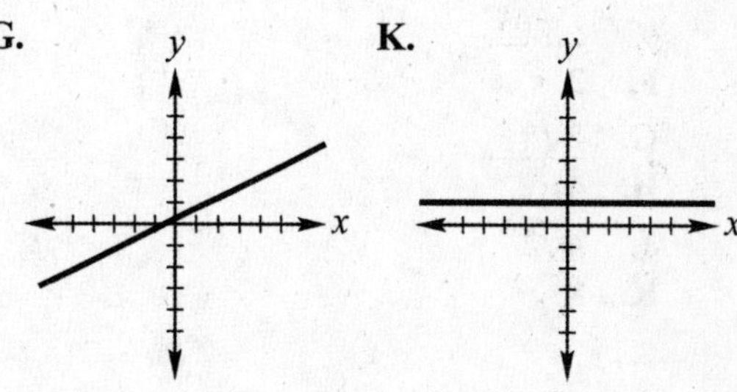

H.

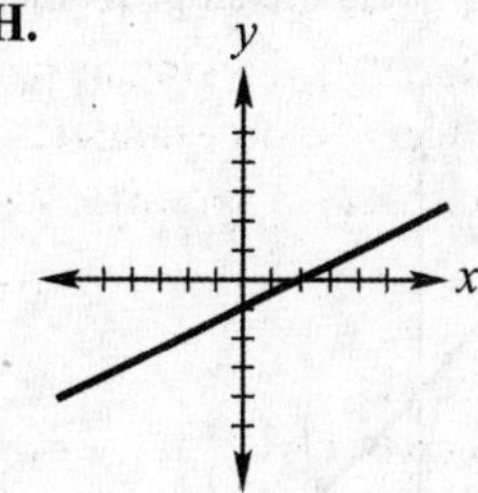

161. In the figure below, what are the coordinates, (x,y), of the point on the semicircle that is farthest from the y-axis?

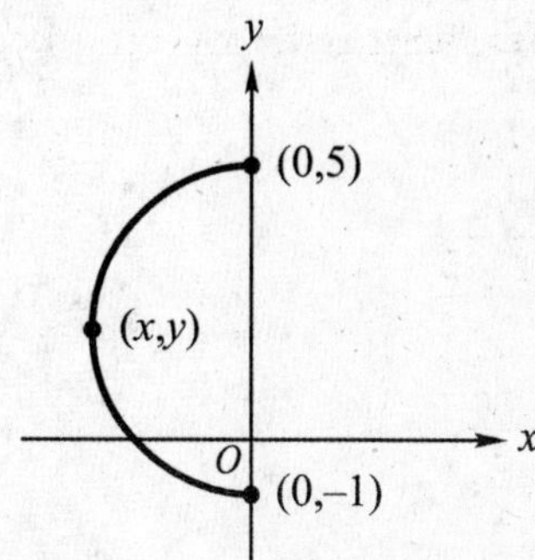

A. (–4,–4)
B. (–3,–3)
C. (–2,–3)
D. (–3,2)
E. (3,2)

162. In the figure below, the area of ΔABC is 8. What is the value of k?

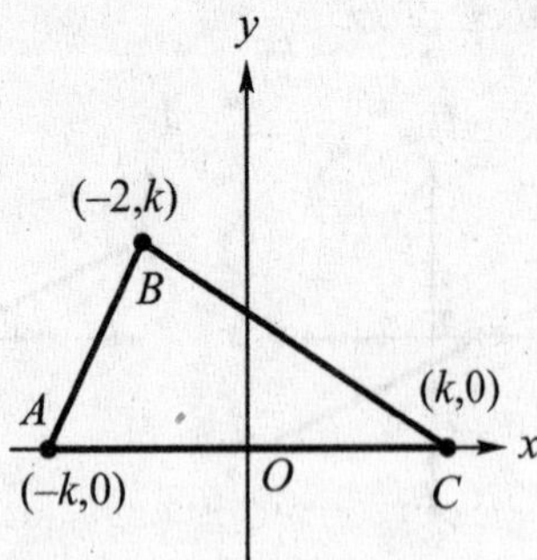

F. 2
G. $2\sqrt{2}$
H. 4
J. $4\sqrt{2}$
K. 8

163. In the figure below, what is the slope of the line?

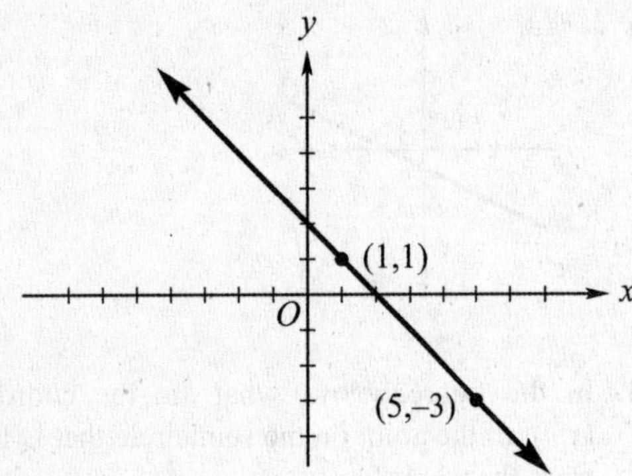

A. –3
B. –2
C. –1
D. 1
E. 2

164. In the figure below, which two sides of polygon $PQRST$ have the same slope?

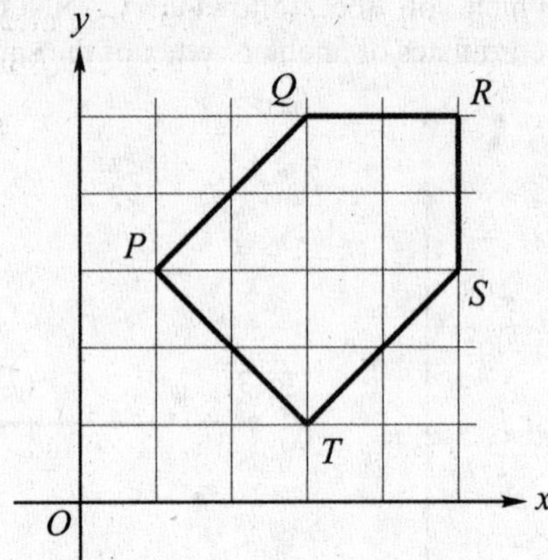

F. $\overline{PQ}$ and $\overline{QR}$
G. $\overline{PQ}$ and $\overline{RS}$
H. $\overline{PQ}$ and $\overline{ST}$
J. $\overline{QR}$ and $\overline{RS}$
K. $\overline{RS}$ and $\overline{ST}$

165. Line l is the graph of the equation $y = \frac{3x}{2} + 2$. The graph of which of the following equations is perpendicular to line l at (0,2)?

A. $y = \frac{3x}{2} - 2$
B. $y = \frac{2x}{3} - 2$
C. $y = -\frac{2x}{3} + 2$
D. $y = -\frac{3x}{2} + 3$
E. $y = -3x + 4$

166. If set $A = \{(-2,3), (-1,1), (-4,-5)\}$, and set $B = \{(3,4), (4,3), (2,-1)\}$, how many lines can be drawn with a positive slope that include exactly one point from set A and one point from set B?

F. 2
G. 3
H. 4
J. 5
K. 6

167. A line includes the points $(2,3)$ and $(3,6)$. What is the equation of the line?

A. $y = 2x - 3$
B. $y = 3x - 3$
C. $y = \frac{3x-3}{2}$
D. $y = 3x + 3$
E. $y = x - 3$

168. Which of the following is the equation for the line with slope of 2 that includes point (0,2)?

F. $y = x - 1$
G. $y = 2x - 1$
H. $y = 2x - 2$
J. $y = 2x + 2$
K. $y = x + 1$

169. Which of the following is the equation for the line that includes points $(-1,1)$ and $(7,5)$?

A. $y = \frac{x}{2} + 2$
B. $y = \frac{x}{2} + \frac{3}{2}$
C. $y = \frac{x}{2} + \frac{2}{3}$
D. $y = 2x + \frac{3}{2}$
E. $y = 2x + 2$

170. If the graph of a line in the coordinate plane includes the points $(2,4)$ and $(8,7)$, what is the y-intercept of the line?

F. 6
G. 4
H. 3
J. –1
K. -3

171. If the slope and y-intercept of a line are -2 and 3, respectively, then the line passes through which of the following points?

A. $(-5,-10)$
B. $(-5,10)$
C. $(-2,3)$
D. $(3,4)$
E. $(4,-5)$

172. What is the distance between the points $(-3,-2)$ and $(3,3)$?

F. $\sqrt{3}$
G. $2\sqrt{3}$
H. 5
J. $\sqrt{29}$
K. $\sqrt{61}$

173. In the coordinate plane below, $\overline{MO} \cong \overline{MN}$ and $\overline{MO} \perp \overline{MN}$. What is the value of y?

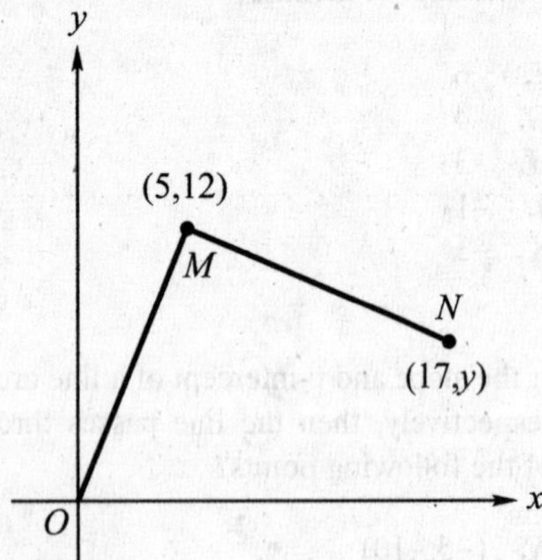

A. 5
B. 7
C. 12
D. 13
E. 17

174. In the figure below, what is the area of the square region?

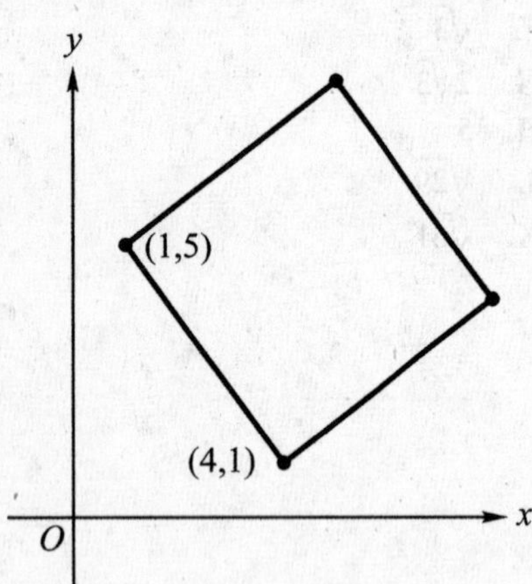

F. 4
G. 8
H. $8\sqrt{2}$
J. 16
K. 25

175. In the coordinate plane, what is the midpoint of the line segment with endpoints $(-3,-5)$ and $(5,7)$?

A. $(1,1)$
B. $(1,6)$
C. $\left(3,\frac{7}{2}\right)$
D. $(4,6)$
E. $(8,12)$

176. The figure below is the graph of which of the following equations?

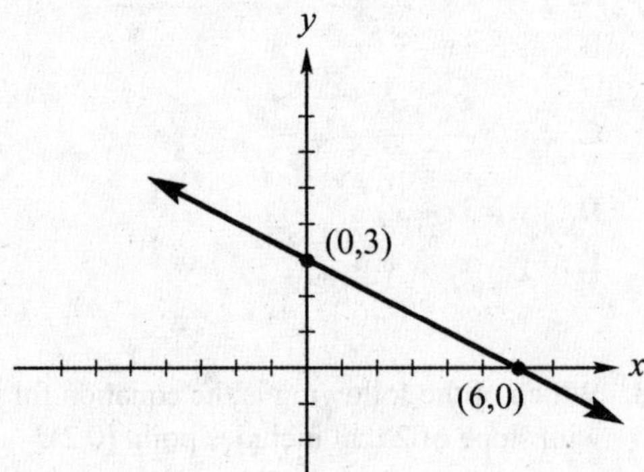

F. $x+2y=6$
G. $2x+y=6$
H. $x+\frac{y}{2}=6$
J. $\frac{x}{2}+y=2$
K. $x-3y=2$

177. A school rented a hotel ballroom for a dance. The cost of the rental is \$1,500 plus \$5.00 per person who attends. Each person who attends will pay an admission charge of \$12.50. If x represents the number of people who attend, which of the graphs can be used to determine how many people must attend for the admission charges to cover exactly the cost of renting the ballroom?

A.

y; Rental Cost (Dollars): 500, 1000, 1,500, 2,000, 2,500; (0,1500); (200,2500); (0,0); x: 50 100 150 200 250; Number of Attendees

B.

y; Rental Cost (Dollars): 500, 1000, 1,500, 2,000, 2,500; (0,1500); (200,2500); (200,500); (0,0); x: 50 100 150 200 250; Number of Attendees

C.

y; Rental Cost (Dollars): 500, 1000, 1,500, 2,000, 2,500; (0,1500); (200,2500); (0,1000); (200,500); x: 50 100 150 200 250; Number of Attendees

D.

y; Rental Cost (Dollars): 500, 1000, 1,500, 2,000, 2,500; (200,2500); (200,1500); (0,0); x: 50 100 150 200 250; Number of Attendees

E.

y; Rental Cost (Dollars): 500, 1000, 1,500, 2,000, 2,500; (0,1500); (200,2500); (0,500); x: 50 100 150 200 250; Number of Attendees

178. Which of the following is the graph of the inequality $y \geq 2x$?

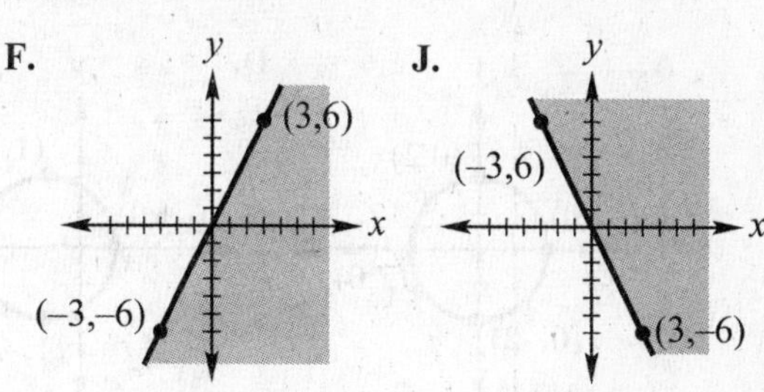

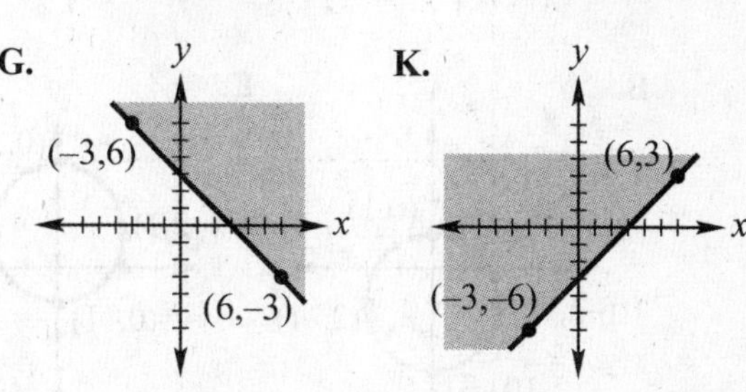

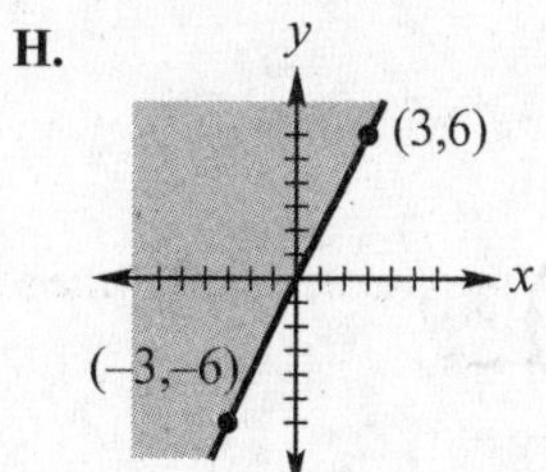

179. Which of the following is the graph of the equation $(x-1)^2 + y^2 = 4$?

A.

D.

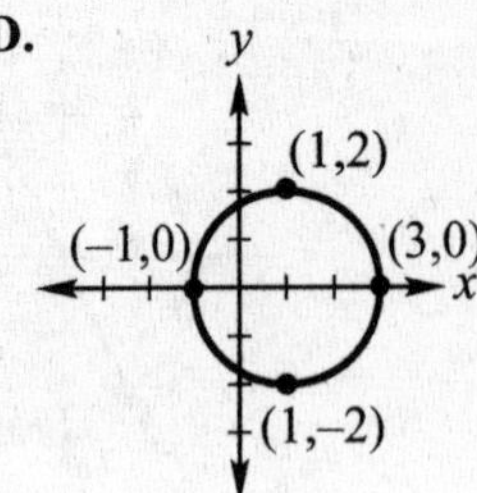

B. **E.**

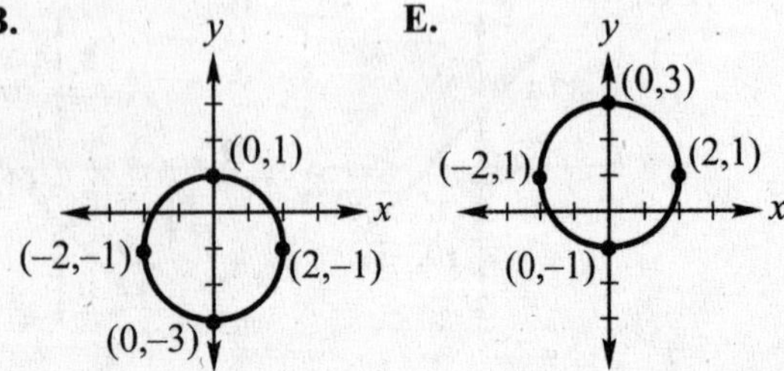

C.

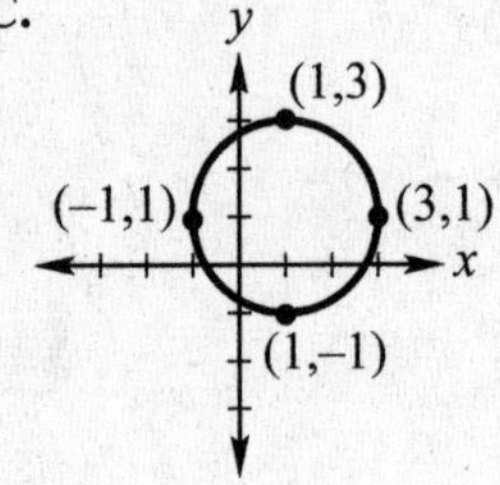

180. Which of the following is the graph of the equation $\frac{x^2}{9} + \frac{y^2}{16} = 1$?

F. **J.**

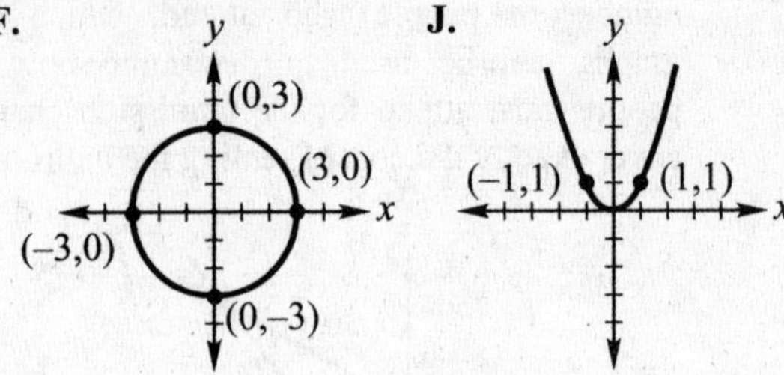

G. **K.**

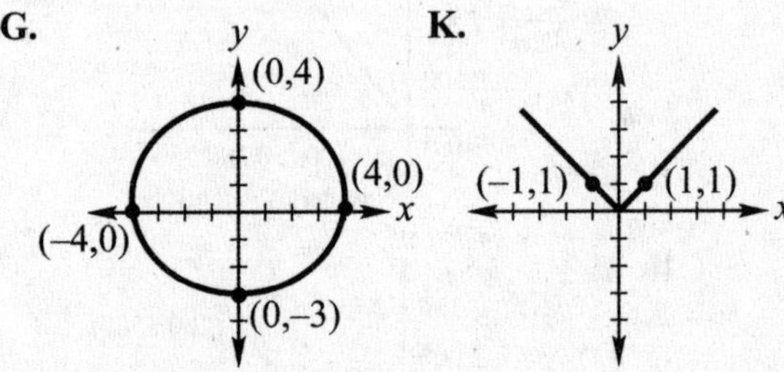

H.

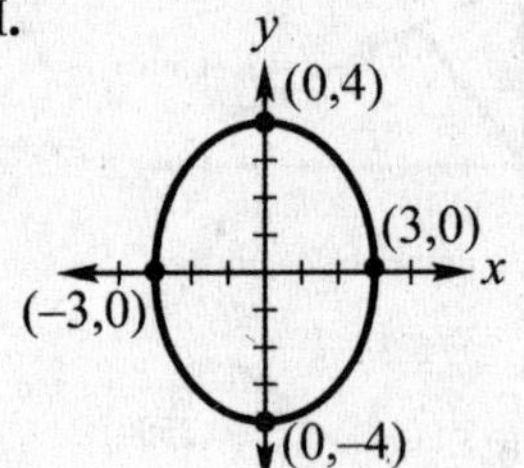

181. The figure below shows the graph of a function $g(x)$. How many times does the graph cross the x-axis?

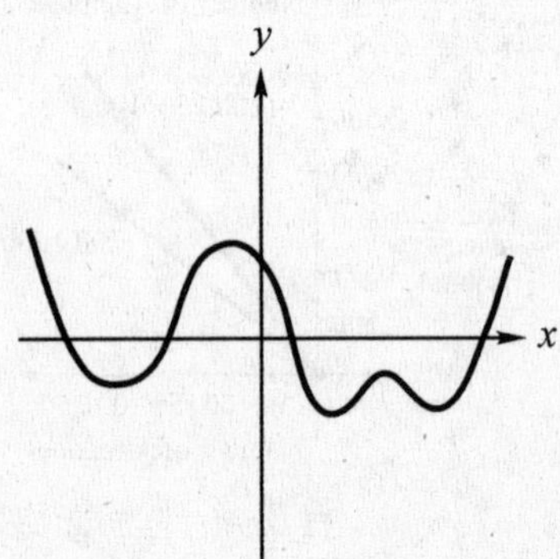

A. 1
B. 2
C. 3
D. 4
E. 5

182. The figure below shows the graph of $f(x)$ in the coordinate plane. For the portion of the graph shown, for how many values of x is $f(x) = 3$?

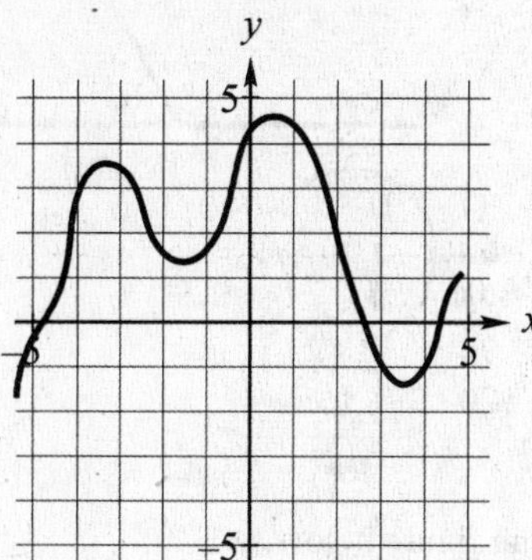

F. 0
G. 1
H. 2
J. 3
K. 4

183. The figure below represents the graph of $y = f(x)$ in the coordinate plane. Which of the graphs that follow is the graph of $y' = f(x-1)$?

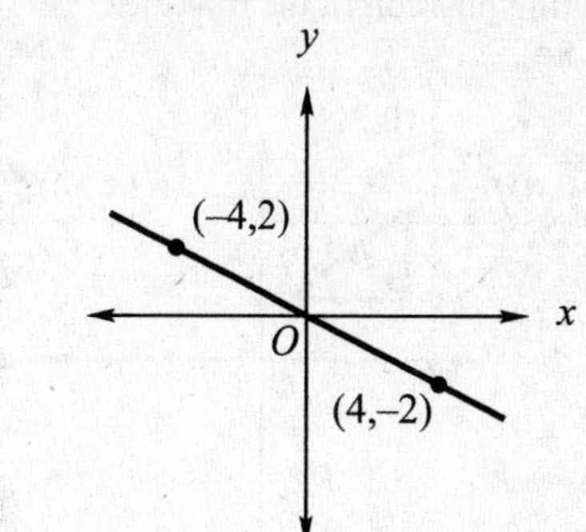

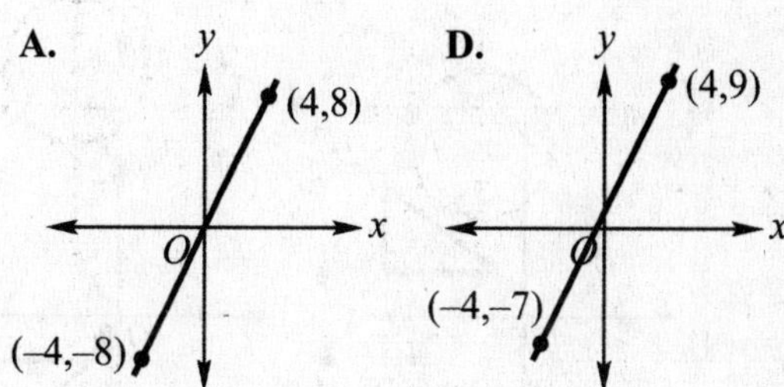

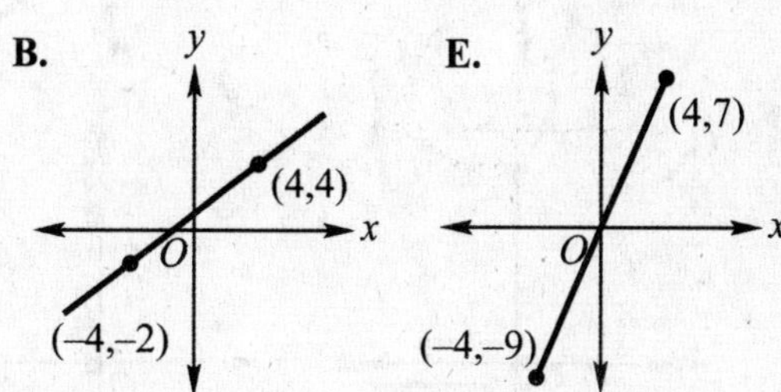

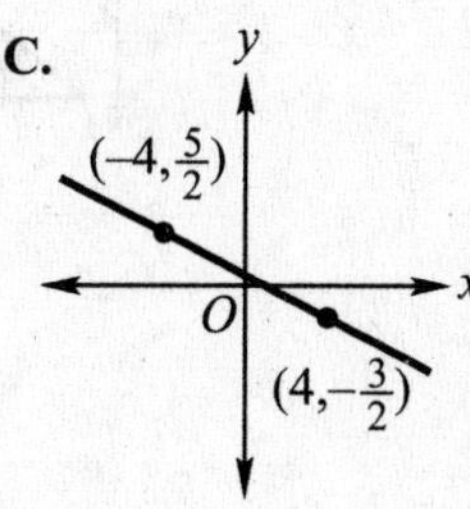

184. If the triangle in the figure below is reflected across the y-axis and then reflected across the x-axis, which of the graphs that follow shows the resulting position of the triangle?

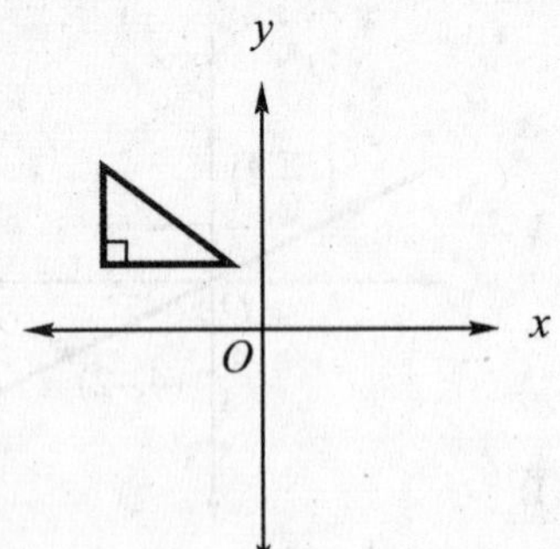

F.

J.

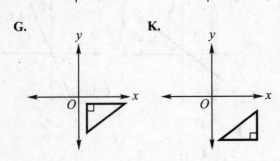

G.

K.

H.

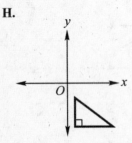

185. In the figure below, $x = ?$

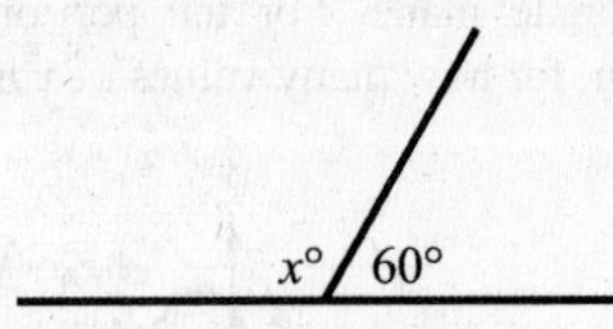

A. 45
B. 60
C. 75
D. 90
E. 120

186. In the figure below, $x = ?$

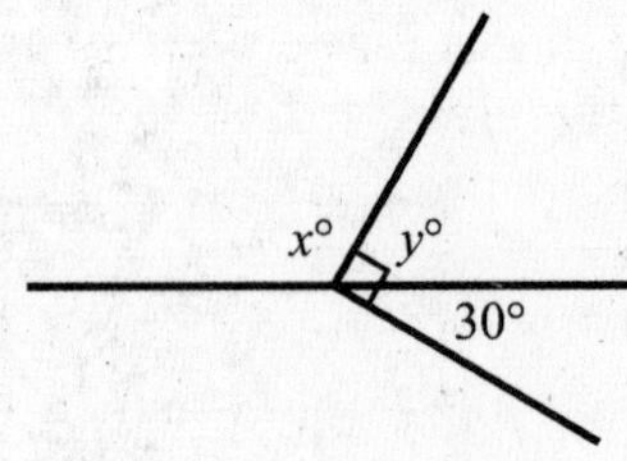

F. 45
G. 60
H. 90
J. 105
K. 120

187. In the figure below, l_1 is parallel to l_2. Which of the following <u>must</u> be true?

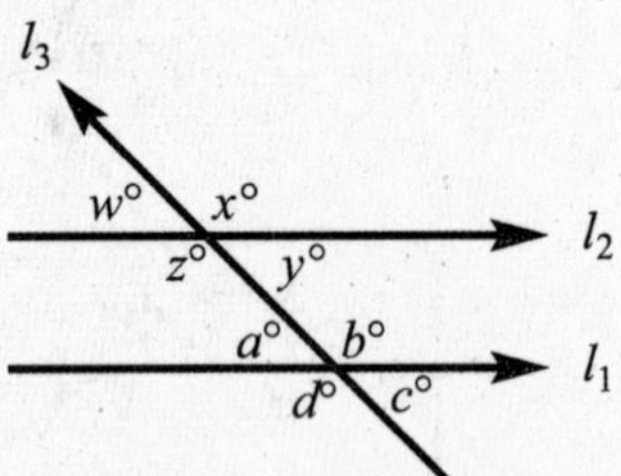

A. $w = a$
B. $y + b = 180$
C. $w = a$ and $y + b = 180$
D. $y + b = 180$ and $x + d = 180$
E. $w = a$, $y + b = 180$, and $x + d = 180$

188. In the figure below, $x = ?$

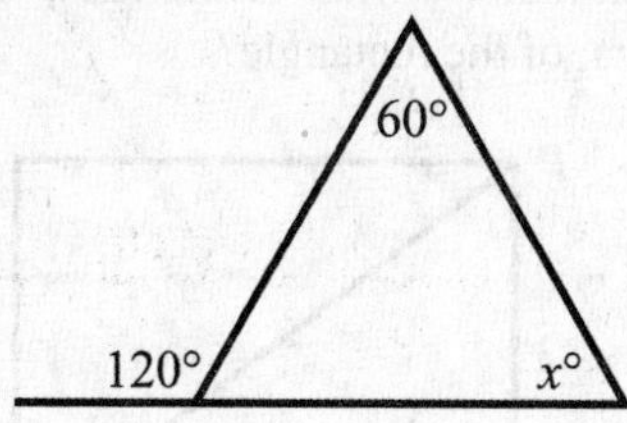

F. 30
G. 45
H. 60
J. 75
K. 90

189. In the figure below, what is the sum of the indicated angles?

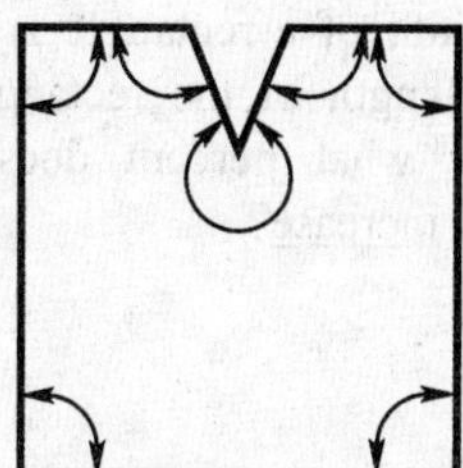

A. 540
B. 720
C. 900
D. 1,080
E. 1,260

190. In the figure below, what is the length of $\overline{AB}$?

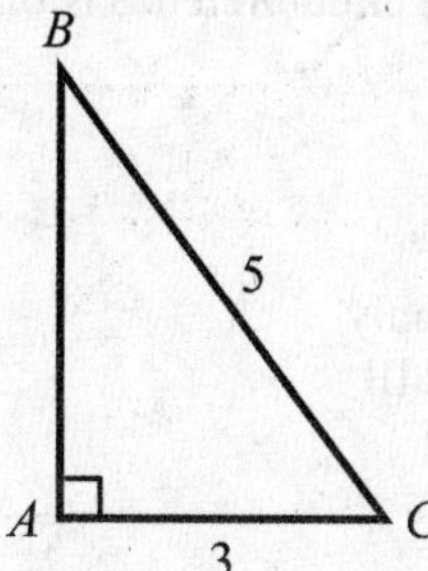

F. 2
G. $2\sqrt{3}$
H. 4
J. $4\sqrt{2}$
K. 8

191. In the figure below, what is the length of $\overline{PQ}$?

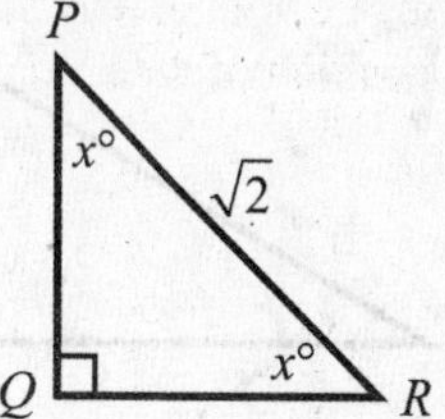

A. 1
B. $\sqrt{2}$
C. $2\sqrt{2}$
D. 4
E. 5

192. In a right isosceles triangle, the hypotenuse is equal to which of the following?

F. Half the length of either of the other sides
G. The length of either of the other sides multiplied by $\sqrt{2}$
H. Twice the length of either of the other sides
J. The sum of the lengths of the other two sides
K. The sum of the lengths of the other two sides multiplied by $\sqrt{2}$

193. In the triangle below, what is the length of $\overline{AC}$?

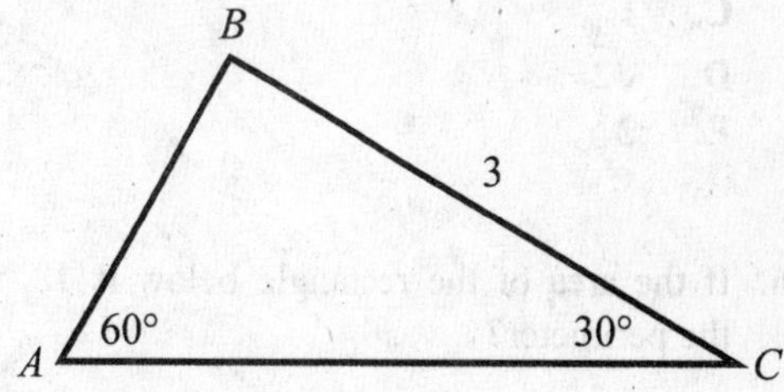

A. 2
B. $\sqrt{3}$
C. $2\sqrt{3}$
D. $3\sqrt{3}$
E. 6

194. In the figure below, the perimeter of ΔPQR = ?

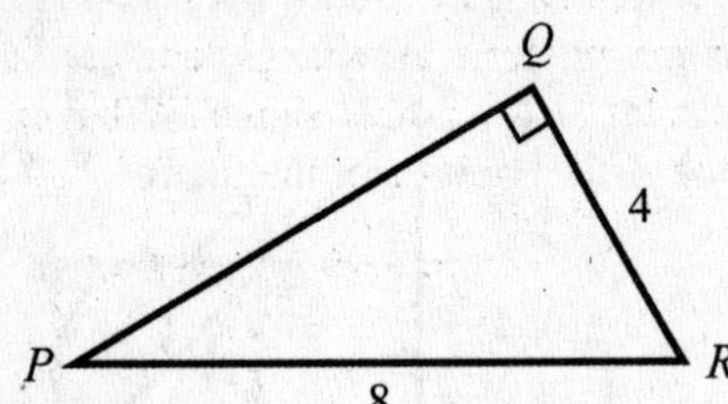

F. $12+\sqrt{3}$
G. $12+2\sqrt{3}$
H. $12+4\sqrt{3}$
J. 28
K. 56

195. In the figure below, what is the area of ΔMNO?

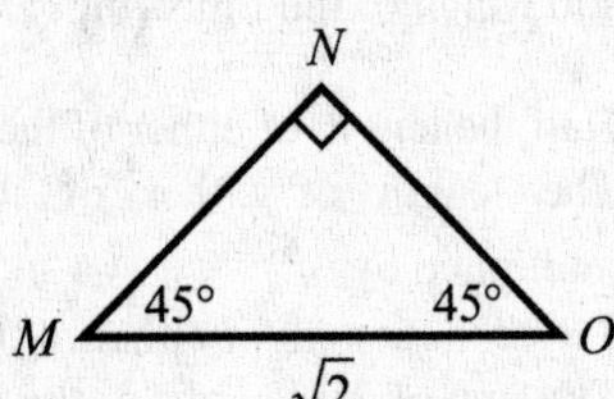

A. $\frac{1}{2}$
B. $\frac{\sqrt{2}}{2}$
C. 1
D. $\sqrt{2}$
E. 2

196. If the area of the rectangle below is 18, what is the perimeter?

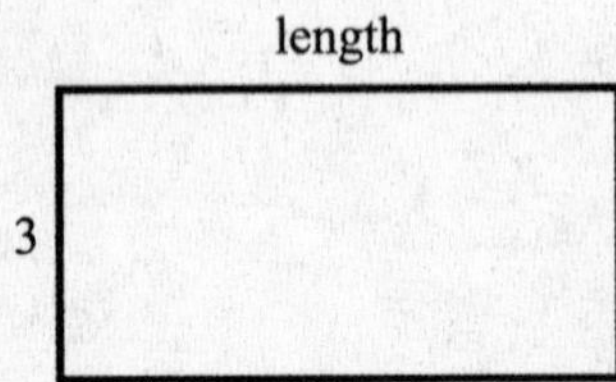

F. 9
G. 12
H. 18
J. 24
K. 30

197. In the figure below, *PQRS* is a rectangle. If $\overline{PR}$ = 5 centimeters, what is the area, in square centimeters, of the rectangle?

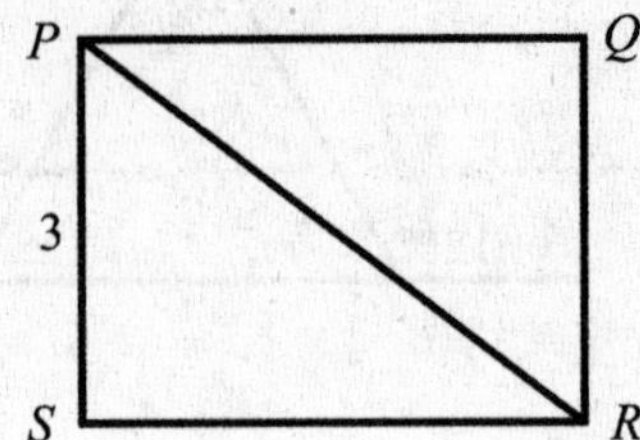

A. 2
B. 3
C. 4
D. 8
E. 12

198. If the width of a rectangle is increased by 10% and the length of the rectangle is increased by 20%, by what percent does the area of the rectangle <u>increase</u>?

F. 2%
G. 10%
H. 15%
J. 32%
K. 36%

199. If the area of a circle is equal to 9π, which of the following is (are) true?

I. The radius is 3.
II. The diameter is 6.
III. The circumference is 6π.

A. I only
B. II only
C. III only
D. I and II only
E. I, II, and III

200. In the figure below, O is the center of the circle, and $\overline{PQ}$ is tangent to the circle at P. If the radius of circle O has a length of 6, what is the area of the shaded portion of the figure?

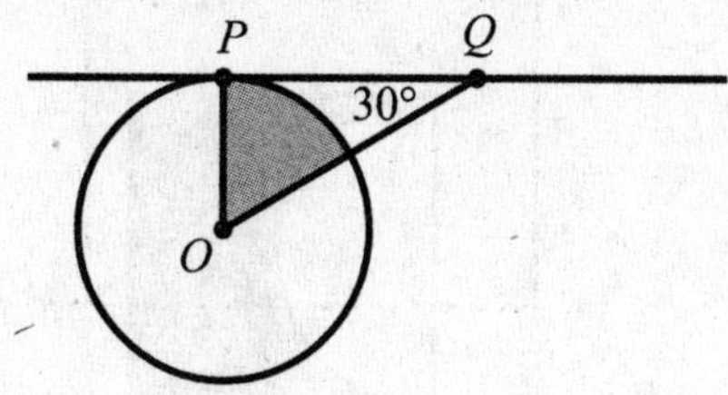

F. π
G. 3π
H. 6π
J. 9π
K. 12π

201. The figure below shows two pulleys connected by a belt. If the centers of the pulleys are 8 feet apart and the pulleys each have a radius of 1 foot, what is the length, in feet, of the belt?

A. 4π
B. 8π
C. $8+\pi$
D. $16+\pi$
E. $16+2\pi$

202. In the figure below, a circle is inscribed in an equilateral triangle. If the radius of the circle is 1, what is the perimeter of the triangle?

F. $\sqrt{3}$
G. $2\sqrt{3}$
H. $3\sqrt{3}$
J. 6
K. $6\sqrt{3}$

203. The figure below shows two circles of diameter 2 that are tangent to each other at point P. The line segments form a rectangle and are tangent to the circles at the points shown. What is the area of the shaded portion of the figure?

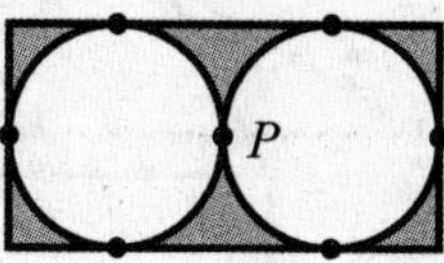

A. $8-2\pi$
B. $8-\pi$
C. $4-2\pi$
D. $4-\pi$
E. 2π

204. If a circle of radius 1 foot is inscribed in a square, what is the area, in square feet, of the square?

F. $\frac{\sqrt{2}}{2}$
G. 1
H. $\sqrt{2}$
J. 2
K. 4

205. An isosceles right triangle is inscribed in a semicircle with a radius of 1 inch. What is the area, in square inches, of the triangle?

A. $\frac{\sqrt{2}}{3}$
B. $\frac{1}{2}$
C. 1
D. $\sqrt{2}$
E. $2\sqrt{2}$

206. In the figure below, $BCDE$ is a square with an area of 4. What is the perimeter of ΔABE?

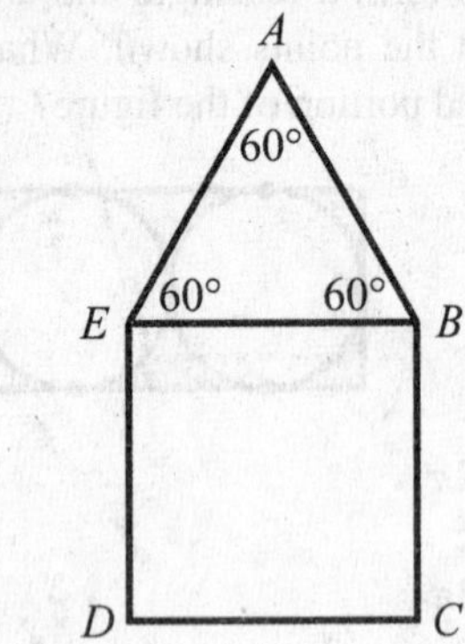

F. 3
G. 4
H. 6
J. 8
K. 12

207. In the figure below, if $QRST$ is a square and the length of $\overline{PQ}$ is $\sqrt{2}$, what is the length of $\overline{RU}$?

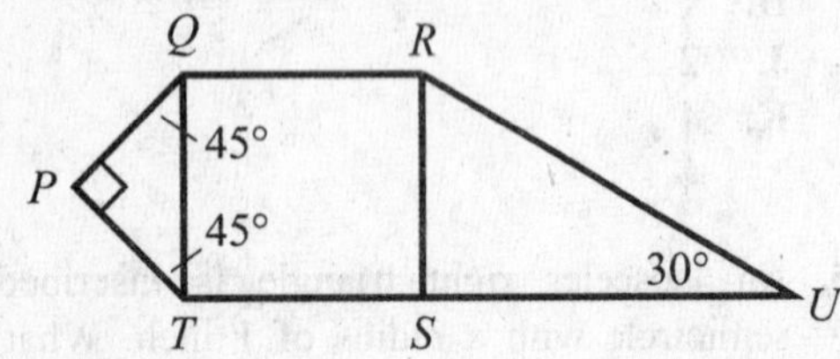

A. $\sqrt{2}$
B. $2\sqrt{2}$
C. $\sqrt{6}$
D. 4
E. $4\sqrt{3}$

208. In the figure below, $PQRS$ is a square, and $\overline{PS}$ is the diameter of a semicircle. If the length of $\overline{PQ}$ is 2, what is the area of the shaded portion of the diagram?

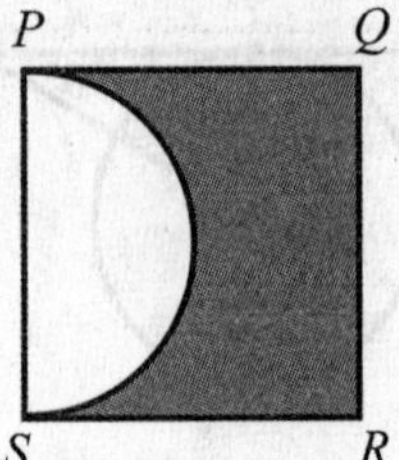

F. $4-2\pi$
G. $4-\pi$
H. $4-\frac{\pi}{2}$
J. $8-\pi$
K. $8-\frac{\pi}{2}$

209. If the lengths of the sides, in inches, are as marked on the figure below, what is the area, in square inches, of the quadrilateral?

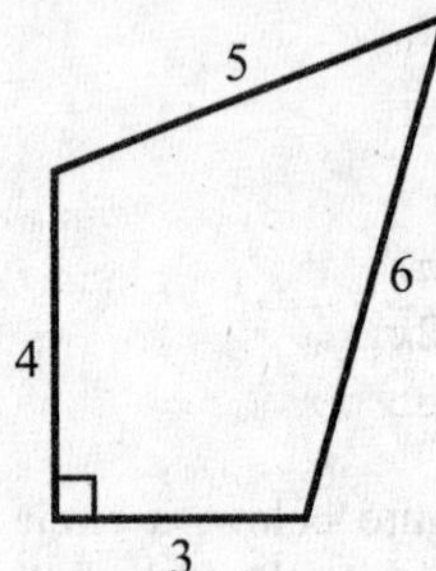

A. 6
B. $6+\sqrt{3}$
C. 12
D. 18
E. 24

210. In the figure below, $x = ?$

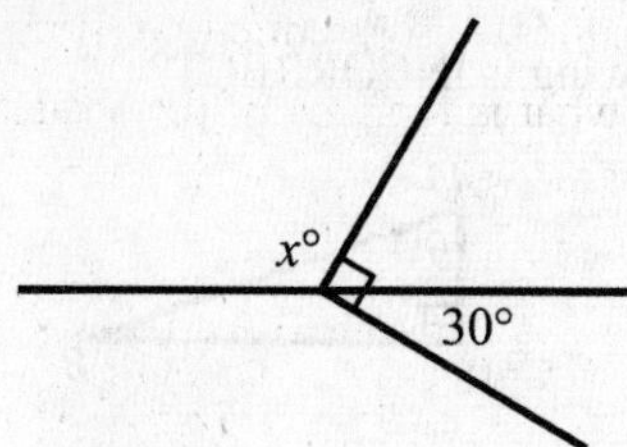

F. 30
G. 65
H. 120
J. 150
K. 170

211. What is the perimeter of the triangle shown below?

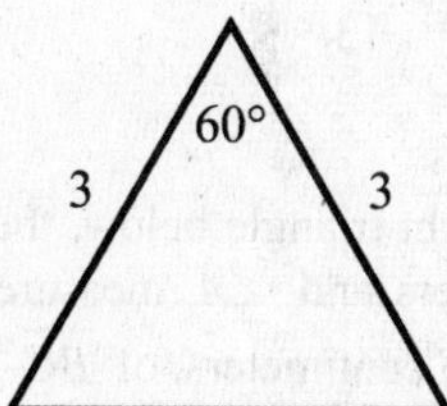

A. $3\sqrt{2}$
B. 6
C. 7.5
D. 9
E. 15

212. In the figure below, $x = ?$

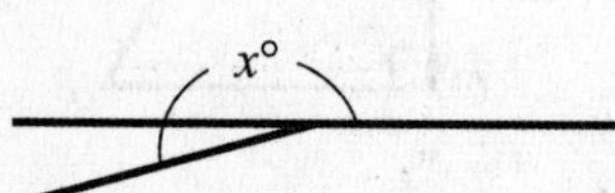

F. 120
G. 150
H. 180
J. 210
K. 240

213. In the figure below, $x = ?$

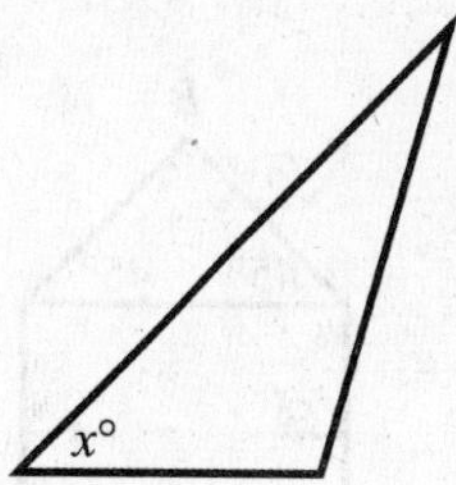

A. 30
B. 45
C. 60
D. 75
E. 90

214. In the figure below, what is the length of $\overline{AC}$?

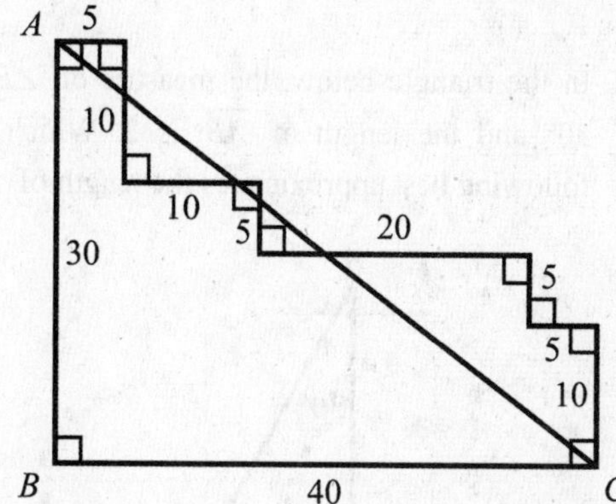

F. $30\sqrt{2}$
G. 50
H. 75
J. $60\sqrt{2}$
K. 100

215. In the figure below, what is the area of square $ABCD$?

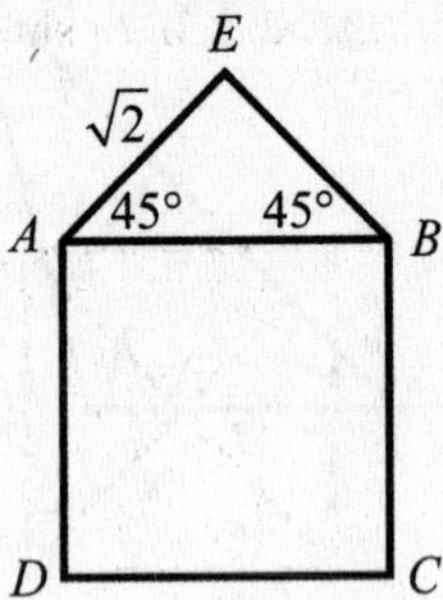

A. 2
B. $2\sqrt{2}$
C. 4
D. $4\sqrt{2}$
E. 8

216. In the triangle below, the measure of $\angle BAC$ is 30° and the length of $\overline{AB}$ is 2. Which of the following best approximates the length of $\overline{AC}$?

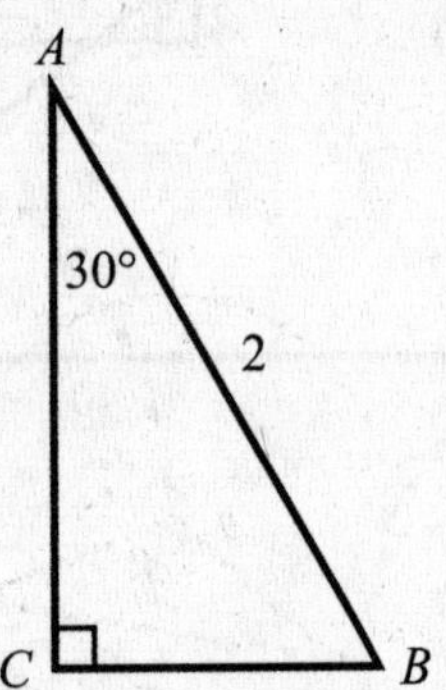

F. 0.8
G. 1.0
H. 1.7
J. 1.9
K. 2.3

217. For the figure below, $\sin\theta = \frac{12}{13}$. Which of the following is INCORRECT?

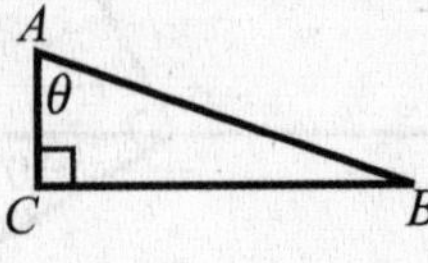

A. $\cos\theta = \frac{5}{13}$

B. $\tan\theta = \frac{12}{5}$

C. $\cot\theta = \frac{5}{12}$

D. $\sec\theta = \frac{13}{5}$

E. $\csc\theta = \frac{12}{13}$

218. In the right triangle below, the length of $\overline{AB}$ is 5 centimeters and $\angle A$ measures 30°. What is the length, in centimeters, of $\overline{BC}$? ($\sin 30° = 0.5$)

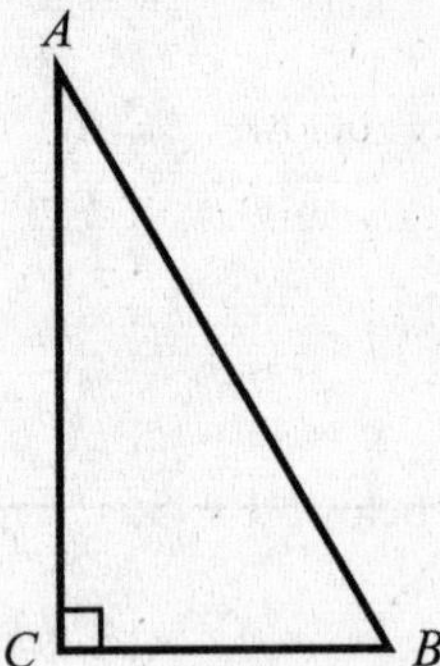

F. 4

G. $3\frac{1}{2}$

H. $2\frac{3}{4}$

J. $2\frac{1}{2}$

K. 2

219. If $\sin 60°$ is equal to $\frac{\sqrt{3}}{2}$, what is the value of $\sin^2 30° + \cos^2 30°$?

A. $\frac{\sqrt{3}+1}{2}$
B. $\sqrt{5}$
C. $\frac{\sqrt{5}}{2}$
D. $\frac{3}{4}$
E. 1

220. Which of the following is equivalent to $\frac{\sin A}{\cos A}$?

F. $\tan A$
G. $\cot A$
H. $\sec A$
J. $\csc A$
K. $\frac{1}{\tan A}$

221. In the figure below, ΔPQR and ΔQRS are isosceles right triangles. If $\overline{QP} = 3$, what is the length of $\overline{QS}$? $\left(\sin 45° = \frac{\sqrt{2}}{2}\right)$

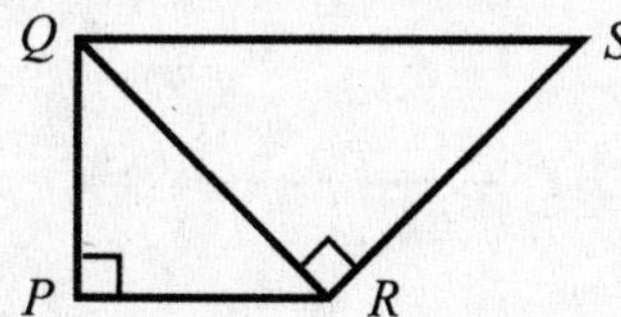

A. $\sqrt{2}$
B. $2\sqrt{2}$
C. 4
D. 6
E. 8

222. If the area of the square $JKLM$ in the figure below is 4, what is the sum of the lengths of the diagonals $\overline{JL}$ and $\overline{KM}$? $\left(\sin 45° = \frac{\sqrt{2}}{2}\right)$

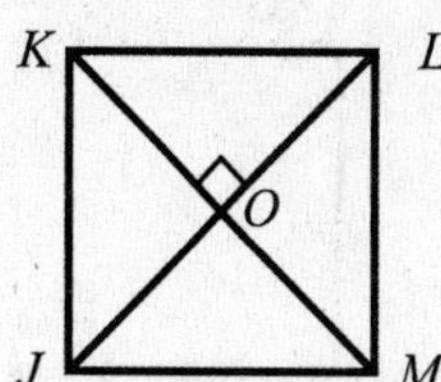

F. $\frac{\sqrt{2}}{2}$
G. $2+\frac{\sqrt{2}}{2}$
H. $4\sqrt{2}$
J. $4+4\sqrt{2}$
K. $8\sqrt{2}$

223. In the figure below, O is the center of the circle with radius 10. What is the area of ΔAOB? $\left(\sin 30° = \frac{1}{2}\ ;\ \sin 60° = \frac{\sqrt{3}}{2}\right)$

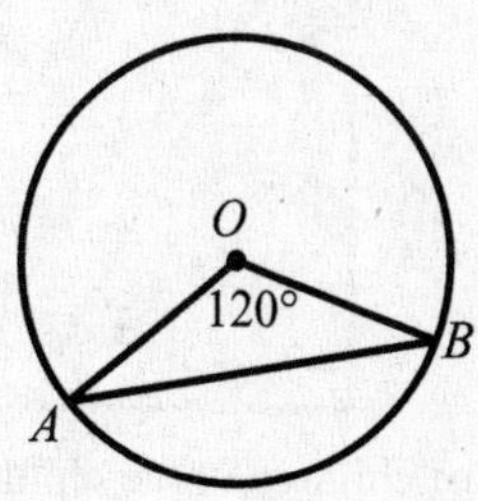

A. $10\sqrt{3}$
B. 10
C. 25
D. $25\sqrt{3}$
E. 50

224. If the average of 35, 38, 41, 43, and x is 37, what is x?

F. 28
G. 30
H. 31
J. 34
K. 36

225. The average weight of 6 packages is 50 pounds per package. Another package is added, making the average weight of the 7 packages 52 pounds per package. What is the weight, in pounds, of the additional package?

A. 2
B. 7
C. 52
D. 62
E. 64

226. The average of 10 test scores is 80. If the high and low scores are dropped, the average is 81. What is the average of the high and low scores?

F. 76
G. 78
H. 80
J. 81
K. 82

227. In Latin 101, the final exam grade is weighted two times as heavily as the mid-term grade. If Leo received a score of 84 on his final exam and 90 on his mid-term, what was his course average?

A. 88
B. 87.5
C. 86.5
D. 86
E. 85

228. In a group of children, three children are 10 years old and two children are 5 years old. What is the average age, in years, of the children in the group?

F. 6
G. 6.5
H. 7
J. 7.5
K. 8

229. The number of employment applications received by All-Star Staffing each month during 2002 was as follows: 8, 3, 5, 3, 4, 3, 1, 0, 3, 4, 0, and 7. What is the median number of applications received in 2002?

A. 3
B. 4
C. 5
D. 6
E. 7

230. William's monthly electric bills for last year were as follows: $40, 38, 36, 38, 34, 34, 30, 32, 34, 37, 39, and 40. What is the mode of the bills?

F. $33
G. $34
H. $35
J. $36
K. $37

231. If set $A = \{1, 2, 3, 4, 5, 6\}$ and set $B = \{1, 2, 3, 4, 5, 6\}$, what is the probability that the sum of one number from set A and one number from set B will total 7?

A. $\frac{1}{12}$
B. $\frac{5}{36}$
C. $\frac{1}{6}$
D. $\frac{1}{5}$
E. $\frac{1}{3}$

232. If a book is selected at random from the collection shown below, which of the following has the greatest probability of being selected?

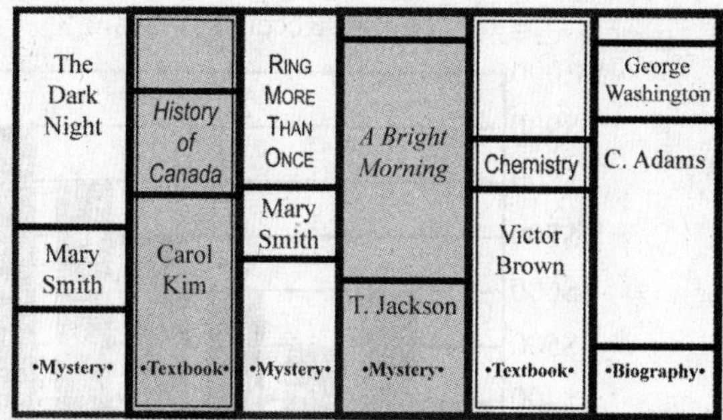

F. A book by Mary Smith
G. A textbook
H. A mystery
J. A book written by either Carol Kim or Victor Brown
K. A biography

233. If a jar contains r red marbles, b blue marbles, and g green marbles, which of the following expresses the probability that a marble drawn at random will NOT be red?

A. $\frac{-r}{r+b+g}$

B. $\frac{r}{r+b+g}$

C. $\frac{b+g-r}{b+g+r}$

D. $\frac{r}{b+g}$

E. $\frac{b+g}{b+g+r}$

234. The figure below shows a dartboard consisting of two concentric circles with center O. The radius of the larger circle is equal to the diameter of the smaller circle. What is the probability that a randomly thrown dart striking the board will score a 3?

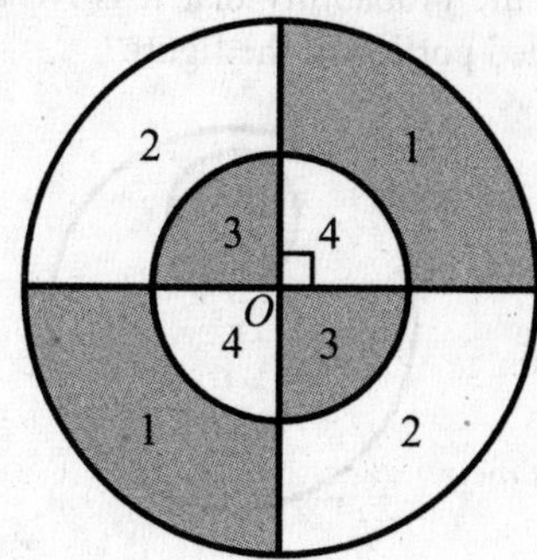

F. $\frac{1}{16}$

G. $\frac{1}{8}$

H. $\frac{1}{4}$

J. $\frac{1}{2}$

K. $\frac{3}{4}$

235. An underwater salvage team is searching the ocean floor for a lost signal device using a large circular search pattern and a smaller circular search pattern with a radius equal to one-third that of the larger pattern. If the device is known to be inside the boundary of the larger search area, what is the probability that it is NOT located in the shaded portion of the figure?

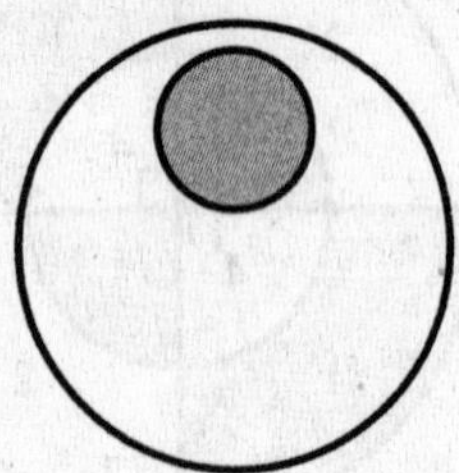

A. $\frac{1}{9}$

B. $\frac{1}{6}$

C. $\frac{1}{3}$

D. $\frac{1}{2}$

E. $\frac{8}{9}$

236. During the week shown in the graph below, what was the greatest increase in sales from one day to the next?

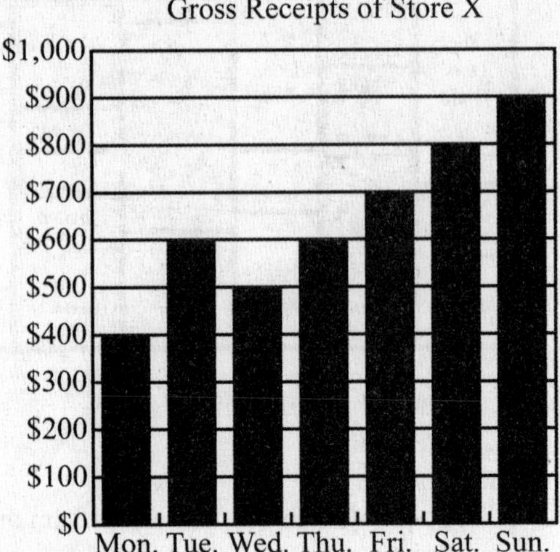

F. $50
G. $100
H. $150
J. $200
K. $250

237. If the graph below represents expenditures by Corporation X in two different years, what was the approximate ratio of expenditures in 2006 to those in 2007?

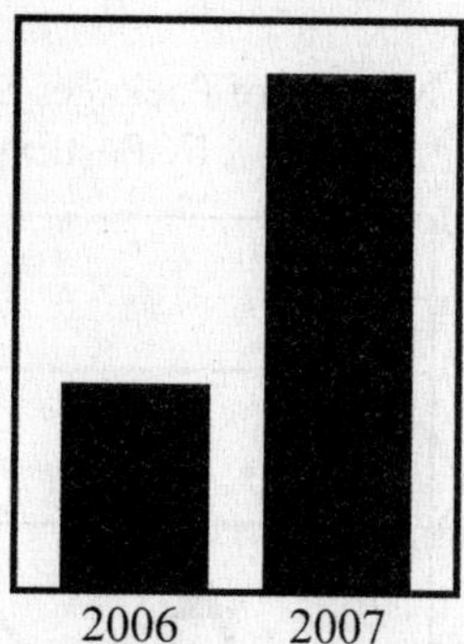

A. $\frac{1}{5}$

B. $\frac{2}{5}$

C. $\frac{1}{2}$

D. $\frac{2}{3}$

E. 2

238. Based on the data presented below, what was the difference, if any, between the number of permanent workers employed by Corporation X on March 1st and the number of permanent workers employed by Corporation X on April 1st?

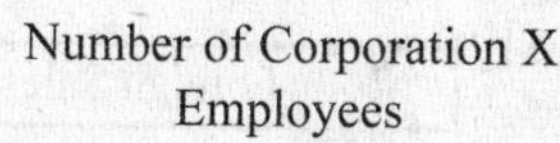

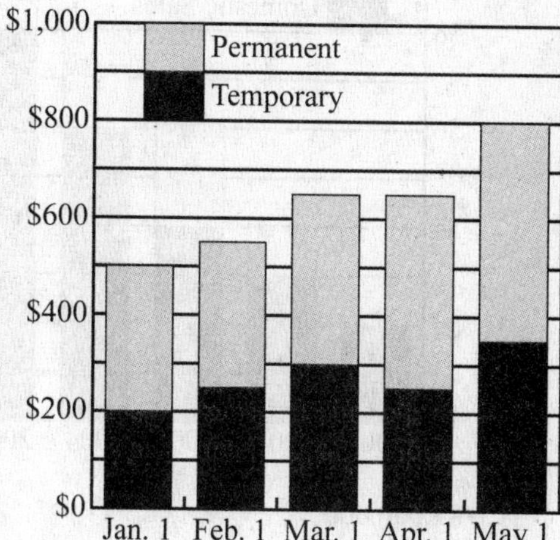

F. 0

G. 50

H. 100

J. 150

K. 200

239. Based on the data presented above, what was the difference in the value of foreign sales by Company T between 2003 and 2005?

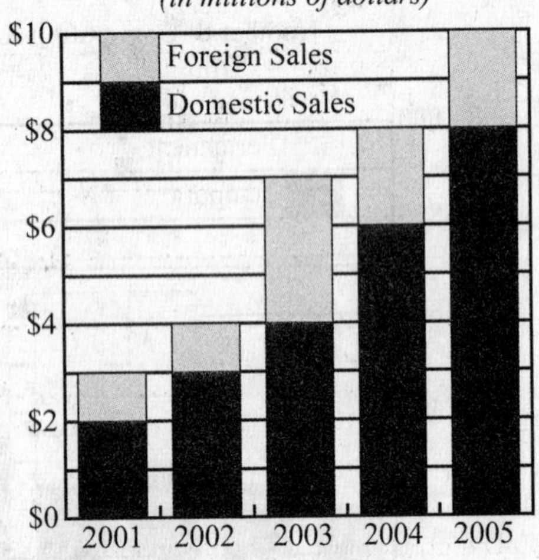

A. $1,000,000
B. $2,000,000
C. $3,000,000
D. $5,000,000
E. $6,000,000

240. Based on the data presented below, what was the approximate total number of packages shipped by PostExpress for the months January, February, and March, inclusive?

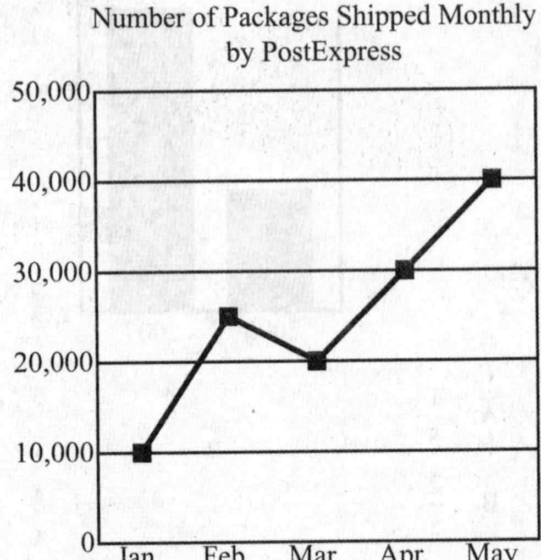

F. 40,000
G. 55,000
H. 60,000
J. 70,000
K. 85,000

241. Based on the data presented below, approximately how much money was spent on the Air Force?

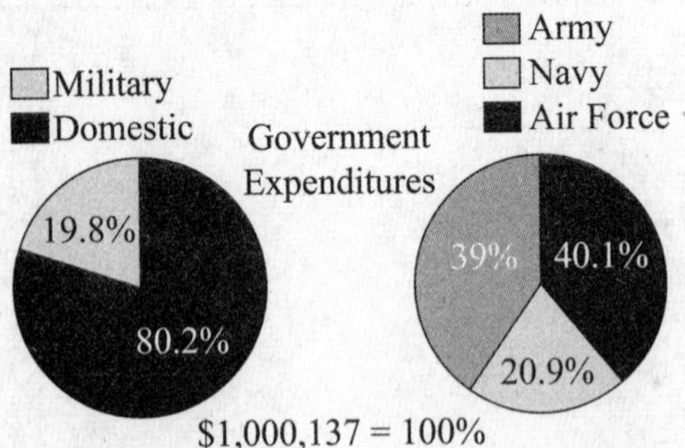

A. $39,704
B. $79,409
C. $96,123
D. $198,027
E. $401,054

242. Based on the data presented below, what was the dollar value of foreign sales to Europe by PetProducts in 2002?

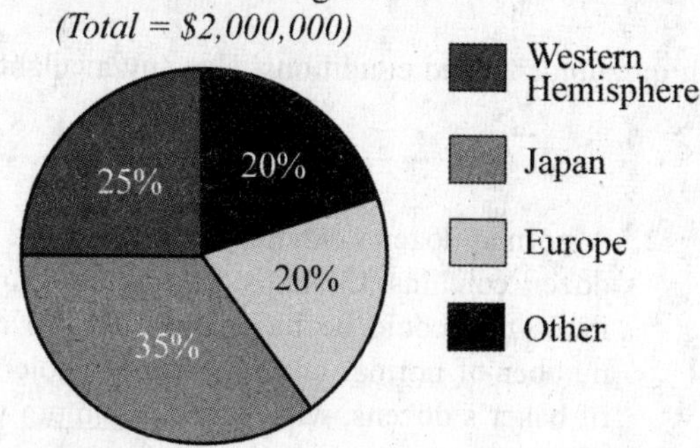

F. $200,000
G. $400,000
H. $1,200,000
J. $1,600,000
K. $2,000,000

243. Based on the data presented below, what is the total cost of 5 large blue t-shirts, 8 small red t-shirts, and 4 extra large white t-shirts?

T-Shirt Prices			
	Blue	*Red*	*White*
Small	$5.00	$6.00	$7.00
Large	$5.75	$6.50	$7.25
Extra Large	$6.50	$7.25	$8.00

A. $56.00
B. $88.25
C. $105.50
D. $108.75
E. $135.00

244. The following scatterplot shows the video-game playing habits of 20 students.

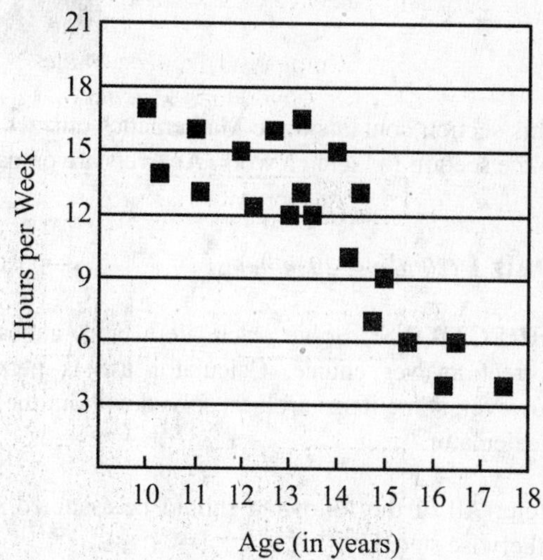

The graph most strongly supports the conclusion that the number of hours per week spent playing video-games:

F. is constant from age 10 to age 18.
G. increases as age increases from 10 to 18.
H. decreases as age increases from 10 to 18.
J. is constant for ages 10 through 14 and then decreases.
K. is constant for ages 10 through 14 and then increases.

This section contains three Mathematics quizzes. Complete each quiz under timed conditions. Use any available space in the section for scratch work. Answers are on page 634.

Quiz I *(20 items; 20 minutes)*

DIRECTIONS: Solve each item and choose the correct answer choice. Calculator use is permitted; however, some items are best solved without the use of a calculator.

Note: All of the following should be assumed, unless otherwise stated.

1. Illustrative figures are NOT necessarily drawn to scale.
2. The word *average* indicates arithmetic mean.
3. The word *line* indicates a straight line.
4. Geometric figures lie in a plane.

1. In the triangle below, $x = ?$

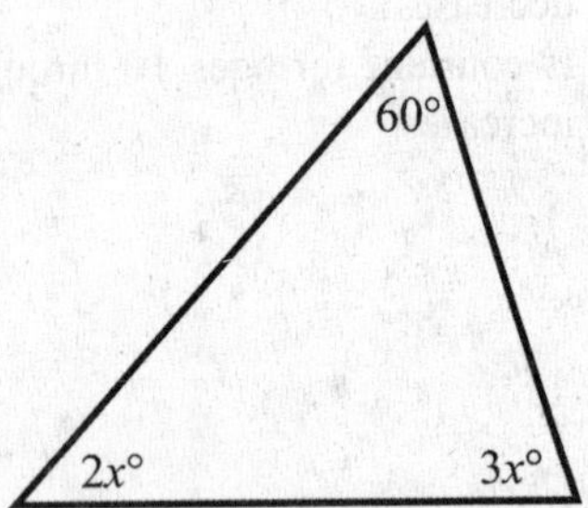

A. 24
B. 20
C. 16
D. 12
E. 10

2. A normal dozen contains 12 items, and a baker's dozen contains 13 items. If x is the number of items that could be measured either in a whole number of normal dozens or in a whole number of baker's dozens, what is the minimum value of x?

F. 1
G. 12
H. 13
J. 25
K. 156

3. In the figure below, what is the degree measure of the smaller of the two angles formed by the hour and minute hands of the clock?

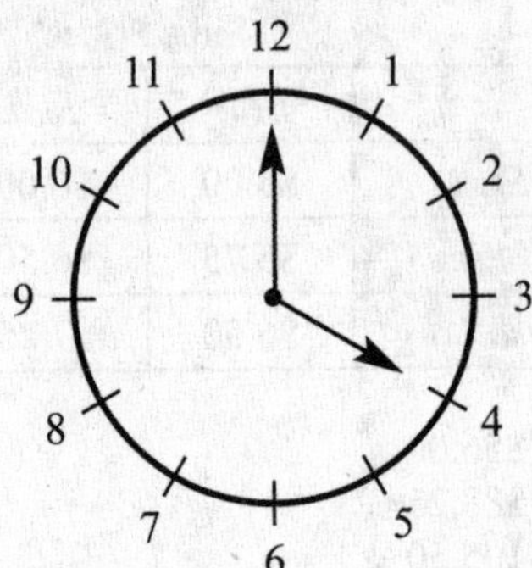

A. 45
B. 60
C. 90
D. 120
E. 240

4. Starting from points that are 200 kilometers apart, two trains travel toward each other along two parallel tracks. If one train travels at 70 kilometers per hour and the other travels at 80 kilometers per hour, how much time, in hours, will elapse before the trains pass each other?

F. $\frac{3}{4}$
G. 1
H. $\frac{4}{3}$
J. $\frac{3}{2}$
K. 2

5. A student begins heating a certain substance with a temperature of 50°C over a Bunsen burner. If the temperature of the substance will rise 20°C for every 24 minutes it remains over the burner, what will be the temperature, in degrees Celsius, of the substance after 18 minutes?

A. 52
B. 56
C. 60
D. 65
E. 72

6. If the ratio of apples to oranges in a salad is 8 to 7, what fractional part of the salad is oranges?

F. $\frac{1}{56}$
G. $\frac{1}{15}$
H. $\frac{1}{7}$
J. $\frac{7}{15}$
K. $\frac{8}{7}$

7. The object of a popular board game is to use clues to identify a suspect and the weapon used to commit a crime. If there are 3 suspects and 6 weapons, how many different solutions to the game are possible?

A. 2
B. 3
C. 9
D. 12
E. 18

8. The average weight of three boxes is $25\frac{1}{3}$ pounds. If each box weighs at least 24 pounds, what is the greatest possible weight, in pounds, of any one of the boxes?

F. 25
G. 26
H. 27
J. 28
K. 29

9. If n subtracted from $\frac{13}{2}$ is equal to n divided by $\frac{2}{13}$, what is the value of n?

A. $\frac{2}{3}$
B. $\frac{13}{15}$
C. 1
D. $\frac{13}{11}$
E. 26

10. In the figure below, what is the area of the quadrilateral?

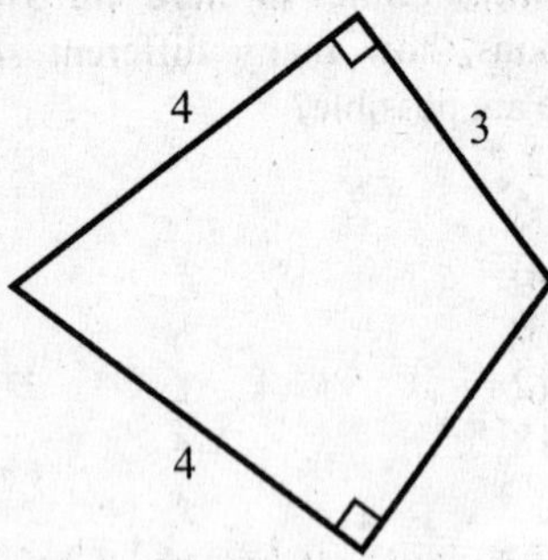

F. 18
G. 15
H. 12
J. 9
K. 8

11. In the figure below, what is the length of $\overline{BC}$? $\left(\sin 30° = \frac{1}{2}\right)$

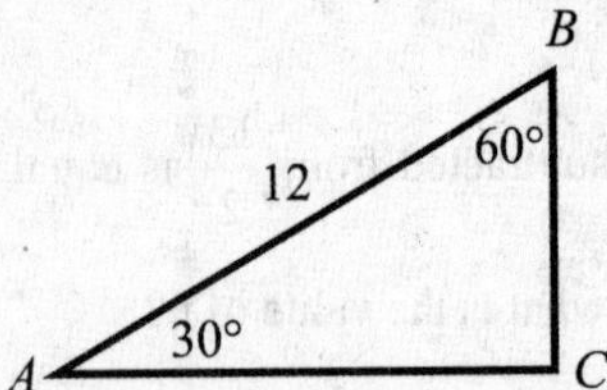

A. 2
B. 3
C. $3\sqrt{3}$
D. 6
E. $6\sqrt{3}$

12. After being dropped from a height of h meters, a ball bounces 3 meters high on the third bounce and $\frac{4}{3}$ meters high on the fifth bounce. What is the value, in meters, of h?

F. $\frac{27}{8}$
G. $\frac{9}{2}$
H. $\frac{27}{4}$
J. $\frac{81}{8}$
K. $\frac{27}{2}$

13. Set $A = \{-2, -1, 0\}$, and set $B = \{-1, 0, 1\}$. If a is an element of set A and b is an element of set B, for how many pairs (a,b) is the product ab a member of both set A and set B?

A. 0
B. 2
C. 4
D. 6
E. 9

14. Which of the following is the complete solution set for $|2x+4| = 12$?

F. {–8, 4}
G. {–4, 8}
H. {0, 8}
J. {4, 8}
K. {6, 8}

15. If $f(x)=\frac{(x-1)^2}{(-2-x)}$, for what value of x is $f(x)$ undefined?

A. –2
B. –1
C. 0
D. 1
E. 2

Items #16–17 refer to the following table:

ANNUAL EXPENDITURES FOR THE JONES FAMILY *(percent of disposable income)*		
Category	*2006*	*2007*
Rent	23.0%	19.3%
Food	17.6%	18.2%
Clothing	14.2%	15.1%
Automobile	11.3%	12.3%
Utilities	10.9%	10.2%
Savings	6.2%	5.1%
Entertainment	5.2%	5.3%
Medical and Dental Care	4.0%	3.7%
Charitable Contributions	3.2%	3.9%
Household Furnishings	2.9%	3.1%
Other	1.5%	3.8%
Total	100.0%	100.0%
Total Expenditures	$34,987.00	$40,012.00

16. Approximately how much money did the Jones family spend on medical and dental care in 2006?

F. $1,200
G. $1,400
H. $1,520
J. $2,250
K. $4,000

17. If the categories in the table are rank ordered from one to eleven in each year, for how many categories would the rank ordering change from 2006 to 2007?

A. 2
B. 3
C. 4
D. 5
E. 6

18. For the figure below, which of the following statements is INCORRECT?

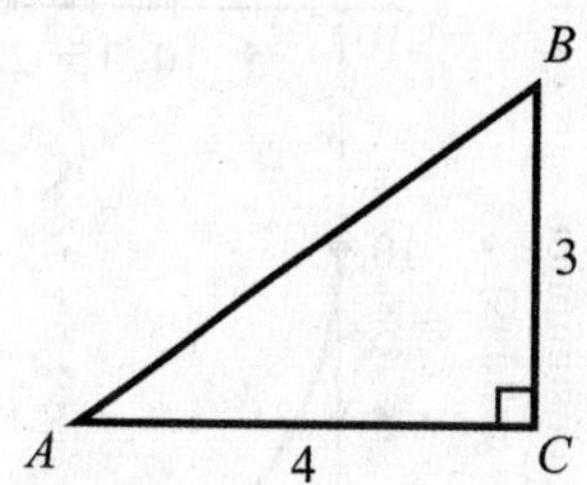

F. $\sin A=\frac{3}{5}$

G. $\cos A=\frac{4}{5}$

H. $\tan A=\frac{3}{4}$

J. $\cot A=\frac{5}{3}$

K. $\sec A=\frac{5}{4}$

19. When the 10-gallon tank of an emergency generator is filled to capacity, the generator operates without interruption for 20 hours, consuming fuel at a constant rate. Which of the graphs below represents the fuel consumption of the generator over time?

A. 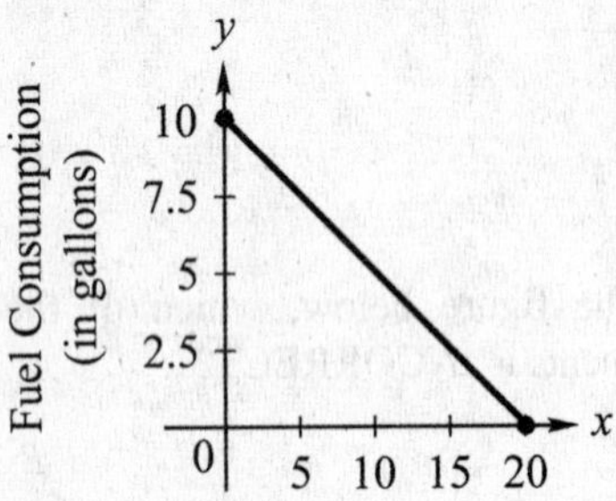

B. 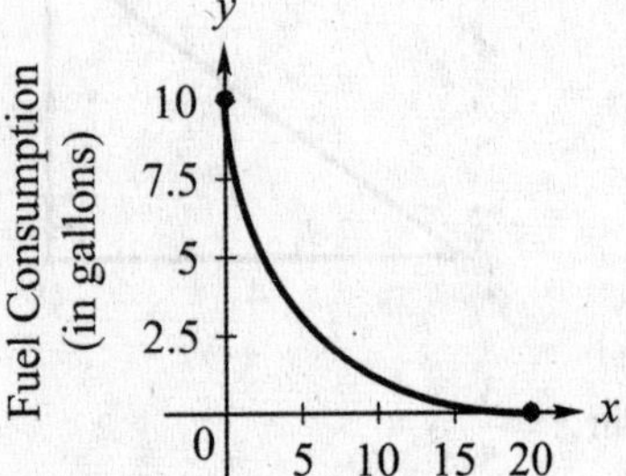

C. 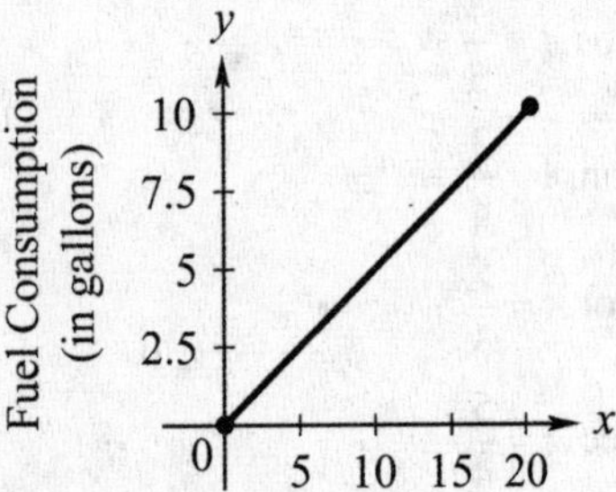

D. 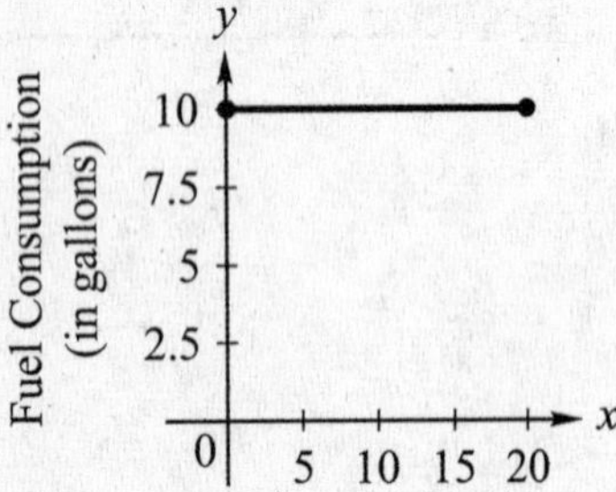

E. 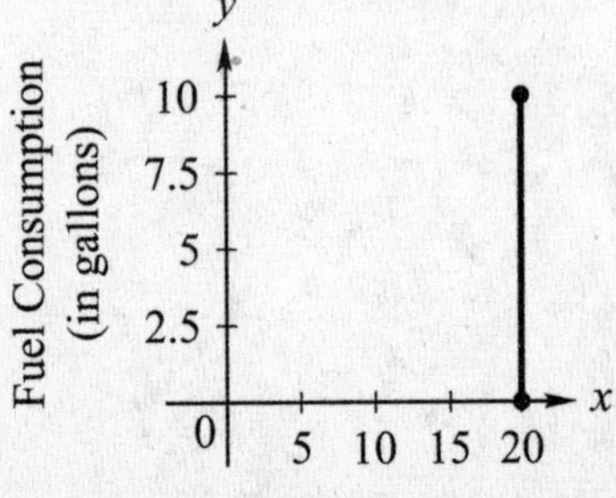

20. In the figure below, $\overline{PQ}$ is tangent to circle O at point S and $\overline{QR}$ is tangent to circle O at point T. If the radius of circle O is 2, what is the area of the shaded portion of the figure?

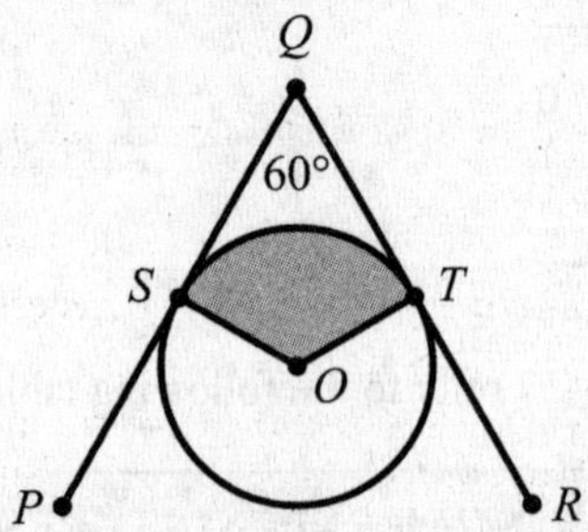

F. $\frac{\pi}{3}$

G. $\frac{2\pi}{3}$

H. π

J. $\frac{4\pi}{3}$

K. 2π

Quiz II *(20 items; 20 minutes)*

DIRECTIONS: Solve each item and choose the correct answer choice. Calculator use is permitted; however, some items are best solved without the use of a calculator.

Note: All of the following should be assumed, unless otherwise stated.

1. Illustrative figures are NOT necessarily drawn to scale.
2. The word *average* indicates arithmetic mean.
3. The word *line* indicates a straight line.
4. Geometric figures lie in a plane.

1. The figure below is a plan that shows a solid set of steps to be constructed from concrete blocks of equal size. How many blocks are needed to construct the steps?

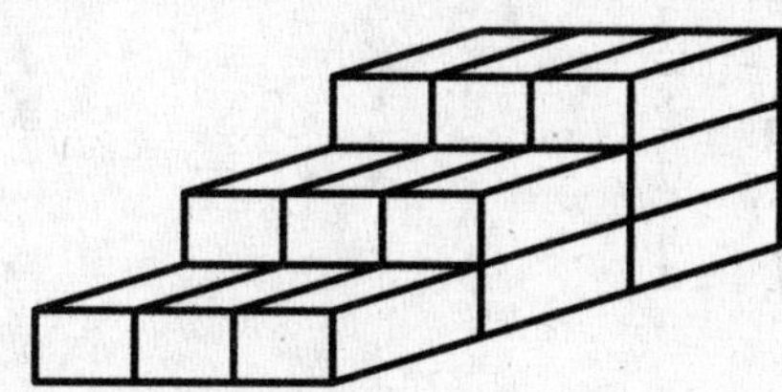

A. 12
B. 15
C. 18
D. 21
E. 24

2. In the figure below, what is the value of x?

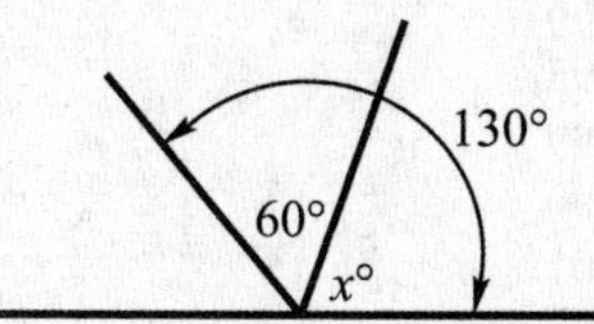

F. 70
G. 60
H. 50
J. 40
K. 30

3. If $2^{x+1} = 4^{x-1}$, what is the value of x?

A. 1
B. 2
C. 3
D. 4
E. 5

4. Of the actors in a certain play, five actors are in Act I, 12 actors are in Act II, and 13 actors are in Act III. If 10 of the actors are in exactly two of the three acts and all of the other actors are in just one act, how many actors are in the play?

F. 17
G. 20
H. 24
J. 30
K. 38

5. In the figure below, $\overline{AB} \cong \overline{BC} \cong \overline{CA}$. What is the value of y?

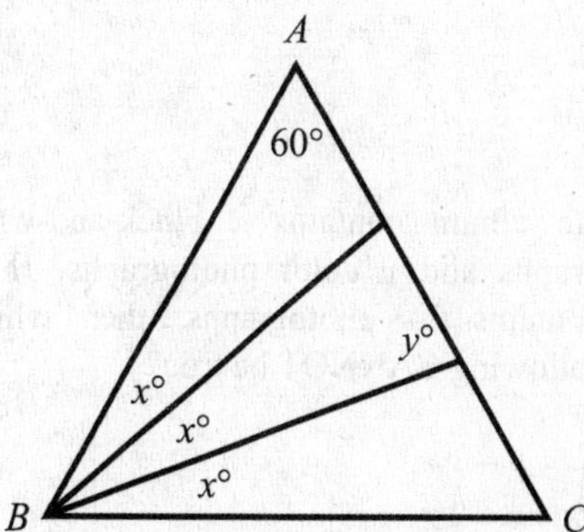

A. 20
B. 60
C. 80
D. 100
E. 120

6. Under certain conditions, a bicycle traveling k meters per second requires $\frac{k^2}{20}+k$ meters to stop. If $k=10$, how many meters does the bicycle need to stop?

F. 10
G. 12
H. 15
J. 20
K. 30

7. What is the slope of a line that passes through the origin and $(-3,-2)$?

A. $\frac{3}{2}$
B. $\frac{2}{3}$
C. 0
D. $-\frac{2}{3}$
E. $-\frac{3}{2}$

8. An album contains x black-and-white photographs and y color photographs. If the album contains 24 photographs, then which of the following CANNOT be true?

F. $x=y$
G. $x=2y$
H. $x=3y$
J. $x=4y$
K. Cannot be determined from the given information

9. If $2a=3b=4c$, then what is the average (arithmetic mean) of a, b, and c, in terms of a?

A. $\frac{13a}{18}$
B. $\frac{13a}{9}$
C. $\frac{8a}{3}$
D. $\frac{4a}{3}$
E. $2a$

10. If $x=6+y$ and $4x=3-2y$, what is the value of x?

F. 4
G. $\frac{11}{3}$
H. $\frac{5}{2}$
J. $-\frac{2}{3}$
K. $-\frac{7}{2}$

11. If $\frac{2}{3}$ is written as a decimal to 101 places, what is the sum of the first 100 digits to the right of the decimal point?

A. 66
B. 595
C. 599
D. 600
E. 601

12. In the figure below, O is the center of the circle with radius 1. What is the area of the shaded region?

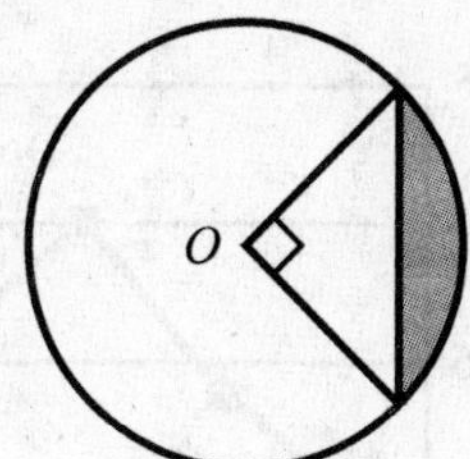

F. $\frac{3\pi}{4}+\frac{1}{2}$

G. $\frac{3\pi}{4}-\frac{1}{2}$

H. $\frac{\pi}{4}+\frac{1}{2}$

J. $\frac{\pi}{4}-\frac{1}{2}$

K. $\pi-1$

13. If $f(3)=5$ and $f(7)=7$, what is the slope of the graph of $f(x)$ in the coordinate plane?

A. -2

B. $-\frac{1}{2}$

C. 1

D. $\frac{1}{2}$

E. 2

14. In a list of the first 100 positive integers, the digit 9 appears how many times?

F. 9
G. 10
H. 11
J. 19
K. 20

15. If $\frac{x}{x+3}=\frac{3}{4}$, and $x \neq -3$, then $x=?$

A. 3
B. 4
C. 5
D. 7
E. 9

16. Which of the following is the complete solution set for $\sqrt{2x+3}+2=5$?

F. {}
G. {–1}
H. {3}
J. {–1, 3}
K. {1, 2}

17. In the figure below, what is the length of $\overline{AC}$? $\left(\sin\angle ABD=\frac{\sqrt{7}}{4}\right)$

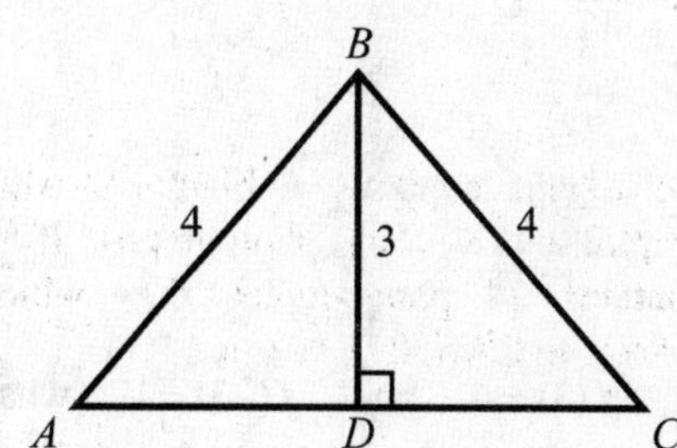

A. 5
B. $2\sqrt{7}$
C. $4\sqrt{3}$
D. 7
E. $3\sqrt{7}$

18. A dartboard has four concentric circles with the center as indicated in the figure below. If the diameter of each circle except for the smallest is twice that of the next smaller circle, what is the probability that a randomly thrown dart will strike the shaded portion of the figure?

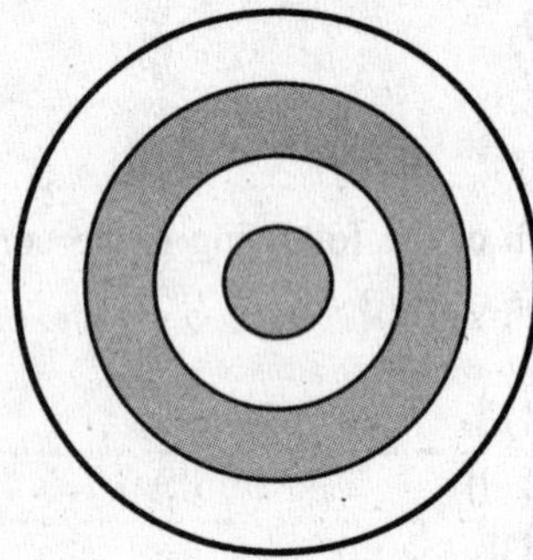

F. $\frac{3}{16}$

G. $\frac{1}{4}$

H. $\frac{13}{64}$

J. $\frac{17}{64}$

K. $\frac{1}{2}$

19. If $f(3)=4$ and $f(-3)=1$, what is the y-intercept of the graph of $f(x)$ in the coordinate plane?

A. $-\frac{5}{2}$

B. $-\frac{2}{5}$

C. 0

D. $\frac{2}{5}$

E. $\frac{5}{2}$

20. The following graph shows the data for domestic and foreign sales for Company X over five years.

Sales of Company X (in millions)

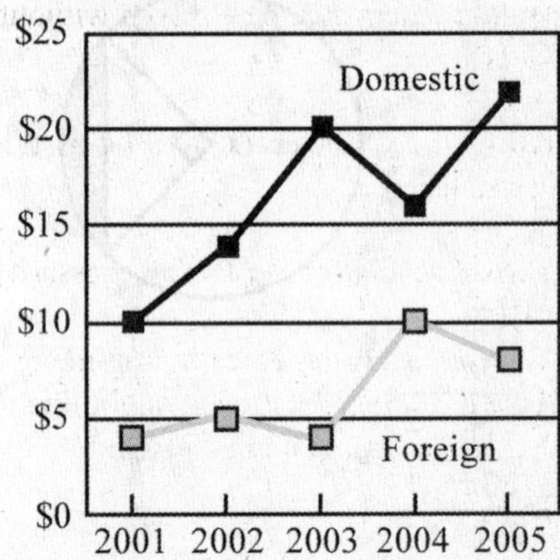

Which of the following pie graphs best represents the division of total sales between foreign and domestic sales for 2004?

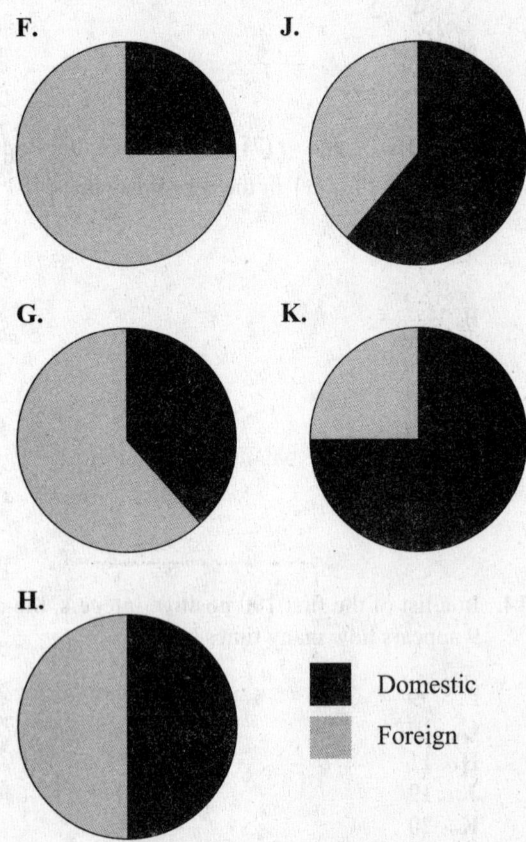

Quiz III *(20 items; 20 minutes)*

DIRECTIONS: Solve each item and choose the correct answer choice. Calculator use is permitted; however, some items are best solved without the use of a calculator.

Note: All of the following should be assumed, unless otherwise stated.

1. Illustrative figures are NOT necessarily drawn to scale.
2. The word *average* indicates arithmetic mean.
3. The word *line* indicates a straight line.
4. Geometric figures lie in a plane.

1. What is the average (arithmetic mean) of all integers 6 through 15 (including 6 and 15)?

A. 6
B. 9
C. 10.5
D. 11
E. 21

2. Which of the following numbers is the largest?

F. 0.08
G. 0.17
H. 0.171
J. 0.1077
K. 0.10771

3. If the rectangle below has an area of 72, then $x = ?$

$x+3$

$x-3$

A. 3
B. 4
C. 6
D. 8
E. 9

4. Machine X produces 15 units per minute, and Machine Y produces 12 units per minute. In one hour, Machine X will produce how many more units than Machine Y?

F. 90
G. 180
H. 240
J. 270
K. 360

5. Which of the following pie charts represents the data shown below?

Team Expenses		
Transportation	$240	■
Lodging	$360	▒
Meals	$120	□

A. **D.**

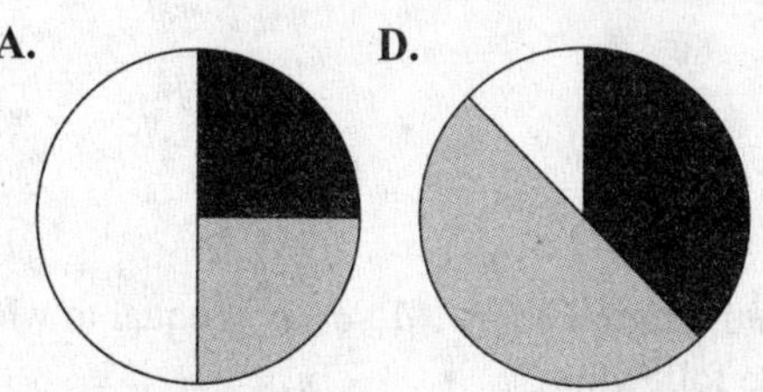

B. **E.**

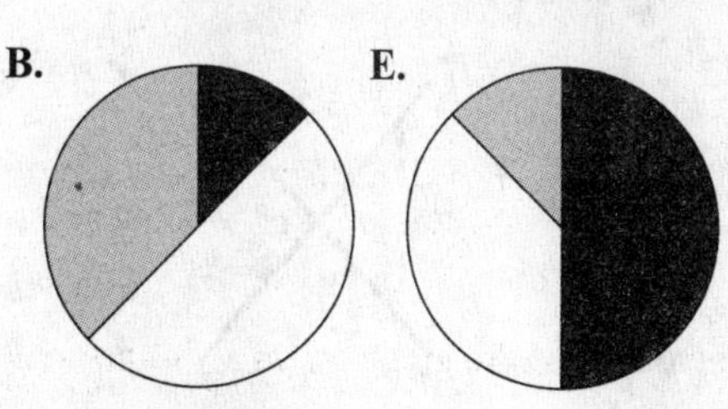

C.

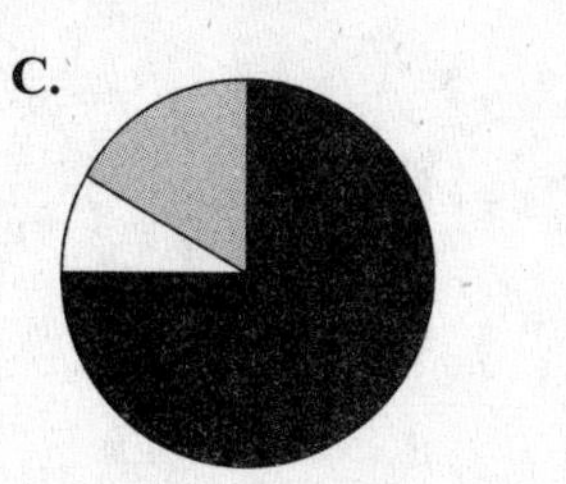

6. On the first day after being given an assignment, a student read $\frac{1}{2}$ the number of pages assigned, and on the second day, the student read 3 more pages. If the student still has 6 additional pages to read, how many pages were assigned?

   F. 15
   G. 18
   H. 24
   J. 30
   K. 36

7. The average (arithmetic mean) of Pat's scores on three tests was 80. If the average of her scores on the first two tests was 78, what was her score on the third test?

   A. 82
   B. 84
   C. 86
   D. 88
   E. 90

8. In the figure below, $a+c-b$ is equal to which of the following?

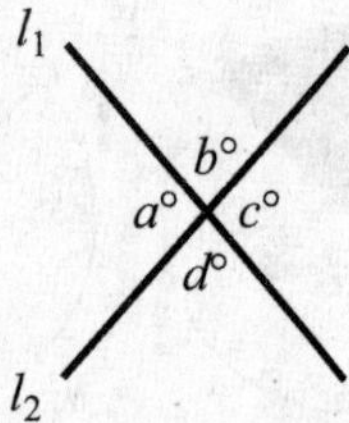

   F. $2a-d$
   G. $2a+d$
   H. $2d-a$
   J. $2a$
   K. 180

9. If $3a+6b=12$, then $a+2b=?$

   A. 1
   B. 2
   C. 3
   D. 4
   E. 6

10. Two circles with radii r and $r+3$ have areas that differ by 15π. What is the radius of the <u>smaller</u> circle?

   F. 4
   G. 3
   H. 2
   J. 1
   K. $\frac{1}{2}$

11. If x, y, and z are integers, $x>y>z>1$, and $xyz=144$, what is the <u>greatest</u> possible value of x?

   A. 8
   B. 12
   C. 16
   D. 24
   E. 36

12. For all integers, $x \Phi y = 2x+3y$. Which of the following must be true?

   I. $3 \Phi 2 = 12$
   II. $x \Phi y = y \Phi x$
   III. $0 \Phi (1 \Phi 2) = (0 \Phi 1) \Phi 2$

   F. I only
   G. I and II only
   H. I and III only
   J. II and III only
   K. I, II, and III

13. In the figure below, what is the slope of line l?

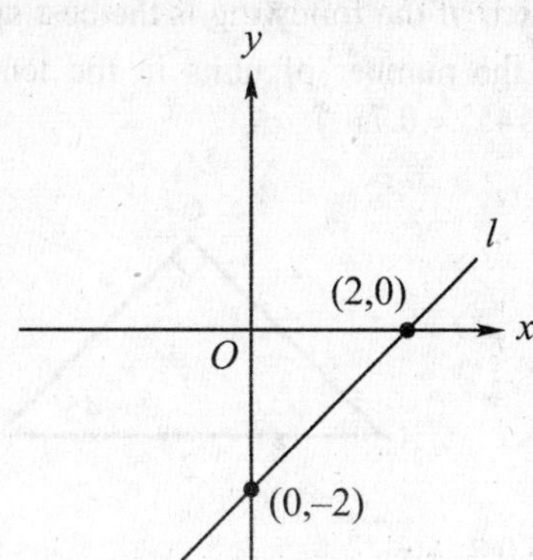

A. 1

B. $\frac{1}{2}$

C. 0

D. $-\frac{1}{2}$

E. –1

14. If Yuriko is now twice as old as Lisa was 10 years ago, how old is Lisa today if Yuriko is now n years old?

F. $\frac{n}{2}+10$

G. $\frac{n}{2}-10$

H. $n-10$

J. $2n+10$

K. $2n-10$

15. In the figure below, $ABCD$ is a rectangle with sides $\overline{AB}$, $\overline{BC}$, and $\overline{CD}$ touching the circle with center O. If the radius of the circle is 2, what is the area of the shaded region?

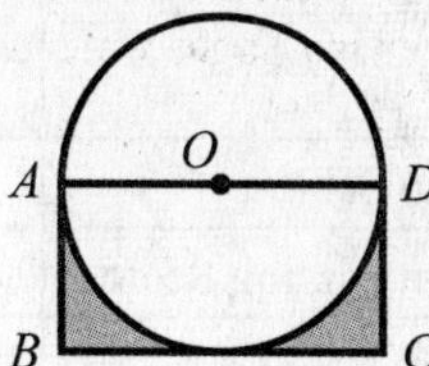

A. $\frac{3\pi}{2}$

B. $\frac{3\pi}{4}$

C. $8-2\pi$

D. $2-\pi$

E. $\pi-1$

16. The sum of two positive consecutive integers is n. In terms of n, what is the value of the larger of the two integers?

F. $\frac{n-1}{2}$

G. $\frac{n+1}{2}$

H. $\frac{n}{2}+1$

J. $\frac{n}{2}-1$

K. $\frac{n}{2}$

17. The table below shows a teacher how to convert scores for a test from the Old Scale to the New Scale. What is the Minimum Passing Score on the New Scale?

	Old Scale	*New Scale*
Minimum Score	0	120
Minimum Passing Score	60	?
Maximum Score	100	180

A. 108
B. 136
C. 156
D. 164
E. 208

18. If a polygon with all equal sides is inscribed in a circle, then the measure in degrees of the minor arc created by adjacent vertices of the polygon could be all of the following EXCEPT:

F. 30
G. 25
H. 24
J. 20
K. 15

19. A jar contains 5 blue marbles, 25 green marbles, and x red marbles. If the probability of drawing a red marble at random is $\frac{1}{4}$, what is the value of x?

A. 25
B. 20
C. 15
D. 12
E. 10

20. In the figure below, the length of $\overline{AB}$ is 2 units. Which of the following is the best approximation for the number of units in the length of $\overline{BC}$? ($\cos 45° \approx 0.7$)

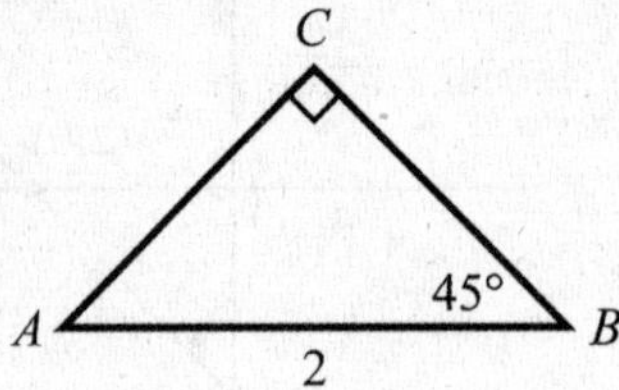

F. 0.7
G. 1.2
H. 1.4
J. 2.9
K. 3.4

REVIEW

This section contains additional Mathematics items for further practice. Answers are on page 634.

DIRECTIONS: Solve each item and choose the correct answer choice. Calculator use is permitted; however, some items are best solved without the use of a calculator.

Note: All of the following should be assumed, unless otherwise stated.

1. Illustrative figures are NOT necessarily drawn to scale.
2. The word *average* indicates arithmetic mean.
3. The word *line* indicates a straight line.
4. Geometric figures lie in a plane.

1. Nine playing cards from the same deck are placed as shown in the figure below to form a large rectangle of area 180 sq. in. How many inches are there in the perimeter of this large rectangle?

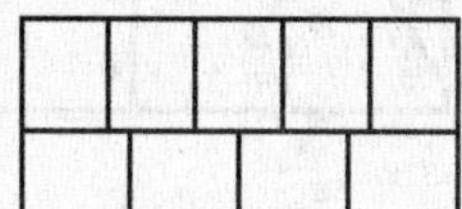

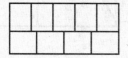

A. 29
B. 58
C. 64
D. 116
E. 210

2. If each of the dimensions of a rectangle is increased by 100%, by what percent is the area increased?

F. 100%
G. 200%
H. 300%
J. 400%
K. 500%

3. What is 10% of $\frac{x}{3}$ if $\frac{2x}{3}$ is 10% of 60?

A. 0.1
B. 0.2
C. 0.3
D. 0.4
E. 0.5

4. In the figure below, M and N are midpoints of sides $\overline{PR}$ and $\overline{PQ}$, respectively, of ΔPQR. What is the ratio of the area of ΔMNS to that of ΔPQR?

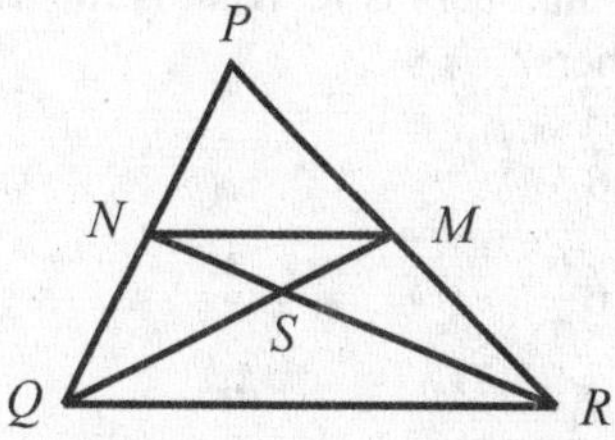

F. 2:5
G. 2:9
H. 1:4
J. 1:8
K. 1:12

5. A cube has an edge that is 4 inches long. If the edge is increased by 25%, which of the following is the best approximation of the percent increase in the volume of the cube?

A. 25%
B. 48%
C. 73%
D. 95%
E. 122%

6. In the figure below is a portion of the (x,y) coordinate plane. If each small square has an area of 1 and the coordinates of point P are (3,7), what are the (x,y) coordinates of point Q?

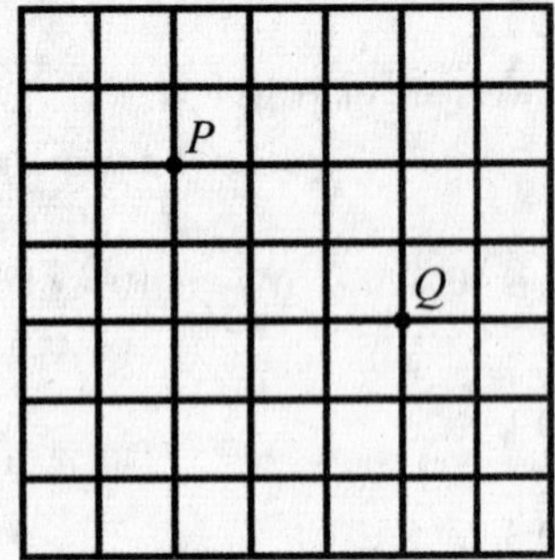

F. (5,6)
G. (1,10)
H. (6,9)
J. (6,5)
K. (5,10)

7. The average of 8 numbers is 6; the average of 6 other numbers is 8. What is the average of all 14 numbers?

A. 6
B. $6\frac{6}{7}$
C. 7
D. $7\frac{2}{7}$
E. $8\frac{1}{7}$

8. The front wheels of a wagon are 7 feet in circumference and the back wheels are 9 feet in circumference. When the front wheels have made 10 more revolutions than the back wheels, what distance, in feet, has the wagon gone?

F. 126
G. 180
H. 189
J. 315
K. 630

9. Doreen can wash her car in 15 minutes, while her younger brother Dave takes twice as long to do the same job. If they work together, how many minutes will the job take them?

A. 5
B. $7\frac{1}{2}$
C. 10
D. $22\frac{1}{2}$
E. 30

10. In the figure below, the sides of the large square are each 14 inches long. Joining the midpoints of each opposite side forms 4 smaller squares. What is the value of y, in inches?

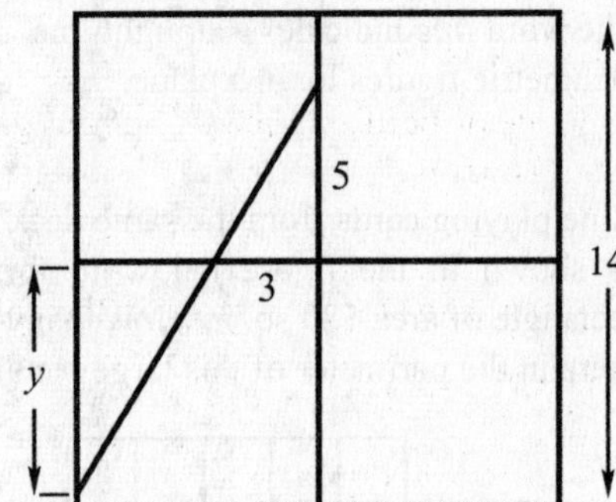

F. 5
G. 6
H. $6\frac{5}{8}$
J. $6\frac{2}{3}$
K. 6.8

11. In the figure below, *PQRS* is a parallelogram, and $\overline{ST} = \overline{TV} = \overline{VR}$. If $\angle PTS = 90°$, what is the ratio of the area of ΔSPT to the area of the parallelogram?

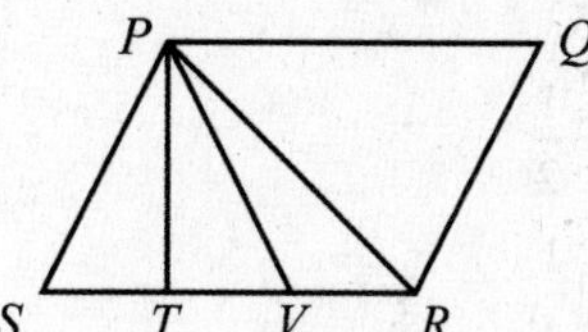

A. $\frac{1}{6}$

B. $\frac{1}{5}$

C. $\frac{2}{7}$

D. $2\frac{1}{3}$

E. Cannot be determined from the given information

12. If $p > q$ and $r < 0$, which of the following is (are) true?

I. $pr < qr$
II. $p + r > q + r$
III. $p - r < q - r$

F. I only
G. II only
H. I and III only
J. I and II only
K. I, II, and III

13. A pound of water is evaporated from 6 pounds of seawater that is 4% salt. What is the percentage of salt in the remaining solution?

A. 3.6%
B. 4%
C. 4.8%
D. 5.2%
E. 6%

14. John is now three times Pat's age. Four years from now, John will be *x* years old. In terms of *x*, how old is Pat now?

F. $\frac{x+4}{3}$

G. $3x$

H. $x + 4$

J. $x - 4$

K. $\frac{x-4}{3}$

15. In the figure below, what percent of the area of rectangle *PQRS* is shaded?

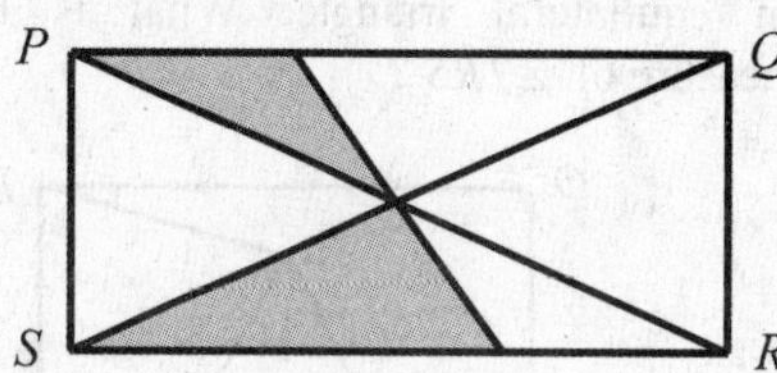

A. 20%
B. 25%
C. 30%
D. $33\frac{1}{3}\%$
E. 35%

16. A cylindrical container has a diameter of 14 inches and a height of 6 inches. Since one gallon equals 231 cubic inches, what is the approximate capacity, in gallons, of the tank?

F. $\frac{2}{3}$

G. $1\frac{1}{7}$

H. $2\frac{2}{7}$

J. $2\frac{2}{3}$

K. 4

17. A train running between two towns arrives at its destination 10 minutes late when it travels at a constant rate of 40 miles per hour and 16 minutes late when it travels at a constant rate of 30 miles per hour. What is the distance, in miles, between the two towns?

A. $8\frac{6}{7}$
B. 12
C. 192
D. 560
E. 720

18. In the figure below, *PQRS* is a square and *PTS* is an equilateral triangle. What is the degree measure of $\angle TRS$?

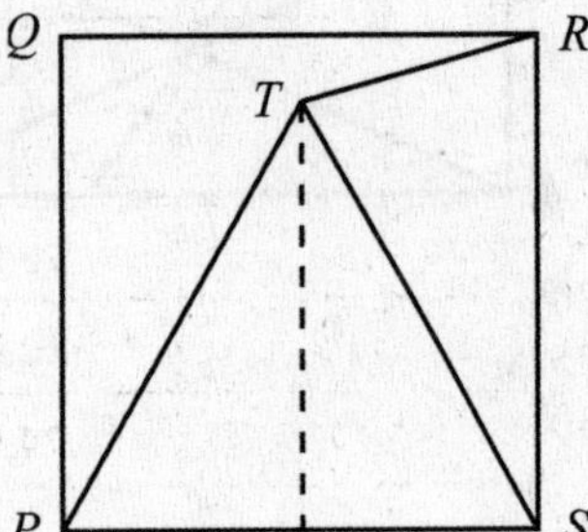

F. 60
G. 75
H. 80
J. 90
K. Cannot be determined from the given information

19. In the figure below, $\overline{PQ}$ is parallel to $\overline{RS}$, $y = 60°$, and $z = 130°$. What is the degree measure of $\angle x$?

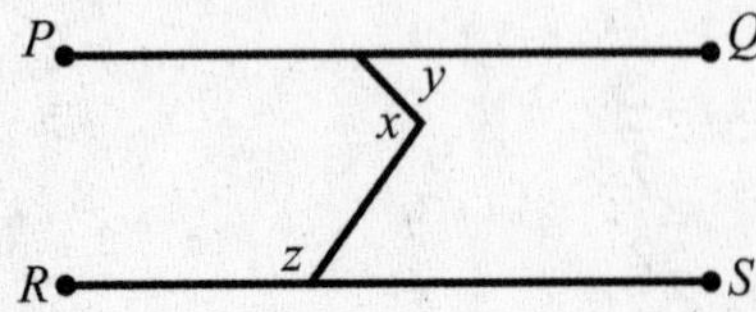

A. 90
B. 100
C. 110
D. 120
E. 130

20. Paul can paint a fence in 2 hours and Fred can paint the same fence in 3 hours. If Paul and Fred work together, how many hours will it take them to paint the fence?

F. 5
G. $2\frac{1}{2}$
H. $1\frac{1}{5}$
J. 1
K. $\frac{5}{6}$

21. A motorist drives 60 miles to her destination at an average speed of 40 miles per hour and makes the return trip at an average speed of 30 miles per hour. What is her average speed, in miles per hour, for the entire trip?

A. 17
B. $34\frac{2}{7}$
C. 35
D. $43\frac{1}{3}$
E. 70

22. An ice cream truck drives down Willy Street 4 times a week. The truck carries 5 different flavors of ice cream bars, each of which comes in 2 different designs. If the truck runs Monday through Thursday, and Monday was the first day of the month, by what day of the month could Zachary, buying 1 ice cream bar each time the truck drives down the street, purchase all of the different varieties of ice cream bars?

F. the 11th day
G. the 16th day
H. the 21st day
J. the 24th day
K. the 30th day

23. If $N! = N(N-1)(N-2)\ldots[N-(N-1)]$, what does $\frac{N!}{(N-2)!}$ equal?

A. $N^2 - N$
B. $N^5 + N^3 - N^2 + \frac{N}{N^2}$
C. $N+1$
D. 1
E. 6

24. In the figure below, *ABC* is an equilateral triangle with a perpendicular line drawn from point *A* to point *D*. If the triangle is "folded over" on the perpendicular line so that points *B* and *C* meet, the perimeter of the new triangle is approximately what percent of the perimeter of the triangle before the fold?

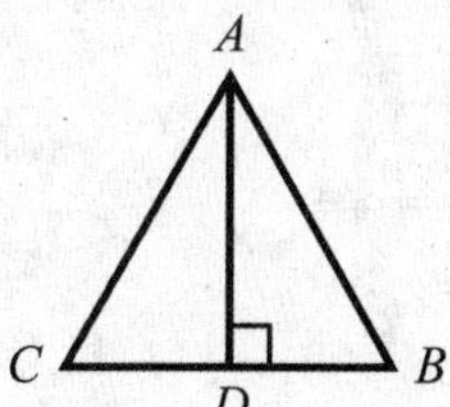

F. 100%
G. 78%
H. 50%
J. 32%
K. Cannot be determined from the given information

25. In the figure below, $\overline{AB}$ is three times longer than $\overline{BC}$, and $\overline{CD}$ is two times longer than $\overline{BC}$. If $\overline{BC}$ is removed from the line and the other two segments are joined to form one line, what is the ratio of the original length of $\overline{AD}$ to the new length of $\overline{AD}$?

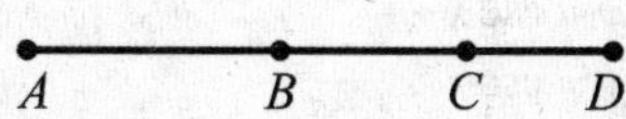

A. 3:2
B. 6:5
C. 5:4
D. 7:6
E. 11:10

26. If $(x+1)(x-2)$ is positive, then which of the following statements is true?

F. $x < -1$ or $x > 2$
G. $x > -1$ or $x < 2$
H. $-1 < x < 2$
J. $-2 < x < 1$
K. $x = -1$ or $x = 2$

27. In the table below, which yearly period had the smallest percent increase in sales?

ABC SOUND STORES Annual Sale of Cassettes	
Year	*Number Sold*
2002	7,000
2003	9,000
2004	12,000
2005	16,000
2006	20,000
2007	24,000

A. 2002–2003
B. 2003–2004
C. 2004–2005
D. 2005–2006
E. 2006–2007

28. For the figure below, which of the following statements is true?

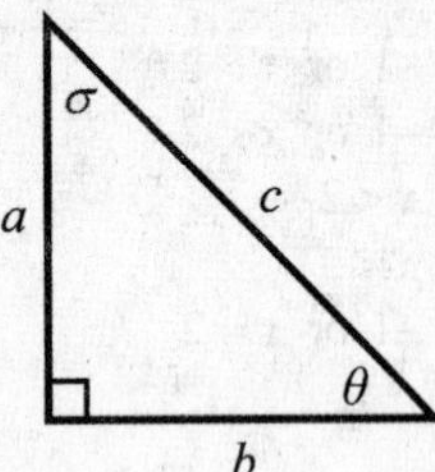

F. $\sin\theta = \frac{b}{c}$
G. $\tan\sigma = \frac{a}{b}$
H. $\cos\theta = \frac{c}{a}$
J. $\sin\theta = \cos\sigma$
K. $\cot\sigma = \tan\sigma$

29. In the figure below, if $\arcsin s = 2(\arcsin d)$, then $x = ?$

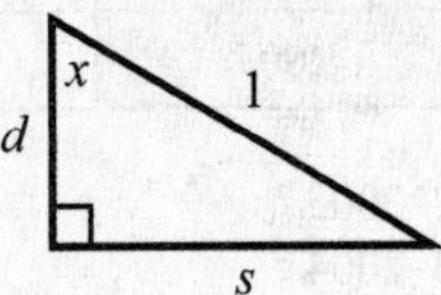

A. 15
B. 30
C. 45
D. 60
E. 75

30. In the figure below, if $\overline{AC}$ is the diameter of the circle, B is a point on the circle, and $\sin\theta = \frac{1}{2}$, then $\sin\phi = ?$

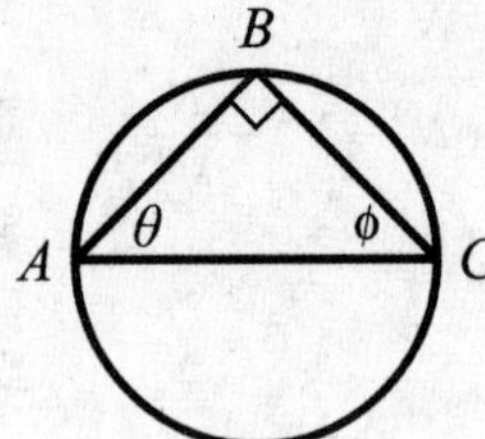

F. $\frac{\sqrt{2}}{3}$
G. $\frac{\sqrt{3}}{3}$
H. $\frac{\sqrt{3}}{2}$
J. $\frac{2\sqrt{2}}{3}$
K. $\frac{2\sqrt{3}}{2}$

31. The figure below is a possible graph of which of the following equations?

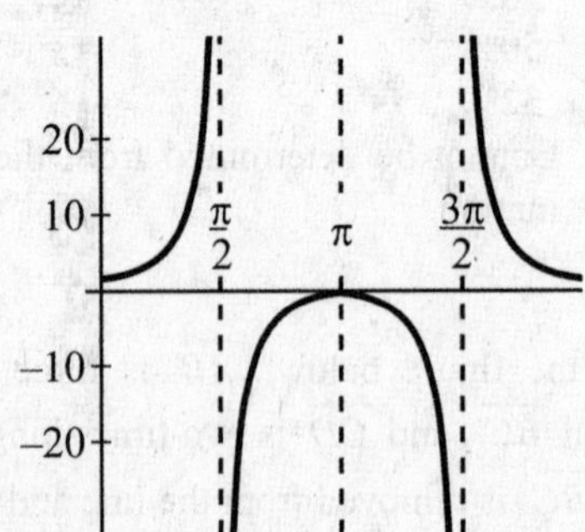

A. $y = 2(\sin x)$
B. $y = \sin x + 2$
C. $y = \csc x + 1$
D. $y = \csc x - 1$
E. $y = \sec x + 1$

32. If θ is an acute angle and $\cos\theta = \frac{b}{c}$, $b > 0$ and $c > 0$ and $b \neq c$, then $\sin\theta$ is equal to which of the following?

F. $\frac{b}{\sqrt{b^2 - c^2}}$

G. $\frac{c}{\sqrt{b^2 - b^2}}$

H. $\frac{\sqrt{b^2 - c^2}}{b}$

J. $\frac{\sqrt{b^2 - c^2}}{c}$

K. $\frac{\sqrt{c^2 - b^2}}{c}$

GENERAL STRATEGIES: When approaching a Mathematics item, there are several things to which you should pay careful attention:

1. *Figures:* Figures are usually, but not always, drawn to scale. When all other options for answering the item fail, try the strategy of assuming the figure *is* drawn to scale. Then, use the figure to help you answer the item.

2. *Answer Choices:* Most answer choices are arranged in order of ascending or descending value and many incorrect answer choices correspond to conceptual errors.

3. *"Signal" Words:* Typically, "signal" words are capitalized (e.g., thought-reversers, such as "NOT," "CANNOT," and "EXCEPT"); however, they may sometimes be underlined or italicized (e.g., specified units). While the specific formatting of these words may vary, they can be critical to correctly understanding the item. Pay careful attention to thought-reversers, as they reverse the apparent meaning of an item.

4. *Ladder of Difficulty:* Difficult Mathematics items tend to be clustered near the end of the section. When solving items that are high on the ladder of difficulty, be wary of simplistic answers and the "Cannot be determined..." response. Remember to pace yourself—difficult, time-consuming items have the same value as the easy items.

5. *Preview Item Stems:* Read the item stem first. Only then should you read the details of the item, keeping this item stem in mind.

6. *Confirm Solutions:* Double-check the solution by confirming that it answers the particular question that is being asked. When applicable, this confirmation includes verifying that the solution is given in the units specified by the item stem.

If you are unable to either find an elegant (quick) solution or solve the item directly based on subject knowledge, the following alternative solutions strategies can be extremely helpful:

1. *"Test-the-Test" Strategy*: The correct answer to any item is always one of five given choices. Sometimes, the easiest and quickest way to solve an item is to test each of the answer choices. The "test-the-test" strategy can mean plugging answer choices back into the item (starting with the middle answer choice) to test the validity of an expression, or it can mean checking each answer choice against any stated conditions. The "test-the-test" strategy is typically useful for items with numerical solutions or variables and values that meet stated conditions.

2. *"Plug-and-Chug" Strategy*: This strategy is similar to the "test-the-test" strategy in that the item stem and answer choices (rather than direct mathematical solution strategies) are used to isolate the correct answer. The difference is that rather than testing the validity of each answer choice against the item stem conditions, the item stem and/or answer choices are evaluated by plugging in chosen numbers: "plug-and-chug." This strategy is especially helpful when solving Algebra items.

3. *"Eliminate-and-Guess" Strategy*: If unable to determine the correct answer directly by using mathematical methods or indirectly by using either the "test-the-test" or "plug-and-chug" strategy, eliminate as many answer choices as possible and then guess from the remaining answer choices. For difficult mathematics items, eliminate answer choices that can be reached either by a single step or by copying a number from the item.

CHECKLIST OF SKILLS AND CONCEPTS:

Arithmetic

___ Simplifying: Fractions, Collecting Terms
___ Factoring
___ Approximation
___ The "Flying-X" Method
___ Decimal/Fraction Equivalents
___ Properties of Numbers (Odd, Even, Negative, Positive, Consecutive)
___ Sets (Union, Intersection, Elements)
___ Absolute Value
___ Percents (Change, Original Amount, Price Increase)
___ Ratios (Two-Part, Three-Part, Weighted)
___ Proportions (Direct, Indirect)

Algebra

___ Evaluation of Expressions (Rational, Radical)
___ Exponents (Integer, Rational, Negative)
___ Factoring
___ Sequence
___ Solving Single Variable Equations and Inequalities
___ Absolute Value
___ Function (Picture) Math
___ Domain and Range
___ Solving Equations (Multi-Variable, Linear, Quadratic, Simultaneous)
___ Story Problems: Work (Joint Effort), Averages

Coordinate Geometry

___ Coordinate Plane
___ Slope of a Line
___ Slope-Intercept Form of a Linear Equation
___ Distance Formula
___ Graphing Linear Equations
___ Graphing First-Degree Inequalities
___ Graphing Quadratic Equations
___ Permutations of Equations and Graphs

Geometry

___ Lines and Angles (Perpendicular, Parallel, Intersecting, Big Angle/Little Angle Theorem)
___ Triangles (Equilateral, Isosceles, Acute, Obtuse, Perimeter, Area, Altitudes, Angles, Bisectors, Pythagorean Theorem)
___ Quadrilaterals (Squares, Rectangles, Rhombuses, Parallelograms, Trapezoids, Perimeter, Area)
___ Polygons (Sum of Interior Angles)
___ Circles (Chords, Tangents, Radius, Diameter, Circumference, Area)
___ Solids (Cubes, Cylinders, Spheres, Volumes, Surface Areas)
___ Complex Figures

Trigonometry

___ Trigonometric Functions
___ Trigonometric Values
___ Trigonometric Relationships

Statistics and Probability

___ Averages (Simple, Weighted), Median, and Mode
___ Probability
___ Graphs (Bar, Cumulative, Line)
___ Pie Charts
___ Tables (Matrices)
___ Scatterplots

NOTES: ____

____

Reading

COURSE CONCEPT OUTLINE

What You Absolutely Must Know

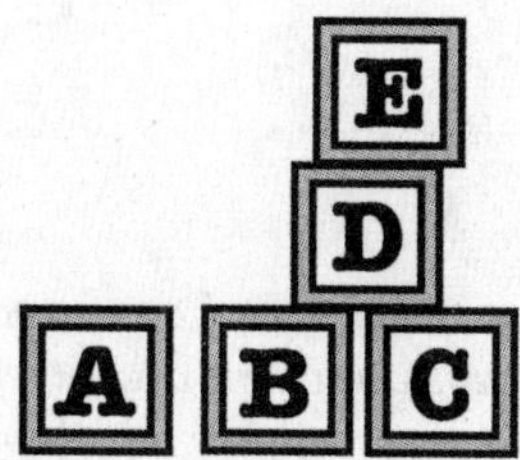

BASICS

The Reading Test consists of four approximately 700-word reading selections, each followed by 10 items. You read a passage and answer the items based upon what is stated or implied in the reading selection.

You'll have one passage from each of the following four categories: Prose Fiction, Social Science, Humanities, and Natural Science. In most cases, the passage will be about a topic with which you are not familiar. The test-writers choose unusual topics so that the Reading Test will be one of reading skill and not of knowledge. Of course, you may find a topic that you know something about, but even so, your knowledge is probably not going to help you very much, though familiarity with a topic is a definite advantage.

The time limit for the 40 items on the Reading Test is 35 minutes. Given the time limit, you obviously need to work quickly. The exam, however, is not a test of "speed-reading." Instead, the exam is a test of reading comprehension.

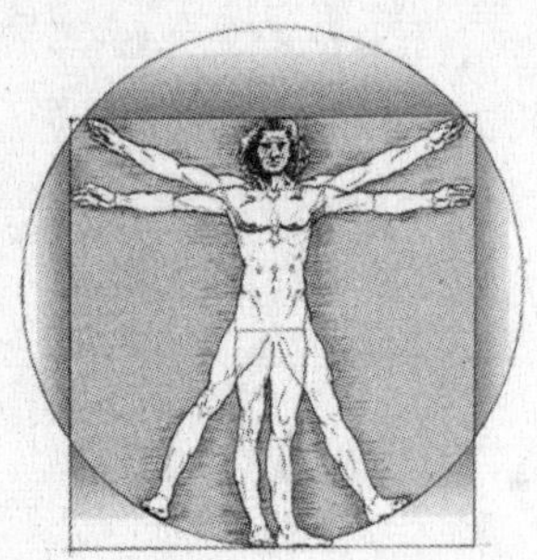

ANATOMY

DIRECTIONS: The passage below is followed by a set of items. Read the passage and choose the best answer for each item. You may refer to the passage as often as necessary to answer the items.

The directions make Reading items sound easy: read this and answer the items. So, the directions aren't very helpful, and you can ignore them from now on. (<u>Note:</u> Given space restrictions, this passage is much shorter than those used by the ACT.)

Passage I

SOCIAL SCIENCE: This passage is adapted from a government publication about the history of alcohol abuse.

Most of the passages include an introductory note telling you where the passage comes from. A note may provide some useful information, so read it.

The movement to prohibit alcohol began in the early years of the nineteenth century with the formation of local societies in New York and Massachusetts to promote temperance in consumption of alcohol. Many of the temperance societies were affiliated with Protestant evangelical denominations and met in local churches. As time passed, most temperance societies modified their goal to call for complete abstinence from all alcoholic beverages.

Typically, reading passages discuss an unfamiliar topic. Even if you know something about Prohibition, that information may or may not be helpful since you'll be asked about this particular passage.

This passage is organized chronologically. The first paragraph talks about the "early years of the nineteenth century," in other words, the early 1800s.

In 1919, largely in response to the lobbying efforts of the Anti-Saloon League, the Eighteenth Amendment to the Constitution was passed banning the production, transportation, and sale of all alcoholic beverages. The Amendment, also known as the Prohibition Amendment, provided for concurrent enforcement by both federal and state law. By January 1920, in addition to the federal Volstead Act, the nation had laws in thirty-three states prohibiting alcohol entirely.

The second paragraph starts with 1919. Then, the passage briefly traces the events leading up to Prohibition.

Prohibition, however, proved unworkable as bootleggers and speakeasies quickly organized to satisfy the public's continuing thirst for alcohol. Thirteen years later, the "Noble Experiment," doomed by the impracticality of enforcement, ended with the repeal of the Prohibition Amendment.

The third paragraph explains why Prohibition failed: people wanted to drink, so bootleggers and illegal clubs satisfied that demand. Eventually, Prohibition was repealed.

1. The passage is primarily concerned with the:

A. social problems caused by alcohol abuse.
B. founding of anti-alcohol temperance societies.
C. origins of Prohibition and its subsequent failure.
D. efforts to enforce Prohibition legislation.

2. According to the passage, in the early nineteenth century, temperance societies originally:

F. encouraged moderation in alcohol use.
G. demanded the repeal of the Eighteenth Amendment.
H. supported efforts to enforce the Volstead Act.
J. refused to align with religious groups.

3. The passage implies that Prohibition failed because:

A. religious organizations withdrew their support for the program.
B. the repeal of the Eighteenth Amendment was only experimental.
C. too many states passed laws prohibiting the sale of alcohol.
D. widespread demand for alcohol made enforcement impossible.

4. In line 15, the word *concurrent* means:

F. unsuccessful.
G. shared.
H. practicable.
J. intermittent.

1. **(C)** *This is a common type of Reading item: the item asks you to identify the main idea of the passage. The passage discusses the origins and failure of Prohibition.*

2. **(F)** *This item asks about something that is specifically stated in the passage. The author clearly states that the temperance societies were originally founded to "promote temperance" as opposed to complete prohibition.*

3. **(D)** *This item requires that you "read between the lines" of the passage. In the third paragraph, the author does not specifically say why Prohibition failed, but you can figure it out from what's said: people simply refused to quit consuming alcohol, even illegally.*

4. **(G)** *This item asks you for the definition of a term in the context of the passage. The passage states that the federal government and the states were given "concurrent" authority and that the states, as well as the federal government, passed laws against alcohol. So, "concurrent" must mean something like "joint" or "shared."*

PACING

The Reading Test has 40 items and a 35-minute time limit. The fact that there are four passages of approximately equal length, each with the same number of items, and a 35-minute time limit leads naturally to the conclusion that you should spend eight minutes and 45 seconds on each passage—and that's a pretty good plan. The following table summarizes the timing for this approach.

Task	*Allotted Time*	*Remaining Time*
Read the first selected passage	2.5 minutes	32.5 minutes
Answer the accompanying items	6.25 minutes*	26.25 minutes
Read the second selected passage	2.5 minutes	23.75 minutes
Answer the accompanying items	6.25 minutes*	17.5 minutes
Read the third selected passage	2.5 minutes	15 minutes
Answer the accompanying items	6.25 minutes*	8.75 minutes
Read the fourth selected passage	2.5 minutes	6.25 minutes
Answer the accompanying items	6.25 minutes*	0 minutes

*Approximately 37 seconds per item

Note that the table refers to "first selected passage," "second selected passage," and so on. These references are to the order in which you decide to do the passages, not to the order in which they are presented in your test booklet. For reasons discussed in the "Game Plan" feature, you might choose to start with the passage that appears last. It's up to you.

TIME TRIAL

3 Items
Time—3 minutes

DIRECTIONS: The passage below is followed by a set of items. Read the passage and choose the best answer for each item. You may refer to the passage as often as necessary to answer the items.

Passage I

NATURAL SCIENCE: This passage is excerpted from an essay exploring the possible reasons for extinction of salmon runs in New England rivers.

Folklore holds that Atlantic salmon were once so abundant in New England rivers that early colonists walked across the backs of the fish as they ran up the rivers in spring. Then, according to the received wisdom, at the turn of the nineteenth century, increasing pollution in the rivers and the construction of large main stem dams across rivers caused salmon to become severely depleted. If this theory were accurate, then there should be considerable archaeological evidence that salmon played a significant role in the diets of the aboriginal peoples of New England; but in site after site, although bones of numerous other fish species have been recovered, no salmon bones have been found. It's more likely that the accounts of salmon were intentionally embellished by early writers.

In fact, salmon did not begin to colonize New England streams until a period of climatic cooling known as the Little Ice Age (C.E. 1550–1800). At the end of this period, the climatic warming created less favorable environmental conditions for salmon, and hence their range retracted. The idea that initial colonization did not occur until this time, and then only as a temporary range expansion, explains the lack of salmon in prehistoric sites and the depletion of the fish at the end of the eighteenth century.

While authorities such as D. W. Lufkin have stated that "the circumstances leading to the demise of *Salmo salar* are relatively simple to identify" and have cited dams, pollution, logging practices, and over-fishing, causes behind its demise are more complex, with ecological and climatological bases. If pollution and dams were the major cause of the extinctions, then why were the runs not made extinct on the Penobscot, a heavily dammed and polluted river in Maine? Why did salmon runs become extinct downstream of the dams on the Connecticut River? The general lack of success in salmon restoration programs over the last two centuries suggests a more fundamental ecological cause for impoverished salmon runs in New England than an anthropogenic one.

1. The primary purpose of the passage is to:
   - **A.** propose a long term plan for restoring salmon runs to the rivers of New England.
   - **B.** undermine the theory that human activity caused the extinction of salmon runs in New England rivers.
   - **C.** demonstrate that anthropogenic factors are often more powerful than natural ones in shaping the environment.
   - **D.** provide evidence that the disappearance of *Salmo salar* was caused by the damming and pollution of the rivers.

2. The author cites the lack of salmon bones in archaeological digs as evidence that:

   F. the salmon population in New England rivers declined sharply after the end of the Little Ice Age.
   G. aboriginal Americans, who consumed other fish species, refused to eat the abundant salmon.
   H. salmon were not available to aboriginal Americans before the time of the arrival of the first colonists.
   J. anthropogenic factors were largely responsible for the extinction of the salmon runs.

3. It can be inferred that D. W. Lufkin would most likely:

   A. agree with the author that the primary causes of the depletion of salmon stocks are climatological.
   B. accept the author's contention that early reports about the abundance of salmon were greatly exaggerated.
   C. reject the author's thesis and insist that the causes of salmon extinction are anthropogenic.
   D. disagree with the author that salmon stocks have declined precipitously since the end of the eighteenth century.

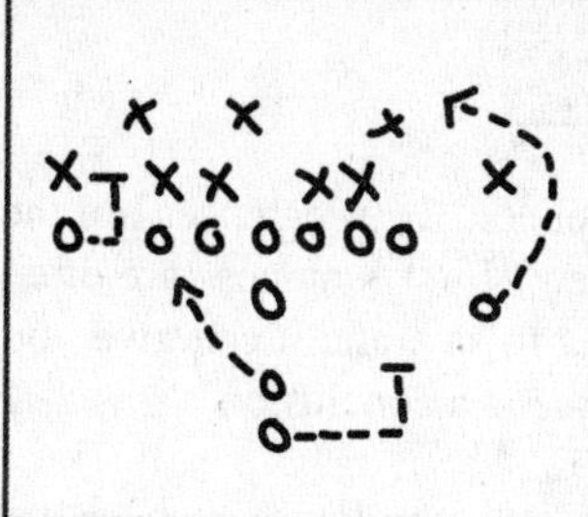

GAME PLAN

Quickly Preview the Test, but Skip the Directions

Last-minute adjustments to the test format are theoretically (but not practically) possible, so check the subject test before you start to work, especially the number of passages, the number of items, and the time limit. And yes, the test-writers always tell you to "read the directions carefully." But they don't tell you that you have to read them during the test. Instead, become familiar with them before test day. That way, you won't waste 30 seconds or more (enough time to answer an item) re-reading directions you are already familiar with.

Personalize the Passage Order

Remember that you don't have to do the items in the order in which they are presented in the booklet. For some sections, like the math section, doing problems in order (more or less) makes good sense. But in Reading, it is a sound strategy to make a choice about the order in which you're going to work through the section. You may decide to do the passages in the order presented, or you may want to change the order.

What factors should you consider? First, you may find a topic that seems familiar to you. Of course, you can't expect that you'll already know the answers to the items, but familiarity is a definite advantage. Second, you'll feel more comfortable with some topics than with others. Do you like biology but hate literature or like social science but hate art? Then do the passages with topics that you like first.

This sets up the following personalized order for completion of the passages:

1. Choose familiar topics to do first.
2. Otherwise, choose your favorite topics to do first.
3. Choose your second favorite topic to do second, and so on.

When you choose your passages, you should number them in the margin of your test booklet. Put a big "1" by the passage you'll do first, and so on.

Read Any Introductory Notes

Most passages on the Reading Test will include an introductory note telling you where the passage comes from and maybe some other information. Sometimes, this information is useful for getting a better understanding of the passage. Therefore, before starting on a passage and items, always read any introductory notes.

Preview the Passage

Before you begin reading a particular passage, take 15 to 30 seconds to preview key sentences. Key sentences are the first and last sentences of the passage and the first sentence of each paragraph. Why preview? First sentences are often topic sentences, so reading a series of topic sentences will tell you what the author is trying to say, and it can give you an outline of the development of the passage. Sometimes, though not always, the last sentence is a conclusion.

To see how this can work, preview the following passage about solar energy, in which only the key sentences are visible.

At the present time, 98 percent of world energy consumption comes from sources such as fossil fuels.

Our energy consumption amounts to about one-ten thousandth of the energy we receive from the sun.

It is often stated that the growth rate will decline or that energy conservation measures will preclude any long-range problem.

The only practical means of avoiding the problem of thermal pollution is the use of solar energy.

To see what you can learn from just a few sentences, think about these questions:

What's the passage about?

- Gas mileage.
- Space exploration.
- Solar energy.

What is a common attitude about energy conservation?

- That it doesn't work.
- That it might work.
- That it will probably work.

What's the author's view on solar energy?

- It doesn't work.
- It's unnecessary.
- It's absolutely essential.

And the answers are that the passage is about solar energy, which the author believes to be necessary, even though a lot of people think conservation could solve all our problems.

Preview the Item Stems

Additionally, before reading a particular passage, you may find it helpful to preview the item stems, which are presented either as questions or incomplete statements. If a stem mentions a key word or phrase, make a mental note and look for it as you read the selection. See what you would learn from the following items, in which only the item stems are visible.

1. According to the passage, the most important disadvantage of nuclear energy is:

   A.
   B.
   C.
   D.

Previewing would tell you to look for certain information in your reading. The first stem uses the phrase "most important disadvantage of nuclear energy." So, you know that the passage will discuss disadvantages of nuclear energy. When you find the "most important" one, mark that reference so that you can answer this item.

2. According to the author, shifting climate patterns will have all of the following effects EXCEPT:

   F.
   G.
   H.
   J.

The second stem tells you that the author discusses "shifting climate patterns," probably in some detail since the passage mentions multiple effects. Each time you find one of the effects, mark it so that when you answer this item you can eliminate those choices that mention such effects. ("EXCEPT" means to look for the one NOT mentioned in the passage.)

3. The author's attitude toward scientists who deny that average temperatures are rising can best be described as:

   A.
   B.
   C.
   D.

The third stem lets you know that the passage discusses average temperatures and a theory advanced by some scientists. If you find that reference in your reading, you'll have the answer to this item.

4. Which of the following best describes the main point of the passage?

   F.
   G.
   H.
   J.

Finally, the last stem tells you to look for the main idea. That, in and of itself, is not particularly helpful because you're always reading for the main idea—even if you don't get a question that asks about it. So, some stems are not very helpful while others are.

Note that some students may not find this technique useful. Try it, and use it if you like it. Otherwise, do not preview the item stems.

Read the Passage

Keep the following points in mind when reading a passage:

- Read the passage quickly but carefully. You'll probably need about two to three minutes to read a passage. This is about 300 to 350 words a minute.
- Read the passage for important themes. Many of the items will ask about important themes of the passage, such as the main point, the purpose of a particular paragraph, or the author's intention.
- Do not try to memorize details. If you need detailed information, you can always go back to the passage to find it. This is an "open-book" test.
- Pause at the end to summarize your reading. One of the most helpful reading techniques is to summarize in your own words what you have just read. What is the main point? What did the author do in the first paragraph? In the second paragraph? What did the author prove?

Answer the Items

Keep the following points in mind when answering the accompanying items:

- Identify the question being asked. Reading items fall into one of seven categories such as "Main Idea," "Explicit Detail," and "Vocabulary." Specific item-types have characteristic kinds of answers. If you identify the category first, it will be easier to find the right answer. You'll learn more about the seven item-types later in the Reading Lesson.
- Answer the question being asked. One of the most common mistakes made by examinees is to read the item stem carelessly and then answer the "wrong" question. That is, they respond to what they think they read rather than what is actually on the page. Since wrong answers often sound plausible, if you make this mistake, you're probably going to find a pretty good answer—to the wrong question.
- Read the answer choices carefully. You'll learn how to recognize the seven Reading item-types and what the correct answer to each should look like. Do this experiment: estimate how many words are in the passage and then how many are in the answer choices. The answer choices are just about as long as the passage itself. That means reading comprehension doesn't stop at the end of the last sentence of the passage. It continues all the way through to the last word of the last answer choice to the last item.
- Pay attention to thought-reversers. Thought-reversers are words in the item stem like "NOT," "BUT," and "EXCEPT." These words turn the question upside down. What is normally the right answer is now a wrong answer, and what is normally a wrong answer is the right answer.
- Do not spend too much time on any one item. Remember that you get +1 for the hardest question and +1 for the easiest. With Reading items, the easiest ones can theoretically be the last in the group and the hardest ones can be the first. So, if you sense that you're spinning your wheels, make a guess and then move along. You should always guess, even if you are unable to eliminate any answer choices, because there is no penalty for guessing on the ACT test. However, your chances improve if you are able to eliminate even one answer choice.

LESSON

The passages and items in this section accompany the in-class review of the skills and concepts tested by the ACT Reading Test. You will work through the items with your instructor in class. Answers are on page 635.

DIRECTIONS: Each passage below is followed by a set of items. Read the passage and choose the best answer for each item. You may refer to the passage as often as necessary to answer the items.

Passage I

SOCIAL SCIENCE: This passage is excerpted from an essay about the presidential election of 1796 in a history book.

To broaden their voting appeal in the Presidential election of 1796, the Federalists selected Thomas Pinckney, a leading South Carolinian, as running mate for the New Englander John Adams. But Pinckney's Southern friends chose to ignore their party's intentions and regarded Pinckney as a Presidential candidate, creating a political situation that Alexander Hamilton was determined to exploit. Hamilton had long been wary of Adams' stubbornly independent brand of politics and preferred to see his running mate, who was more pliant and over whom Hamilton could exert more control, in the President's chair.

The election was held under the system originally established by the Constitution. At that time, there was but a single tally, with the candidate receiving the largest number of electoral votes declared President and the candidate with the second largest number declared Vice President. Hamilton anticipated that all the Federalists in the North would vote for Adams and Pinckney equally in an attempt to ensure that Jefferson would not be either first or second in the voting. Pinckney would be solidly supported in the South while Adams would not. Hamilton concluded if it were possible to divert a few electoral votes from Adams to Pinckney, Pinckney would receive more than Adams, yet both Federalists would outpoll Jefferson.

Various methods were used to persuade the electors to vote as Hamilton wished. In the press, anonymous articles were published attacking Adams for his monarchical tendencies and Jefferson for being overly democratic, while pushing Pinckney as the only suitable candidate. In private correspondence with state party leaders, the Hamiltonians encouraged the idea that Adams' popularity was slipping, that he could not win the election, and that the Federalists could defeat Jefferson only by supporting Pinckney.

Had sectional pride and loyalty not run as high in New England as in the deep South, Pinckney might well have become Washington's successor. New Englanders, however, realized that equal votes for Adams and Pinckney in their states would defeat Adams; therefore, eighteen electors scratched Pinckney's name from their ballots and deliberately threw away their second votes to men who were not even running. It was fortunate for Adams that they did, for the electors from South Carolina completely abandoned him, giving eight votes to Pinckney and eight to Jefferson.

In the end, Hamilton's interference in Pinckney's candidacy lost him even the Vice Presidency. Without New England's support, Pinckney received only 59 electoral votes, finishing third to Adams and Jefferson. He might have been President in 1797, or as Vice President a serious contender for the Presidency in 1800; instead, stigmatized by a plot he had not devised, he served a brief term in the United States Senate and then dropped from sight as a national influence.

1. The main purpose of the passage is to:

   A. propose reforms of the procedures for electing the President and Vice President.
   B. condemn Alexander Hamilton for interfering in the election of 1796.
   C. describe the political events that led to John Adams' victory in the 1796 Presidential election.
   D. contrast the political philosophy of the Federalists to that of Thomas Jefferson.

2. Which of the following titles best describes the content of the passage?

   F. The Failure of Alexander Hamilton's Plan for Thomas Pinckney to Win the 1796 Presidential Election
   G. The Roots of Alexander Hamilton's Distrust of John Adams and New England's Politics
   H. Important Issues in the 1796 Presidential Campaign as Presented by the Federalist Candidates
   J. The Political Careers of Alexander Hamilton, John Adams, and Thomas Pinckney

3. According to the passage, which of the following was true of the Presidential election of 1796?

   A. Thomas Jefferson received more electoral votes than did Thomas Pinckney.
   B. John Adams received strong support from the electors of South Carolina.
   C. Alexander Hamilton received most of the electoral votes of New England.
   D. Thomas Pinckney was selected by Federalist party leaders to be the party's Presidential candidate.

4. According to the passage, Hamilton's plan included all of the following EXCEPT:

   F. articles published in newspapers to create opposition to John Adams.
   G. South Carolina's loyalty to Thomas Pinckney.
   H. private contact with state officials urging them to support Thomas Pinckney.
   J. John Adams' reputation as a stubborn and independent New Englander.

5. The passage supplies information that answers which of the following questions?

   A. How many electoral votes were cast for John Adams in the 1796 Presidential election?
   B. Under the voting system originally set up by the Constitution, how many votes did each elector cast?
   C. Who was Jefferson's running mate in the 1796 Presidential election?
   D. What became of Alexander Hamilton after his plan to have Thomas Pinckney elected President failed?

6. In line 11, the word *pliant* most nearly means:

   F. assertive.
   G. public.
   H. national.
   J. yielding.

7. Why does the author refer to the election procedure established by the original Constitution?

   A. To prove to the reader that New England as a whole had more electoral votes than the state of South Carolina
   B. To persuade the reader that Thomas Pinckney's defeat could have been avoided
   C. To alert the reader that the procedure used in 1796 was unlike that presently used
   D. To encourage the reader to study Constitutional history

8. The overall development of the passage can best be described as:

   F. refuting possible explanations for certain phenomena.
   G. documenting a thesis with specific examples.
   H. offering an explanation of a series of events.
   J. making particular proposals to solve a problem.

9. The passage implies that some electors voted for John Adams because they were:

A. in favor of a monarchy.
B. persuaded to do so by Hamilton.
C. afraid South Carolina would not vote for Pinckney.
D. anxious to have a President from their geographical region.

10. Which of the following can be inferred from the passage?

F. Thomas Pinckney had a personal dislike for Jefferson's politics.
G. The Federalists regarded themselves as more democratic than Jefferson.
H. The Hamiltonians contacted key Southern leaders to persuade them to vote for Adams.
J. Electors were likely to vote for candidates from their own geographical region.

11. It can be inferred that had South Carolina not cast any electoral votes for Jefferson, the outcome of the 1796 election would have been a:

A. larger margin of victory for John Adams.
B. victory for Thomas Jefferson.
C. Federalist defeat in the Senate.
D. victory for Thomas Pinckney.

12. The electors who scratched Pinckney's name from their ballots behaved most like which of the following people?

F. A newspaper publisher who adds a special section to the Sunday edition to review the week's political events
G. A member of the clergy who encourages members of other faiths to meet to discuss solutions to the community's problems
H. An artist who saves preliminary sketches of an important work even after the work is finally completed
J. A general who orders his retreating troops to destroy supplies they must leave behind so the enemy cannot use the supplies

13. Hamilton's strategy can best be summarized as:

A. divide and conquer.
B. retreat and regroup.
C. feint and counterattack.
D. hit and run.

14. The tone of the passage can best be described as:

F. witty.
G. comical.
H. scholarly.
J. frivolous.

15. The author's attitude toward Hamilton's plan can best be described as:

A. angry.
B. approving.
C. analytical.
D. regretful.

Passage II

HUMANITIES: This passage is adapted from an essay on citizenship in a philosophy textbook.

The liberal view of democratic citizenship that developed in the seventeenth and eighteenth centuries was fundamentally different from that of the classical Greeks. The pursuit of private interests with as little interference as possible from government was seen as the road to human happiness and progress rather than the public obligations and involvement in the collective community that were emphasized by the Greeks. Freedom was to be realized by limiting the scope of governmental activity and political obligation and not through immersion in the collective life of the *polis*. The basic role of the citizen was to select governmental leaders and keep the powers and scope of public authority in check. On the liberal view, the rights of citizens against the state were the focus of special emphasis.

Over time, the liberal democratic notion of citizenship developed in two directions. First, there was a movement to increase the proportion of members of society who were eligible to participate as citizens—especially through extending the right of suffrage—and to ensure the basic political equality of all. Second, there was a broadening of the legitimate activities of government and a use of governmental power to redress imbalances in social and economic life. Political citizenship became an instrument through which groups and classes with sufficient numbers of votes could use the state's power to enhance their social and economic well-being.

Within the general liberal view of democratic citizenship, tensions have developed over the degree to which government can and should be used as an instrument for promoting happiness and well-being. Political philosopher Martin Diamond has categorized two views of democracy as follows. On the one hand, there is the "libertarian" perspective that stresses the private pursuit of happiness and emphasizes the necessity for restraint on government and protection of individual liberties. On the other hand, there is the "majoritarian" view that emphasizes the "task of the government to uplift and aid the common man against the malefactors of great wealth." The tensions between these two views are very evident today. Taxpayer revolts and calls for smaller government and less government regulation clash with demands for greater government involvement in the economic marketplace and the social sphere.

16. The author's primary purpose is to:

F. study ancient concepts of citizenship.
G. contrast different notions of citizenship.
H. criticize modern libertarian democracy.
J. describe the importance of universal suffrage.

17. It can be inferred from the passage that the Greek word *polis* (line 11) means:

A. family life.
B. military service.
C. marriage.
D. political community.

18. The author cites Martin Diamond in the last paragraph because the author:

F. regards Martin Diamond as an authority on political philosophy.
G. wishes to refute Martin Diamond's views on citizenship.
H. needs a definition of the term "citizenship."
J. is unfamiliar with the distinction between libertarian and majoritarian concepts of democracy.

19. According to the passage, all of the following are characteristics that would distinguish the liberal idea of government from the Greek idea of government EXCEPT:

A. the emphasis on the rights of private citizens.
B. the activities that government may legitimately pursue.
C. the obligation of citizens to participate in government.
D. the size of the geographical area controlled by a government.

20. A majoritarian would be most likely to favor legislation that would:

F. eliminate all restrictions on individual liberty.
G. cut spending for social welfare programs.
H. provide greater protection for consumers.
J. lower taxes on the wealthy and raise taxes on the average worker.

Passage III

HUMANITIES: This passage is adapted from an article about John Dewey and his theories of education.

The place of public education within a democratic society has been widely discussed and debated through the years. Perhaps no one has written more widely on the subject in the United States than John Dewey, sometimes called "the father of public education," whose theories of education have a large social component; that is, he places an emphasis on education as a social act and the classroom or learning environment as a replica of society.

Dewey defined various aspects or characteristics of education. First, it was a necessity of life inasmuch as living beings needed to maintain themselves through a process of renewal. Therefore, just as humans needed sleep, food, water, and shelter for physiological renewal, they also needed education to renew their minds, assuring that their socialization kept pace with physiological growth.

A second aspect of education was its social component, which was to be accomplished by providing the young with an environment that would provide a nurturing atmosphere to encourage the growth of their, as yet, undeveloped social customs.

A third aspect of public education was the provision of direction to youngsters, who might otherwise be left in uncontrolled situations without the steadying and organizing influences of school. Direction was not to be of an overt nature, but rather indirect through the selection of the school situations in which the youngster participated.

Finally, Dewey saw public education as a catalyst for growth. Since the young came to school capable of growth, it was the role of education to provide opportunities for that growth to occur. The successful school environment is one in which a desire for continued growth is created—a desire that extends throughout one's life beyond the end of formal education. In Dewey's model, the role of education in a democratic society is not seen as a preparation for some later stage in life, such as adulthood. Rather, education is seen as a process of growth that never ends, with human beings continuously expanding their capacity for growth. Neither did Dewey's model see education as a means by which the past was recapitulated. Instead, education was a continuous reconstruction of experiences, grounded very much in the present environment.

Since Dewey's model places a heavy emphasis on the social component, the nature of the larger society that supports the educational system is of paramount importance. The ideal larger society, according to Dewey, is one in which the interests of a group are all shared by all of its members and in which interactions with other groups are free and full. According to Dewey, education in such a society should provide members of the group a stake or interest in social relationships and the ability to negotiate change without compromising the order and stability of the society.

Thus, Dewey's basic concept of education in a democratic society is based on the notion that education contains a large social component designed to provide direction and assure children's development through their participation in their school group.

21. Which of the following best states the main idea of this passage?

A. The role of education is extremely complex.
B. Dewey's notion of education contains a significant social component.
C. Dewey's model of education is not relevant today.
D. Direction provided in education must not be overt.

22. The phrase "a continuous reconstruction of experiences" (line 44) used in reference to education means that education is:

F. based in life experiences.
G. a never-ending process.
H. a meaning-based endeavor.
J. an individual pursuit.

23. The passage implies that:

A. true education fosters the desire for lifelong learning.
B. a truly educated person understands physics.
C. Dewey was a radical philosopher.
D. education must cease at some point.

24. The tone of this passage can best be described as:

F. humorous.
G. serious.
H. dramatic.
J. informal.

Passage IV

SOCIAL SCIENCE: This passage is adapted from an article on Aleut language and culture.

The Aleuts, residing on several islands of the Aleutian Chain, the Pribilof Islands, and the Alaskan Peninsula, have possessed a written language since 1825, when the Russian missionary Ivan Veniaminov selected appropriate characters of the Cyrillic alphabet to represent Aleut speech sounds, recorded the main body of Aleut vocabulary, and formulated grammatical rules. The Czarist Russian conquest of the proud, independent sea hunters was so devastatingly thorough that tribal traditions, even tribal memories, were almost obliterated. The slaughter of the majority of an adult generation was sufficient to destroy the continuity of tribal knowledge, which was dependent upon oral transmission. Consequently, the Aleuts developed a fanatical devotion to their language as their only cultural heritage.

The Russian occupation placed a heavy linguistic burden on the Aleuts. Not only were they compelled to learn Russian to converse with their overseers and governors, but they had to learn Old Slavonic to take an active part in church services as well as to master the skill of reading and writing their own tongue. In 1867, when the United States purchased Alaska, the Aleuts were unable to break sharply with their immediate past and substitute English for any one of their three languages.

To communicants of the Russian Orthodox Church, knowledge of Slavonic remained vital, as did Russian, the language in which one conversed with the clergy. The Aleuts came to regard English education as a device to wean them from their religious faith. The introduction of compulsory English schooling caused a minor renaissance of Russian culture as the Aleut parents sought to counteract the influence of the schoolroom. The harsh life of the Russian colonial rule began to appear more happy and beautiful in retrospect.

Regulations forbidding instruction in any language other than English increased its unpopularity. The superficial alphabetical resemblance of Russian and Aleut linked the two tongues so closely that every restriction against teaching Russian was interpreted as an attempt to eradicate the Aleut tongue. From the wording of many regulations, it appears that American administrators often had not the slightest idea that the Aleuts were clandestinely reading and writing in their own tongue or that they even had a written language of their own. To many officials, anything in Cyrillic letters was Russian and something to be stamped out. Bitterness bred by abuses and the exploitations that the Aleuts suffered from predatory American traders and adventurers kept alive the Aleut resentment against the language spoken by Americans.

Gradually, despite the failure to emancipate the Aleuts from a sterile past by relating the Aleut and English languages more closely, the passage of years has assuaged the bitter misunderstandings and caused an orientation away from Russian toward English as their second language, but Aleut continues to be the language that molds their thought and expression.

25. The author is primarily concerned with describing:

A. the Aleuts' loyalty to their language and American failure to understand the language.
B. Russian and American treatment of Alaskan inhabitants both before and after 1867.
C. how the Czarist Russian occupation of Alaska created a written language for the Aleuts.
D. American government attempts to persuade the Aleuts to use English as a second language.

26. The author is primarily concerned with:

F. describing the Aleuts' loyalty to their language and American failure to understand the language.
G. criticizing Russia and the United States for their mistreatment of the Aleuts.
H. praising the Russians for creating a written language for the Aleuts.
J. condemning Russia for its mistreatment of the Aleuts during the Czarist Russian occupation.

27. Which of the following titles best fits the passage?

A. Aleut Loyalty to Their Language: An American Misunderstanding
B. Failure of Russian and American Policies in Alaska
C. Russia's Gift to the Aleuts: A Written Language
D. Mistreatment of Aleuts During Russian Occupation

28. According to the passage, the most important reason for the Aleuts' devotion to their language was:

F. the invention of a written version of their language.
G. the introduction of Old Slavonic for worship.
H. the disruption of oral transmission of tribal knowledge.
J. the institution of compulsory English education.

29. In line 17, the word *linguistic* infers relation to:

A. orthodoxy.
B. commerce.
C. language.
D. laws.

30. In line 33, the word *renaissance* most nearly means:

F. resurgence.
G. rejection.
H. repeal.
J. reassessment.

31. In line 45, the word *clandestinely* most nearly means:

A. secretly.
B. reliably.
C. openly.
D. casually.

32. In line 54, the word *sterile* most nearly means:

F. germ-free.
G. unproductive.
H. fortunate.
J. ill-timed.

33. In line 56, the word *assuaged* most nearly means:

A. failed.
B. created.
C. intensified.
D. eased.

34. The passage is developed primarily by:

F. testing the evidence supporting a theory.
G. describing causes and effects of events.
H. weighing the pros and cons of a plan.
J. projecting the future consequences of a decision.

35. The author mention that the Russians killed the majority of adult Aleuts to:

A. call attention to the immorality of foreign conquest.
B. urge Russia to make restitution to the children of those killed.
C. stir up outrage against the Russians for committing such atrocities.
D. explain the extreme loyalty that Aleuts feel to their language.

36. Which of the following statements about the religious beliefs of the Aleuts can be inferred from the passage?

F. Prior to the Russian occupation they had no religious beliefs.
G. American traders and adventurers forced them to abandon all religious beliefs.
H. At no time in their history have the Aleuts had an organized religion.
J. The Russians forced Aleuts to become members of the Russian Orthodox Church.

37. The passage implies that:

A. the Cyrillic alphabet was invented for the Aleut language.
B. all of the Cyrillic characters were used in writing the Aleut language.
C. Russian and the Aleut language have some similar speech sounds.
D. English is also written using the Cyrillic alphabet.

38. Distributing which of the following publications would be most likely to encourage Aleuts to make more use of English?

F. Russian translations of English novels
G. English translations of Russian novels
H. An English-Russian bilingual text devoted to important aspects of Aleutian culture
J. An Aleut-English bilingual text devoted to important aspects of Aleutian culture

39. The author's attitude toward the Aleuts can best be described as one of:

A. understanding and sympathy.
B. callousness and indifference.
C. condemnation and reproof.
D. ridicule and disparagement.

Passage V

PROSE FICTION: This passage is adapted from the short story "Mrs. Gay's Prescription" by Louisa May Alcott.

The poor little woman looked as if she needed rest but was not likely to get it; for the room was in a chaotic state, the breakfast table presented the appearance of having been devastated by a swarm of locusts, the baby began to fret, little Polly set up her usual whine of "I want sumpin to do," and a pile of work loomed in the corner waiting to be done.

"I don't see how I ever shall get through it all," sighed the despondent matron as she hastily drank a last cup of tea, while two great tears rolled down her cheeks, as she looked from one puny child to the other, and felt the weariness of her own tired soul and body more oppressive than ever.

"A good cry" was impending, when there came a brisk ring at the door, a step in the hall, and a large, rosy woman came bustling in, saying in a cheery voice as she set a flower-pot down upon the table, "Good morning! Nice day, isn't it? Came in early on business and brought you one of my Lady Washingtons, you are so fond of flowers."

"Oh, it's lovely! How kind you are. Do sit down if you can find a chair; we are all behind hand today, for I was up half the night with poor baby, and haven't energy enough to go to work yet," answered Mrs. Bennet, with a sudden smile that changed her whole face, while baby stopped fretting to stare at the rosy clusters, and Polly found employment in exploring the pocket of the newcomer, as if she knew her way there.

"Let me put the pot on your stand first, girls are so careless, and I'm proud of this. It will be an ornament to your parlor for a week," and opening a door Mrs. Gay carried the plant to a sunny bay window where many others were blooming beautifully.

Mrs. Bennet and the children followed to talk and admire, while the servant leisurely cleared the table.

"Now give me that baby, put yourself in the easy chair, and tell me all about your worries," said Mrs. Gay, in the brisk, commanding way which few people could resist.

"I'm sure I don't know where to begin," sighed Mrs. Bennet, dropping into the comfortable seat while baby changed bearers with great composure.

"I met your husband and he said the doctor had ordered you and these chicks off to Florida for the winter. John said he didn't know how he should manage it, but he meant to try."

"Isn't it dreadful? He can't leave his business to go with me, and we shall have to get Aunt Miranda to come and see to him and the boys while I'm gone, and the boys can't bear her strict, old-fashioned ways, and I've got to go that long journey all alone and stay among strangers, and these heaps of fall work to do first, and it will cost an immense sum to send us, and I don't know what is to become of me."

Here Mrs. Bennet stopped for breath, and Mrs. Gay asked briskly, "What is the matter with you and the children?"

"Well, baby is having a hard time with his teeth and is croupy, Polly doesn't get over scarlet fever well, and I'm used up; no strength or appetite, pain in my side and low spirits. Entire change of scene, milder climate, and less work for me, is what we want, the doctor says. John is very anxious about us, and I feel regularly discouraged."

"I'll spend the day and cheer you up a bit. You just rest and get ready for a new start tomorrow; it is a saving of time to stop short now and then and see where to begin next. Bring me the most pressing job of work. I can sew and see to this little rascal at the same time."

40. The phrase "little woman" (line 1) refers to:

F. Lady Washington.
G. a servant.
H. Mrs. Bennet.
J. Mrs. Gay.

41. When Alcott compares the breakfast table to something "devastated by a swarm of locusts" (lines 4–5), she means:

A. that it is a mess left by an uncaring mob.
B. that children are no more meaningful than insects to Mrs. Bennet.
C. to illustrate the horror of Mrs. Bennet's life.
D. that the Bennets are pests.

42. Had Mrs. Gay not arrived when she did, the author leads us to suspect that:

F. Mrs. Bennet would have gone back to bed.
G. the children would have continued to cry.
H. Mrs. Bennet would have accomplished little all day.
J. sickness would have overtaken the entire family.

43. The phrase "rosy clusters" (lines 26–27) refers to:

A. Mrs. Gay's cheeks.
B. Mrs. Bennet's cheeks.
C. candies from Mrs. Gay's pockets.
D. flowers.

44. In lines 29–33, the author:

F. reveals Mrs. Bennet's only talent.
G. uses the sunny parlor as a symbol of hope.
H. contrasts Mrs. Gay's sunniness with Mrs. Bennet's dullness.
J. contrasts Mrs. Bennet's plants with her children.

45. When Mrs. Bennet says that she's "used up" (line 60), she means that she:

A. has no energy.
B. is abused.
C. is exploited.
D. has spent all her money.

46. The word *pressing* (line 68) means:

F. heavy.
G. ardent.
H. forceful.
J. important.

47. The disposition of Mrs. Bennet's friend is indicated by:

I. her name.
II. her speech.
III. her clothing.

A. I only
B. III only
C. I and II only
D. I and III only

48. The author implies that Mrs. Bennet's real problem is:

F. her inability to cope.
G. a touch of fever.
H. the cold winter weather.
J. a lack of common sense.

49. Mrs. Gay's primary quality seems to be her:

A. lethargy.
B. anxiety.
C. dignity.
D. practical nature.

Passage VI

PROSE FICTION: This passage is adapted from the memoir series "Old Times on the Mississippi" by Mark Twain that appeared in *Atlantic Monthly*.

At the end of what seemed a tedious while, I had managed to pack my head full of islands, towns, bars, "points," and bends; and a curiously inanimate mass of lumber it was, too. However, inasmuch as I could shut my eyes and reel off a good long string of these names without leaving out more than ten miles of river in every fifty, I began to feel that I could make her skip those little gaps. But of course my complacency could hardly get started enough to lift my nose a trifle into the air, before Mr. Bixby would think of something to fetch it down again. One day he turned on me suddenly with this settler:

"What is the shape of Walnut Bend?"

He might as well have asked me my grandmother's opinion of protoplasm. I reflected respectfully, and then said I didn't know it had any particular shape. My gunpowdery chief went off with a bang, of course, and then went on loading and firing until he was out of adjectives.

I had learned long ago that he only carried just so many rounds of ammunition, and was sure to subside into a very placable and even remorseful old smoothbore as soon as they were all gone. That word "old" is merely affectionate; he was not more than thirty-four. I waited. By and by he said:

"My boy, you've got to know the *shape* of the river perfectly. It is all there is left to steer by on a very dark night. Everything else is blotted out and gone. But mind you, it hasn't the same shape in the night that it has in the daytime."

"How on earth am I ever going to learn it, then?"

"How do you follow a hall at home in the dark? Because you know the shape of it. You can't see it."

"Do you mean to say that I've got to know all the million trifling variations of shape in the banks of this interminable river as well as I know the shape of the front hall at home?"

"On my honor, you've got to know them *better* than any man ever did know the shapes of the halls in his own house."

"I wish I was dead!"

"Now I don't want to discourage you, but…"

"Well, pile it on me; I might as well have it now as another time."

"You see, this has got to be learned; there isn't any getting around it. A clear starlight night throws such heavy shadows that, if you didn't know the shape of a shore perfectly, you would claw away from every bunch of timber, because you would take the black shadow of it for a solid cape; and you see you would be getting scared to death every fifteen minutes by the watch. You would be fifty yards from shore all the time when you ought to be within fifty feet of it. You can't see a snag in one of those shadows, but you know exactly where it is, and the shape of the river tells you when you are coming to it. Then there's your pitch-dark night; the river is a very different shape on a pitch-dark night from what it is on a starlit night. All shores seem to be straight lines, then, and mighty dim ones, too; and you'd *run* them for straight lines, only you know better. You boldly drive your boat right into what seems to be a solid straight wall (you knowing very well that in reality there is a curve there), and that wall falls back and makes way for you. Then there's your gray mist. You take a night when there's one of these grisly, drizzly, gray mists, and then there isn't any particular shape to a shore. A gray mist would tangle the head of the oldest man that ever lived. Well, then different kinds of *moonlight* change the shape of the river in different ways."

50. In line 12, the word *settler* is used to mean:

F. a pioneer.
G. a perch on the railing.
H. a remark that decides the issue.
J. a humbling problem.

51. When the narrator compares Bixby's question to asking his "grandmother's opinion of protoplasm" (line 15), he means that:

A. the question is inane.
B. the speaker is very old.
C. he does not know the answer.
D. his grandmother would be able to respond.

52. Comparing the chief to a gun (lines 17–19) points out the chief's:

F. accuracy.
G. peppery temper.
H. love of hunting.
J. violent past.

53. When Twain writes that Mr. Bixby "carried just so many rounds of ammunition," he means that:

A. Bixby used a pistol to settle arguments.
B. Bixby loaded and fired his gun at random.
C. Bixby was an impossible employer.
D. Bixby's hot temper would soon subside.

54. The narrator's reaction to Mr. Bixby's insistence on the need to know the river at night is:

F. despair.
G. elation.
H. puzzlement.
J. anger.

55. In the phrase "pile it on me" (line 43), "it" refers to:

A. clothing.
B. information.
C. the river.
D. the shoreline.

56. The word *cape* (line 50) means:

F. cloak.
G. robe.
H. peninsula.
J. waterway.

57. Mr. Bixby is shown to be extremely:

A. knowledgeable.
B. rude.
C. condescending.
D. fearful.

58. What is the purpose of including the lengthy explanation provided in the last paragraph of the selection?

I. To show how well Bixby speaks
II. To show how much a riverboat captain must know
III. To show the many modes of the river

F. I only
G. II only
H. I and III only
J. II and III only

59. According to the passage, which of the following is true?

A. A riverboat should always be within 100 feet of the shore.
B. On a clear, starlit night, the shoreline is easy to see.
C. On a pitch-dark night, the pilot cannot discern the curve of the shoreline.
D. The river's shape gives no hint of underwater snags.

Passage VII

PROSE FICTION: This passage is adapted from Nathaniel Hawthorne's *The House of the Seven Gables*.

It still lacked a half hour of sunrise when Miss Hepzibah—we will say awoke, it being doubtful whether the poor old lady had so much as closed her eyes during the brief night of midsummer—but, at all events, arose from her solitary pillow, and began the adornment of her person. She was alone in the old house—quite a house by itself, indeed—with locks, bolts, and oaken bars on all the intervening doors. Inaudible, consequently, were poor Miss Hepzibah's gusty sighs, inaudible the creaking joints of her stiffened knees, as she knelt down by the bedside. And inaudible too, by mortal ear, that almost agony of prayer—now whispered, now a groan, now a struggling silence—wherewith she sought the Divine assistance through the day! Evidently this is to be the day of more than ordinary trial to Miss Hepzibah, who for above a quarter of a century gone by has dwelt in strict seclusion, taking no part in the business of life, and just as little in its intercourse and pleasures.

Here comes Miss Hepzibah. Forth she steps into the dusky, time-darkened passage a tall figure, clad in black silk, with a long and shrunken waist, feeling her way towards the stair like a nearsighted person, which in truth she is.

Her scowl—as the world persisted in calling it—her scowl had done Miss Hepzibah every ill office, in establishing her character as an ill-tempered old maid; nor does it appear improbable that, by often gazing at herself in a dim looking glass, and perpetually encountering her own frown within its ghostly sphere, she had been led to interpret the expression almost unjustly as the world did. But her heart never frowned.

60. According to the passage, Miss Hepzibah is all of the following EXCEPT:

F. elderly.
G. reclusive.
H. religious.
J. vain.

61. The author's portrait of Miss Hepzibah is:

A. critical and disparaging.
B. loving and intimate.
C. sarcastic and mocking.
D. interested and sympathetic.

62. It can be inferred that Miss Hepzibah views the day's coming events with:

F. apprehension.
G. confidence.
H. eagerness.
J. boredom.

63. Which of the following correctly describes the scene as set by the passage?

I. The season is summer.
II. The weather is threatening.
III. The time is morning.

A. I only
B. III only
C. I and II only
D. I and III only

64. In the last paragraph, the author implies that Miss Hepzibah is:

F. old and wicked.
G. affable and outgoing.
H. good-hearted but misunderstood.
J. sincere but blasphemous.

Passage VIII

SOCIAL SCIENCE: This passage discusses the contest over the vice presidency in the 1792 election.

In 1792, there was no contest for the presidency. George Washington received the unanimous vote of the electors, Federalist and Republican alike. But the struggle over the vice presidency hinted at the rekindling of old divisions and antagonisms sparked by Alexander Hamilton's system. Southern planters who in 1789 had been ready, in fact eager, to cooperate with the monied men of the North, parted with them when they realized that the policies designed to benefit Northern merchants and bankers brought no profit to them as landed aristocrats. Even more, they saw themselves paying for a system that contributed to another section's prosperity. Although in 1792 they were willing to continue with Washington, they were not as willing to go along with Vice President John Adams, who represented the commerce, shipbuilding, fisheries, and banking institutions of New England and the North. If the Federalists were to have the first office, then the followers of Jefferson—who had already come to call themselves Republicans in contradistinction to the unpopular term anti-Federalist, insisted that they were to command the second office.

Appealing to the shopkeepers, artisans, laboring men, and farmers of the North based on their sympathy with the French Revolution, and to the Southern planters with their agrarian bias, the Republicans waged a gallant but losing campaign for the second office. However, the campaign served notice to the overconfident Federalists that when the Republicans became better organized nationally, they would have to be more seriously considered. This did not take long. In 1793, England went so far as to declare war with republican France over the guillotining of Louis XVI, and in 1794, John Jay's treaty terminating the United States' difficulties with Britain seemed to suggest a sympathetic policy toward monarchical and conservative England, instead of republican, liberty-loving France. The treaty intensified party spirit and gave the Republicans a sense of mission that legitimized their existence. The contest was now between the Republican "lovers of liberty" and the Monocrats.

65. Which of the following titles best describes the content of the passage?

A. The Origins of Jefferson's Republican Party
B. Jefferson's Defeat in the 1792 Election
C. The Legacy of Hamilton's Political System
D. Political Differences Between the Rich and the Poor

66. According to the passage, all of the following are true of the Republicans EXCEPT:

F. they opposed the monied interests of the North.
G. they were led by Thomas Jefferson.
H. they disapproved of the French Revolution.
J. they and the Federalists supported the same candidate for president in 1792.

67. It can be inferred from the passage that the term *Monocrats* (line 42) was:

A. used by John Jay in his treaty to refer to France's King Louis XVI.
B. invented by the Federalists to refer to the aristocratic landowners of the South.
C. coined by the Republicans to disparage the Federalists' support of England.
D. employed by Republicans to describe their leader, Thomas Jefferson.

68. The passage implies that Thomas Jefferson was unsuccessful in his 1792 bid for the vice presidency because the Republican Party:

F. did not have a presidential candidate.
G. was not as well organized as the Federalists.
H. refused to support John Adams.
J. appealed to workers in the North.

69. The tone of the passage can best be described as:

A. enthusiastic and impassioned.
B. scholarly and neutral.
C. opinionated and dogmatic.
D. argumentative and categorical.

Passage IX

SOCIAL SCIENCE: This passage is adapted from a policy article about attempts to change the healthcare system.

Considerable advances have been made in healthcare services since World War II. These include better access to healthcare (particularly for the poor and minorities), improvements in physical plants and facilities, and increased numbers of physicians and other health personnel. All have played a part in the recent improvement in life expectancy. But there is mounting criticism of the large remaining gaps in access, unbridled cost inflation, the further fragmentation of service, excessive indulgence in wasteful high-technology "gadgeteering," and breakdowns in doctor-patient relationships. In recent years, proposed panaceas and new programs, small and large, have proliferated at a feverish pace, and disappointments have multiplied at almost the same rate. This has led to an increased pessimism—"everything has been tried and nothing works"—that sometimes borders on cynicism or even nihilism.

It is true that the automatic "pass through" of rapidly spiraling costs to government and insurance carriers produced for a time a sense of unlimited resources and allowed a mood to develop whereby every practitioner and institution could "do his own thing" without undue concern for the "Medical Commons." The practice of full-cost reimbursement encouraged capital investment, and now the industry is overcapitalized. Many cities have hundreds of excess hospital beds; hospitals have proliferated a superabundance of high-technology equipment; and structural ostentation and luxury were the order of the day. In any given day, one-fourth of all community beds are vacant; expensive equipment is underused or, worse, used unnecessarily. Capital investment brings rapidly rising operating costs.

Yet, in part, this pessimism derives from expecting too much of healthcare. Care is often a painful experience accompanied by fear and unwelcome results; although there is room for improvement, it will always retain some unpleasantness and frustration. Moreover, the capacities of medical science are limited. Humpty Dumpty cannot always be put back together again. Too many physicians are reluctant to admit their limitations to patients; too many patients and families are unwilling to accept such realities. Nor is it true that everything has been tried and nothing works, as shown by the prepaid group practice plans at the Kaiser Foundation and Puget Sound. However, typically such undertakings have been drowned by a veritable flood of public and private moneys that have supported and encouraged the continuation of conventional practices and subsidized their shortcomings on a massive, almost unrestricted scale. Except for the most idealistic and dedicated, there were no incentives to seek change or to practice self-restraint or frugality. In this atmosphere, it is not fair to condemn as failures all attempted experiments; it may be more accurate to say that many never had a fair trial.

70. In line 14, the word *feverish* most nearly means:

F. diseased.
G. rapid.
H. controlled.
J. timed.

71. According to the author, the pessimism mentioned in line 35 is partly attributable to the fact that:

A. there has been little real improvement in healthcare services.
B. expectations about healthcare services are sometimes unrealistic.
C. large segments of the population find it impossible to get access to healthcare services.
D. advances in technology have made healthcare service unaffordable.

72. The author cites the prepaid plans (line 47) as:

F. counterexamples to the claim that nothing has worked.
G. examples of healthcare plans that were overfunded.
H. evidence that healthcare services are fragmented.
J. proof of the theory that no plan has been successful.

73. It can be inferred that the sentence "Humpty Dumpty cannot always be put back together again" (lines 41–42) means that:

A. the cost of healthcare services will not decline.
B. some people should not become doctors.
C. medical care is not really essential to good health.
D. medical science cannot cure every ill.

74. With which of the following descriptions of the system for the delivery of healthcare services would the author most likely agree?

F. It is biased in favor of doctors and against patients.
G. It is highly fragmented and completely ineffective.
H. It has not embraced new technology rapidly enough.
J. It is generally effective but can be improved.

75. Which of the following best describes the logical structure of the selection?

A. The third paragraph is intended as a refutation of the first and second paragraphs.
B. The second and third paragraphs are intended as a refutation of the first paragraph.
C. The second and third paragraphs explain and put into perspective the points made in the first paragraph.
D. The first paragraph describes a problem, and the second and third paragraphs present two horns of a dilemma.

76. The author's primary concern is to:

F. criticize physicians and healthcare administrators for investing in technologically advanced equipment.
G. examine some problems affecting delivery of healthcare services and assess the severity of those problems.
H. defend the medical community from charges that healthcare has not improved since World War II.
J. analyze the reasons for the healthcare industry's inability to provide quality care to all segments of the population.

Passage X

HUMANITIES: This passage is adapted from an article that discusses literary genre.

When we speak casually, we call *Nineteen Eighty-Four* a novel, but to be more exact we should call it a political fable. This requirement is not refuted by the fact that the book is preoccupied with an individual, Winston Smith, who suffers from a varicose ulcer, or by the fact that it takes account of other individuals, including Julia, Mr. Charrington, Mrs. Parsons, Syme, and O'Brien. The figures claim our attention, but they exist mainly in their relation to the political system that determines them. It would indeed be possible to think of them as figures in a novel, though in that case they would have to be imagined in a far more diverse set of relations. They would no longer inhabit or sustain a fable, because a fable is a narrative relieved of much contingent detail so that it may stand forth in an unusual degree of clarity and simplicity. A fable is a structure of types, each of them deliberately simplified lest a sense of difference and heterogeneity reduce the force of the typical. Let us say, then, that *Nineteen Eighty-Four* is a political fable, projected into a near future and incorporating historical references mainly to document a canceled past.

Since a fable is predicated upon a typology, it must be written from a certain distance. The author cannot afford the sense of familiarity that is induced by detail and differentiation. A fable, in this respect, asks to be compared to a caricature, not to a photograph. It follows that in a political fable there is bound to be some tension between a political sense dealing in the multiplicity of social and personal life, and a fable sense committed to simplicity of form and feature. If the political sense were to prevail, the narrative would be drawn away from fable into the novel, at some cost to its simplicity. If the sense of fable were to prevail, the fabulist would station himself at such a distance from any imaginary conditions in the case that his narrative would appear unmediated, free or bereft of conditions. The risk would be considerable: a reader might feel that the fabulist has lost interest in the variety of human life and fallen back upon an unconditioned sense of its types, that he has become less interested in lives than in a particular idea of life. The risk is greater still if the fabulist projects his narrative into the future: The reader cannot question by appealing to life conditions already known. He is asked to believe that the future is another country and that "they just do things differently there."

In a powerful fable, the reader's feeling is likely to be mostly fear: He is afraid that the fabulist's vision of any life that could arise may be accurate. The fabulist's feeling may be more various. A fable such as *Nineteen Eighty-Four* might arise from disgust, despair, or world-weariness induced by evidence that nothing, despite one's best efforts, has changed and that it is too late now to hope for the change one wants.

77. In line 15, the word *contingent* most nearly means:

A. dependent.
B. essential.
C. boring.
D. unnecessary.

78. In drawing an analogy between a fable and a caricature (lines 26–27), the author would most likely regard which of the following pairs of ideas as also analogous?

F. The subject of a caricature and the topic of a fable
G. The subject of a caricature and the main character in *Nineteen Eighty-Four*
H. The subject of a fable and the artist who draws the caricature
J. The artist who draws the caricature and a novelist

79. Which of the following would be the most appropriate title for the passage?

A. A Critical Study of the Use of Characters in *Nineteen Eighty-Four*
B. *Nineteen Eighty-Four*: Political Fable Rather Than Novel
C. *Nineteen Eighty-Four*: Reflections on the Relationship of the Individual to Society
D. The Use of Typology in the Literature of Political Fables

80. According to the passage, which of the following are characteristics of a political fable?

F. It is widely popular at its time of development.
G. The reader is unlikely to experience fear as his reaction to the political situation described.
H. Its time frame must treat events that occur at some point in the future.
J. Its characters are defined primarily by their relationship to the social order.

81. The author mentions that Winston Smith suffers from a varicose ulcer to:

A. demonstrate that a political fable must emphasize type over detail.
B. show that Winston Smith has some characteristics that distinguish him as an individual.
C. argue that Winston Smith is no more important than any other character in *Nineteen Eighty-Four.*
D. illustrate one of the features of the political situation described in *Nineteen Eighty-Four.*

82. The tension that the author mentions in line 29 refers to the:

F. necessity of striking a balance between the need to describe a political situation in simple terms and the need to make the description realistic.
G. reaction the reader feels because he is drawn to the characters of the fable as individuals but repulsed by the political situation.
H. delicate task faced by a literary critic who must interpret the text of a work while attempting to describe accurately the intentions of the author.
J. danger that too realistic a description of a key character will make the reader feel that the fable is actually a description of his own situation.

83. The author's attitude toward *Nineteen Eighty-Four* can best be described as:

A. condescending.
B. laudatory.
C. disparaging.
D. scholarly.

84. The author uses the phrase "another country" (line 46) to describe a political fable in which:

F. political events described in a fable occur in a place other than the country of national origin of the author.
G. a lack of detail makes it difficult for a reader to see the connection between his own situation and the one described in the book.
H. too many minor characters create the impression of complete disorganization, leading the reader to believe he is in a foreign country.
J. the author has allowed his personal political convictions to infect his description of the political situation.

85. The author's primary concern is to:

A. define and clarify a concept.
B. point out a logical inconsistency.
C. trace the connection between a cause and an effect.
D. illustrate a general statement with examples.

Passage XI

HUMANITIES: This passage is adapted from the speech "Is it a Crime for a Citizen of the United States to Vote?" by Susan B. Anthony.

Friends and fellow citizens: I stand before you tonight under indictment for the alleged crime of having voted at the last presidential election without having a lawful right to vote. It shall be my work this evening to prove to you that in thus voting, I not only committed no crime, but, instead, simply exercised *my citizen's rights*, guaranteed to me and all United States citizens by the National Constitution, beyond the power of any State to deny. The preamble of the Federal Constitution says: "We, the people of the United States, in order to form a more perfect union, establish justice, insure *domestic* tranquility, provide for the common defense, promote the general welfare, and secure the blessings of liberty to ourselves and our posterity, do ordain and establish this Constitution for the United States of America."

It was we, the people, not we, the white male citizens; but we, the whole people, who formed the Union. And we formed it, not to give the blessings of liberty, but to secure them; not to the half of ourselves and the half of our posterity but to the whole people—women as well as men. And it is a downright mockery to talk to women of their enjoyment of the blessings of liberty while they are denied the use of the only means of securing them provided by this democratic-republican government—the ballot.

For any State to make sex a qualification that must ever result in the disfranchisement of one entire half of the people is a violation of the supreme law of the land. By it the blessings of liberty are forever withheld from women and their female posterity. To them this government has no just powers derived from the consent of the governed. To them this government is not a democracy. It is not a republic. It is a hateful oligarchy of sex. An oligarchy of learning, where the educated govern the ignorant, might be endured; but this oligarchy of sex, which makes father, brothers, husband, sons, the oligarchs or rulers over the mother and sisters, the wife and daughters of every household—which ordains all men sovereigns, all women subjects, carries dissension, discord and rebellion into every home of the nation.

Webster's Dictionary defines a citizen as a person in the United States, entitled to vote and hold office.

The only question left to be settled now is, Are women persons? And I hardly believe any of our opponents will have the hardihood to say we are not. Being persons, then, women are citizens; and no State has a right to make any law, or to enforce any old law, that shall abridge their privileges or immunities. Hence, every discrimination against women in the constitutions and laws of the several States is today null and void.

86. The nineteenth-century feminist leader Susan B. Anthony fought long and hard to guarantee women the right to vote. In this speech, she talks as if she were a:

F. defendant on trial.
G. chairperson of a committee.
H. legislator arguing for a new law.
J. judge ruling at a trial.

87. Anthony broadens her appeal to her audience by showing how her case could affect all:

A. existing laws.
B. United States citizens.
C. women.
D. uneducated persons.

88. Anthony quotes the preamble to the Constitution (lines 10–16) in order to:

F. impress the audience with her intelligence.
G. utilize a common legalistic trick.
H. point out which part of the preamble needs to be changed.
J. add force to her argument.

89. According to Anthony, who formed the Union?

A. Only one-half of the people
B. The whole people
C. White male citizens only
D. White female citizens

90. When Anthony says that the blessings of liberty are forever withheld from women and their female posterity, she means that:

- **F.** all classes of women are discriminated against.
- **G.** women of the past have been victimized.
- **H.** female children of the poor will be the only ones affected.
- **J.** women of the present and the future will suffer.

91. Anthony argues that a government that denies women the right to vote is not a democracy because its powers do not come from:

- **A.** the Constitution of the United States.
- **B.** the rights of the states.
- **C.** the consent of the governed.
- **D.** the vote of the majority.

92. According to this speech, an "oligarchy of sex" would cause:

- **F.** women to rebel against the government.
- **G.** men to desert their families.
- **H.** problems to develop in every home.
- **J.** the educated to rule the ignorant.

93. In this speech, a citizen is defined as a person who has the right to vote and also the right to:

- **A.** acquire wealth.
- **B.** speak publicly.
- **C.** hold office.
- **D.** pay taxes.

94. Anthony argues that state laws that discriminate against women are:

- **F.** being changed.
- **G.** null and void.
- **H.** helpful to the rich.
- **J.** supported by the Constitution.

Passage XII

HUMANITIES: This passage is adapted from an essay by Oliver Goldsmith that appeared in *The Citizen of the World.*

Were we to estimate the learning of the English by the number of books that are every day published among them, perhaps no country, not even China itself, could equal them in this particular. I have reckoned not less than twenty-three new books published in one day, which, upon computation, makes eight thousand three hundred and ninety-five in one year. Most of these are not confined to one single science, but embrace the whole circle. History, politics, poetry, mathematics, metaphysics, and the philosophy of nature are all comprised in a manual not larger than that in which our children are taught the letters. If then, we suppose the learned of England to read but an eighth part of the works which daily come from the press (and surely none can pretend to learning upon less easy terms), at this rate every scholar will read a thousand books in one year. From such a calculation, you may conjecture what an amazing fund of literature a man must be possessed of, who thus reads three new books every day, not one of which but contains all the good things that ever were said or written.

And yet I know not how it happens, but the English are not, in reality, so learned as would seem from this calculation. We meet but few who know all arts and sciences to perfection; whether it is that the generality are incapable of such extensive knowledge, or that the authors of those books are not adequate instructors. In China, the Emperor himself takes cognizance of all the doctors in the kingdom who profess authorship. In England, every man may be an author that can write; for they have by law a liberty, not only of saying what they please, but also of being as dull as they please.

Yesterday, I testified my surprise, to the man in black, where writers could be found in sufficient number to throw off the books I daily saw crowding from the press. I at first imagined that their learned seminaries might take this method of instructing the world. But, to obviate this objection, my companion assured me that the doctors of colleges never wrote, and that some of them had actually forgotten their reading. "But if you desire," continued he, "to see a collection of authors, I fancy I can introduce you to a club, which assembles every Saturday at seven...." I accepted his invitation; we walked together, and entered the house some time before the usual hour for the company assembling.

My friend took this opportunity of letting me into the characters of the principal members of the club....

"The first person," said he, "of our society is Doctor Nonentity, a metaphysician. Most people think him a profound scholar, but, as he seldom speaks, I cannot be positive in that particular; he generally spreads himself before the fire, sucks his pipe, talks little, drinks much, and is reckoned very good company. I'm told he writes indexes to perfection: he makes essays on the origin of evil, philosophical inquiries upon any subject, and draws up an answer to any book upon 24 hours' warning...."

95. Goldsmith's disdainful attitude toward English authors is best explicated in:

A. lines 1–4.
B. lines 12–17.
C. lines 30–33.
D. lines 42–44.

96. Goldsmith believes that:

F. we can tell how knowledgeable English authors are by counting the number of books they publish.
G. the number of books published in England is not up to standards set in China.
H. the number of books published in England says nothing about English scholarship.
J. every English scholar reads a thousand books a year.

97. Goldsmith calculates the number of books published in England to:

A. impress his readers with English erudition.
B. make the point that anyone can be an author.
C. make a defense for his argument that England is better than China.
D. make a comparison with publication quotas in other lands.

98. The tone of the second paragraph may best be described as:

F. self-satisfied.
G. awestruck.
H. affectionate.
J. sardonic.

99. Goldsmith first assumes that English writers come from:

A. foreign lands.
B. seminaries.
C. China.
D. clubs.

100. The word *obviate* (line 39) means:

F. clarify.
G. obscure.
H. turn.
J. negate.

101. Goldsmith's opinion of the first member of the club is illuminated by which of the following?

I. His conversation with the character
II. The given name for the character
III. His friend's description of the character

A. I only
B. II only
C. I and III only
D. II and III only

102. One of Goldsmith's major objections to English authors is to their:

F. deficiency in language skills.
G. inclination to drink.
H. tendency to write about everything at once.
J. inability to retain information.

Passage XIII

HUMANITIES: This passage discusses the impact of Southwestern environment and culture on twentieth-century artists.

Georgia O'Keeffe, whose death at age 98 closed one of the most fertile chapters of American artistic creativity, flourished as a maverick in her life and work. While other painters spent a season or two in the country trying to come to terms with the scenes and settings of the Southwest, O'Keeffe stayed a lifetime. When the canvases of other artists working in the region faded from view, and then were neglected in the chronicle of American visual history, her stylized images, skeletal, floral, and geological motifs made an indelible impression on countless eyes.

Between 1900 and 1945, the region now called New Mexico both fascinated and perplexed two generations of American artists—luminaries such as Stuart Davis, Marsden Hartley, and John Sloan, whose reputations were built largely on depictions of gritty, modern life in Eastern urban centers. Despite successes, many of these artists wearied of the industrial world of the East. The vast expanse of the American West offered a promise for inspiration. It was an ancient yet new world to their eyes—an enchanted land far removed from urban conventions.

For these artists, life and art, so separate in New York and Paris, seemed inextricably bound in Southwestern cultures. Painters of every persuasion were convinced that sampling this mysterious phenomenon would strengthen and enrich their own work. Most were touched by what D.H. Lawrence called the "spirit of the place." Besides the scenic possibilities bathed in clear golden light, the rich traditions of New Mexico's Native American and Latino people—their dress, crafts, adobe pueblos, plaza life, rituals, and simple dignity—became frequent subjects of the artists who traveled to Taos and Santa Fe.

Some of the artists were traditionalists—local color realists; some were modernists—like O'Keeffe, avant-garde painters of the abstract. Their varied talents coupled with the attractions of the land gave New Mexico's art centers a status unrivaled among other American summer colonies and contributed to their heyday in the early twentieth century.

103. This passage deals primarily with:

A. the life of Georgia O'Keeffe.
B. the major trends of American modern art.
C. the mystery and spirit of the Southwest.
D. artists in the American Southwest.

104. The author implies that the Southwest attracted artists for all of the following reasons EXCEPT:

F. the quality of life was different from that of large urban centers.
G. the inhabitants and culture provided interesting subject matter.
H. New Mexico was the only state to support young, avant-garde painters.
J. the region offered unusual geological features and landscapes.

105. The author implies that most of the artists who painted in the Southwest:

A. originally studied in Paris.
B. lived there only temporarily.
C. painted only landscapes.
D. received considerable recognition.

106. The author mentions which of the following facts about Georgia O'Keeffe?

I. She resided permanently in the Southwest.
II. She enjoyed considerable and lasting fame.
III. She created modern, abstract paintings.

F. I only
G. II only
H. I and III only
J. I, II, and III

107. Stuart Davis, Marsden Hartley, and John Sloan were painters who painted mainly in:

A. Paris.
B. New Mexico.
C. cities in the Eastern United States.
D. Rome.

Passage XIV

NATURAL SCIENCE: This passage discusses the development of basic inheritance theories and the role of DNA in genetic mutation processes.

In 1866, Gregor Mendel published the results of his studies on the breeding of different races of pea plants. Through his experiments, Mendel discovered a pattern of inheritance and subsequently developed the concept of a "unit of inheritance."

Mendel started with a pure stock of pea plants that had recognizably different characteristics. He artificially cross-pollinated the different races of plants and noted the characteristics of the different offspring over several generations. Mendel concluded that a pair of discrete "factors" governed each trait and that they segregated upon the formation of the gametes. This pair of factors is now known as the maternally and paternally derived alleles on homologous chromosomes that first come together at fertilization and later segregate during meiosis.

Subsequent studies have shown that new genes could appear as mutations of existing genes and that crossing over and recombination could redistribute maternal and paternal characteristics. Genes can occur in a linear sequence, and groups of genes that segregate together are called "linkage groups." The chromosome is the carrier of the linear array of genes and the physical basis of the linkage groups.

It was originally thought that proteins were the genetic carrier. In contrast to nucleic acids, proteins were known to mediate complex reactions and to be composed of a variety of different building blocks. There are approximately 20 different amino acids in a protein, but only 4 different nucleotides in a nucleic acid molecule. It was not until 1944 that Avery et al. noted that deoxyribonucleic acid (DNA) was the genetic carrier, not protein. Avery and his co-workers conducted experiments on the transformation in pneumococcus. Two strains of the bacteria had been isolated: one produced colonies having a smooth (S) appearance and was able to cause pneumonia in a suitable host; the other grew into rough (R) colonies because of a defect in its capsule and was non-virulent. When a cell-free extract of the S bacteria was added to the medium in which the R strain was growing, a few of the R bacteria grew into smooth colonies and were virulent. They had become transformed. From the time of transformation, the progeny of that cell continued to have the properties of the S strain. The transformation was a stable genetic change. Avery and his co-workers purified the contents of cells in detergent after their disruption and found that among the contents of the cells, only the purified DNA was capable of causing the transformation. As a result of these and future experiments, it was determined that in order for transformation to occur, DNA fragments entered the recipient cell intact and substituted in the bacterial chromosome for the original DNA, which was eliminated. This process resulted in the creation of a genetically different microorganism.

DNA is a very long, fibrous molecule with a backbone composed of alternate sugar and phosphate groups joined by 3'-5'-phosphodiester linkages. Attached to each sugar is one of four possible nitrogenous bases. There are two types of bases: the pyrimidines, cytosine (C) and thymine (T); and the purines, adenine (A) and guanine (G). The amount of purine equals the amount of pyrimidine, and, more specifically, the amount of adenine equals the amount of thymine, and the amount of guanine equals the amount of cytosine.

In 1953, Watson and Crick proposed that DNA was made of two chains of nucleotides coiled around a common axis, with the sugar-phosphate backbone on the outside and the bases pointing in toward the axis, and that the two chains were held together by hydrogen bonds. The hydrogen bonds occur between each base of one chain and an associated base on the other chain. Based on the 20-angstrom width of the fiber, a pyrimidine from one chain is always paired with a purine from the other chain. Adenine is the only purine capable of bonding to thymine and guanine is the only purine capable of bonding to cytosine.

Watson and Crick proposed that the information in DNA was coded for by the linear sequence of the base pairs. They theorized that a mutation could be accounted for by a chance mistake in the formation of the sequence during duplication. Another major aspect of the Watson and Crick model was the proposed complementarity between hydrogen-bonded nucleotides. For example, adenine is complementary to thymine, AGC is complementary to TCG, and one chain is complementary to the other. If the base sequence of one chain is known, then the base sequence of the complementary chain can be derived. The concept of complementarity of nucleic acids in DNA and RNA chains is the basis of most research in which these classes of molecules are involved.

108. Mendel conducted his studies using the method known as:

F. cloning.
G. genetic mapping.
H. cross-pollination.
J. transformation.

109. Mendel's findings were important because they indicated which of the following?

I. DNA fragments can replace original DNA.
II. Specific units, handed down from one generation to the next, govern traits in organisms.
III. Proteins are composed of approximately 20 different amino acids.

A. I only
B. II only
C. I and III only
D. I, II, and III

110. Contrary to earlier beliefs, Avery et al. discovered that:

F. there are only four nucleotides in DNA.
G. pneumonia can be passed from host to host.
H. genes can mutate.
J. DNA, not protein, carries genetic information.

111. If you witnessed R strain pneumococcus infected with S extract and saw a few R strain pneumococcus transformed to S strain, you would expect:

A. the remaining R strain pneumococcus to transform later.
B. only the new S strain cells to survive.
C. offspring of those transformed cells to be S strain as well.
D. a few S strain pneumococcus to transform to R strain.

112. The author uses the word *non-virulent* (line 39) to mean:

F. harmless.
G. toxic.
H. bacterial.
J. sweet.

113. In contrast to the paragraphs before, the fifth paragraph is intended primarily to:

A. give historical genetic research information .
B. describe the results of Mendel's experiments.
C. speculate on the future of genetic research.
D. provide a definition for an essential element in genetic research.

114. A chain of DNA with the pattern CAG would bond with a chain with the pattern:

F. GAC.
G. TGA.
H. GTC.
J. Cannot be determined from the given information

115. Which of the following is (are) classified as a purine?

I. Cytosine
II. Guanine
III. Thymine

A. I only
B. II only
C. III only
D. I and II only

116. Which of the following was Watson and Crick's contribution to the study of genetics?

I. Information about the transfer of genes across membranes
II. The notion that pairs of genes could work together
III. A suggestion about the structure of DNA

F. I only
G. II only
H. III only
J. I, II, and III

117. The concept of complementarity in DNA is apparently important because:

A. it contradicts the notion that proteins are the basis for genetic transformation.
B. hydrogen bonds connect the nucleotides.
C. if maternally and paternally derived alleles were not complementary, life could not exist.
D. if you know one chain's sequence, you can determine that of the other.

Passage XV

NATURAL SCIENCE: This passage is adapted from a science magazine article about galaxies.

Galaxies come in a variety of sizes and shapes: majestic spirals, ruddy disks, elliptically shaped dwarfs and giants, and a menagerie of other, more bizarre forms. Most currently, popular theories suggest that conditions prior to birth—mass of the protogalactic cloud, its size, its rotation—determine whether a galaxy will be large or small, spiral or elliptical; but about ten percent of all galaxies are members of rich clusters of thousands of galaxies. The gravitational forces of fields of nearby galaxies constantly distort galaxies in the crowded central region of rich clusters. In addition, rich clusters of galaxies are pervaded by a tenuous gas with a temperature of up to 100 million degrees. Galaxies are blasted and scoured by a hot wind created by their motion through the gas. In crowded conditions such as these, environment becomes a more important determinant of the size and shape of a galaxy than heredity. In fact, if our galaxy had happened to form well within the core of a cluster such as Virgo, the Sun would probably never have formed, because the Sun, a second- or third-generation star located in the disk of the galaxy, was formed from leftover gas five billion years or so after the initial period of star formation. By that time, in a rich cluster, the galaxy may well have already been stripped of its gas.

As a galaxy moves through the core of a rich cluster, it is not only scoured by hot gas; it encounters other galaxies as well. If the collision is one-on-one at moderate to high speeds of galaxies of approximately the same size, both galaxies will emerge relatively intact, if a little distorted and ragged about the edges. If, however, a galaxy coasts by a much larger one in a slow, grazing collision, the smaller one can be completely disrupted and assimilated by the larger.

Under the right conditions, these cosmic cannibals can consume 50 to 100 galaxies. The accumulative effect of these collisions is to produce a dynamic friction on the large galaxy, slowing it down. As a result, it gradually spirals in toward the center of the cluster. Eventually, the gravitational forces that bind the stars to the infalling galaxy are overwhelmed by the combined gravity of the galaxies in the core of the cluster—just as the ocean is pulled away from the shore at ebb tide by the Moon, the stars are pulled away from their infalling parent galaxy. If there is a large galaxy at the center of the cluster, it may ultimately capture these stars. With the passage of time, many galaxies will be torn asunder in the depths of this gravitational maelstrom and be swallowed up in the ever-expanding envelope of the central cannibal galaxy.

Galactic cannibalism also explains why there are few if any bright galaxies in these clusters other than the central supergiant galaxy. That is because the bright galaxies, which are the most massive, experience the greatest dynamical friction. They are the first to go down to the gravitational well and be swallowed up by the central galaxies.

Over the course of several billion years, 50 or so galaxies may be swallowed up, leaving only the central supergiant and the 51st, the 52nd, etc., brightest galaxies. Given time, all the massive galaxies in the cluster will be absorbed, leaving a sparse cluster of a supergiant galaxy surrounded by clouds of small, dim galaxies.

118. In line 3, the word *menagerie* most nearly means:

F. odd mixture.
G. open environment.
H. uniform collection.
J. flat area.

119. It can be inferred from the passage that the physical features of a galaxy that does not belong to a rich cluster are determined primarily by the:

A. size and rotation of the protogalactic cloud.
B. intensity of light emanating from the galaxy.
C. temperature of the interstellar gas.
D. age of the protogalactic cloud.

120. The author implies that the currently accepted theories on galaxy formation are:

F. completely incorrect and misguided.
G. naive and out-of-date.
H. speculative and unsupported by observation.
J. substantially correct but in need of modification.

121. According to the passage, a cluster with a central, supergiant galaxy will:

A. contain no intermediately bright galaxies.
B. have 50–100 galaxies of all sizes and intensities.
C. consist solely of third- and fourth-generation stars.
D. produce only spiral and disk-shaped galaxies.

122. According to the passage, the outcome of a collision between galaxies depends on:

F. the relative velocities of the galaxies.
G. the relative ages of the galaxies.
H. the relative sizes of the galaxies.
J. the relative velocities and sizes of the galaxies.

123. According to the passage, as a galaxy falls inward toward the center of a cluster, it:

A. collides with the central core and emerges relatively intact.
B. absorbs superheated gases from the interstellar medium.
C. is broken apart by the gravitational forces of the core.
D. is transformed by collisions into a large, spiral galaxy.

124. The passage provides information that will answer which of the following questions?

F. What is the age of our sun?
G. What proportion of all galaxies are found in clusters?
H. Approximately how many galaxies would be found in a rich cluster?
J. What type of galaxy is ours?

125. The tone of the passage can best be described as:

A. light-hearted and amused.
B. objective but concerned.
C. detached and unconcerned.
D. cautious but sincere.

Passage XVI

NATURAL SCIENCE: This passage reviews the basic physical chemistry of atoms and radioactive decay.

An atom consists of a nucleus (containing protons and neutrons) surrounded by electrons. Each proton has a positive charge of +1, and each electron has a negative charge of –1. A neutron has no charge. The number of protons in their nuclei determines the identities of the different elements. For example, hydrogen atoms have only one proton, while oxygen atoms have eight protons. The total number of protons in the nucleus is the "atomic number" of that element. The total number of protons and neutrons in the nucleus is the "atomic mass" of the atom. Different atoms of the same element may contain a different number of neutrons, and so have different atomic masses. (But they will have the same number of protons and the same atomic number.) Atoms of the same element with different atomic masses are called isotopes of that element.

Certain elements are radioactive—they emit various types of radiation from their atomic nuclei. Two common types of radiation are alpha particles and beta particles. An alpha particle, which is the equivalent of a helium nucleus, consists of two protons and two neutrons. It is written ${}^{4}_{2}\text{He}$ (the superscript 4 is the mass number of the particle, and the subscript 2 is its atomic number). A beta particle is an electron traveling at high speed. It is written ${}^{0}_{-1}\text{e}$. Both types of radiation are emitted at a very high speed and can easily penetrate other substances.

When atoms of a substance emit radiation, they are said to undergo radioactive decay. The result is a different element with a different atomic number and a different mass number. For example, when a radium atom emits an alpha particle, it decays into an atom of radon. This reaction is shown in the following equation:

$$^{226}_{88}\text{Ra} \rightarrow {}^{4}_{2}\text{He} + {}^{222}_{86}\text{Rn}$$

Note that the equation is balanced. That is, the atomic number of the original atom on the left side of the equation equals the sum of the atomic numbers of the products on the right side of the equation. Similarly, the mass number of the original atom equals the sum of the mass numbers of the products. Every nuclear reaction balances in this same manner.

Some types of nuclear radiation take place very slowly; other types are very rapid. The rate of radiation is measured in half-lives. A half-life is the time required for one-half the amount of a given radioactive substance to decay.

126. As radium emits alpha particles, the mass of radium will:

F. increase.
G. decrease.
H. stay the same.
J. either increase or decrease, depending on the conditions.

127. In nuclear chemistry notation, two isotopes, or forms, of cobalt are written ${}^{59}_{27}\text{Co}$ and ${}^{60}_{27}\text{Co}$. The difference between the two isotopes is:

A. an alpha particle.
B. a beta particle.
C. a proton.
D. a neutron.

128. An alpha particle has:

F. no electric charge.
G. a positive electric charge.
H. a negative electric charge.
J. a variable electric charge.

129. A beta particle has:

A. no electric charge.
B. a positive electric charge.
C. a negative electric charge.
D. a variable electric charge.

130. When an atom emits a beta particle, the atomic mass number will:

F. increase.
G. decrease.
H. stay the same.
J. either increase or decrease, depending on the conditions.

QUIZZES

This section contains three Reading quizzes. Complete each quiz under timed conditions. Answers are on page 635.

Quiz I *(18 items; 15 minutes)*

DIRECTIONS: Each passage below is followed by a set of items. Read the passage and choose the best answer for each item. You may refer to the passage as often as necessary to answer the items.

Passage I

SOCIAL SCIENCE: This passage discusses the economic structure of current healthcare policy.

The healthcare economy is replete with unusual and even unique economic relationships. One of the least understood involves the peculiar roles of producer or "provider" and purchaser or "consumer" in the typical doctor-patient relationship. In most sectors of the economy, the seller attempts to attract a potential buyer with various inducements of price, quality, and utility, and the buyer makes the decision. Where circumstances permit the buyer no choice because there is effectively only one seller and the product is relatively essential, government usually asserts monopoly and places the industry under price and other regulations. Neither of these conditions prevail in most of the healthcare industry.

In the healthcare industry, the doctor-patient relationship is the mirror image of the ordinary relationship between producer and consumer. Once an individual has chosen to see a physician—and even then there may be no real choice—it is the physician who usually makes all significant purchasing decisions: whether the patient should return "next Wednesday," whether X-rays are needed, whether drugs should be prescribed, etc. It is a rare and sophisticated patient who will challenge such professional decisions or raise in advance questions about price, especially when the ailment is regarded as serious.

This is particularly significant in relation to hospital care. The physician must certify the need for hospitalization, determine what procedures will be performed, and announce when the patient may be discharged. The patient may be consulted about some of these decisions, but in the main it is the doctor's judgments that are final. Little wonder, then, that in the eyes of the hospital, the physician is the real "consumer." Consequently, the medical staff represents the "power center" in hospital policy and decision-making, not the administration.

Although usually there are in this situation four identifiable participants—the physician, the hospital, the patient, and the payer (generally an insurance carrier or government)—the physician makes the essential decisions for all of them. The hospital becomes an extension of the physician; the payer generally meets most of the bona fide bills generated by the physician/hospital; and for the most part the patient plays a passive role. In routine or minor illnesses, or just plain worries, the patient's options are, of course, much greater with respect to use and price. In illnesses that are of some significance, however, such choices tend to evaporate, and it is for these illnesses that the bulk of the healthcare dollar is spent. We estimate that about 75 to 80 percent of healthcare expenditures are determined by physicians, not patients. For this reason, economy measures directed at patients or the public are relatively ineffective.

1. In line 1, the phrase "replete with" most nearly means:

   A. filled with.
   B. restricted by.
   C. enriched by.
   D. damaged by.

2. The author's primary purpose is to:

F. speculate about the relationship between a patient's ability to pay and the treatment received.
G. criticize doctors for exercising too much control over patients.
H. analyze some important economic factors in healthcare.
J. urge hospitals to reclaim their decision-making authority.

3. It can be inferred that doctors are able to determine hospital policies because:

A. it is doctors who generate income for the hospital.
B. most of a patient's bills are paid by health insurance.
C. hospital administrators lack the expertise to question medical decisions.
D. a doctor is ultimately responsible for a patient's health.

4. According to the author, when a doctor tells a patient to "return next Wednesday," the doctor is in effect:

F. taking advantage of the patient's concern for his health.
G. instructing the patient to buy more medical services.
H. warning the patient that a hospital stay might be necessary.
J. advising the patient to seek a second opinion.

5. The author is most probably leading up to:

A. a proposal to control medical costs.
B. a discussion of a new medical treatment.
C. an analysis of the causes of inflation in the United States.
D. a study of lawsuits against doctors for malpractice.

6. The tone of the passage can best be described as:

F. whimsical.
G. cautious.
H. analytical.
J. inquisitive.

7. With which of the following statements would the author be likely to agree?

A. Few patients are reluctant to object to the course of treatment prescribed by a doctor or to question the cost of the services.
B. The payer, whether an insurance carrier or the government, is less likely to acquiesce to demands for payment when the illness of the patient is regarded as serious.
C. Today's patients are more informed as to what services and procedures they will need from their healthcare providers.
D. The more serious the illness of a patient, the less likely it is that the patient will object to the course of treatment prescribed or to question the cost of services.

8. The author's primary concern is to:

F. define a term.
G. clarify a misunderstanding.
H. refute a theory.
J. discuss a problem.

Passage II

HUMANITIES: This passage discusses the voyages to North American continents by Leif Ericsson and Biarni and debates the veracity of the varied accounts.

In the summer of 999, Leif Ericsson voyaged to Norway and spent the following winter with King Olaf Tryggvason. Substantially the same account is given by both the Saga of Eric the Red and the Flat Island Book. Of Leif's return voyage to Greenland the latter says nothing, but according to the former it was during this return voyage that Leif discovered America. The Flat Island Book, however, tells of another and earlier landfall by Biarni, the son of a prominent man named Heriulf, and makes this Leif's inspiration for the voyage to the new land. In short, like Leif, Biarni and his companions sight three countries in succession before reaching Greenland, and to come upon each new land takes one "doegr" more than the last until Biarni comes to land directly in front of his father's house in the last-mentioned country.

Most later writers have rejected this narrative, and they may be justified. Possibly, Biarni was a companion of Leif when he voyaged from Norway to Greenland via America, or it may be that the entire tale is but a garbled account of that voyage and Biarni another name for Leif. It should be noted, however, that the stories of Leif's visit to King Olaf and Biarni's to that king's predecessor are in the same narrative in the Flat Island Book, so there is less likelihood of duplication than if they were from different sources. Also, Biarni landed on none of the lands he passed, but Leif apparently landed on one, for he brought back specimens of wheat, vines, and timber. Nor is there any good reason to believe that the first land visited by Biarni was Wineland. The first land was "level and covered with woods," and "there were small hillocks upon it." Of forests, later writers do not emphasize them particularly in connection with Wineland, though they are often noted incidentally; and of hills, the Saga says of Wineland only "wherever there was hilly ground, there were vines."

Additionally, if the two narratives were from the same source, we should expect a closer resemblance of Helluland. The Saga says of it: "They found there hellus" (large flat stones). According to the Biarni narrative, however, "this land was high and mountainous." The intervals of one, two, three, and four "doegr" in both narratives are suggestive, but mythic formulas of this kind may be introduced into narratives without altogether destroying their historicity. It is also held against the Biarni narrative that its hero is made to come upon the coast of Greenland exactly in front of his father's home. But it should be recalled that Heriulfsness lay below two high mountains that served as landmarks for navigators.

I would give up Biarni more readily were it not that the story of Leif's voyage, contained in the supposedly more reliable Saga, is almost as amazing. But Leif's voyage across the entire width of the North Atlantic is said to be "probable" because it is documented in the narrative of a preferred authority, while Biarni's is "improbable" or even "impossible" because the document containing it has been condemned.

9. The author's primary concern is to demonstrate that:

A. Leif Ericsson did not visit America.
B. Biarni might have visited America before Leif Ericsson.
C. Biarni did not visit Wineland.
D. Leif Ericsson visited Wineland first.

10. The passage provides information that defines which of the following terms?

I. Doegr
II. Hellus
III. Heriulfsness

F. I only
G. II only
H. I and II only
J. II and III only

11. It can be inferred from the passage that scholars who doubt the authenticity of the Biarni narrative make all of the following objections EXCEPT:

A. Biarni might have accompanied Leif Ericsson on the voyage to America, and that is why a separate, erroneous narrative was invented.
B. the similarity of the voyages described in the Saga and in the Flat Island Book indicates that there was but one voyage, not two voyages.
C. it seems very improbable that a ship, having sailed from America to Greenland, could have found its way to a precise point on the coast of Greenland.
D. both the Saga of Eric the Red and the Flat Island Book make use of mythic formulas, so it is probable that the same person wrote them both.

12. The author mentions the two high mountains (lines 50–51) in order to show that it is:

F. reasonable for Biarni to land precisely at his father's home.
G. possible to sail from Norway to Greenland without modern navigational equipment.
H. likely that Biarni landed on America at least 100 years before Leif Ericsson.
J. probable that Leif Ericsson followed the same course as Biarni.

13. All of the following are mentioned as similarities between Leif Ericsson's voyage and Biarni's voyage EXCEPT:

A. both visited Norway.
B. on the return voyage, both visited three different lands.
C. both returned to Greenland.
D. both sighted Wineland.

14. It can be inferred that the author regards the historicity of the Biarni narrative as:

F. conclusively proved.
G. almost conclusively proved.
H. possibly true.
J. highly unlikely.

15. In the final paragraph, the author suggests that some authorities who regard the Saga as authentic are guilty of which of the following errors in reasoning?

A. Oversimplification
B. Logical contradiction
C. False analogy
D. Circular reasoning

16. According to the passage, Heriulf is:

F. Leif Ericsson's son.
G. one of Leif Ericsson's sailors.
H. Biarni's father.
J. King Olaf Tryggvason's son.

17. According to the author, most authorities regard the Biarni narrative as:

A. conclusively demonstrated.
B. probably true.
C. probably untrue.
D. an attempted fraud.

18. Biarni's home was in:

F. Norway.
G. Greenland.
H. Wineland.
J. Flat Island.

Quiz II *(17 items; 15 minutes)*

DIRECTIONS: Each passage below is followed by a set of items. Read the passage and choose the best answer for each item. You may refer to the passage as often as necessary to answer the items.

Passage I

SOCIAL SCIENCE: This passage discusses the 1796 presidential election between Thomas Jefferson and John Adams.

"Heartily tired" from the brutal, almost daily, conflicts that erupted over questions of national policy between himself and Alexander Hamilton, Thomas Jefferson resigned his position as Secretary of State in 1793. Although his Federalist opponents were convinced that this was merely a strategic withdrawal to allow him an opportunity to plan and promote his candidacy for the presidency should Washington step down in 1796, Jefferson insisted that this retirement from public life was to be final.

But even in retirement, the world of politics pursued him. As the election grew nearer and it became apparent that Washington would not seek a third term, rumors of Jefferson's presidential ambitions grew in intensity. Reacting to these continuous insinuations in a letter to James Madison, Jefferson admitted that while his enemies, to impugn his political motives, had originated the idea that he coveted the office of chief executive, he had been forced to examine his true feelings on the subject for his own peace of mind. In so doing he concluded that his reasons for retirement—the desire for privacy, and the delight of family life—coupled with his now failing health were insuperable barriers to public service. The "little spice of ambition" he had in his younger days had long since evaporated and the question of his presidency was forever closed.

Jefferson did not actively engage in the campaign on his own behalf. The Republican Party, presaging modern campaign tactics, created a grass roots sentiment for their candidate by directing their efforts toward the general populace. In newspapers, Jefferson was presented as "the uniform advocate of equal rights among the citizens" while Adams was portrayed as the "champion of rank, titles, heredity, and distinctions."

Jefferson was not certain of the outcome of the election until the end of December. Under the original electoral system established by the Constitution, each presidential elector cast his ballot for two men without designating between them as to office. The candidate who received the greater number of votes became the president; the second highest, the vice president. Based on his own calculations, Jefferson foresaw that the electoral vote would be close. He wrote to Madison that in the event of a tie, he wished for the choice to be in favor of Adams. The New Englander had always been his senior in public office, he explained, and the expression of public will being equal, he should be preferred for the higher honor. Jefferson, a shrewd politician, realized that the transition of power from the nearly mythical Washington to a lesser luminary in the midst of the deep and bitter political divisions facing the nation could be perilous, and he had no desire to be caught in the storm that had been brewing for four years and was about to break. "This is certainly not a moment to covet the helm," he wrote to Edward Rutledge. When the electoral vote was tallied, Adams emerged as the victor. Rejoicing at his "escape," Jefferson was completely satisfied with the decision. Despite their obvious and basic political differences, Jefferson genuinely respected John Adams as a friend and compatriot. Although he believed that Adams had deviated from the course set in 1776, Jefferson never felt a diminution of confidence in Adams' integrity and was confident he would not steer the nation too far off its Republican tack. Within two years, Jefferson's views would be drastically altered as measures such as the Alien and Sedition Acts of 1798 convinced him of the need to wrest control of the government from the Federalists.

1. The phrase "heartily tired" (line 1) is most probably a quotation from:

A. Alexander Hamilton.
B. Thomas Jefferson.
C. George Washington.
D. John Adams.

2. The "escape" mentioned in line 57 refers to the fact that Jefferson:

F. was no longer Secretary of State.
G. would not be burdened with the problems of the presidency.
H. fled the country following the election.
J. was hoping that the votes would be recounted.

3. According to the passage, the Republican Party appealed primarily to:

A. wealthy landowners.
B. ordinary people.
C. prosperous merchants.
D. high society.

4. The author states that all of the following were reasons Jefferson resigned as Secretary of State EXCEPT:

F. Jefferson disliked Madison.
G. Jefferson wanted to spend time with his family.
H. Jefferson was weary of the demands of public service.
J. Jefferson wished for greater privacy.

5. The author is primarily concerned with revealing:

A. the feud between Alexander Hamilton and Thomas Jefferson.
B. the difference between the Federalists and the Republicans.
C. the strategies used by early American political parties.
D. Thomas Jefferson's character and personality.

6. The author relies on which of the following in developing the selection?

I. Personal correspondence
II. Newspapers
III. Voter registration rolls

F. I only
G. II only
H. I and II only
J. I and III only

7. One reason for Jefferson's retirement was his disagreement with:

A. Alexander Hamilton.
B. George Washington.
C. James Madison.
D. Edward Rutledge.

8. In the context of the passage, the phrase "covet the helm" (line 55) means:

F. to aspire to be President.
G. to desire to purchase a boat.
H. to wish to be left in peace.
J. to hope to become wealthy.

9. The passage suggests that two years after the 1796 election, Jefferson would:

A. ally himself with Alexander Hamilton.
B. ally himself with John Adams.
C. disagree with John Adams.
D. disagree with Edward Rutledge.

10. The newspaper depicted Jefferson and Adams as:

F. conservative and liberal, respectively.
G. liberal and conservative, respectively.
H. conservatives.
J. liberals.

Passage II

NATURAL SCIENCE: This passage discusses human social evolution and adaptation.

Man, so the truism goes, lives increasingly in a man-made environment. This puts a special burden on human immaturity, for it is plain that adapting to such variable conditions must depend very heavily on opportunities for learning, or whatever the processes are that are operative during immaturity. It must also mean that during immaturity, man must master knowledge and skills that are neither stored in the gene pool nor learned by direct encounter, but that are contained in the culture pool—knowledge about values and history, skills as varied as an obligatory natural language or an optional mathematical one, as mute as levers or as articulate as myth telling.

Yet, it would be a mistake to leap to the conclusion that because human immaturity makes possible high flexibility, therefore anything is possible for the species. Human traits were selected for their survival value over a four- to five-million-year period with a great acceleration of the selection process during the last half of that period. There were crucial, irreversible changes during that final man-making period: the recession of formidable dentition, a 50-percent increase in brain volume, the obstetrical paradox—bipedalism and strong pelvic girdle, larger brain through a smaller birth canal—an immature brain at birth, and creation of what Washburn has called a "technical-social way of life," involving tool and symbol use.

Note, however, that hominidization consisted principally of adaptations to conditions in the Pleistocene. These preadaptations, shaped in response to earlier habitat demands, are part of man's evolutionary inheritance. This is not to say that close beneath the skin of man is a naked ape, that civilization is only a veneer. The technical-social way of life is a deep feature of the species adaptation. But we would err if we assumed *a priori* that man's inheritance placed no constraint on his power to adapt. Some of the preadaptations can be shown to be presently maladaptive. Man's inordinate fondness for fats and sweets no longer serves his individual survival well. Furthermore, the human obsession with sexuality is plainly not fitted for survival of the species now, however well it might have served to populate the upper Pliocene and the Pleistocene. Nevertheless, note that the species responds typically to these challenges by technical innovation rather than by morphological or behavioral change. Contraception dissociates sexuality from reproduction. Of course, we do not know what kinds and what range of stresses are produced by successive rounds of such technical innovation. Dissociating sexuality and reproduction, for example, surely produces changes in the structure of the family, which in turn redefines the role of women, which in turn alters the authority pattern affecting the child, etc. Continuing and possibly accelerating change seems inherent in such adaptation. This, of course, places an enormous pressure on man's uses of immaturity, preparing the young for unforeseeable change—the more so if there are severe restraints imposed by human preadaptations to earlier conditions of life.

11. The primary purpose of the passage is to:

A. refute some misconceptions about the importance of human immaturity.
B. introduce a new theory of the origins of the human species.
C. describe the evolutionary forces that formed the physical appearance of modern humans.
D. discuss the importance of human immaturity as an adaptive mechanism.

12. It can be inferred that the obstetrical paradox is puzzling because:

F. it occurred very late during the evolution of the species.
G. evolutionary forces seemed to work at cross purposes to each other.
H. technological innovations have made the process of birth easier.
J. an increase in brain size is not an ordinary evolutionary event.

13. Which of the following statements can be inferred from the passage?

A. Human beings are today less sexually active than were our ancestors during the Pleistocene era.
B. During the Pleistocene era, a fondness for fats and sweets was a trait that contributed to survival of humans.
C. Mathematics was invented by human beings during the latter half of the Pleistocene era.
D. The use of language and tools is a trait that is genetically transmitted from one generation to the next.

14. As used in line 31, the word *preadaptations* refers to traits that:

F. were useful to earlier human beings but have since lost their utility.
G. appeared in response to the need to learn a natural language and the use of tools.
H. humans currently exhibit but that developed in response to conditions of an earlier age.
J. are disadvantageous to creatures whose way of life is primarily technical and social.

15. The author mentions contraception to demonstrate that:

A. human beings may adapt to new conditions by technological invention rather than by changing their behavior.
B. sexual promiscuity is no longer an aid to the survival of the human species.
C. technological innovation is a more important adaptive mechanism than either heredity or direct encounter.
D. conditions during the upper Pliocene and Pleistocene eras no longer affect the course of human evolution.

16. With which of the following statements would the author LEAST likely agree?

F. The technical-social way of life of humans is an adaptive mechanism that arose in response to environmental pressures.
G. The possibility of technical innovation makes it unlikely that the physical appearance of humans will change radically in a short time.
H. Technological innovations can result in changes in the social structures in which humans live.
J. The fact that humans have a technical-social way of life makes the species immune from evolutionary pressures.

17. The author is most probably addressing which of the following audiences?

A. Medical students in a course on human anatomy
B. College students in an introductory course on archaeology
C. Psychologists investigating the uses of human immaturity
D. Biologists trying to trace the course of human evolution

Quiz III *(18 items; 15 minutes)*

DIRECTIONS: Each passage below is followed by a set of items. Read the passage and choose the best answer for each item. You may refer to the passage as often as necessary to answer the items.

Passage I

SOCIAL SCIENCE: This passage is adapted from an article that discusses Japanese culture and civilization.

The uniqueness of the Japanese character is the result of two, seemingly contradictory forces: the strength of traditions, and selective receptivity to foreign achievements and inventions. As early as the 1860s, there were counter movements to the traditional orientation. Yukichi Fukuzawa, the most eloquent spokesman of Japan's "Enlightenment," claimed "The Confucian civilization of the East seems to me to lack two things possessed by Western civilization: science in the material sphere and a sense of independence in the spiritual sphere." Fukuzawa's great influence is found in the free and individualistic philosophy of the Education Code of 1872, but he was not able to prevent the government from turning back to the canons of Confucian thought in the Imperial Rescript of 1890. Another interlude of relative liberalism followed World War I, when the democratic idealism of President Woodrow Wilson had an important impact on Japanese intellectuals and, especially, students; but more important was the Leninist ideology of the 1917 Bolshevik Revolution. Again, in the early 1930s, nationalism and militarism became dominant, largely because of failing economic conditions.

Following the end of World War II, substantial changes were undertaken in Japan to liberate the individual from authoritarian restraints. The new democratic value system was accepted by many teachers, students, intellectuals, and old liberals, but it was not immediately embraced by the society as a whole. Japanese traditions were dominated by group values, and notions of personal freedom and individual rights were unfamiliar. Today, democratic processes are evident in the widespread participation of the Japanese people in social and political life; yet, there is no universally accepted and stable value system. Values are constantly modified by strong infusions of Western ideas, both democratic and Marxist. School textbooks espouse democratic principles, emphasizing equality over hierarchy and rationalism over tradition; but in practice these values are often misinterpreted and distorted, particularly by youth who translate the individualistic and humanistic goals of democracy into egoistic and materialistic ones.

Most Japanese people have consciously rejected Confucianism, but vestiges of the old order remain. An important feature of relationships in many institutions such as political parties, large corporations, and university faculties is the *oyabun-kobun* or parent-child relation. A party leader, supervisor, or professor, in return for loyalty, protects those subordinate to him and takes general responsibility for their interests throughout their entire lives, an obligation that sometimes even extends to arranging marriages. The corresponding loyalty of the individual to his patron reinforces his allegiance to the group to which they both belong. A willingness to cooperate with other members of the group and to support without qualification the interests of the group in all its external relations is still a widely respected virtue. The *oyabun-kobun* creates ladders of mobility that an individual can ascend, rising as far as abilities permit, so long as he maintains successful personal ties with a superior in the vertical channel, the latter requirement usually taking precedence over a need for exceptional competence. Consequently, there is little horizontal relationship between people even within the same profession.

1. As used in line 45, the word *vestiges* most nearly means:

A. institutions.
B. superiors.
C. traces.
D. subordinates.

2. Which of the following is most like the relationship of the *oyabun-kobun* described in the passage?

F. A political candidate and the voting public
G. A gifted scientist and his protégé
H. Two brothers who are partners in a business
J. A judge presiding at the trial of a criminal defendant

3. According to the passage, Japanese attitudes are NOT influenced by which of the following?

   A. Democratic ideals
   B. Elements of modern Western culture
   C. Remnants of an earlier social structure
   D. Confucianism

4. The author implies that:

   F. decisions about promotions within the vertical channel are often based on personal feelings.
   G. students and intellectuals do not understand the basic tenets of Western democracy.
   H. Western values have completely overwhelmed traditional Japanese attitudes.
   J. respect for authority was introduced into Japan following World War II.

5. In developing the passage, the author does which of the following?

   A. Introduces an analogy
   B. Defines a term
   C. Presents statistics
   D. Cites an authority

6. It can be inferred that the Imperial Rescript of 1890:

   F. was a protest by liberals against the lack of individual liberty in Japan.
   G. marked a return in government policies to conservative values.
   H. implemented the ideals set forth in the Education Code of 1872.
   J. was influenced by the Leninist ideology of the Bolshevik Revolution.

7. Which of the following is the most accurate description of the organization of the passage?

   A. A sequence of inferences in which the conclusion of each successive step becomes a premise in the next argument
   B. A list of generalizations, most of which are supported by only a single example
   C. A chronological analysis of historical events leading up to a description of the current situation
   D. A statement of a commonly accepted theory that is then subjected to a critical analysis

8. Which of the following best states the central thesis of the passage?

   F. The value system of Japan is based upon traditional and conservative values that have, in modern times, been modified by Western and other liberal values.
   G. Students and radicals in Japan have used Leninist ideology to distort the meaning of democratic, Western values.
   H. The notions of personal freedom and individual liberty did not find immediate acceptance in Japan because of the predominance of traditional group values.
   J. Modern Japanese society is characterized by hierarchical relationships in which a personal tie to a superior is often more important than merit.

Passage II

NATURAL SCIENCE: This passage reviews the basic physics of electromagnetic waves and radar specifically.

Whether used to control airplane traffic, detect speeding automobiles, or track a hurricane, radar is a very useful tool. Developed during World War II, this technology allows for remote sensing, that is, locating objects that are not seen directly. The word "radar" is a contraction of "radio detection and ranging." It works in much the same way as an echo. When you shout toward a cliff or a large building, part of the sound bounces back. In radar, waves of electromagnetic radiation are sent out. When they strike an object, they bounce back and are picked up by a receiver. The returning signal indicates the direction of the object; the time it takes for the signal to return indicates the distance to the object. Radar waves detect objects by their varying densities. They are not deflected by atmospheric layers and therefore always travel in a straight line—in all weather, both day and night.

Radar waves are electromagnetic waves, as are light waves, electric waves, X-rays, cosmic rays, and radio waves. All electromagnetic waves travel at 300,000 kilometers per second—the speed of light. Waves differ from each other in the number of times they vibrate per second; this variable is known as frequency and is usually expressed as cycles per second. Waves also differ in their size, or wavelength. The speed, frequency, and wavelength of a wave are related by the wave equation in which:

$$\text{speed} = \text{frequency} \bullet \text{wavelength}$$

This shows that the product of the frequency and wavelength of any given wave is always a constant—the speed of light. To find the wavelength of a wave, knowing the frequency, this formula is used:

$$\text{wavelength} = \frac{\text{speed}}{\text{frequency}}$$

For example, if a radio station broadcasts waves at 600,000 cycles per second (cps), the wavelength would be calculated this way:

$$\text{wavelength} = \frac{300{,}000 \text{ km per sec}}{600{,}000 \text{ cps}} = 0.5 \text{ km} = 500 \text{ m}$$

If the frequency of the wave is doubled to 1,200,000 cycles per second, its wavelength would be cut in half to 250 meters. Since frequencies are so high, the unit "megahertz" is usually used; 1 megahertz = 1,000,000 cycles per second.

Wavelengths within the electromagnetic spectrum vary greatly. Radar has wavelengths that measure from approximately one centimeter (0.01 meters) up to one meter. Each kind of wave has a range of wavelengths. The table compares some sample wavelengths of several kinds of electromagnetic waves.

Type of Wave (meters)	*Sample Wavelength*
cosmic rays	0.0000000000000001
X-rays	0.0000000001
ultraviolet rays	0.00000001
visible light	0.000001
infrared heat	0.0001
microwaves	0.001
radar	0.1
television	1.0
radio	100
long radio waves	10,000
electric power	1,000,000

9. Radio waves and radar waves have the same:

A. frequency.
B. wavelength.
C. cycles per second.
D. speed.

10. A radar signal having a frequency of 3,000 megahertz would have a wavelength of:

F. 0.001 km.
G. 0.01 km.
H. 10 m.
J. 0.1 m.

11. A radar set could not locate an airplane if it were flying:

A. faster than the speed of sound.
B. above a heavy storm.
C. above the atmosphere.
D. below the horizon.

12. It is possible to find the distance to an object from a radar set because the:

F. wavelength of radar is known.
G. frequency of radar is known.
H. speed of radar is 300,000 kilometers per second.
J. set operates at 10 megahertz.

13. The relationship between the frequency and wavelength of a wave is:

A. constant.
B. directly proportional.
C. exponential.
D. inverse.

14. An antenna picks up a signal that has a wavelength of about one meter. It is likely to be:

F. in the visible spectrum.
G. an ultraviolet ray.
H. a television signal.
J. an X-ray.

15. Radio waves will not penetrate the ionosphere, but microwaves will. Would you expect X-rays to penetrate the ionosphere?

A. Yes, because they have a shorter wavelength than microwaves and radio waves.
B. Yes, because they have a lower frequency than microwaves and radio waves.
C. No, because they travel more slowly than microwaves.
D. No, because they have fewer cycles per second than microwaves or radio waves.

16. Compared to cosmic rays, the frequency value of visible light waves is:

F. higher.
G. lower.
H. the same.
J. Cannot be determined from the given information

17. Which of the following factors would be most important in order for radar to detect and track storms?

A. Radar signals travel in straight lines.
B. The densities of moist air masses are different from those of dry air masses.
C. The atmosphere does not deflect radar signals.
D. Radar signals travel much faster than storm tracks.

18. Like a radar reflection, an echo can be used to determine the distance of an object. This must be because:

F. sound is a form of radar.
G. sound travels at a relatively fixed rate.
H. sound waves have different frequencies.
J. sound waves are invisible.

This section contains additional Reading items for further practice. Answers are on page 636.

DIRECTIONS: Each passage below is followed by a set of items. Read the passage and choose the best answer for each item. You may refer to the passage as often as necessary to answer the items.

Passage I

NATURAL SCIENCE: This passage discusses systems for reporting and investigating adverse drug effects.

A fundamental principle of pharmacology is that all drugs have multiple actions. Actions that are desirable in the treatment of disease are considered therapeutic, while those that are undesirable or pose risks to the patient are called "effects." Adverse drug effects range from the trivial, for example, nausea or dry mouth, to the serious, such as massive gastrointestinal bleeding or thromboembolism; and some drugs can be lethal. Therefore, an effective system for the detection of adverse drug effects is an important component of the healthcare system of any advanced nation. Much of the research conducted on new drugs aims at identifying the conditions of use that maximize beneficial effects and minimize the risk of adverse effects. The intent of drug labeling is to reflect this body of knowledge accurately so that physicians can properly prescribe the drug or, if it is to be sold without prescription, so that consumers can properly use the drug.

The current system of drug investigation in the United States has proved very useful and accurate in identifying the common side effects associated with new prescription drugs. By the time a new drug is approved by the Food and Drug Administration, its side effects are usually well described in the package insert for physicians. The investigational process, however, cannot be counted on to detect all adverse effects because of the relatively small number of patients involved in pre-marketing studies and the relatively short duration of the studies. Animal toxicology studies are, of course, done before marketing in an attempt to identify any potential for toxicity, but negative results do not guarantee the safety of a drug in humans, as evidenced by such well known examples as the birth deformities due to thalidomide.

This recognition prompted the establishment in many countries of programs to which physicians report adverse drug effects. The United States and other countries also send reports to an international program operated by the World Health Organization. These programs, however, are voluntary reporting programs and are intended to serve a limited goal: alerting a government or private agency to adverse drug effects detected by physicians in the course of practice. Other approaches must be used to confirm suspected drug reactions and to estimate incidence rates. These other approaches include conducting retrospective control studies, for example, the studies associating endometrial cancer with estrogen use, and systematically monitoring hospitalized patients to determine the incidence of acute common side effects, as typified by the Boston Collaborative Drug Surveillance Program.

Thus, the overall drug surveillance system of the United States is composed of a set of information bases, special studies, and monitoring programs, each contributing in its own way to our knowledge about marketed drugs. The system is decentralized among a number of governmental units and is not administered as a coordinated function. Still, it would be inappropriate at this time to attempt to unite all of the disparate elements into a comprehensive surveillance program. Instead, the challenge is to improve each segment of the system and to take advantage of new computer strategies to improve coordination and communication.

1. In line 63, the word *disparate* most nearly means:

A. useless.
B. expensive.
C. temporary.
D. unconnected.

2. The author's primary concern is to discuss:

F. methods for testing the effects of new drugs on humans.
G. the importance of having accurate information about the effects of drugs.
H. procedures for determining the long-term effects of new drugs.
J. attempts to curb the abuse of prescription drugs.

3. The author implies that a drug with adverse side effects:

A. will not be approved for use by consumers without a doctor's prescription.
B. must wait for approval until lengthy studies prove the effects are not permanent.
C. should be used only if its therapeutic value out-weighs its adverse effects.
D. should be withdrawn from the marketplace pending a government investigation.

4. Which of the following can be inferred from the passage?

F. The decentralization of the overall drug surveillance system results in it being completely ineffective in any attempts to provide information about adverse drug effects.
G. Drugs with serious adverse side effects are never approved for distribution.
H. Some adverse drug effects are discovered during testing because they are very rare.
J. Some adverse drug effects cannot be detected prior to approval because they take a long time to develop.

5. The author introduces the example of thalidomide in the last sentence of the second paragraph to show that some:

A. drugs do not have the same reactions in humans that they do in animals.
B. drug testing procedures are ignored by careless laboratory workers.
C. drugs have no therapeutic value for humans.
D. drugs have adverse side effects as well as beneficial actions.

6. It can be inferred that the estrogen study mentioned in the last sentence of the third paragraph:

F. uncovered long-term side effects of a drug that had already been approved for sale by the Food and Drug Administration.
G. discovered potential side effects of a drug that was still awaiting approval for sale by the Food and Drug Administration.
H. revealed possible new applications of a drug that had previously been approved for a different treatment.
J. is an example of a study that could be more efficiently conducted by a centralized authority than by volunteer reporting.

7. The author is most probably leading up to a discussion of some suggestions about how to:

A. centralize authority for drug surveillance in the United States.
B. centralize authority for drug surveillance among international agencies.
C. coordinate better the sharing of information among the drug surveillance agencies.
D. eliminate the availability and sale of certain drugs now on the market.

8. The author makes use of which of the following devices in the passage?

F. Definition of terms
G. Examples
H. Analogy
J. Definition of terms and examples

Passage II

NATURAL SCIENCE: This passage is adapted from a science magazine article that discusses lightning.

Lightning is an electrical discharge of immense proportions. Some 80 percent of lightning occurs within clouds; about 20 percent is cloud-to-ground lightning; and an extremely small percentage is cloud-to-sky lightning.

Cloud-to-ground lightning begins when complex meteorological processes cause a tremendous electrostatic charge to build up within a cloud. Typically, the bottom of the cloud is negatively charged. When the charge reaches 50 to 100 million volts, air is no longer an effective insulator, and lightning occurs within the cloud itself. Ten to 30 minutes after the onset of intracloud lightning, negative charges called stepped leaders emerge from the bottom of the cloud, moving toward the earth in 50-meter intervals at speeds of 100 to 200 kilometers per second and creating an ionized channel. As the leaders near the Earth, their strong electric field causes streamers of positively charged ions to develop at the tips of pointed objects that are connected directly or indirectly to the ground. These positively charged streamers flow upward.

When the distance, known as the striking distance, between a stepped leader and one of the streamers reaches 30 to 100 meters, the intervening air breaks down completely and the leader is joined to the Earth via the streamer. Now a pulse of current known as a return stroke ranging from thousands to hundreds of thousands of amperes moves at one tenth to one third the speed of light from the Earth through the object from which the streamer emanated and up the ionized channel to the charge center within the cloud. An ionized channel remains in the air and additional negative charges called dart leaders will quickly move down this path resulting in further return strokes. This multiplicity causes the flash to flicker. The entire event typically lasts about one second.

The return stroke's extremely high temperature creates the visible lightning and produces thunder by instantly turning moisture into steam. Most direct damage results from the heavy return stroke current because it produces high temperatures in the channel, or from arcing at the point of ground contact. If the lightning current is carried by an enclosed conductor (e.g., within a jacketed cable, through a concrete wall, or beneath a painted surface), entrapped moisture is turned into high-pressure steam that can cause a cable, wall, or painted object to explode. Arcing frequently ignites combustibles.

Lightning causes hundreds of millions of dollars in property losses annually and the majority of forest fires. Lightning is also the leading weather-related killer in the U.S., causing from 100 to 200 deaths each year.

9. In line 13, the word *intracloud* most nearly means:

A. between clouds.
B. within a cloud.
C. from cloud to sky.
D. from ground to cloud.

10. The selection defines the striking distance as the distance between:

F. the ground and the cloud.
G. a stepped leader and a dart leader.
H. a dart leader and a return stroke.
J. a streamer and a stepped leader.

11. According to the selection, the flickering appearance of a lightning strike is created by:

A. the stepped movement of leaders.
B. multiple return strokes.
C. water being vaporized.
D. arcing at ground contact.

12. What topic might the author logically address in a continuation of the passage?

F. Precautions to minimize lightning damage
G. Other weather phenomena that cause injury
H. Basic principles governing electricity
J. Identifying different types of clouds

13. According to the passage, which of the following is NOT true of stepped leaders?

A. They develop 10 to 30 minutes after intra-cloud lightning.
B. As they traverse the distance from cloud to ground, they create an ionized channel.
C. Their powerful positive charge causes streamers to develop in grounded objects.
D. They emerge from the bottom of the cloud and move downward in intervals of 50 meters.

14. The passage answers which of the following questions?

F. How does lightning produce the associated thunder?
G. How far above the ground is the bottom of the typical lightning-producing cloud?
H. How frequently will lightning strike a given object?
J. How long does it take a cloud to build up an electrostatic charge?

15. The author's primary concern is to:

A. warn about the dangers posed by lightning strikes.
B. describe the sequence of events that make up a lightning strike.
C. discuss fundamental scientific laws pertaining to electricity.
D. support the commonly held view that lightning strikes the ground.

Passage III

SOCIAL SCIENCE: This passage discusses the history of hospitals.

Public general hospitals originated in the almshouse infirmaries established as early as colonial times by local governments to care for the poor. Later, in the late eighteenth and early nineteenth centuries, the infirmary separated from the almshouse and became an independent institution supported by local tax money. At the same time, private charity hospitals began to develop. Both private and public hospitals mainly provided food and shelter for the impoverished sick, since there was little that medicine could actually do to cure illness, and the middle class was treated at home by private physicians.

Late in the nineteenth century, private charity hospitals began trying to attract middle-class patients. Although the depression of 1890 stimulated the growth of charitable institutions and an expanding urban population became dependent on assistance, there was a decline in private contributions to these organizations that forced them to look to local government for financial support. Since private institutions had also lost benefactors, they began to charge patients. In order to attract middle-class patients, private institutions provided services and amenities that distinguished between paying and nonpaying patients, making the hospital a desirable place for private physicians to treat their own patients. As paying patients became more necessary to the survival of the private hospital, the public hospitals slowly became the only place for the poor to get treatment. By the end of the nineteenth century, cities were reimbursing private hospitals for their care of indigent patients and the public hospitals remained dependent on the tax dollars.

The advent of private hospital health insurance, which provided middle-class patients with the purchasing power to pay for private hospital services, guaranteed the private hospital a regular source of income. Private hospitals restricted themselves to revenue-generating patients, leaving the public hospitals to care for the poor. Although public hospitals continued to provide services for patients with communicable diseases and outpatient and emergency services, the Blue Cross plans developed around the needs of the private hospitals and the inpatients they served. Thus, reimbursement for ambulatory care has been minimal under most Blue Cross plans, and provision of outpatient care has not been a major function of the private hospital, in part because private patients can afford to pay for the services of private physicians. Additionally, since World War II, there has been a tremendous influx of federal money into private medical schools and the hospitals associated with them. Further, large private medical centers with expensive research equipment and programs have attracted the best administrators, physicians, and researchers. Because of the greater resources available to the private medical centers, public hospitals have increasing problems attracting highly qualified research and medical personnel. With the mainstream of health care firmly established in the private medical sector, the public hospital has become a "dumping ground."

16. In line 31, the word *indigent* most nearly means:

F. without the means to pay.
G. having emergency medical needs.
H. lacking health insurance.
J. reimbursed by the government.

17. According to the passage, the very first private hospitals:

A. developed from almshouse infirmaries.
B. provided better care than public infirmaries.
C. were established mainly to service the poor.
D. were supported by government revenues.

18. It can be inferred that the author believes the differences that currently exist between public and private hospitals are primarily the result of:

F. political considerations.
G. economic factors.
H. ethical concerns.
J. legislative requirements.

19. It can be inferred that the growth of private health insurance:

A. relieved local governments of the need to fund public hospitals.
B. guaranteed that the poor would have access to medical care.
C. forced middle-class patients to use public hospitals.
D. reinforced the distinction between public and private hospitals.

20. Which of the following would be the most logical topic for the author to introduce in the next paragraph?

    F. A plan to improve the quality of public hospitals
    G. An analysis of the profit structure of health insurance companies
    H. A proposal to raise taxes on the middle class
    J. A discussion of recent developments in medical technology

21. The author's primary concern is to:

    A. describe the financial structure of the healthcare industry.
    B. demonstrate the importance of government support for healthcare institutions.
    C. criticize wealthy institutions for refusing to provide services to the poor.
    D. identify the historical causes of the division between private and public hospitals.

22. The author cites all of the following as factors contributing to the decline of public hospitals EXCEPT:

    F. government money was used to subsidize private medical schools and hospitals to the detriment of public hospitals.
    G. public hospitals are not able to compete with private institutions for top-flight managers and doctors.
    H. large private medical centers have better research facilities and more extensive research programs than public hospitals.
    J. blue Cross insurance coverage does not reimburse subscribers for medical expenses incurred in a public hospital.

23. The author's attitude toward public hospitals can best be described as:

    A. contemptuous and prejudiced.
    B. apprehensive and distrustful.
    C. concerned and understanding.
    D. enthusiastic and supportive.

24. The author implies that any outpatient care provided by a hospital is:

    F. paid for by private insurance.
    G. provided in lieu of treatment by a private physician.
    H. supplied primarily by private hospitals.
    J. a source of revenue for public hospitals.

Passage IV

SOCIAL SCIENCE: This passage discusses a historical argument that emerged following U.S. military unification.

The National Security Act of 1947 created a national military establishment headed by a single Secretary of Defense. The legislation had been a year-and-a-half in the making—beginning when President Truman first recommended that the armed services be reorganized into a single department. During that period, the President's concept of a unified armed service was torn apart and put back together several times; the final measure to emerge from Congress was a compromise. Most of the opposition to the bill came from the Navy and its numerous civilian spokesmen, including Secretary of the Navy James Forrestal. In support of unification (and a separate air force that was part of the unification package) were the Army air forces, the Army, and, most importantly, the President of the United States.

Passage of the bill did not end the bitter interservice disputes. Rather than unify, the act served only to federate the military services. It neither halted the rapid demobilization of the armed forces that followed World War II nor brought to the new national military establishment the loyalties of officers steeped in the traditions of the separate services. At a time when the balance of power in Europe and Asia was rapidly shifting, the services lacked any precise statement of United States foreign policy from the National Security Council on which to base future programs. The services bickered unceasingly over their respective roles and missions, already complicated by the Soviet nuclear capability that, for the first time, made the United States subject to devastating attack. Not even the appointment of Forrestal as First Secretary of Defense allayed the suspicions of naval officers and their supporters that the role of the U.S. Navy was threatened with permanent eclipse. Before the war of words died down, Forrestal himself was driven to resignation and then suicide.

By 1948, the United States military establishment was forced to make do with a budget approximately 10 percent of what it had been at its wartime peak. Meanwhile, the cost of weapons procurement was rising geometrically as the nation came to put more and more reliance on the atomic bomb and its delivery systems. These two factors inevitably made adversaries of the Navy and the Air Force as the battle between advocates of the B-36 and the supercarrier so amply demonstrates. Given severe fiscal restraints on the one hand, and on the other the nation's increasing reliance on strategic nuclear deterrence, the conflict between these two services over roles and missions was essentially a contest over slices of an ever-diminishing pie.

Yet if in the end neither service was the obvious victor, the principle of civilian dominance over the military clearly was. If there had ever been any danger that the United States military establishment might exploit, to the detriment of civilian control, the goodwill it enjoyed as a result of its victories in World War II, that danger disappeared in the interservice animosities engendered by the battle over unification.

25. In line 20, the word *demobilization* most nearly means:

A. shift to a unified military.
B. realignment of allies.
C. change from war to peace.
D. adoption of new technology.

26. According to the passage, the interservice strife that followed unification occurred primarily between the:

F. Army and Army air forces.
G. Army and Navy.
H. Army air forces and Navy.
J. Air Force and Navy.

27. It can be inferred from the passage that Forrestal's appointment as Secretary of Defense was expected to:

A. placate members of the Navy.
B. result in decreased levels of defense spending.
C. outrage advocates of the Army air forces.
D. win Congressional approval of the unification plan.

28. According to the passage, President Truman supported:

F. elimination of the Navy.
G. a unified military service.
H. establishment of a separate air force.
J. a unified military service and establishment of a separate air force.

29. With which of the following statements about defense unification would the author most likely agree?

A. Unification ultimately undermined United States military capability by inciting interservice rivalry.
B. The unification legislation was necessitated by the drastic decline in appropriations for the military services.
C. Although the unification was not entirely successful, it had the unexpected result of ensuring civilian control of the military.
D. In spite of the attempted unification, each service was still able to pursue its own objectives without interference from the other branches.

30. According to the selection, the political situation following the passage of the National Security Act of 1947 was characterized by all of the following EXCEPT:

F. a shifting balance of power in Europe and in Asia.
G. fierce interservice rivalries.
H. lack of strong leadership by the National Security Council.
J. a lame-duck President who was unable to unify the legislature.

31. The author cites the resignation and suicide of Forrestal in order to:

A. underscore the bitterness of the interservice rivalry surrounding the passage of the National Security Act of 1947.
B. demonstrate that the Navy eventually emerged as the dominant branch of service after the passage of the National Security Act of 1947.
C. suggest that the nation would be better served by a unified armed service under a single command.
D. provide an example of a military leader who preferred to serve his country in war rather than in peace.

32. The author is primarily concerned with:

F. discussing the influence of personalities on political events.
G. describing the administration of a powerful leader.
H. criticizing a piece of legislation.
J. analyzing a political development.

Passage V

HUMANITIES: This passage is adapted from an article about early American education ideology.

The founders of the American Republic viewed their revolution primarily in political rather than economic or social terms. Furthermore, they talked about education as essential to the public good—a goal that took precedence over knowledge as occupational training or as a means to self-fulfillment or self-improvement. Over and over again, the Revolutionary generation, both liberal and conservative in outlook, asserted its conviction that the welfare of the Republic rested upon an educated citizenry and that schools, especially free public schools, would be the best means of educating the citizenry in civic values and the obligations required of everyone in a democratic republican society. All agreed that the principal ingredients of a civic education were literacy and the inculcation of patriotic and moral virtues, some others adding the study of history and the study of principles of the republican government itself.

The founders, as was the case with almost all their successors, were long on exhortation and rhetoric regarding the value of civic education, but they left it to the textbook writers to distill the essence of those values for schoolchildren. Texts in American history and government appeared as early as the 1790s. The textbook writers turned out to be largely of conservative persuasion, more likely Federalist in outlook than Jeffersonian, and they almost universally agreed that political virtue must rest upon moral and religious precepts. Since most textbook writers were New Englanders, this meant that the texts were infused with Protestant, and above all Puritan, outlooks.

In the first half of the Republic, civic education in the schools emphasized the inculcation of civic values and made little attempt to develop participatory political skills. That was a task left to incipient political parties, town meetings, churches, and the coffee or ale houses where men gathered for conversation. Additionally, as a reading of certain Federalist papers of the period would demonstrate, the press probably did more to disseminate realistic as well as partisan knowledge of government than the schools. The goal of education, however, was to achieve a higher form of *unum* for the new Republic. In the middle half of the nineteenth century, the political values taught in the public and private schools did not change substantially from those celebrated in the first fifty years of the Republic. In the textbooks of the day, their rosy hues if anything became golden. To the resplendent values of liberty, equality, and a benevolent Christian morality were now added the middle-class virtues—especially of New England—of hard work, honesty, integrity, the rewards of individual effort, and obedience to parents and legitimate authority. But of all the political values taught in school, patriotism was preeminent; and whenever teachers explained to schoolchildren why they should love their country above all else, the idea of liberty assumed pride of place.

33. In line 5, the phrase "took precedence over" most nearly means:

A. set an example for.
B. formulated a policy of.
C. enlightened someone on.
D. had greater importance than.

34. The passage deals primarily with the:

F. content of textbooks used in early American schools.
G. role of education in late eighteenth- and early to mid-nineteenth-century America.
H. influence of New England Puritanism on early American values.
J. origin and development of the Protestant work ethic in modern America.

35. According to the passage, the founders of the Republic regarded education primarily as:

A. a religious obligation.
B. a private matter.
C. an unnecessary luxury.
D. a political necessity.

36. The author states that textbooks written in the middle part of the nineteenth century:

F. departed radically in tone and style from earlier textbooks.
G. mentioned for the first time the value of liberty.
H. treated traditional civic virtues with even greater reverence.
J. were commissioned by government agencies.

37. Which of the following would LEAST likely have been the subject of an early American textbook?

A. Basic rules of English grammar
B. The American Revolution
C. Patriotism and other civic virtues
D. Vocational education

38. The author's attitude toward the educational system discussed in the passage can best be described as:

F. cynical and unpatriotic.
G. realistic and analytical.
H. pragmatic and frustrated.
J. disenchanted and bitter.

39. The passage provides information that would be helpful in answering which of the following questions?

A. Why was a disproportionate share of early American textbooks written by New England authors?
B. Was the Federalist Party primarily a liberal or conservative force in early American politics?
C. How many years of education did the founders believe were sufficient to instruct young citizens in civic virtue?
D. What were the names of some of the Puritan authors who wrote early American textbooks?

40. The author implies that an early American Puritan would likely insist that:

F. moral and religious values are the foundation of civic virtue.
G. textbooks should instruct students in political issues of vital concern to the community.
H. textbooks should give greater emphasis to the value of individual liberty than to the duties of patriotism.
J. private schools with a particular religious focus are preferable to public schools with no religious instruction.

Passage VI

SOCIAL SCIENCE: This passage discusses the interrelationship of the United States economy and international commerce.

International commerce is woven thoroughly into the fabric of the American economy. Exports and imports amounted to more than 11 percent of the U.S. gross domestic product (GDP) in 1991, up dramatically from 7.5 percent just five years before. More than 7 million American jobs are related to exports, and millions more depend on the overall economic activity generated by export trade. Export-related jobs pay more—almost 17 percent more than the average American job.

Exports are vital to the economic health of many key sectors of the manufacturing economy. For instance, makers of computers, aerospace and heavy earthmoving equipment, and farm implements are increasingly dependent on export markets. For these exports, slow growth abroad translates to declining vitality at home. The same picture is true of agriculture, where roughly one in four farm acres is now harvested for the export market. International sales of business-related services—construction, finance, insurance, and engineering, among others—amount to tens of billions of dollars each year.

In the early years of the post-World War II era, the United States stood virtually alone as the industrial and technological leader of the world. At that time, the U.S. produced almost half of the world's GDP, including much of the world's manufactured goods, and had roughly 80 percent of the world's hard currency reserves. Today, while the U.S. remains the world's leading economy, its share of world GDP has shrunk to about 24 percent, and its share of world manufacturers is even lower. Experts agree that, relative to the size of the economy and the diversity of its industrial and technological base, the U.S. has lagged far behind its export potential.

Meanwhile, the potential for growth in U.S. exports is enormous. Markets in Europe and Japan are huge and relatively stable. There is growing promise in Asia's \$5.7 trillion economy and Latin America's \$1 trillion economy. These markets are generating a rapidly growing demand for infrastructure investment, aircraft, and high-technology capital goods—all areas in which the U.S. has real or potential strengths. In addition, new entrants into the world economy, such as Central and Eastern Europe and the countries of the former Soviet Union, show real promise as potential markets for U.S. exports.

Growing world markets, however, do not automatically translate into U.S. export sales. The fierce competition for international markets comes primarily from the more innovative firms in Europe and Japan. In particular, Japanese companies have set the pace with a mix of aggressive business practices and a virtually economy-wide commitment to quality, rapid time to market, ongoing innovation, and customer satisfaction. American companies are beginning to try to meet the competition abroad, as well as to view their success as a benchmark for improvement, whether that best is in Chicago, Frankfurt, or Osaka.

The new realities of international competition yield lessons for the U.S. government as well. Persistent economic diplomacy and high-level advocacy, competitive and well-focused export financing, and improved efforts at information-gathering have become necessary components of an export promotion policy. Many foreign governments have been more aggressive and more focused than the U.S. government in working with their firms to secure export sales. Senior government officials, up to and including the President or Prime Minister, often will travel to support the sale of their home country's goods and services. The U.S. government needs to begin to measure its export strategy against the flexibility and effectiveness of the competition. Exports are central to growth, jobs, and a rising standard of living for all Americans. Our role in building a better America at home and acting as an economic leader abroad is dependent on our ability to develop a coherent, aggressive, and effective national export strategy.

41. Which of the following U.S. economic sectors has declined most seriously since World War II?

A. Agriculture
B. Manufacturing
C. High-technology products
D. Business-related services

42. Which of the following best expresses the central point of the passage?

F. Exports drive the U.S. economy.
G. U.S. exports have declined since shortly after World War II.
H. Exports are so important to the U.S. economy that steps should be taken to increase U.S. exports worldwide.
J. The U.S. government should encourage U.S. corporations to expand into markets in Asia and Latin America.

43. Which of the following areas is NOT mentioned in the passage as a potential market for U.S. goods abroad?

A. Asia
B. Latin America
C. Central Europe
D. Northern Africa

44. The passage suggests that both U.S. corporations and the U.S. government should:

F. discourage imports in favor of exports.
G. focus on improving the quality of American products.
H. try to meet the competition abroad.
J. take steps to reduce the economy's dependence on exports.

45. With which of the following explanations for the decline in the United States' share of world GDP would the author be most likely to agree?

I. Other countries are relatively uninterested in purchasing the goods and services the U.S. has to offer.
II. Other governments have done more to encourage their countries' exports than has the U.S. government.
III. Companies in some other countries have been more enterprising in producing high-quality goods and services.

A. II only
B. I and II only
C. I and III only
D. II and III only

46. According to the passage, an increase in U.S. exports abroad would generate:

F. more high-paying jobs for American workers.
G. increased profits for American farmers.
H. greater diversity in American industry.
J. resentment among foreign competitors.

Passage VII

NATURAL SCIENCE: This passage details lake regions, the conditions under which the regions occur, and how various interactions between these regions create different types of lakes.

Lakes arise from sources that are almost entirely geologic in nature. Once they have formed, lakes are doomed. Because of the concave nature of the lake basin, there is a trend toward demise as the basin fills in with sediment. A lake lives through youthful stages to maturity, senescence, and death when the basin is finally full. This procedure does not always follow a direct course. Periods of rejuvenation occasionally occur in some lakes. Eventually, marshes, swampy meadows, and forests appear where lakes once existed. Large lakes may be far from death as a result of shoaling, but climatic changes or geologic events that result in drying out or drainage eventually lead to their ends.

The littoral zone of a lake is the region of the shallows. The shallows are subject to fluctuating temperatures and erosion of the shoreline through wave action and the effects of weather. The shallows are usually well lit and serve as home to rooted aquatic plants. The littoral region is the region from the shoreline to the depth where the weeds disappear. Sometimes, wave action is so extreme that most aquatic vegetation is absent and only algae are present, marking the outer regions of the littoral region. The littoral benthos is the bottom region of the littoral region. This region contains many species and taxonomic groups. A high diversity and high annual production set this community apart from other regions of the lake.

The sublittoral zone extends from the outer region of the littoral region. Sediments in the sublittoral zone are finer grained than those of the littoral zone. Although this region is dimly lit, it is usually well oxygenated. The sublittoral zone community contains fewer species than does the littoral zone. This is due mainly to the reduced number of habitats.

In some lakes, the old shells of gastropods and pelecypods that inhabit the littoral zone are found accumulated in the sublittoral zone. These shell zones are thought to mark the place where weather interactions and currents have carried and dropped these remains.

The profundal zone is defined as the region of a lake where summer temperature stratification is apparent. Under such conditions a deep cold region is formed where currents are at a minimum and where light is greatly reduced. The temperature is mostly uniform throughout this region, and under some conditions, oxygen is almost completely absent, but CO_2 and methane are prevalent. The hydrogen ion concentration is high because of the presence of carbonic acid. This stratum of water is characterized by the existence of decayed matter rather than by the production of organic matter.

As solar radiation passes down from the surface of the lake, it disappears exponentially, and the heating wavelengths are usually absorbed very fast. At the end of the yearly heating period, one might expect the temperature stratum to resemble the light curve; however, due to weather conditions—for example, wind—the temperature profiles of lakes are altered. The temperature difference is readily explained by the wind mixing the upper layers of water and distributing downward the heat that has been absorbed by the surface layers of water.

Direct stratification occurs when dense cold water lies beneath lighter warm layers of water. Direct stratification divides a lake into three regions. The upper warm region, mixed completely by wind to produce a region that is almost at a uniform temperature throughout, is called the epilimnion. At the bottom is a colder, heavier region of water, which is unaffected by wind action and therefore remains stagnant. This region is called the hypolimnion. Separating these two regions is the thermocline, a region of water where temperature drops quickly with increasing depth.

Dimictic lakes are lakes that have two mixing periods: vernal and autumnal. The typical dimictic lake stratifies directly during the warm months. When the cold months arrive, the surface water starts to cool, which eventually destroys the stratification and initiates complete circulation. During the fall mixing, chilling of the entire water mass continues until the water mass achieves a uniform temperature of about 4 degrees Celsius.

Polymictic lakes are lakes that have many mixing periods or which have continuous circulation throughout the year. Polymictic lakes are influenced more by fluctuations in temperature from day to night than by seasonal changes.

Meromictic lakes circulate at times, but incompletely. The entire water mass does not participate in the mixing. A dense region of water at the bottom remains stagnant and anaerobic. The three regions of a meromictic lake have their own names. The bottom layer, which is basically stagnant and contains a greater concentration of dissolved substances, is called the monimolimnion. The upper layer is mixed by the wind, is more dilute, and shows seasonal changes. This region is called the mixolimnion. Between the monimolimnion and the mixolimnion is a region where salinity increases quickly with depth. This region is called the chemocline.

47. The author uses the word *doomed* in line 3 to indicate that:

I. He regrets the event.
II. The lakes have a limited future.
III. People will destroy the lakes.

A. I only
B. II only
C. II and III only
D. I, II, and III

48. Unlike the sublittoral zone, the littoral zone:

F. has fine-grained sediment.
G. contains many varied habitats.
H. contains aquatic vegetation.
J. is well oxygenated.

49. Why is aquatic vegetation absent in some lakes?

A. Extreme wave action might uproot plants.
B. Some lakes have no littoral or sublittoral regions.
C. Algae take over the littoral region.
D. The lakes are fully mature.

50. Which of the following were responsible for depositing remains of gastropods in the sublittoral zone?

I. Currents
II. Wind
III. Animals

F. I only
G. II only
H. I and II only
J. I and III only

51. The profundal zone is marked by:

A. shells of organisms, low vegetation, and high diversity.
B. solar radiation and a vernal mixing period.
C. increased temperatures in summer and production of organic matter.
D. cold temperatures, low light, and a lack of oxygen.

52. In October, you would expect a northern dimictic lake to:

F. be warmer on the surface than it was in May.
G. cool from the surface to achieve a uniform temperature.
H. begin to stratify directly.
J. slowly freeze across the surface.

53. A polymictic lake might be coldest:

A. at night.
B. in autumn.
C. after sunrise.
D. in spring.

54. The chemocline in a meromictic lake is equivalent to:

F. the littoral zone in a senescent lake.
G. the profundal zone in a dimictic lake.
H. the thermocline in a dimictic lake.
J. the epilimnion in a polymictic lake.

55. Which of the following conclusions CANNOT be drawn from this passage?

A. Deep lakes are unaffected by weather.
B. Lakes have geologic derivations.
C. Lakes vary in temperature.
D. All lakes will eventually die.

Passage VIII

NATURAL SCIENCE: This passage discusses home and building construction in the Appalachian region of North America.

For nearly a century, the houses and other artificial structures of the Appalachian region have played a prominent role in its representation in books, magazines, and film. From nineteenth century magazine illustrations of single-room log cabins to twentieth century television programs focusing on unpainted, one- or two-room company houses, the dominant image of the region has been the dilapidated, weather-beaten Appalachian home. While some of these presentations are authentic, some are contrived, and nearly all are selective. Interpreters of Appalachian culture have tended to focus on extremes and, as a result, have misrepresented Appalachian life. A survey of the New River Gorge area in West Virginia revealed a much more diverse landscape than has been described in the past. While project researchers did locate log cabins and abandoned coal towns, they also found considerable architectural variety. Contrary to past reports, the New River Gorge cultural landscape reflects the history of a community that designed, built, and used its buildings according to individual tastes and principles.

The territory is dotted with homes that have had the original appearances altered to suit the occupant. These individually styled facades may appear quirky to the outsider, but their meaning is revealed through an understanding of the local history. Coal companies originally constructed many of the homes for their workers. Whole towns of box houses (cheap, fast to build, and temporary) were constructed at one time. While the floor plans varied, the basic construction technique did not. Vertical boards attached to sills and plates formed both the interior and exterior walls, as well as the buildings' weight-bearing supports. Today, West Virginians commonly call box houses "Jinn Linns." One local resident related a story concerning the origin of the term. Jenny Lynn, a coal camp resident, decided to distinguish her home from the other identical box houses in her camp by nailing narrow strips over the spaces between the vertical boards, creating the board and batten siding now characteristic of these houses. Soon, many others followed her example and eventually named the house type after her.

Unlike Jenny Lynn, most coal camp residents were required to maintain their box houses according to strict company standards or risk eviction. As the coal boom declined, however, companies began selling the homes to their tenants. Having obtained the freedom to maintain their homes according to their own standards, residents altered facades or added rooms or porches, resulting in the variety of box houses visible in the region today. Others decided to leave the company camps altogether. Many purchased modern prefabricated houses, for example, the Lustron, an all-steel factory-made home manufactured in Ohio between 1948 and 1950. The Lustron was a one-story, gable-roof ranch house with an exterior and interior skin of enameled steel panels bolted to a structural-steel frame and a concrete slab foundation. Unlike the Jinn Linn, the home was durable, easy to maintain, and strong.

Innovative construction materials are also produced locally. Bluish cinder blocks and "red dog" blocks, both by-products of the coal industry, have been used to construct homes, churches, gymnasiums, and barns throughout the Gorge. These and other colorful materials, including glazed tile, are often used in striking combinations, and an unusual amount of care is given to decorative detail. For example, yellow and red bricks and stones are often used for window and door trims, quoins, and belt courses (projecting horizontal strips around the outside of a building).

The complex balance between formal design and personal expression is a striking feature of the New River Gorge landscape. Like the quilts made in the region, much of the architecture is pieced together from locally made and recycled materials. Materials rarely used in combination in other areas are carefully pieced together into a landscape filled with personal meaning.

56. The author uses the word *selective* (line 11) when describing the popular representations of Appalachian architecture to indicate that they:

F. present only one facet of Appalachian architecture.
G. focus on public buildings rather than on private homes.
H. show only the most attractive side of Appalachian architecture.
J. represent the perceptions only of the residents themselves.

57. The aspect of New River Gorge houses that the interpreters mentioned in line 11 would be most surprised by is:

A. their uniformity.
B. their unusually large size.
C. the ease with which they were built and maintained.
D. the attention given to decorative detail in constructing them.

58. Which of the following best expresses the author's main point in telling the story of Jenny Lynn (lines 37–44)?

F. Residents of the coal camps modified their originally identical homes to suit their own preferences.
G. The person who most influenced architecture in the New River Gorge was Jenny Lynn.
H. Box houses are the most common type of house in the New River Gorge because they were inexpensive to construct.
J. Coal companies had a great deal of control over the architecture of the New River Gorge.

59. Which of the following is NOT a difference between Lustron houses and Jinn Linn houses?

A. Lustron houses were tougher than were Jinn Linn houses.
B. Lustron houses were easier to keep up than were Jinn Linn houses.
C. Lustron houses were made of steel while Jinn Linn houses were made of wood.
D. Lustron houses came in several different floor plans while Jinn Linn houses always had the same plan.

60. According to the passage, Lustron houses were:

F. less expensive than box houses.
G. more common in Ohio than in West Virginia.
H. ready-made in one place to be put up elsewhere.
J. extremely popular among former coal-camp residents.

61. In what way is the architecture of the New River Gorge like the quilts made there?

I. Both use designs or plans that originally come from outside the region.
II. Both are made from available materials used in innovative ways.
III. Both express the personal tastes of the makers or users.

A. I and II only
B. II only
C. II and III only
D. I, II, and III

62. The aspect of Appalachian architecture that the author appears to value most highly is its:

F. beauty.
G. diversity.
H. practicality.
J. durability.

STRATEGY SUMMARY SHEET

READING STRATEGIES: Understanding the three levels of reading comprehension and how they relate to the seven Reading item-types will help you to identify quickly the question that is being asked by a particular item.

1. *Level 1—General Theme*: The first level of reading, appreciation of the general theme, is the most basic. Main Idea items test whether you understand the passage at the most general level. The first sentence of a paragraph—often the topic sentence—may provide a summary of the content of that paragraph. Also, the last sentence of a paragraph usually provides concluding material that may also be helpful in understanding the general theme of the passage.

   Main Idea items ask about the central theme that unifies the passage(s):

   - *Which of the following is the main point of the passage?*
   - *The primary purpose of the passage is to....*

2. *Level 2—Specific Points*: The second level of reading, understanding of specific points, takes you deeper into the selection. Explicit Detail, Vocabulary, and Development items all test your ability to read carefully. Since this is an "open-book" test, you can always return to the selection. Therefore, if something is highly technical or difficult to understand, do not dwell on it for too long—come back later if necessary.

   Explicit Detail items ask about details that are specifically mentioned in the passage. This type of item differs from a Main Idea item in that explicit details are points provided by the author in developing the main idea of the passage. Explicit Detail items provide "locator words" that identify the required information in the passage.

   - *The author mentions which of the following?*
   - *According to the passage,...?*

   Vocabulary items test the understanding of a word or phrase in context. The nature of the Vocabulary items indicates two points. First, the correct answer choice will make sense when it is substituted for the referenced word. Second, the correct answer choice may not be the most commonly used meaning of the word; in fact, if it were, then what would be the point of including the item on the test? Thus, the general strategy for this type of item is to favor the less commonly used meaning.

   - *The word ------- in line ## means....*
   - *In line ##, what is the best definition of the word -------?*

   Development items ask about the overall structure of the passage or about the logical role played by a specific part of the passage.

   - *The author develops the passage primarily by....*
   - *The author mentions...in order to....*

3. *Level 3—Evaluation*: The third level of reading, evaluation of the text, takes you even deeper into the selection. Implied Idea, Application, and Voice items ask not just for understanding, but require a judgment or an evaluation of what you have read. This is why these items are usually the most difficult.

   Implied Idea items don't ask about what is specifically stated in the passage; rather, Implied Idea items ask about what can be logically inferred from what is stated in the passage. For example, the passage might explain that a certain organism (*X*) is found only in the presence of another organism (*Y*). An accompanying Implied Idea item might ask the following question: "If organism *Y* is not present, what can be inferred?" Since the passage implies that in the absence of *Y*, *X* cannot be present, the answer would be "*X* is not present." Since this type of item generally builds on a specific detail, "locator words" for identifying information in the passage are often provided in the item stem.

- *The passage implies that....*
- *The author uses the phrase "..." to mean....*

Application items are similar to Implied Idea items, but they go one step further: Examinees must apply what they have learned from the passage to a new situation.

- *With which of the following statements would the author most likely agree?*
- *The passage is most probably taken from which of the following sources?*

Voice items ask about the author's attitude toward a specific detail or the overall tone of the passage.

- *The tone of the passage can best be described as....*
- *The author regards...as....*

GENERAL STRATEGIES: Reading strategies are not an exact science. Practice is essential to mastering the following techniques:

1. *Read the first sentence of each passage in the Reading Test.* After reading the first sentence of each passage, label each passage as either "Easy" or "Hard" based on your initial understanding of the material and your level of interest. Analyze the easier passages first.

2. *Preview the first and last sentences of each paragraph.* There is usually an introductory paragraph for excerpted passages that identifies the author and provides a brief description of the selection. First, read this introductory material to gain clues as to the author's point of view. Then, preview the first and last sentences of each paragraph, as they often provide paragraph summaries.

3. *Preview the item stems for a given passage.* Code each item stem as one of the following three levels of reading comprehension: GT (Level 1—General Theme); SP (Level 2—Specific Points); or E (Level 3—Evaluation).

4. *Read the passage.* Ask what the author is attempting to describe, especially in the case of Evaluation items. Also, read the first sentence in each paragraph prior to reading the entire selection. This step is optional, depending on the ease of the selection, your personal preference, and the time available. Bracket difficult material, either mentally or with some sort of a mark, and then simply revisit it if necessary or if time permits. Instead of wasting time re-reading, attempt to understand the context in which the author introduces a particular concept.

5. *Circle the answers to the items in the test booklet, and transcribe the answers to all the items for a passage to the answer sheet after finishing each passage.* This approach helps increase accuracy and makes checking your work easier and more efficient. For each selection, transcribe the answers to the answer sheet together as a group. Only when the time limit approaches should you transcribe each answer individually.

NOTES: ____

Science

COURSE CONCEPT OUTLINE

What You Absolutely Must Know

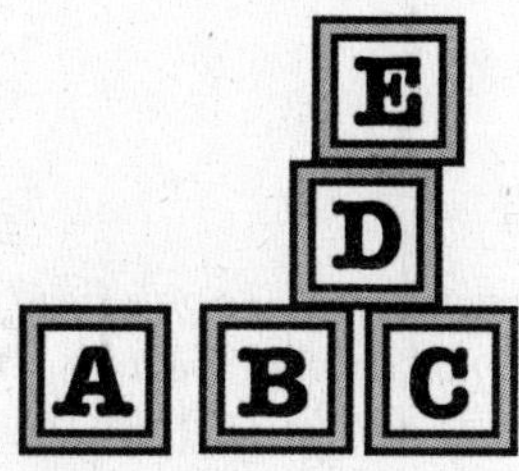

BASICS

The Science Test consists of 40 multiple-choice items divided into seven groups. Each group of items is based on a report of data findings, a description of an experiment, or the presentation of a debate on different scientific theories. The time limit for the Science Test is 35 minutes.

We'll call the initial presentation a "passage," whether it is a report of data (Data Representation), a description of an experiment (Research Summary), or a debate of a theory (Conflicting Viewpoints). So, just as the English and Reading Tests have passages with associated items, the Science Test has passages (of the three types) with associated items. We'll use this terminology even though "passage" doesn't quite fit here since the Science Test uses a lot of diagrams, pictures, tables, and graphs.

The Science Test roughly follows the content of science courses taught in grades 7 through 12. Passages use content from the following areas:

- **Biology:** botany, cellular biology, ecology, evolution, genetics, microbiology, zoology
- **Chemistry:** biochemistry, organic chemistry, nuclear chemistry, thermo-chemistry, acids and bases, kinetics and equilibria, properties of matter
- **Earth/Space Sciences:** astronomy, environmental science, geology, meteorology, oceanography
- **Physics:** mechanics, thermodynamics, fluids, solids, electromagnetism, optics

Although these are obviously "science" subjects, you don't really need to know any science—beyond some basic concepts—to do well on this part of the exam. In fact, the ACT Science Test would be more accurately labeled "Science Reasoning" Test because that phrase would emphasize that the items test reasoning ability and not the mastery of some specific body of scientific knowledge.

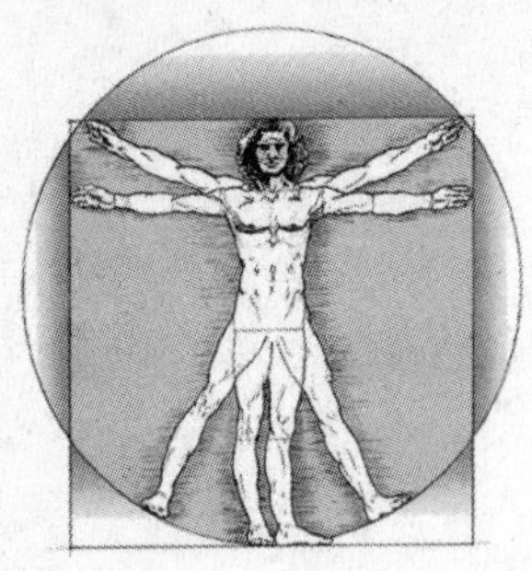

ANATOMY

DIRECTIONS: The passage below is followed by several items. After reading the passage, choose the best answer to each item. You may refer to the passage as often as necessary. You are NOT permitted the use of a calculator.

Passage I

A student studied the process by which malodorzane is produced by heated protocrud in a closed system and then released into the surrounding atmosphere.

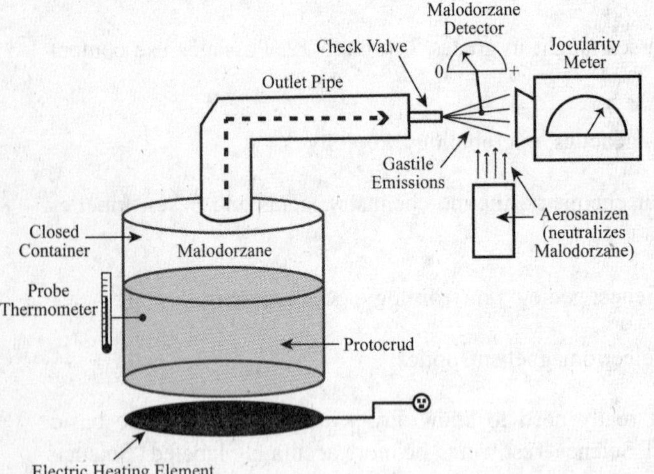

Experiment 1

The concentration of malodorzane produced by the protocrud at various temperatures was measured by determining how much aerosanizen was needed to neutralize the malodorzane (Table 1).

Now that you've read the directions, you don't need to read them again, especially not during the test. The only thing of real significance is that you CANNOT use your calculator on this part, even though you might think it would be nice. But you should be able to remember that one point without re-reading the directions.

In this Science passage, there is a single device and a series of tables that report data from the operation of the device. You'll see examples of other types of passages later in the Science Lesson.

Table 1	
Temperature of Protocrud	Aerosanizen (spritz/min.)
20°C	46–198
22.5°C	199–377
25°C	378–612

Experiment 2

The student observed that the release of gastiles, whether or not the malodorzane was counteracted by aerosanizen, produced primary and secondary jocularities. The intensity of the jocularities was measured and recorded by different durations of gastiles (Table 2).

Table 2		
	Intensity of Jocularities	
Gastiles (seconds)	Primary Jocularities (decibels)	Secondary Jocularities (decibels)
1.0	30 dB	—*
2.0	35 dB	—*
5.0	40 dB	30 dB
12.0	60 dB	40 dB
19.0	120 dB	60 dB

*Intensity was below measurable levels.

Experiment 3

The student measured and recorded the duration of the jocularities for different durations of gastiles (see Table 3).

Table 3		
	Duration of Jocularities	
Gastiles (seconds)	Primary Jocularities (seconds)	Secondary Jocularities (seconds)
0.2	3	2
1.0	7	6
2.5	13	11
5.0	25	9
12.0	51	4

1. Data from the passage indicate that duration was greatest for secondary jocularities produced by gastiles of what duration?

   A. 1.0 seconds
   B. 2.5 seconds
   C. 5.0 seconds
   D. 12.0 seconds

1. **(B)** *Data for the duration of jocularities is given in Table 3, and the greatest entry, 11 seconds, corresponds to gastiles of 2.5 seconds.*

2. Gastiles with a duration of 13.0 seconds would probably produce primary jocularities of a duration:

   F. between 3 and 7 seconds.
   G. between 7 and 13 seconds.
   H. between 13 and 25 seconds.
   J. greater than 51 seconds.

2. **(J)** *Again, the answer is in Table 3, but this time there is no entry for 13 seconds. The largest entry is 12.0 seconds. Therefore, the corresponding entry in the "Primary Jocularities" column, if one existed, would have to be greater than 51 seconds.*

3. A primary jocularity of 90 decibels would most likely be produced by a gastile of:

   A. less than 1.0 seconds.
   B. between 1.0 and 2.0 seconds.
   C. between 12.0 and 19.0 seconds.
   D. greater than 5.0 seconds.

3. **(C)** *The relevant information is located in Table 2, but there is no entry in the table for 90 dB. However, that value is between 60 dB and 120 dB. The most likely conclusion, then, is that the corresponding entry in the first column, if one existed, would be between 12.0 and 19.0 seconds.*

4. The data in Table 1 would be most useful in determining whether:

   F. the temperature of aerosanizen affects the chemical's ability to neutralize malodorzane.
   G. the volume of malodorzane varies with the chemical composition of the protocrud.
   H. the closed system produces a greater volume of malodorzane than aerosanizen.
   J. the temperature of the protocrud affects the rate of malodorzane production.

4. **(J)** *Table 1 shows the amount of aerosanizen needed to neutralize the quantity of malodorzane at various temperatures. So, the data in that table would provide information about how the temperature of the protocrud affects the rate of malodorzane production.*

PACING

The Science Test presents seven passages, with a total of 40 items, to be completed in 35 minutes. The table below establishes the time that you can afford to spend on various parts of the Science Test if your goal is to complete the entire test. For many people, completing the entire test may be an unrealistic goal, and it would be better to have the goal of doing just six of the seven passages. Or perhaps even only five passages. If you choose to define your goal differently than completing the entire test, then you can adjust the timing for the remaining passages so that you'll have more time (e.g., four minutes for five items equals 48 seconds per item).

Passage	*Time to Spend*	*Remaining Time*
I	5 minutes	30 minutes
II	5 minutes	25 minutes
III	5 minutes	20 minutes
IV	5 minutes	15 minutes
V	5 minutes	10 minutes
VI	5 minutes	5 minutes
VII	5 minutes	0 minutes

You should begin work on each passage by reading the passage itself and familiarizing yourself with the main purpose of the data reports or experiments or the focus of the debate. This should be an overview of the information, not a detailed study. You are reading primarily to learn where information is located so that you can retrieve it—if an item asks about it.

If you allow yourself one minute to learn about the passage, then you have four minutes left to answer the five or six items, which is somewhere between 40 and 50 seconds per item. So, on the Science Test (perhaps more so than on any other test) time is of the essence.

TIME TRIAL

6 Items
Time—5 minutes

DIRECTIONS: The passage below is followed by several items. After reading the passage, choose the best answer to each item. You may refer to the passage as often as necessary. You are NOT permitted the use of a calculator.

Passage I

How old is the Earth? Two opposing views are presented.

Scientist 1

The Earth is approximately five billion years old. We know this to be true because of radioactive dating. Some chemical elements are unstable and will fall apart into smaller pieces over time. This disintegration occurs over a period of time that is very regular for the particular element. In general, we talk about the half-life of the element, which is the time necessary for one-half of the material to disintegrate. This time is constant whether we have an ounce or a ton of the material. So, by measuring the relative amounts of the material left and the disintegration products, we can form an accurate idea of how old the Earth is by determining how many half-lives have occurred.

Scientist 2

The argument that supports the hypothesis that the Earth is only five billion years old is seriously flawed. What the argument fails to take into account is that the Earth is the constant recipient of a shower of cosmic debris in the form of meteorites. These meteorites replenish the stock of radioactive material on the surface of the Earth, making it seem as though the Earth has gone through fewer half-lives than it really has. Therefore, all estimates of the age of the Earth based on radioactive dating are too low.

1. Which of the following is a major assumption of Scientist 1?

A. The Earth has life that recycles carbon-14.
B. The half-life of all radioactive elements is five billion years.
C. The radioactive material was formed at the same time as the Earth.
D. There is no longer any radioactivity on the Earth.

2. Which of the following is a major assumption of Scientist 2?

F. The meteorites that land on the Earth are radioactive.
G. Few meteorites have landed on the Earth.
H. The Earth is more than five billion years old.
J. The Earth is highly radioactive.

3. Which of the following, if true, would best refute Scientist 2's argument?

A. Recent meteorites have been found to be radioactive.
B. The Earth has a greater amount of radioactive material on the surface than in the mantle.
C. The Earth's orbit intersects the orbits of a number of meteorites.
D. Few meteorites have been found to contain radioactive material.

4. Which of the following would be most likely if Scientist 2's hypothesis were correct?

F. The amount of radioactive material and its disintegration products on the Earth has decreased over time.
G. The amount of radioactive material and its disintegration products has increased over time.
H. The amount of radioactive material and its disintegration products has stayed essentially the same over time.
J. The Earth will reach a critical mass and explode.

5. Which of the following would be most likely if Scientist 1's hypothesis were correct?

A. The amount of radioactive material and its disintegration products has decreased over time.
B. The amount of radioactive material and its disintegration products has increased over time.
C. The amount of radioactive material and its disintegration products has stayed essentially the same over time.
D. The Earth will reach a critical mass and explode.

6. Which of the following conditions, if true, would prevent an estimation of the Earth's age by Scientist 1's method?

F. No radioactive disintegration has occurred.
G. Only some of the radioactive material has disintegrated.
H. Eighty percent of the radioactive material has disintegrated.
J. All of the radioactive material has disintegrated.

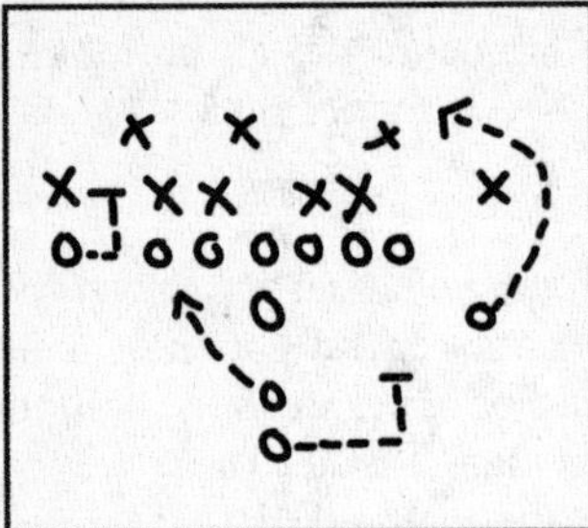

GAME PLAN

Quickly Preview the Test, but Skip the Directions

Last-minute adjustments to the test format are theoretically (but not practically) possible, so check the subject test before you start to work, especially the number of passages, the number of items, and the time limit. And yes, the test-writers always tell you to "read the directions carefully." But they don't tell you that you have to read them during the test. Instead, become familiar with them before test day. That way, you won't waste 30 seconds or more (enough time to answer an item) re-reading directions you are already familiar with.

Personalize the Passage Order

You are not required to do the passages in the order in which they appear in the test booklet. You can do the first passage second, or fourth, or last; and you can do the last passage first or third. So, you have the flexibility of choosing which ones you will do before the others, and you'll want to do first those passages that seem easier. "Easier," in this context, is really a subjective matter; it means the ones with which you are most comfortable, either because of the type of presentation or the subject matter.

- First, do those passage formats that you find easiest to handle.
- Then, of the remaining passages, do the familiar ones.
- Finally, do the rest of the passages, from the simplest to the most complicated.

Put large numbers in the margins of the test booklet beside each passage to indicate where the passage comes in the order.

Read the Passage

For the Science Test, "reading the passage" means "reading through" the passage. You can't afford to study the passage, and don't forget that this is an "open-book" test. So, learn generally what is going on and where things are located. Then, let the items tell you where to look more carefully.

- Read any introductory paragraph(s). Not only does this material usually explain why an experiment is being conducted or data are being collected, but it often defines a key term that is essential to understanding the connections of the various parts of the passage.

- Examine any diagrams or schematics. The focus of a passage is often a device that includes beakers, tubing, switches, pulleys, test tubes, and other paraphernalia associated with science. Try to understand what the device is designed to accomplish and how the various parts work together.
- Look at the various subparts of the passage. The subparts are things such as experiments that change initial conditions, tables of data, and graphs. Do not try to fully understand these. Just get a general notion of what they do. For example, for a graph, read the title and the labels of the *x*- and *y*-axes. For tables, read the column heads and the titles of the rows. Do not, however, read specific values on a graph or in a table. There are too many of them, and only one or two are likely to be relevant to answering one of the few items based on that passage (compared to all the different questions that the test-writers could have chosen).

Answer the Items

Answer the question that is being asked. One of the most commonly made mistakes is to read the item stem carelessly and then answer the "wrong" question. It's just a matter of inattention, in which you respond to what you think you read rather than what is actually there on the page. Since wrong answers often correspond to wrong readings, if you make this mistake, you are probably going to find a pretty good answer—to the wrong question.

Pay attention to thought-reversers. "Thought-reversers" are words in the item stem like "NOT," "BUT," and "EXCEPT." These words turn the question upside-down. What is normally the right answer is now a wrong answer, and what is normally a wrong answer is the right answer. Circle these words or put stars beside them so that they get your attention again.

Locate the relevant information. The first and often last step in answering an item is to locate the information you need. Most item stems use a key word or phrase to tell you where to look. For example, "in Table 2" tells you that the information you need is located in Table 2; "the troposphere…" tells you that you need the graph, table, or description that supplies information about the troposphere; and "lowering the temperature" indicates that the answer is in the subpart of the passage that provides information about temperature.

Use the Answer Choices

Study the answer choices for guidance. The answer choices, like an item stem, can direct you to the subpart of the passage that contains the information you need. Consider the following item, in which only the answer choices are visible:

Example:

A. Sodium
B. Potassium
C. Lithium
D. Oxygen

With this array, you know to look at that table or graph or paragraph that includes that list of terms. The choices will also give you guidance as to what degree of precision is required by the item.

Often, the choices are ranges of values, such as $0.015w$ to $0.018w$, rather than specific values, such as simply $0.018w$. Do not look for more precision than the choices allow.

Read the answer choices carefully. The test-writers love to put in wrong answers that look right. For example, if a particular value doubles with a decrease in temperature from 40° to 20° (it doesn't matter what scale; this is just a sketch of a question), a question might ask: "Assuming the temperature rises from 20° to 40°, what happens to the value?" The correct answer is, of course: "The value is reduced by half." But you can bet that the wrong answers will include ideas like "doubles," "increases by one-fourth," and "decreases by four"—or some other variation on those ideas.

Eliminate Choices, Guess (If Necessary), and Move On

Do NOT spend too much time on any one item. Remember that you get +1 for the hardest item and +1 for the easiest item. The items that correspond to a Science passage tend to be arranged from easiest to most difficult. (This is not an absolute rule; it is just a useful tool.) The first item may ask you to find a single number in a table. The second item may ask for a value that is the largest or smallest in a series. And the third item may require you to interpolate a value. Then, the going might get considerably more difficult. So, try the next item, and if it is completely whack, blow off the others and go to the next passage where the difficulty resets to the lowest setting. And don't forget: the ACT test has no penalty for guessing. If you find yourself stuck on a difficult item, eliminate as many choices as possible, guess, and move on!

LESSON

The passages and items in this section accompany the in-class review of the skills and concepts tested by the ACT Science Test. You will work through the items with your instructor in class. Answers are on page 637.

DIRECTIONS: Each passage below is followed by several items. After reading a passage, choose the best answer to each item. You may refer to the passages as often as necessary. You are NOT permitted the use of a calculator.

Passage I

The kinetic energy of an object with mass m (measured in grams) after a fall from a height h (measured in centimeters) was recorded for different heights. A graph was made representing the kinetic energy versus height.

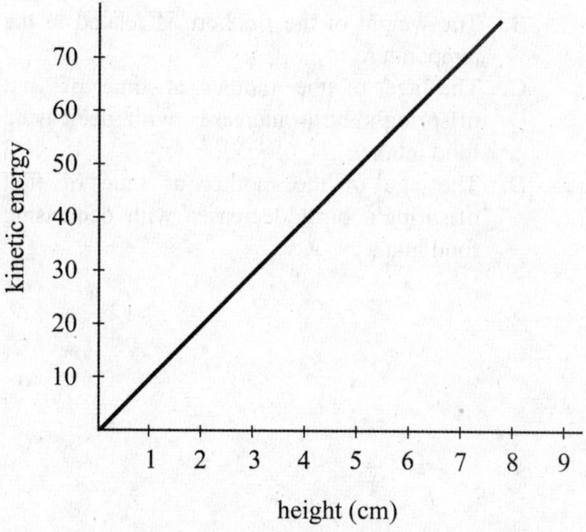

1. If the kinetic energy is given in units of $g \cdot cm^2/s^2$ what units must the slope have?

A. $g \cdot cm/s$
B. $g \cdot cm/s^2$
C. $s \cdot cm/g$
D. $s^2/(g \cdot cm)$

2. It is discovered that if we redo the experiment with an object with twice the mass, the kinetic energy obtained for every height is doubled. The slope of the new set of experiments can be obtained by doing what to the old slope?

F. Multiplying by 2
G. Dividing by 2
H. Squaring
J. Taking the square root

3. What would be the kinetic energy (in $g \cdot cm^2/s^2$) of an object of mass m if it were dropped from a height of 4.5 cm?

A. 4.5
B. 9.0
C. 45
D. 90

Passage II

A scientist investigated the variables that affect the age at which a female of the animal species *taedi periculum* first gives birth. Some of the results of this study are summarized in the table below.

Experiment	Temperature (°C)	Average food intake (grams)	Age when first gave birth (months)
1	25	15	7
2	25	30	6
3	25	45	4
4	35	15	5
5	35	30	3
6	35	45	3

4. Which of the following would be good animals to use for the experiment?

F. Adult females
G. Newborn females
H. Newborn males
J. Adult males

5. Which of the pairs of experiments listed below would be useful for studying the effect of temperature on the age of first birth?

A. 1 and 2
B. 1 and 5
C. 1 and 4
D. 2 and 6

6. If all other variables are kept constant, which of the following will result in an increase in the age at which the animals give birth?

F. Increase in temperature from 25°C to 35°C
G. Increase in food from 15 grams to 45 grams
H. Decrease in food from 30 grams to 15 grams
J. Increase in temperature from 25°C to 30°C

7. Which experiment was the control for temperature for Experiment 5?

A. Experiment 1
B. Experiment 2
C. Experiment 3
D. Experiment 6

8. If an experiment was set up with the temperature set at 30°C and the food intake at 30 grams, which of the following would be a reasonable prediction of the age in months of the animals when they first gave birth?

F. 7.5
G. 6.0
H. 4.5
J. 2.5

9. Which of the following conclusions is consistent with the data presented in the table?

A. The weight of the firstborn is proportional to the food intake.
B. The weight of the firstborn is related to the temperature.
C. The age of the mother at time of first offspring's birth increases with decreasing food intake.
D. The age of the mother at time of first offspring's birth decreases with decreasing food intake.

Passage III

The chart below shows the average blood pressure and relative total surface area associated with the different types of human blood vessels.

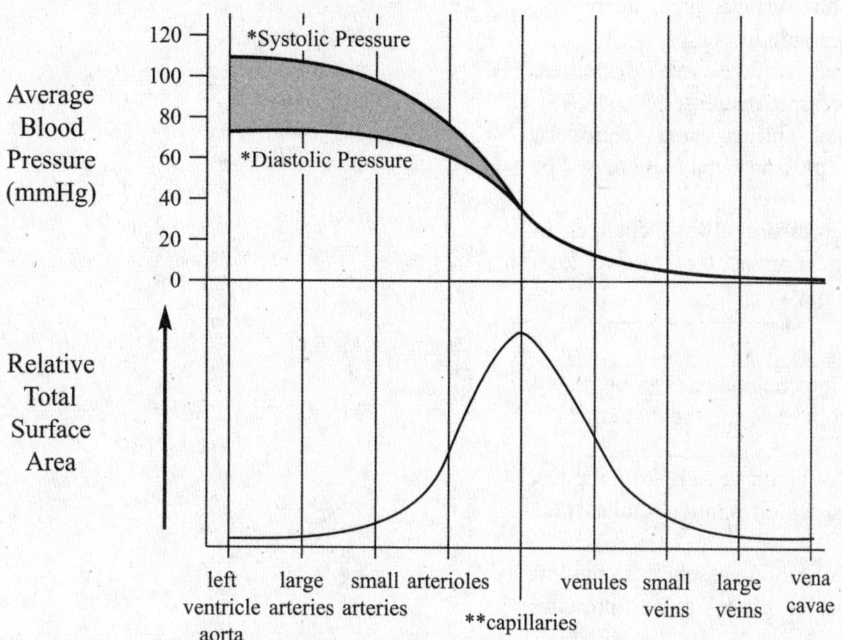

*Pulse pressure is the difference between systolic and diastolic pressure.
**Blood velocity is lowest in the capillaries (averaging 3 cm/sec).

10. According to the diagram, pulse pressure can be detected:

F. in large arteries only.
G. in large arteries as well as in large veins.
H. in blood vessels between the aorta and the capillaries.
J. primarily in the arterioles, capillaries, and venules.

11. Based on the information in the diagram, which of the following conclusions about average blood pressure is correct?

A. The average blood pressure decreases continuously as it gets further away from the left ventricle.
B. The average blood pressure remains approximately the same as it passes through the different blood vessels of the body.
C. Starting at the aorta, average blood pressure first increases and then decreases.
D. The average blood pressure is highest in the blood vessels with the greatest relative total surface area.

12. Which of the following correctly states the relationship between the relative total surface area of different blood vessels and their average blood pressure?

    F. As relative total surface area decreases, average blood pressure increases.
    G. As relative total surface area decreases, average blood pressure decreases.
    H. As relative total surface area decreases, average blood pressure may increase or decrease.
    J. Average blood pressure always changes in the opposite direction as the relative total surface area changes.

13. Which of the following conclusions can be drawn from the information provided in the diagram?

    A. As the distance of blood vessels from the left ventricle increases, their relative total surface area decreases.
    B. As the distance of blood vessels from the left ventricle increases, their pulse pressure increases.
    C. Blood vessels with the greatest relative total surface area have the highest pulse pressure.
    D. Blood vessels closest to and farthest away from the left ventricle have the smallest relative total surface area.

14. A physician examining a newly discovered tribe of people deep in the Amazon jungles found that the relative total surface area of their capillaries was greater than that previously reported for any other group of people. If the physician were to predict the average velocity of blood through the capillaries of these people, which of the following values would be most reasonable?

    F. 2 cm/sec
    G. 3 cm/sec
    H. 4 cm/sec
    J. 5 cm/sec

Passage IV

Ocean water contains "salt"—actually a mixture of ions, primarily sodium, chloride, potassium, calcium, magnesium, bicarbonate, and sulfate. The solid-line graph below indicates the percentage of these ions ("salinity") in a slab of ice that lies over seawater on a cold ocean surface. The arrow and dashed line indicate the salinity of the water beneath the ice.

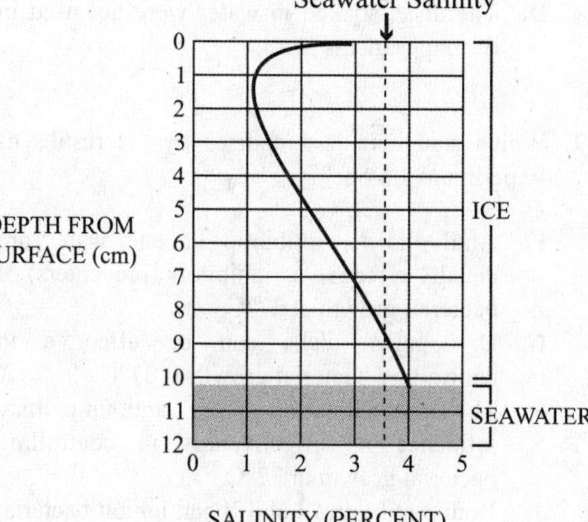

15. According to this figure, the salt content of the ice above the ocean water:

A. equals 0.
B. is constant at all depths.
C. generally decreases with greater depth.
D. generally increases with greater depth.

16. Compared to the ocean water below it, the salinity of the ice is:

F. generally lower.
G. about the same.
H. generally higher.
J. unable to be determined.

17. The salinity of the ice at the surface of the slab is equal to the salinity of:

A. the ice at a depth of approximately 1.5 cm.
B. the ice at a depth of approximately 7.0 cm.
C. the ice at a depth of approximately 9.0 cm.
D. the water beneath the ice.

18. A researcher wants to take a sample of ice that is one half the salinity of the seawater below. At what depth should the researcher sample?

F. Between 1 and 2 cm
G. Between 4 and 5 cm
H. Either between 0 and 1 cm or between 3 and 4 cm
J. Between 5 and 6 cm

19. The researcher takes a 1-gram sample of ice from a depth of 10 cm, and wishes to take a sample of ice from 1.3 cm depth that will contain the same weight of total salts. How large a sample is needed?

A. 0.25 grams
B. 1.0 grams
C. 4.0 grams
D. 10.0 grams

Passage V

To test the hypothesis that all antibiotics are equally effective in preventing bacterial growth, the following three experiments were carried out using clear plastic plates filled with nutrient agar (a mixture of ingredients that supports the growth of bacteria).

Experiment 1

Three plates (A, B, and C) of agar were set up, each with an equal amount of bacterial culture (Bacterium X) spread over the agar surface and with a paper disk placed in the center. Plate A's disk was soaked in Antibiotic I; Plate B's disk was soaked in Antibiotic II; Plate C's disk was soaked in plain water. After incubation overnight at 37°C (body temperature), Plates A and B had a clear area, 2" in diameter surrounding the paper disk, but beyond this 2" region, the plates were cloudy. Plate C was entirely cloudy, including the area adjacent to the paper disk. When bacteria reproduce successfully, colonies form on the agar, giving it a cloudy appearance.

Experiment 2

Identical procedures were followed except that Plates A, B, and C were incubated overnight at 22°C (room temperature). After incubation, Plate A had a clear area, 2" in diameter, surrounding the paper disk. Plates B and C were entirely cloudy.

Experiment 3

Identical procedures were followed except that the concentrations of Antibiotic I (Plate A) and Antibiotic II (Plate B) were made twice as strong. After incubation overnight at 22°C, Plates A and B both had clear, 2" areas around the paper disk, while Plate C remained entirely cloudy.

20. After incubation, a clear area around a previously soaked paper disk represents a region where:

F. agar had washed away.
G. decomposition had occurred due to high incubation temperatures.
H. bacterial growth did not occur.
J. bacteria grew best.

21. Which of the following results would indicate that the antibiotics being tested have nothing to do with the control of bacterial growth?

A. A clear, 2" region was always observed around the disks soaked in water.
B. All results remained the same at the two experimental temperatures and at the two antibiotic concentration levels.
C. Plates A and B always remained clear.
D. The disks soaked in water were not used in the experiments at all.

22. Which statement is supported by the results of Experiment 1 alone?

F. Antibiotic I, Antibiotic II, and water are equally effective as inhibitors (preventers) of bacterial growth at 37°C.
G. Dry paper disks can be effective in controlling bacterial growth at 37°C.
H. The concentration of an antibiotic may influence its effectiveness in controlling bacterial growth at 37°C.
J. Both Antibiotics I and II can inhibit bacterial growth at 37°C.

23. The results of both Experiment 2 and Experiment 3 lead to which of the following conclusions?

A. Antibiotics I and II have similar effects on bacterial growth, regardless of concentrations.
B. Antibiotic II and water have similar effects on bacterial growth, regardless of concentrations.
C. The effectiveness of Antibiotic I at 22°C depends on its concentration.
D. The effectiveness of Antibiotic II at 22°C depends on its concentration.

24. Which hypothesis best explains the observation that the agar plates never appear clear beyond a 2" area surrounding the soaked paper disks?

F. The bacteria cannot grow well within 2" of any moist paper disks.
G. The antibiotics cannot seep through the agar beyond a distance of 2".
H. At the experimental incubation temperatures used, the two antibiotics interfere with each other's effectiveness.
J. The paper disks can absorb nutrients out of the agar from the distance of 2".

25. If either Antibiotic I or II could be prescribed for internal use to prevent the spread of Bacterium X infections, which recommendation, based on the experimental results, is appropriate if the cost due to the amount of antibiotic used per dose is the most critical factor (the antibiotics are equal in cost for equal concentrations)?

A. Either Antibiotic I or II can be taken at equal cost.
B. Antibiotic I would be less expensive.
C. Antibiotic II would be less expensive.
D. Neither Antibiotic I nor II would be effective in preventing the spread of Bacterium X.

Passage VI

To investigate the hypothesis that the quality of the detail of a fossil depends on the size of the particles that make up the rock surrounding the fossil, three experiments were performed using a particular type of leaf with many fine veins.

Experiment 1

A leaf was placed on a flat bed made of paste from extra-fine plaster and then completely covered with more of the same paste. A glass cover with a 5-lb weight was placed on top of the paste for one hour, until the plaster set. The plaster was then baked for 30 minutes at 25°C. When the cast was opened, the imprint of the leaf showed all of the veins, including the finest ones.

Experiment 2

A leaf was placed on a flat bed made of paste from fine-grade plaster and then completely covered with more of the same paste. A glass cover with a 5-lb weight was placed on top of the plaster for one hour, until the plaster set. The plaster was then baked for 30 minutes at 25°C. When the cast was opened, all the main veins were visible, but only isolated traces of the finer veins were found.

Experiment 3

A leaf was placed on a flat bed made of paste from coarse-grain plaster and then completely covered with more of the same paste. A glass cover with a 5-lb weight was placed on top of the plaster for one hour, until the plaster set. The plaster was then baked for 30 minutes at 25°C. When the cast was opened, only the thickest veins were visible, and some of the leaf edge was difficult to discern.

26. Should the investigator have used a different type of leaf in each experiment?

F. Yes: different types of structure could be studied.
G. Yes: in real life, many different types of fossils are found.
H. No: the leaf served as a controlled variable.
J. No: the nature of the leaf is not important.

27. When a fossil is formed, the sediment that surrounds it is normally compressed by the tons of earth deposited over it. What part of the model simulates this compressing element?

A. The 5-lb weight
B. The glass
C. The upper layer of paste
D. The baking oven

28. A fourth experiment was set up the same way as the previous three, except the paste was made by mixing equal amounts of very coarse sand with the extra-fine plaster. The investigator is likely to discover:

F. no change from Experiment 1 because only the plaster counts.
G. no change because the same kind of leaf is used.
H. the imprint is better than Experiment 1 because the sand provides air pockets.
J. the imprint is worse than Experiment 1 because the average particle size is bigger.

29. Which of the following hypotheses is supported by the results of Experiment 1 alone?

A. The finer the sediment the greater the detail of the resulting fossil.
B. Hardened sediment can preserve the imprint of a specimen.
C. All fossils must have been baked at high temperatures.
D. Only organic material can leave imprints in sediment.

30. Which of the following changes in the experiments would have permitted a test of the hypothesis that the quality of a fossil imprint depends on the pressure applied?

F. Repeat the experiments except for using a 10-lb weight in Experiment 2, and a 20-lb weight in Experiment 3.
G. Choose one of the plasters, and run experiments using the same plaster in all trials while varying the weights.
H. Rerun all the experiments without the glass.
J. Vary the depth of the leaf in each new trial, because in nature increased pressure means the fossil is at a greater depth.

Passage VII

Erosion refers to processes that wear down rocks and soil, as well as processes that transport the worn-away materials to other locations. Although these processes usually cause effects gradually (over geologic time), laboratory models can be designed to investigate which environmental factors affect erosion rate.

Three experimental sandboxes were set up that were identical in size (10-feet-by-10-feet), had identical types of soil and rocks, and were filled to equal depths (3 feet). The sandboxes were kept for two weeks in large environmental chambers, each maintained at a constant temperature, with a continuous wind flow of 5 mph.

Sandbox 1

One half was kept bare (just soil and rocks), while the other half had a variety of grasses and weeds planted among the soil and rocks. After two weeks, the bare half had small channels (ruts) running along its length that averaged 1 inch in width. The planted half had few channels, and those that were found averaged less than 1 inch wide.

Sandbox 2

The conditions were identical to those of Sandbox 1, with the addition that both halves were subjected to light, 15-minute showers of water every twelve hours. After two weeks, the bare half had channels averaging 4 inches wide, while the planted half had fewer channels averaging 2 inches wide.

Sandbox 3

The conditions were identical to those of Sandbox 2, but the entire box was mechanically raised to rest at an angle of 15° to simulate a steep slope. After two weeks, the bare half had channels averaging 7 inches wide, while channels in the planted half were less common and averaged 4 inches in width.

31. Results from all three sandboxes indicate that:

A. different types of soils and rocks are affected differently by environmental factors.
B. under all tested conditions, plants reduce erosion.
C. changing wind and temperature conditions can affect erosion patterns.
D. water from short periods of rain has little or no effect on erosion patterns.

32. Which of the following claims does the design and results of the experiments NOT support?

F. Light winds have no erosive effect.
G. Slopes have more erosion than level surfaces.
H. Water has major erosive effects.
J. The effects of changing temperature remain unanswered.

33. Sudden cloudbursts are known to cause more erosion than longer periods of mild rains. How could the present experiments be changed to examine this idea?

A. Raise the angle in Sandbox 3 to produce a steeper slope.
B. Add the "rain conditions" from Sandbox 2 to the conditions in Sandbox 1.
C. Include light, 15-minute showers every six hours instead of every twelve hours.
D. Every twelve hours allow the same total volume of water to fall in a 5-minute span rather than in a 15-minute span.

34. Should the investigator have used different soil types in each sandbox experiment?

F. Yes, because different soils may erode differently.
G. Yes, because a different group of plants could have been used in each sandbox as well.
H. No, because some soils can be washed completely away within the 2-week experiment.
J. No, because the soil type was a controlled variable in all three experiments.

35. Sandbox 3 specifically demonstrates the role of which particular variable in the set of experiments?

A. Rain
B. Wind
C. Gravity
D. Temperature

36. If another sandbox were set up, which of the following conditions would probably cause wider and deeper channels in the soil of the new sandbox than those in Sandbox 3?

I. Steeper angles for the sandbox
II. A greater volume of water during the 15-minute showers every twelve hours
III. Removal of plants from soil

F. I only
G. I and II only
H. II and III only
J. I, II, and III

Passage VIII

Theory 1

Early in the twentieth century, many chemists believed that the stability of the molecule methane, CH_4, could be explained by the "octet" rule, which states that stability occurs when the central atom, in this case carbon, is surrounded by eight "valence," or outer, electrons. Four of these originally came from the outer electrons of the carbon itself, and four came from the four surrounding hydrogen atoms (the hydrogen atom was considered an exception to the rule since it was known to favor a closed shell of two electrons as helium has.) According to the octet rule, neither CH_3 nor CH_5 should exist as stable compounds, and this prediction has been borne out by experiment.

Theory 2

While the octet rule predicted many compounds accurately, it also had shortcomings. Ten electrons, for example, surround the compound PC_{15}. The greatest shock to the octet rule concerned noble gases such as krypton and xenon, which have eight electrons surrounding them in their atomic states, and therefore should not form compounds since no more electrons would be needed to make an octet. The discovery in 1960 that xenon could form compounds such as XeF_4 forced consideration of a new theory, which held that (a) compounds formed when electrons were completely paired, either in bonds or in non-bonded pairs; (b) the total number of shared electrons around a central atom varied, and could be as high as twelve; (c) the shapes of compounds were such as to keep the pairs of electrons as far from each other as possible.

For example, since six electrons in the atomic state surround sulfur, in the compound SF_6 it acquired six additional shared electrons from the surrounding fluorines for a total of twelve electrons. The shape of the compound is "octahedral," as shown below, since this conformation minimizes the overlap of bonding pairs of electrons.

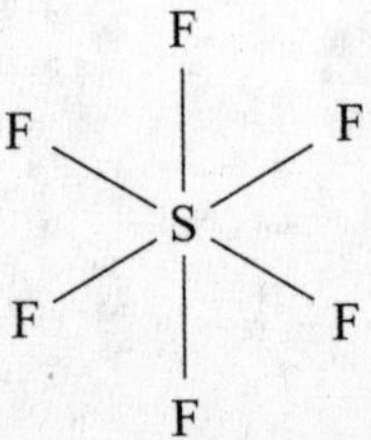

37. According to Theory 1, the compound CH_2Cl_2:

A. should have eight electrons surrounding the carbon atom.
B. cannot exist since the original carbon atom does not have eight electrons.
C. should have eight electrons surrounding each hydrogen atom.
D. requires more electrons for stability.

38. According to Theory 1, the compound XeF_4:

F. exists with an octet structure around the xenon.
G. should not exist since more than eight electrons surround the xenon.
H. will have similar chemical properties to CH_4.
J. exists with the xenon surrounded by twelve electrons.

39. The atom boron has three outer electrons, and in bonding to boron, a fluorine atom donates one electron. The BF_3 molecule is known to exist. Which of the following is true?

A. BF_3 obeys Theory 1.
B. The existence of BF_3 contradicts Theory 2.
C. According to Theory 2, the structure of BF_3 is a pyramid:

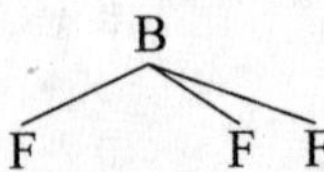

D. According to Theory 2, the structure of BF_3 is triangular and planar:

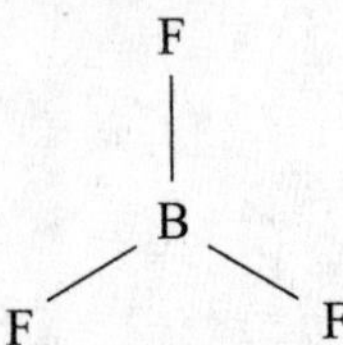

40. A scientist seeking to explain why Theory 2 has more predictive power than Theory 1 might argue that:

F. eight electrons shall represent a "closed shell."

G. while eight electrons represent a "closed shell" for some atoms, for others the closed shell may be six, ten, or twelve.

H. it is incorrect to assume that a given atom always has the same number of electrons around it.

J. CH_4 is not as important a compound as XeF_4.

41. Theory 2 could be threatened by evidence of:

A. the existence of SF_4.

B. the existence of XeF_5.

C. molecules with stable octets.

D. the existence of SF_6.

Passage IX

Scientist 1

The atmosphere of the Earth was at one time almost totally lacking in oxygen. One piece of evidence supporting this assertion is the very fact that life got started at all. The first chemical reactions that are necessary for the origin of life, the formation of amino acids, require ultraviolet light. Most of the ultraviolet light coming from the Sun is now absorbed by oxygen in the atmosphere. If there were as much oxygen in the atmosphere then as there is now, there would have been too little ultraviolet light available to enable life to begin. Also, the oldest bacteria, the ones that have the shortest DNA, are almost all anaerobes—they either do not need oxygen or die if exposed to oxygen. Most of the oxygen that exists now entered the atmosphere later from volcanic fumes.

Scientist 2

The prevailing opinion is that the atmosphere, though thicker now than it was in the past, is not essentially different in composition. The argument that the Earth must originally have been deficient in oxygen is flawed. First of all, the presence of iron and other oxides in the rocks from this time indicates that there was oxygen available. Secondly, the requirement for a great deal of ultraviolet light holds only if there is a low concentration of the starting materials in the water. If the water in some prehistoric lake began to freeze, the starting materials would be concentrated in a small volume of unfrozen water. The high concentration of the starting materials would offset the so-called deficiency of ultraviolet light, and life could begin.

42. According to the hypothesis of Scientist 1, which of the following would have been among the last living things to evolve?

F. Anaerobes
G. Plants
H. Insects
J. Viruses

43. According to the information presented by Scientist 1, if his theory of the origin of oxygen in the atmosphere is correct, the total amount of oxygen in the air over the next million years, on the average, should:

A. decrease, then increase.
B. increase, then decrease.
C. increase.
D. decrease.

44. Underlying the argument of Scientist 2 is the assumption that the oxygen in the oxides in the rocks was:

F. always tied up in the rocks.
G. involved in biological reactions.
H. all gaseous during the early days of the atmosphere.
J. proportional to the oxygen in the atmosphere at the time.

45. Underlying Scientist 1's suggestion that the evolutionary record supports the idea of an oxygen deficiency on the early Earth is the assumption that the oldest living things:

A. have the shortest DNA.
B. have the most fragmented DNA.
C. have changed radically.
D. must have died out.

46. Which of the following is the strongest argument Scientist 1 could use to counter Scientist 2's suggested mechanism for the origin of life?

F. There was not enough ultraviolet light available.
G. Chemical reactions occurred differently then.
H. The temperature at the surface of the Earth at that time was always above 35°C because of geothermal heat release.
J. Most lakes would not have covered large enough areas to guarantee that all the essential building blocks were present.

47. To refute Scientist 1's hypothesis, Scientist 2 might best show that:

A. the amount of oxide in rocks has changed little over the past four billion years.
B. there are ways of making the biologically important molecules without ultraviolet light.
C. there are complex anaerobic bacteria.
D. the atmospheric pressure has not changed over the Earth's history.

Passage X

In the 1940s, 1950s, and 1960s, the growing field of animal behavior maintained an ongoing debate about the origin of observed behavior in many different animal species. Two extreme viewpoints were at the center of this "Nature vs. Nurture" debate.

Viewpoint 1 (Nature)

Many behaviors or instincts are literally programmed by one or more genes. Genes serve as "blueprints" that enable an individual to carry out a particular stereotyped behavior (Fixed Action Pattern) as soon as the appropriate stimulus (releaser) is observed. Other individuals do not have to be observed performing the behavior. The releasing stimulus need never have been seen before. At first view of the releaser and every time thereafter, the Fixed Action Pattern will be carried out to completion in the exact same way—even if the releaser is removed before the Fixed Action Pattern is finished! Examples include: a) the pecking of baby gulls at the red spot on their mother's bill (which causes the mother gull to regurgitate food), b) song birds producing their species song without ever having heard it before, and c) a male stickle-back fish defending its territory by attacking anything red because other breeding males always have red underbellies.

Viewpoint 2 (Nurture)

Many behaviors are determined by experience and/or learning during an individual's lifetime. Genes provide the limits of the "blank slate" that each individual starts out as, but then various experiences will determine the actual behavior patterns within the individual genetic range of possibilities. In other words, behavior can be modified. Examples include: a) positive ("reward") reinforcement and punishment causing a behavior to increase and decrease (respectively), and b) songbirds producing their species song only after having heard it performed by other individuals of their species.

48. The red spot on a mother gull's bill is called a(n):

F. Fixed Action Pattern.
G. instinct.
H. releaser.
J. stereotyped response.

49. To refute the strict "genetic blueprint" ideas of Viewpoint 1, a scientist could show that:

A. baby gulls peck at a stick with a red spot.
B. baby gulls will peck at mother gulls' red spot as soon as they hatch out of their eggs.
C. baby gulls pecking at the red spot happens exactly the same way each time.
D. baby gulls' accuracy in pecking at mother gulls' red spot improves with practice.

50. A food-seeking blue jay captured a distinctively colored butterfly that had a bad-tasting substance in its tissues. After spitting out the butterfly, it never again tried to capture a similarly colored butterfly. This incident seems to support:

F. Viewpoint 1.
G. Viewpoint 2.
H. both viewpoints.
J. neither viewpoint (the incident is irrelevant).

51. Which of the following supports Viewpoint 1?

A. A rat reaches the end of a maze by the same route, but finishes faster after each trip.
B. Monkey A watches other monkeys wash sweet potatoes before they eat them; then, he washes sweet potatoes before he eats them.
C. A male stickleback fish attacks a picture of a red mailbox held in front of his aquarium.
D. A bird performs its species song after hearing the song only once.

52. If baby chickens peck at grains of food on the ground when hungry, but not as much after they have recently eaten, then this:

F. supports Viewpoint 1.
G. supports Viewpoint 2.
H. does not refer to behavior.
J. is irrelevant to the Nature vs. Nurture debate.

53. It is thought that some species of birds "learn" to fly. This belief is based on observations of young birds fluttering and flapping their wings at the nest until they reach the age when flight is possible. In Species X, nestlings were kept in harmless, but tight plastic tubes in which they could not carry out such "practice movements." They were released when they reached the age of flight. Viewpoint 1 predicts that the birds will fly:

A. after fluttering their wings for a time.
B. after watching other birds flutter their wings.
C. after watching other birds flutter and fly.
D. immediately.

54. A songbird can sing its species song after it hears other birds of its own species singing. Yet, if it hears the song from another species, the bird will not sing the "foreign" song. This suggests that:

F. genetic "programming" and experience play a role in this species' ability to sing its song.
G. this species' song is a Fixed Action Pattern.
H. song development in this species is strictly a learned behavior with no genetic component.
J. genes appear to be far more important than experience in this example.

This section contains three Science quizzes. Complete each quiz under timed conditions. Answers are on page 637.

Quiz I *(10 items; 9 minutes)*

DIRECTIONS: Each passage below is followed by several items. After reading a passage, choose the best answer to each item. You may refer to the passages as often as necessary. You are NOT permitted the use of a calculator.

Passage I

The ecological pyramid below shows the relative biomass* of organisms at each trophic feeding level of a marine food chain.

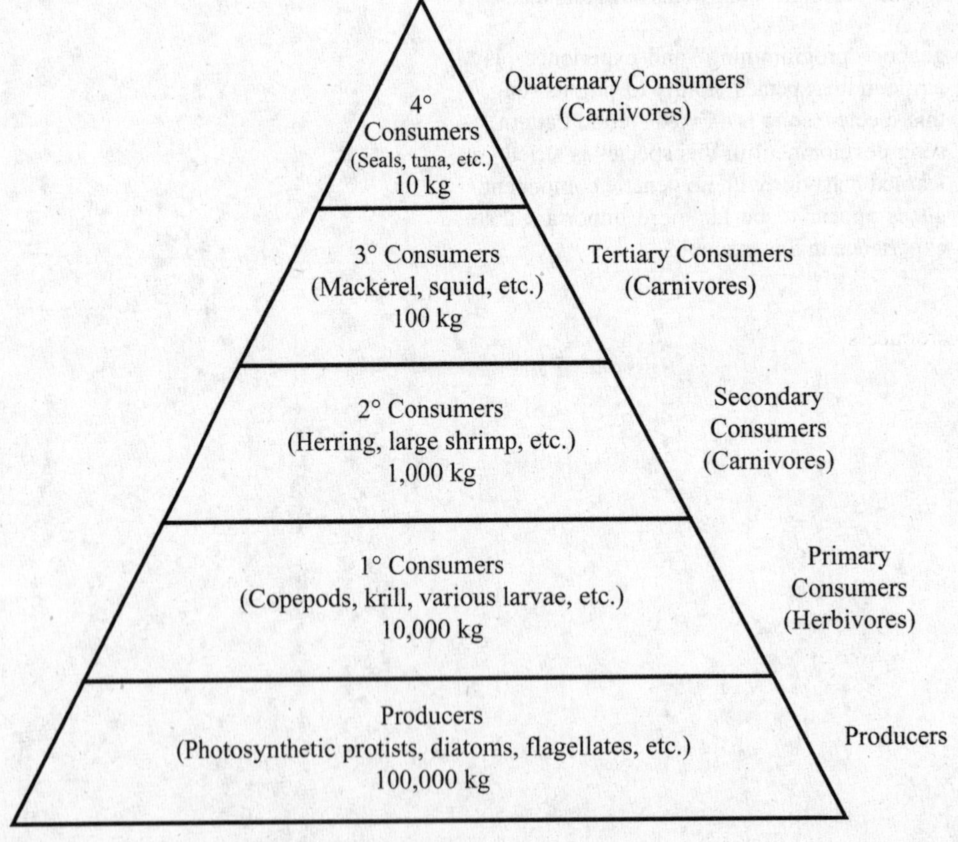

*Biomass is the total dry weight of organisms (useable chemical energy stored in organic matter) at each trophic level at any given time.

1. According to the diagram, the trophic level with the largest relative biomass is the:

   A. 4° consumers.
   B. 3° and 2° consumers.
   C. 1° consumers.
   D. producers.

2. From the information in the diagram, one can conclude that at any given time:

   F. 10 seals may be found for every mackerel.
   G. the relative dry weight of all carnivores combined is far greater than that of the herbivores alone.
   H. only 1 percent of all producers live long enough to be eaten by a mackerel.
   J. the relative dry weight of every consumer trophic level is usually less than that of the trophic level on which they feed.

3. Organisms from which trophic level are most likely to be found near the water surface where light can penetrate?

   A. 4° consumers
   B. 2° consumers
   C. 3° consumers
   D. producers

4. If there were an additional trophic level of carnivores (5° consumers), its relative biomass at any given time would be approximately:

   F. 1 kg.
   G. 11 kg.
   H. 111 kg.
   J. 1,000,000 kg.

5. The best explanation for biomass being measured as dry weight is:

   A. if water weight were included, efficiency ratios at each trophic level would be unpredictable.
   B. body fluids contribute little to the mass of marine organisms.
   C. water molecules contain little or no usable chemical energy.
   D. each trophic level contains a different amount of water.

Passage II

The table below shows various characteristics of different layers of the atmosphere.

Approximate Altitude (km)	Layers of the Atmosphere	Approximate Mean Temperature (°C)	Clouds
60,000			
6,000			
	THERMOSPHERE		
600		1200	
80		–90	
	MESOSPHERE		
50		–3	
	STRATOSPHERE		Cirrus
12		–50	
			Cirrostratus
5	TROPOSPHERE		Altostratus
0		18	Nimbostratus

6. Which statement accurately describes the relationship between the approximate altitude and the approximate mean temperature of the layers of the atmosphere?

   F. As altitude increases, temperature increases.
   G. As altitude increases, temperature decreases.
   H. As altitude increases, temperature first decreases then continuously increases.
   J. As altitude increases, temperature first decreases, then increases, then decreases, and then increases.

7. Based on the information in the table, the atmospheric layer with the narrowest range of altitude is the:

   A. thermosphere.
   B. troposphere.
   C. mesosphere.
   D. stratosphere.

8. The type of cloud(s) most likely to consist of ice crystals is (are):

   F. nimbostratus only.
   G. nimbostratus and altostratus.
   H. cirrus and cirrostratus.
   J. cirrostratus only.

9. The absorption of solar heat energy increases as the gases of the atmosphere become less dense, or rarefied. The layer of the atmosphere that appears most rarefied is the:

   A. thermosphere.
   B. mesosphere.
   C. stratosphere.
   D. troposphere.

10. According to the table, which atmospheric layer shows a decrease in temperature of approximately 3°C for every 1-kilometer increase in altitude?

 F. thermosphere
 G. mesosphere
 H. stratosphere
 J. troposphere

Quiz II *(10 items; 9 minutes)*

DIRECTIONS: Each passage below is followed by several items. After reading a passage, choose the best answer to each item. You may refer to the passages as often as necessary. You are NOT permitted the use of a calculator.

Passage I

The chart below shows in outline form a common means of analyzing a sample solution for various cations (positive ions). Ions above the horizontal arrows are those that are suspected to be present in the sample solution; the substances in the boxes are the reagents added as tests (0.3 M H^+ is acidic, NH_4OH is alkaline); the products shown next to the arrows pointing downward are solid precipitates resulting from the tests. Tests for specific ions need not always start from the beginning of the sequence.

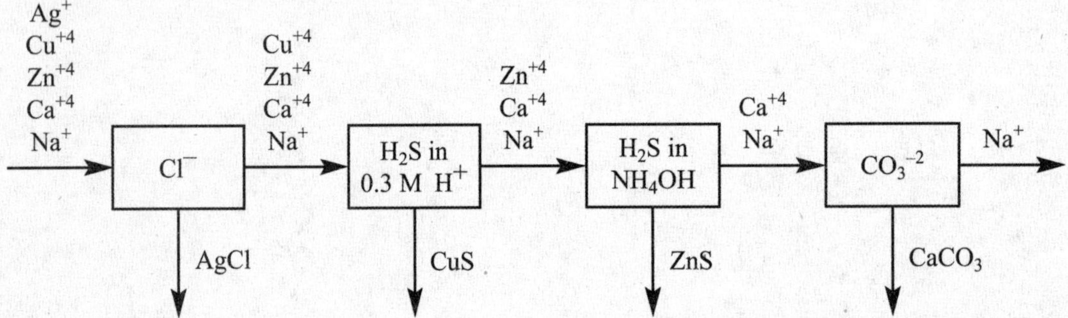

1. According to the chart, which precipitate indicates if silver (Ag) is present in the sample?

   A. AgCl
   B. Ag
   C. CuS
   D. ZnS

2. If a solution containing silver (Ag) nitrate and cupric (Cu) nitrate is tested according to this scheme, an experimenter will:

   F. first observe AgCl on treatment with Cl^-, and next observe CuS on treatment with H_2S.
   G. first observe CuS on treatment with Cl^-, and next observe AgCl on treatment with H_2S.
   H. first observe $CaCO_3$ on treatment with CO_3^{-2}, and next observe AgCl on treatment with Cl^-.
   J. observe no reactions, since the scheme does not test for nitrate.

3. What is the minimum number of tests necessary to confirm the composition of an unknown solution that contains no other positive ions except Cu^{+2} or Zn^{+2}, but not both?

   A. 1
   B. 2
   C. 3
   D. 4

4. Which statement is most correct concerning the separation of Cu^{+2} from Zn^{+2} in the same solution?

   F. Completely different test reagents are used in each of the two steps.
   G. The same test reagents are used in each of the two steps.
   H. The same test reagents are used, but the first step must be in an alkaline environment while the second step must be in an acidic environment.
   J. The same test reagents are used, but the first step must be in an acidic environment while the second step must be in an alkaline environment.

5. A clear solution is found, by a method not discussed here, to contain chloride ion (Cl^-). From the information given here, what ion could not be present in the solution?

A. Carbonate (CO^{-2})
B. Cupric (Cu^{+2})
C. Silver (Ag^+)
D. Zinc (Zn^{+2})

Passage II

The chart below shows the flavor preferences of white-tailed deer when offered various fluids to drink at different ages.

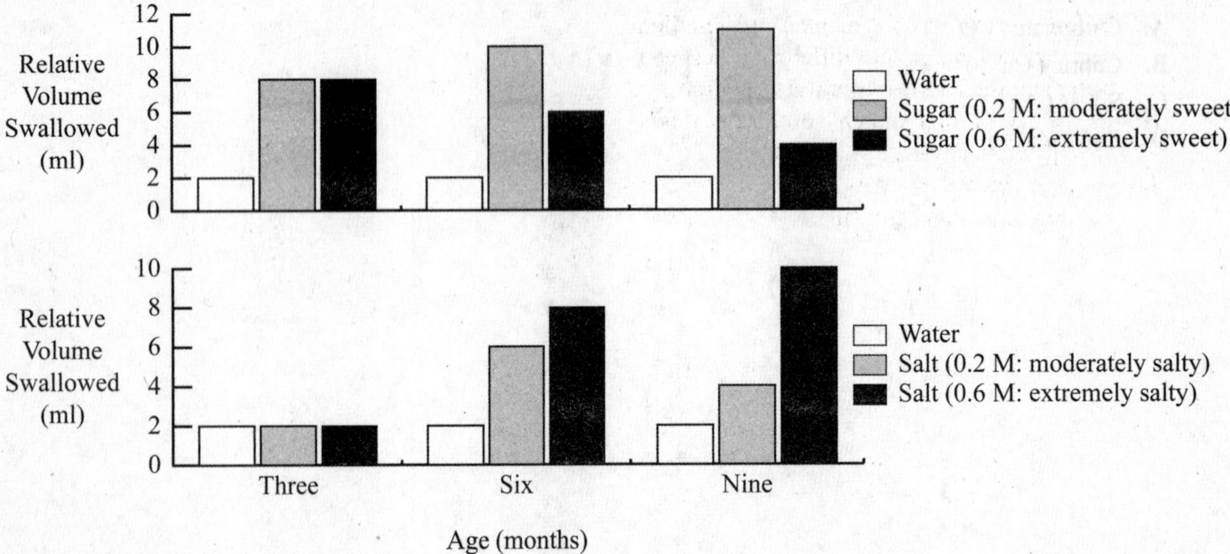

6. Which category on the chart shows no preference between water and the experimental flavor?

   F. Three months of age/sugar
   G. Six months of age/salt
   H. Three months of age/salt
   J. Nine months of age/sugar

7. Which statement about white-tailed deer is supported by the information in the chart?

   A. As age increases, the preference for all tested sugars increases.
   B. As age increases, the preference for all tested salts increases.
   C. As age increases, differences between sugars cannot be detected, and differences between salts cannot be detected.
   D. As age increases, differences between sugars can be detected, and differences between salts can be detected.

8. The flavor preference that fluctuates most irregularly with age is:

   F. moderately salty.
   G. moderately sweet.
   H. extremely salty.
   J. extremely sweet.

9. Based on the trends shown in the chart, which of the following predictions is most reasonable for one-year-old white-tailed deer?

   A. Moderately sweet and moderately salty will be most preferred.
   B. Extremely sweet and extremely salty will be most preferred.
   C. Moderately sweet and extremely salty will be most preferred.
   D. Extremely sweet and moderately salty will be most preferred.

10. Which of the following conclusions about water is NOT consistent with the data in the chart?

    F. Water is never preferred over any tested flavors.
    G. Before the age of six months, white-tailed deer cannot taste the difference between water and sugar or between water and salt.
    H. At the age of three months, both salty fluids are equal to the water swallowed.
    J. As age increases, the volume of water swallowed remains the same.

Quiz III *(11 items; 9 minutes)*

DIRECTIONS: Each passage below is followed by several items. After reading a passage, choose the best answer to each item. You may refer to the passages as often as necessary. You are NOT permitted the use of a calculator.

Passage I

The table below shows the first three ionization energies for the atoms hydrogen through potassium. The first ionization energy, E_1, is the energy (in kilocalories per mole of atoms) that must be added in order to remove the first electron. E_2 is the energy required to remove a second electron once the first has been removed, and E_3 is the energy needed to remove a third electron. If an atom lacks a second or third electron, no value is given in the table.

IONIZATION ENERGIES OF THE ELEMENTS (kcal/mole)

Atomic No.	Element	E_1	E_2	E_3
1	H	313.6	-	-
2	He	566.8	1254	-
3	Li	124.3	1744	2823
4	Be	214.9	419.9	3548
5	B	191.3	580	874.5
6	C	259.6	562.2	1104
7	N	335.1	682.8	1094
8	O	314	810.6	1267
9	F	401.8	806.7	1445
10	Ne	497.2	947.2	1500
11	Na	118.5	1091	1652
12	Mg	176.3	346.6	1848
13	Al	138	434.1	655.9
14	Si	187.9	376.8	771.7
15	P	241.8	453.2	695.5
16	S	238.9	540	807
17	Cl	300	548.9	920.2
18	Ar	363.4	637	943.3
19	K	100.1	733.6	1100

1. For a given element, the ionization energies increase in the order:

A. E_3, E_2, E_1.
B. E_2, E_1, E_3.
C. E_1, E_2, E_3.
D. Order varies.

2. A student suspects that there may be an atom for which the second ionization energy is roughly twice that of the first, and the third is roughly twice that of the second. Which of the following atoms best fits this relationship?

F. Be
G. C
H. Ne
J. Ar

3. As atomic number increases, the trend in the values of E_2 is:

A. generally upward.
B. generally downward.
C. upward for a few values, then suddenly downward, followed by another increase, etc.
D. downward for a few values, then suddenly upward, followed by a decrease again, etc.

4. If the chart were continued to the element having atomic number 20, its value for E_1 would be expected to be closest to:

F. 20.
G. 90.
H. 140.
J. 730.

5. An experimenter has at her disposal a means of providing an atom with any energy up to 200 kcal/mole. From how many different atoms could she remove one electron?

A. 7
B. 8
C. 11
D. 12

Passage II

A physics student performed two sets of experiments designed to examine the factors that influence the motion of falling objects.

Experiment 1

A stone was dropped from a steep cliff while a camera, mounted on a tripod on the ground, took photographs at 1-second intervals. Back in the laboratory, the same procedure was repeated in the absence (nearly) of air inside a huge vacuum chamber.

Experiment 2

The experiments were repeated (on the cliff and inside the vacuum chamber) using a stone and a cork with identical masses dropped at the same time. At the cliff, the stone hit the ground first. In the vacuum chamber, both objects hit the ground together.

6. Assuming that air acts to resist the downward acceleration of the stone, how will the total time required to reach the ground in the vacuum chamber compare to the time required to reach the ground from the cliff?

   F. Longer time in air than in vacuum chamber
   G. Longer time in vacuum chamber than in air
   H. Same time in each
   J. Cannot be determined from the given information

7. If part of Experiment 1 were repeated on the moon, where the pull of gravity is one sixth that of the Earth, the stone's downward speed would increase as it falls (i.e., it would accelerate) but the rate of increase in speed would only be one sixth as great as on the Earth. When the photos taken at 1-second intervals on the moon are compared to the photos taken on Earth, the series of moon pictures of the stone will be:

   A. closer together.
   B. farther apart.
   C. identical.
   D. closer at some times and farther apart at others.

8. In Experiment 2, the observed results can be explained by the hypothesis that:

   F. heavier objects fall more rapidly than lighter ones.
   G. a cork of the same mass as a stone is smaller than the stone, and it encounters more air resistance.
   H. a cork of the same mass as a stone is larger than the stone, and it encounters more air resistance.
   J. the gravitational acceleration of objects toward the ground diminishes when air is not present.

9. In Experiment 1, gravity accelerates the stone as it falls from the cliff, causing it to pick up speed as it drops. Which of the following series of pictures most resembles how the stone appears as it drops?

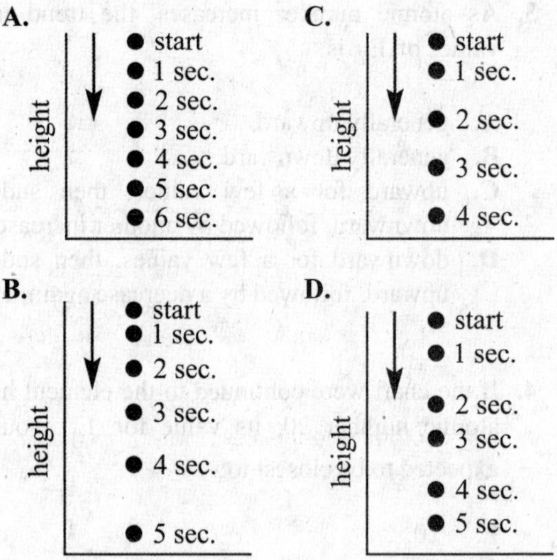

10. The experimenter devises a means of suspending the Earth's gravity for short periods of time. Armed with this technique, he drops the stone (on Earth, in air, under conditions of normal gravity), and then suspends gravity 2 seconds after the stone has been falling and leaves it off for the next minute. Recalling that gravity causes the stone's downward speed to increase continually, choose the "photo" that best illustrates, in 1-second intervals, this experiment.

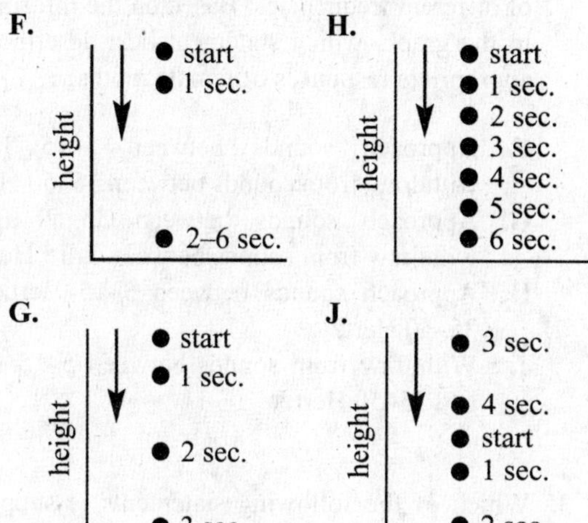

11. If Experiment 2 were repeated on the airless moon, which prediction would be correct?

   A. The cork would fall more slowly than on the Earth.
   B. The cork would fall as rapidly as the stone.
   C. Both predictions are correct.
   D. Neither prediction is correct.

This section contains additional Science items for further practice. Answers are on page 637.

DIRECTIONS: Each passage below is followed by several items. After reading a passage, choose the best answer to each item. You may refer to the passages as often as necessary. You are NOT permitted the use of a calculator.

Passage I

The graph of the thin line below shows the hearing sensitivity of female moths. The auditory characteristics of certain sounds important to moth survival are also included.

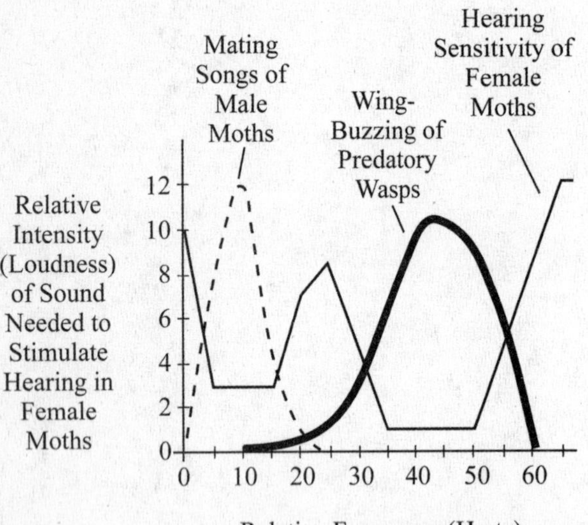

1. According to the graph, female moths are most sensitive to sounds between:

   A. 0–5 Hertz.
   B. 5–15 Hertz.
   C. 20–25 Hertz.
   D. 35–50 Hertz.

2. The nervous system of female moths may be set up to allow them to respond differently to sounds of different frequencies. Based on the information in the graph, which statement best describes the appropriate responses of female moths?

   F. Approach sounds between 5–15 Hertz, withdraw from sounds between 35–50 Hertz
   G. Approach sounds between 35–50 Hertz, withdraw from sounds between 5–15 Hertz
   H. Approach sounds between 5–15 Hertz and 35–50 Hertz
   J. Withdraw from sounds between 5–15 Hertz and 35–50 Hertz

3. Which of the following statements is supported by the information in the graph?

   A. The wing-buzzing sounds of wasps occur at a narrower range of frequencies than the range of the male moth mating song.
   B. The frequency range of the male moth mating song is narrower than the range of wasp wing-buzzing sounds.
   C. Female moths cannot hear sounds with relative intensities less than 3.
   D. Male moths are less sensitive to sounds than predatory wasps.

4. Which of the following statements accurately describes the relationship between the male moth mating song and female moth hearing sensitivity?

   F. The frequency range of the male song coincides with the frequency range at which females are maximally sensitive to any sound.
   G. Females need not be maximally sensitive at the frequency range of the male song because of the extremely high intensity of the song.
   H. Females cannot hear the male song if its intensity level is less than 10.
   J. The male song does not extend to an intensity level above 10.

5. If a new species of wasp were introduced into the moths' environment, which of the following wing-buzzing characteristics would make it the most successful predator of female moths?

   A. Extremely high intensity at relative frequencies between 35–50 Hertz
   B. An intensity level of 7–8 at relative frequencies between 20–25 Hertz
   C. Low intensity at relative frequencies above 60 Hertz
   D. Extremely high intensity at relative frequencies above 60 Hertz

6. A "new male" comes to town having a mating song with a frequency range between 20–25 Hertz and an intensity level of 4. What are his chances of finding a mate?

   F. Excellent
   G. Poor
   H. Good, if no wasps are present
   J. Cannot be determined from the given information

Passage II

A chemistry student wishes to study weight relationships between compounds before and after they take part in reactions. Two experiments were conducted to investigate two different reactions. The reactions are shown below, together with the amount (grams) of each substance before and after each reaction has proceeded. Equations are balanced to show the number of each type of atom before and after the reactions.

Experiment 1				
	$NaBr$ +	$AgNO_3$ ⇒	$AgBr$ +	$NaNO_3$
Initial Wt.	103	170	0	0
Final Wt.	0	0	188	85

Experiment 2					
	Na_2CO_3 +	$2HCl$ ⇒	$2NaCl$ +	$H_2O(g)$ +	CO_2
Initial Wt.	106	72	0	0	(?)
Final Wt.	0	0	117	18	(?)

(The student has measured the quantities he could, but was unable to weigh the CO_2 because it is a gas. Since it is a gas, he assumes it has negligible weight.)

7. In Experiment 1, the data indicate that after the reaction has proceeded:

A. all of the Na originally present has been converted to Ag.
B. there are fewer molecules of $NaNO_3$ than there were molecules of $AgNO_3$ at the outset.
C. no NaBr remains.
D. no AgBr remains.

8. Which of the following is (are) conserved in the reaction in Experiment 1?

I. mass
II. number of atoms
III. amount of $AgNO_3$

F. I only
G. I and II only
H. I and III only
J. I, II, and III

9. In Experiment 2, the mass of the weighed products is:

A. 0.
B. less than the mass of reactants.
C. equal to the mass of reactants.
D. greater than the mass of reactants.

10. Experiment 2 differs from Experiment 1 in that:

F. the number of atoms is not conserved.
G. the reaction does not go to completion.
H. there are no ionic compounds involved.
J. gas is produced.

11. Assuming the student is right in neglecting the weight of one of the products in Experiment 2, he can conclude from the data that:

A. mass is consumed as the reaction proceeds.
B. mass is produced as the reaction proceeds.
C. energy is consumed as the reaction proceeds.
D. mass is conserved as the reaction proceeds.

12. The student is advised of a means to weigh the CO_2 gas produced in the reaction, and finds this weight to be 43 grams. The student can now state that the two experiments:

F. lead to similar conclusions: neither mass nor atoms are conserved.
G. lead to similar conclusions: both mass and atoms are conserved.
H. lead to different conclusions: the number of molecules is not the same for the reactants as for the products.
J. lead to different conclusions: gases have negligible weight.

Passage III

Jean Baptiste Lamarck hypothesized the process of biological evolution before Charles Darwin was born. Some aspects of Lamarck's ideas and Darwin's ideas are presented below.

Lamarckism

Observations of the fossil record led Lamarck to believe that several lines of descent led to nature's broad diversity of organisms. Old fossils and recent fossils showed patterns leading to the characteristics of modern species. He believed that newer forms were more complex and more "perfectly" adapted to their environment. New adaptations could arise as the environment changed. Body organs that were used to cope with the environment became stronger and larger, while those not used deteriorated. For example, giraffes stretching their necks to reach higher leaves would develop longer necks. In addition, such changes in structure could then be passed on to offspring (these acquired characteristics could be inherited).

Darwinism

Based on the fossil and geologic record, Darwin also came to believe that various modern species were related through descent from common ancestors. He also noted that the great diversity of organisms that he observed during his travels were all very well adapted to their environments. The adaptations, however, did not come about through "coping" or usage. Instead, individuals from a population can each show slight genetic or "heritable" differences (variability) in a trait. If such differences, by chance alone, give the individual some reproductive advantage (he or she can successfully produce more offspring than other members of the population), then more individuals with that trait will make up the next generation. Through this "natural selection" of individuals with characteristics that give them a slight advantage in their particular environment, species appear to become very well suited to their natural world. However, "perfection" is not a useful term since the environment is constantly changing. The adaptations that are advantageous "today" may not be advantageous "tomorrow" under different conditions.

13. A major difference between Lamarck and Darwin relates to their views on:

A. the diversity of organisms in the natural world.
B. the significance of fossils.
C. the importance of adaptations to the environment.
D. the way adaptations come about.

14. Which viewpoint supports the idea that present-day species are descended from earlier forms?

F. Lamarckism
G. Darwinism
H. Both viewpoints
J. Neither viewpoint

15. Which statement might be used by a Darwinist to explain the extinction of a species?

A. The environment changed, and not enough individuals had traits or adaptations well suited to the new conditions.
B. The environment changed, and body parts could not be manipulated enough to adapt to new conditions.
C. As the environment changed, the individuals present were not "perfect" enough.
D. As the environment changed, there was no "natural selection."

16. Darwin might dispute the Lamarckian idea of inheriting acquired characteristics by pointing out that:

F. giraffes with short necks may do just as well as those with long necks.
G. giraffes that break a leg and walk around on three legs all their lives still do not produce three-legged offspring.
H. giraffes had shorter necks millions of years ago.
J. giraffes that break a leg would not be able to reach the highest leaves.

17. Many species of moles live underground, in the dark. These species often have small, almost dysfunctional eyes. Which of the following statement(s) would a Lamarckian thinker use to explain this phenomenon?

    I. Moles without eyesight are better adapted for survival underground and therefore produce more offspring.
    II. Disuse of eyes in the dark led to their deterioration in mole species.
    III. Eye deterioration can be transferred to a mole's genes, which are then passed on to the next generation.

    A. I only
    B. II only
    C. II and III only
    D. I, II, and III

18. Which factor is vital to Darwin's ideas, but not to those of Lamarck?

    F. The fossil record
    G. An examination of modern species
    H. The inheritance of adaptations
    J. Chance

19. A few individuals in a population have an adaptation that enables them to tolerate extremely cold temperatures. In their lifetimes, the environment never reaches such extremes. If all other traits are the same among individuals, what would a Darwinist predict about the number of offspring left in the next generation by these individuals, compared to the number left by other members of the population?

    A. These individuals will leave approximately the same number of offspring.
    B. These individuals will leave more offspring.
    C. These individuals will leave fewer offspring.
    D. These individuals will probably not leave any offspring.

Passage IV

Graph I shows the relationship between the relative rates of activity of enzymes A and B and temperature. Graph II shows the relationship between the relative rates of activity of enzymes A and B and pH.

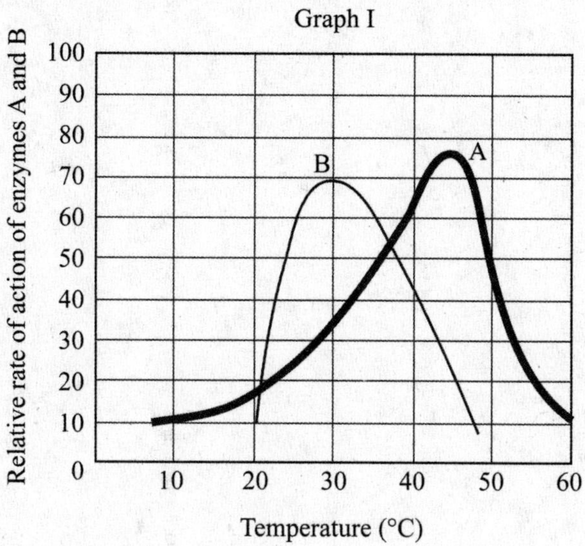

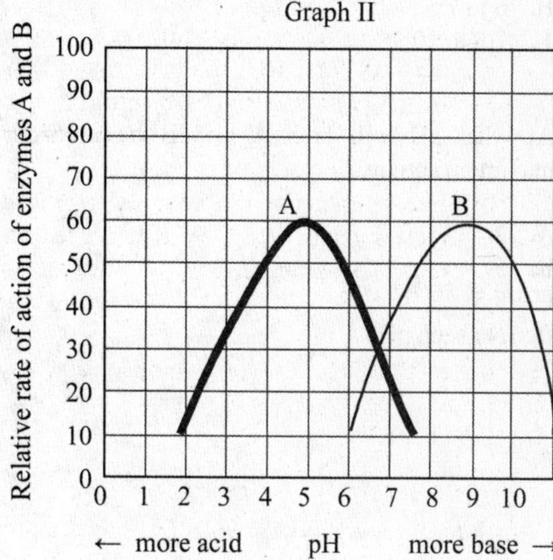

20. Under which conditions is enzyme A most effective?

F. 40°C and a pH of 5
G. 45°C and a pH of 5
H. 45°C and a pH of 9
J. 50°C and a pH of 9

21. The optimum environment for enzyme B is:

A. acidic.
B. basic.
C. either acidic or basic.
D. neutral.

22. At which one of the following temperatures do A and B exhibit the same relative rate of action?

F. 6.9°C
G. 10°C
H. 37°C
J. 47°C

23. At which pH do both A and B exhibit the same relative rate of action?

A. 6.7
B. 10
C. 37
D. 47

24. At what temperature does A have half the activity of B?

F. 20°C
G. 25°C
H. 42°C
J. 53°C

25. At what temperature does B have about half the activity of A?

A. 20°C
B. 30°C
C. 42°C
D. 53°C

26. Over which of the following pH ranges will both A and B be active?

    F. 1 to 3
    G. 3 to 6
    H. 6 to 7.5
    J. 7.5 to 10

27. At what pH will both A and B be at their maximum activity?

    A. 2
    B. 5
    C. 8.5
    D. No such pH

Passage V

A series of three experiments was designed to investigate the interrelationships between various factors known to influence gases: temperature (Kelvin), pressure (atmospheres), volume (liters), and the number of moles of gas.

Experiment 1

A gas at 200 K and a volume of 0.30 liters was found to have a pressure of 0.40 atm. After the temperature was raised to 400 K while keeping the volume the same, the pressure was found to be 0.80 atm.

Experiment 2

A gas at 200 K had a pressure of 0.50 atm. when its volume was 1 liter. Its volume was then increased to 2 liters at constant temperature. The resulting pressure was 0.25 atm.

Experiment 3

Two moles of a gas were found to occupy 44.8 liters at 1 atm. pressure and 273 K. Four moles of the same gas are added to the system with temperature and pressure held constant, resulting in a new volume of 134.4 liters.

28. Which of the following hypotheses is (are) supported by the results of Experiment 1?

I. The pressure of the gas is proportional to its volume at constant temperature.
II. The volume of the gas is proportional to its temperature at constant pressure.
III. The pressure of a gas is proportional to its temperature at constant volume.

F. I only
G. I and II only
H. III only
J. II and III only

29. The results of Experiment 2 support the hypothesis that if the temperature of a gas is held constant, then the pressure:

A. increases as the volume increases.
B. decreases as the volume increases.
C. does not depend strongly on the volume.
D. Cannot be determined from the given information

30. The result of Experiment 3 supports the hypothesis that if both the pressure and the temperature of a gas are held constant, then the volume:

F. varies inversely with the number of moles of gas.
G. varies directly with the number of moles of gas.
H. is raised to a maximum value of 134.4 liters when additional gas is added.
J. does not depend on the number of moles of gas.

31. An experimenter put 0.08 moles of gas into a 4-liter flask at 273 K and 0.448 atm. pressure. She allowed 0.02 moles of the gas to escape, and she put the remaining gas into a smaller flask that caused the pressure to remain at 0.448 atm. pressure, while the temperature was kept constant as well. According to Experiment 3, the volume of the smaller flask must be:

A. 0.06 liter.
B. 0.448 liters.
C. 3 liters.
D. Cannot be determined from the given information

32. Six moles of a gas originally at 0.1 atm. pressure and 273 K occupy a volume of 13.4 liters. The temperature is then changed to 300 K and the volume changed to 10.0 liters. To predict the final pressure on the six moles of gas, a student should use the results of:

    I. Experiment 1.
    II. Experiment 2.
    III. Experiment 3.

    F. I only
    G. II only
    H. I and II only
    J. I and III only

33. The final pressure of the gas described in the previous question will be:

    A. less than 0.1 atm. pressure.
    B. equal to 0.1 atm. pressure.
    C. greater than 0.1 atm. pressure.
    D. Cannot be determined from the given information

Passage VI

How did life originate on the planet Earth? Two opposing views are presented.

Scientist 1

The idea that Earth could have given rise to life independently is mistaken. Life on this planet must have come from elsewhere for several reasons. First of all, complex life appears very suddenly in the geological record. Secondly, all life on Earth has a very similar biochemistry. If life originated on Earth, one would expect regional variations in biochemistry, similar to the variations in species spread over large areas. Finally, the time when life first appeared in the geological record was also a time when large numbers of meteorites struck the Earth. The meteorites must have caused life to appear on the Earth. The simplest hypothesis is that the meteorites brought life with them.

Scientist 2

Life need not have been imported from outer space. The chemicals required for life existed on the surface of the Earth at the time life first appeared. The fact that all life has a similar biochemistry can be explained by considering that any group of chemicals that won the race to life would probably have used the "almost-living" as food. Since we can offer explanations for what happened without relying on a meteorite of unknown composition that might have fallen to Earth, we should stick to hypotheses that have fewer unknowns.

34. Which of the following is an assumption of Scientist 1?

F. Complex life forms can develop quickly.
G. Meteorites burn up as soon as they hit the Earth's atmosphere.
H. There is a cause-and-effect relationship between meteors falling and the origin of life.
J. The changes on the Earth's surface due to the presence of life attracted meteor showers.

35. Which of the following, if true, strengthens Scientist 2's argument the most?

A. Only five percent more meteors than normal fell on the Earth during the time life began.
B. Only five percent of the meteorites studied contained organic molecules.
C. A simulation of early Earth chemistry showed the spontaneous formation of complex biomolecules.
D. Meteorites containing amoebas have been found.

36. Which of the following, if true, strengthens Scientist 1's argument the most?

F. Only five percent more meteors than normal fell on the Earth during the time life began.
G. Only five percent of the meteorites studied contained organic molecules.
H. A simulation of early Earth chemistry showed the spontaneous formation of complex biomolecules.
J. Meteorites containing amoebas have been found.

37. With which explanation of the similar biochemistry of all life on Earth would Scientist 1 most likely agree?

A. A single chemical pathway to life exists.
B. Life arose from a single source.
C. Life is not varied.
D. Meteors are simple.

38. With which explanation of the similar biochemistry of all life on Earth would Scientist 2 most likely agree?

F. A single chemical pathway to life exists.
G. Life arose from a single source.
H. Life is not varied.
J. Meteors are simple.

39. Which scientist would be likely to disagree with the idea that life on different planets could have different biochemistries?

A. Scientist 1
B. Scientist 2
C. Both scientists
D. Neither scientist

40. Which of the following questions would be the most difficult for Scientist 1 to defend his theory against?

F. Why was there more meteorite activity earlier in Earth's history?
G. Why have other meteors not brought other life based on a different biochemistry?
H. Why did complex life emerge suddenly?
J. Why should meteor activity have any connection to the origin of life?

41. Could Scientist 2 believe that life exists on other planets without affecting his hypothesis?

A. Yes, as long as he believes that life elsewhere has a different biochemistry.
B. Yes, because wherever the chemicals required for life exist, life can begin.
C. No, because then he has to admit that meteorites brought life from these planets.
D. No, because then he has to admit that meteorites that came from pieces of similar planets brought life to the Earth.

Passage VII

A seismographic station can detect how far away an earthquake occurred, but it cannot determine the direction of the earthquake. Any given station can therefore report that the epicenter of an earthquake occurred somewhere on the circumference of a circle. The map below shows the data recorded for an earthquake at three different seismic stations (A, B, and C). Intersections of the three seismic stations' curves are marked by Roman numerals.

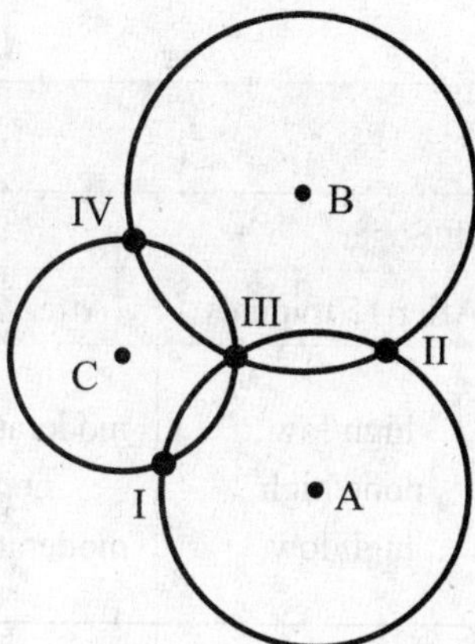

42. Which station was closest to the earthquake epicenter?

    F. A
    G. B
    H. C
    J. Cannot be determined from the given information

43. Given the information from stations A and B only, which site(s) is (are) possible for the earthquake epicenter?

    A. I only
    B. III only
    C. II and III only
    D. I and III only

44. Given the information from stations A and C only, which site(s) is (are) possible for the earthquake epicenter?

    F. I only
    G. III only
    H. II and III only
    J. I and III only

45. Given the information from all three stations, which site(s) is (are) possible for the epicenter?

    A. I only
    B. III only
    C. I and III only
    D. II and III only

46. If a fourth seismic station gave a report, at what point must its curve meet A's curve?

    F. I
    G. II
    H. III
    J. IV

47. If a fourth seismic station gave a report, at what point must its curve meet C's curve?

    A. I
    B. II
    C. III
    D. IV

48. What is the minimum number of points where two circumferences from two seismic stations, both measuring the same earthquake, can meet?

    F. 1
    G. 2
    H. 3
    J. Infinite

Passage VIII

To investigate the factors affecting the rate at which starch is broken down to sugar by the digestive enzyme salivary amylase, two experiments were performed. In both experiments, starch (in the form of a cracker) was mixed in a beaker with the enzyme, and the samples were removed every three minutes. Dipping special sugar indicators in the sample revealed the presence of starch in a sample (indicating that the cracker had not yet been completely digested).

Experiment 1

To test the effects of different pH levels on enzyme activity rate, one cracker and a standard amount of enzyme were placed in three beakers, each containing buffers of different pH. This procedure was repeated using standard amounts of water in place of the enzyme. All tests were carried out at optimal temperature. Starch and sugar levels (starch/sugar) from selected samples are shown in Table 1.

Table 1

Contents of Beakers	Approximate pH Levels	Levels of Starch/Sugar			
		After 3 minutes	After 9 minutes	After 15 minutes	After 60 minutes
cracker + enzyme + buffer	5 7 9	high/none moderate/moderate high/none	high/none low/high high/none	high/low none/high high/low	moderate/moderate none/high moderate/moderate
cracker + water + buffer	5 7 9	high/none high/none high/none	high/none high/none high/none	high/none high/none high/none	high/none high/none high/none

Experiment 2

To test the effects of temperature on enzyme activity rate, one cracker and a standard amount of enzyme were placed in three beakers, each kept at different temperatures. This was also repeated using standard amounts of water in place of the enzyme. All tests were carried out at optimal pH. Starch and sugar levels (starch/sugar) from selected samples are shown in Table 2.

Table 2

Contents of Beakers	Temperatures	Levels of Starch/Sugar			
		After 3 minutes	After 9 minutes	After 15 minutes	After 60 minutes
cracker + enzyme	25°C 37°C 45°C	high/none moderate/moderate high/none	high/none low/high high/none	high/low none/high high/low	moderate/moderate none/high moderate/moderate
cracker + water	25°C 37°C 45°C	high/none high/none high/none	high/none high/none high/none	high/none high/none high/none	high/none high/none high/none

49. Under what conditions does salivary amylase appear to work best?

A. Any pH level greater than 5 and any temperature greater than 25°C
B. Any pH level greater than 5 and any temperature less than 45°C
C. pH level of 9 and temperature equals 37°C
D. pH level of 7 and temperature equals 37°C

50. The ingredient used as a control for both experiments is the:

F. cracker.
G. water.
H. enzyme.
J. starch/sugar level.

51. Which of the following hypotheses is supported by the results of Experiment 1?

A. At the appropriate pH, water can break down starch, but at a slower rate than salivary amylase can.
B. At any one-time interval, no differences in the effects of the three buffers on salivary amylase activity should be detectable.
C. Salivary amylase can show activity at each of the three pH levels tested.
D. The duration of time in which starch and enzyme remain in the beakers should have no effect on the amount of sugar produced.

52. Which of the following experimental designs would test the hypothesis that enzyme concentration can affect the rate of starch digestion?

F. Using the same pH, temperature, and enzyme levels in all beakers, test additional samples at 90 minutes, 120 minutes, and 240 minutes.
G. Using different pH, temperature, and enzyme levels in all beakers, test additional samples at 90 minutes, 120 minutes, and 240 minutes.
H. Using the same pH and temperatures in all beakers, test additional samples with the enzyme at one-half the strength, two times the strength, and four times the strength.
J. Using the same pH, temperature, and enzyme levels in all beakers, test additional samples after stirring for 3 minutes, 9 minutes, 15 minutes, and 60 minutes.

53. In Experiment 2, an additional beaker was tested at 70°C (cracker + enzyme). After 60 minutes, the sample showed high levels of starch and no sugar. Which of the following best explains this result?

A. All the starch was destroyed at this high temperature.
B. The enzyme does not work at all at this high temperature.
C. Starch cannot be detected at this high temperature.
D. Iodine and sugar indicators cannot function properly at this high temperature.

54. On the basis of the results of Experiment 1, what would probably occur if Experiment 2 were carried out at a pH level of 5?

F. Digestion of starch to sugar would slowly begin in the beakers containing crackers plus water.
G. Overall, digestion of starch to sugar would probably take place less efficiently.
H. Overall, digestion of starch to sugar would probably take place more efficiently.
J. Results would not change.

Passage IX

What will the end of the universe be like? Two opposing views are presented.

Scientist 1

The universe will die out with a whimper because the energy of the big bang that created the universe will spread itself out over larger and larger regions of space. Since there is only so much energy in the universe, every cubic foot must hold, on the average, less energy as time goes on. In the end everything will get so cold that all motion will stop. That will be the true end of time.

Scientist 2

The idea that the universe will spread itself too thin and freeze is seriously flawed. Such theories do not take into account the gravitational attractions of the bits of matter in the universe for each other. Gravity can act as a cosmic glue to keep the universe from dissolving into nothingness.

55. Which of the following is a major assumption of Scientist 1?

A. All matter consists of atoms.
B. There is a limited amount of energy in the universe.
C. Gravity does not exist in interstellar space.
D. The universe is contracting.

56. Which of the following facts, if true, does not help Scientist 2's hypothesis?

F. It is shown that the galaxies are moving away from each other with a constant speed.
G. It is shown that the galaxies are moving towards each other with a constant speed.
H. It is shown that the galaxies are moving towards each other with a constant acceleration.
J. It is shown that the galaxies are not moving at all relative to each other.

57. It has been calculated that if the universe has a mass greater than or equal to m, then the universe will eventually collapse on itself. Scientist 1 would likely say that the mass of the universe:

A. is equal to m.
B. is less than or equal to m.
C. is greater than m.
D. is less than m.

58. If Scientist 2 claims that the universe is contracting, what would he expect the average temperature of the universe to be in 10 billion years?

F. Higher than now
G. Lower than now
H. Same as now
J. No comparison is possible

59. What must be true about the energy content of the universe if Scientist 1 is correct?

A. It is increasing.
B. It is decreasing.
C. It is a constant.
D. It increased at the moment of the big bang, and decreased afterwards.

60. What would happen if the forces moving the galaxies farther out were exactly balanced by the forces pulling them together?

F. The galaxies would stop moving.
G. The galaxies would move in a straight line with constant speed.
H. The galaxies would move in a straight line with constant acceleration.
J. The galaxies would move back and forth in a straight line.

Passage X

A scientist investigated the number of fossils per cubic foot through several feet in a quarry. The results are presented below.

Layer	Fish	Shells	Plants	Land Reptile
1 (TOP)	0	0	3	1
2	0	1	8	2
3	1	10	4	0
4	5	18	1	0
5	7	20	0	0

61. When was the site most likely above water?

A. During the formation of Layers 1 and 2
B. During the formation of Layers 2 and 3
C. During the formation of Layers 1 and 4
D. During the formation of Layer 3

62. Was the quarry site most recently above or below water?

F. Above
G. Below
H. Borderline
J. Cannot be determined from the given information

63. What assumption is made to relate the fossil record to the surrounding environment?

A. No assumption
B. That fossils do not affect the environment
C. That the fossils are mostly from plants and animals that lived in the region
D. That only animal fossils are important

64. No trilobite fossils were found. This proves:

F. that no trilobites were in the region.
G. that the layers were formed before trilobites existed.
H. that the layers were formed after the trilobites died out.
J. nothing about the presence of the trilobite in the region.

65. A nautilus shell was found in Layer 3. This proves that:

A. Layer 3 formed while the nautilus still existed.
B. Layer 3 is newer than Layer 2.
C. Layer 3 is older than Layer 2.
D. the nautilus once lived on land.

66. Where will the newest layer form?

F. Under Layer 4
G. Over Layer 1
H. Across all the layers
J. Layers no longer form

Passage XI

Using electrical circuits, three experiments were performed to investigate the relationship between voltage (olts), resistance (ohms) (total resistance equals sum of individual resistances), and current (amperes). Each experiment was set up with the following circuit design:

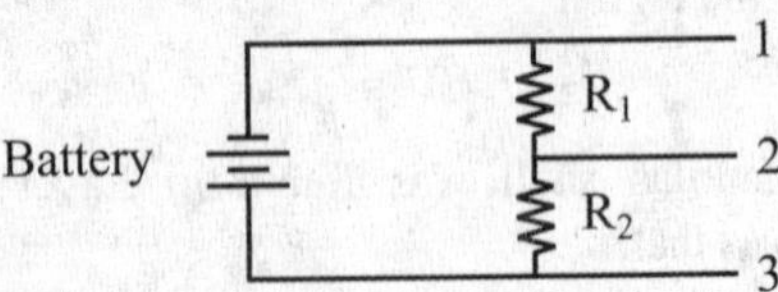

Experiment 1

Using a 6-volt battery (far left), and two 1,000-ohm resistors (R_1 and R_2), the measured voltages between points 1 and 2 and between points 2 and 3 were 3 volts each.

Experiment 2

When the battery voltage was increased to 12 volts, and the resistors were kept the same (1,000 ohms each), the measured voltages between points 1 and 2 and between points 2 and 3 were 6 volts each.

Experiment 3

Using the original 6-volt battery, R_1 was replaced with a 2,000-ohm resistor. The voltages measured between points 1 and 2 and between points 2 and 3 were 4 volts and 2 volts, respectively.

67. Judging from the results in Experiment 1 and Experiment 2, if the battery voltage were changed to 1.5 volts, what voltage would be expected between point 1 and point 2?

A. 0.75 volts
B. 1.5 volts
C. 3.0 volts
D. 6.0 volts

68. The experimenter studies the measurement made in the previous question, as well as those made earlier in Experiments 1, 2, and 3, and hypothesizes that:

F. voltage measured across a resistor is inversely proportional to the value of that resistor.
G. voltage measured across a resistor is directly proportional to the value of that resistor.
H. voltage measured across a resistor is not related to the value of that resistor.
J. voltage measured across a resistor equals the battery voltage.

69. When the experimenter recorded the current in the circuit of Experiment 1, it measured 0.003 amperes. In Experiment 3, however, the current measured 0.002 amperes. These results show that current and total resistances are:

A. directly proportional.
B. inversely proportional.
C. equal.
D. unrelated.

70. Which of the following formulas for the current in the circuit best summarizes the above results? (The battery voltage is given by V_b and the total resistance is given by R.)

F. $V_b R$

G. $\frac{R}{V_b}$

H. $\frac{V_b}{R}$

J. $V_b + R$

71. A new circuit is set up, similar in design to those in the experiments. The battery voltage and the size of the resistors are unknown, but the current measures 0.001 amperes. If the battery voltage is doubled and one of the two resistors is replaced with one having a smaller value, which answer most accurately describes the new current?

A. It will be smaller than 0.001.
B. It will be unchanged.
C. It will be greater than 0.001.
D. Cannot be determined from the given information

72. Which of the following single changes to Experiment 2 would produce a current of 0.004 amperes?

F. Decrease the voltage to 8 volts.
G. Increase the resistance to 3,000 ohms.
H. Neither change will create a current of 0.004 amperes.
J. Either change will create a current of 0.004 amperes.

STRATEGY SUMMARY SHEET

GENERAL STRATEGIES: Science items test your reasoning skills, not your scientific knowledge. So, most of the passages have all of the information that you will need to answer the items. In some cases, background information at the level of your high school general science courses is required, but do not assume data that is not given. The following are general strategies for the Science Test:

1. Before reading any Science passage, *quickly glance over all of the passages and code them according to passage-type* in order to determine the order in which you will attack them. Identifying and coding the passages should take no more than five seconds each.

2. *Do NOT preview the item stems.* Since the Science item stems tend to be confusing without having first read the corresponding passage, previewing them will only confuse you and slow you down.

3. It is important to only *read the passage thoroughly once*, rather than to skim over it several times. The material can be difficult to understand; thus, it is important to read thoughtfully and carefully. *Be an active reader.* Use your pencil to underline key words and points of information. That way, you will be able to locate them easily when answering the items.

4. When a Science passage includes tables or graphs, make sure that you *read and understand the labels* on axes, columns, and rows. You need to know what information is being presented and what units of measure are being used.

5. Many passages will contain much more information than you need to answer a particular item. In your search for a logical conclusion, *do not be misled by data that does not relate to the item at hand.*

6. In Data Representation passages, tables and graphs present results, often of observations or experiments. Corresponding items will usually ask you to spot patterns in the data, so *look for trends*, such as upward movement, downward movement, inverse variation, etc.

7. The experiments described in Research Summary passages are based on scientific assumptions. However, if an assumption is faulty, the experiment may not prove what it claims, and conclusions drawn from it may therefore be invalid. So, for items that ask about the validity of a scientific conclusion, *consider the validity of any underlying assumptions.*

8. The arguments presented in Conflicting Viewpoints passages are also based on scientific assumptions. Again, *if the assumption is wrong, the entire argument is open to challenge.* Assumptions that are based on scientific fact add strength to an argument; faulty assumptions weaken an argument.

9. Offering the assumptions that you started with as proof of your argument is called circular reasoning, and this type of proof is not acceptable. For that reason, any conclusions discussed in Science passages or offered as answer choices must be based on additional evidence (e.g., experiments) to be valid. *Beware of any conclusions that are nothing more than a restatement of an underlying premise.*

10. All of the information that you need to answer the items is provided in the passage—do not infer any information that is not given or relate any previous experience to the passage. *Pay attention to material noted with an asterisk.*

11. *Transcribe your answers from the test booklet to the answer sheet in groups (by passage).* However, when you arrive at the last passage, transcribe each answer as it is determined.

STRATEGIES FOR EACH PASSAGE-TYPE:

- **Data Representation Passages:** When given data in the form of a graph or a chart, pay particular attention to the scale, units, legend, and other noted information.
- **Research Summary Passages:** When given multiple experiments, identify the controls and variables. Note that the controls must remain the same and that variables can only change one at a time in all experiments.
- **Conflicting Viewpoints Passages:** When given two points of view on a topic, identify the main points of difference and the logical value of each argument. After you understand the nature of the passage, attack the items.

STRATEGIES FOR EACH ITEM-TYPE:

- **Comprehension Items:** Recognize basic concepts. Read carefully. Make sure that your answers consider appropriate scales and units. Also, note the difference between absolute and percentage changes.
- **Analysis Items:** Identify relationships and trends. Pay particular attention to direct and inverse relationships.
- **Application Items:** Draw conclusions, predict outcomes, and synthesize new information. In answering Application items, beware of the following terms: "all," "none," "always," and "never." Remember that a single case of contradictory evidence is all that is necessary to disprove an absolute theory.

NOTES: ____________________

Writing

COURSE CONCEPT OUTLINE

What You Absolutely Must Know

7. Punctuate and Spell Correctly
8. Write Clearly, Concisely, and Legibly
9. Proofread the Essay

III. Quizzes (p. 306)

A. Quiz I (Essay Prompt, p. 306)

B. Quiz II (Essay Prompt, p. 310)

C. Quiz III (Essay Prompt, p. 314)

IV. Strategy Summary Sheet (p. 318)

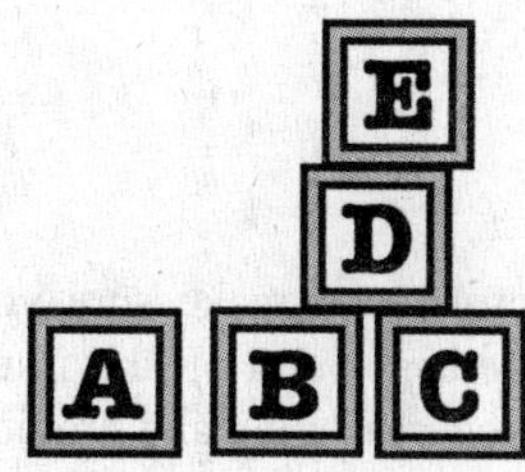

BASICS

The Writing Test will assess in broad terms your ability to develop and express ideas in writing. It is not intended to evaluate if you'd be a good novelist or how well you'd write if given time to do research in a library or on the web, writing several drafts before submitting a final version. In short, you will produce an on-demand piece of writing that will likely be of rough draft quality.

The Writing Test is also not intended to test your mastery of any body of knowledge. The topic will be sufficiently broad so that arguments and explanations can be drawn from personal experience; for example, the topic might ask you to express your opinions about sports, music, psychology, current events, or even modern technology such as "twittering" or video games.

The essay topic will be described as a "prompt." The word "prompt" was chosen because it indicates that the topic is really just an *excuse* or *opportunity* for you to write something. The test could just as easily say, "During the next thirty minutes, write an essay on anything of interest to you." However, the readers would then have to deal with essays on an unwieldy number of topics; the prompt keeps everyone more or less on the same page.

Essays are scored *holistically*, which means they are given a grade based on the overall impression created. Bonus points are not awarded for a well-turned phrase, and specific points are not deducted for specific grammatical mistakes (though consistently poor grammar that interferes with meaning will affect the essay score). All essays are read by two graders, and each grader assigns a score of "1" to "6" (an essay will receive a "0" if it is off-topic or does not respond to the prompt). The two scores are combined to produce a subscore between "2" and "12." The essay score is then combined with your English Test score to produce a Combined English/Writing scale score from "1" to "36." Your Essay score will not affect your English Test score. The Combined English/Writing score and the Writing Test score will be reported in addition to the English, Math, Reading, and Science scores.

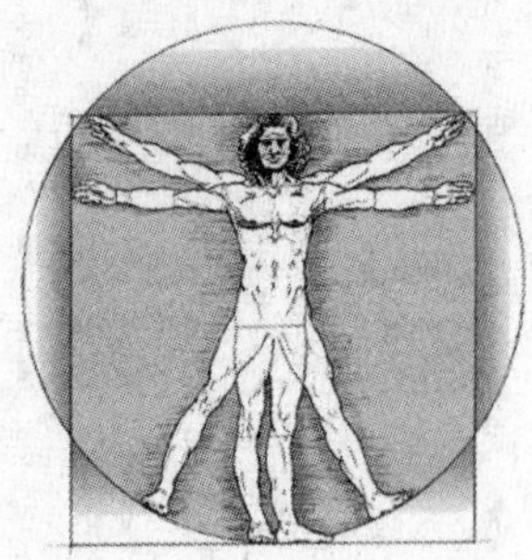

ANATOMY

DIRECTIONS: You have 30 minutes to plan and write an essay. Read the prompt carefully and make sure you understand the instructions. A successful essay will have the following features: it will take a position on the issue presented in the writing prompt; it will maintain a consistent focus on the topic; it will use logical reasoning and provide supporting ideas; it will present ideas in an organized manner; and, finally, it will include clear and effective language in accordance with the conventions of standard written English.

> In some schools, teachers are debating whether students should be given "must read" lists for summer break. These lists would include a number of books, plays, and/or short stories, and students would be required to submit reports upon returning to school for the fall semester. Some educators think this would be a good idea because students would be exposed to additional readings in literature. They also believe that the less-structured summer break would provide students with the opportunity to enjoy reading more than they would during the school year, thereby encouraging students to read more on their own. Other educators think the requirement would not be a good idea because students would perceive the requirement as burdensome and, therefore, be unlikely to enjoy the reading. Additionally, these educators argue that students' summer breaks already have too many activities and too much structure. Do you think that schools should assign summer reading to their students?
>
> In your essay, take a position on this issue. You can write about either point of view presented here, or you can present a different point of view on this topic. Support your position with relevant reasons and/or examples from your own experience, observations, or reading.

Notice that the prompt does not test a specific body of knowledge. For example, it does not ask "What were the causes of World War II?" or "What is the best recipe for chocolate cake?" Also, notice that the prompt is constructed so you can provide a very successful response based simply on your own personal experience. Specifically, you're a student who reads books and who has a summer break; and, most importantly, you certainly have an opinion about whether you think required reading during the summer is a good idea. Finally, notice that the prompt provides you with encouragement and points you in the right direction. It asks you a question, and all you need to do is respond to the question and meet the requirements outlined above. These requirements will be discussed in more detail later in the Writing Lesson.

PACING

There is one essay prompt, and there is a 30-minute time limit. During the 30 minutes, you must read the prompt, formulate a position, outline your argument or analysis, write your essay, and proofread your essay. Here is a suggested breakdown for those tasks:

Task	*Time to Execute*	*Time Remaining*
Read the prompt	1 minute	29 minutes
Formulate your position	1 minute	28 minutes
Outline your essay	2 minutes	26 minutes
Write the introduction	2 minutes	24 minutes
Write the first paragraph	6-7 minutes	17-18 minutes
Write the second paragraph	6-7 minutes	10-12 minutes
Write the third paragraph	6-7 minutes	3-6 minutes
Write the conclusion	2 minutes	1-4 minutes
Proofread your essay	1-4 minutes	0 minutes

If you follow this approximate schedule, it is likely your essay will score at least an "8." After all, your essay will include an introduction that states your position, three supporting paragraphs (each of which will provide a specific reason in support of your position), and a brief conclusion that clearly expresses your point of view. Obviously, if your essay is also expressed in clear and precise language, and if it does not include any major grammatical errors, you will likely receive an even higher score.

TIME TRIAL

Essay
Time—10 minutes

DIRECTIONS: Read the following topic, and write a brief response.

In some high schools, many teachers and parents have encouraged the school to adopt a dress code that sets guidelines for what students can wear in the school building. Some teachers and parents support a dress code because they think it will improve the learning environment in the school. Other teachers and parents do not support a dress code because they think it restricts the individual student's freedom of expression. In your opinion, should high schools adopt dress codes for students?

In your essay, take a position on this issue. You can write about either point of view presented here, or you can present a different point of view on this topic. Support your position with relevant reasons and/or examples from your own experience, observations, or reading.

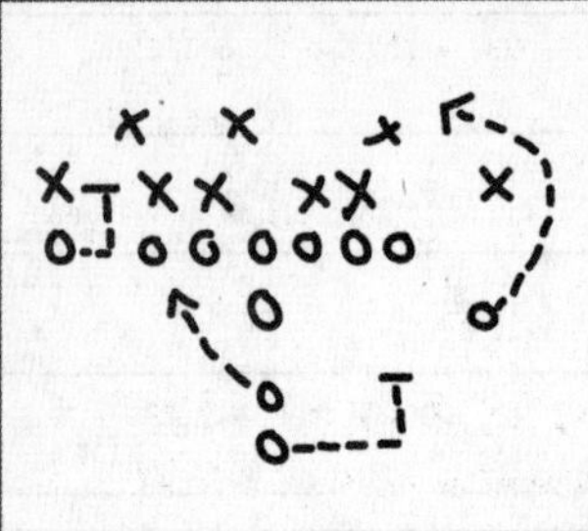

GAME PLAN

Respond to the Specific Prompt

Write on the topic that is presented. If you write an essay that is off-topic, your essay will automatically receive a "0" because it will be considered "not responsive."

Write Legibly

Write clearly and legibly. If you write an essay that is illegible, your essay will automatically receive a "0." Readers cannot give a grade to what they cannot read. So, if your handwriting is hard to read, take a little extra time and try printing.

Don't Copy the Prompt

Do not copy the prompt onto the lined paper. The readers know the topic, and it is already written on the page. If you copy the prompt onto the lined paper, it looks like you're simply trying to fill up space.

Don't Skip Lines

Do not skip lines when writing your essay on the lined paper. You should be able to make your essay legible without skipping lines. If you skip lines, it looks like you're trying to "pad" your essay to make it look longer.

Use a Pencil

Write your essay in pencil. Do not use a pen. Any essay written in pen will automatically receive a "0."

Be Specific

When writing your essay, be specific. Avoid vague generalizations. For example, here are a few sentences that are weak because they are too vague:

"Perfection in house painting is very time-consuming and requires a lot of hard work. You just can't do it in a short time; you've got to invest a lot of effort."

If you include specific details, the same point can be made much more persuasively. For example, here is the same argument about house painting but made with specific details:

"House painting requires attention to details. You have to prepare the surface by scraping away all old and loose paint and carefully washing it. You have to put down hundreds of strips of masking tape to protect those areas that should not receive paint, like glass panes, trim to be painted a second color, and fixtures. You have to apply a primer, then a base coat, and then the finish coat. Finally, you have to apply the second color and clean up all the mistakes. A perfect paint job would take 6 months or longer, and the cost would be prohibitive. That is why when you look closely you will always see imperfections."

As you can see, the response is much more compelling because the point of view is supported by specific details. Specific details are frequently the difference between an essay that receives a "2" or "3" and an essay that receives a "4" or "5."

The following essay topic will be used during the Writing Lesson to illustrate proper essay development and writing skills. Follow along with your instructor to outline and develop sample responses to the prompts. Sample essay responses begin on page 638.

DIRECTIONS: Read the following prompt and assignment. Then use the space provided below to create an outline for an essay that responds to the prompt. Your outline should include a thesis statement, a topic sentence for each paragraph of your essay, and examples or details that will appear in each paragraph. After your outline is complete, use the lined pages that follow to write an essay that responds to the assignment. Use your outline as a guide.

> Residents of rural areas often wonder why people would voluntarily choose to live in a large city, and they insist that rural life—with its open spaces, relative freedom from worries about crime, and healthful living conditions—is preferable. Conversely, residents of urban areas say that city life—with access to public transportation, cultural amenities, and many entertainment opportunities—is preferable. Which do you find more compelling—the belief that the quality of life is greater in urban areas, or the belief that the quality of life is greater in rural areas?
>
> In your essay, take a position on this issue. You can write about either point of view presented here, or you can present a different point of view on this topic. Support your position with relevant reasons and/or examples from your own experience, observations, or reading.

ESSAY OUTLINE

This section contains three Writing quizzes. Complete each quiz under timed conditions. Sample essay responses begin on page 639.

Quiz I *(1 prompt; 30 minutes)*

DIRECTIONS: You have 30 minutes to plan and write an essay. Read the prompt carefully and make sure you understand the instructions. A successful essay will have the following features: it will take a position on the issue presented in the writing prompt; it will maintain a consistent focus on the topic; it will use logical reasoning and provide supporting ideas; it will present ideas in an organized manner; and, finally, it will include clear and effective language in accordance with the conventions of standard written English.

Some schools and districts have eliminated study hall for their students. In general, schools and districts have taken this step so students can take additional electives and substantive subjects. Though students might have slightly more work to complete at home, it is argued that they will leave school as more well-rounded individuals due to the additional knowledge learned in these extra classes. Proponents of study hall argue that study hall provides an environment that is conducive to learning for students who suffer from time constraints at home. They argue that some students may not have the luxury to complete homework assignments at home due to work or extra-curricular activities. Finally, they argue that the core classes are more important than elective courses in developing a student's future prospects; therefore, they argue, it is important to provide a quiet learning environment for students who cannot complete core class assignments at home. In your opinion, should schools and districts eliminate study hall for their students?

In your essay, take a position on this issue. You can write about either point of view presented here, or you can present a different point of view on this topic. Support your position with relevant reasons and/or examples from your own experience, observations, or reading.

ESSAY OUTLINE

Quiz II *(1 prompt; 30 minutes)*

DIRECTIONS: You have 30 minutes to plan and write an essay. Read the prompt carefully and make sure you understand the instructions. A successful essay will have the following features: it will take a position on the issue presented in the writing prompt; it will maintain a consistent focus on the topic; it will use logical reasoning and provide supporting ideas; it will present ideas in an organized manner; and, finally, it will include clear and effective language in accordance with the conventions of standard written English.

> In some countries, upon graduating from or leaving high school, young people are required to perform 24 months of compulsory service. A choice is offered between military service and community service. Some people think universal compulsory service is a good idea because young people learn valuable lessons from the experience. Other people think that required service engenders resentment so that no important civic lesson is learned. In your opinion, should all young people be required to participate in some form of universal compulsory service?
>
> In your essay, take a position on this issue. You can write about either point of view presented here, or you can present a different point of view on this topic. Support your position with relevant reasons and/or examples from your own experience, observations, or reading.

ESSAY OUTLINE

Quiz III *(1 prompt; 30 minutes)*

DIRECTIONS: You have 30 minutes to plan and write an essay. Read the prompt carefully and make sure you understand the instructions. A successful essay will have the following features: it will take a position on the issue presented in the writing prompt; it will maintain a consistent focus on the topic; it will use logical reasoning and provide supporting ideas; it will present ideas in an organized manner; and, finally, it will include clear and effective language in accordance with the conventions of standard written English.

> Some schools, notably military academies, have honor codes that not only prohibit cheating but that also require students to inform authorities of any cheating of which they might be aware. Some teachers and administrators think that all schools should have similar honor codes because these codes teach the virtue of personal integrity and reinforce a sense of responsibility among students toward one another. Other teachers and administrators argue that honor codes are often ineffective and that they require students to make impossible choices between loyalty to friends and the demands of a code. In your opinion, should schools adopt honor codes that cover all students?
>
> In your essay, take a position on this issue. You can write about either point of view presented here, or you can present a different point of view on this topic. Support your position with relevant reasons and/or examples from your own experience, observations, or reading.

ESSAY OUTLINE

STRATEGY SUMMARY SHEET

GENERAL STRATEGIES:

1. Begin with the prompt.
2. Write only on the assigned topic. Writing on any other topic will result in a score of 0.
3. Do not try to do too much. Try to mentally limit the scope of your topic.
4. Organize your thoughts and write an outline before beginning the essay. Do not spend more than two minutes writing the outline.
   a) Familiarize yourself with the essay prompt and assignment.
   b) Develop a point of view.
   c) Develop a thesis.
   d) Identify two to four important points.
   e) Decide on the order of presentation of the major points.
5. Organize ideas into paragraphs.
   a) Introduction
   b) Two to Four Body Paragraphs
   c) Conclusion
6. Write grammatically.
7. Write clearly, concisely, and legibly.
8. Punctuate and spell correctly.
9. Spend a few minutes proofreading your essay.

NOTES: ____________________

Practice Test Reinforcement

Objectives:

Complete four full-length ACT® tests to reinforce everything you've learned in your course.

Work through the tests either all at once or by section to highlight specific skills and concepts.

Snapshot of Practice Test Reinforcement:

In this part of the book, you will have the opportunity to apply everything that you have learned throughout the course. Each of the four practice tests has been arranged in an order and with a frequency that approximates the real ACT® test. The Self-Guided Practice Test will allow you to work through the test with some guidance before tackling a practice test that functions like the real exam. Timed Practice Tests I-III will help reinforce the test content, help you become more comfortable with timing and pacing, reduce your test anxiety, and give you the chance to practice using alternative test-taking strategies.

Self-Guided Practice Test

1 1 1 1 1 1 1 1 1 1 1 1

ENGLISH TEST

75 Items

DIRECTIONS: In the passages below, certain parts of the sentences have been underlined and numbered. In the right-hand column, you will find different ways of writing each underlined part; the original version is indicated by the "NO CHANGE" option. For each item, select the choice that best expresses the intended idea, is most acceptable in standard written English, or is most consistent with the overall tone and style of the passage.

There are also items that ask about a section of the passage or the passage as a whole. These items do not refer to an underlined portion of the passage; these items are preceded by statements that are enclosed in boxes.

Read the passage through once before you begin to answer the accompanying items. Finding the answers to certain items may depend on looking at material that appears several sentences beyond the item. So, be sure that you have read far enough ahead before you select your answer choice.

PASSAGE I

An American Christmas

As befits a nation made up of immigrants from all over the Christian world, Americans have no distinctive Christmas symbols we (1) have taken the symbols of all the nations and made them our own. The Christmas tree, the holly and the ivy, the mistletoe, the exchange of gifts, the myth of Santa Claus, the carols of all nations, the plum pudding, and the wassail bowl are all elements in the American Christmas of the early

1. **A.** NO CHANGE
   B. symbols but, we
   C. symbols; but we
   D. symbols: but we

1. **(C)** ***English/Usage and Mechanics/Punctuation/Semicolons.*** The original sentence is incorrect because two independent clauses are spliced together. The two clauses could be split into separate sentences; but if they are going to be a single sentence, they must be joined with a conjunction and appropriate punctuation. (C) uses the second approach. In this case, a semicolon is a good choice for punctuation because the first clause already includes a dependent element joined by a comma. The stronger semicolon will alert the reader to the main break in the logic of the sentence. In (B), a commas, if used, would have to come before, not after, the conjunction "but." Finally, (D) is not the appropriate use of a colon.

twenty-first century as we know it today. Though we have no Christmas symbols of our own, the American Christmas still has a distinctive aura by virtue of two character elements.

2. F. NO CHANGE
G. as it is known today
H. known as it is today
J. OMIT the underlined portion.

2. (J) ***English/Rhetorical Skills/Style/Conciseness.*** The original sentence is incorrect because the underlined portion provides information that is simply unnecessary. It adds no new or required information to the sentence; and, most importantly, the sentence is improved if it is removed. (J) is the correct answer choice because it omits the underlined portion.

3. A. NO CHANGE
B. characters
C. characterized
D. characteristic

3. (D) ***English/Usage and Mechanics/Grammar and Usage/Adjectives versus Adverbs.*** The original sentence is incorrect because it includes a usage error. As currently written, the sentence has "character" (a noun) modifying "elements" (a noun). However, a noun cannot modify a noun; only an adjective can modify a noun. (D) is the correct answer choice because it supplies the correct adjective ("characteristic," which means distinctive) for modifying "elements."

The first of these is when, as might be expected in a nation as dedicated to the carrying on of business as the American nation, the dominant role of the Christmas festivities has come to serve as a stimulus to retail business. The themes of Christmas advertising begin to appear as early as September, and the open

4. F. NO CHANGE
G. is that
H. is which
J. is where

4. (G) ***English/Usage and Mechanics/Grammar and Usage/Diction.*** The original sentence is incorrect because it is not idiomatic. Specifically, the phrase "is when" is not an acceptable idiom. The correct, idiomatic phrase is "is that." (G) is the correct answer because it supplies the required phrase.

5. A. NO CHANGE
B. have come
C. having come
D. comes

5. (A) ***English/Usage and Mechanics/No Change.*** The original sentence is correct. The singular

verb phrase ("has come") agrees with the singular subject ("the dominant role") of the sentence. In addition, it also supplies the past tense verb form required here. As for the other answer choices, (B) is incorrect because a plural verb phrase ("have come") does not agree with a singular subject ("the dominant role"). (C) is incorrect because a gerund verb phrase ("having come") cannot serve as the main verb of an independent clause. (D) is incorrect because a present tense verb ("comes") is not needed here; instead, a past tense verb is required.

season on Christmas shopping began[6] in November.

6. **F.** NO CHANGE
   G. beginning
   H. begins
   J. will begin

6. **(H)** ***English/Usage and Mechanics/Grammar and Usage/Verb Tense.*** The original sentence is incorrect because it includes a verb tense error. The past tense "began" is inconsistent with the time frame of the sentence, as indicated by the present tense "begin" used earlier. (The author is describing the current situation and how things are now.) (H) corrects the error by using the present tense verb "begins." (J) is incorrect because "will begin" is the future tense and fails to correct the verb tense inconsistency. Finally, as for (G), "beginning" is the participle of the verb "to begin." The participle, or "-ing" form, cannot be used as the main verb of the clause.

Fifty years ago, Thanksgiving Day was regarded like it was[7] the opening day of the season for Christmas shopping; today, the season opens immediately after Halloween. Thus, virtually a whole month has been

7. **A.** NO CHANGE
   B. like as
   C. as
   D. like

7. **(C)** ***English/Usage and Mechanics/Grammar and Usage/Diction.*** The original sentence is incorrect because it includes a word choice error. Specifically, "like it was" is an awkward, needlessly wordy, and non-standard phrase that means the same thing as "as." (C) is the correct answer choice because it supplies the simple and more direct word that is required here. As for the other answer choices, (B) and (D) are both incorrect because they are simply not idiomatic phrases; in other words, neither "regarded like…" nor "regarded like as" are recognized as acceptable ways of making a comparison.

added to the Christmas season—for shopping purposes.
8

8. Which of the following would NOT be an acceptable way of punctuating the underlined part?

F. season—for (NO CHANGE)
G. season. For
H. season, for
J. season: for

8. (G) ***English/Usage and Mechanics/Sentence Structure/Fragments.*** The original sentence is acceptable as are (H) and (J). (G), however, is not acceptable because the period would create a sentence fragment of the word grouping introduced by "For." Notice that each acceptable punctuation alternative gives the sentence a slightly difference emphasis. The dash strongly emphasizes the point that the purpose is "shopping," while no punctuation makes the same point with relatively little emphasis. Using a comma stresses the point to a degree somewhere between the dash and no punctuation at all. All are acceptable with the difference being the author's intended meaning.

Second, the nations season of Christmas festivities has insensibly combined with the New Year's celebration into one lengthened period of Saturnalia. This starts with office parties a few days
9

9. A. NO CHANGE
B. nation's
C. nations'
D. nation

9. (B) ***English/Usage and Mechanics/Punctuation/Apostrophes.*** The original sentence is incorrect because it includes a punctuation error. Specifically, an apostrophe is required to show possession. In this instance, the celebration belongs to the nation. As for the other answer choices, (C) is incorrect because the apostrophe makes "nation" plural when the singular is intended by the author. (D) is incorrect for the same reason as the original.

before Christmas continues on Christmas Eve, now the occasion in America of one of two large-scale revels that mark the season, and continues in spirited euphoria until New Year's Eve, the second of the large-scale revels. New Year's Day is spent resting, possibly
10

10. F. NO CHANGE
G. Christmas, continues
H. as Christmas continues
J. Christmas as continues

10. (G) ***English/Usage and Mechanics/Punctuation/Commas.*** The original sentence is incorrect because it includes a punctuation error. Specifically, the sentence includes a series of singular verbs ("starts…continues…continues")

which all agree with the singular subject ("This") of the sentence. The second and third verbs should be preceded by a comma. (G) is the correct answer choice because it supplies the required punctuation. As for the other answer choices, (H) and (J) are both incorrect because they result in sentences that are grammatically incorrect as well as incomprehensible.

regretting <u>somebody's</u> [11] excesses, and <u>watching football games on television</u> [12].

11. A. NO CHANGE
B. everyone's
C. someone's
D. one's

11. (D) ***English/Usage and Mechanics/Grammar and Usage/Pronoun Usage.*** The original sentence is incorrect because it includes a pronoun usage error. Specifically, according to the logic of the sentence, New Year's day would not be spent regretting the excesses of some unidentified person ("somebody's excesses"); instead, it would be spent regretting one's own excesses ("one's excesses"). (D) is the correct answer choice because it supplies the correct possessive pronoun. As for the other answer choices, (B) and (C) are incorrect for the same reason as the original.

12. F. NO CHANGE
G. watching, football games on television
H. watching, football games, on television
J. watching football, games on television

12. (F) ***English/Usage and Mechanics/Punctuation/Commas.*** The original sentence is correct. The comma after "excesses" correctly completes the series. No comma is needed in the underlined portion. (H) is incorrect because the pattern of commas suggests that "football games" is an appositive of "watching," but the two are not synonymous. (G) and (J) are both incorrect because the commas in these choices disrupt the logical flow of the sentence.

PASSAGE II

The Myth of a Criminal Physique

[1]

Can you spot a criminal by his physical characteristics? [13] When the science of criminology was founded in the nineteenth century, an imaginative Italian observer decided that criminals are

13. Is the use of a question appropriate to begin Paragraph 1?

    A. No, because questions are not used in formal writing.
    B. No, because the question is not answered.
    C. Yes, because it varies sentence structure and interests the reader.
    D. Yes, because an essay should always begin with a question.

13. **(C)** ***English/Rhetorical Skills/Strategy/Effective Opening Sentence.*** (C) is the correct answer choice. The question clearly introduces the main subject of the essay; in addition, it piques the reader's interest and establishes a high level of interest in the topic. As for the other answer choices, (A) is incorrect because questions are frequently used in formal writing. (B) is incorrect for two reasons: first, the passage does answer the question asked here; second, even if the passage did not answer the question, formal writing can include unanswered or unanswerable questions. Finally, (D) is incorrect because an essay does not have to begin with a question.

born that way and are distinguished by <u>certainly physical</u>[14] characteristics. They are, he claimed, "a special species, a subspecies having distinct physical mental characteristics. In general, all criminals have and long, large, protruding ears; abundant hair; a thin beard; prominent front sinuses; a protruding chin; and

14. **F.** NO CHANGE
    G. certain physically
    H. certain physical
    J. certainly physically

14. **(H)** ***English/Usage and Mechanics/Grammar and Usage/Adjectives versus Adverbs.*** The original sentence is incorrect because "certain" is intended to modify the noun phrase "physical characteristics." (H) correctly provides the adjective form "certain." (G) is incorrect because "physical" modifies the noun "characteristics" and so the adjective form is needed. As for (J), it fails to correct the original and changes "physical" to the adverb form "physically."

large cheekbones." According to his theory, murderers have [15] cold, glassy eyes, strong jaws, large cheekbones, and curly hair.

15. **A.** NO CHANGE.
B. theory murderers, have
C. theory, murderers, have
D. theory, murderers have,

15. **(A)** ***English/Usage and Mechanics/Punctuation/Commas.*** The original is correct. (B) is wrong because it deletes the commas used to signal the end of the introductory phrase and it inserts a comma between the subject and the verb (a commonly tested error). (C) also makes this second error. Finally, (D) inserts an unnecessary comma between the verb and the direct object (another commonly tested error).

[2]

But the myth does not die easily. [16] During the 1930s, a German criminologist, Gustav Aschaffenburg, declared that stout, squat people with large abdomens

16. **F.** NO CHANGE
G. easy
H. easiest
J. easier

16. **(F)** ***English/Usage and Mechanics/No Change.*** The original sentence is correct. "Easily" is an adverb that properly modifies the verb "die." As for the other answer choices, they are all incorrect because they are adjectives. Adjectives cannot modify verbs; so, (G), (H), and (J) must be incorrect.

are more like [17] to be occasional offenders, while slender builds and slight muscular development are common among habitual offenders. In the 1940s, according to writer Jessica Mitford, a group of Harvard sociologists

17. **A.** NO CHANGE
B. likely
C. likely apt
D. possible

17. **(B)** ***English/Usage and Mechanics/Grammar and Usage/Diction.*** The original sentence is incorrect due to a diction error. Specifically, "like" means "similar" or "comparable" and does not provide the meaning required here. (B) is the correct answer choice because "likely" provides the required meaning; in short, it means "probable" or "apt." As for the other answer choices, (C) is incorrect because "likely apt" is a redundant phrase; "likely" and "apt" are synonyms, so there is no reason to include both in the same phrase. Finally, (D) is incorrect because "possible" does not provide the required meaning.

who study sociology, decided that criminals are most likely to be "mesomorphs," muscular types with large trunks who walk assertively, talk noisily, and behave aggressively. The Harvard scholars warned readers to watch out for people with them.

[3]

Around about the turn of the century, a British physician made a detailed study of the faces of three

18. **F.** NO CHANGE
G. whom study sociological changes,
H. who studied sociology,
J. OMIT the underlined portion.

18. **(J)** ***English/Rhetorical Skills/Style/Conciseness.*** The original sentence is incorrect because the underlined portion is redundant. Sociologists are people "who study sociology," so there is no reason to include the underlined portion in the sentence. (J) is the correct answer choice because it makes the required correction. As for the other answer choices, (G) is incorrect for three reasons: first, it is incorrect for the same reason as the original; second, an objective pronoun ("whom") should not be used when referring to the subject ("sociologists") in a sentence; third, the comma after "changes" introduces a comma splice into the sentence. Finally, (H) is incorrect for two reasons: first, it is incorrect for the same reason as the original; second, the comma after "sociology" introduces a comma splice into the sentence.

19. **A.** NO CHANGE
B. them characteristics
C. them kind of characteristics
D. those characteristics

19. **(D)** ***English/Usage and Mechanics/Grammar and Usage/Pronoun Usage.*** The original sentence is incorrect because the pronoun "them" does not have a clear antecedent. The sentence means to refer to the characteristics listed, and for that the writer needs a plural reference. The correct choice, (D), uses the demonstrative adjective "those," which is plural, to modify the plural "characteristics." (B) and (C) both use the plural "characteristics" but exhibit low-level usage not acceptable in formal writing.

20. **F.** NO CHANGE
G. At about
H. Around
J. OMIT the underlined portion.

20. **(H)** ***English/Rhetorical Skills/Style/Idiomatic Expression.*** The original sentence is incorrect because it includes an example of non-standard English. Specifically, the phrase "Around about"

is a non-accepted or low-level substitute for "around." (H) is the correct answer choice because "around" successfully completes the sentence. As for the other answer choices, (G) is incorrect for the same reason as the original. (J) is incorrect because the initial clause would then become a fragment (rather than a fully formed introductory adverbial clause).

thousand convicts and compared[21] them with a like number of English college students, measuring the

21. **A.** NO CHANGE
B. compare
C. compares
D. comparing

21. **(A)** ***English/Usage and Mechanics/No Change.*** The original sentence is correct. "Compared" (a past tense verb) is consistent with the past tense verb ("made") used earlier in the sentence. As for the other answer choices, they are all incorrect because they are not consistent with the past tense verb used earlier in the sentence.

noses ears eyebrows and chins[22] of both groups. He could find no correlation among physical types and criminal behavior.

22. **F.** NO CHANGE
G. noses ears and eyebrows and chins
H. noses; ears; eyebrows and chins
J. noses, ears, eyebrows, and chins

22. **(J)** ***English/Usage and Mechanics/Punctuation/Commas.*** The original sentence is incorrect due to a punctuation error. Specifically, items in a list should be separated by commas (unless the items in a list themselves include commas, in which case the items should be separated by semicolons. (J) is the correct answer choice because it supplies the required punctuation. As for the other answer choices, (G) is incorrect for two reasons: first, it is incorrect for the same reason as the original; second, it inserts "and" between the second and third items in the list, whereas "and" should only appear between the third and fourth items. (H) is incorrect because, as mentioned above, items in a list should be separated by semicolons only if the items themselves include commas.

Items #23–24 ask about the preceding passage as a whole.

23. This essay was most probably excerpted from a:

A. college textbook on the history of criminology.
B. manual of techniques for forensic investigators.
C. news article on recent discoveries in police science.
D. biography of Gustav Aschaffenburg.

23. (A) ***English/Rhetorical Skills/Strategy/Audience.*** (A) is the correct answer choice. The level of detail is consistent with a textbook, and the subject is clearly the history of the study of criminals. (B) is wrong because there is not a lot of technical detail in the essay and because the writer discredits the theories discussed. (C) is wrong because the theories discussed are old, not new. (D) is incorrect because the essay focuses on criminology in general and not on Aschaffenburg specifically.

24. Choose the order of paragraph numbers that will make the essay's structure most logical.

F. NO CHANGE
G. 3, 2, 1
H. 1, 3, 2
J. 2, 3, 1

24. (H) ***English/Rhetorical Skills/Organization/ Passage-Level Structure.*** (H) is the correct answer choice. The most logical ordering of the paragraphs will put them in chronological order. Paragraph 1 refers to the nineteenth century. Paragraph 3 refers to the "turn of the century." Paragraph 2 refers to the 1930s and the 1940s.

PASSAGE III

Scientific Advances Pose Global Risks

[1]

The history of modern pollution problems <u>show</u> 25 that most have resulted from negligence and ignorance. We have an appalling tendency to interfere with nature before all of the possible consequences of our actions

25. **A.** NO CHANGE
B. show
C. shows
D. showed

25. **(C)** ***English/Usage and Mechanics/Grammar and Usage/Subject-Verb Agreement.*** The original sentence is incorrect due to an error involving agreement. Be certain to identify the actual subject of the sentence: "history," not "problems." In this sentence, "show" (a plural verb) does not agree with "history" (a singular subject). (C) is the correct answer choice because it supplies a singular verb ("shows") that agrees with the singular subject ("history") of the sentence. As for the other answer choices, (B) and (D) are incorrect because neither a passive, past tense verb ("shown") nor an active, past tense verb ("showed") are appropriate in this context. Only an active, present tense verb ("shows") is appropriate here.

have been studied <u>into completeness</u> 26. We produce and distribute radioactive substances, synthetic chemicals and fibers, and many other potent compounds before

26. **F.** NO CHANGE
G. as completely as possible
H. for completeness
J. a lot

26. **(G)** ***English/Rhetorical Skills/Style/Idiomatic Expression.*** The original sentence is incorrect because it is not idiomatic. The correct, idiomatic phrase is "as completely as possible." So, (G) is the correct answer choice. As for the other answer choices, (H) is incorrect for the same reason as the original. (J) is incorrect because the phrase "studied a lot" is an example of non-accepted or low-level usage.

fully comprehending their <u>effects</u> 27 on living organisms.

27. **A.** NO CHANGE
B. effectiveness
C. affect
D. affects

27. **(A)** ***English/Usage and Mechanics/No Change.*** The original sentence is correct. "Effects" is a plural noun which means "results," and it

supplies the meaning required in this context. As for the other answer choices, (B) is incorrect because "effectiveness" means "efficiency," which does not supply the required meaning. (C) and (D) are both incorrect because, when used as a noun, "affect" means "manner" or "attitude"; neither of those meanings is appropriate here.

Synthetic means manmade. Many of today's fashions are made with synthetic fibers. (28) Our education is dangerously incomplete.

28. **F.** NO CHANGE
G. Synthetic fibers are manmade.
H. Many of today's fashions are made with synthetic fibers.
J. OMIT the underlined portion.

28. (J) ***English/Rhetorical Skills/Strategy/Appropriate Supporting Material.*** The original sentence is incorrect because the underlined portion is redundant. It is commonly understood that "synthetic" means "artificial" or "manmade"; in addition, there is no logical reason to include the information about current fashions and synthetic fibers. (J) is the correct answer choice because it omits the unnecessary information. As for the other answer choices, (G) and (H) are both incorrect for the same reason as the original.

[2]

It will be argued that the purpose of science is to move into unknown territory; (29) to explore, and to discover. It can be said that similar risks have been taken before and that these risks are necessary to

29. **A.** NO CHANGE
B. territory:
C. territory,
D. territory

29. (C) ***English/Usage and Mechanics/Punctuation/Commas.*** The original sentence is incorrect because it includes a punctuation error. Specifically, phrases or clauses in a series should be separated by commas unless the phrases or clauses themselves contain commas; in that case, the phrases or clauses should be separated by semicolons. In this sentence, the phrases themselves do not include commas; so, commas should be used to separate them. Therefore, (C) is the correct answer choice.

technological progress. [30]

[3]

These arguments overlook an important element. [31] In the past, risks taken in the name of scientific progress were restricted to a small place and brief period of time. The effects of the processes we now

30. The writer could most effectively bolster the essay at this point by:

F. including an example of one of the risks argued by some to be necessary for technological progress.
G. adding rhetorical emphasis with the sentence "The risks are necessary."
H. briefly describing an unknown territory.
J. defining the word *science.*

30. (F) ***English/Rhetorical Skills/Strategy/Appropriate Supporting Material.*** (F) is the correct answer choice. At this point, it would be best to add a specific example of a risk that it is necessary to undertake in order to achieve technological progress. Such an example would make the author's argument more concrete and vivid for the reader. As for the other answer choices, (G) is incorrect because a rhetorical device would be less effective than a concrete example. (H) is incorrect because the topic at hand is risk and its relationship to technological progress. Finally, (J) is incorrect because the definition of "science" is commonly understood; it is not necessary to define it.

31. A. NO CHANGE
B. a important
C. importance
D. important

31. (A) ***English/Usage and Mechanics/No Change.*** The original sentence is correct. "An" is used before singular nouns or adjectives that begin with a vowel. As for the other answer choices, (B) is incorrect because "a" is used only before singular nouns or adjectives that begin with consonants. (C) is incorrect because a noun ("importance") cannot modify a noun ("element"). Finally, (D) is incorrect because an adjective that modifies a singular noun must always be preceded by an article (i.e., "a," "an," or "the").

strive to master are <u>not either</u> [32] localized nor brief. Air pollution covers vast urban areas. Ocean pollutants have been discovered in nearly every part of the world. Synthetic chemicals spread over huge stretches of

32. **F.** NO CHANGE
    G. either
    H. not neither
    J. neither

32. (J) ***English/Usage and Mechanics/Grammar and Usage/Diction.*** The original sentence is incorrect because it is not idiomatic. The correct, idiomatic phrase is "neither…nor." So, (J) is the correct answer choice. As for the other answer choices, (G) and (H) are both incorrect for the same reason as the original.

forest and farmland may remain in the soil <u>for decades and years to come</u> [33]. Radioactive pollutants will be found in the biosphere for generations. The size and

33. **A.** NO CHANGE
    B. for decades
    C. for years to come in decades
    D. for decades and years

33. (B) ***English/Rhetorical Skills/Style/Conciseness.*** The original sentence is incorrect because the underlined portion includes redundant information. Specifically, the phrase "and years to come" is unnecessary since it adds no information beyond what's already communicated by the phrase "for decades." (B) is the correct answer choice since it eliminates the superfluous phrase. As for the other answer choices, (C) is incorrect for two reasons: first, it is incorrect for the same reason as the original; second, it is also grammatically incorrect. (D) is incorrect for the same reason as the original.

<u>persistent</u> [34] of these problems have grown with the expanding power of modern science.

34. **F.** NO CHANGE
    G. persistence
    H. persevering
    J. persisting

34. (G) ***English/Usage and Mechanics/Grammar and Usage/Nouns and Noun Clauses*** and ***Sentence Structure/Faulty Parallelism.*** The original sentence is incorrect due to a lack of parallelism. Specifically, "persistent" (an adjective) is not the same part of speech as "size" (a noun). (G) is the correct answer choice because it makes the needed correction ("The size and the persistence of these problems…"). As for the other answer choices, (H) and (J) are incorrect for the same reason as the original.

[4]

One might also argue that the hazards of modern pollutants are small <u>comparison for</u> [35] the dangers associated with other human activity. No estimate of the actual harm done by smog, fallout, or chemical residues can obscure the reality that the risks are being taken before being fully understood.

[5]

The importance of these issues lies in the failure of science to predict and <u>control. Human</u> [36] intervention into natural processes. The true measure of the danger is represented by the hazards we will encounter if we enter the new age of technology without first evaluating our responsibility to the environment.

35. **A.** NO CHANGE
B. consideration for
C. comparing with
D. compared to

35. **(D)** ***English/Usage and Mechanics/Grammar and Usage/Diction.*** The original sentence is incorrect due to a word choice error. Specifically, the sentence requires a past tense verb to complete it successfully. (D) is the correct answer choice because it supplies the required verb. As for the other answer choices, (B) and (C) are both incorrect for the same reason as the original.

36. **F.** NO CHANGE
G. control human
H. control; human
J. control and human

36. **(G)** ***English/Usage and Mechanics/Sentence Structure/Fragments.*** The original is incorrect because the word grouping following the period is a fragment. (G) solves the problem by integrating the fragment into the main part of the sentence as a direct object. As for the other answer choices, (H) is incorrect for the same reason as the original. (J) is incorrect because the conjunction "and" should not appear between a verb phrase ("predict and control") and the object of that verb phrase ("human intervention into natural processes").

Items #37–38 ask about the preceding passage as a whole.

37. Choose the order of paragraph numbers that will make the essay's structure most logical.

A. NO CHANGE
B. 2, 4, 3, 1, 5
C. 1, 3, 2, 4, 5
D. 5, 1, 2, 3, 4

37. **(A)** ***English/Rhetorical Skills/Organization/ Passage-Level Structure.*** The original order is correct. Paragraph 1 introduces the topic of the entire essay. Only (A) and (C) have Paragraph 1 as the first paragraph, so eliminate (B) and (D). The only difference between (A) and (C) is whether Paragraph 2 or Paragraph 3 should come next. Paragraph 3 begins with "These arguments overlook an important element," so it should be preceded by a paragraph where arguments are made, and this is Paragraph 2. So, (A) is correct.

38. This essay was probably intended for readers who:

F. lack an understanding of the history of technology.
G. are authorities on pollution and its causes.
H. are interested in becoming more aware of our environmental problems and the possible solutions to these problems.
J. have worked with radioactive substances.

38. **(H)** ***English/Rhetorical Skills/Strategy/Audience.*** (H) is the correct answer choice. The topic of the essay is pollution problems in general, and the level of detail suggests that the essay is aimed at the average reader who is interested in becoming more aware. As for the other answer choices, (F) is incorrect because the topic of the essay is pollution problems in general (and not a history of technology). (G) is incorrect because authorities on this subject would expect a much more technical and specialized level of detail. Finally, (J) is incorrect because the topic of the essay is pollution problems in general (and not just problems related to radioactive substances).

PASSAGE IV

The Changing Scientific Workplace

[1]

Many researchers can be of greatest service to a company by <u>sticking around</u> [39] in the laboratory. A single outstanding discovery <u>may of had</u> [40] a far greater impact on the company's five-year profit picture than the activities of even the <u>most able</u> [41] administrator. It is simply good sense—and good economics—to allow qualified researchers to continue their work. Granting these researchers maximum freedom to explore their scientific ideas is also eminently good sense.

39. **A.** NO CHANGE
B. remaining
C. remaining around
D. sticking up

39. (B) ***English/Rhetorical Skills/Style/Idiomatic Expression.*** The original sentence is incorrect due to an idiomatic expression error. Specifically, "sticking around" is a non-standard or low-level usage substitute for "remaining." (B) is the correct answer choice because it supplies the word required here. As for the other answer choices, (C) and (D) are incorrect for the same reason as the original.

40. **F.** NO CHANGE
G. maybe
H. might of had
J. may have

40. (J) ***English/Usage and Mechanics/Grammar and Usage/Diction.*** The original sentence is incorrect because it confuses "of" with "have." In conversation, people often make the mistake of saying "I should of stayed in bed" but they mean "I should have stayed in bed." The error is likely due to the similarity of the sounds in spoken English, but it should not come up in writing.

41. **A.** NO CHANGE
B. most ablest
C. more ablest
D. most abled

41. (A) ***English/Usage and Mechanics/No Change.*** The original sentence is correct. The correct, superlative form of "able" is "most able." As for the other answer choices, (B), (C), and (D) are all incorrect because they do not supply the correct, superlative form of "able."

[2]

In recent <u>years however</u>[42] this theory has fallen into wide <u>disrepair</u>[43]. Companies find that many researchers continue to be highly productive throughout their careers. There is every reason to allow these researchers to continue their pioneering work.

[3]

Some years ago, the theory was rampant that after the age of about 40, the average researcher began losing <u>their</u>[44] creative spark. The chance of one making a major discovery was believed to drop off sharply. Hence, there really wasn't much point to

42. **F.** NO CHANGE
G. years, however
H. years, however,
J. years however,

42. **(H)** ***English/Usage and Mechanics/Punctuation/Commas.*** The original sentence is incorrect due to a punctuation error. Specifically, conjunctive phrases ("however," "meanwhile," and "instead") should be set off by commas when they are inserted into the sentence to signal the reader of a continuation or a reversal of thought. As for the other answer choices, they are all incorrect because they do not supply the necessary pair of commas.

43. **A.** NO CHANGE
B. argument
C. ill repute
D. disrepute

43. **(D)** ***English/Usage and Mechanics/Grammar and Usage/Diction.*** The original sentence is incorrect due an error involving word choice. Specifically, a word is required here which can be used to describe the status or reputation of an idea ("this theory"). (D) is the correct answer choice because "disrepute" means "having a bad reputation" and is commonly used to describe ideas. As for the other answer choices, (A) is incorrect because "disrepair" is not a word used to describe ideas; instead, it is used to describe physical objects (i.e., a building, a bridge, etc). (B) is incorrect because the phrase "fallen into…argument" is simply not idiomatic. Finally, (C) is incorrect because "ill repute" is not a phrase used to describe ideas; instead, it is used to describe people ("a woman of ill repute").

44. **F.** NO CHANGE
G. its
H. his or her
J. theirs

44. **(H)** ***English/Usage and Mechanics/Grammar and Usage/Pronoun Usage.*** The original sentence is incorrect due to an error in pronoun-antecedent agreement. Specifically, "their" (a

plural pronoun) does not agree with "researcher" (a singular noun). (H) is the correct answer choice because it supplies a pair of singular pronouns ("his or her") that agrees with "researcher" (a singular noun). As for the other answer choices, (G) is incorrect because "its" (an impersonal pronoun) does not agree with "researcher" (a personal noun). (J) is incorrect for the same reason as the original.

encouraging a person of 45 or 50 to do research. [45]

[4]

Companies are also convinced that the traditional guideposts in establishing salaries are not completely

45. If, at this point in the essay, the writer wanted to increase the information about creative contributions from researchers, which of the following additions would be most relevant to the passage as a whole?

A. A bibliography of books about retirement
B. A description of a few of the contributions older researchers have made to science
C. A list of today's most prominent researchers
D. A brief description of a model retirement benefits plan

45. (B) ***English/Rhetorical Skills/Strategy/Appropriate Supporting Material.*** (B) is the correct answer choice. In this paragraph, the writer presents a theory related to whether researchers make valuable discoveries after age 40. Therefore, it would be appropriate here to introduce a few contributions that older researchers have made to science. As for the other answer choices, (A) and (D) are both incorrect because they are simply irrelevant. (C) is incorrect because it is too general; again, the paragraph is about older researchers (and not researchers in general).

valid. In former years of previous times,[46] the size of a person's paycheck was determined primarily by the size of that person's annual budget. On this basis, the

46. **F.** NO CHANGE
G. of times previous
H. previously
J. OMIT the underlined portion.

46. (J) ***English/Rhetorical Skills/Style/Conciseness.*** The original sentence is incorrect because the underlined portion is redundant. Specifically, "of previous times" has a similar meaning to "in former years." (J) is the correct answer choice because it eliminates this unnecessary phrase. As for the other answer choices, (G) and (H) are incorrect for the same reason as the original.

researcher—no matter how <u>brilliant, with</u> [47] only one assistant and a limited budget made an extremely poor showing. Companies now realize that the two very

47. **A.** NO CHANGE
B. brilliant with
C. brilliant—with
D. brilliant; with

47. **(C)** ***English/Usage and Mechanics/Punctuation/Dashes.*** Dashes can be used to set off a thought to give it special emphasis. They are not used very extensively, but when they are used, the come in pairs. (C) correctly provides the following dash for the opening dash earlier in the sentence.

important criteria that must also <u>be considerable</u> [48] are a researcher's actual contributions to the company and creative potential.

48. **F.** NO CHANGE
G. be considered
H. most considerable
J. considerable of

48. **(G)** ***English/Usage and Mechanics/Grammar and Usage/Diction.*** The original sentence is incorrect due to a word choice error. Specifically, the verb phrase "be considerable" has a meaning which is not appropriate in this context: "be substantial" or "be large." (G) is the correct answer choice since the verb phrase "be considered" has the appropriate meaning: "thought about" or "considered." As for the other answer choices, (H) and (J) are incorrect because they are not verb phrases ("be considered" or "be substantial"); a verb phrase is required to complete the sentence successfully.

[5]

With today's shortage of qualified scientists, companies have more reason than ever to encourage scientists to do the work for which they are most qualified. They also have greater reason than ever to provide a laboratory environment <u>in which</u> [49] the creative processes of research can be carried out most effectively.

49. **A.** NO CHANGE
B. about which
C. of which
D. into which

49. **(A)** ***English/Usage and Mechanics/No Change.*** The original sentence is correct. "In" is the correct preposition because the creative processes take place *in* the laboratory environment. As for the other answer choices, (B) is incorrect because the creative processes do not take place *about* the laboratory environment. (C) is incorrect because the creative processes do not take place *of* the laboratory environment. (D) is incorrect because the creative processes do not take place *into* the laboratory environment.

Item #50 asks about the preceding passage as a whole.

50. Choose the order of paragraph numbers that will make the essay's structure most logical.

F. NO CHANGE
G. 1, 2, 4, 3, 5
H. 1, 2, 3, 5, 4
J. 3, 2, 1, 4, 5

50. (J) ***English/Rhetorical Skills/Organization/Passage-Level Structure.*** (J) is the correct answer choice. The most logical order will involve presenting the two main topics in a compare and contrast format. Specifically, the most logical order would present an earlier view of creativity (Paragraph 3), a contemporary view of creativity (Paragraphs 1 and 2), an earlier view of salary guideposts (Paragraph 4), and then a contemporary view of salary guideposts (Paragraph 5).

PASSAGE V

An Argument in Favor of Scientific Contributions

[1]

What are those of us <u>who</u> [51] have chosen careers in science and engineering able to do about meeting

51. A. NO CHANGE
B. we
C. we ones
D. us ones

51. (B) ***English/Usage and Mechanics/Grammar and Usage/Pronoun Usage.*** The original sentence is incorrect due to a pronoun error. Specifically, an objective pronoun ("us") should not be used when as a subject in a sentence. Instead, a subjective pronoun ("we") should be used. So, (B) is the correct answer choice. As for the other answer choices, (C) and (D) are incorrect because both "we ones" and "us ones" are low-level usage.

our current problems? [52]

[2]

Second, we can identify the many areas in which science and technology, more considerately used, can

52. **F.** NO CHANGE
G. problems.
H. problems!
J. problems;

52. **(F)** ***English/Usage and Mechanics/Punctuation/End-Stop Punctuation.*** The original sentence is correct. A question mark should always be used after a direct question. As for the other choices, (G), (H), and (J) are all incorrect because they include incorrect punctuation.

be of greatest [53] service in the future than in the past to improve the quality of life. While we can make many speeches and pass many laws, the quality of our

53. **A.** NO CHANGE
B. great
C. more great
D. greater

53. **(D)** ***English/Usage and Mechanics/Grammar and Usage/Faulty or Illogical Comparisons*** and ***Diction.*** The original sentence is incorrect due to a word choice error involving a comparison. Specifically, the superlative form of an adjective ("greatest") is not typically used when comparing two ideas or concepts ("service in the future" and "service in the past"). Instead, the comparative form ("greater") is used. So, (D) is the correct answer choice. As for the other answer choices, (B) is incorrect because it is not the comparative form of an adjective. (C) is incorrect because it is a faulty version of "greater."

environment will be improved only in [54] better knowledge and better application of that knowledge.

54. **F.** NO CHANGE
G. through
H. until
J. inside

54. **(G)** ***English/Usage and Mechanics/Grammar and Usage/Diction.*** The original sentence is incorrect due to a word choice error. Specifically, The preposition "in" does not fit the context; "through," however, does. And neither "until" nor "inside" has an acceptable meaning.

[3]

Third, we can recognize that much of the dissatisfaction we suffer today results from our very successes of former years in the past. [55] We have been so eminently successful in attaining material goals that

55. **A.** NO CHANGE
B. of the past
C. being in the past
D. OMIT the underlined portion.

55. **(D)** ***English/Rhetorical Skills/Style/Conciseness.*** The original sentence is incorrect because

the underlined portion is redundant. Specifically, "in the past" has the same meaning as "of former years." (D) is the correct answer choice as it eliminates the unnecessary phrase. As for the other answer choices, (B) and (C) are both incorrect for two reasons: first, they have the same error as the original; second, they both introduce grammatical errors into the sentence.

we are deeply dissatisfied <u>of the fact that</u> [56] we cannot attain other goals more rapidly. We have achieved a better life for most people, but we are unhappy that we have not spread it to all people. We have illuminated

56. F. NO CHANGE
G. in the fact that
H. about
J. that

56. (J) ***English/Rhetorical Skills/Style/Conciseness.*** As written, the original sentence is redundant. The phrase "of the fact" adds no meaning to the sentence; and, in fact, it makes the sentence harder to understand. (J) is the correct answer because it omits the unnecessary language. As for the other answer choices, (G) is incorrect for the same reason as the original. (H) is incorrect because "dissatisfied about" is a low-level or non-standard substitute for "dissatisfied that."

many sources of environmental deterioration, <u>because of</u> [57] we are unhappy that we have not conquered all of

57. A. NO CHANGE
B. despite
C. but
D. also

57. (C) ***English/Usage and Mechanics/Sentence Structure/Problems of Coordination and Subordination*** and ***Grammar and Usage/Diction.*** The original sentence is incorrect due to a word choice error involving coordination and subordination. Specifically, the phrase "because of" incorrectly suggests that the state of things in the first clause ("We have illuminated...") was motivated by the state of things in the second clause ("we are unhappy..."). In fact, the author intends to suggest a contrast between the two ideas ("We have illuminated...but we are unhappy"). (C) is the correct answer choice because it supplies the required conjunction; the resulting sentence also mirrors the construction of the previous sentence. As for the other answer choices, (B) and (D) are incorrect because they create sentences that include grammatical errors and that are not logical.

them. It is our raising expectations rather than our failures that now cause our distress.
58

[4]

First, we can help destroy the false impression that science and engineering have caused the current world troubles. To the contrary, science and engineering have made vast contributions to better
59

58. F. NO CHANGE
G. arising
H. rising
J. raised

58. (H) ***English/Usage and Mechanics/Grammar and Usage/Diction.*** The original sentence is incorrect due to an error involving word choice. Specifically, "raising" cannot be used as an adjective to modify a noun. "Rising," which means "moving upward," can be used as an adjective to modify a noun; in addition; it also supplies the meaning required here. So, (H) is the correct answer choice. As for the other answer choices, (G) is incorrect because "arising" means "as a result of"; it does not provide the required meaning. (J) is incorrect because "raised" means "fully elevated" and incorrectly suggests that expectations have reached their highest levels. As the passage states, though, expectations continue to rise as accomplishments continue to be made; so, "raised" is not the best choice here.

59. A. NO CHANGE
B. Contrary to,
C. Contrasted with,
D. In contrast with,

59. (A) ***English/Rhetorical Skills/No Change.*** The original sentence is correct. The phrase "To the contrary" provides an elegant and grammatically correct transition from the previous sentence. As for the other answer choices, (B), (C), and (D) are incorrect because they are incomplete phrases; they require additional language (e.g., "Contrary to popular opinion" or "Contrasted with popular opinion") in order to be grammatically and logically correct.

living for more people. [60]

[5]

Although many of our current problems must be cured more by social, political, and economic instruments rather than by science and technology, science and technology must still be the tools to make further <u>advances in</u> [61] such things as clean air, clean water, better transportation, better housing, better medical care, more adequate welfare programs, purer food, conservation of resources, and many other areas.

60. Suppose, at this point, that the writer wanted to add more information about the benefits of science and engineering. Which of the following additions would be most relevant?

F. A list of the colleges with the best science and engineering degree programs
G. Specific examples of contributions from the areas of science and engineering that have improved the standard of living
H. A brief explanation of the current world troubles
J. The names of several famous scientists and engineers

60. (G) ***English/Rhetorical Skills/Strategy/Appropriate Supporting Material.*** (G) is the correct answer choice. The writer makes a general claim that science and engineering have helped to improve people's lives. Therefore, it would be appropriate to support that claim with specific examples. As for the other answer choices, (F) and (J) are both incorrect because they are simply irrelevant. (H) is incorrect because it is too general; the paragraph is about only those global problems where science and engineering have made contributions towards improving people's lives (and not global problems in general).

61. A. NO CHANGE
B. advances, in
C. advances. In
D. advances: in

61. (A) ***English/Usage and Mechanics/No Change.*** The original sentence is correct. No punctuation is required between "advances" and "in." As for the other answer choices, (B) is incorrect because the comma disrupts the logical flow of the sentence. (C) is incorrect because "In such things…" would create a sentence fragment. (D) is incorrect the semicolon creates a fragment out of the word grouping that follows.

Items #62–63 ask about the preceding passage as a whole.

62. This essay was probably written for readers who:

F. are retired scientists and engineers.
G. are interested in a career in the "green" sector of the economy.
H. are in a career or contemplating a career in science or engineering.
J. are dissatisfied with the lack of progress in solving various scientific problems.

62. (H) ***English/Rhetorical Skills/Strategy/Audience.*** (H) is the correct answer choice. First, the passage's topic is how science and engineering can help to solve the world's problems; this topic would be of interest to scientists, engineers, and anyone considering a career as either. Second, the passage explicitly addresses scientists and engineers ("What are those of us who have chosen careers in science and engineering able to do about meeting our current problems?"). As for the other choices, (F) is wrong because the emphasis on making continued efforts doesn't seem to speak to people who are no longer active in the field. (J) is too general; the intended audience is more specific than anyone frustrated by a general lack of progress in the field of science. (G) is incorrect because it is too narrow; the author addresses areas and issues of interest to all scientists and engineers, not just those interested in becoming environmental scientists.

63. Choose the order of paragraph numbers that will make the essay's structure most logical.

A. NO CHANGE
B. 1, 4, 2, 3, 5
C. 5, 4, 2, 3, 1
D. 4, 2, 3, 1, 5

63. (B) ***English/Rhetorical Skills/Organization/ Passage-Level Structure.*** (B) is correct. Paragraph 1 introduces the passage's main topic. Paragraphs 4, 2, and 3 then begin with "First…," "Second…," and "Third…" respectively. Finally, Paragraph 5 summarizes the author's point of view and provides a conclusion.

PASSAGE VI

Youth Market of Europe

With increasing prosperity, West European youth am[64] having a fling that is creating distinctive consumer and cultural patterns. The result has been the increasing emergence in Europe of that phenomenon well known in America as the "youth market." This here[65] is a market in which enterprising businesses cater to the demands of teenagers and older youths in all their rock mania and pop art forms. The evolving European youth market has both similarities[66] and differences from the American youth market.

64. F. NO CHANGE
G. youths is
H. youth be
J. youth are

64. (J) ***English/Usage and Mechanics/Grammar and Usage/Subject-Verb Agreement.*** The original is incorrect due to an agreement error. Specifically, a third person plural subject ("youth") requires a plural verb that agrees with it. "Am" is a verb that can only be used with first person singular subjects. (J) is the correct choice because it provides the verb that is required here. As for the other answer choices, (G) is incorrect because a plural subject ("youths") does not agree with a singular verb ("is"). (H) is incorrect because it results in a verb phrase ("be having") that is not grammatically correct.

65. A. NO CHANGE
B. here idea
C. here thing
D. OMIT the underlined portion.

65. (D) ***English/Usage and Mechanics/Grammar and Usage/Pronoun Usage*** and ***Rhetorical Skills/Style/Idiomatic Expression.*** The original sentence is incorrect because "this here" is a non-standard or low-level variation on the pronoun "this." (D) is the correct answer choice because it eliminates "here" and leaves the correct pronoun. As for the other answer choices, (B) and (C) are incorrect for the same reason as the original.

66. F. NO CHANGE
G. similarity
H. similarities to
J. similar

66. (H) ***English/Usage and Mechanics/Grammar and Usage/Diction.*** The original sentence is incorrect due to a diction error involving prepositions. As written, "from" completes both "similarities" and "differences." However,

"from" is not the proper preposition to use with "similarities." The proper preposition is "to" ("similarities to..."). (H) is correct because it provides the required preposition. As for the other answer choices, (G) is incorrect for two reasons: first, it is incorrect for the same reason as the original; second, the singular noun "similarity" is not parallel with the plural noun "differences." (J) is also incorrect for two reasons: first, it is incorrect for the same reason as the original; second, the adjective "similar" is not parallel with the plural noun "differences."

The markets [67] basis is essentially the same—more spending power and freedom to use it in the hands of teenagers and older youths. Young consumers also

67. **A.** NO CHANGE
B. markets'
C. market's
D. market

67. (C) ***English/Usage and Mechanics/Punctuation/Apostrophes.*** The original sentence is incorrect due to a punctuation error. Specifically, an apostrophe is required in the phrase "the market's basis." An apostrophe should always be used to show possession. Here, the basis belongs to the market; so, an apostrophe should be used. As for the other answer choices, (B) is incorrect because the apostrophe is used in the wrong place. The "market" is singular; so the apostrophe should appear before the "s." An apostrophe is placed after the "s" only when possession belonging to a plural group is to be established ("After they came in, I cleaned the boys' shoes"). (D) is incorrect for the same reason as the original.

make up an increasing high [68] proportion of the population. Youthful tastes in the United States and Europe include a similar range of products—records and record players, tapes and CDs, VCRs and DVD players, leather jackets, "trendy" clothing, cosmetics,

68. **F.** NO CHANGE
G. increasingly high
H. increasing higher
J. high increasing

68. (G) ***English/Usage and Mechanics/Grammar and Usage/Adjectives versus Adverbs.*** The original sentence is incorrect due to a usage error involving modification. Specifically, an adjective ("increasing") cannot modify an adjective ("high"). Only an adverb ("increasingly") can modify an adjective ("high"). (G) is the correct answer because it makes the required correction. As for the other answer choices, (H) and (J) are incorrect for the same reason as the original.

and soft drinks, generally [69] it now is difficult to tell in which direction transatlantic teenage influences are flowing.

69. A. NO CHANGE
B. drinks. Generally,
C. drinks, in general
D. drinks generally

69. (B) ***English/Usage and Mechanics/Sentence Structure/Run-On Sentences*** and ***Punctuation/End-Stop Punctuation.*** The original sentence is incorrect because it includes a run-on sentence: two or more complete sentences joined together without the necessary punctuation or conjunctions. The first clause in the sentence ("Youthful tastes…cosmetics and soft drinks") is a complete sentence by itself. The second clause ("generally…teenage influences are flowing") is also a complete sentence by itself. For the sake of correctness and clarity, it would be best to put a piece of end-stop punctuation at the end of the first clause and then start an entirely new sentence. (B) is the correct answer choice because it accomplishes this task. As for the other answer choices, (C) and (D) are incorrect because they also result in run-on sentences.

As in the United States, where "teen" and "teenager" becomed [70] merchandising terms,

70. F. NO CHANGE
G. become
H. will become
J. have become

70. (J) ***English/Usage and Mechanics/Grammar and Usage/Verb Tense.*** "Becomed" is neither the past tense nor the past participle of "to become." (J) correctly provides the past tense form ("have become") needed to show the same time frame as "Europeans also have adapted." As for the other answer choices, (G) is the present tense, and (H) is the future tense.

Europeans also have adapted [71] similar terminology. In Flemish and Dutch, it is "tiener" for "teenagers." The French have simply adopted the English word "teenager." In West Germany, the key word in advertising addressed to teenagers is "freizeit," meaning "holidays" or "time off."

71. A. NO CHANGE
B. picked up
C. added
D. adopted

71. (D) ***English/Usage and Mechanics/Grammar and Usage/Diction.*** The original sentence is incorrect due to a word choice error. Specifically, "adapted" means "adjusted" or "modified." However, the sentence requires a word that means "to have taken up and used as one's own." (D) is the correct answer choice because "adopted" has that meaning. As for the

other answer choices, (B) and (C) are incorrect because they do not provide the required meaning.

The most obvious difference <u>among</u> 72 the youth market in Europe and that in the United States is in size. In terms of volume and variety of sales, the market in Europe is only a shadow of its American counterpart, <u>but it</u> 73 is a growing shadow.

72. **F.** NO CHANGE
G. with
H. by
J. between

72. (J) ***English/Usage and Mechanics/Grammar and Usage/Diction.*** The original sentence is incorrect due to a word choice error. Specifically, "among" is only used when describing more than two persons or things ("Her departure caused a stir among the many who were present."). "Between" is used when talking about two persons or things. So, (J) is the correct answer choice. As for (G) and (H), those prepositions have meanings that are not appropriate in this sentence.

73. **A.** NO CHANGE
B. it
C. it being
D. as it

73. (A) ***English/Usage and Mechanics/No Change.*** The original is correct as written. You have two independent clauses correctly joined by a conjunction ("but") and punctuated with a comma. (B) and (C) are wrong because they turn the word group that follows into a fragment. (D) is wrong because "as" creates a dependent clause where an independent clause is intended.

Items #74–75 ask about the preceding passage as a whole.

74. Is the author's use of quotation marks appropriate in this essay?

F. No, because quotation marks are only used to set off a direct quote.
G. No, because the essay has no dialogue.
H. Yes, because quotation marks are used to set off words used in a special sense.
J. Yes, because quotation marks indicate a conversation.

74. (H) ***English/Usage and Mechanics/Punctuation/Quotation Marks.*** (H) is the correct answer choice. The author uses several words that have meanings specific to the context of this essay (for example, "freizeit" is a German word meaning "holidays" or "time off" and is not a misspelled English word). Quotation marks are properly used to set off those words so they are easily identifiable. As for the other answer choices, (F) and (G) are incorrect because quotation marks can be used for several reasons in addition to setting off a direct quote or dialogue. (J) is incorrect because quotation marks are not used in this essay to set off the dialogue in a conversation.

75. This essay was probably written for readers who:

A. are interested in new trends in the consumer patterns of the world's youth.
B. are parents of teenagers.
C. are teenagers.
D. are interested in the different cultural patterns of West Germany.

75. (A) ***English/Rhetorical Skills/Strategy/Audience.*** (A) is the correct answer choice. The passage focuses solely on the topic of youth markets in Western Europe and America; given this single subject, we can assume it was written for readers who are interested in the consumer habits of young people. As for the other answer choices, (B) and (C) are incorrect because there is a level of detail included in the essay (for example, German and Dutch terms for words commonly used in youth advertising) that would not be of interest to a general readership such as parents or teenagers in general. (D) is incorrect because the essay discusses the youth market across Europe; in other words, it takes in more than just cultural patterns within Germany.

2 2 2 2 2 2 2 2 2 2 2 2

MATHEMATICS TEST

60 Items

DIRECTIONS: Solve each item and choose the correct answer choice. Calculator use is permitted on this test; however, some items are best solved without the use of a calculator.

Note: All of the following should be assumed, unless otherwise stated.

1. Illustrative figures are NOT necessarily drawn to scale.
2. The word *average* indicates arithmetic mean.
3. The word *line* indicates a straight line.
4. Geometric figures lie in a plane.

---

1. What is the additive inverse of $-\frac{2}{3}$?

A. $-\frac{3}{2}$
B. 0
C. $\frac{2}{3}$
D. 1
E. $\frac{3}{2}$

2. In the figure below, if O is the center of the circle and $\angle AOC$ is a central angle equal to 70°, what is the measure of $\angle ABC$?

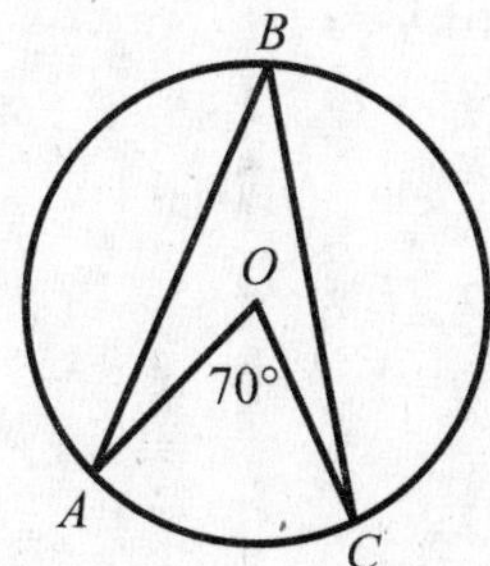

F. 140°
G. 70°
H. 50°
J. 35°
K. 22°

1. (C) ***Mathematics/Arithmetic/Simple Manipulations.*** Two numbers that add up to zero are additive inverses. $(a)+(-a)=0$. The additive inverse is the opposite of the original value: $\frac{2}{3}$ is the additive inverse of $-\frac{2}{3}$.

2. (J) ***Mathematics/Geometry/Lines and Angles*** and ***Circles.*** $\angle AOC$ is a central angle and equals 70°. A central angle is equal to its intercepted arc. $\overparen{AC} = 70°$. An inscribed angle is equal to one-half the measure of its intercepted arc. The measure of $\angle ABC$ is:

$$\angle ABC = \frac{1}{2} m \bullet (\overparen{AC}) = 35°$$

3. Which of the following is an element of the solution set of the equation $x^2 + 6x + 8 = 0$?

A. 8
B. 6
C. 4
D. –2
E. –8

3. (D) ***Mathematics/Algebra/Solving Quadratic Equations.*** Factor the quadratic equation:

$$x^2 + 6x + 8 = 0$$
$$(x+4)(x+2) = 0$$
$$x+4 = 0 \text{ or } x+2 = 0$$

Therefore, $x = -4$ or -2.

4. In the figure below $l_1 \parallel l_2$. If $x = 70$ and $y = 105$, what is the value of r?

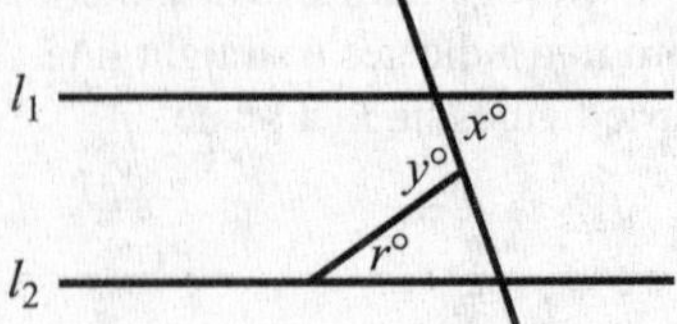

F. 35
G. 45
H. 85
J. 145
K. 175

4. (F) ***Mathematics/Geometry/Lines and Angles.*** Fill in the given information:

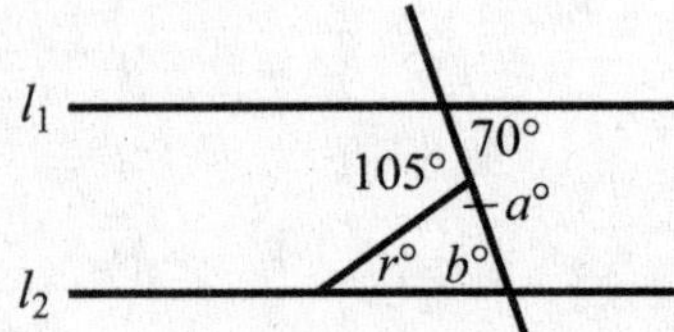

$b = 70$ because it is an alternate interior angle with $x°$. $a = 75$ because it is the supplement of $y°$. The three angles form a triangle: $r + a + b = 180$. Thus:

$$r + 75 + 70 = 180$$
$$r = 35$$

5. $A = \frac{2gr}{g+r}$. What is the value of g when $r = 1$ and $A = 4$?

A. –2
B. $\frac{4}{7}$
C. $\frac{8}{5}$
D. 2
E. 4

5. (A) ***Mathematics/Algebra/Manipulating Algebraic Expressions/Evaluating Expressions.*** Plug in the given values for A and r and solve for g:

$$A = \frac{2gr}{g+r}$$
$$4 = \frac{2g(1)}{g+(1)}$$
$$4 = \frac{2g}{g+1}$$
$$4(g+1) = 2g$$
$$4g + 4 = 2g$$
$$2g = -4$$
$$g = -2$$

6. The figure below represents which of the following equations?

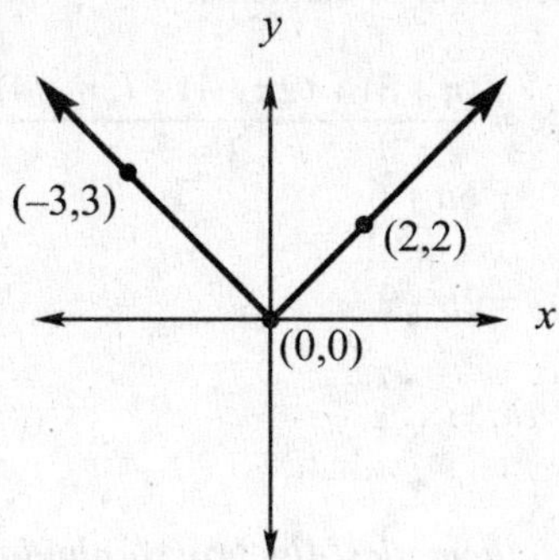

F. $y = x$
G. $y = -x$
H. $y = |x|$
J. $|y| = x$
K. $y = x^2$

6. (H) ***Mathematics/Coordinate Geometry/Graphs of Linear Equations.*** V-shaped graphs usually indicate absolute value functions. Substitute the given coordinates $(2,2)$, $(0,0)$, and $(-3,3)$ into the answer choices: only $y = |x|$ satisfies all the ordered pairs.

7. Which of the following is an illustration of the distributive property?

A. $(12 \cdot 25)(4) = 12(25 \cdot 4)$
B. $7n + 2 - 3n = 7n - 3n + 2$
C. $(17)(b^2)(5) = (17)(5)(b)^2$
D. $x(x+2) = x^2 + 2x$
E. $ab + ac = ba + ca$

7. (D) ***Mathematics/Algebra/Manipulating Algebraic Expressions/Basic Algebraic Manipulations.*** The distributive property indicates multiplication over addition $[a(b+c) = ab + ac]$ and multiplication over subtraction $[a(b-c) = ab - ac]$. Thus, $x(x+2) = x^2 + 2x$.

8. Joshua buys a television that costs \$600. If the sales tax is 7%, what is the total cost of the purchase?

F. \$4.20
G. \$42.00
H. \$420.00
J. \$604.20
K. \$642.00

8. (K) ***Mathematics/Arithmetic/Common Arithmetic Items/Percents.*** The sales tax is 7% of \$600: $0.07(600) = \$42$. Thus, the total cost is $\$600 + \$42 = \$642$.

9. What is the value of $-x^2 - 2x^3$ when $x = -1$?

A. –3
B. –1
C. 0
D. 1
E. 3

9. (D) ***Mathematics/Algebra/Expressing and Evaluating Algebraic Functions/Function Notation.*** Substitute the value –1 for *x*:

$$\begin{aligned} -x^2 - 2x^3 &= -(-1)^2 - 2(-1)^3 \\ &= -(1) - 2(-1) \\ &= -1 + 2 \\ &= 1 \end{aligned}$$

10. What is the average of $n+3$, $2n-1$, and $3n+4$?

F. $\frac{5n+6}{3}$
G. $2n+2$
H. $3n+3$
J. $\frac{6n+7}{3}$
K. $6n+6$

10. (G) ***Mathematics/Statistics and Probability/Averages.*** The average is the sum of the numbers divided by the number of elements:

$$\begin{aligned}\text{average} &= \frac{(n+3)+(2n-1)+(3n+4)}{3}\\ &= \frac{6n+6}{3}\\ &= 2n+2\end{aligned}$$

11. If $x=9$, what is the value of $x^0+x^{\frac{1}{2}}+x^{-2}$?

A. $77\frac{1}{2}$
B. $76\frac{1}{2}$
C. $5\frac{7}{18}$
D. $4\frac{1}{81}$
E. $3\frac{1}{81}$

11. (D) ***Mathematics/Algebra/Manipulating Algebraic Expressions/Evaluating Expressions.*** Substitute 9 for x:

$$\begin{aligned}x^0+x^{\frac{1}{2}}+x^{-2} &= 9^0+9^{\frac{1}{2}}+9^{-2}\\ &= 1+\sqrt{9}+\frac{1}{9^2}\\ &= 1+3+\frac{1}{81}\\ &= 4\frac{1}{81}\end{aligned}$$

12. $4\sqrt{3}+3\sqrt{27}=$?

F. $7\sqrt{30}$
G. $10\sqrt{3}$
H. $13\sqrt{3}$
J. 63
K. 108

12. (H) ***Mathematics/Arithmetic/Simple Manipulations.*** In order to add radicals, the number in the square root must be the same:

$$\begin{aligned}4\sqrt{3}+3\sqrt{27} &= 4\sqrt{3}+3\left(3\sqrt{3}\right)\\ &= 4\sqrt{3}+9\sqrt{3}\\ &= 13\sqrt{3}\end{aligned}$$

13. Jessica Dawn received marks of 87, 93, and 86 on 3 successive tests. What grade must she receive on a fourth test in order to have an average grade of 90?

A. 90
B. 92
C. 93
D. 94
E. 95

13. (D) ***Mathematics/Statistics and Probability/Averages.*** The average is the sum of the test scores divided by the number of tests:

$$\begin{aligned}\text{average} = 90 &= \frac{87+93+86+x}{4}\\ 4(90) &= 87+93+86+x\\ 360 &= 266+x\\ x &= 94\end{aligned}$$

14. In terms of x, what is the total number of cents in $4x$ dimes?

F. $0.04x$
G. $0.4x$
H. $4x$
J. $40x$
K. $400x$

14. (J) ***Mathematics/Algebra/Manipulating Algebraic Expressions/Creating Algebraic Expressions.*** Each dime is 10 cents. Three dimes would be $3(10) = 30$ cents. $4x$ dimes would be $4x(10) = 40x$ cents.

15. Which of the following is shown by the graph below?

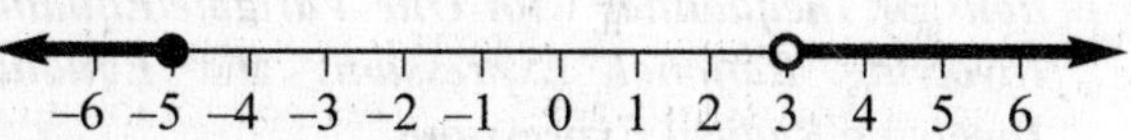

A. $-5 \le x < 3$
B. $-5 < x$ or $x < 3$
C. $-5 \le x$ or $x > 3$
D. $-5 \le x \le 3$
E. $-5 \ge x$ or $x > 3$

15. (E) ***Mathematics/Arithmetic/Simple Manipulations.*** The shaded circle at –5 indicates either ≥ or ≤, and the unshaded circle at 3 indicates either > or <, without the equal sign. The arrow pointing to the left, <, indicates "less than," and the arrow pointing to the right, >, indicates "greater than." The graph indicates $x \le -5$ or $x > 3$. The answers are connected by "or." Therefore, the answer is $x \le -5$ or $x > 3$.

16. $2\frac{2}{5} - 1\frac{7}{8} = ?$

F. $\frac{11}{40}$
G. $\frac{19}{40}$
H. $\frac{21}{40}$
J. $\frac{7}{13}$
K. $1\frac{5}{40}$

16. (H) ***Mathematics/Arithmetic/Simple Manipulations.*** First, convert the mixed numbers to improper fractions:

$$2\frac{2}{5} - 1\frac{7}{8} = \frac{12}{5} - \frac{15}{8}$$

Since the lowest common denominator is 40, we have:

$$\frac{12}{5} - \frac{15}{8} = \frac{96}{40} - \frac{75}{40} = \frac{21}{40}$$

17. In a circle with a radius of 6, what is the measure (in degrees) of an arc whose length is 2π?

A. 20°
B. 30°
C. 60°
D. 90°
E. 120°

17. (C) ***Mathematics/Geometry/Circles.*** Use the equation for circumference of a circle:

$$C_{circle} = 2\pi r = 2\pi(6) = 12\pi$$

Therefore, 2π is $\frac{2\pi}{12\pi} = \frac{1}{6}$ of the circumference. In turn, the measure (in degrees) of the arc is $\frac{1}{6}(360°) = 60°$ or:

$$\frac{\text{arc length}}{\text{circumference}} = \frac{x°}{360°}$$
$$\frac{2\pi}{12\pi} = \frac{x}{360}$$
$$\frac{1}{6} = \frac{x}{360}$$
$$6x = 360$$
$$x = 60$$

18. If $\frac{2x}{3\sqrt{2}} = \frac{3\sqrt{2}}{x}$, what is the positive value of x?

F. $\sqrt{3}$
G. $\sqrt{6}$
H. $2\sqrt{3}$
J. 3
K. 9

18. (J) ***Mathematics/Algebra/Solving Algebraic Equations or Inequalities with One Variable/Equations Involving Rational Expressions*** and ***Equations Involving Radical Expressions.***

$$\frac{2x}{3\sqrt{2}} = \frac{3\sqrt{2}}{x}$$
$$2x(x) = (3\sqrt{2})(3\sqrt{2})$$
$$2x^2 = 9(2) = 18$$
$$x^2 = 9$$
$$x = \pm 3$$

Therefore, the positive value of x is 3.

19. If $f(x) = 2x - x^2$ and $g(x) = x - 4$, what is the value of $g(f(2))$?

A. –8
B. –4
C. –2
D. 0
E. 3

19. (B) ***Mathematics/Algebra/Expressing and Evaluating Algebraic Functions/Function Notation.*** Begin with the part that is inside the inner parentheses, $f(2)$:

$$f(x) = 2x - x^2$$
$$f(2) = 2(2) - (2)^2 = 4 - 4 = 0$$

$$g(x) = x - 4$$
$$g(0) = 0 - 4 = -4$$

Therefore:

$$g(f(2)) = g(0) = -4$$

20. What is the solution set of the equation $|5 - 2x| = 7$?

F. $\{-1, 6\}$
G. $\{-1\}$
H. $\{1\}$
J. $\{6\}$
K. The empty set

20. (F) ***Mathematics/Algebra/Solving Algebraic Equations or Inequalities with One Variable/Equations Involving Absolute Value.*** Since $|5 - 2x| = 7$, we know that $5 - 2x = 7$ or $-(5 - 2x) = 7$. Solve each for possible values of x:

$$5 - 2x = 7$$
$$-2x = 2$$
$$x = -1$$

21. When $\frac{3-\frac{3}{x}}{x(x-1)}$ is defined, it is equivalent to which of the following expressions?

A. $\frac{1}{x-1}$

B. $\frac{1}{3}$

C. $x+1$

D. $\frac{3}{x}$

E. 3

And:

$$-(5-2x)=7$$
$$-5+2x=7$$
$$2x=12$$
$$x=6$$

Double-check each possible value for x in the original equation:

$$|5-2x|=7$$
$$|5-2(-1)|=7$$
$$|5+2|=7$$
$$|7|=7 \checkmark$$

And:

$$|5-2x|=7$$
$$|5-2(6)|=7$$
$$|5-12|=7$$
$$|-7|=7 \checkmark$$

Therefore, the solution set is $\{-1, 6\}$, (F).

21. **(D)** ***Mathematics/Algebra/Manipulating Algebraic Expressions/Evaluating Expressions.*** Multiply the top and bottom of the fraction by the lowest common denominator, which is x:

$$\frac{3-\frac{3}{x}}{x(x-1)}=\frac{x(3)-x\left(\frac{3}{x}\right)}{x(x-1)}$$
$$=\frac{3x-3}{x(x-1)}$$
$$=\frac{3(x-1)}{x(x-1)}$$
$$=\frac{3}{x}$$

22. What is the slope of the line that passes through the points (–3,5) and (4,7)?

F. $\sqrt{53}$
G. $\frac{7}{2}$
H. 2
J. $\frac{1}{2}$
K. $\frac{2}{7}$

23. In the figure below, diameter $\overline{AB}$ is perpendicular to chord $\overline{CD}$ at point E. If chord $\overline{CD} = 8$ inches and $\overline{OE} = 3$ inches, what is the length of the radius of the circle, in inches?

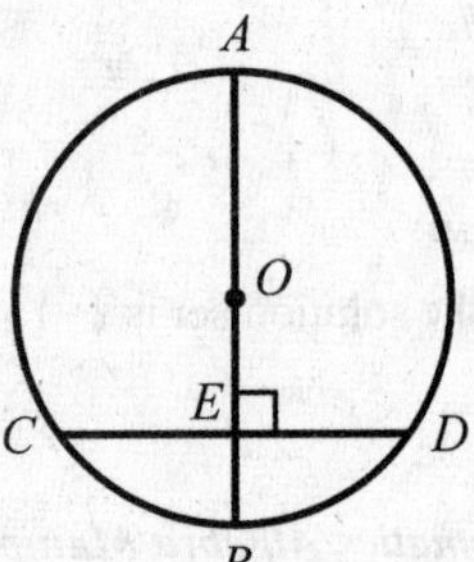

A. $\sqrt{3}$
B. $\sqrt{5}$
C. $\sqrt{7}$
D. $\sqrt{15}$
E. 5

22. **(K)** ***Mathematics/Coordinate Geometry/Slope of a Line.*** Use the equation for finding the slope of a line, where m is the slope and (x_1, y_1) and (x_2, y_2) are the two given points:

$$m = \frac{y_2 - y_1}{x_2 - x_1}$$
$$= \frac{7-5}{4-(-3)}$$
$$= \frac{2}{7}$$

23. **(E)** ***Mathematics/Geometry/Circles*** **and** ***Triangles/Pythagorean Theorem.***

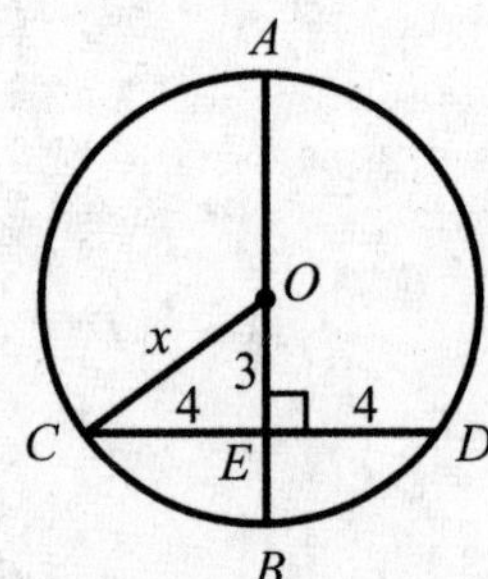

A diameter drawn perpendicular to the chord bisects the chord. Therefore, $\overline{AB}$ bisects $\overline{CD}$. A constructed radius $\overline{OC}$ forms right ΔOEC with $\overline{OC}$ as the hypotenuse. Since $\overline{OE} = 3$ inches and $\overline{CE} = 4$ inches, use the Pythagorean theorem:

$$(\text{Hypotenuse})^2 = (\text{Leg}_1)^2 + (\text{Leg}_2)^2$$
$$(\overline{OC})^2 = (\overline{OE})^2 + (\overline{CE})^2$$
$$x^2 = 3^2 + 4^2$$
$$x^2 = 25$$
$$x = \pm 5$$

Since length must be positive, the radius is 5.

24. In the figure below, the diagonals of parallelogram $ABCD$ intersect at point E. If $\overline{DB} = 4x + 2$ and $\overline{DE} = x + 4$, what is the value of x?

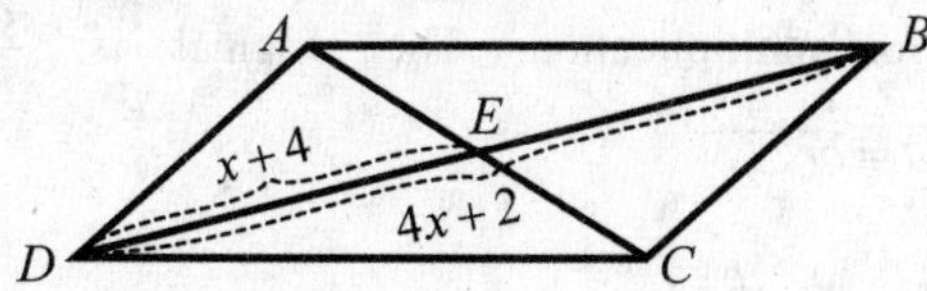

F. 3
G. 2
H. 1
J. $\frac{2}{3}$
K. 0

24. (F) ***Mathematics/Geometry.*** The diagonals of a parallelogram bisect each other; therefore:

$$\overline{DB} = 2(\overline{DE})$$
$$4x + 2 = 2(x + 4)$$
$$4x + 2 = 2x + 8$$
$$2x = 6$$
$$x = 3$$

25. If the measure of the central angle of a sector of a circle is 120°, what is the area, in square units, of the sector if the radius is 6 units long?

A. 4π
B. 6π
C. 8π
D. 10π
E. 12π

25. (E) ***Mathematics/Geometry/Lines and Angles*** and ***Circles.*** Since a figure isn't provided, draw one:

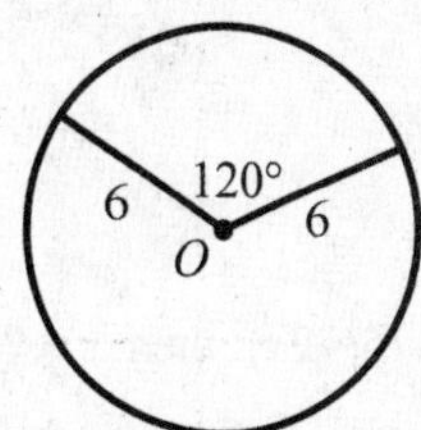

$$\frac{\text{area of sector}}{\text{area of circle}} = \frac{\text{central angle}}{360°}$$
$$\frac{x}{\pi r^2} = \frac{120°}{360°}$$
$$\frac{x}{36\pi} = \frac{1}{3}$$
$$3x = 36\pi$$
$$x = 12\pi$$

26. If the statement "if two triangles are red, then they are equal in area" is true, then which of the following *must* be true?

F. If the two triangles are not equal in area, then they are not red.
G. If the two triangles are equal in area, then they are red.
H. If the two triangles are equal in area, then they are not red.
J. If the two triangles are not red, then they are not equal in area.
K. If the two triangles are red, then they are not equal in area.

26. (F) ***Mathematics/Geometry/Triangles.*** By the principle of transposition, "If p, then q" is equivalent to "If not-q, then not-p."

27. If $\frac{a}{b}=\frac{r}{t}$, then which of the following is NOT necessarily true?

A. $\frac{a}{r}=\frac{b}{t}$
B. $\frac{a}{t}=\frac{b}{r}$
C. $\frac{a+b}{b}=\frac{r+t}{t}$
D. $\frac{b}{a}=\frac{t}{r}$
E. $at=br$

28. If $-2x+5=2-(5-2x)$, then $x=$?

F. 6
G. 5
H. 4
J. 3
K. 2

29. $\frac{(1+\sin x)(1-\sin x)}{(1+\cos x)(1-\cos x)}$ is equivalent to which of the following?

A. $\cos x$
B. $\tan x$
C. $\tan^2 x$
D. $\cos^2 x$
E. $\cot^2 x$

27. **(B)** ***Mathematics/Algebra/Manipulating Algebraic Expressions/Basic Algebraic Manipulations.*** Compare all the answer choices to the original using cross-multiplication. The original is: $\frac{a}{b}=\frac{r}{t}\Rightarrow at=br$.

A. $\frac{a}{r}=\frac{b}{t}$
$at=br$ ✓

B. $\frac{a}{t}=\frac{b}{r}$
$ar=bt$ ✗

C. $\frac{a+b}{b}=\frac{r+t}{t}$

$$t(a+b)=b(r+t)$$
$$at+bt=br+bt$$
$$at=br \quad ✓$$

D. $\frac{b}{a}=\frac{t}{r}$
$at=br$ ✓

E. $at=br$ ✓

28. **(K)** ***Mathematics/Algebra/Solving Algebraic Equations or Inequalities with One Variable/Simple Equations.*** Simply solve the given equation for x:

$$\begin{aligned}-2x+5&=2-(5-2x)\\&=2-5+2x\\&=-3+2x\\5&=-3+4x\\8&=4x\\x&=2\end{aligned}$$

29. **(E)** ***Mathematics/Trigonometry/Trigonometric Relationships.*** Use the trigonometric relationships to evaluate the given expression:

$$\frac{(1+\sin x)(1-\sin x)}{(1+\cos x)(1-\cos x)}=\frac{1-\sin x+\sin(x)-\sin^2 x}{1-\cos(x)+\cos(x)-\cos^2 x}=\frac{1-\sin^2 x}{1-\cos^2 x}$$

Using the identity $\sin^2 x+\cos^2 x=1$, we have:

$$\sin^2 x+\cos^2 x=1$$
$$\cos^2 x=1-\sin^2 x$$
$$\sin^2 x=1-\cos^2 x$$

30. In the figure below, ΔACB is a right triangle. $\overline{CE}$ is the median to hypotenuse $\overline{AB}$, and $\overline{AB} = 14$ centimeters. What is the length, in centimeters, of $\overline{CE}$?

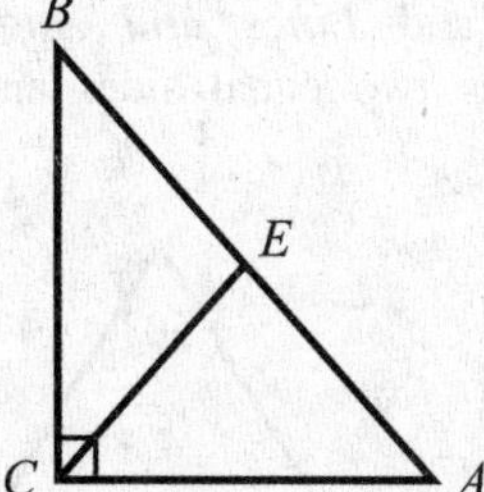

F. 5
G. 6
H. 7
J. 8
K. Cannot be determined from the given information

31. If y varies directly as x, and $y = 10$ when $x = \frac{1}{5}$, what is the value of y when $x = \frac{1}{2}$?

A. 1
B. 4
C. 7
D. 16
E. 25

32. $\frac{(-1)(2)(-3)(4)(-5)}{(5)(-4)(3)(-2)(1)} = ?$

F. −2
G. −1
H. 1
J. 2
K. 3

Therefore, by substitution:

$$\frac{1-\sin^2 x}{1-\cos^2 x} = \frac{\cos^2 x}{\sin^2 x} = \cot^2 x$$

30. (H) ***Mathematics/Geometry/Triangles/Working with Triangles.*** The median to the hypotenuse of a right triangle is equal in length to half the hypotenuse: $\overline{BE} = \overline{AE} = \overline{CE}$:

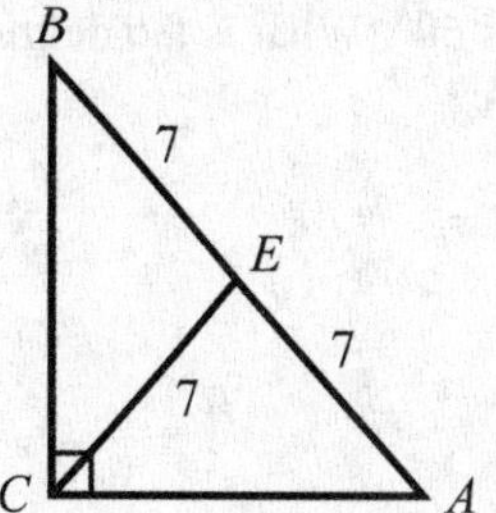

31. (E) ***Mathematics/Arithmetic/Common Arithmetic Items/Proportions and Direct-Inverse Variation.*** Since y varies directly as x, we have: $\frac{y_1}{x_1} = \frac{y_2}{x_2}$.

Therefore:

$$\frac{10}{\frac{1}{5}} = \frac{y}{\frac{1}{2}}$$
$$10(5) = y(2)$$
$$50 = 2y$$
$$y = 25$$

32. (G) ***Mathematics/Arithmetic/Complicated Manipulations/Simplifying.*** Cancel out like terms until the given expression is simplified:

$$\frac{(-1)(\not{2})(-\not{3})(\not{4})(-\not{5})}{(\not{5})(-\not{4})(\not{3})(-\not{2})(1)} = \frac{(-1)(\not{-1})(\not{-1})}{(\not{-1})(\not{-1})} = -1$$

33. How many positive prime factors does the number 36 have?

A. 2
B. 3
C. 4
D. 5
E. 6

34. The measure of the vertex angle of an isosceles triangle is 50°. What is the degree measure of each base angle?

F. 40°
G. 50°
H. 65°
J. 75°
K. 130°

35. Using the table below, what is the median of the following data?

Score	Frequency
20	4
30	4
50	7

A. 20
B. 30
C. 40
D. 50
E. 60

33. (A) ***Mathematics/Arithmetic/Common Arithmetic Items/Properties of Numbers.*** The factors of 36 are: 1 and 36, 2 and 18, 3 and 12, 4 and 9, 6 and 6. Of 1, 2, 3, 4, 6, and 9, only 2 and 3 are primes.

34. (H) ***Mathematics/Geometry/Triangles/Working with Triangles*** and ***Lines and Angles.*** An isosceles triangle has two equal sides and two equal base angles:

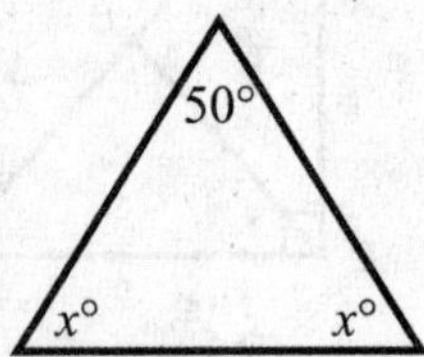

$$\begin{aligned} 50 + x + x &= 180 \\ 50 + 2x &= 180 \\ 2x &= 130 \\ x &= 65 \end{aligned}$$

35. (B) ***Mathematics/Statistics and Probability/Median.*** The median is the "middle" data element when the data are arranged in numerical order: 20, 20, 20, 20, 30, 30, 30, 30, 50, 50, 50, 50, 50, 50, 50. The "middle" data element is 30.

36. Which of the following number lines represents the solution set of $x^2 - 2x - 3 > 0$?

F. 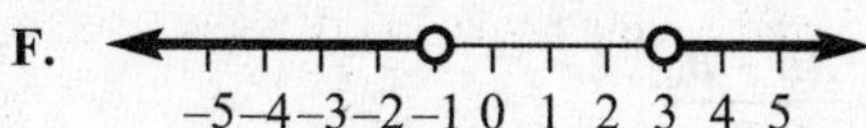

G. –5–4–3–2–1 0 1 2 3 4 5

H. –5–4–3–2–1 0 1 2 3 4 5

J. –5–4–3–2–1 0 1 2 3 4 5

K. –5–4–3–2–1 0 1 2 3 4 5

37. The expression $\sin x + \dfrac{\cos^2 x}{\sin x}$ is equal to which of the following?

A. 1
B. $\sin x$
C. $\cos x$
D. $\dfrac{1}{\sin x}$
E. $\dfrac{1}{\cos x}$

38. The value of $\left(2.5 \times 10^5\right)^2$ is equal to which of the following?

F. 6.25×10^7
G. 6.25×10^{10}
H. 2.5×10^7
J. 2.7×10^{10}
K. 5×10^7

36. (F) ***Mathematics/Algebra/Solving Quadratic Equations.*** Factor the given quadratic inequality:

$$x^2 - 2x - 3 > 0$$
$$(x-3)(x+1) > 0$$

This is true for two situations: (+)(+) and (–)(–). $|x-3|$ is positive for $x > 3$ and negative for $x < 3$. $x+1$ is positive for $x > -1$ and negative for $x < -1$. Thus, the two situations for which $(x-3)(x+1) > 0$ are:

$(x > 3)$ and $(x > -1)$, which simplifies to $(x > 3)$

And:

$(x < 3)$ and $(x < -1)$, which simplifies to $(x < -1)$

To keep both parentheses true in each situation, x must be larger than 3 or less than -1. This is two intervals: numbers less than –1 and numbers greater than +3, (F).

37. (D) ***Mathematics/Trigonometry/Trigonometric Relationships.*** To evaluate $\dfrac{\sin x}{1}$, a common denominator is required in order to add the fractions. The lowest common denominator is $\sin x$:

$$\frac{\sin x}{1} \bullet \frac{\sin x}{\sin x} + \frac{\cos^2 x}{\sin x} = \frac{\sin^2 x}{\sin x} + \frac{\cos^2 x}{\sin x}$$
$$= \frac{\sin^2 x + \cos^2 x}{\sin x}$$

Since $\sin^2 x + \cos^2 x = 1$, the expression reduces to $\dfrac{1}{\sin x}$.

38. (G) ***Mathematics/Arithmetic/Simple Manipulations.*** Perform the indicated operations:

$$\left(2.5 \times 10^5\right)^2 = \left(2.5 \times 10^5\right)\left(2.5 \times 10^5\right)$$
$$= (2.5)^2 \left(10^5\right)^2$$
$$= (2.5)(2.5)\left(10^{5+5}\right)$$
$$= 6.25 \times 10^{10}$$

39. If $A * B$ is defined as $\frac{AB - B}{-B}$, what is the value of $-2 * 2$?

A. −3
B. −1
C. 0
D. 1
E. 3

39. **(E)** ***Mathematics/Algebra/Expressing and Evaluating Algebraic Functions/Function Notation.***

$$A * B = \frac{AB - B}{-B}$$
$$-2 * 2 = \frac{(-2)(2) - 2}{-2} = \frac{-4 - 2}{-2} = \frac{-6}{-2} = 3$$

40. If one of the roots of the equation $x^2 + kx - 12 = 0$ is 4, what is the value of k?

F. −1
G. 0
H. 1
J. 3
K. 7

40. **(F)** ***Mathematics/Algebra/Solving Quadratic Equations.*** Substitute the root into the equation for the value of x:

$$x^2 + kx - 12 = 0$$
$$(4)^2 + k(4) - 12 = 0$$
$$16 + 4k - 12 = 0$$
$$4k + 4 = 0$$
$$4k = -4$$
$$k = -1$$

41. In the figure below, D is a point on $\overline{AB}$ and E is a point on $\overline{BC}$ such that $\overline{DE} \parallel \overline{AC}$. If $\overline{DB} = 4$ units long, $\overline{AB} = 10$ units long, and $\overline{BC} = 20$ units long, how many units long is $\overline{EC}$?

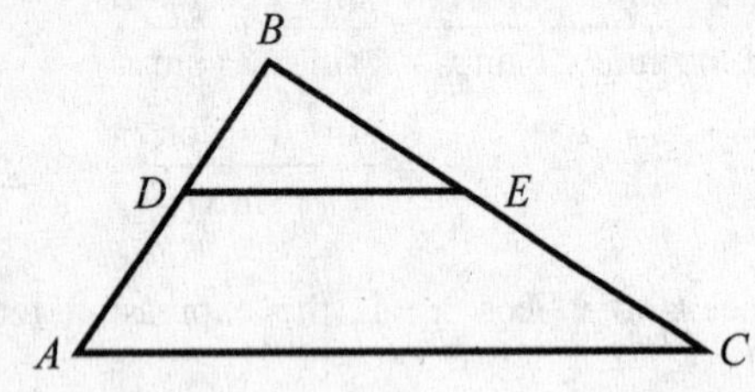

A. 4
B. 6
C. 8
D. 10
E. 12

41. **(E)** ***Mathematics/Geometry/Triangles/Working with Triangles.*** ΔABC and ΔDBE are similar; create a proportion between the sides of the two triangles. If $\overline{AB} = 10$ and $\overline{DB} = 4$, $\overline{DA} = 6$; if $\overline{BC} = 20$ and $\overline{EC} = x$, $\overline{BE} = 20 - x$.

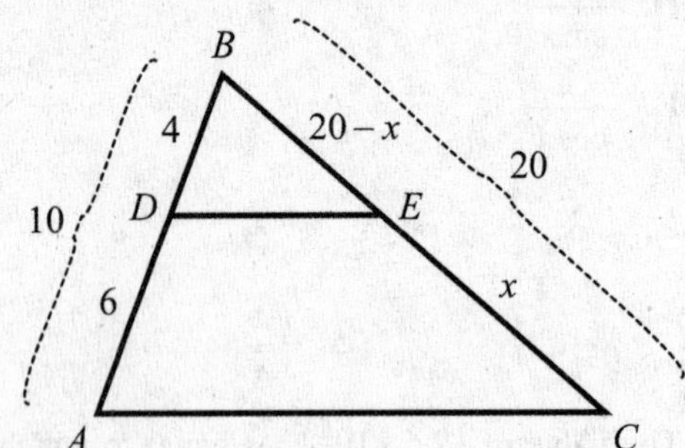

Therefore:

$$\frac{4}{10} = \frac{20 - x}{20}$$
$$80 = 200 - 10x$$
$$10x = 120$$
$$x = 12$$

42. $(x+2)(x-4)-(x+4)(x-2) = ?$

F. 0
G. $2x^2+4x-16$
H. $-4x$
J. $4x$
K. $-4x-16$

43. If the sum of the measures of the interior angles of a polygon equals the sum of the measures of the exterior angles, how many sides does the polygon have?

A. 3
B. 4
C. 5
D. 6
E. 7

44. If the perimeter of an equilateral triangle is 12 inches, what is its area, in square inches?

F. $2\sqrt{3}$
G. $4\sqrt{3}$
H. 8
J. $6\sqrt{3}$
K. $36\sqrt{3}$

42. (H) ***Mathematics/Algebra/Manipulating Algebraic Expressions/Basic Algebraic Manipulations.*** Evaluate each part of the expression using the FOIL (First, Outer, Inner, Last) method:

$$\begin{aligned}(x+2)(x-4) &= x^2-4x+2x-8\\ &= x^2-2x-8\end{aligned}$$

And:

$$\begin{aligned}(x+4)(x-2) &= x^2-2x+4x-8\\ &= x^2+2x-8\end{aligned}$$

Now, subtract the second from the first:

$$x^2-2x-8-(x^2+2x-8) = -2x-2x = -4x$$

43. (B) ***Mathematics/Geometry/Lines and Angles.*** The sum of the measures of the exterior angles of a polygon is 360° for all polygons. The sum of the measures of the interior angles of a polygon can be expressed as $180°(n-2)$, where n is the number of sides. Therefore:

$$\begin{aligned}180(n-2) &= 360\\ n-2 &= 2\\ n &= 4\end{aligned}$$

44. (G) ***Mathematics/Geometry/Triangles/Working with Triangles.*** If the perimeter is 12, then each side of the triangle is: $\frac{12}{3}=4$. $\text{Area}_{\text{triangle}} = \frac{bh}{2}$, where b is the base and h is the height. So, draw a figure:

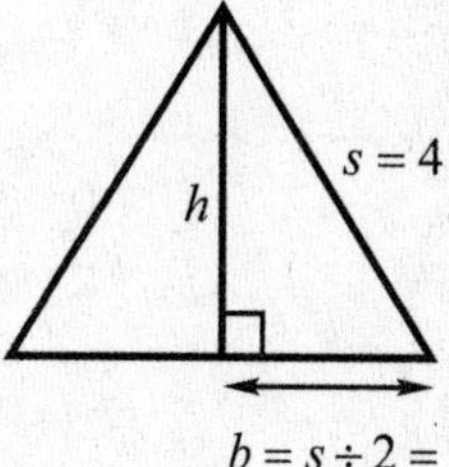

Use the Pythagorean theorem to solve for h:

$$\begin{aligned}2^2+h^2 &= 4^2\\ h^2 &= 16-4\\ &= 12\\ h &= \pm\sqrt{12} = 2\sqrt{3} \text{ (distance is positive)}\end{aligned}$$

Therefore:

$$\text{Area}_{\text{triangle}} = \frac{bh}{2} = \frac{4\left(2\sqrt{3}\right)}{2} = 4\sqrt{3}$$

Alternatively, if you remember the formula for the area of an equilateral triangle, you can use that:

$$\text{Area}_{\text{equilateral triangle}} = \frac{s^2\sqrt{3}}{4} = \frac{4^2\sqrt{3}}{4} = \frac{16\sqrt{3}}{4} = 4\sqrt{3}$$

45. If the ratio of 2 complementary angles is 8:1, what is the degree measure of the smaller angle?

A. 10°
B. 20°
C. 30°
D. 40°
E. 80°

45. (A) ***Mathematics/Geometry/Lines and Angles.*** Let $8x$ equal one angle and x equal the other angle. Since complementary angles add to 90°, we have:

$$8x + x = 90^\circ$$
$$9x = 90^\circ$$
$$x = 10^\circ$$

46. Given a square, a rectangle, a trapezoid, and a circle, if one figure is selected at random, what is the probability that the figure has four right angles?

F. 1
G. $\frac{3}{4}$
H. $\frac{1}{2}$
J. $\frac{1}{4}$
K. 0

46. (H) ***Mathematics/Statistics and Probability/Probability.*** A square has four right angles; a rectangle has four right angles; a trapezoid does not have four right angles; a circle has no angles. Thus, the probability of four right angles is:

$$\frac{\#\text{ of successes}}{\#\text{ of possibilities}} = \frac{2}{4} = \frac{1}{2}$$

47. A man travels 320 miles in 8 hours. If he continues at the same rate, how many miles will he travel in the next 2 hours?

A. 6
B. 40
C. 80
D. 120
E. 240

48. $\frac{\sin x}{\cos x}+\frac{\cos x}{\sin x}=?$

F. 1
G. $\sin x$
H. $\frac{1}{(\sin x)(\cos x)}$
J. $\tan x$
K. $\frac{\sin x+\cos x}{(\sin x)(\cos x)}$

49. The average temperatures for 5 days were 82°, 86°, 91°, 79°, and 91°. What is the mode of these temperatures?

A. 79°
B. 82°
C. 85.8°
D. 86°
E. 91°

50. A booklet contains 30 pages. If 9 pages in the booklet have drawings, what percentage of the pages in the booklet has drawings?

F. 30%
G. 9%
H. 3%
J. 1%
K. $\frac{3}{10}$%

47. (C) ***Mathematics/Arithmetic/Common Arithmetic Items/Proportions and Direct-Inverse Variation.*** Set up a direct proportion:

$$\frac{320 \text{ miles}}{x \text{ miles}}=\frac{8 \text{ hours}}{2 \text{ hours}}$$

$$x \text{ miles}=\frac{320 \text{ miles} \bullet 2 \cancel{\text{hours}}}{8 \cancel{\text{hours}}}$$

$$=80 \text{ miles}$$

48. (H) ***Mathematics/Trigonometry/Trigonometric Relationships.*** Use the common denominator, $(\sin x)(\cos x)$, to simplify the expression:

$$\frac{\sin x}{\cos x}\left(\frac{\sin x}{\sin x}\right)+\frac{\cos x}{\sin x}\left(\frac{\cos x}{\cos x}\right)$$

$$=\frac{\sin^2 x}{(\sin x)(\cos x)}+\frac{\cos^2 x}{(\sin x)(\cos x)}$$

$$=\frac{\sin^2 x+\cos^2 x}{(\sin x)(\cos x)}$$

$$=\frac{1}{(\sin x)(\cos x)}$$

49. (E) ***Mathematics/Statistics and Probability/Mode.*** The mode is the data element with the greatest frequency: 91°.

50. (F) ***Mathematics/Arithmetic/Common Arithmetic Items/Percents.*** Simplify the stem: "9 is what percent of 30?" Set up the "is-over-of" equation and solve for the missing value:

$$\frac{\text{is}}{\text{of}}=\frac{\%}{100}$$

$$\frac{9}{30}=\frac{x}{100}$$

$$x=\frac{9(100)}{30}$$

$$=30\%$$

51. Which of the following represents $-7t+6t^2-3$ when it is completely factored?

A. $(3t-1)(2t+3)$
B. $(3t+1)(2t-3)$
C. $(6t-1)(t+3)$
D. $(6t+1)(t-3)$
E. $(2t-1)(3t+3)$

52. What is the solution set of $2^{x^2+2x}=2^{-1}$?

F. {1}
G. {−1}
H. {1, −1}
J. {2}
K. The empty set

53. Jessica is 3 years younger than Joshua. If x represents Joshua's age now, what was Jessica's age four years ago in terms of x?

A. $x-1$
B. $x-3$
C. $x-4$
D. $x-6$
E. $x-7$

54. In a drama club, x students contributed y dollars each to buy an $18 gift for their advisor. If three more students had contributed, each student could have contributed one dollar less to buy the same gift. Which of the following sets of equations expresses this relationship?

F. $xy=18$ and $(x+3)(y-1)=18$
G. $xy=18$ and $(x-3)(y+1)=18$
H. $xy=18$ and $(x+3)(y+1)=18$
J. $xy=18$ and $(x-3)(y-1)=18$
K. $xy=18$ and $(x+1)(y-3)=18$

51. (B) ***Mathematics/Algebra/Manipulating Algebraic Expressions/Factoring Expressions.*** Rearrange the expression and then factor:

$$-7t+6t^2-3=6t^2-7t-3$$
$$=(3t+1)(2t-3)$$

52. (G) ***Mathematics/Algebra/Solving Algebraic Equations or Inequalities with One Variable/Equations Involving Integer and Rational Exponents.*** If $2^{x^2+2x}=2^{-1}$, then $x^2+2x=-1$. Thus:

$$x^2+2x+1=(x+1)(x+1)=0$$

This equation holds true only if $x=-1$.

53. (E) ***Mathematics/Algebra/Manipulating Algebraic Expressions/Evaluating Expressions.*** If Joshua is x years old now and Jessica is 3 years younger, then Jessica is now $x-3$ years old. Four years ago she was $(x-3)-4=x-7$ years old.

54. (F) ***Mathematics/Algebra/Manipulating Algebraic Expressions/Creating Algebraic Expressions.*** The amount collected is equal to the number of students multiplied by the amount that each student contributed. Therefore:

$$(x)(y)=18$$

And:

$$(x+3)(y-1)=18$$

55. $\frac{1}{2}\sqrt{112}-\sqrt{28}+2\sqrt{63}=?$

A. $6\sqrt{7}$
B. $7\sqrt{7}$
C. $8\sqrt{7}$
D. $9\sqrt{7}$
E. $10\sqrt{7}$

56. What is the value of x for the following set of simultaneous equations?

$$\frac{1}{x}+\frac{1}{y}=\frac{1}{4}$$
$$\frac{1}{x}-\frac{1}{y}=\frac{3}{4}$$

F. 4
G. 2
H. $\frac{1}{2}$
J. $\frac{1}{4}$
K. –4

57. Which set could represent the lengths of the sides of a triangle?

A. {1, 3, 6}
B. {2, 4, 7}
C. {2, 10, 12}
D. {4, 6, 8}
E. {4, 4, 10}

55. (A) ***Mathematics/Arithmetic/Complicated Manipulations/Simplifying.*** First, evaluate each part of the expression:

$$\frac{1}{2}\sqrt{112}=\frac{1}{2}\left(\sqrt{16}\right)\left(\sqrt{7}\right)=\frac{1}{2}(4)\left(\sqrt{7}\right)=2\sqrt{7}$$

$$\sqrt{28}=\sqrt{4}\sqrt{7}=2\sqrt{7}$$

$$2\sqrt{63}=2\left(\sqrt{9}\right)\left(\sqrt{7}\right)=2(3)\left(\sqrt{7}\right)=6\sqrt{7}$$

Now, combine the parts as indicated in the stem:

$$\frac{1}{2}\sqrt{112}-\sqrt{28}+2\sqrt{63}=2\sqrt{7}-2\sqrt{7}+6\sqrt{7}=6\sqrt{7}$$

56. (G) ***Mathematics/Algebra/Solving Simultaneous Equations.*** Add the two equations:

$$\begin{array}{rl} & \frac{1}{x}+\frac{1}{y}=\frac{1}{4} \\ + & \frac{1}{x}-\frac{1}{y}=\frac{3}{4} \\ \hline & \frac{2}{x}=1 \Rightarrow x=2 \end{array}$$

57. (D) ***Mathematics/Geometry/Triangles/Working with Triangles.*** The sum of the lengths of any two sides of a triangle must exceed the length of the third side. Check each of the answer choices:

A. $1+3>6$ ✗
B. $2+4>7$ ✗
C. $2+10>12$ ✗
D. $4+6>8$
$4+8>6$
$6+8>4$ ✓
E. $4+4>10$ ✗

58. What is the solution set, in terms of a and b, for the following system of equations?

$$ax + y = b$$
$$2ax + y = 2b$$

F. $\left\{\left(-\frac{b}{a}, -1\right)\right\}$

G. $\{(-a, b)\}$

H. $\left\{\left(\frac{b}{a}, 0\right)\right\}$

J. $\left\{\left(\frac{b}{a}, \frac{a}{b}\right)\right\}$

K. $\left\{\left(\frac{2a}{b}, \frac{2b}{a}\right)\right\}$

59. In the figure below, $\sin\theta = \frac{r}{4}$. What is the value of $\cos\theta$?

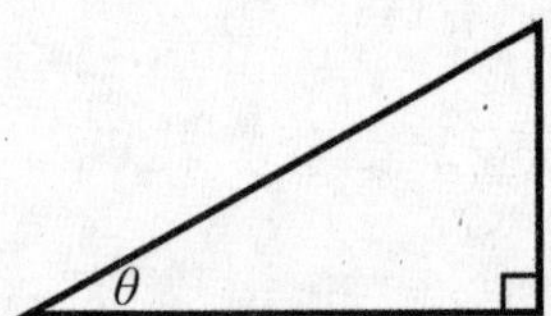

A. $\frac{\sqrt{16 - r^2}}{4}$

B. $\frac{4 - r}{4}$

C. $\frac{16 - r^2}{2}$

D. $\frac{4 - r}{2}$

E. $\frac{16 - r^2}{r}$

58. (H) ***Mathematics/Algebra/Solving Simultaneous Equations.*** To eliminate the variable y, multiply the first equation by -1 and add the equations:

$$\begin{aligned} -1(ax + y &= b) \\ +\ 2ax + y &= 2b \\ \hline ax &= b \\ x &= \frac{b}{a} \end{aligned}$$

Substitute the value of x into the first equation and solve for y:

$$\begin{aligned} ax + y &= b \\ a\left(\frac{b}{a}\right) + y &= b \\ b + y &= b \\ y &= 0 \end{aligned}$$

The solution set is $\left\{\left(\frac{b}{a}, 0\right)\right\}$.

59. (A) ***Mathematics/Trigonometry/Determining Trigonometric Values*** and ***Geometry/Triangles/Pythagorean Theorem.*** From the given information, draw a figure:

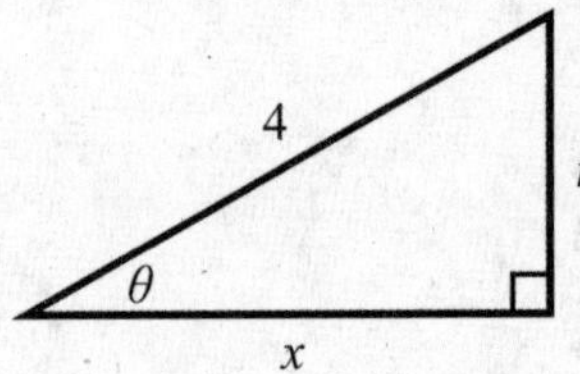

The third side of the triangle, x, is found using the Pythagorean theorem:

$$\begin{aligned} x^2 + r^2 &= 4^2 \\ &= 16 \\ x^2 &= 16 - r^2 \\ x &= \pm\sqrt{16 - r^2} \\ &= \sqrt{16 - r^2} \text{ (length is positive)} \end{aligned}$$

Since $\cos\theta = \frac{\text{side adjacent to } \theta}{\text{hypotenuse}}$, we have:

$$\cos\theta = \frac{\sqrt{16 - r^2}}{4}$$

60. If 3 copier machines can copy 300 sheets in 3 minutes, assuming the same rate, how long, in minutes, will it take 6 such copiers to copy 600 sheets?

F. 2
G. 3
H. 4
J. 6
K. 9

60. (G) ***Mathematics/Arithmetic/Common Arithmetic Items/Proportions and Direct-Inverse Variation.*** The number of sheets is directly proportional to the number of machines, as well as directly proportional to the amount of time. Thus:

$$\left(\frac{\text{sheets}}{\text{\# of machines} \bullet \text{time}}\right)_1 = \left(\frac{\text{sheets}}{\text{\# of machines} \bullet \text{time}}\right)_2$$

$$\frac{300}{3(3)} = \frac{600}{6(t)}$$

$$\frac{300}{9} = \frac{600}{6t}$$

$$\frac{100}{3} = \frac{100}{t}$$

$$100t = 300$$

$$t = 3$$

3 3 3 3 3 3 3 3 3 3 3 3

READING TEST

40 Items

DIRECTIONS: Each passage below is followed by a set of items. Read each passage and choose the best answer for each item. You may refer to the passage as often as necessary to answer the items.

Passage I

PROSE FICTION: This passage is adapted from the short story "Paul's Case: A Study in Temperament" by Willa Cather.

It was Paul's afternoon to appear before the faculty of Pittsburgh High School to account for his various misdemeanors. He had been suspended a week ago, and his father had called at the Principal's office and confessed his perplexity about his son. Paul entered the faculty room suave and smiling. His clothes were a trifle outgrown, and the tan velvet on the collar of his open overcoat was frayed and worn; but for all that there was something of the dandy in him, and he wore an opal pin in his neatly knotted black four-in-hand, and a red carnation in his buttonhole. This latter adornment the faculty somehow felt was not properly significant of the contrite spirit befitting a boy under the ban of suspension.

Paul was tall for his age and very thin, with high, cramped shoulders and a narrow chest. His eyes were remarkable for a certain hysterical brilliancy, and he continually used them in a conscious, theatrical sort of way, peculiarly offensive in a boy. The pupils were abnormally large, as though he was addicted to belladonna, but there was a glassy glitter about them, which that drug does not produce.

When questioned by the Principal as to why he was there Paul stated, politely enough, that he wanted to come back to school. This was a lie, but Paul was quite accustomed to lying; he found it, indeed, indispensable for overcoming friction. His teachers were asked to state their respective charges against him, which they did with such a rancor and aggrievement as evinced that this was not a usual case. Disorder and impertinence were among the offenses named, yet each of his instructors felt that it was scarcely possible to put into words the real cause of the trouble, which lay in a sort of hysterically defiant manner of the boy's, in the contempt which they all knew he felt for them, and which he seemingly made not the least effort to conceal. Once, when he had been making a synopsis of a paragraph at the blackboard, his English teacher had stepped to his side and attempted to guide his hand. Paul had started back with a shudder and thrust his hands violently behind him. The astonished woman could scarcely have been more hurt and embarrassed had he struck at her. The insult was so involuntary and definitely personal as to be unforgettable. In one way or another he had made all his teachers, men and women alike, conscious of the same feeling of physical aversion. In one class he habitually sat with his hand shading his eyes; in another he always looked out of the window during the recitation; in another he made a running commentary on the lecture, with humorous intention.

His teachers felt this afternoon that his whole attitude was symbolized by his shrug and his flippant red carnation flower, and they fell upon him without mercy, his English teacher leading the pack. He stood through it smiling, his pale lips parted over his white teeth. (His lips were continuously twitching, and he had a habit of raising his eyebrows that was contemptuous and irritating to the last degree.) Older boys than Paul had broken down and shed tears under that baptism of fire, but his set smile did not once desert him, and his only sign of discomfort was the nervous trembling of the fingers that toyed with the buttons of his overcoat, and an occasional jerking of the other hand that held his hat. Paul was always smiling, always glancing about him, seeming to feel that people might be watching him and trying to detect something. This conscious expression, since it was as far as possible from boyish mirthfulness, was usually attributed to insolence or "smartness."

1. This short story is subtitled "A Study in Temperament," which suggests that the author wants to examine:

A. a certain type of character.
B. reactions under pressure.
C. how people change over time.
D. people and their settings.

1. (A) ***Reading/Prose Fiction/Main Idea.*** A person's temperament is their usual mood or attitude towards the world, and it is an outgrowth of a person's character. For this reason, (A) is the correct answer choice. Cather's general purpose is to dramatize and examine how a certain type of character, or a person of a certain mood or attitude, responds to the world around him. As for the other answer choices, (B) and (C) are incorrect because they are not broad enough to encompass Cather's general purpose; how a person reacts under pressure, (B), and how a person changes over time, (C), are aspects of temperament, but Cather is interested in more than just these single aspects. Finally, (D) is incorrect because it is too general; as explained above, Cather is interested in a topic much more specific than people in general and their settings.

2. The introductory phrases "something of the dandy" (line 9), "hysterical brilliancy" (line 17), and "peculiarly offensive" (line 19):

I. describe Paul's reaction to his peers.
II. show the narrator's distaste for Paul.
III. reveal Paul as an unpleasant character.

F. I only
G. III only
H. I and II only
J. II and III only

2. (J) ***Reading/Prose Fiction/Implied Idea.*** These introductory phrases, as well as several other details throughout the passage, show Paul in a very unsympathetic light. Paul is shown to be an unpleasant character, (III), and the unrelenting nature of the negative description reveals that the narrator finds Paul to be unpleasant as well, (II). These introductory phrases do not describe Paul's reactions to his peers, (I), though, so (J) is the correct answer choice.

3. The passage makes it clear in the first paragraph that the faculty of the high school:

A. is perplexed by Paul's actions.
B. finds Paul's demeanor inappropriate.
C. cannot understand Paul's words.
D. wants only the best for Paul.

3. (B) ***Reading/Prose Fiction/Explicit Detail.*** At the end of the first paragraph, Cather describes a red carnation that Paul wears in his buttonhole. She says "This latter adornment the faculty somehow felt was not properly significant of the contrite spirit befitting a boy under the ban of suspension" (lines 11–14). In other words, the faculty does not find Paul's demeanor appropriate to the situation at hand. So, (B) is the correct answer choice. As for the other answer choices, (A) is incorrect because it is Paul's father that is described as perplexed (lines 4–5). (C) and (D) are both incorrect because there is simply no evidence to support either idea.

4. The words *hysterical* and *hysterically*, as used in lines 17 and 34, respectively, seem to imply:

F. delirium.
G. raving.
H. uncontrolled behavior.
J. frothing.

5. The author implies that the most serious flaw Paul has is his:

A. inability to complete his work.
B. flippant sense of humor.
C. drug use.
D. failure to hide his contempt for others.

6. In the fourth paragraph (lines 52–55), the author indicates that the faculty behaved like a pack of:

F. cowards.
G. predators.
H. liars.
J. scholars.

7. The author uses the phrase "baptism of fire" (line 61) to denote the:

A. challenge faced by students in a faculty inquisition.
B. youthfulness of Paul and his fellow students.
C. obstacles adolescents confront while growing up.
D. fury with which Paul faced the faculty.

8. The word *smartness* (line 70) is used to mean:

F. wit.
G. intelligence.
H. impudence.
J. reasonableness.

4. (H) ***Reading/Prose Fiction/Vocabulary.*** Although the descriptions in lines 17 and 34 suggest that Paul is unable to control his odd mannerisms, there is no concrete evidence that he suffers from delirium, (F), raving, (G), or frothing, (J). These are all conditions which one normally associates with intense physical illness or psychosis, and these are diagnoses that seem too severe for the behavior that Paul exhibits. So, (H) is the correct answer choice.

5. (D) ***Reading/Prose Fiction/Implied Idea.*** Paul's most serious flaw is vividly described and analyzed in lines 37–51. In these lines, Cather shows Paul's violent interaction with his English teacher, his habit of ignoring teachers during class, and his tendency to mock these teachers who now sit in judgment of him. In short, it is Paul's inability to hide his contempt for others that has landed him in trouble. So, (D) is the correct answer choice. As for the other answer choices, they are all incorrect simply because there is no evidence to support these ideas.

6. (G) ***Reading/Prose Fiction/Explicit Detail.*** In lines 54–55, Cather compares the faculty to a pack of predators. Specifically, she writes that they "fell upon him without mercy, his English teacher leading the pack." So, (G) is the correct answer choice.

7. (A) ***Reading/Prose Fiction/Implied Idea.*** In lines 59–61, Cather writes that "Older boys than Paul had broken down and shed tears under that baptism of fire." The "baptism of fire" is the inquisition performed by the faculty into student misbehaviors. So, (A) is the correct answer choice. As Cather says, most students broke down during such inquisitions. However, Paul manages the entire experience without any visible show of emotion at all.

8. (H) ***Reading/Prose Fiction/Vocabulary.*** Cather writes that Paul was always smiling, and the faculty attributed his constant smiling to "insolence or 'smartness'" (line 70). "Insolence" means "disrespect" or "rudeness." So, it is logical that "smartness" has a negative connotation in this context. Therefore, (H) is the correct answer choice since "impudence" also means "rudeness" or "disrespect." As for the other answer choices, they are all incorrect because they do not have the negative connotations required here.

9. Which adjective does NOT describe Paul as he is presented in this story?

A. Defiant
B. Proud
C. Flippant
D. Candid

10. By the end of the selection, we find that the faculty:

F. resents and loathes Paul.
G. admires and trusts Paul.
H. struggles to understand Paul.
J. is physically revolted by Paul.

9. (D) ***Reading/Prose Fiction/Implied Idea.*** In lines 25–27, Cather focuses on Paul's tendency to lie. As she writes, "Paul was quite accustomed to lying" (lines 25–26). A person who lies cannot be described as "candid" or honest, so (D) is the correct answer choice. As for the other answer choices, Paul is shown to be defiant, (A), proud, (B), and flippant, (C), throughout the passage.

10. (F) ***Reading/Prose Fiction/Implied Idea.*** Although it is evident throughout the passage that Paul's teachers dislike him, it is only in the final paragraph that the ferocity of their hatred for him receives full expression. Cather compares the faculty to a pack of wild wolves that finally "fell upon him without mercy, his English teacher leading the pack" (lines 54–55). The faculty loathes and resents Paul. So, (F) is the correct answer choice. As for the other answer choices, (G) and (H) are incorrect because there is simply no evidence to support either idea. Finally, (J) is incorrect because Paul is physically revolted by the faculty (lines 46–47) and not vice versa.

Passage II

SOCIAL SCIENCE: This passage discusses the history of African Americans in Congress.

Only with the enforcement of the Reconstruction Act of 1867 and the ratification of the Fifteenth Amendment to the Constitution—nearly 70 years after the ratification of the U.S. Constitution—did African Americans first win seats in Congress. Hiram Revels of Mississippi became the first African American to serve in Congress when he took his seat in the Senate on February 25, 1870. Joseph Rainey of South Carolina became the first African American member of the House of Representatives later in 1870. In the next 80 years, nearly seventy African Americans served in Congress.

African Americans throughout the South became politically active soon after emancipation and the close of the Civil War. State conventions and local political societies such as the Union League provided an opportunity for freed African Americans to articulate their vision of full participation in the political and economic life of the former slave states. Out of this broad-based political mobilization emerged a generation of African American leaders who nearly unanimously adhered to the Republican Party because it had championed the rights of African Americans. African Americans elected to Congress during Reconstruction found the national legislature an effective forum for the advocacy of political equality. Following the end of federal Reconstruction in 1877, African Americans continued to win election to Congress and they carried on the struggle for civil rights and economic opportunity. The African American congressional representatives of the late nineteenth century were the most prominent indication of the persistence of political organization on a local level in the South.

During the 1890s and early 1900s, no African American won election to Congress, in part because of restrictive state election codes in some southern states. During World War I and in the following decade, however, African American migration to northern cities established the foundation for political organization in urban centers. Oscar DePriest's election in 1928 as a representative from Chicago began a slow but steady succession of political victories in the North. Over the next three decades African Americans won congressional seats in New York City, Detroit, and Philadelphia. In the wake of the civil rights movement and the enforcement of the Voting Rights Act of 1965, African Americans regained seats in the South. Since the 1930s, nearly all African American representatives have been Democrats.

Since the nineteenth century, African American members of Congress have served as advocates for all African Americans as well as representatives for their constituencies. During Reconstruction and the late nineteenth century, African American representatives called on their colleagues to protect the voting rights of African Americans. These members of Congress, many of them former slaves, also called for expanded educational opportunities and land grants for freed African Americans. In the mid-twentieth century, African American representatives turned to the needs of urban communities and urged federal programs for improved housing and job training. As the most prominent African American office-holders of the time, these representatives served as defenders of the civil rights movement and proponents of legislation to end segregation. In 1971, the establishment of the Congressional Black Caucus offered a formal means of representing the combined interests of African Americans. The caucus has demonstrated a special concern for the protection of civil rights; the guarantee of equal opportunity in education, employment, and housing; and a broad array of foreign and domestic policy issues.

African Americans in Congress have been further united by their shared experience in the African American community. Many of the early Black representatives were born in slavery. The political and economic opportunities of Reconstruction offered these representatives the hope that African Americans might achieve genuine equality in American society, while the opposition of some white Southerners reminded them of the need for federal protection of the liberties won in the aftermath of the Civil War.

Since the victories of the civil rights movement in the 1960s, African American men and women have won election to Congress from increasingly diverse regions of the country. Whether from largely urban districts, suburban areas, or more recently from rural Mississippi, these members of Congress have maintained their common concern with economic issues that affect African Americans and with the protection of civil rights.

The collected biographies of African Americans who served in the House and Senate provide an important perspective on the history of the Congress and the role of African Americans in American politics. Their stories offer eloquent testimony to the long struggle to extend the ideals of the founders to encompass all citizens of the United States.

11. According to the passage, the first African American to serve in the House of Representatives was:

A. Hiram Revels.
B. Joseph Rainey.
C. from Chicago.
D. a former slave.

11. (B) ***Reading/Social Science/Explicit Detail.*** The correct answer choice is (B). In lines 8–10, the author says Joseph Rainey was the first African American elected to the House. As for the other answer choices, (A) is incorrect because Hiram Revels was the first African American in the Senate. (C) is incorrect because Joseph Rainey was from South Carolina. Finally, (D) is incorrect because there is no evidence in the passage that Rainey was a former slave.

12. The passage suggests that, in contrast to African Americans elected to Congress during and shortly after Reconstruction, African Americans elected to Congress today are more likely to:

F. be Democrats.
G. be members of the Republican Party.
H. work for full political equality for all African Americans.
J. come from districts in which the majority is African American.

12. (F) ***Reading/Social Science/Explicit Detail.*** The correct answer choice is (F). In the last sentence of the third paragraph, the author states that since "the 1930s, nearly all African American representatives have been Democrats."

13. One difference between African American congressional representatives in the nineteenth century and those in the mid-twentieth century was:

A. the political party to which they were likely to belong.
B. their commitment to education for African Americans.
C. the strength of their ties to the African American community as a whole.
D. the extent to which they represented all African Americans and not just their constituents.

13. (A) ***Reading/Social Science/Explicit Detail.*** In lines 19–23, the author says African American leaders after the Civil War "nearly unanimously adhered to the Republican Party." In lines 47–49, the author then says that "Since the 1930s, nearly all African American representatives have been Democrats." So, (A) is the correct answer choice. As for the other answer choices, they are all contradicted by the fourth paragraph where the author details the activities of African American members of Congress during both the nineteenth and the twentieth century.

14. When the African American representatives "turned to" (line 60) certain issues in the mid-twentieth century, they:

F. became antagonistic toward those issues.
G. reversed their positions on those issues.
H. devoted themselves to those issues.
J. referred to those issues.

14. (H) ***Reading/Social Science/Implied Idea.*** In lines 59–62, the author writes that "In the mid-twentieth century, African American representatives turned to the needs of urban communities and urged federal programs for improved housing and job training." Given the use of the word "urged" and the context of this sentence, it is clear that "turned to" means "concentrated" or "devoted themselves to." So, (H) is correct. As for the other choices, (F) and (G) are incorrect because they are the exact opposite of what the author intends to say in the above sentence. (J) is incorrect because the African American representatives did more than just "refer" to these issues; they dedicated themselves and took action to achieve specific goals related to these issues.

15. According to the passage, one reason African Americans began to be elected to Congress from cities in the northern United States after the 1930s was that:

A. more African Americans lived in northern cities at that time than had been the case previously.
B. African Americans in northern cities had better political organizations than did African Americans in the rural South.
C. African American politicians in the North were more likely to be members of the Democratic Party than were those in the South.
D. African American politicians in the North were more likely to focus on voting rights for African Americans than were those in the South.

15. (A) ***Reading/Social Science/Explicit Detail.*** In lines 38–40, the author writes that an "African American migration to northern cities established the foundation for political organization in urban centers" after World War I and in the following decade. So, (A) is the correct answer choice. As for the other answer choices, (B) and (D) are both incorrect because there is no evidence in the passage to support these ideas. (C) is incorrect because lines 47–49 indicate African American representatives from all regions of America were nearly all Democrats.

16. Which one of the following is NOT mentioned in the passage as a common concern of African American congressional representatives?

F. Enforcing voting rights for African Americans
G. Increasing educational opportunities for African Americans
H. Ensuring opportunities for employment for African Americans
J. Protecting people of African descent in other countries

16. (J) ***Reading/Social Science/Explicit Detail.*** Voting rights, (F), are mentioned or implied in lines 29, 55, and 70. Educational opportunities, (G), are mentioned or implied in lines 58 and 71. Finally, employment (H) is mentioned or implied in lines 62 and 71. Only the issue of protecting people of African descent in other countries is not mentioned in the passage. So, (J) is the correct answer choice.

17. One reason cited in the passage for the election of African Americans to Congress from both southern states after Reconstruction and northern states after World War I is the:

A. success of the civil rights movement.
B. passage and enforcement of the Fifteenth Amendment.
C. strength of local African American political organizations.
D. predominance of African Americans in certain districts.

17. (C) ***Reading/Social Science/Explicit Detail.*** In lines 15–19 and lines 30–33, the author discusses the strength of African American political organizations in southern states during the nineteenth century. In lines 37–40, the author mentions the strength of African American political organizations in northern states during the twentieth century. So, (C) is correct. As for the other answer choices, (A) is incorrect because the civil rights movement did not occur until the second half of the twentieth century. (B) is incorrect because, while the Fifteenth Amendment is mentioned in lines 2–3, it is not cited as a reason why African Americans won congressional seats during these two time periods. Finally, (D) is incorrect since there is no evidence to support this idea.

18. According to the passage, the Congressional Black Caucus:

F. focused its attention almost exclusively on domestic issues.
G. was the first organization founded exclusively for African American congressional representatives.
H. was intended to replace local African American political organizations with one large national organization.
J. provided a forum in which African American representatives could deal with issues of concern to all African Americans.

19. The last paragraph suggests that this passage might serve as:

A. a call to political involvement on the part of African Americans.
B. an introduction to biographies of African American members of Congress.
C. the conclusion of a history of African Americans in the United States.
D. part of a longer work on the history of the United States Congress.

20. The author expresses admiration toward the African American congressional representatives discussed in the passage for their:

F. political acumen.
G. attempts to ensure the rights of all Americans.
H. single-minded devotion to the struggle for civil rights.
J. focus on providing economic opportunity for African Americans.

18. (J) ***Reading/Social Science/Explicit Detail.*** In lines 66–73, the author discusses the Congressional Black Caucus. Specifically, the author says that the caucus "offered a formal means of representing the combined interests of African Americans." So, (J) is the correct answer choice. As for the other answer choices, (F) is incorrect because it is contradicted by line 72. (G) and (H) are incorrect because there is no evidence in the passage to support these ideas.

19. (B) ***Reading/Social Science/Main Idea.*** In the last paragraph, the author specifically mentions the "collected biographies of African Americans who served in the House and Senate" (lines 93–94) as well as "their stories" (line 97). Based on these details, it is logical to assume that this passage could serve as the introduction to a collection of biographies of African American members of Congress. So, (B) is the correct answer choice. As for the other answer choices, they are all incorrect because there is no evidence in the final paragraph to support these ideas.

20. (G) ***Reading/Social Science/Implied Idea.*** In lines 98–99, the author praises African American members of Congress for their "long struggle to extend the ideals of the founders to encompass all citizens of the United States." In other words, they are praised for their efforts to ensure the rights of all Americans. So, (G) is the correct answer choice. As for the other answer choices, (F) is incorrect because it is never mentioned in the passage. (H) and (J) are incorrect because they are contradicted by the above quotation.

Passage III

HUMANITIES: This passage is adapted from Thomas Bulfinch's *Mythology.*

Minerva was the goddess of wisdom, but on one occasion she did a very foolish thing; she entered into competition with Juno and Venus for the prize of beauty. It happened thus: at the nuptials of Peleus and Thetis all the gods were invited with the exception of Eris, or Discord. Enraged at her exclusion, the goddess threw a golden apple among the guests, with the inscription, "For the fairest." Thereupon Juno, Venus, and Minerva each claimed the apple. Jupiter, not willing to decide in so delicate a matter, sent the goddesses to Mount Ida, where the beautiful shepherd Paris was tending his flocks, and to him was committed the decision. The goddesses accordingly appeared before him. Juno promised him power and riches, Minerva glory and renown in war, and Venus the fairest of women for his wife, each attempting to bias his decision in her own favour. Paris decided in favour of Venus and gave her the golden apple, thus making the two other goddesses his enemies. Under the protection of Venus, Paris sailed to Greece, and was hospitably received by Menelaus, king of Sparta. Now Helen, the wife of Menelaus, was the very woman whom Venus had destined for Paris, the fairest of her sex. She had been sought as a bride by numerous suitors, and before her decision was made known, they all, at the suggestion of Ulysses, one of their number, took an oath that they would defend her from all injury and avenge her cause if necessary. She chose Menelaus, and was living with him happily when Paris became their guest. Paris, aided by Venus, persuaded her to elope with him, and carried her to Troy, whence arose the famous Trojan War, the theme of the greatest poems of antiquity, those of Homer and Virgil.

Menelaus called upon his brother chieftains of Greece to fulfill their pledge, and join him in his efforts to recover his wife. They generally came forward, but Ulysses, who had married Penelope, and was very happy in his wife and child, had no disposition to embark in such a troublesome affair. He therefore hung back and Palamedes was sent to urge him. When Palamedes arrived at Ithaca, Ulysses pretended to be mad. He yoked an ass and an ox together to the plough and began to sow salt. Palamedes, to try him, placed the infant Telemachus before the plough, whereupon the father turned the plough aside, showing plainly that he was no madman, and after that could no longer refuse to fulfill his promise. Being now himself gained for the undertaking, he lent his aid to bring in other reluctant chiefs, especially Achilles. This hero was the son of that Thetis at whose marriage the apple of Discord had been thrown among the goddesses. Thetis was herself one of the immortals, a sea-nymph, and knowing that her son was fated to perish before Troy if he went on the expedition, she endeavored to prevent his going. She sent him away to the court of King Lycomedes, and induced him to conceal himself in the disguise of a maiden among the daughters of the king. Ulysses, hearing he was there, went disguised as a merchant to the palace and offered for sale female ornaments, among which he had placed some arms. While the king's daughters were engrossed with the other contents of the merchant's pack, Achilles handled the weapons and thereby betrayed himself to the keen eye of Ulysses, who found no great difficulty in persuading him to disregard his mother's prudent counsels and join his countrymen in the war.

21. By describing Jupiter as "not willing to decide in so delicate a matter" (lines 9–10), the author implies that:

A. Jupiter is usually heavy-handed.
B. any decision is bound to offend someone.
C. Jupiter is overly sensitive.
D. the problems are so obscure that no one can judge them.

22. The word *disposition* (line 38) is used to mean:

F. inclination.
G. nature.
H. integrity.
J. value.

23. All of the following assertions are examples of the author's inserting himself into the narrative EXCEPT:

A. Minerva did a foolish thing.
B. The poems of Homer and Virgil were great.
C. Helen was the fairest of her sex.
D. The greatest poems of antiquity were about the Trojan War.

24. Ulysses pretended to be mad by planting salt because salt:

F. does not grow.
G. is nearly worthless.
H. was used for money.
J. is used in battle.

21. (B) ***Reading/Humanities/Implied Idea.*** Jupiter is asked to decide which of three goddesses is the fairest—Juno, Minerva, or Venus. Regardless of which goddess he selects, he will anger the other two because he did not choose them. It is a no-win proposition in that he is bound to offend someone. So, (B) is the correct answer choice. As for the other answer choices, they are all incorrect since there is no evidence to support these ideas.

22. (F) ***Reading/Humanities/Vocabulary.*** The passage tells us that "Ulysses, who had married Penelope, and was very happy in his wife and child, had no disposition to embark in such a troublesome affair" (lines 37–39). Given the context, it is clear that "disposition" means "inclination." In other words, Ulysses had no inclination to embark on the adventure since he is happy at home with his family. So, (F) is the correct answer choice. As for the other answer choices, they are all incorrect because they cannot substitute for "disposition" and create a sentence with the same meaning as the original.

23. (C) ***Reading/Humanities/Voice.*** In lines 1–2, the author asserts that Minerva once did a foolish thing, (A). In lines 32–33, the author asserts that the poems of Homer and Virgil were great, (B), as well as that the greatest poems of antiquity were about the Trojan War, (D). Nowhere in the passage, though, does the author claim that Helen was the fairest of her sex. Instead, it is Venus who identifies Helen as "the fairest of her sex" (lines 23–24) and destines her for a relationship with Paris. So, (C) is the correct answer choice.

24. (F) ***Reading/Humanities/Implied Idea.*** In lines 41–42, the author says "Ulysses pretended to be mad" in order to avoid going off to war. The author then says Ulysses attempted to prove his madness by hitching a mismatched pair of animals together ("an ass and an ox") and sowing into the ground something that could never grow—salt. So, (F) is the correct answer choice. As for the other answer choices, they are all incorrect since there no evidence to support these ideas.

25. When Palamedes tries Ulysses (lines 43–47), he:

A. finds him guilty.
B. judges him.
C. tests him.
D. attempts to help him.

26. The author reveals that Thetis is a sea-nymph in order to explain:

F. why she married Peleus.
G. why she dislikes the idea of war.
H. the effect of the apple of Discord.
J. her ability to predict the future.

27. Among the chieftains of Greece apparently are:

A. Juno, Venus, and Minerva.
B. Paris and Lycomedes.
C. Ulysses, Achilles, and Menelaus.
D. Eris and Thetis.

28. Why does Ulysses display arms among the ornaments?

F. To trick Achilles into revealing himself
G. As a declaration of war
H. To mislead the daughters of the king
J. To complete his disguise as a merchant

25. (C) ***Reading/Humanities/Implied Idea.*** In lines 43–47, Palamades visits Ulysses to take him to war. Ulysses does not wish to go and pretends to be insane. Palamades is skeptical of Ulysses' act, though, and thinks up a way to test him. He puts Ulysses' child in the path of a sharp plow that Ulysses steers across a field. Ulysses steers the plow so his young child's life is spared, proving that he is indeed sane. (C) is the correct answer choice because Palamades tries Ulysses in this manner to test him. As for the other answer choices, they are all incorrect because there is no evidence to support these ideas.

26. (J) ***Reading/Humanities/Implied Idea.*** In lines 51–54, the author explains how Thetis, "one of the immortals, a sea nymph" tried to prevent her son Achilles from going off to war because she knew "that her son was fated to perish before Troy if he went on the expedition." Instead of stating explicitly that Thetis could read the future, the author merely mentions her immortal status and expects the reader to understand that this means she can see into the future. So, (J) is the correct answer choice. As for the other answer choices, they are all incorrect because there is no evidence to support these ideas.

27. (C) ***Reading/Humanities/Explicit Detail.*** Juno, Venus, and Minerva, (A), are the goddesses mentioned in the first paragraph. Paris, (B), is "the beautiful shepherd" (line 11) who is asked to decide which of the goddesses is fairest. Eris and Thetis, (D), are the goddess of Discord (line 6) and a sea-nymph (line 52) respectively. Finally, in lines 34–35, the author says "Menelaus called upon his brother chieftains of Greece to fulfill their pledge." The author then explains how Ulysses and Achilles were gathered for the impending war; in other words, they too are chieftains of Greece. So, (C) is the correct answer choice.

28. (F) ***Reading/Humanities/Implied Idea.*** Readers are expected to understand Ulysses' clever ploy at King Lycomedes' court even though it is not entirely spelled out. In short, Ulysses visits the court because he knows Achilles is hiding there. Ulysses disguises himself as a merchant and pretends to sell "female ornaments" (lines 59–60) to the women at the court. Mixed into this collection of ornaments, though, are several weapons ("some arms"). Now Achilles, who has disguised himself as a woman so he won't be recognized, comes to look through the wares being offered by this new merchant. Achilles looks only at the weapons and ignores the "female ornaments"

29. According to the passage, the events described will ultimately lead to:

I. the death of Achilles.
II. the advent of war.
III. the downfall of Paris.

A. I only
B. II only
C. I and II only
D. II and III only

30. A reasonable title for this narrative might be:

F. "Achilles and Ulysses"
G. "The Apple of Discord Leads to War"
H. "Beauty and the Beast"
J. "The Pettiness of the Gods"

entirely. In this manner, Achilles betrays himself "to the keen eye of Ulysses" (lines 63–64) and is discovered. (F) is the correct answer choice because, as shown above, the purpose of Ulysses' clever ploy is to trick Achilles into revealing himself.

29. (C) ***Reading/Humanities/Development.*** In lines 51–54, the passage foreshadows the death of Achilles by telling us that Thetis knows "her son was fated to perish before Troy if he went on the expedition." So, (I) is true. In lines 28–33, the author describes Helen's elopement with Paris from "whence arose the famous Trojan War"; in addition, the second paragraph describes the gathering of chieftains in preparation for war. So, (II) is true. Nowhere in the passage, though, is the downfall of Paris mentioned. So, only (I) and (II) are true. Therefore, (C) is the correct answer choice.

30. (G) ***Reading/Humanities/Main Idea.*** The correct answer choice is (G). "The Apple of Discord Leads to War" is a title that accurately and fully summarizes all of the events, characters, and themes in this passage. As for the other answer choices, (F) is incorrect because Achilles and Ulysses are only two of several important characters here. (H) is incorrect because it is not clear who "Beauty and the Beast" would be. Finally, (J) is incorrect because the title only relates to part of the passage; in short, the pettiness of the gods precipitates the chain of events in this passage, but much happens in the latter part that is unrelated to the gods' pettiness.

Passage IV

NATURAL SCIENCE: This passage discusses the production of electromagnetic radiation.

When you run a comb through your hair, you disturb electrons in both your hair and the comb, producing static electricity. You can do a simple experiment to confirm this. Stand near an AM radio and comb your hair. You'll hear static. The scientific principle that you've just proved is: whenever you disturb electrons, you generate electromagnetic waves.

The principle also applies to heated objects. The atoms in a heated object are vibrating rapidly, and the hotter the object becomes, the faster the atoms vibrate. The vibrating atoms collide with the electrons in the material. Each time the motion of an electron is disturbed, it emits a photon. Therefore, heated objects emit electromagnetic radiation. This type of radiation, called black body radiation, is very common and is responsible for the light emitted from an ordinary incandescent light bulb.

The light coming from the bulb that your eye can detect is called visible light, but the visible spectrum is just a small segment of the much larger electromagnetic spectrum. The average wavelength of visible light is about 0.0005 mm, so small that 50 light waves could be lined up end to end across the thickness of ordinary plastic wrap. For this reason, scientists measure wavelengths in Angstroms. One Angstrom (Å) is 10^{-10} meters or 0.0000000001 meters.

Visible light ranges from 4,000 Å to 7,000 Å. Light near the short wavelength end of the visible spectrum (4,000 Å) looks violet, and light near the long wavelength end (7,000 Å) looks red. Beyond the red end of the visible spectrum lies infrared radiation, where wavelengths range from 7,000 Å to 1 mm. At wavelengths shorter than violet, there is ultraviolet radiation. These wavelengths range from 4,000 Å down to about l00 Å. At wavelengths shorter than these are X-rays and gamma rays.

Although we cannot see it, our skin senses long wavelength radiation (7,000 Å to 1 mm) as warmth. This is the principle on which "heat lamps" work. These lower-energy photons can warm us without being dangerous. In contrast, the short wavelengths contain a large amount of energy, and these wavelengths can be quite dangerous.

When a bulb's filament is heated, three sorts of collisions take place among the electrons. Gentle collisions produce low-energy photons with long wavelengths, and violent collisions produce high-energy photons with short wavelengths. Most collisions are of moderate intensity, producing photons of intermediate wavelengths.

The wavelength at which an object emits the maximum amount of energy is called the wavelength of maximum. The wavelength of maximum depends on the object's temperature. As an object is heated, the average collision between electrons becomes more violent, producing high-energy, shorter-wavelength photons. The hotter the object is, the shorter the wavelength of maximum.

This is a very important point in astronomy, since it is possible to determine the temperature of a star from its light. It is also possible to estimate the temperature of a star from the color of light it emits. For a hot star the wavelength of maximum lies in the ultraviolet spectrum and most of the radiation cannot be seen, but in the visible range the star emits more blue than red. Thus, a hot star looks blue. In contrast, a cooler star radiates its maximum energy in the infrared. In the visible range of the spectrum it radiates more red than blue and therefore looks red.

31. According to the passage, which of the following types of radiation has the shortest wavelength?

A. infrared light
B. visible light
C. ultraviolet light
D. X-rays

31. (D) ***Reading/Natural Science/Explicit Detail.*** Lines 35–36 state that X-rays are found at wavelengths shorter than 100 Å, which is the lower end of ultraviolet radiation. The correct answer choice is (D).

32. It can be inferred that radiation of very short wavelengths can be dangerous because the radiation:

F. has no wavelength of maximum.
G. has very high energy.
H. originated in a black body.
J. is visible to the eye.

32. (G) ***Reading/Natural Science/Explicit Detail.*** Lines 41–43 explain that short wavelengths contain a high amount of energy, which makes them more dangerous than long wavelengths. So, the correct answer choice is (G).

33. According to the passage, the wavelength of maximum is:

A. the maximum temperature at which a body emits light.
B. visible radiation with the longest wavelength.
C. the wavelength of light at the red end of the spectrum.
D. the wavelength at which a body emits the maximum amount of energy.

33. (D) ***Reading/Natural Science/Explicit Detail.*** The definition appears in lines 51–53. In short, it is the wavelength at which an object emits the maximum amount of energy. So, (D) is the correct answer choice.

34. The main purpose of the second paragraph is to:

F. introduce a new theory of electromagnetic radiation.
G. define the scientific concept of black body radiation.
H. contrast black body radiation with incandescence.
J. illustrate the different kinds of radiation that make up the spectrum.

34. (G) ***Reading/Natural Science/Main Idea.*** The last sentence of the second paragraph states the main point of the paragraph, which is to define for the reader the concept of black body radiation. So, (G) is the correct answer choice.

35. According to the passage, ultraviolet radiation has wavelengths:

A. shorter than 100 Å.
B. between 100 Å and 4,000 Å.
C. between 4,000 Å and 7,000 Å.
D. longer than 7,000 Å.

35. (B) ***Reading/Natural Science/Explicit Detail.*** According to the fourth paragraph, ultraviolet radiation is the radiation with wavelengths from 4,000 Å down to 100 Å.

36. The passage implies that "heat lamps" utilize:

F. X-rays.
G. gamma rays.
H. visible wavelengths.
J. infrared radiation.

37. An astronomer views two stars of different temperatures. Which is hotter?

A. The one that is larger.
B. The one that is smaller.
C. The one that is redder.
D. The one that is bluer.

38. According to the sixth paragraph (lines 44–50), most of the electron collisions in the filament of a light bulb are:

F. gentle and emit photons with long wavelengths.
G. violent and emit photons with short wavelengths.
H. violent and emit photons with long wavelengths.
J. moderate and emit photons of intermediate wavelengths.

39. It can be inferred from the information that an incandescent bulb emits light because:

A. electricity heats the bulb's filament.
B. high-energy radiation surrounds the filament.
C. non-visible radiation bombards the filament.
D. high-energy photons collide with the atoms.

40. According to the information provided, heating an object results in electron collisions that produce:

F. higher energy photons with shorter wavelengths.
G. photons of intermediate wavelengths.
H. no net effect on the wavelength of the radiation emitted.
J. more red light than blue light.

36. (J) ***Reading/Natural Science/Explicit Detail.*** In lines 37–41, the passage states that we cannot see the radiation from a heat lamp but do experience it as warmth. Radiation of wavelengths 7,000 Å to 1 mm is infrared radiation. So, (J) is the correct answer choice.

37. (D) ***Reading/Natural Science/Explicit Detail.*** In lines 59–69, the author discusses the temperature of stars. In line 66, the author states that "a hot star looks blue." So, (D) is the correct answer choice.

38. (J) ***Reading/Natural Science/Explicit Detail.*** The sixth paragraph describes three types of collisions: gentle, violent, and moderate. Lines 48–50 state that most of the collisions are of moderate intensity and produce photons of intermediate wavelengths. There are fewer gentle, (F), and violent, (G) and (H), collisions.

39. (A) ***Reading/Natural Science/Implied Idea.*** The passage states that the incandescent light bulb is a heated object (lines 13–17). The light is emitted when electrons collide in the filament because the filament is heated (lines 44–50).

40. (F) ***Reading/Natural Science/Application.*** The information is explicitly stated in lines 44–48.

4 4 4 4 4 4 4 4 4 4 4 4

SCIENCE TEST

40 Items

DIRECTIONS: Each passage below is followed by several items. After reading a passage, choose the best answer for each item. You may refer to the passage as often as necessary. You are NOT permitted the use of a calculator on this test.

Passage I

The solubility of materials in liquids depends not only on the nature of the solute and the solvent, but also on temperature. A graph showing the solubilities of several substances in water is presented below.

Solubility Curves

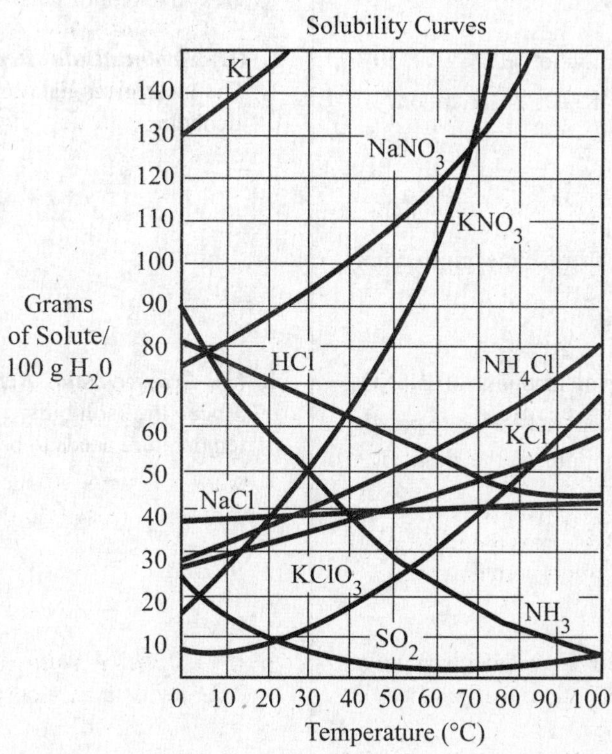

Note: NH_3 is a gas

1. Which of the following has the most temperature sensitive solubility throughout the range shown?

A. KNO_3
B. $NaNO_3$
C. NaCl
D. NH_3

1. **(A)** ***Science/Data Representation/Comprehension.*** The sharpest sloping curve is for potassium nitrate (KNO_3).

2. The solubility of sodium (Na) salts is:

F. high because sodium is an alkali metal.
G. low because sodium combines with anions to make salts.
H. dependent on what salt it forms.
J. always greater than 20 grams per 100 grams of water.

2. **(H)** ***Science/Data Representation/Analysis.*** The sodium salts, NaCl and $NaNO_3$, have different solubilities, indicating that solubility depends on more than the nature of sodium. Thus, (F) and (G) must be incorrect. (J) is incorrect because it is not known whether the solubility curves for all sodium compounds have been given. (H) is correct because it takes into account the differences in solubilities of different sodium salts.

3. A 250 ml alcoholic solution of KNO_3 at 50°C contains how many grams KNO_3 at saturation?

A. 200
B. 80
C. 30
D. Cannot be determined from the given information

3. **(D)** ***Science/Data Representation/Comprehension.*** The table gives data only for aqueous solutions, not alcoholic.

4. A solution containing equal amounts of $NaNO_3$ and KNO_3 is allowed to cool until a white powder begins to appear at the bottom of the flask. That powder is:

F. KNO_3.
G. $NaNO_3$.
H. a mixture of both.
J. Cannot be determined from the given information

4. **(J)** ***Science/Data Representation/Comprehension.*** Since the solubility curves cross at 71°F, the temperature needs to be known.

5. The solubility curve of NH_3 suggests an explanation of why:

A. divers get the bends (nitrogen bubbles in the blood) if they rise too quickly.
B. soda goes flat.
C. warm lemonade is sweeter than cold lemonade.
D. hot air balloons rise.

5. **(B)** ***Science/Data Representation/Application.*** Soda goes flat as gas (carbon dioxide) leaves the liquid. The warmer the soda, the faster it goes flat. (A) shows the effect of pressure, not temperature, on solubility. (C) shows the solubility of a solid (sugar), which has nothing to do with the solubility characteristics of a gas. (D) deals with relative densities of gases and not with solubilities.

Passage II

Part of our understanding of Earth comes from a consideration of its physical properties. Selected properties of Earth are presented in Table 1.

Table 1

Property	*Value*
Mass	6×10^{24} kg
Diameter	6×10^{6} m
Orbital Radius	1.5×10^{11} m
Period of Revolution	365.3 days
Period of Rotation	24 hours

Table 2 compares the properties of the other planets of the solar system relative to Earth's properties.

Table 2

Property	Earth	Jupiter	Mars	Mercury	Neptune	Pluto	Saturn	Uranus	Venus
Diameter	1	10	0.55	0.38	4.3	?	9.4	4.1	0.98
Mass	1	320	0.10	0.58	17	?	95	14	0.83
Surface Gravity	1	2.7	0.40	0.40	1.2	?	1.2	1.1	0.90
Volume	1	1,320	0.15	0.58	42	0.729	760	50	0.90
Average Distance to Sun	1	5.3	1.5	0.40	30	40	10	19	0.70
Period of Revolution	1	12	2	0.25	165	248	30	84	0.60
Period of Rotation	1	0.40	1	60	0.50	0	0.40	0.50	240

The following are a few basic equations:

(1) $\text{density} = \dfrac{\text{mass}}{\text{volume}}$

(2) distance = rate • time

(3) $\text{volume}_{\text{sphere}} = \dfrac{4}{3}\pi r^3$, where r is the radius of the sphere

6. Based on the information given in Table 1 and Table 2, what is the approximate ratio of the period of revolution in days to the period of rotation in days for Mercury?

F. 240
G. $\frac{3}{2}$
H. $\frac{2}{3}$
J. $\frac{1}{240}$

6. **(G)** ***Science/Data Representation/Comprehension.*** Mercury's period of revolution equals $0.25 \bullet$ period of Earth's revolution $= 0.25 \bullet 365.3$ days ≈ 90 days. Mercury's period of rotation equals $60 \bullet$ period of Earth's rotation $= 60 \bullet 1$ day $= 60$ days. The ratio of revolution to rotation $= \frac{90}{60} = \frac{3}{2}$.

7. Which planet is as dense as the planet Earth?

A. Mercury
B. Venus
C. Mars
D. None

7. **(A)** ***Science/Data Representation/Comprehension.*** Mercury's density equals that of the Earth. Density is mass divided by volume:

$$\begin{aligned} \text{density}_{\text{Mercury}} &= \frac{\text{mass}_{\text{Mercury}}}{\text{volume}_{\text{Mercury}}} \\ &= \frac{0.58 \bullet \text{mass}_{\text{Earth}}}{0.58 \bullet \text{volume}_{\text{Earth}}} \\ &= \frac{\text{mass}_{\text{Earth}}}{\text{volume}_{\text{Earth}}} \\ &= \text{density}_{\text{Earth}} \end{aligned}$$

8. Which planet orbits the sun at the slowest rate?

F. Mercury
G. Jupiter
H. Neptune
J. Pluto

8. **(J)** ***Science/Data Representation/Comprehension.*** Rate is distance divided by time. Divide the average distance to the sun by the period of revolution to get the relative rate. The smallest relative rate is the slowest. In this specific case, the planet with the greatest relative period of revolution orbits the sun at the slowest rate.

9. Analysis of Table 1 and Table 2 shows that surface gravity most likely depends on:

A. mass alone.
B. distance and mass.
C. density alone.
D. density of the planet and proximity to the sun.

9. **(B)** ***Science/Data Representation/Analysis.*** Gravity depends on both the distance between the centers of objects (and thereby the volume—assuming the planets are roughly spherical in shape) and on the mass of the objects. Compare Mars and Mercury to see the effect of volume (by considering their diameters). Mars is more massive, but the smaller size of Mercury gives it an equivalent surface gravity. Density, a ratio of mass and volume, is not enough because gravity depends on the amount of mass and the amount of distance, not their ratio.

10. Assuming that both Earth and Pluto are spherical, the diameter of Pluto is:

F. 0.729 times the Earth's radius.
G. 0.9 times the Earth's radius.
H. 1.8 times the Earth's radius.
J. 2.7 times the Earth's radius.

10. (H) ***Science/Data Representation/Comprehension.***

$$\frac{\text{volume}_{\text{Pluto}}}{\text{volume}_{\text{Earth}}} = 0.729$$

$$\frac{\frac{4}{3}\pi r^3_{\text{Pluto}}}{\frac{4}{3}\pi r^3_{\text{Earth}}} = 0.729$$

$$\frac{r^3_{\text{Pluto}}}{r^3_{\text{Earth}}} = 0.729$$

$$\frac{r_{\text{Pluto}}}{r_{\text{Earth}}} = \sqrt[3]{0.729} = 0.9$$

Therefore:

$$\text{diameter}_{\text{Pluto}} = 2(0.9)(\text{radius}_{\text{Earth}}) = 1.8(\text{radius}_{\text{Earth}})$$

11. How many meters separate the orbits of the farthest apart planetary neighbors?

A. 40 times the Earth's orbital radius.
B. 11 times the Earth's orbital radius.
C. 10 times the Earth's orbital radius.
D. 9 times the Earth's orbital radius.

11. (B) ***Science/Data Representation/Comprehension.*** The neighbors that are farthest from each other are Uranus and Neptune. Relative distances to the sun are as follows:

$$\frac{\text{Mercury}}{0.4} < \frac{\text{Venus}}{0.7} < \frac{\text{Earth}}{1} <$$

$$\frac{\text{Mars}}{1.5} < \frac{\text{Jupiter}}{5.3} < \frac{\text{Saturn}}{10} <$$

$$\frac{\text{Uranus}}{19} < \frac{\text{Neptune}}{30} < \frac{\text{Pluto}}{40}$$

The largest difference is $30 - 19 = 11$.

Passage III

Four groups of 1,000 men each were placed on strict diets that contained different intakes of cholesterol. The men stayed on the diet for 40 years, and their history of illness over that time is recorded below.

	Death rate, standardized/1,000			
		Men taking in a daily average of		
Illness	No cholesterol	0–5 grams	6–20 grams	20+ grams
Cancer				
Colon	0.01	0.03	0.04	0.02
Prostate	2.02	0.06	1.03	4.01
Lung	0.03	0.06	0.40	0.20
Coronary				
Thrombosis	5.02	1.01	4.00	10.05
Arrest	6.00	0.98	5.09	11.00
Cardiovascular	5.96	0.65	4.97	9.08
Cerebral Clot	4.01	0.02	0.50	4.01
Depression	5.01	0.30	0.30	0.30

12. Which of the following statements is best supported by the data?

F. A man ingesting no cholesterol is approximately twice as likely to die of prostate cancer as a man ingesting 10 grams per day.
G. Any ingestion of cholesterol decreases the risk of dying from all three forms of cancer listed here.
H. Ingestion of cholesterol seems unrelated to the probability of coronary disease.
J. Cerebral clots are the most prevalent form of death among the group consuming the most cholesterol.

12. (F) ***Science/Data Representation/Analysis.*** The death rate for the 6–20 grams/day cholesterol eater from prostate cancer is 1.03, while that for a non-cholesterol eater is 2.02. Thus, (F) is correct. (G) contradicts the data for colon cancer; (H) ignores the direct relationship between coronary deaths and cholesterol intake; and cardiac arrest is a more common form of death than cerebral clots for the 20+ eaters.

13. What might one conclude about the relationship between cholesterol ingestion and depression based on the information above?

A. Cholesterol causes depression.
B. Ingestion of cholesterol has no effect on the occurrence of depression.
C. Small amounts of cholesterol are most effective in combating depression.
D. Large and small amounts of cholesterol are equally effective in reducing the depression death rate.

13. (D) ***Science/Data Representation/Analysis.*** The death rate for all three groups of cholesterol-eaters from depression is 0.30. This number is lower than for non-cholesterol-eaters, so (A) and (B) are both wrong. According to the data, large amounts of cholesterol are just as effective in combating depression as small amounts, so (C) is incorrect.

14. For which of the following diseases does the highest cholesterol diet increase the probability of death most, compared relatively to the non-cholesterol diets?

F. Cerebral clots
G. Coronary arrest
H. Cardiovascular disease
J. Coronary thrombosis

14. (J) ***Science/Data Representation/Comprehension.*** Although the 20+ diet increases coronary arrest to the highest absolute death rate, the percentage increase is less than 100 percent (from 6.00 to 11.00). The percentage increase for coronary thrombosis is greater than 100 percent (from 5.02 to 10.05).

15. For which of the following groups of diseases does a daily intake of 0–5 grams of cholesterol reduce the probability of death?

A. Cerebral clot, coronary thrombosis, and lung cancer
B. Cerebral clot, depression, and colon cancer
C. Depression, coronary arrest, and prostate cancer
D. Depression, coronary thrombosis, and colon cancer

15. (C) ***Science/Data Representation/Comprehension.*** (C) is the only group in which low intake of cholesterol decreases the death rate from all three diseases. Intake of 0–5 grams raises the probability of death for lung and colon cancer only. This question is probably best answered by recognizing that fact and eliminating those choices that include either lung or colon cancer.

16. What might be involved in determining a standardized death rate for men?

F. Ignoring deaths that do not conform to the average results
G. Adjusting death rates according to discrepancies in age
H. Assuming that the natural death rate is 0 deaths per 1,000 men
J. Comparing data with a similar experiment involving women

16. (G) ***Science/Data Representation/Application.*** Standardizing the death rate involves correcting for variables inherent in the subject groups but not involved in the experiment. Age, weight, genetic histories, and accidental deaths are just some of the variables that the scientist must consider. However, (F) does not correct for intrinsic variables; rather, it ignores results that might not conform to a "neat" result. This does not standardize the death rate so much as "fudge" it. (H) involves an arbitrary assumption that is in fact incorrect. Assuming a zero death rate in the male population distorts the result of this experiment and does not correct for variations within the subject groups. (J) is incorrect because this experiment does not consider women at all. It might be valid to compare results with a different experiment involving women, but the actual death rates for men and women for different diseases are not necessarily similar (e.g., the gender-related differences for breast cancer).

Passage IV

The resistance (R) of a material is directly proportional to the resistivity (r) of the material, resistivity is measured in ohm-meters. The voltage (V, measured in volts) in a circuit is directly proportional to both the resistance (R, measured in ohms) and the current (I, measured in amperes). Resistors in series act as one resistor according to the formula:

$$R_s = R_1 + R_2 + R_3 + \ldots$$

and resistors in parallel act as one resistor according to the formula:

$$\frac{1}{R_p} = \frac{1}{R_1} + \frac{1}{R_2} + \frac{1}{R_3} + \ldots$$

The resistivities of several materials are listed in Table 1.

Table 1

Substance	Resistivity, r (ohm-meters)
Aluminum	2.63×10^{-8}
Copper	1.72×10^{-8}
Germanium	6.00×10^{-1}
Silicon	2.30×10^{3}
Silver	1.47×10^{-8}
Sulfur	1.00×10^{15}

17. According to the information provided, the best formula for the voltage in a circuit, where voltage is V, current is I, and resistance is R, is:

 A. $V = \frac{I}{R}$.
 B. $V = I + R$.
 C. $V = IR$.
 D. $V = I - R$.

17. **(C)** ***Science/Data Representation/Analysis.*** Since voltage is directly related to current, voltage increases by the same factor as current if other variables are held constant. The same applies for resistance; therefore, the only correct formula is (C).

18. Two resistors with $R = 2$ are placed in series. How does the voltage in the circuit compare with the voltage in a circuit with only one resistor, $R = 2$? (Assume current remains constant.)

 F. The voltage is doubled.
 G. The voltage is halved.
 H. The voltage is the same.
 J. The voltage is zero.

18. **(F)** ***Science/Data Representation/Application.*** The total resistance R_s of the series resistors is $R_1 + R_2 = 2 + 2 = 4$. This resistance is double that of the circuit where $R = 2$. If R doubles, then the voltage doubles as long as the current remains the same.

19. According to the information provided, how would the voltage in a circuit with a silver resistor compare to the voltage in a circuit with a germanium resistor of the same size? (Current is the same in both circuits.)

A. The voltage in the germanium circuit would be greater.
B. The voltage in the silver circuit would be greater.
C. The voltage would be the same in both circuits.
D. Cannot be determined from the given information

19. (A) ***Science/Data Representation/Analysis.*** The passage states that the voltage is directly proportional to the both the resistance and the current ($V = IR$), so the circuit with the greater resistance would have the greater voltage. Since resistance is directly proportional to resistivity, the germanium circuit would have the greater resistance and voltage.

20. A resistor with $R = 4$ is put in parallel with an identical resistor with $R = 4$. What is R_p?

F. 0
G. $\frac{1}{2}$
H. 1
J. 2

20. (J) ***Science/Data Representation/Application.*** Use the given formula for resistors in parallel:

$$\frac{1}{R_p} = \frac{1}{4} + \frac{1}{4}$$
$$= \frac{2}{4}$$
$$= \frac{1}{2}$$
$$R_p = 2$$

21. Power is defined as $P = I^2R$. If R is a constant, then power would increase ______ with an increase in the current. (Fill in the blank space with the best answer choice.)

A. exponentially
B. logarithmically
C. directly
D. inversely

21. (A) ***Science/Data Representation/Application.*** If R is constant, then P increases with I^2; this is the definition of exponential growth.

22. In order to keep the current in a circuit constant, if one increases the voltage, one must:

F. lengthen the circuit.
G. shorten the circuit.
H. decrease the resistance.
J. increase the resistance.

22. (J) ***Science/Data Representation/Analysis.*** Based on the information given in the passage, we have:

$$V = IR$$
$$I = \frac{V}{R}$$

Therefore, to keep I constant if V increases, R must be increased.

Passage V

In order to discover the steps by which a chemical reaction occurs, the dependence of the initial rate of reaction on the concentration of the reactants is determined. Three experiments exploring the mechanism of a reaction are presented below.

Experiment 1

Compound A is injected into a rapidly stirred solution of B in hexamethyl phosphor-amide. As A and B react, they form a compound that has a characteristic absorption at 520 nanometers. The concentration of product, and therefore the rate of reaction, can be calculated by measuring the strength of the absorption. Results are presented below:

Table 1

Trial	Concentration A	Concentration B	Rate
1	4	4	60
2	2	2	30
3	4	2	30
4	4	8	120

Experiment 2

Compound A is injected into a rapidly mixed solution of B in carbon tetrachloride. The product of the reaction is identical to the product in Experiment 1. The course of the reaction is followed by spectrophotometric methods as in Experiment 1.

Table 2

Trial	Concentration A	Concentration B	Rate
1	3	3	27
2	6	6	108
3	6	3	54
4	12	6	216

Experiment 3

Compound A is injected in a swirling solution of B in a 1:1-by-volume mixture of carbon tetrachloride and hexamethyl phosphoramide. The formation of product, as before, is followed by spectrophotometry.

Table 3

Trial	Concentration A	Concentration B	Rate
1	9	9	54
2	9	4.5	27
3	4	4.5	18
4	4	9	36

23. Which of the following statements best describes the effect of Concentration A on the rate of reaction in Experiment 1?

A. Rate increases with increasing A.
B. Rate increases by the square of A's concentration.
C. Rate increases by the square root of A's concentration.
D. Rate is independent of A's concentration.

23. (D) ***Science/Research Summary/Analysis.*** Compare Trials 2 and 3 to see what changing the concentration of only one component has on rate. In this case, there is no change in rate with change in concentration of A, so rate is independent of concentration.

24. Which of the following statements best describes the effect of Concentration A on the rate of reaction in Experiment 2?

F. Rate increases with increasing A.
G. Rate increases by the square of A's concentration.
H. Rate increases by the square root of A's concentration.
J. Rate is independent of A's concentration.

24. (F) ***Science/Research Summary/Analysis.*** Compare Trials 2 and 4 or Trials 1 and 3 to see what changing the concentration of only one component has on rate. In this case, rate increases with increasing A.

25. Which of the following statements best describes the effect of Concentration A on the rate in Experiment 3?

A. Rate increases with increasing A.
B. Rate increases by the square of A's concentration.
C. Rate increases by the square root of A's concentration.
D. Rate is independent of A's concentration.

25. (C) ***Science/Research Summary/Analysis.*** Compare Trials 1 and 4 or Trials 2 and 3 to see what changing the concentration of only one component has on rate. In this case, rate increases by the square of the starting concentration of A.

26. What is the likeliest explanation for the results obtained in Experiment 3?

F. A mechanism intermediates between the ones found in Experiments 1 and 2.
G. Some of the molecules react by Experiment 1's mechanism, others by Experiment 2's mechanism.
H. A different mechanism is responsible.
J. There is an averaging of the mechanisms.

26. (H) ***Science/Research Summary/Analysis.*** Averaging or intermediate mechanisms do not work because one mechanism has no dependence on A with regard to rate. (G) is unlikely because a well-mixed solution should be homogeneous and have no pockets for mechanisms 1 and 2.

27. What is the best conclusion that can be drawn from this set of experiments?

   A. Rate is increased by changing solvents.
   B. Reactions may depend on solvent effects as well as on the nature of the reactants.
   C. Mechanisms can always be changed by use of an appropriate solvent.
   D. Reactions depend on solvent effects as well as on the nature of the reactants.

27. **(B)** ***Science/Research Summary/Analysis.*** This is a subtle question. (C) and (D) are incorrect because they over-generalize from a single case. It cannot be said that mechanisms can always be changed, (C), or that in every case the mechanism depends on solvent effects, (D). (A) is a special case of (D), where the claim is made that all reactions are solvent dependent. (B) alone allows for the possibility that solvents need not have an effect (note the word "may").

Passage VI

Acceleration is defined as the change in the velocity of an object divided by the length of time during which that change took place. Contrary to popular belief, Galileo did not base his conclusion of the acceleration of gravity on experiments done with cannonballs dropped from the Leaning Tower of Pisa. Instead, he used the motion of objects moving down an inclined plane to develop his theory. In the following sets of experiments, a student studies the motion of bodies on an inclined plane.

For all of the following experiments, time is measured in seconds, distance in meters, and velocity in meters per second. The distance (d) an object travels at a constant acceleration (a) in time (t), assuming it starts from rest, is given by the equation: $d = \frac{1}{2}at^2$.

Experiment 1

A student set up a smooth wooden board at an angle of 30° from horizontal. The board had a length of 10 meters. Using a stroboscope, the student was able to determine the position of a 100-gram steel ball that was rolled down the incline. Velocity was determined by means of a radar gun. The results are presented in Table 1.

Table 1

Time	Distance (m)	Velocity (m/sec)
0	0	0
0.5	0.44	1.75
1.0	1.75	3.5
1.5	3.94	5.25
2.0	7.00	7.00

Experiment 2

The same 10-meter wooden board was used in Experiment 2. The angle used was again 30°. The object used this time was a 100-gram sled made of the same material as the ball in Experiment 1. The stroboscope and the radar gun were used to determine its position and velocity as it slid down the inclined plane. The results are presented in Table 2.

Table 2

Time	Distance (m)	Velocity (m/sec)
0	0	0
0.5	1.13	2.45
1.0	2.45	4.90
1.5	5.51	7.35
2.0	9.80	9.80

Experiment 3

The same board at the same angle was used in the third experiment as in the previous two. In this experiment, a 100-gram box made of the same material as the ball and the sled was used. The same recording devices were used, and the results are presented in Table 3.

Table 3

Time	Distance (m)	Velocity (m/sec)
0	0	0
1.0	0.33	0.66
2.0	1.31	1.32
3.0	2.97	1.98
4.0	5.28	2.64
5.0	8.25	3.30

Experiment 4

The board in the previous experiments was carefully oiled. Once again, the board was placed at an angle of 30° from horizontal. Each of the objects was then allowed to move down the inclined plane, and the time required to reach the bottom of the plane is recorded in Table 4.

Table 4

Object	Time
sled	2.02
ball	2.39
box	4.08

28. Which object in the first three experiments has the greatest acceleration?

F. Ball
G. Sled
H. Box
J. Ball and sled are equal.

29. The acceleration of the ball relative to that of the sled is due to the ball's:

A. rolling.
B. friction.
C. rolling and friction.
D. being the same mass as the sled, and therefore having the same acceleration.

28. (G) ***Science/Research Summary/Comprehension.*** The first sentence of the passage tells us that:

$$\text{acceleration} = \frac{\text{change in velocity}}{\text{change in time}} = \frac{\Delta v}{\Delta t}$$

Experiment 1 (steel ball): The acceleration is constant at 3.5 m/sec^2. This can be demonstrated by choosing a time interval and dividing the corresponding velocity change during the time interval by the length of the time interval. For example, between 1 and 2 seconds, the velocity changes from 3.5 m/sec to 7 m/sec; therefore, the acceleration is equal to:

$$\frac{\Delta v}{\Delta t} = \frac{7-3.5}{2-1} = \frac{3.5}{1} = 3.5 \text{ m/sec}^2$$

For a time interval from 0.5 seconds to 1 second, the corresponding velocity would change from 1.75 m/sec to 3.5 m/sec; therefore, the acceleration is equal to:

$$\frac{\Delta v}{\Delta t} = \frac{3.5-1.75}{1-0.5} = \frac{1.75}{0.5} = 3.5 \text{ m/sec}^2$$

Experiment 2 (sled): The acceleration is a constant 4.9 m/sec^2. For example, the change in velocity corresponding to the time interval from 0.5 seconds to 1 second is 4.90 m/sec − 2.45 m/sec = 2.45 m/sec; therefore, the acceleration is equal to:

$$\frac{\Delta v}{\Delta t} = \frac{4.90-2.45}{1-0.5} = \frac{2.45}{0.5} = 4.9 \text{ m/sec}^2$$

Experiment 3 (box): The acceleration is constant at 0.66 m/sec^2.

29. (A) ***Science/Research Summary/Analysis.*** When friction is reduced in Experiment 4, the sled and the ball still travel at about the same accelerations as in the previous experiments. This can be demonstrated by using the equation $d = 0.5at^2$, which relates the distance that an object travels starting from rest to the time (traveling at constant acceleration) it takes to travel the indicated distance. Since the board is 10 meters in length, the distance that each travels is 10 meters. Therefore, for the sled:

$$d = \frac{1}{2}at^2$$

$$10 = \frac{1}{2}a(2.02)^2$$

$$\approx \frac{1}{2}(a)(4)$$

$$a = 5 \text{ m/sec}^2$$

For the ball:

$$d = \frac{1}{2}at^2$$

$$10 = \frac{1}{2}a(2.39)^2$$

$$\approx \frac{1}{2}(a)(5.7)$$

$$a = 3.5 \text{ m/sec}^2$$

The ball and sled travel at about the same accelerations before and after oiling, so the differences in their relative accelerations must be due to something other than friction. The difference is the rolling of the ball.

30. The acceleration of the ball relative to that of the box is due to:

F. the ball's rolling only.
G. the ball's friction only.
H. the ball's rolling and the box's friction.
J. the ball's having the same mass as the box, and therefore having the same acceleration.

30. (H) ***Science/Research Summary/Analysis.*** Experiment 4 shows that friction affects the relative acceleration between the box and either the sled or ball. Calculate the acceleration for the box:

$$d = \frac{1}{2}at^2$$

$$10 = \frac{1}{2}a(4.08)^2$$

$$\approx \frac{1}{2}a(16)$$

$$a = 1.25 \text{ m/sec}^2$$

Because the oiling in Experiment 4 caused a change in the box's acceleration, friction is a factor. Rolling must also be a factor as per the answer explanation to item #29.

31. Based on these four experiments, the ratio of the acceleration of the ball to the acceleration of the sled is:

A. 1.
B. $\frac{5}{7}$.
C. dependent on the amount of friction.
D. dependent on time.

31. (B) ***Science/Research Summary/Comprehension.*** The acceleration of the ball is constant at 3.5 m/sec^2 (either Experiment 1 or 4). The acceleration of the sled is constant at 4.9 m/sec^2 (Experiment 2 or 4). Therefore, the ratio of the ball's acceleration to the sled's acceleration is: $\frac{3.5}{4.9} = \frac{5}{7}$.

32. Based on these four experiments, the ratio of the acceleration of the ball to the acceleration of the box is:

F. 1.
G. $\frac{5}{7}$.
H. dependent on the amount of friction.
J. dependent on time.

32. (H) ***Science/Research Summary/Comprehension.*** Although the acceleration of the ball is relatively insensitive to the amount of friction, the acceleration of the box is very sensitive to friction. Therefore, in a ratio, the effect of changing the amount of friction will change the numerator (ball acceleration) only slightly, whereas the denominator (box acceleration) will change significantly depending on friction. (J) is not correct because the acceleration remains constant within each experiment.

Passage VII

What was the fate of Neanderthal man? Two differing views are presented below.

Scientist 1

Neanderthals were very similar to modern humans in appearance. It is true that Neanderthals were somewhat more muscular than modern humans and that the way the muscles seem to have been arranged on the skeleton was, in a few minor ways, different. This we are able to deduce from the places on the surviving bones that mark where the ligaments were once attached. For example, the neck and wrists of Neanderthals were far thicker than is natural to modern humans. Some of the facial structure was also different, especially the protrusion of the brow. But differences between the appearance of Neanderthals and modern humans have been exaggerated since they are based on the skeleton of one individual who was later discovered to have been suffering from severe arthritis. It is not unlikely that, because of the low population density and the nomadic lifestyle that spread the few individuals over ever-larger areas, Neanderthal and early modern humans interbred and eventually merged into one species. The notion that some sort of "war" broke out between these different species (or, more likely, subspecies) of humans is an attempt to look out of early human eyes with a modern perspective.

Scientist 2

Whenever two species compete for the same niche there is a conflict. In this conflict the loser either moves to a different niche or dies out. It is unusual for two species to interbreed. The difference between early modern humans and Neanderthals physically may not appear great to an anatomist, but to the average man on the street, or prehistoric man in the forest, the differences are not subtle. And it was these individuals, not the anatomists, who had to decide whether or not to mate. Even if early modern humans and Neanderthals did mate, the result—us—would look more like a mix of the two rather than like modern humans. Early modern humans and Neanderthals, because they were so close to each other physically, must have been deadly enemies. The population was thinly dispersed at that time because the resources available would not support a greater population density. There literally was not room enough on the planet for the two species. They could not combine because they were so different in appearance, so only one answer remained. We survived because we killed our cousin.

33. Underlying the hypothesis of Scientist 1 is the assumption that:

A. Neanderthals were more likely than early modern humans to suffer from diseases such as arthritis.
B. early modern humans and Neanderthals were sufficiently alike to allow them to interbreed.
C. Neanderthals and early modern humans lived in geographically distinct regions.
D. in combat a group of Neanderthals was likely to defeat a similar grouping of early modern humans.

33. (B) ***Science/Conflicting Viewpoints/Analysis.*** Scientist 1 concludes by saying that Neanderthals and early modern humans merged into a single species by interbreeding, so Scientist 1 assumes that the two groups were sufficiently similar to permit interbreeding of the members. (A) distorts the position of Scientist 1. Scientist 1 says that the picture we have of the Neanderthals is based upon one individual, an individual who was not entirely representative of his species. In other words, the one Neanderthal with arthritis was the exception, not the rule. (C) also misreads the passage. Scientist 1 says that populations were spread out geographically, not that the two groups were separated physically from one another. (Indeed, they must have lived pretty close to each other to permit the interbreeding that Scientist 1 believes occurred.) Finally, as for (D), though Scientist 1 says that Neanderthals were apparently more muscular than early modern humans, this does not automatically mean that they would win a fight. Speed, intelligence, weapons, and a lot of other factors might affect the outcome.

34. Underlying the hypotheses of both scientists is the assumption that:

F. early modern humans and Neanderthals understood the consequences of their actions.
G. early modern humans and Neanderthals both lived in exactly the same type of environment.
H. early modern humans and Neanderthals both lived in the same geographical regions.
J. early modern humans were more intelligent than Neanderthals.

34. (H) ***Science/Conflicting Viewpoints/Analysis.*** For early modern humans to completely replace Neanderthals, there could not have been a region containing Neanderthals that did not also contain early modern humans.

35. If an isolated community of Neanderthals was discovered, whose hypothesis would be more damaged?

A. Scientist l's because his theory does not allow for such a community to survive
B. Scientist 2's because the descendants of early modern humans inhabit all the Earth and therefore there should be no community of Neanderthals
C. Both hypotheses are disproved.
D. Neither hypothesis is affected.

35. (D) ***Science/Conflicting Viewpoints/Analysis.*** The discovery of evidence of an isolated community of Neanderthals would not necessarily weaken either hypothesis. When the two scientists talk about populations being dispersed, they are not saying that the individuals were perfectly distributed—like so many salt and chlorine atoms in a water solution. A pocket of Neanderthals here or a concentration of early modern humans there would not be inconsistent with the general distribution pattern described.

36. Which of the following, if true, would most support the hypothesis of Scientist 2?

F. The camps of early modern humans are often close to the camps of Neanderthals.
G. The camps of early modern humans are never close to Neanderthal camps.
H. Bones of Neanderthals and early modern humans are often found near each other.
J. Chipped Neanderthal bones are found with early modern human weapons.

37. The fact that lions and tigers fight when brought together even though they can be interbred supports which hypothesis to the greater extent?

A. Scientist 1's hypothesis, because it proves two species can interbreed
B. Scientist 1's hypothesis, because two species still exist that share the same niche
C. Scientist 2's hypothesis, because it suggests that two species that can interbreed may not do so under natural conditions
D. Scientist 2's hypothesis, because lions and tigers fight when brought together

38. According to the hypothesis of Scientist 2, what should be the result of interbreeding lions and tigers?

F. The offspring should be infertile.
G. The offspring will resemble one parent only.
H. The offspring will possess a mixture of traits.
J. Scientist 2's hypothesis makes no conjectures on the point because lions and tigers would not interbreed.

39. What other assumption do both Scientist 1 and Scientist 2 make about Neanderthals and early modern humans?

A. That early modern humans were directly involved in the disappearance of Neanderthals
B. That early modern humans were the more intelligent of the two
C. That Neanderthals differed little from early modern humans
D. That early modern humans only inhabited regions that were hospitable for Neanderthals

36. (J) ***Science/Conflicting Viewpoints/Analysis.*** This information suggests that early modern humans killed Neanderthals, which supports Scientist 2.

37. (C) ***Science/Conflicting Viewpoints/Analysis.*** This fact shows that even if two species can breed, they may not do so voluntarily. Scientist 2 can therefore use this case as an example of the fact that two genetically compatible but dissimilar-looking animals choose not to interbreed. (D) is not readily relevant because lions and tigers are brought together artificially. No one disputed the notion that animals can interbreed, so (A) does not enter the argument. (B) is incorrect because lions and tigers do not share the same niche (tigers are solitary forest hunters while lions are group-hunting plains dwellers), and their ranges rarely overlap.

38. (H) ***Science/Conflicting Viewpoints/Comprehension.*** The mixing of traits is part of Scientist 2's objections to Scientist 1's hypothesis.

39. (A) ***Science/Conflicting Viewpoints/Analysis.*** Both hypotheses attribute the disappearance of Neanderthals to early modern humans.

40. If a burial site containing over one hundred early modern humans and Neanderthal remains was discovered, and if two Neanderthal skeletons were found with early modern human spearpoints in them, which hypothesis would be the most strengthened?

F. Scientist 1's hypothesis, because spearpoints need not have been what killed the two Neanderthals
G. Scientist 2's hypothesis, because two Neanderthals were killed by early modern humans
H. Scientist 2's hypothesis, because the spearpoints prove that the early modern humans had more developed weapons
J. Scientist 1's hypothesis, because only a couple of the individuals buried together died violently

40. (G) ***Science/Conflicting Viewpoints/Analysis.*** (F) is a perfectly logical argument but it does not strengthen the position of Scientist 1. (J) does not strengthen the position of Scientist 1 since there is no way to prove from the given information whether others also died violently (clubs may have been used, or spearpoints that were used may have been valuable and were taken by the victors). Even if (J) is acceptable, it does not strengthen the position of Scientist 1. It only casts doubt on the position of Scientist 2. (H) is true in general. The only possible answer that strengthens a scientist's argument is (G).

5 5 5 5 5 5 5 5 5 5 5

WRITING TEST (OPTIONAL)

1 Essay Prompt

DIRECTIONS: You have 30 minutes to plan and write an essay. Read the prompt carefully and make sure you understand the instructions. A successful essay will have the following features: it will take a position on the issue presented in the writing prompt; it will maintain a consistent focus on the topic; it will use logical reasoning and provide supporting ideas; it will present ideas in an organized manner; and, finally, it will include clear and effective language in accordance with the conventions of standard written English.

Writing Test Prompt

Some people believe that schools do not emphasize enough the concept of public service. They point out that volunteer service is a tradition in America and mention organizations such as the Girl and Boy Scouts, volunteer fire departments and rescue squads, and Big Brother and Sister. They believe that high schools should encourage volunteerism by offering students academic credit for such activities. They state that allowing academic credit would release students from studies to do volunteer work and further that such service would strengthen the sense of community. Other people say that volunteer service should be voluntary and that release time from school is a form of compensation for students. Students who receive such compensation would not really be doing volunteer work. Opponents of release time point out that students have opportunities to volunteer after school, on weekends, and during the summer months.

In your essay, take a position on this issue. You can write about either point of view presented here, or you can present a different point of view on this topic. Support your position with relevant reasons and/or examples from your own experience, observations, or reading.

Above Average Response

Volunteerism is an important American tradition, and schools should do more to encourage it. In today's world, most students are very busy. They attend classes for most of the day, and then may participate in one or two after school activities. Many students also manage to hold down part-time jobs such as working at a fast-food restaurant. Because they are so busy, most of them don't have time to volunteer to help others. Schools could encourage volunteering by giving students release time from school to participate in such activities.

In the first place, volunteerism is important. During emergencies, the Boy Scouts stuffing sandbags on the levee as the river rises are volunteers hoping to help their neighbors save their homes and businesses. The rescue workers the television shows walking through the woods all night with flashlights searching for a lost child are volunteers. The people who pass out cold drinks to marathon runners are volunteers. Without these volunteers, these efforts could not take place. While students may not be eligible to fight fires, they can do many other jobs, and the way to get involved is to join an organization that helps out.

Unfortunately, many students find it difficult to find time to join. To really be of service in an emergency, you need to have some sort of training, and that means going to meetings and learning what role to play in a rescue or disaster. Less dramatic, you can join a group that does things like visit sick people or clean up roads. You need to be an active member of the club or organization that is doing the public service. But if your day is booked solid with classes, there may just not be time left over to do meaningful volunteer work. If schools gave one or two hours a week off, say Friday after lunch, then many other students could volunteer.

Some people might say that release time is not really volunteering because you get something for your effort. But having free time that has to be used for volunteering isn't good for anything else. If you are working to clean up a public park, then you can't be making money at your job. So you really are giving up something by volunteering.

There are many other reasons why release time would work. But the most important one is that it gives students time to do some volunteer work.

Position on issue: The writer clearly states a position in the first paragraph.

Topic development and essay organization: The essay has several features related to good topic development and essay organization. First, the essay includes an introductory paragraph with a clearly stated position. Second, the essay includes separate paragraphs for each separate point to be made. Third, these separate paragraphs begin with topic sentences that summarize or preview the contents of the paragraph.

At the same time, the essay does have some weaknesses. For example, the essay has a paragraph that mentions a possible objection to the argument being made. Specifically, the writer says some people might argue that volunteerism shouldn't involve "release time" because the latter is a form of compensation. The writer responds that "release time" is not compensation because, under the terms of a school-run volunteer program, it could not be used for anything except volunteer work. On the one hand, this is a legitimate point. On the other hand, this point does not fully address the objection raised in the prompt, namely that "release time" minimizes the sacrifice that one ordinarily associates and expects with volunteerism. A more successful essay would address this objection in greater detail.

The third paragraph is also under-developed. In general, it is just a restatement of the problem mentioned in the prompt (i.e., students may not have a lot of time to volunteer). It is unlikely that anyone would seriously dispute this point. No one has unlimited time, and everyone has many things they'd like to do. A more successful essay would introduce more substantial arguments in favor of "release time." For example, there is an ethical argument that could be made in favor of "release time"; in other words, the ethical benefits that would follow from increased volunteerism (i.e., the actual good that would be done in the world) outweigh any philosophical objections to be made against "release time."

Language usage, sentence structure, and punctuation: In general, the essay is free from any significant errors.

Summary and conclusions: This essay has several positive features: it clearly states a position in response to the prompt; it is well-organized; and, not unimportantly, it is free from any significant errors. At the same time, for the reasons mentioned above, it is somewhat under-developed and unoriginal. For these reasons, the essay would likely receive a "4."

Below Average Response

It is my opinion that they should let students ought of schooll, to do some volunteering. In America, volunteering is a good idea, and everyone should be ready, willing, and able to help other people. But you can't always help someone else if you're to busy helping yourself. One way of avoiding this problem is to give students time to help other people. Once students learn that they will be allowed to volunteer instead of going to class, they will volunteer more. And more volunteers will help people more.

Position on issue: The writer's position is stated in the first sentence. However, the first sentence also contains several errors related to spelling, punctuation, and clarity that prevent it from being a strong opening sentence.

Topic development and essay organization: This essay lacks any kind of development. In order to improve the essay, the writer would need to make several changes. First, a fully developed introductory paragraph is needed; in this paragraph, the writer would state his or her position and list the main points that will be advanced in support of this position. Second, separate paragraphs for the supporting points are needed; in these paragraphs, the writer would present arguments and details related to the supporting points. Finally, a conclusion is needed where the writer summarizes his or her argument and outlines the benefits of following a plan of action based on the argument just made. As currently written, the essay does not provide any of these features. As a result, the essay is underdeveloped and unconvincing.

Language usage, sentence structure, and punctuation: The essay contains several errors related to punctuation, spelling, and clarity. As a result, the essay does not flow well.

Summary and conclusions: This essay would likely receive a "1." It lacks organization and structure; it fails to include examples or details in support of the points to be made; and it includes multiple errors related to punctuation, spelling, and clarity.

Timed Practice Test I*

*The bubble and essay response sheets for Timed Practice Test I are located in Appendix B.

DIRECTIONS

Timed Practice Test I includes five subject tests: English, Mathematics, Reading, Science, and Writing. Calculator use is permitted on the Mathematics Test only.

The items in each multiple-choice test are numbered and the answer choices are lettered. The bubble sheet provided in Appendix B (p. 731) has numbered rows that correspond to the items on the test. Each row contains lettered ovals to match the answer choices for each item on the test. Each numbered row on the bubble sheet has a corresponding item on the test.

For each item, first decide on the best answer choice. Then, locate the row number that corresponds to the item. Next, find the oval in that row that matches the letter of the chosen answer. Then, use a soft lead pencil to fill in the oval. DO NOT use a ballpoint pen.

Mark only one answer for each item. If you change your mind about an answer choice, thoroughly erase your first mark before marking your new answer.

Note that only responses marked on your bubble sheet will be scored. Your score on each test will be based only on the number of items that are correctly answered during the time allowed for that test. Guessing is not penalized. Therefore, it is to your best advantage to answer every item on the test, even if you must guess.

On the Writing Test, use the essay response sheets provided in Appendix B (pp. 733–736) to write your response to the prompt. (Note that the Writing Test is optional.)

You may work on each test only during the time allowed for that test. If you finish a test before time is called, use the time to review your answer choices or work on items about which you are uncertain. You may not return to a test on which time has already been called and you may not preview another test. You must lay down your pencil immediately when time is called at the end of each test. You may not for any reason fill in or alter ovals for a test after time has expired for that test. Violation of these rules will result in immediate disqualification from the exam.

GO ON TO THE NEXT PAGE.

1 1 1 1 1 1 1 1 1 1 1 1

ENGLISH TEST

45 Minutes—75 Items

DIRECTIONS: In the passages below, certain parts of the sentences have been underlined and numbered. In the right-hand column, you will find different ways of writing each underlined part; the original version is indicated by the "NO CHANGE" option. For each item, select the choice that best expresses the intended idea, is most acceptable in standard written English, or is most consistent with the overall tone and style of the passage.

There are also items that ask about a section of the passage or the passage as a whole. These items do not refer to an underlined portion of the passage; these items are preceded by statements that are enclosed in boxes.

Read the passage through once before you begin to answer the accompanying items. Finding the answers to certain items may depend on looking at material that appears several sentences beyond the item. So, be sure that you have read far enough ahead before you select your answer choice. Answers are on page 643.

PASSAGE I

Basic Principles of Nuclear Weapons

The challenge to start to begin to make (1) timely progress toward removing the threat of nuclear war is the most important challenge in international relations today. Three general principles guide our defense and negotiating policies toward such a goal, principles based on the technical realities of nuclear war.

First, nuclear weapons are fundamentally different than (2) non-nuclear weapons. These weapons of mass destruction that could do a lot of harm (3) have a

1. **A.** NO CHANGE
   B. to begin making
   C. to begin the making of
   D. of beginning the making of

2. **F.** NO CHANGE
   G. different than fundamentally
   H. different from fundamentally
   J. fundamentally different from

3. **A.** NO CHANGE
   B. (and they could also do a great deal of harm)
   C. (owing to the fact that they could do a lot of harm)
   D. OMIT the underlined portion.

GO ON TO THE NEXT PAGE.

long and deadly radioactive memory, the unknowns of
4
nuclear conflict dwarf the predictable consequences.

4. F. NO CHANGE
G. memory. The
H. memory the
J. memory and the

The number of deaths resulting from injuries and the
5
unavailability of medical care and the economic
5

5. A. NO CHANGE
B. from injuries and also from the unavailability of medical care
C. from the unavailability of injuries and medical care
D. both from injuries and also from the unavailability of medical care as well

damage as a result from disruption and disorganization
6

6. F. NO CHANGE
G. as a result to
H. resulting from
J. with a result of

would be even more devastating than the direct loss of
7
life and property. [8]

7. A. NO CHANGE
B. is even more devastating than
C. are even more devastating as
D. might be more devastating even as

8. Which of the following would be an appropriate final sentence for this paragraph?

F. And so I believe nuclear weapons to be a challenge.
G. Nuclear war could have no winners.
H. Nuclear conflict is very dangerous.
J. Nuclear conflict would be rather wasteful.

Second, the sole purpose of nuclear weapons
9

9. A. NO CHANGE
B. solely, the purpose
C. the solely purpose
D. the purpose solely

must be to deter nuclear war, it is neither a substitute
10
for maintaining adequate conventional military forces

10. F. NO CHANGE
G. war. They are
H. war they are
J. war; it is

GO ON TO THE NEXT PAGE.

to meet vital national security goals <u>but</u> [11] an effective defense against the almost total mutual annihilation and devastation that results from a full-scale nuclear war. <u>Third,</u> [12] arms control is an essential part of our national security. Thus far, we have had no effective controls on offensive nuclear weaponry, and it is clear that each step forward in the arms race toward more and improved weapons <u>has made less</u> [13] our security. Before deploying additional weapons, <u>they must develop</u> [14] a coherent arms control strategy.

11. **A.** NO CHANGE
    B. and
    C. nor
    D. including

12. **F.** NO CHANGE
    G. Third
    H. (Begin a new paragraph) Third
    J. (Begin a new paragraph) Third,

13. **A.** NO CHANGE
    B. has lessened
    C. have lessened
    D. have made less of

14. **F.** NO CHANGE
    G. the development is necessary of
    H. it is necessary to develop
    J. it is necessarily to be developed,

Items #15–16 ask about the preceding passage as a whole.

15. Which of the following best describes the overall structure of the essay?

    A. A three-part argument
    B. A two-part narrative
    C. A three-part comparison
    D. A four-part argument

16. Which of the following is the thesis of this essay?

    F. Nuclear weapons are fundamentally different from non-nuclear weapons.
    G. The sole purpose of nuclear weapons must be to deter nuclear war.
    H. There are three principles that guide our effort to remove the threat of nuclear war.
    J. Nuclear war is a frightening possibility.

GO ON TO THE NEXT PAGE.

PASSAGE II

Education for a New Republic

The founders of the Republic viewing their [17] revolution primarily in political terms rather as [18] in economic terms. Therefore, [19] they viewed the kind of education needed for the new Republic largely in political terms instead of as a means to [20] academic excellence or individual self-fulfillment. Talking about [21] education as a bulwark for liberty, equality, popular consent, and devotion to the public good goals [22] that took precedence over [23] the uses of knowledge for self-improvement or occupational preparation. Over and over again, the Revolutionary generation, both liberal and conservative in outlook—assert their [24] faith that the welfare of the Republic rested upon an educated citizenry.

17. A. NO CHANGE
B. having viewed its
C. viewed its
D. viewed their

18. F. NO CHANGE
G. rather than
H. but
J. OMIT the underlined portion.

19. A. NO CHANGE
B. Since
C. However
D. On the contrary

20. F. NO CHANGE
G. as a means or a way to
H. to
J. as

21. A. NO CHANGE
B. Talking
C. They talked about
D. With the talking about

22. F. NO CHANGE
G. good. Goals
H. good, goals
J. good; goals

23. A. NO CHANGE
B. precede
C. precede over
D. took precedence on

24. F. NO CHANGE
G. outlook, asserted its
H. outlook; asserted its
J. outlook asserts their

GO ON TO THE NEXT PAGE.

All agreed that the principal ingredients of a civic education was [25] literacy and inculcation of patriotic and moral virtues some [26] others added the study of history and the study of the principles of the republican government itself. The founders, as was the case of almost all their successors, were long on exhortation and rhetoric regarding the value of civic education; since [27] they left it to the textbook writers to distill the essence of those values for school children. Texts in American history and government appeared as early as the 1790s. The textbook writers turned out being [28] very largely of conservative persuasion, more likely Federalist in outlook than Jeffersonian, and universally almost agreed [29] that political virtue must rest upon moral and religious precepts. Since most textbook writers were New Englanders, this meant that the texts had a decidedly Federalist slant.

In the first half of the Republic, civic education in the schools emphasized the inculcation of civic values, put less emphasis on political knowledge, and no attempt to develop [30] political skills. The development of political skills was left to the local parties, town meetings, churches, coffeehouses, and ale houses

25. **A.** NO CHANGE
B. being
C. were
D. were like

26. **F.** NO CHANGE
G. virtues—some
H. virtues, some
J. virtues; some

27. **A.** NO CHANGE
B. education. And
C. education. Since
D. education, but

28. **F.** NO CHANGE
G. turned out to be
H. turning out to be
J. having turned out to be

29. **A.** NO CHANGE
B. almost, agreed universally
C. almost universally agreed
D. almost universally, agreed

30. **F.** NO CHANGE
G. made no attempt to develop
H. none at all on the development of
J. none was put at all on developing

GO ON TO THE NEXT PAGE.

where men gathered to talk. [31]

31. Which of the following correctly describes how the last paragraph of the essay functions?

A. It contradicts much of what was said before.
B. It continues the logical development of the essay.
C. It reiterates what was said in the first paragraph.
D. It is a transitional paragraph to introduce a new topic.

Item #32 asks about the preceding passage as a whole.

32. This essay would most likely be published in a:

F. history textbook.
G. political science journal.
H. journal for educators.
J. biography of Jefferson.

PASSAGE III

Women and World War I

[1]

The contribution of women [33] on the home front during World War I was varied. It included a large range of activities—from knitting and the operation of [34] drill presses—and engaged a cross section of the female population, from housewives to society girls. World War I marked the first time [35] in the history of the United States that a systematic effort was made, through organizations like the League for Women's

33. **A.** NO CHANGE
B. Women, their contribution
C. The contribution of woman
D. Woman's contribution

34. **F.** NO CHANGE
G. from knitting with the operation of
H. from knitting and operating
J. from knitting to operating

35. **A.** NO CHANGE
B. has marked the first time
C. is the first time it is marked
D. was marked, the first time

GO ON TO THE NEXT PAGE.

Service, to utilize[36] the capabilities of women in all regions of the country.

[2]

While much of this volunteer work falls within[37] the established bounds of women's club work, many women entered areas of industrial work previously reserved by[38] the male population. Women put on the uniforms of elevator operators, streetcar conductors, postmen, and industrial workers. However, they were employed[39] in aircraft and munitions plants as well as in shipbuilding yards and steel mills.

[3]

Much of the work fell into the traditional realm of volunteer activity knitting[40] garments for the boys overseas, canning for Uncle Sam, planting Victory gardens, etc. Through these activities, every homemaker could demonstrate their[41] patriotism while still fulfilling her role as homemaker. Women with more time volunteered to hostess at canteens: make[42] bandages, and organize food and clothing drives. The Women's Land Army, dressed in bloomer uniforms and armed with such slogans as "The Woman with the

36. **F.** NO CHANGE
G. being able to utilize
H. utilizing
J. and utilize

37. **A.** NO CHANGE
B. fell within
C. having fallen within
D. fell in

38. **F.** NO CHANGE
G. having previously been reserved
H. previously reserved for
J. reserved previous to then

39. **A.** NO CHANGE
B. workers. They were employed
C. workers, but they were employed
D. workers. Since they were employed

40. **F.** NO CHANGE
G. activity—knitting
H. activity: knitting
J. activity, knitting

41. **A.** NO CHANGE
B. be demonstrating
C. have demonstrated their
D. demonstrate her

42. **F.** NO CHANGE
G. canteens make
H. canteens, make
J. canteens; make

GO ON TO THE NEXT PAGE.

Hoe Must Defend the Man with the Musket," was dispatched[43] to assist farmers in processing crops.

[4]

Women performed ably during the war and laid the foundation[44] for more specialized jobs, increased wages, better working conditions, and a more competitive job status in the labor market.

43. **A.** NO CHANGE
B. Musket," which was then dispatched
C. Musket," and it was dispatched
D. Musket," and it got dispatched

44. **F.** NO CHANGE
G. the foundation was laid
H. the foundation was lain
J. laying the foundation

Items #45–46 ask about the preceding passage as a whole.

45. Which of the following represents the most logical order for the paragraphs?

A. 1, 4, 3, 2
B. 1, 3, 4, 2
C. 1, 3, 2, 4
D. 2, 4, 3, 1

46. Is the use of the sample slogan appropriate to the essay?

F. Yes, because it helps the reader to understand one of the points being made.
G. Yes, because all general statements should be illustrated with an example.
H. No, because it does not help the reader to understand the point being made.
J. No, because it is needlessly distracting.

PASSAGE IV

Democracy in Japan

Following the end of World War II, substantial changes undertaken[47] in Japan to liberate the individual from authoritarian restraints. The new democratic

47. **A.** NO CHANGE
B. will be undertaken
C. have been undertaken
D. were undertaken

GO ON TO THE NEXT PAGE.

value system was acceptable by (48) many teachers,

48. **F.** NO CHANGE
G. excepted to
H. excepted by
J. accepted by

students, intellectuals, and old liberals, and (49) it was not immediately embraced by the society as a whole.

49. **A.** NO CHANGE
B. liberals, since
C. liberals, but
D. liberals; consequently

Japanese traditions were dominated by group values, (50) and notions of personal freedom and individual rights

50. **F.** NO CHANGE
G. Dominated by group values were the Japanese traditions
H. Group values were always dominating the Japanese traditions
J. Dominating Japanese traditions were group values

being (51) unfamiliar.

51. **A.** NO CHANGE
B. were
C. was
D. are

Today, the triumph of (52) democratic processes

52. **F.** NO CHANGE
G. (Do NOT begin a new paragraph) Today the triumph, of
H. Today, the triumph, of
J. (Do NOT begin a new paragraph) Today, owing to the fact that

is clear (53) evident in the widespread participation of the

53. **A.** NO CHANGE
B. is
C. is clear and also
D. are clearly

Japanese in social and political life. Furthermore, (54) there is no universally accepted and stable value

54. **F.** NO CHANGE
G. Therefore,
H. So,
J. Yet,

GO ON TO THE NEXT PAGE.

system, values being constantly modified by strong infusions of Western ideas. School textbooks expound democratic principles, and so emphasizing equality over hierarchy and rationalism over tradition, but in practice, these values are often sometimes distorted, particularly by the youth that translated the individualistic and humanistic goals of democracy into egoistic and materialistic ones.

55. A. NO CHANGE
B. system with that values are
C. system since that values are
D. system since values are

56. F. NO CHANGE
G. principles, emphasizing
H. principles and the emphasis of
J. principles with the emphasis that

57. A. NO CHANGE
B. had been misinterpreted and distorted often
C. often misinterpreted and distorted
D. are often misinterpreted and distorted

58. F. NO CHANGE
G. that translate
H. who translate
J. translate

59. What type of discussion might logically follow this last paragraph?

A. A discussion of goals of Japanese youth
B. A discussion of democratic principles
C. A discussion of Western education
D. A discussion of World War II

PASSAGE V

Zoological Nature

From the beginning, humankind always has shared some sort of link with the animal world. The earliest and most primitive was surely that of hunter and prey—with humans possibly playing the fatal role of victim. Later, of course, humans reversed the roles

60. F. NO CHANGE
G. have always shared
H. is always sharing
J. has always shared

GO ON TO THE NEXT PAGE.

as they became more skillful <u>and intelligenter</u>.[61]

61. A. NO CHANGE
B. so intelligent
C. and more intelligent
D. but intelligent

The later domestication of certain <u>animals and also</u>[62] the discovery of agriculture, made for a more settled and stable existence and was an essential step in the not-so-orderly <u>and very chaotic</u>[63] process of becoming civilized. However, the intellectual distance between regarding an animal as the source of dinner or of material comfort and <u>to consider them</u>[64] a worthy subject for study is considerable.

62. F. NO CHANGE
G. animals, also
H. animals, along with
J. animals; along with

63. A. NO CHANGE
B. (and very chaotic)
C. yet very chaotic
D. OMIT the underlined portion.

64. F. NO CHANGE
G. considering it
H. considering them
J. then to consider them

Not until Aristotle did the animal world become a subject for serious scientific study. Although <u>he seemingly writes on</u>[65] every <u>subject, Aristotle's work</u>[66] in zoology—studying animals as animals—is considered his most successful. He seemed to have had a natural affinity for and curiosity about all the living creatures of the world, <u>and</u>[67] he took special interest in marine life.

65. A. NO CHANGE
B. he wrote (seemingly) on
C. writing seemingly on
D. he wrote on seemingly

66. F. NO CHANGE
G. subject; Aristotles work
H. subject Aristotles' work
J. subject: Aristotle's work

67. A. NO CHANGE
B. so
C. but
D. because

Aristotle's zoological writings reveal him to be a remarkably astute observer of the natural world, <u>wedding his</u>[68] observations to what might be called speculative reason. He was therefore a theorist as well.

68. F. NO CHANGE
G. who was wedded to
H. in that he wedded
J. with the wedding of

GO ON TO THE NEXT PAGE.

His overall theory was simple. In[69] the works of Nature," he said, "purpose and not accident is predominant." A thing is known then when we know what it is for. He linked and combined[70] theory and practice by saying that interpretation of an observed phenomenon must always be made in light of its purpose[71]. His zoological theory was thus a reflection of the essentially teleological nature of his overall philosophy. [72]

69. A. NO CHANGE
B. simple—in
C. simple. "In
D. simply. "In

70. F. NO CHANGE
G. combining
H. to combine
J. OMIT the underlined portion.

71. A. NO CHANGE
B. always keeping its purpose in mind
C. without ever forgetting what its purpose is
D. given an understanding of what its purpose is

72. Is the quote from Aristotle in the last paragraph appropriate?

F. Yes, because it is important to quote the works of people you are talking about.
G. Yes, because it is a succinct statement of Aristotle's theory.
H. No, because the quote is irrelevant to what the author is talking about in that paragraph.
J. No, because it is wrong to quote when you can express the idea in your own words.

Items #73–75 ask about the preceding passage as a whole.

73. The author probably had which of the following audiences in mind for this essay?

A. Zoologists
B. Students who are studying Aristotle
C. The average person interested in science
D. Teachers of marine biology

GO ON TO THE NEXT PAGE.

74. What is the actual thesis of this essay?

F. People have always liked animals.
G. Animals and people reversed roles.
H. Aristotle was interested in the natural world.
J. The animal world became a source of serious study because of Aristotle.

75. How does the first paragraph of this essay function?

A. It poses questions to be answered.
B. It provides general background for the rest of the passage.
C. It introduces an argument.
D. It provides an anecdote related to the rest of the passage.

END OF TEST 1
STOP! DO NOT TURN THE PAGE UNTIL TOLD TO DO SO.

NO TEST MATERIAL ON THIS PAGE

MATHEMATICS TEST

60 Minutes—60 Items

DIRECTIONS: Solve each item and choose the correct answer choice. Then, fill in the corresponding oval on the bubble sheet.

Allocate time wisely. Try to solve as many items as possible, returning to skipped items if time permits.

Calculator use is permitted on this test; however, some items are best solved without the use of a calculator.

Note: All of the following should be assumed, unless otherwise stated.

1. Illustrative figures are NOT necessarily drawn to scale.
2. The word *average* indicates arithmetic mean.
3. The word *line* indicates a straight line.
4. Geometric figures lie in a plane.

Answers are on page 643.

DO YOUR FIGURING HERE.

1. If $\frac{1}{x}+\frac{1}{x}=8$, then $x=$?

A. $\frac{1}{4}$
B. $\frac{1}{2}$
C. 1
D. 2
E. 4

2. If $x=2$ and $y=-1$, then $3x-4y=$?

F. –5
G. –1
H. 0
J. 2
K. 10

GO ON TO THE NEXT PAGE.

DO YOUR FIGURING HERE.

3. In a certain school, there are 600 boys and 400 girls. If 20% of the boys and 30% of the girls are on the honor roll, how many of the students are on the honor roll?

A. 120
B. 175
C. 240
D. 250
E. 280

4. If p, q, r, s, and t are whole numbers, the expression $t[r(p+q)+s]$ must be an even number when which of the 5 numbers is even?

F. p
G. q
H. r
J. s
K. t

5. A student conducting a lab experiment finds that the population of flies in a bottle increases by a certain multiple from week to week. If the pattern shown in the table continues, how many flies can the student expect to find in the bottle in Week 5?

Results of Biology Project Conducted by Student X					
Week	1	2	3	4	5
# of flies in bottle	3	12	48	192	?

A. 195
B. 240
C. 384
D. 564
E. 768

GO ON TO THE NEXT PAGE.

DO YOUR FIGURING HERE.

6. At a school assembly, 3 students are each scheduled to give a short speech. In how many different orders can the speeches be scheduled?

F. 12
G. 9
H. 6
J. 4
K. 3

7. If points P and Q lie in the xy-plane and have the coordinates shown below, what is the midpoint of $\overline{PQ}$?

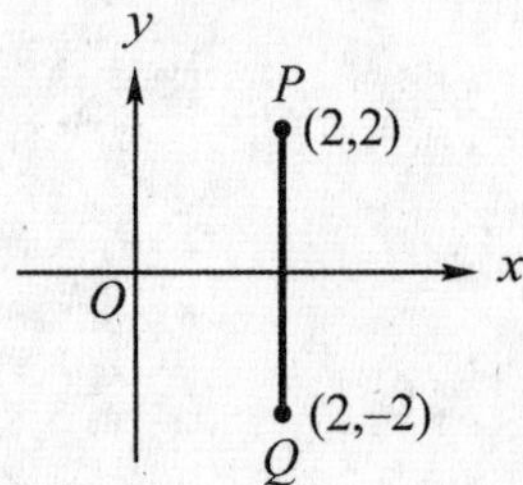

A. (–2,0)
B. (–2,2)
C. (0,2)
D. (2,0)
E. (2,2)

8. If $xy = |xy|$ and $xy \neq 0$, which of the following CANNOT be true?

F. $x > y > 0$
G. $y > x > 0$
H. $x > 0 > y$
J. $0 > x > y$
K. $0 > y > x$

GO ON TO THE NEXT PAGE.

DO YOUR FIGURING HERE.

9. In the scale drawing of the floor of a rectangular room shown below, the scale used was 1 cm = 4 m. What is the actual area, in square meters, of the floor of the room?

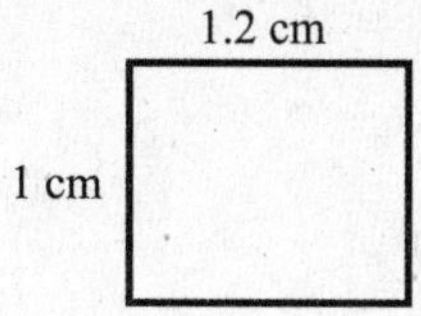

1.2 cm

1 cm

A. 9.6
B. 13.6
C. 15
D. 19.2
E. 38.4

10. If $30,000 \times 20 = 6 \times 10^n$, then $n = ?$

F. 4
G. 5
H. 6
J. 7
K. 8

11. Karen purchased 4 pounds of candy, which was a mix of chocolates and caramels. If chocolates cost \$3 per pound and caramels cost \$2 per pound, and if Karen spent a total of \$10.00, how many pounds of chocolates did she buy?

A. 1
B. 2
C. 2.5
D. 3
E. 3.5

12. The average of Al's scores on 3 tests was 80. If the average of his scores on the first 2 tests was 77, what was his score on the third test?

F. 86
G. 83
H. 80
J. 77
K. 74

GO ON TO THE NEXT PAGE.

13. A book contains 10 photographs, some in color and some in black-and-white. Each of the following could be the ratio of color to black-and-white photographs EXCEPT:

A. 9:1
B. 4:1
C. 5:2
D. 3:2
E. 1:1

DO YOUR FIGURING HERE.

14. If $\frac{4}{5} = \frac{x}{4}$, then $x = ?$

F. 5
G. $\frac{16}{5}$
H. $\frac{5}{4}$
J. $\frac{4}{5}$
K. $\frac{5}{16}$

15. In the figure below, three equilateral triangles have a common vertex. How many degrees is $x + y + z$?

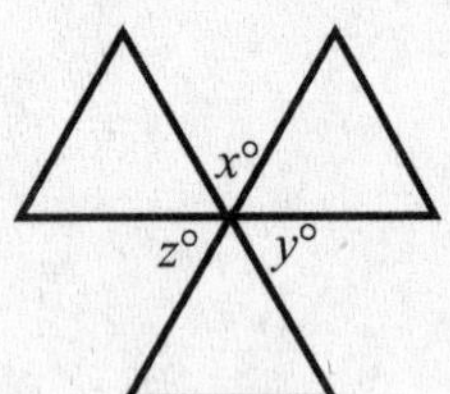

A. 60
B. 90
C. 120
D. 180
E. 240

GO ON TO THE NEXT PAGE.

16. Peter spent $\frac{1}{4}$ of his allowance on Monday and $\frac{1}{3}$ of the remainder on Tuesday. What part of the allowance does Peter still have?

F. $\frac{1}{12}$

G. $\frac{1}{4}$

H. $\frac{1}{2}$

J. $\frac{3}{4}$

K. $\frac{11}{12}$

17. If 100 identical bricks weigh p pounds, then how many pounds do 20 of the identical bricks weigh in terms of p?

A. $\frac{p}{20}$

B. $\frac{p}{5}$

C. $20p$

D. $\frac{5}{p}$

E. $\frac{20}{p}$

DO YOUR FIGURING HERE.

GO ON TO THE NEXT PAGE.

DO YOUR FIGURING HERE.

18. If the distances between points P, Q, and R are equal, which of the following could be true?

I. P, Q, and R are points on a circle with center O.
II. P and Q are points on a circle with center R.
III. P, Q, and R are vertices of an equilateral triangle.

F. I only
G. I and II only
H. I and III only
J. II and III only
K. I, II, and III

19. In the table below, the percent increase in the price of the item was greatest during which of the following periods?

Year	1980	1985	1990	1995	2000	2005
Price	\$2	\$4	\$7	\$12	\$20	\$30

A. 1980–1985
B. 1985–1990
C. 1990–1995
D. 1995–2000
E. 2000–2005

20. Which of the following is a factorization of $x^2 + 4x - 12$?

F. $(x-2)(x+6)$
G. $(x-4)(x+3)$
H. $(x-6)(x+2)$
J. $(x+2)(x+6)$
K. $(x+3)(x+4)$

GO ON TO THE NEXT PAGE.

DO YOUR FIGURING HERE.

21. Two cartons weigh $3x-2$ and $2x-3$. If the average weight of the cartons is 10, the heavier carton weighs how much more than the lighter carton?

A. 2
B. 4
C. 5
D. 6
E. 10

22. A group of 15 students took a test that was scored from 0 to 100. If 10 students scored 75 or more on the test, what is the lowest possible value for the average score of all 15 students?

F. 25
G. 50
H. 70
J. 75
K. 90

23. For all real numbers x, 16^x is equal to which of the following expressions?

A. x^{16}
B. 2^{3x}
C. 4^{2x}
D. 8^{2x}
E. 8^{4x}

24. If the figure below is a square, what is the perimeter of the figure?

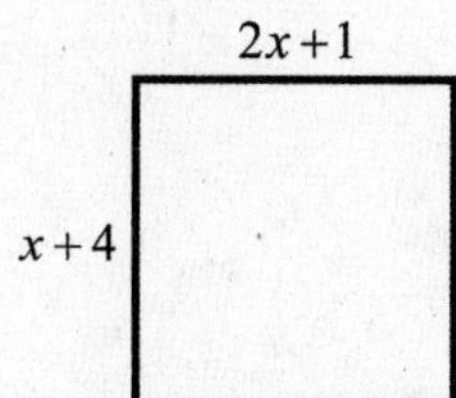

F. 28
G. 16
H. 9
J. 3
K. 2

GO ON TO THE NEXT PAGE.

DO YOUR FIGURING HERE.

25. If a certain rectangle has a length that is 2 times its width, what is the ratio of the area of the rectangle to the area of an isosceles right triangle with a hypotenuse equal to the width of the rectangle?

A. $\frac{1}{8}$

B. $\frac{1}{4}$

C. $\frac{1}{2}$

D. $\frac{4}{1}$

E. $\frac{8}{1}$

26. In the coordinate plane, what is the shortest distance between the point with (x, y) coordinates $(1,3)$ and the line with the equation $x = -2$?

F. 1
G. 3
H. 4
J. 6
K. 9

27. If 5 pounds of coffee cost $12, how many pounds of coffee can be purchased for $30?

A. 7.2
B. 10
C. 12.5
D. 15
E. 18

GO ON TO THE NEXT PAGE.

28. If the 2 triangles below are equilateral, what is the ratio of the perimeter of the smaller to that of the larger?

DO YOUR FIGURING HERE.

F. $\frac{1}{36}$

G. $\frac{1}{15}$

H. $\frac{1}{9}$

J. $\frac{1}{4}$

K. $\frac{1}{3}$

29. If $f(x) = -3x^3 + 3x^2 - 4x + 8$, then $f(-2) = ?$

A. 16
B. 22
C. 28
D. 36
E. 52

30. A merchant pays \$120 wholesale for a dress and then adds a 30% markup. Two weeks later, the dress is put on sale at 40% off the retail price. What is the sale price of the dress?

F. \$108.00
G. \$97.30
H. \$93.60
J. \$89.40
K. \$87.00

GO ON TO THE NEXT PAGE.

DO YOUR FIGURING HERE.

31. If $\frac{1}{3}$ of a number is 2 more than $\frac{1}{5}$ of the number, then which of the following equations can be used to find the number x?

A. $\frac{1}{3}x - \frac{1}{5}x = 2$

B. $\frac{1}{3}x - \frac{1}{5}x = -2$

C. $\frac{1}{3}x - 2 = -\frac{1}{5}x$

D. $\frac{1}{3}x + 2 = -\frac{1}{5}x$

E. $5\left(\frac{1}{3}x + 2\right) = 0$

32. In the figure below, the triangle is equilateral and has a perimeter of 12 centimeters. What is the perimeter, in centimeters, of the square?

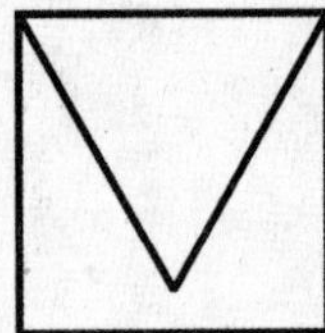

F. 9
G. 12
H. 16
J. 20
K. 24

33. If one solution of the equation $12x^2 + kx = 6$ is $\frac{2}{3}$, then $k = ?$

A. 1

B. $\frac{3}{2}$

C. 2
D. 5
E. 9

GO ON TO THE NEXT PAGE.

DO YOUR FIGURING HERE.

34. If a 6-sided polygon has 2 sides of length $x-2y$ each and 4 sides of length $2x+y$ each, what is its perimeter?

F. $6x-6y$
G. $6x-y$
H. $5x$
J. $6x$
K. $10x$

35. At the first stop on her route, a driver unloaded $\frac{2}{5}$ of the packages in her van. After she unloaded another 3 packages at her next stop, $\frac{1}{2}$ of the original number of packages in the van remained. How many packages were in the van before the first delivery?

A. 10
B. 20
C. 25
D. 30
E. 50

36. For all x and y, $12x^3y^2-8x^2y^3=$?

F. $2x^2y^2(4x-y)$
G. $4x^2y^2(2xy)$
H. $4x^2y^2(3xy)$
J. $4x^2y^2(3x-2y)$
K. $x^3y^3(12xy-8xy)$

GO ON TO THE NEXT PAGE.

37. When $\dfrac{1}{1+\dfrac{1}{x}}$ is defined, it is equivalent to which of the following expressions?

A. $x+1$

B. $\dfrac{1}{x+1}$

C. $\dfrac{x}{x+1}$

D. $\dfrac{x+1}{x}$

E. x^2+x

38. If S is 150% of T, what percent of $S+T$ is T?

F. $33\frac{1}{3}\%$
G. 40%
H. 50%
J. 75%
K. 80%

39. In ΔPQR, the lengths of $\overline{PQ}$ and $\overline{QR}$ are equal, and the measure of $\angle Q$ is 3 times that of $\angle P$. What is the measure of $\angle R$?

A. 24°
B. 30°
C. 36°
D. 45°
E. 60°

DO YOUR FIGURING HERE.

GO ON TO THE NEXT PAGE.

DO YOUR FIGURING HERE.

40. If the cost of b books is d dollars, which of the following equations can be used to find the cost, C, in dollars, of x books at the same rate?

F. $C = xd$

G. $C = \frac{dx}{b}$

H. $C = \frac{bd}{x}$

J. $C = bx$

K. $C = \frac{bx}{d}$

41. An article is on sale for 25% off its regular price of \$64. If the merchant must also collect a 5% sales tax on this reduced price, what is the total cost of the article including sales tax?

A. \$42.10
B. \$44.20
C. \$49.60
D. \$50.40
E. \$56.70

42. If $\frac{x}{z} = k$ and $\frac{y}{z} = k - 1$, then $x = ?$

F. $\frac{y}{z}$
G. $z - y$
H. $y - 1$
J. $y + 1$
K. $y + z$

43. If x is 25% of y, then y is what percent of x?

A. 400%
B. 300%
C. 250%
D. 125%
E. 75%

GO ON TO THE NEXT PAGE.

44. If x is an integer that is a multiple of both 9 and 5, which of the following *must* be true?

DO YOUR FIGURING HERE.

I. x is equal to 45.
II. x is a multiple of 15.
III. x is odd.

F. I only
G. II only
H. III only
J. II and III only
K. I, II, and III

45. If each edge of a cube is 2 units long, what is the distance from any vertex to the cube's center?

A. $\frac{\sqrt{2}}{2}$
B. $\sqrt{3}$
C. $2\sqrt{2}$
D. $2\sqrt{3}$
E. $\frac{3}{2}$

46. The figure below shows 2 circular cylinders, C and C'. If $r = kr'$ and $h = kh'$, what is the ratio of $\frac{\text{volume of } C'}{\text{volume of } C}$? $\left(\text{volume}_{\text{cylinder}} = \pi r^2 h\right)$

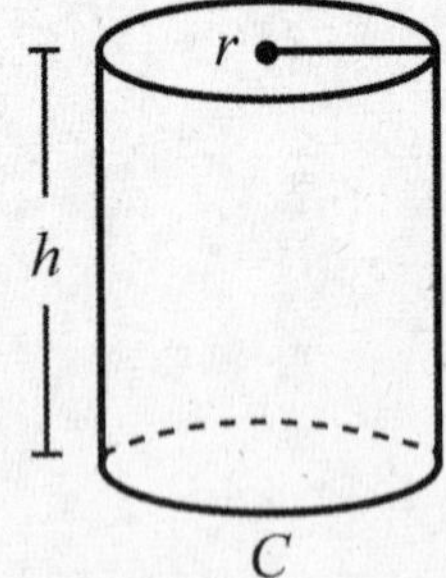

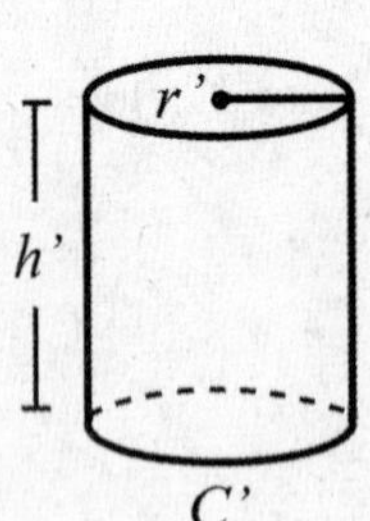

F. $1:\pi$
G. $\pi:1$
H. $k\pi:1$
J. $1:k^3$
K. $k^3:1$

GO ON TO THE NEXT PAGE.

DO YOUR FIGURING HERE.

47. In the figure below, if the triangle has an area of 1 square unit, what is the area of the circle, in square units?

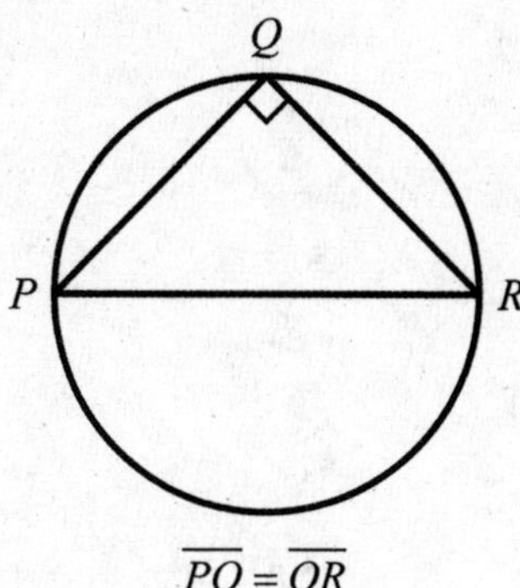

$\overline{PQ} = \overline{QR}$

A. π
B. 2π
C. $2\sqrt{3}\pi$
D. 4π
E. $4\sqrt{3}\pi$

48. In the figure below, P and Q are the centers of their respective circles and the radius of each circle is 1 inch. What is the perimeter, in inches, of the shaded part of the figure?

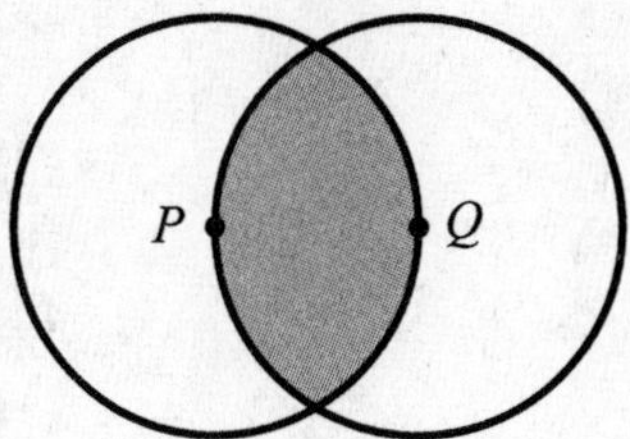

F. $\frac{4\pi}{3}$
G. π
H. $\frac{2\pi}{3}$
J. $\frac{\pi}{3}$
K. $\frac{\pi}{6}$

GO ON TO THE NEXT PAGE.

49. A student's final grade in a certain course is the average of his scores on 10 tests graded on a scale of 0 to 100, inclusive. For the first 6 tests, the student's scores averaged 83. If x is the student's final grade for the course, then which of the following is true?

A. $8.3 \le x \le 83.0$
B. $49.8 \le x \le 83.0$
C. $49.8 \le x \le 89.8$
D. $54.7 \le x \le 89.8$
E. $83.0 \le x \le 89.8$

DO YOUR FIGURING HERE.

50. What is the multiplicative inverse of the complex number $2-i$?

F. $2+i$
G. $i-2$
H. $\frac{2+i}{3}$
J. $\frac{2-i}{3}$
K. $\frac{2+i}{5}$

51. $\log_3 \sqrt{3} = ?$

A. -1
B. $\frac{1}{3}$
C. $\frac{1}{2}$
D. $\frac{2}{3}$
E. 2

52. If $f(x) = (x-1)^2 + 2$, then what value for x creates the minimum value for $f(x)$?

F. -3
G. -2
H. 0
J. 1
K. 2

GO ON TO THE NEXT PAGE.

53. If, for all n, $2^n + 2^n + 2^n + 2^n = x\left(2^{n+1}\right)$, then $x = ?$

A. 2
B. 4
C. 2^n
D. 2^{2n}
E. 2^{n+1}

DO YOUR FIGURING HERE.

54. If $f(k) = k^2 + 2k + 1$, then what is the set of all k for which $f(k) = f(-k)$?

F. $\{0\}$
G. $\{1\}$
H. $\{2\}$
J. $\{1, 2\}$
K. All real numbers

55. What is $\lim_{x \to 1} \frac{x^2 - 1}{x - 1}$?

A. −1
B. 0
C. 1
D. 2
E. The limit does not exist.

56. If $0 \le x \le \pi$ and $\cos x = -1$, then $\cos \frac{x}{2} = ?$

F. $-\frac{\sqrt{3}}{2}$
G. $-\frac{1}{2}$
H. 0
J. $\frac{1}{2}$
K. $\frac{\sqrt{3}}{2}$

GO ON TO THE NEXT PAGE.

DO YOUR FIGURING HERE.

57. Which of the following defines the range of the function $f(x) = \dfrac{1-x}{x}$?

A. All real numbers
B. All real numbers except -1
C. All real numbers except 0
D. All real numbers except 1
E. All real numbers greater than -1

58. Which of the following graphs represents the equations $x = 3(\sin\theta)$ and $y = 2(\cos\theta)$?

F.

y
(2,3)
x
O

J.

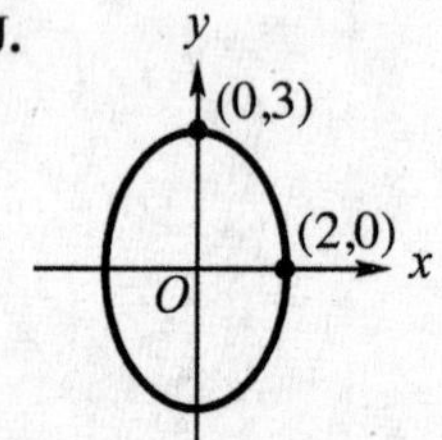

G.

y
(0,3)
x
O
(3,0)

K.

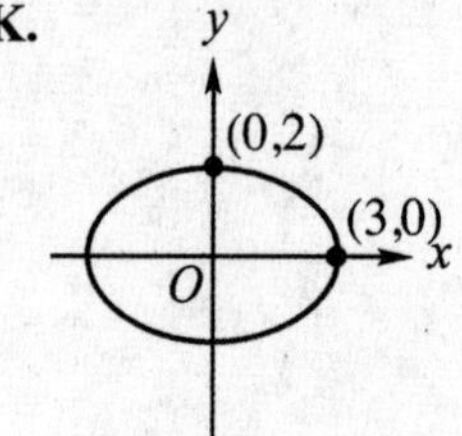

H.

y
(2,3)
x
O

59. For all θ such that $0° < \theta < 90°$, which of the following is equal to $(\sin\theta)(\csc\theta)$?

A. 1
B. $\sqrt{2}$
C. $\tan\theta$
D. $\cot\theta$
E. $\sec\theta$

GO ON TO THE NEXT PAGE.

60. In ΔABC below, the measures of $\angle ABC$, $\angle BCA$, and $\angle CAB$ are 90°, 40°, and 50°, respectively. If $\overline{AB}$ is 3 units long, how many units long is $\overline{BC}$?

DO YOUR FIGURING HERE.

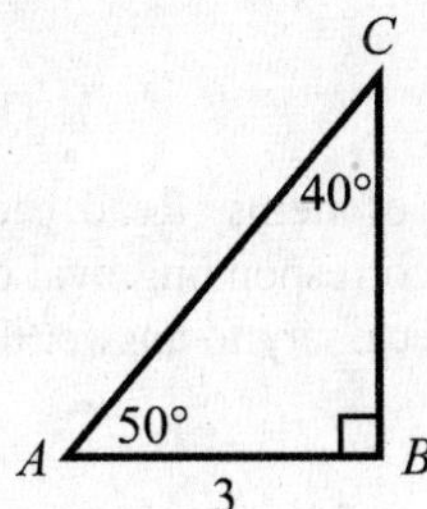

F. 4
G. 5
H. sin 10°
J. 3(tan 50°)
K. 3(tan 40°)

END OF TEST 2
STOP! DO NOT TURN THE PAGE UNTIL TOLD TO DO SO.
DO NOT RETURN TO THE PREVIOUS TEST.

3 3 3 3 3 3 3 3 3 3 3 3

READING TEST

35 Minutes—40 Items

DIRECTIONS: Each passage below is followed by a set of items. Read each passage and choose the best answer for each item. Fill in the corresponding oval on your bubble sheet. You may refer to the passage as often as necessary to answer the items. Answers are on page 644.

Passage I

PROSE FICTION: In this passage, a young country man, alone in town for the first time, tries to find a relative, Major Molineux.

It was near nine o'clock of a moonlight evening, when a boat crossed the ferry with a single passenger, who had obtained his conveyance at that unusual hour by the promise of extra fare. He was a youth of barely eighteen years, evidently country-bred, and now upon his first visit to town. The youth finally drew from his pocket a little province bill of five shillings, which, in depreciation in that sort of currency, satisfied the ferryman's demand with the addition of a sex-angular piece of parchment, valued at three pence. He then walked forward into the town with as light a step as if his day's journey had not already exceeded thirty miles and with as eager an eye as if he were entering London city, instead of the little metropolis of a New England colony. However, before Robin had proceeded far, it occurred to him that he knew not whither to direct his steps; so he paused, and looked up and down the narrow street, scrutinizing the small and mean wooden buildings that were scattered on either side.

"This low hovel cannot be my kinsman's dwelling," thought he, "nor yonder old house; and truly I see none hereabouts that might be worthy of him. It would have been wise to inquire my way of the ferryman and doubtless he would have gone with me, and earned a shilling from the Major for his pains. But the next man I meet will do as well."

He resumed his walk, and was glad to perceive that the street now became wide, and the houses were more respectable in their appearance. He soon discerned a figure moving on moderately in advance, and he hastened his steps to overtake it. Robin laid hold of the skirt of the man's old coat, just when the light from the open door and windows of a barber's shop fell upon both their figures.

"Good evening to you, honored sir," said he, making a low bow, and still retaining hold of the skirt. "I pray you tell me whereabouts is the dwelling of my kinsman, Major Molineux."

The citizen answered him in a tone of excessive anger and annoyance. "Let go my garment, fellow! I tell you, I know not the man you speak of. What! I have the authority, I have—hem, hem—authority; and if this be the respect you show for your betters, your feet shall be brought acquainted with the stocks by daylight, tomorrow morning!"

Robin released the old man's skirt, and hastened away, pursued by an ill-mannered roar of laughter from the barber's shop. He was at first considerably surprised by the result of his question, but, being a shrewd youth, he soon thought himself able to account for the mystery.

"This is some country representative," was his conclusion, "who has never seen the inside of my kinsman's door, and lacks the breeding to answer a stranger civilly. Ah, Robin, Robin! Even the barber's boys laugh at you for choosing such a guide! You will be wiser in time, friend Robin."

GO ON TO THE NEXT PAGE.

1. In the final paragraph, the young man is talking to:

A. the Major.
B. the man in the coat.
C. the barbers.
D. himself.

2. The total cost of the young man's passage on the ferryboat was:

F. five shillings.
G. three pence.
H. five shillings less three pence.
J. five shillings plus three pence.

3. The young man believes that his relative is a:

A. barber.
B. wealthy person.
C. constable.
D. builder.

4. The incidents described in the passage take place:

F. in the late morning.
G. in the early afternoon.
H. in the late afternoon.
J. at night.

5. The passage suggests that thirty miles is:

A. a long distance to travel in one day.
B. easily traveled in a single day.
C. easily traveled in an hour.
D. a long ferryboat ride.

6. The young man believes that the barbers laughed at him because:

F. his clothes clearly show that he is from the country.
G. he asked a question of a stranger who obviously would not know the answer.
H. he badly needs a haircut and a shave.
J. the stranger he questioned is actually the man he is looking for.

7. The scenes in the passage are most likely set in which of the following time periods?

A. Eighteenth century
B. Nineteenth century
C. Early twentieth century
D. Present time

8. The young man approaches the stranger in the coat:

F. respectfully.
G. rudely.
H. coyly.
J. stealthily.

9. The young man is the only passenger on the ferryboat because:

A. he paid the ferryman extra for a private charter.
B. no one else was traveling at that hour.
C. the Major had sent the boat especially for him.
D. the ferryman was a good friend of the young man.

10. Just after he gets off the ferry, the young man finds himself in a:

F. poorer neighborhood.
G. wealthy neighborhood.
H. forest.
J. large city.

GO ON TO THE NEXT PAGE.

Passage II

SOCIAL SCIENCE: This passage discusses Frederick Turner's hypothesis of the American Frontier.

In July of 1893, Frederick Jackson Turner, a historian from the University of Wisconsin, presented a paper to a group of historians convening in Chicago during the Columbian Exposition. Entitled "The Significance of the American Frontier in History," Turner's paper drew little immediate reaction. Yet no theory of history has had a greater influence on the direction and methodology of inquiry and the issues of debate in American history. Later historians took issue with some of Turner's interpretations; some of his own students were among those whose research proved certain of his views wrong. Yet these debates merely serve to illustrate the importance of Turner's hypothesis.

Turner's was an overarching hypothesis about how the settlement of the frontier had shaped the American experience and character. As with all general hypotheses in any field of study, it gave a coherent interpretation to many facts that had been largely ignored by historians up to that time.

Turner used statistical evidence from the 1880 census as the basis for a startling conclusion: prior to 1880 there had been a frontier to be settled. By 1890, Turner pointed out, there was no longer any area of wilderness completely untouched by settlements. The frontier had disappeared. The passing of the frontier, Turner concluded, was a historic moment.

Turner further claimed that the frontier experience had produced a distinctively American character, which was not explainable simply as the predictable behavioral traits molded by English political institutions. Frontier settlers developed inquisitiveness, inventiveness, energy, and a great passion for freedom. These attributes defined a new American character—one evidenced in nationalism, independence, and democracy. This new sense of national identity derived from the fact that people from every section of the country mixed at the Western frontier. Economic independence could be traced to the fact that the settlers no longer depended on England for goods but had become self-sufficient. In addition, the frontier settlers, whose basic social unit was the family, enjoyed freedom from direct governmental interference. Frontier life thus reinforced the fundamental ideals of populist democracy.

In addition, Turner argued that the frontier fostered democracy in the cities of the East. The availability of free land at the frontier provided a "safety-valve" against possible social unrest: those discontented with social inequities and economic injustice could strike out and settle the free land available in frontier territories.

Turner's thesis was thus original in both what it said and in the methodology that Turner used in formulating it. Up to the time of Turner's essay, history had been essentially the history of politics. A Midwesterner, Turner challenged this traditional approach of Eastern historians by incorporating techniques of the social sciences, showing how factors of geography, economics, climate, and society influenced the development of the American West. Although now common among historians, at the time this interdisciplinary approach was novel.

11. Turner's essay challenged the views of:

A. frontier writers such as Mark Twain.
B. other American historians of his time.
C. sociologists.
D. European critics of America.

12. Turner's methods were original in that he:

F. utilized research techniques from a variety of other academic fields.
G. insulted other historians.
H. refused to encourage further research.
J. ignored the need for a unifying view.

13. Turner's evidence for the disappearance of the American frontier drew on:

A. interviews with settlers.
B. his reading of Karl Marx.
C. diaries.
D. the census of 1880.

GO ON TO THE NEXT PAGE.

14. Turner's essay affected:

F. the reputations of American historians in Europe.
G. future settlements in the West.
H. the way in which population was counted.
J. the subsequent focus of inquiry in American history.

15. One fact that would cast a doubtful light on Turner's view that the West was settled by individuals looking for escape from the pressures of Eastern city life would be if:

A. many Western towns had few inhabitants.
B. few people settled in mountain country.
C. much of the land in the West and Midwest was actually bought by wealthy land speculators from the East.
D. many people chose to settle along the banks of the Mississippi.

16. Which of the following, if true, would prove that Turner's "safety-valve" theory was false?

F. Population movements showed that more people actually left the farms for the cities than left cities to move to the frontier.
G. Much of the West had a desert climate.
H. The transcontinental railroad was completed in 1869.
J. The numbers of buffalo dropped markedly during the late nineteenth century.

17. A theory would best be defined as:

A. a foolish notion founded on questionable data.
B. an idle speculation that may have no basis in fact.
C. a hypothesis that explains a large number of isolated facts.
D. a somewhat questionable view of factual data.

18. America's frontier line moved essentially from:

F. the South to the East.
G. the West to the East.
H. the East to the West.
J. the North to the South.

19. The economic independence of Americans arose, Turner said, from the fact that:

A. Americans rarely bought anything.
B. many pioneers had few relatives left in Europe.
C. few settlers ever voted in local elections.
D. Americans were buying American goods rather than English goods.

20. Which of the following quotations captures the approach of historians at the time when Turner read his paper?

F. "This history of the world is but the biography of great men."
G. "History is past politics and politics is present history."
H. "Those who do not heed the lessons of history are doomed to repeat them."
J. "Anybody can make history. Only a great man can write it."

GO ON TO THE NEXT PAGE.

Passage III

HUMANITIES: In this passage, the author expresses his opinion regarding the role of philosophy.

The service of philosophy towards the human spirit is to startle it into sharp and eager observation. Every moment, and for that moment only, some form grows perfect in hand or face; some tone on the hills or the sea is choicer than the rest. Not the fruit of experience, but experience itself is the end. Only a counted number of pulses are given to us of a variegated, dramatic life. How shall we pass most quickly from point to point and be present always at the focus where the greatest number of vital forces unite in their purest energy?

To burn always with this hard, gemlike flame, to maintain this ecstasy, is success in life. It is only the roughness of the eye that makes any two persons, things, or situations seem alike. While all melts under our feet, we may well catch at any exquisite passion, or any knowledge that seems by a lifted horizon to set the spirit free for a moment, or any stirring of the senses, strange dyes, strange colors, curious odors, or work of the artist's hands or the faces of one's friends. Not to discriminate every moment some passionate attitude in those about us, and in the brilliancy of their gifts some tragic dividing of forces of their ways is, on this short day of the frost and sun, to sleep before evening. With this sense of the splendor of our experience and of its awful brevity, gathering all we are into one desperate effort to see and touch, we shall hardly have time to make theories about the things we see and touch.

We are all under sentence of death but with a sort of indefinite reprieve; we have an interval and then our place knows us no more. Some spend this interval in listlessness, others in high passions, the wisest—at least among the "children of this world"—in art and song. Our one chance lies in expanding this interval—in getting as many pulsations as possible into the given time. Great passions may give us this quickened sense of life, ecstasy, sorrow, and love, the various forms of enthusiastic activity. Of this wisdom, the poetic passion, the desire of beauty, the love of art for art's sake has most; for art comes to you professing frankly to give nothing but the highest quality to your moments as they pass, and simply for the sake of those moments.

21. Which of the following best describes the overall structure of the passage?

- **A.** The author raises a question and then provides an answer.
- **B.** The author presents a theory, which he then proves.
- **C.** The author studies a widely held belief and then rejects it.
- **D.** The author defines a term and then provides examples.

22. In the passage, the author uses the word *pulsations* (line 35) to mean:

- **F.** children.
- **G.** lives.
- **H.** death.
- **J.** experiences.

23. According to the author, the function of art is to:

- **A.** depict reality accurately.
- **B.** stimulate strong emotions.
- **C.** encourage social reform.
- **D.** express the artist's feelings.

24. With which of the following statements would the author most likely agree?

- **F.** A person's lifetime is merely preparation for what comes after death.
- **G.** Only an artist can truly enjoy life.
- **H.** The original experience is more important than the memory of it.
- **J.** A perceptive person understands that all experience is repetitious.

25. The tone of the passage can best be described as:

- **A.** impassioned.
- **B.** scholarly.
- **C.** informative.
- **D.** speculative.

GO ON TO THE NEXT PAGE.

26. In the context of this passage, the phrase "short day of the frost and sun" (lines 23–24) refers to:

F. the transient effect of poetry.
G. a brief moment of passion.
H. the life of a person.
J. stimulation of the senses.

27. The phrase "awful brevity" (line 26) means that:

A. philosophy is not really useful.
B. art may not satisfy everyone.
C. life is short.
D. passion is the greatest virtue.

28. The "children of this world" (line 33) are NOT:

F. passionate.
G. wise.
H. lovers of art and song.
J. listless.

29. According to the author, the greatest passion is the love of:

A. beauty.
B. one's spouse.
C. wealth.
D. security.

30. The phrase "then our place knows us no more" (lines 30–31) means that we:

F. move to another town.
G. have children.
H. die.
J. divorce.

GO ON TO THE NEXT PAGE.

Passage IV

NATURAL SCIENCE: This passage explains how energy becomes usable through photosynthesis.

Every living cell must acquire energy in a usable form. According to the First Law of Thermodynamics, energy, which is the capacity for doing work, can be converted from one form into another without any net gain or loss. An organism must have an outside source of usable energy. The Second Law of Thermodynamics states that every energy transformation reduces the free (usable) energy of the system. Living cells primarily use chemical energy derived from complex organic compounds.

Photosynthesis is the process by which green plants transform sunlight into a usable energy source. Green plants utilize the energy of light to combine carbon dioxide with water to form organic material (sugar) and oxygen.

$$6CO_2 + 12H_2O + \text{light} \overset{\text{chlorophyll}}{\Rightarrow} 6O_2 + C_6H_{12}O_6 + 6H_2O$$

Photosynthesis is a reduction reaction. Reduction is the addition of one or more electrons to an atom or molecule. Oxidation is the removal of electrons from an atom or molecule. Reduction stores energy, while oxidation releases it. Biological systems rely on the addition or removal of an electron from hydrogen. Photosynthesis is based on two key processes. Light energy is trapped and stored, and hydrogen atoms are transformed from water to carbon dioxide to form carbohydrate.

Photosynthesis takes place within the chloroplasts. The pigments within the chloroplasts are precisely arranged within the membranes of flattened sacs called thylakoids. Thylakoids often lie close together in sacks called grana. The light reactions of photosynthesis take place within the thylakoid membranes, while the dark reactions take place in the colorless matrix (stroma) surrounding the thylakoids.

Different wavelengths of light, especially red and blue light, are trapped by various pigment molecules contained within chloroplasts. When a photon of light strikes a pigment molecule and is absorbed, the energy is transferred to an electron, which is raised to a high-energy state. A specialized form of chlorophyll passes the energized electron to an acceptor molecule, X, which has a high affinity for electrons. X passes the electron to a series of acceptor molecules, each at a slightly lower energy level. After being passed from molecule to molecule, the electron may return to the chlorophyll from which it started. Some of the energy released as the electron is passed down the energy gradient is used to synthesize the compound ATP from ADP and inorganic phosphate.

ATP is a universal energy packet used by cells to do work. ATP is synthesized from ADP and inorganic phosphate in a process called phosphorylation. Phosphorylation is a very high energy demanding process. *Cyclic photophosphorylation* occurs when the energy used for ATP synthesis comes from light-energized electrons as they are returned to the chlorophyll molecules from which they originated.

Another process that occurs in green plants is noncyclic photophosphorylation. In this reaction, some electrons are passed from the chlorophyll to a different type of acceptor molecule called $NAPD_{ox}$, which retains the electron and is therefore reduced to become $NAPD_{re}$.

The ATP and $NAPD_{re}$ produced in the light reaction are used to reduce carbon dioxide to carbohydrate in a series of reactions called the *Calvin cycle* (dark reaction). Basically, a five-carbon sugar, ribulose diphosphate (RuDP), is combined with CO_2. This process is called carboxyilation. The products are then phosphorylated by ATP and reduced by $NAPD_{re}$ to form PGAL, a three-carbon sugar.

Under certain conditions, the very same enzyme that under more agreeable conditions would facilitate its carboxyilation oxidizes RuDP. This process, called photorespiration, is seemingly a wasteful process since no ATP is created. Photorespiration predominates over photosynthesis when CO_2 levels are low and O_2 levels are high.

Some tropical angiosperm plants have a unique leaf structure known as *Kranz* anatomy (C_4 plants). In Kranz plants, the bundle-sheath cells have numerous chloroplasts (other plants usually do not), and the mesophyll cells are clustered in a ring-like arrangement around the bundle sheath. These plants can carry out photosynthesis under conditions of high temperature and concentrated light, when loss of water induces

GO ON TO THE NEXT PAGE.

closure of the stomata. When the stomata close, the concentration of CO_2 in the air spaces inside the leaf falls, and the concentration of O_2 rises. Under these conditions most plants (C_3) would experience a net loss of CO_2 because of photorespiration. Kranz plants (C_4) do not because of their specialized way of initially fixing CO_2. They combine CO_2 with a three-carbon compound in the mesophyll cells to form a four-carbon compound that passes into the bundle-sheath cells, where the CO_2 is regenerated. Therefore, Kranz plants can maintain a CO_2 level in the bundle-sheath cells that allows carboxyilation of RuDP in the Calvin cycle to predominate over its oxidation in photorespiration.

31. According to this passage, "the capacity for doing work" (line 3) is the definition of:

A. photosynthesis.
B. energy.
C. oxidation.
D. thermodynamics.

32. In the equation in line 16, $C_6H_{12}O_6$ apparently names:

F. oxygen.
G. carbon dioxide.
H. a sugar.
J. photosynthesis.

33. Which of these could be considered the reverse of reduction?

A. Oxidation
B. Photosynthesis
C. Transformation
D. Phosphorylation

34. Which of the following conclusions is (are) suggested by the third paragraph?

I. Photosynthesis involves the addition of electrons.
II. Photosynthesis involves action on hydrogen.
III. Photosynthesis is a form of energy release.

F. I only
G. II only
H. III only
J. I and II only

35. The fifth paragraph deals mainly with:

A. defining terms related to plant growth.
B. comparing one reduction reaction to another.
C. explaining the process of photosynthesis.
D. expressing the author's opinion.

36. Which of the following statements is NOT true about ATP?

F. It mixes with phosphate to make ADP.
G. It is created through phosphorylation.
H. It serves a purpose in the Calvin cycle.
J. It is used by cells to do work.

37. The Calvin cycle involves:

A. the combination of carbon dioxide and a five-carbon sugar, with a three-carbon sugar as the result.
B. the combination of oxygen and a three-carbon sugar, with a five-carbon sugar as the result.
C. a mix of ATP and sugar to create carbon dioxide.
D. a reduction of carbohydrate to form carbon dioxide.

GO ON TO THE NEXT PAGE.

38. By "more agreeable conditions" (line 73), the author probably means:

F. conditions that produce higher levels of oxygen.
G. conditions that produce higher levels of CO_2.
H. conditions with higher temperatures.
J. conditions with longer growing periods.

39. Which of the following statements names a difference between photorespiration and photosynthesis?

I. Photorespiration involves RuDP.
II. In photosynthesis, ATP is synthesized.
III. Photorespiration is a reduction reaction.

A. I only
B. I and II only
C. II and III only
D. I, II, and III

40. Unlike the preceding paragraphs, the final paragraph discusses:

F. plants that do not photosynthesize.
G. living matter other than plants.
H. plants with an unusual structure.
J. plants that transform carbon dioxide into carbohydrate.

END OF TEST 3
STOP! DO NOT TURN THE PAGE UNTIL TOLD TO DO SO.
DO NOT RETURN TO THE PREVIOUS TEST.

NO TEST MATERIAL ON THIS PAGE

4 4 4 4 4 4 4 4 4 4 4 4

SCIENCE TEST

35 Minutes—40 Items

DIRECTIONS: Each passage below is followed by several items. After reading a passage, choose the best answer for each item. Fill in the corresponding oval on your bubble sheet. You may refer to the passage as often as necessary. You are NOT permitted the use of a calculator on this test. Answers are on page 644.

Passage I

The chart below shows several physical properties of compounds called alkanes, which are long "chains" of carbons to which hydrogen atoms are attached. As an example, the compound propane, which has three carbons, has the structural formula:

$$CH_3—CH_2—CH_3$$

Physical Properties of Straight-Chain Alkanes				
Name	# of Carbons	Boiling Point (°C)	Melting Point (°C)	Density
methane	1	−162	−183	0.47
ethane	2	−89	−183	0.57
propane	3	−42	−188	0.50
butane	4	0	−138	0.58
pentane	5	36	−130	0.56
hexane	6	69	−95	0.66
heptane	7	98	−91	0.68
octane	8	126	−57	0.70
nonane	9	151	−54	0.72
decane	10	174	−30	0.74

1. The general trends shown in the chart are:

A. as the number of carbons increases, all properties increase in value (with occasional exceptions).
B. as the number of carbons increases, boiling points and melting points decrease, while density increases.
C. as the number of carbons increases, density decreases and other properties increase.
D. as the number of carbons increases, all properties decrease.

2. The change in boiling point is greatest:

F. from methane to ethane.
G. from propane to butane.
H. from butane to pentane.
J. from nonane to decane.

3. For alkanes with more than one carbon, the change in melting point from one alkane to the next:

A. tends to be greater from an even number of carbons to the next odd number.
B. tends to be greater from an odd number of carbons to the next even number.
C. is similar, whether from an even number of carbons to the next odd number, or from an odd number of carbons to the next even number.
D. Cannot be determined from the given information

GO ON TO THE NEXT PAGE.

4. Considering the alkane properties listed, if alkane X has a higher boiling point than alkane Y, then without exception, it must also have a:

   F. higher melting point.
   G. higher density.
   H. higher number of carbons.
   J. longer name.

5. The greatest percentage increase in density occurs from:

   A. ethane to propane.
   B. propane to butane.
   C. pentane to hexane.
   D. hexane to heptane.

GO ON TO THE NEXT PAGE.

Passage II

A student performs a set of physics laboratory experiments, in which objects of different masses glide "frictionlessly" along a smooth surface, collide, and then continue to glide. The momentum of each object is defined as its "mass • velocity." The momentum of a system of objects is the sum of the individual momentums.

Experiment 1

The light mass moves toward the stationary, heavy mass, and both stick together and continue to move. Table 1 shows the relevant information.

Table 1		
	Object 1	Object 2
Mass	2 kg	5 kg
Initial velocity	4 m/sec	0 m/sec
Final velocity	1.14 m/sec	1.14 m/sec

Experiment 2

The student performs a similar experiment in which the objects do not stick together, but collide "elastically"—that is, rebound from each other with no loss in energy. Table 2 shows the results.

Table 2		
	Object 1	Object 2
Mass	2 kg	5 kg
Initial velocity	4 m/sec	0 m/sec
Final velocity	−1.71 m/sec	2.29 m/sec

(Note that positive velocities indicate motion to the right, negative velocities indicate motion to the left.)

6. In Experiment 1, the momentum of Object 1 before the collision is:

F. 0 kg • m/sec.
G. 2 kg • m/sec.
H. 4 kg • m/sec.
J. 8 kg • m/sec.

7. After the collision in Experiment 1, the momentum of the combined masses is:

A. much less than the initial total momentum of the two masses.
B. about equal to the initial total momentum of the two masses.
C. much greater than the initial total momentum of the two masses.
D. Cannot be determined from the given information

8. After the collision in Experiment 2:

F. both objects are moving to the right.
G. both objects are moving to the left.
H. Object 1 is moving to the left and Object 2 to the right.
J. Object 1 is moving to the right and Object 2 to the left.

9. In Experiment 2, if Object 2 were replaced by another object that was far more massive than Object 1, its final velocity would be closest to:

A. 4.0 m/sec.
B. 2.3 m/sec.
C. −1.7 m/sec.
D. 0 m/sec.

10. Under the conditions described in the previous item, the final velocity of Object 1 would be closest to:

F. −2 m/sec.
G. −1.7 m/sec.
H. 0 m/sec.
J. 2 m/sec.

GO ON TO THE NEXT PAGE.

11. Kinetic energy is defined as $\frac{mv^2}{2}$. During the collision described in Experiment 1, the kinetic energy of Object 1:

A. increases.
B. remains the same.
C. decreases.
D. Cannot be determined from the given information

GO ON TO THE NEXT PAGE.

Passage III

The table below shows how an increase (+) or a decrease (–) in one or more plant hormones and environmental factors can affect various plant activities. The activities listed on the left occur when the combinations of conditions to the right exist at the same time. Hormones (H) are numbered; e.g., H_1, H_2, etc.

Activities	H_1	H_2	H_3	H_4	H_5	Day Length	Temperature
Plant growth	++		++				
No plant growth (1)	++		++	++			
No plant growth (2)	++		++		++		
Seed germination			++				
Flowering			++		++	(++ *or* – –)*	++
Flower drop-off	– –	++					
Fruit drop-off	– –	++					
Leaf drop-off	– –	++					– –

*Different species of plants require different combinations of light and darkness to stimulate flowering.

12. Based on the information in the table, a drop in temperature will help cause:

F. flowering.
G. loss of leaves, fruit, and flowers.
H. loss of leaves only.
J. seed germination.

13. The hormones that can inhibit (prevent) plant growth are:

A. 1 and 3.
B. 1, 3, and 4.
C. 1, 3, and 5.
D. 4 and 5.

14. Which conclusion is correct about the various factors affecting plant activities?

F. Hormone 3 influences more plant activities than any other factor.
G. Seed germination is influenced by the fewest factors, whereas flowering is influenced by the most.
H. For Hormone 1 to have an effect on any plant activity, it must be changing in the opposite direction of at least one other hormone.
J. Temperature changes can affect all plant activities.

15. Which activity would most likely be affected by changing a houseplant's growing conditions from 12 hours of light per 12 hours of darkness to constant light?

I. Plant growth
II. Loss of leaves
III. Flowering

A. I only
B. II only
C. III only
D. I and III only

GO ON TO THE NEXT PAGE.

16. Which statement best describes the relationship between Hormone 1 and Hormone 2?

F. Hormone 2 must change in the opposite direction of Hormone 1 for plant growth to occur.
G. When Hormone 1 and Hormone 2 affect a plant activity together, no other factors influence that activity.
H. As Hormone 1 increases, Hormone 2 always decreases; and as Hormone 1 decreases, Hormone 2 always increases.
J. Hormone 2 only affects plant activities when Hormone 1 is also involved.

GO ON TO THE NEXT PAGE.

Passage IV

In order to examine the factors that affect the flow of substances across cell membranes, three experiments were carried out. In each experiment, semi-permeable bags (bags with small pores that allow some substances to pass through, but not others) were partially filled with a fluid, tied, and then weighed (first weighing). The bags were then submerged into a large beaker of water, and at 10-minute intervals, removed from the beaker of water and re-weighed.

Experiment 1

A bag containing a 30% red dye solution (30% red dye and 70% water) weighed 100 grams. The bag was then submerged in a beaker of pure water. After 20 minutes, the bag weighed 110 grams. The beaker water remained clear.

Experiment 2

A second bag containing 40% red dye solution (40% red dye and 60% water) weighed 100 grams before being submerged in a beaker of pure water. After only 10 minutes, the bag weighed 110 grams. The beaker water remained clear.

Experiment 3

A third bag containing only pure water and weighing 100 grams was submerged in a beaker of 50% red dye solution (50% red dye and 50% water). After 20 minutes, the bag weighed 70 grams. The bag water remained clear.

17. In Experiment 1, a gain in bag weight suggests that:

A. material passed out from bag to beaker faster than it passed in from beaker to bag.
B. material passed in from beaker to bag faster than it passed out from bag to beaker.
C. material passed in and out of the bag at approximately the same rate.
D. material did not move at all.

18. Which of the following hypotheses is supported by the results of all three experiments?

F. Red dye can leave the bag but not enter.
G. Red dye can enter the bag but not leave.
H. Red dye can enter or leave the bag.
J. Red dye cannot enter or leave the bag.

19. Which of the following represents the best approximation for the weight of the bag in Experiment 2 after 20 minutes?

A. 90 grams
B. 100 grams
C. 110 grams
D. 120 grams

20. Which of the following questions is the entire set of experiments designed to answer?

F. How does concentration of red dye affect rate and direction of water flow?
G. How does concentration of water affect rate and direction of red dye flow?
H. How does rate of red dye flow affect direction of water movement?
J. How does direction of red dye movement affect rate of water flow?

21. A control experiment was set up to confirm the investigation's conclusion. A bag containing pure water and weighing 100 grams was submerged in a beaker of pure water. What is expected to occur?

A. The bag will slowly gain weight.
B. The bag will slowly lose weight.
C. The bag will remain approximately the same weight.
D. The bag will eventually become empty, and the water level in the beaker will rise.

GO ON TO THE NEXT PAGE.

22. Assuming that salts cannot freely pass across a cell's membrane, what would happen to human red blood cells (approximately 1% salt and 99% water) submerged in sea water (approximately 5% salt and 95% water)?

    F. The cells would shrink due to a loss of water.
    G. The cells would shrink due to a loss of salt.
    H. The cells would swell up due to a gain of water.
    J. The cells would swell up due to a gain of salt.

GO ON TO THE NEXT PAGE.

Passage V

The chart below shows various physical characteristics of different types of soil.

Physical Characteristics of Soil				
Types of Soil	Diameter of Particles (μm)	Relative Ability* to Hold Positively Charged Minerals (Ca^{+2}, K^{+}, Mg^{+2})	Relative Ability* to Maintain Air Spaces	Relative Ability* to Retain Water
Clay	less than 2	1	4	1
Silt	2–20	2	3	2
Sand	20–200	3	2	3
Coarse Sand	200–2,000	4	1	4

*Relative abilities are rated from 1, indicating the best (most able), to 4, indicating the worst (least able).

23. The soil type that is LEAST able to hold substances such as magnesium (Mg^{+2}) is:

A. sand.
B. coarse sand.
C. silt.
D. clay.

24. Based on the information in the chart, which of the following statements best describes the relationship between a soil's particle size and its other physical characteristics?

F. As particle size increases, the ability to hold positively charged minerals increases.
G. As particle size decreases, the ability to retain water decreases.
H. As particle size decreases, the ability to maintain air spaces increases.
J. As particle size increases, the ability to retain water decreases.

25. The size of particles in the soil type that is neither best nor worst at any of the listed abilities must be:

A. less than 20 micrometers.
B. more than 20 micrometers.
C. between 2 and 200 micrometers.
D. between 2 and 2,000 micrometers.

GO ON TO THE NEXT PAGE.

26. Loam is a type of soil that is mostly clay, but it also contains some sand and silt particles. Which prediction is most likely to be accurate about the ability of loam to support plant growth?

F. Plants will grow well because loam primarily has small particles that can hold minerals and retain water, yet it also has enough large particles to provide air spaces containing oxygen.
G. Plants will grow well because loam primarily has large particles that can provide air spaces containing oxygen, yet it also has enough small particles that can hold minerals and retain water.
H. Plants will not grow well because although loam is excellent at maintaining air spaces for oxygen, it will not hold enough minerals or water.
J. Plants will not grow well because although loam has enough minerals and air spaces for oxygen, it cannot retain enough water.

27. Based on the information provided in the chart, which of the following conclusions about soil types is NOT correct?

A. Soils best at retaining water are also best at holding positively charged minerals.
B. No two soil types have the exact same combination of relative abilities.
C. Clay and coarse sand are the soil types that are most different in every physical characteristic.
D. At each listed ability, a different type of soil is best.

GO ON TO THE NEXT PAGE.

Passage VI

Theory 1

The rate of a chemical reaction is defined as the number of moles of a specified reactant consumed in one second. Reactants must collide in order for a reaction to occur, so it might seem that rates would depend upon the concentration of reactants—the more reactants that are present, the greater the likelihood of a collision. In fact, this is the case; a concrete example makes this clear. For the reaction: $2NO + O_2 \Rightarrow 2NO_2$, the rate is proportional to the amount of NO and O_2 present. This fact is expressed in the following "rate law": $\text{rate} = k[NO]^2[O_2]^1$, where k is the rate constant, and the exponents reflect the coefficients in front of the reactants in the reaction. The relationship between numbers of reactant molecules and exponents in the rate law is a general one.

Theory 2

Theory 1 is very often true, for it expresses the reasonable insight that the greater the concentration of reactants, the greater the likelihood of a reaction. It has a great shortcoming, however, in its assumption that all reactions proceed in one fell swoop rather than in several skirmishes.

For example, let letters A, B, and C stand for molecules. In the reaction $A + 2B \Rightarrow C$, Theory 1 predicts a rate law as follows: $\text{rate} = k[A][B]^2$. However, if the reaction actually proceeds in two stages, the first one would be $A + B \Rightarrow AB$ and the second one would be $AB + B \Rightarrow C$.

Thus, Theory 2 implies that one must understand the details of the reaction, including the relative speeds of the sub-reactions, in order to predict a rate law. Theory 1 is not completely wrong, just incomplete.

28. Theory 1 relates:

F. reaction rate to the concentration of products.
G. reaction rate to the concentration of reactants.
H. the relative amounts of products to one other.
J. reaction rate to the individual rates of various stages of the reaction.

29. According to a proponent of Theory 2, Theory 1:

A. can never give a correct prediction for a rate law.
B. will give a correct result if the reactant coefficients are all equal to 1.
C. will give a correct result for a single-stage reaction.
D. is in error because it claims that collisions are required for reactions to occur.

30. According to Theory 1, the rate of the reaction $3M + 2N \Rightarrow 4P$ will be given by:

F. $k[M][N]$.
G. $k[M]^3[N]^2$.
H. $k[M]^3[N]^2[P]^4$.
J. $k([M]^3 + [N]^2)$.

31. A chemist studies the rate of the reaction $2NO_2 + F_2 \Rightarrow 2NO_2F$. According to Theory 1, the rate of the reaction is proportional to:

A. the first power of NO_2 and the first power of F_2.
B. the second power of NO_2 and the second power of NO_2F.
C. the second power of NO_2 and the second power of F_2.
D. the second power of NO_2 and the first power of F_2.

32. Supporters of Theory 2 would best be able to defend their positions if:

F. they could show that the reaction occurs in more than one stage.
G. they slowed the reaction down by cooling the reactants.
H. they sped the reaction up with additional heat.
J. they eliminated all collisions.

GO ON TO THE NEXT PAGE.

33. According to Theory 2, if in a two-stage reaction Stage 1 is much slower than Stage 2, then the overall reaction rate will be:

A. primarily determined by the rate of Stage 1.
B. primarily determined by the rate of Stage 2.
C. undeterminable unless all collisions are counted.
D. undeterminable unless the rate law is measured experimentally.

34. When discussing the rates of reactions that have more than one stage, Theory 2 would not be necessary if:

F. all stages went quickly.
G. all stages had different rates.
H. the sum of the rates of each stage always equaled the rate of the reaction as a whole.
J. the sum of the rates of each stage was never equal to the rate of the reaction as a whole.

GO ON TO THE NEXT PAGE.

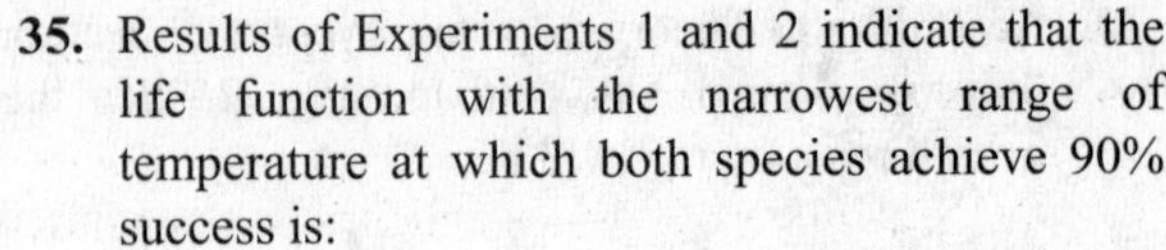

Passage VII

Closely related species of butterflies are often found living in very different environments. A pair of experiments was performed in which butterfly species previously captured in either desert areas or mountain areas were tested in laboratory incubators to determine the conditions at which they could carry out important life functions such as mating, oviposition (egg-laying), and pupation (the stage in which the stationary cocoon undergoes its final development into an adult).

Experiment 1

Under conditions of 100% relative humidity (maximum moisture content of the air), 100 desert butterflies (Species D) and 100 mountain butterflies (Species M) were tested at temperature intervals of 2°C (from 0°C to 40°C) to determine if they could mate, oviposit, and pupate. Each species achieved at least 90% success at the following ranges of temperatures:

Table 1

	Temperature Ranges (°C)		
	Mating	Oviposition	Pupation
Species D	10–34	14–34	4–38
Species M	6–30	10–28	4–34

Experiment 2

The experiment was repeated at 0% relative humidity (minimum moisture content of the air). The species achieved at least 90% success at the following ranges of temperatures:

Table 2

	Temperature Ranges (°C)		
	Mating	Oviposition	Pupation
Species D	10–34	14–34	4–38
Species M	6–24	10–22	4–28

35. Results of Experiments 1 and 2 indicate that the life function with the narrowest range of temperature at which both species achieve 90% success is:

A. mating.
B. oviposition.
C. pupation.
D. different in Experiment 1 than it is in Experiment 2.

36. Which condition has the most detrimental effects on Species M for mating, oviposition, and pupation?

F. Moist air at low temperatures
G. Moist air at high temperatures
H. Dry air at low temperatures
J. Dry air at high temperatures

37. A third experiment was conducted at 100% relative humidity in which the temperature range for caterpillar survival (another life function) was tested in Species D and Species M. Species D achieved 90% success at 12–36 (°C), while Species M achieved 90% success at 8–30 (°C). Which temperature range is a good prediction of survival in Species D under dry conditions?

A. 8°C–30°C
B. 8°C–24°C
C. 12°C–36°C
D. 12°C–30°C

38. If an investigator wanted to set up an experiment to determine the effects of light and dark on mating ability in Species D and Species M at 100% relative humidity, which set of conditions would provide the most complete results?

F. Test both species at 6°C in the light and 6°C in the dark.
G. Test both species at 20°C in the light and 20°C in the dark.
H. Test both species at 34°C in the light and 34°C in the dark.
J. Test both species at 34°C in the light and 30°C in the dark.

GO ON TO THE NEXT PAGE.

39. Which hypothesis is NOT supported by the results of Experiment 1 and Experiment 2?

A. For all tested life functions, dry conditions only affect Species M at the high end of its temperature ranges.
B. For all tested life functions, dry conditions have no effects on the temperature ranges of the desert species.
C. Species D does better than Species M at high temperatures in all tested life functions.
D. Species M does better than Species D at low temperatures for pupation.

40. Which of the following statements best explains the broad range of temperatures for pupation observed in both butterfly species?

F. Since the cocoon is stationary, it must be able to survive changing temperature conditions until the adult butterfly emerges.
G. Deserts can get very hot and mountains can get very cold.
H. Mountain butterflies would not survive long in the desert, and desert butterflies would not survive long in the mountains.
J. The stationary cocoon must be able to survive under light and dark conditions until the adult butterfly emerges.

END OF TEST 4
STOP! DO NOT TURN THE PAGE UNTIL TOLD TO DO SO.
DO NOT RETURN TO THE PREVIOUS TEST.

5 5 5 5 5 5 5 5 5 5 5 5

WRITING TEST (OPTIONAL)

30 Minutes—1 Essay Prompt

DIRECTIONS: You have 30 minutes to plan and write an essay. Read the prompt carefully and make sure you understand the instructions. A successful essay will have the following features: it will take a position on the issue presented in the writing prompt; it will maintain a consistent focus on the topic; it will use logical reasoning and provide supporting ideas; it will present ideas in an organized manner; and, finally, it will include clear and effective language in accordance with the conventions of standard written English. Sample essay responses begin on page 670.

Writing Test Prompt

Some educators and parents advocate changing from the traditional nine-month school year to a twelve-month program. They point out that the nine-month school year was first adopted when students were needed to work on family farms during the summer months, a need that no longer exists. They also state that year-round school would improve academic achievement because it would eliminate the need to review each previous year's work at the beginning of a new school year and allow teachers to cover material in greater detail. Other teachers and parents are opposed to such a change. They point out that summer is the traditional time for family vacations and that in addition to giving students a needed break from academic work, the summer vacation is the time for part-time jobs, summer camp, and special trips, all of which are also learning experiences. Do you think that schools should change from a nine-month school year to a twelve-month school year?

In your essay, take a position on this issue. You can write about either point of view presented here, or you can present a different point of view on this topic. Support your position with relevant reasons and/or examples from your own experience, observations, or reading.

END OF TEST 5
STOP! DO NOT RETURN TO ANY OTHER TEST.

Timed Practice Test II*

*The bubble and essay response sheets for Timed Practice Test II are located in Appendix B.

DIRECTIONS

Timed Practice Test II includes five subject tests: English, Mathematics, Reading, Science, and Writing. Calculator use is permitted on the Mathematics Test only.

The items in each multiple-choice test are numbered and the answer choices are lettered. The bubble sheet provided in Appendix B (p. 737) has numbered rows that correspond to the items on the test. Each row contains lettered ovals to match the answer choices for each item on the test. Each numbered row on the bubble sheet has a corresponding item on the test.

For each item, first decide on the best answer choice. Then, locate the row number that corresponds to the item. Next, find the oval in that row that matches the letter of the chosen answer. Then, use a soft lead pencil to fill in the oval. DO NOT use a ballpoint pen.

Mark only one answer for each item. If you change your mind about an answer choice, thoroughly erase your first mark before marking your new answer.

Note that only responses marked on your bubble sheet will be scored. Your score on each test will be based only on the number of items that are correctly answered during the time allowed for that test. Guessing is not penalized. Therefore, it is to your best advantage to answer every item on the test, even if you must guess.

On the Writing Test, use the essay response sheets provided in Appendix B (pp. 739–742) to write your response to the prompt. (Note that the Writing Test is optional.)

You may work on each test only during the time allowed for that test. If you finish a test before time is called, use the time to review your answer choices or work on items about which you are uncertain. You may not return to a test on which time has already been called and you may not preview another test. You must lay down your pencil immediately when time is called at the end of each test. You may not for any reason fill in or alter ovals for a test after time has expired for that test. Violation of these rules will result in immediate disqualification from the exam.

GO ON TO THE NEXT PAGE.

1 1 1 1 1 1 1 1 1 1 1 1

ENGLISH TEST

45 Minutes—75 Items

DIRECTIONS: In the passages below, certain parts of the sentences have been underlined and numbered. In the right-hand column, you will find different ways of writing each underlined part; the original version is indicated by the "NO CHANGE" option. For each item, select the choice that best expresses the intended idea, is most acceptable in standard written English, or is most consistent with the overall tone and style of the passage.

There are also items that ask about a section of the passage or the passage as a whole. These items do not refer to an underlined portion of the passage; these items are preceded by statements that are enclosed in boxes.

Read the passage through once before you begin to answer the accompanying items. Finding the answers to certain items may depend on looking at material that appears several sentences beyond the item. So, be sure that you have read far enough ahead before you select your answer choice. Answers are on page 672.

PASSAGE I

The Philosophy of Botany

[1]

Botany is surely the more gentler of[1] sciences. The careful observation of a flower is a calm, ostentatious[2] action—the peaceful contemplation of a beautiful object. Reduced to its essentials, it[3] requires no laboratory and the natural world is needed,[4] a few tools and the naked eye. Botany in its most scientific or

1. A. NO CHANGE
   B. the most gentle of
   C. the gentler of
   D. the gentlest in the

2. F. NO CHANGE
   G. unobtrusive
   H. violent
   J. chaotic

3. A. NO CHANGE
   B. essentials; it
   C. essentials, botany
   D. essentials; botany

4. F. NO CHANGE
   G. but you do need the natural world
   H. but the natural world
   J. but the natural world is necessary

GO ON TO THE NEXT PAGE.

purest form <u>consists about</u> [5] seeking to know more about the plant simply for the sake of that knowledge. Plants have not always been regarded as worthy <u>of knowing</u> [6] or studying in and of themselves, not on their merits as sources of food or drugs but as life-forms. In fact, the history of botany can be viewed in terms of repeated rediscoveries of this one theme—that plants are worthy of study <u>in and of themselves</u>, [7] quite apart from any use they might have for mankind.

[2]

[8] The practical motives behind plant study should not be <u>disparaging—the</u> [9] bulk of our medical history, for instance, is made up of accounts of herbal remedies. <u>Nonetheless</u>, [10] the study of the medicinal properties of plants contained a self-limiting mechanism: if a plant seemed to have no utilitarian value, it was disregarded, and no further study of it <u>is made</u>. [11] The Renaissance attitude towards nature changed this overly practical bent and initiated the scientific study of plants.

5. A. NO CHANGE
B. consists of
C. consists in
D. consist of

6. F. NO CHANGE
G. for knowledge
H. of knowledge
J. to know

7. A. NO CHANGE
B. by themselves
C. themselves
D. by and for themselves

8. Beginning Paragraph 2 with which of the following might make the transition from Paragraph 1 to Paragraph 2 clearer?

F. Since
G. Heretofore
H. However,
J. Hence

9. A. NO CHANGE
B. disparaged—the bulk
C. disparaged; the bulk
D. disparaging, the bulk

10. F. NO CHANGE
G. Consequently
H. Thus
J. Moreover

11. A. NO CHANGE
B. had been made
C. was made
D. were made

GO ON TO THE NEXT PAGE.

[3]

Botany, as a pure science, has certain characteristics and makes certain assumptions that prove thought provoking and interesting. One of its unspoken or[12] basic assumptions is an implicit respect and regard for all living things. The botanist who studies a plant's structure or tries to have understood their[13] functions confronts nature on its own terms. Investigations of how a plant thrives or reproduces, or studies of the purposefulness of a flower's coloration and structure, are almost implicitly egalitarian and tautological. The botanist studies the flower because they exist, but[14] because it exists, it is worthy of study.

12. **F.** NO CHANGE
G. because
H. and thus
J. yet

13. **A.** NO CHANGE
B. to understand its
C. understanding their
D. having understood its

14. **F.** NO CHANGE
G. it exists, but
H. it exists and
J. it exists, and

Item #15 asks about the preceding passage as a whole.

15. The last sentence of the essay is actually a restatement of which of the following ideas?

A. The study of the medicinal properties of plants has a self-limiting mechanism.
B. The botanist who tries to understand a plant's function confronts nature on its own terms.
C. The study of plants and flowers is tautological.
D. Botany is a gentle science.

GO ON TO THE NEXT PAGE.

PASSAGE II

Poverty in America

The main characteristic of poverty is, <u>of course,</u> [16] lack of money. A family is defined as poor when its annual income <u>falls below a certain dollar amount,</u> [17] calculated by the U.S. Federal Government to be the minimum a family of <u>their</u> [18] size would need to maintain a minimally decent standard of living. In certain areas of rural America, <u>consequently,</u> [19] poverty is the rule rather than the exception. As many as 50 percent of the families may earn <u>less than</u> [20] the poverty level, and some may manage to subsist somehow on amounts even less than half the official poverty level income. [21]

16. The use of the phrase "of course" is:
    F. appropriate because it is not obvious that someone who is poor lacks money.
    G. appropriate because it disrupts the flow of the sentence.
    H. appropriate because someone who is poor obviously lacks money.
    J. questionable since someone might be poor in spirit.

17. **A.** NO CHANGE
    B. falls and is under a certain dollar amount,
    C. is under a certain specified dollar amount,
    D. OMIT the underlined portion.

18. **F.** NO CHANGE
    G. there
    H. its
    J. it's

19. **A.** NO CHANGE
    B. and therefore, as a result of this,
    C. moreover, due to this fact,
    D. OMIT the underlined portion.

20. **F.** NO CHANGE
    G. lower than
    H. less as
    J. lower as

21. The first paragraph provides which of the following?
    A. An argument
    B. A comparison
    C. A definition
    D. A narrative

GO ON TO THE NEXT PAGE.

Although lack of money is the defining characteristic of poverty, poverty is more than simply lack of money. Poverty is an entire complex of symptoms. Low levels of formal schooling among adults parallel low-income levels. Additionally, in families below the poverty level, the number of children and aged who depend on those who work is in general higher than the national average for all families. As a consequence, fewer workers support a greater number of non-workers than in other, more prosperous families.

22 — Although

23 — parallel

24 — As a consequence,

Often, the schooling provided in low-income areas are as inadequate like incomes. In particular, rural children get poorer schooling than city children, and many rural poor are severely handicapped by it. The general rural average is only 8.8 years of school completed. Moreover, low educational levels seem to just keep repeating and repeating themselves. If the head of a rural poor family have little schooling, the children are often handicapped in their efforts to get an education. It is especially difficult for people who are handicapped educationally to acquire new skills, get new jobs, or otherwise adjust to an increasingly

25 — are as inadequate like incomes

26 — it

27 — just keep repeating and repeating themselves

28 — have

22. **F.** NO CHANGE
G. (Do NOT begin a new paragraph) Although
H. Since
J. (Do NOT begin a new paragraph) Since

23. **A.** NO CHANGE
B. go along with
C. are a lot like
D. very often go together with

24. **F.** NO CHANGE
G. However,
H. Surprisingly,
J. Fortunately,

25. **A.** NO CHANGE
B. is—like family income, inadequate
C. is so inadequate as family income
D. is, like family income, inadequate

26. **F.** NO CHANGE
G. education
H. their education
J. their lack of education

27. **A.** NO CHANGE
B. be self-perpetuating of themselves
C. be self-perpetuating
D. cause the same thing to happen all over again

28. **F.** NO CHANGE
G. have had
H. has had
J. was to have

GO ON TO THE NEXT PAGE.

urbanized society. This is as true on the farm rather than (29) in urban industry, since modern farming of the present day (30) requires skills that poor educated (31) people lack. Lacking in education, the rural poor either take low-paying jobs on the farm or elsewhere in rural areas or swell the ranks of the unemployed or under-employed.

29. **A.** NO CHANGE
B. rather as
C. as they are
D. as it is

30. **F.** NO CHANGE
G. of the present
H. presently
J. OMIT the underlined portion.

31. **A.** NO CHANGE
B. poorly educated
C. educated poor
D. poor education

Item #32 asks about the preceding passage as a whole.

32. The author does NOT use which of the following in the development of the essay?

F. Definitions
G. Personal experience
H. Statistics
J. Explanation

PASSAGE III

School Dropouts

One out of every four children who entered the fifth grade in the fall of 1966 fail to graduate (33) with his or her class. The total number that should of (34) graduated was 4.1 million, but approximately 900,000 fell by the wayside.

33. **A.** NO CHANGE
B. failed to graduate
C. failed graduation
D. fails to graduate

34. **F.** NO CHANGE
G. that should of been
H. who should of
J. who should have

GO ON TO THE NEXT PAGE.

Those who do not make it are called school dropouts. (Official statistics define a dropout as a person who has not yet attained the age of 16 and leaves school before graduation for any reason except transfer.) School officials who work with dropouts <u>who leave school</u> [35] say a student <u>will usually starting thinking</u> [36] about dropping out about two years before he or she ceases to attend <u>school: roughly</u> [37] at age 14. Absenteeism, class cutting, lack of motivation, and lack of interest in school <u>is often</u> [38] early signs of the potential <u>dropout. Also,</u> [39] many students drop out mentally very early in their school career, despite their physical presence until graduation.

The dropout is most often a boy who <u>mostly, frequently</u> [40] leaves school at the age of 16 while in the tenth grade. He is <u>most likely than those</u> [41] who stay in school to score low on an intelligence test and is likely

35. **A.** NO CHANGE
B. who have left school
C. who are leaving school
D. OMIT the underlined portion.

36. **F.** NO CHANGE
G. usually will be starting thinking
H. starts usually thinking
J. usually starts to think

37. **A.** NO CHANGE
B. school but roughly
C. school and roughly
D. school, roughly

38. **F.** NO CHANGE
G. is oftentimes
H. are often
J. were often

39. **A.** NO CHANGE
B. dropout also
C. dropout many
D. dropout but also

40. **F.** NO CHANGE
G. frequently and often
H. frequently
J. sometimes often

41. **A.** NO CHANGE
B. more likely than those
C. most likely as one
D. more likely than one

GO ON TO THE NEXT PAGE.

to be failing in school at the time <u>of him dropping out</u>.
42

Yet most dropouts <u>are really not less bright</u> than
43
students who remain in school until graduation. The dropout typically comes from the lower-income class and most often leaves school for financial reasons. His absences from school <u>increasing noticeably</u> during the
44
eighth grade and he participates little <u>or none</u> in extra-
45
curricular activities. The reasons a student drops out of school <u>goes deeper as</u> a mere desire to be rid of school.
46
Dropping out is a symptom; the roots of the problem are usually below the surface. [47]

42. F. NO CHANGE
G. he drops out
H. of his having dropped out
J. he dropped out

43. A. NO CHANGE
B. really they are no less bright than are the students who remain
C. are, than the students who remain, really no less bright
D. than the students who remain are really no less bright

44. F. NO CHANGE
G. increase so that
H. increase noticeably
J. increased to the point where it was noticed

45. A. NO CHANGE
B. and not at all
C. or not much
D. or not at all

46. F. NO CHANGE
G. go more deeply than
H. go deeper as
J. go deeper than

47. A logical continuation of the essay would be a discussion of:

A. the financial reasons a student might leave school.
B. a student's lack of motivation.
C. possible extracurricular activities.
D. why students might drop out of school.

GO ON TO THE NEXT PAGE.

Item #48 asks about the preceding passage as a whole.

48. Is the use of the official definition of dropout in the second paragraph appropriate?

F. Yes, because without a definition, the article would not be understandable.
G. Yes, because the nature of a "dropout" is one of the central themes of the passage.
H. No, because the definition has nothing to do with what the author is discussing in the second paragraph.
J. No, because the author then redefines the word.

PASSAGE IV

Wind Machines

The idea of generating electricity with wind power is not new. But the kind of attention that idea is getting today, in terms of research and development, are [49] both new and encouraging to planners looking for renewable energy sources satisfying [50] growing national demands. An effort is being made in the United States to use one of humankind's oldest energy sources to

49. **A.** NO CHANGE
B. development, is
C. developing, is
D. development are

50. **F.** NO CHANGE
G. that would have satisfied
H. to satisfy
J. with the satisfaction of

GO ON TO THE NEXT PAGE.

solve one of <u>its</u> [51] most modern <u>problems, to find</u> [52] reliable and cost-effective ways to harness the wind to produce electricity.

51. **A.** NO CHANGE
    B. their
    C. it's
    D. your

52. **F.** NO CHANGE
    G. problems: to find
    H. problems, finding
    J. problems. To find

Wind machines are not the simple devices <u>that they may be appearing to be,</u> [53] and the lessons they teach seldom come easy. <u>On the other hand,</u> [54] the potential reward to a nation that needs more energy from a renewable source is beyond calculation. Rewards for using wind power <u>have been gathered</u> [55] by civilizations and cultures since early in recorded history.

53. **A.** NO CHANGE
    B. they may be
    C. it may seem to be
    D. they may appear to be

54. **F.** NO CHANGE
    G. Therefore,
    H. As a consequence
    J. This means that

55. **A.** NO CHANGE
    B. has been gathering
    C. is gathering
    D. will have been gathered

No record survives of the earliest wind machine. It <u>may have been built</u> [56] in China more than three thousand years ago. It may have been built on the windy plains of Afghanistan. History hints at some sort of wind power used in the Pharaoh's Egypt <u>for the drawing of water</u> [57] for agriculture, long before the birth of Christ. Hammurabi may have taken time out from developing a legal code about 2,000 BC to sponsor development of some sort of wind machine. The earliest confirmed wind machines are in that same

56. **F.** NO CHANGE
    G. may have been
    H. was being built
    J. has been building

57. **A.** NO CHANGE
    B. to draw water
    C. in order that water be drawn
    D. in order to draw water

GO ON TO THE NEXT PAGE.

region. Persian writers described gardens <u>irrigated through the means of</u>[58] wind-driven water <u>lifts several</u>[59]

58. **F.** NO CHANGE
G. irrigated by means of
H. which were then irrigated by means of
J. irrigated by

59. **A.** NO CHANGE
B. lifts several,
C. lifts but several
D. lifts and several

centuries BCE. Ultimately, <u>we can only guess at the origin of the windmill</u>[60].

60. **F.** NO CHANGE
G. the origin of the windmill can only be guessed at
H. the origin of the windmill can only be guessed at by us
J. the origin of the windmill could only be guessed at

<u>Persian machines were horizontal devices,</u>[61] carousel-like contraptions that revolved around a center pole and caught the wind with bundles of reeds. The carousel is perhaps the <u>more simple design for capturing</u>[62] the wind; it cares nothing for the direction of the breeze, but revolves no matter where on the compass the wind may originate. From the Middle East, wind-machine technology may have been carried to Europe by returning Crusaders. Accurate records do not exist, but soon after the Crusades, windmills appeared in northern Europe and soon were found on the British Isles.

61. **A.** NO CHANGE
B. (Do NOT begin a new paragraph) Persian machines were horizontal devices,
C. Since Persian machines were
D. It was discovered that Persian machines were horizontal devices,

62. **F.** NO CHANGE
G. most simplest design for capturing
H. simpler design to capture
J. simplest design for capturing

GO ON TO THE NEXT PAGE.

For a while, windmills flourished in Europe, but with the advent of steam power, they come close to [63] extinction for the wind is real iffy [64]. It can fail to blow just when it is needed the most, or it can rage into a gale [65] when it is not needed at all.

63. A. NO CHANGE
B. came close to
C. are coming closer to
D. come close upon

64. F. NO CHANGE
G. likely to blow sometimes and not to others
H. here today and gone tomorrow isn't
J. capricious

65. The author's use of the phrase "rage into a gale" is:

A. inappropriate because images are out of place in scientific writing.
B. inappropriate because wind is sometimes calm.
C. appropriate because it creates a vivid image.
D. appropriate because it minimizes the importance of weather.

PASSAGE V

The Development of Television Programming

Television and its programs do not just happen. It is [66] planned products of a huge, wealthy, and highly competitive commercial enterprise. The television industry, which includes stations, networks, production companies, actors, and writers, are [67] responsible for selecting, creating, and distributing programs. The three most popular programs are the episodic series, the [68] made-for-television movie, and the mini-series.

66. F. NO CHANGE
G. They are
H. They would be
J. It was

67. A. NO CHANGE
B. writers, is
C. writers are
D. writers—is

68. F. NO CHANGE
G. episodic series the
H. episodic, series the
J. episodic series the,

GO ON TO THE NEXT PAGE.

In the 1970s, the episodic series, both dramatic and comic, was the most [69] popular of these. With the advent [70] of cable and pay television and of video disks and tapes, the television movie is rapidly gaining in [71] popularity. The past ten years have seen [72] several changes in television drama. The action-adventure police drama has lost and the situation comedy has grew [73] in popularity. Topics previously considered taboo emerged. Unmarried [74] couples living together, divorces, and single parents. Even topics that are politically controversy [75] can now be the focus of programs.

69. **A.** NO CHANGE
B. was the more
C. were the most
D. were the more

70. **F.** NO CHANGE
G. Including the advent
H. Notwithstanding the advent
J. With the beginning of the advent

71. **A.** NO CHANGE
B. has rapidly gained in
C. is rapidly gaining
D. will rapidly gain in

72. **F.** NO CHANGE
G. see
H. will see
J. would be seeing

73. **A.** NO CHANGE
B. has grown
C. grew
D. grow

74. **F.** NO CHANGE
G. emerged, unmarried
H. emerged unmarried
J. emerged: unmarried

75. **A.** NO CHANGE
B. politically controversial
C. politics controversy
D. political controversy

END OF TEST 1
STOP! DO NOT TURN THE PAGE UNTIL TOLD TO DO SO.

NO TEST MATERIAL ON THIS PAGE

2 2 2 2 2 2 2 2 2 2 2 2

MATHEMATICS TEST

60 Minutes—60 Items

DIRECTIONS: Solve each item and choose the correct answer choice. Then, fill in the corresponding oval on the bubble sheet.

Allocate time wisely. Try to solve as many items as possible, returning to skipped items if time permits.

Calculator use is permitted on this test; however, some items are best solved without the use of a calculator.

Note: All of the following should be assumed, unless otherwise stated.

1. Illustrative figures are NOT necessarily drawn to scale.
2. The word *average* indicates arithmetic mean.
3. The word *line* indicates a straight line.
4. Geometric figures lie in a plane.

Answers are on page 672.

DO YOUR FIGURING HERE.

1. $121{,}212+\left(2\times10^4\right)=?$

A. 121,232
B. 121,412
C. 123,212
D. 141,212
E. 312,212

2. If $6x+3=21$, then $2x+1=?$

F. 1
G. 2
H. 3
J. 6
K. 7

3. At a recreation center, it costs $3 per hour to rent a ping pong table and $12 per hour to rent a lane for bowling. For the cost of renting a bowling lane for 2 hours, it is possible to rent a ping pong table for how many hours?

A. 4
B. 6
C. 8
D. 18
E. 36

GO ON TO THE NEXT PAGE.

DO YOUR FIGURING HERE.

4. If j, k, l, and m are natural numbers and $j < k < l < m$, which of the following could be true?

F. $k = k + l$
G. $j = l + m$
H. $j + k = l + m$
J. $j + k + m = l$
K. $j + m = k + l$

5. Which of the following is greater than $\frac{1}{2}$?

A. $\frac{6}{11}$
B. $\frac{9}{19}$
C. $\frac{7}{15}$
D. $\frac{4}{9}$
E. $\frac{3}{7}$

6. Out of a group of 360 students, exactly 18 are on the track team. What percent of the students are on the track team?

F. 5%
G. 10%
H. 12%
J. 20%
K. 25%

GO ON TO THE NEXT PAGE.

7. In the figure below, 3 lines intersect as shown. Which of the following *must* be true?

DO YOUR FIGURING HERE.

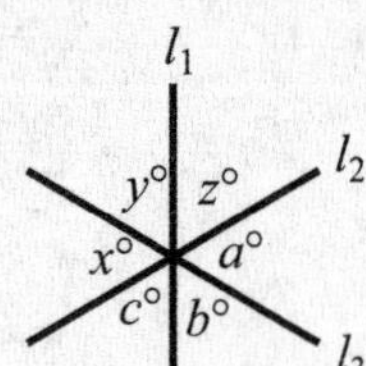

I. $a = x$
II. $y + z = b + c$
III. $x + a = y + b$

A. I only
B. II only
C. I and II only
D. I and III only
E. I, II, and III only

8. In the figure below, $x = ?$

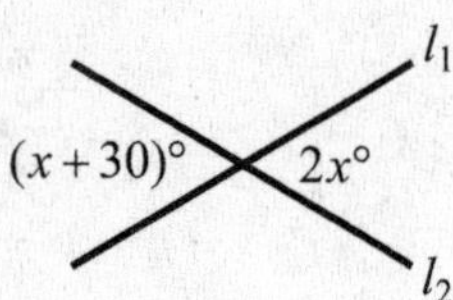

F. 15
G. 30
H. 45
J. 60
K. 90

9. Which of the following is the prime factorization of 60?

A. (2)(3)(10)
B. (3)(4)(5)
C. (2)(2)(3)(5)
D. (2)(2)(3)(6)
E. (3)(3)(3)(5)

GO ON TO THE NEXT PAGE.

10. The average height of 4 buildings is 20 meters. If 3 of the buildings are each 16 meters tall, what is the height, in meters, of the fourth building?

DO YOUR FIGURING HERE.

F. 32
G. 28
H. 24
J. 22
K. 18

11. In the figure below, what is the value of x?

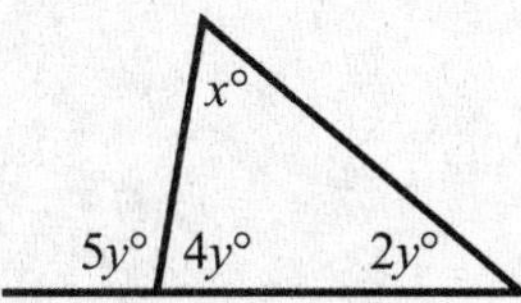

A. 15
B. 20
C. 30
D. 45
E. 60

12. In the figure below, what is the length of $\overline{PQ}$?

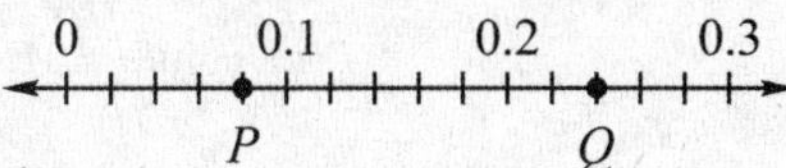

F. 0.09
G. 0.11
H. 0.12
J. 0.13
K. 0.16

13. What is the perimeter of the rectangle below?

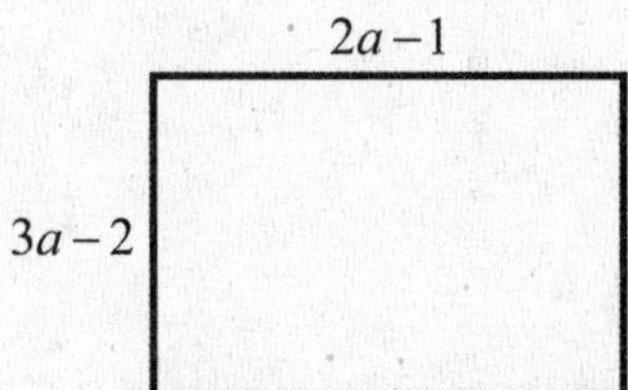

A. $10a-6$
B. $10a-3$
C. $6a-3$
D. $5a-6$
E. $5a-3$

GO ON TO THE NEXT PAGE.

DO YOUR FIGURING HERE.

14. If the average of x, x, x, 56, and 58 is 51, then $x = ?$

F. 43
G. 47
H. 49
J. 51
K. 53

15. For how many integers x is $-2 \leq 2x \leq 2$?

A. 1
B. 2
C. 3
D. 4
E. 5

16. For all real numbers x, 8^x equals which of the following?

F. $8x$
G. x^8
H. 2^{2x}
J. $x^{\frac{2}{3}}$
K. 2^{3x}

17. What is the sum of the areas of 2 squares with sides of 2 and 3 unit lengths, respectively?

A. 1
B. 5
C. 13
D. 25
E. 36

GO ON TO THE NEXT PAGE.

18. If the rectangular solid shown below has a volume of 54 cubic inches, what is the value of x, in inches?

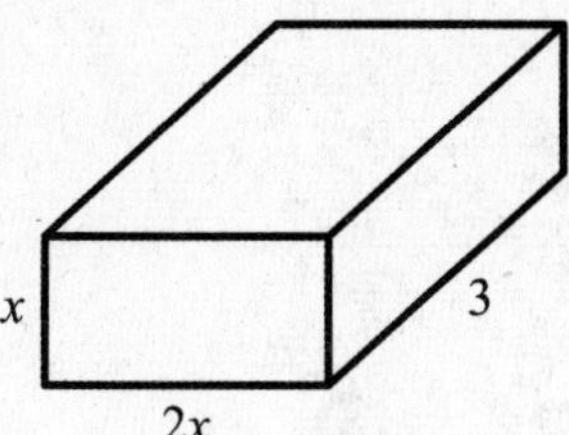

F. 2
G. 3
H. 6
J. 9
K. 12

DO YOUR FIGURING HERE.

19. If x is 80% of y, then y is what percent of x?

A. $133\frac{1}{3}\%$
B. 125%
C. 120%
D. 90%
E. 80%

20. From which of the following statements can it be deduced that $m > n$?

F. $m+1=n$
G. $2m=n$
H. $m+n>0$
J. $m-n>0$
K. $mn>0$

21. If $f(x)=x^2+x$, then what is the value of $f(f(2))$?

A. 42
B. 38
C. 32
D. 18
E. 4

GO ON TO THE NEXT PAGE.

22. The circle below with center O has a radius with a length of 2. If the total area of the shaded regions is 3π, then $x = ?$

DO YOUR FIGURING HERE.

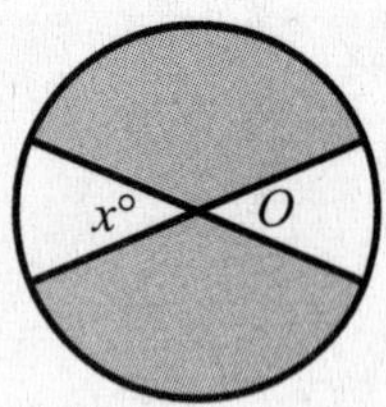

F. 270
G. 180
H. 120
J. 90
K. 45

23. If a bar of metal alloy consists of 100 grams of tin and 150 grams of lead, what percent of the entire bar, by weight, is tin?

A. 10%
B. 15%
C. $33\frac{1}{3}\%$
D. 40%
E. $66\frac{2}{3}\%$

24. If $\frac{1}{x}+\frac{1}{y}=\frac{1}{z}$, then $z = ?$

F. $\frac{1}{xy}$
G. xy
H. $\frac{x+y}{xy}$
J. $\frac{xy}{x+y}$
K. $\frac{2xy}{x+y}$

GO ON TO THE NEXT PAGE.

25. $|-5|+|-12|-|-2|+(-6)=?$

A. 2
B. 3
C. 6
D. 9
E. 14

DO YOUR FIGURING HERE.

26. If the average of $2x$, $2x+1$, and $2x+2$ is $x-1$, which of the following equations could be used to find x?

F. $6x+3=x-1$
G. $6x+3=3(x-1)$
H. $3(6x+3)=x-1$
J. $(6x+3)+(x-1)=3$
K. $(6x+3)(x-1)=3$

27. Members of a civic organization purchase boxes of candy for \$1 each and sell them for \$2 each. If no other expenses are incurred, how many boxes of candy must they sell to earn a net profit of \$500?

A. 250
B. 500
C. 1,000
D. 1,500
E. 2,000

28. $(-2)^2-(-2)^3=?$

F. 16
G. 12
H. 2
J. –2
K. –8

GO ON TO THE NEXT PAGE.

DO YOUR FIGURING HERE.

29. The sum, the product, and the average of 3 different integers are equal. If 2 of the integers are x and $-x$, the third integer is:

A. $\frac{x}{2}$
B. $2x$
C. -1
D. 0
E. 1

30. In a school with a total enrollment of 360, 90 students are seniors. What percent of all students enrolled in the school are seniors?

F. 25%
G. $33\frac{1}{3}\%$
H. 50%
J. $66\frac{2}{3}\%$
K. 75%

31. The perimeter of the square below is:

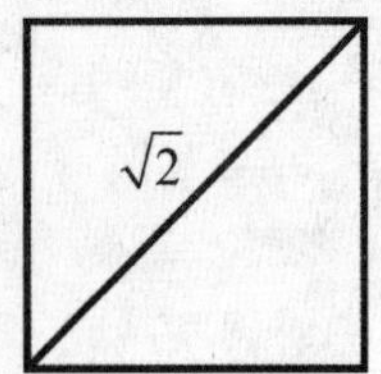

A. 1
B. $\sqrt{2}$
C. 4
D. $4\sqrt{2}$
E. 8

GO ON TO THE NEXT PAGE.

DO YOUR FIGURING HERE.

32. If 2 straight lines intersect as shown, what is the value of x?

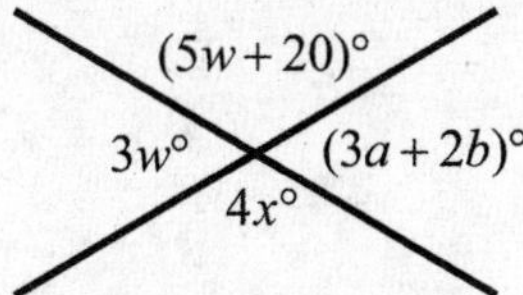

F. 15
G. 30
H. 45
J. 60
K. 75

33. The figure below is a scale drawing of the floor of a dining hall. If 1 centimeter on the drawing represents 5 meters, what is the area, in square meters, of the floor?

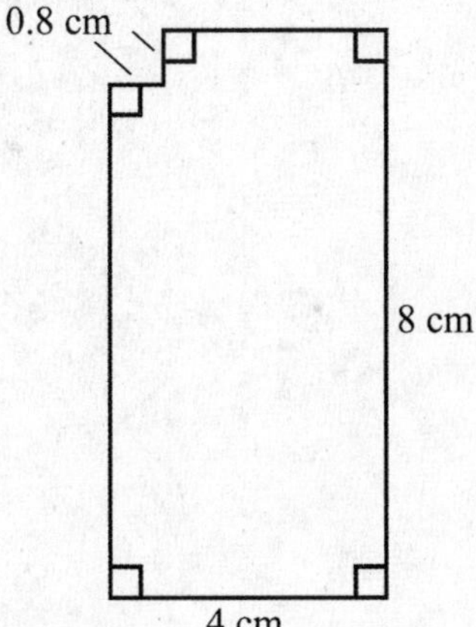

A. 144
B. 156
C. 784
D. 796
E. 844

GO ON TO THE NEXT PAGE.

34. A triangle has one side with a length of 4 and another side with a length of 11. What are the *greatest* and *least* possible integer values for the length of the remaining side?

DO YOUR FIGURING HERE.

F. 7 and 4
G. 11 and 4
H. 14 and 8
J. 15 and 7
K. 16 and 7

35. Which of the following is the solution set for the equation $-x^2 = 3 - 4x$?

A. $\{-3, -1\}$
B. $\{-3, 1\}$
C. $\{1, 3\}$
D. $\{1, 4\}$
E. $\{3, 5\}$

36. A school club spends $\frac{2}{5}$ of its budget for one project and $\frac{1}{3}$ of what remains for another project. If the club's entire budget is \$300, how much of the budget is left after the 2 projects?

F. \$60
G. \$90
H. \$120
J. \$180
K. \$240

GO ON TO THE NEXT PAGE.

DO YOUR FIGURING HERE.

37. If the cost of n nails is c cents, which of the following equations could be used to determine d, the cost in dollars, of x nails?

A. $d = 100cnx$

B. $d = 100\frac{cx}{n}$

C. $d = \frac{100nx}{c}$

D. $d = \frac{nx}{100c}$

E. $d = \frac{cx}{100n}$

38. If a, b, and c are real numbers and $a^2b^3c < 0$, which of the following inequalities *must* be true?

F. $b^3 < 0$
G. $b^2 < 0$
H. $b < 0$
J. $c < 0$
K. $bc < 0$

39. If the figure below is an equilateral triangle, what is its perimeter?

$2x+1$ $y+2$ $2x+y$

A. 1
B. 3
C. 9
D. 12
E. 15

40. In the coordinate plane, what is the distance between the point with (x, y) coordinates $(2,1)$ and the point with (x, y) coordinates $(5,5)$?

F. $\sqrt{3}$
G. $2\sqrt{3}$
H. $3\sqrt{2}$
J. 5
K. 6

GO ON TO THE NEXT PAGE.

41. $\sqrt{45}-\sqrt{20}+\sqrt{5}=?$

DO YOUR FIGURING HERE.

A. 0
B. $2-\sqrt{5}$
C. $2+\sqrt{5}$
D. $2\sqrt{5}$
E. 10

42. What is the least positive integer x for which $12-x$ and $15-x$ will yield non-zero results with opposite signs?

F. 3
G. 4
H. 11
J. 12
K. 13

43. The solution set to the pair of equations $mx+ny=15$ and $nx+my=13$ is $x=3$ and $y=1$. What are the values of m and n?

A. $m=5;\ n=3$
B. $m=4;\ n=3$
C. $m=3;\ n=4$
D. $m=3;\ n=5$
E. $m=2;\ n=6$

44. In the figure below, line segments intersecting each other at 90° join equally spaced points. If the total length of all the small line segments joining two of these equally spaced points in the figure is 24, what is the area of the shaded part?

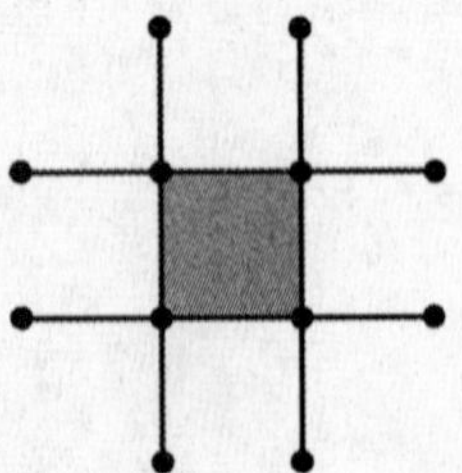

F. 1
G. 4
H. 8
J. 12
K. 16

GO ON TO THE NEXT PAGE.

45. All of the following are true for all real numbers EXCEPT:

A. $|a-b|=-|b-a|$
B. $|a-b|=|b-a|$
C. $|a-b|\leq|a|+|b|$
D. $|a+b|\leq|a|+|b|$
E. $|a|=|-a|$

46. $\text{Arccos}\left(\cos\frac{\pi}{2}\right)=?$

F. 0
G. $\frac{\pi}{4}$
H. $\frac{\pi}{2}$
J. π
K. $\frac{3\pi}{2}$

47. ΔABC has coordinates $A\ (-1,-2)$, $B\ (0,4)$, and $C\ (3,-1)$. If $\Delta A'B'C'$ is the reflection of ΔABC across the line $y=-x$, which of the following provides the coordinates of $\Delta A'B'C'$, respectively?

A. $(2,1)$, $(-4,0)$, $(1,-3)$
B. $(1,2)$, $(0,-4)$, $(-3,1)$
C. $(2,1)$, $(4,0)$, $(1,-3)$
D. $(3,2)$, $(5,1)$, $(2,-2)$
E. $(4,0)$, $(3,-1)$, $(-1,-2)$

48. If $\sin x=\cos x$, then x terminates only in the:

F. first quadrant
G. first or third quadrants
H. second quadrant
J. second or third quadrants
K. second or fourth quadrants

DO YOUR FIGURING HERE.

GO ON TO THE NEXT PAGE.

49. If the line $x = k$ is tangent to the circle $(x-2)^2 + (y+1)^2 = 4$, then which of the following is the point of tangency?

A. $(-6,-1)$ or $(2,-1)$
B. $(-2,-1)$ or $(6,-1)$
C. $(0,-1)$ or $(4,-1)$
D. $(0,1)$ or $(4,1)$
E. $(2,1)$ or $(6,1)$

DO YOUR FIGURING HERE.

50. What is the last term in the expansion $(2x+3y)^4$?

F. y^4
G. $9y^4$
H. $27y^4$
J. $81y^4$
K. $(xy)^4$

51. Which of the following could be a graph of the equation $y = ax^2 + bx + c$, where $b^2 - 4ac = 0$?

A.
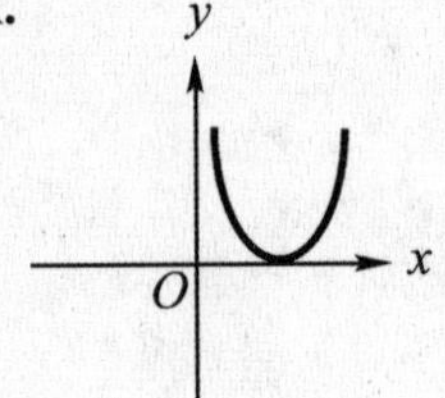

D.
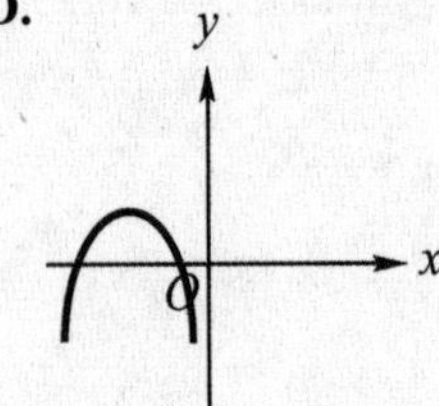

B.
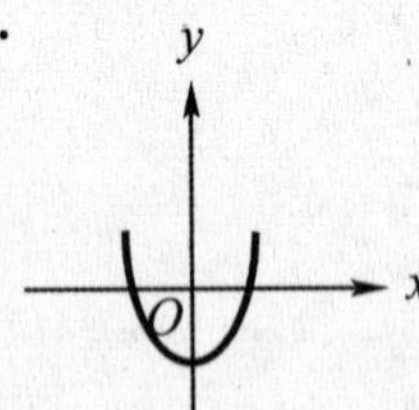

E.
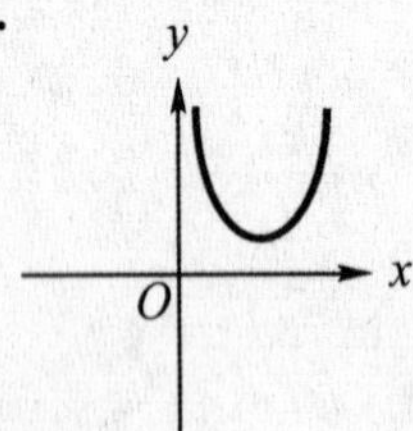

C.
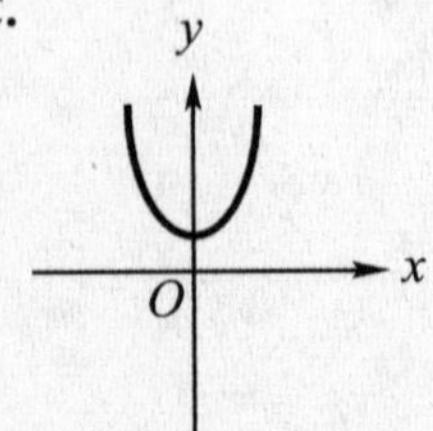

GO ON TO THE NEXT PAGE.

52. For any acute angle θ, which of the following is equal to $\frac{\sin\theta}{\cos\theta}$?

F. $\tan\theta$
G. $\cot\theta$
H. $\sec\theta$
J. 1
K. 0.5

DO YOUR FIGURING HERE.

53. An angle that measures $\frac{3}{2}\pi$ radians measures how many degrees?

A. 60
B. 90
C. 120
D. 180
E. 270

54. What is the solution set for $|2x-1|=3$?

F. All real numbers
G. The empty set
H. $\{-1\}$
J. $\{2\}$
K. $\{-1, 2\}$

55. The end points of a line have coordinates of $(2,5)$ and $(2,-4)$. What are the coordinates of the midpoint of the line?

A. $(0,1)$
B. $\left(2,\frac{1}{2}\right)$
C. $(2,1)$
D. $(2,9)$
E. $(4,9)$

GO ON TO THE NEXT PAGE.

56. What is the slope of the line with the equation $2x+3y-2=0$?

DO YOUR FIGURING HERE.

F. $-\frac{3}{2}$
G. $-\frac{2}{3}$
H. $\frac{2}{3}$
J. 4
K. 6

57. $\frac{1}{\sqrt{3}-1}=?$

A. $\frac{\sqrt{3}-1}{4}$
B. $\frac{\sqrt{3}-1}{3}$
C. $\frac{\sqrt{3}-1}{2}$
D. $\frac{\sqrt{3}+1}{2}$
E. $\sqrt{3+1}$

58. $(-2)^2-2^{-2}=?$

F. -5
G. -3
H. 3
J. $3\frac{3}{4}$
K. $4\frac{1}{4}$

GO ON TO THE NEXT PAGE.

DO YOUR FIGURING HERE.

59. $\frac{-3+\sqrt{5}}{2}$ is 1 root of the equation $x^2+3x+1=0$. What is the other root?

A. $\frac{-3-\sqrt{5}}{2}$
B. $\frac{3-\sqrt{5}}{2}$
C. $\frac{3+\sqrt{5}}{2}$
D. $3-\frac{\sqrt{5}}{2}$
E. $3+\frac{\sqrt{5}}{2}$

60. The figure below represents which of the following equations?

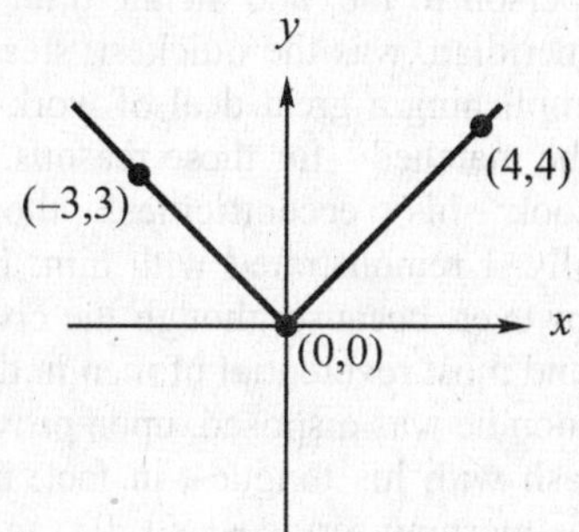

F. $y=x$
G. $y=-x$
H. $y=|x|$
J. $y=2x$
K. $y=x^2$

END OF TEST 2
STOP! DO NOT TURN THE PAGE UNTIL TOLD TO DO SO.
DO NOT RETURN TO THE PREVIOUS TEST.

3 3 3 3 3 3 3 3 3 3 3 3

READING TEST

35 Minutes—40 Items

DIRECTIONS: Each passage below is followed by a set of items. Read each passage and choose the best answer for each item. Fill in the corresponding oval on your bubble sheet. You may refer to the passage as often as necessary to answer the items. Answers are on page 673.

Passage I

PROSE FICTION: In this passage, the narrator shares his exasperation with and sympathy for an employee.

Turkey was a short, pursy Englishman, of about my own age—that is, somewhere not far from sixty. In the morning, one might say, his face was of a fine florid hue, but after twelve o'clock, meridian—his dinner hour—it blazed like a grate full of Christmas coals; and continued blazing—but, as it were, with a gradual wane—till six o'clock p.m., or thereabouts; after which, I saw no more of the proprietor of the face, which, gaining its meridian with the Sun, seemed to set with, to rise, culminate, and decline the following day, with the like regularity and undiminished glory. There are many singular coincidences I have known in the course of my life, not the least among which was the fact that, exactly when Turkey displayed his fullest beams from his red and radiant countenance, just then, too, at that critical moment, began the daily period when I considered his business capacities as seriously disturbed for the remainder of the twenty-four hours.

Not that he was absolutely idle, or averse to business then; far from it. The difficulty was he was apt to be altogether too energetic. There was a strange, inflamed, flurried, flighty recklessness of activity about him. He would be incautious in dipping his pen into his inkstand. All his blots upon my documents were dropped there after twelve o'clock, meridian. Indeed, not only would he be reckless, and sadly given to making blots in the afternoon, but, some days, he went further, and was rather noisy. At such times, too, his face flamed with augmented blazonry, as if cannel coal had been heaped upon anthracite. He made an unpleasant racket with his chair; spilled his sand box; in mending his pens, impatiently split them all to pieces, and threw them on the floor in a sudden passion; stood up, and leaned over his table, boxing the papers about in a most indecorous manner, very sad to behold in an elderly man like him.

Nevertheless, as he was in many ways a most valuable person to me, and all the time before twelve o'clock, meridian, was the quickest, steadiest creature, too, accomplishing a great deal of work in a style not easily to be matched—for these reasons, I was willing to overlook his eccentricities, though, indeed, occasionally, I remonstrated with him. I did this very gently, however, because, though the civilest, nay, the blandest and most reverential of men in the morning, in the afternoon he was disposed, upon provocation, to be slightly rash with his tongue—in fact, insolent. Now, valuing his morning services as I did, and resolved not to lose them—yet, at the same time, made uncomfortable by his inflamed ways after twelve o'clock—and being a man of peace, unwilling by my admonitions to call forth unseemly retorts from him, I took upon me, one Saturday noon (he was always worse on Saturdays) to hint to him, very kindly, that perhaps, now that he was growing old, it might be well to abridge his labors; in short, he need not come to my chambers after twelve o'clock, but, dinner over, had best go home to his lodgings, and rest himself till teatime. But no; he insisted upon his afternoon devotions. His countenance became intolerably fervid, as he oratorically assured me—gesticulating with a long ruler at the other end of the room—that if his services in the morning were useful, how indispensable, then, in the afternoon?

"With submission, sir," said Turkey, on this occasion, "I consider myself your right-hand man. In the morning I but marshal and deploy my columns; but in the afternoon I put myself at their head, and gallantly

GO ON TO THE NEXT PAGE.

charge the foe, thus"—and he made a violent thrust with the ruler.

"But the blots, Turkey," intimated I.

"True; but, with submission sir, behold these hairs! I am getting old. Surely, sir, a blot or two of a warm afternoon is not to be severely urged against gray hairs. Old age—even if it blot the page—is honorable. With submission, sir, we *both* are getting old."

This appeal to my fellow-feeling was hardly to be resisted. At all events, I saw that go he would not. So, I made up my mind to let him stay, resolving, nevertheless, to see to it that, during the afternoon, he had to do with my less important papers.

1. The narrator is Turkey's:

A. older brother.
B. physician.
C. co-worker.
D. employer.

2. The passage suggests that Turkey is a:

F. copyist.
G. painter.
H. fencing instructor.
J. sales clerk.

3. A logical explanation for Turkey's behavior is that he:

A. becomes fatigued.
B. is growing old.
C. drinks alcohol.
D. dislikes the narrator.

4. The fellow-feeling mentioned in the final paragraph is based on the fact that:

F. Turkey is the narrator's right-hand man.
G. Turkey and the narrator are the same age.
H. the narrator also makes ink blots.
J. the ink blots are not very serious.

5. The narrator's final resolution of the problem is to:

A. find a replacement for Turkey.
B. give Turkey Saturdays off.
C. give Turkey afternoons off.
D. give Turkey less important work after noon.

6. According to the narrator, Turkey's face is reddest:

F. in early morning.
G. shortly after noon.
H. in midafternoon.
J. in early evening.

7. It can be inferred that when cannel coal is heaped on anthracite, a fire:

A. burns more intensely.
B. burns less intensely.
C. goes out altogether.
D. begins to sputter and spit.

8. The narrator's attitude toward Turkey's afternoon behavior is one of:

F. amusement.
G. discomfort.
H. indifference.
J. outrage.

9. The narrator finds Turkey's work in the mornings to be:

A. entirely satisfactory.
B. frequently unsatisfactory.
C. almost always unsatisfactory.
D. inconsistent.

10. Which of the following does NOT characterize Turkey's behavior in the afternoon?

F. Frenzied activity
G. Excessive carelessness
H. Idleness
J. Verbal insolence

GO ON TO THE NEXT PAGE.

Passage II

SOCIAL SCIENCE: This passage discusses punishment for individuals who have violated the law.

Justice in society must include both a fair trial to the accused and the selection of an appropriate punishment for those proved guilty. Because justice is regarded as one form of equality, we find in its earlier expressions the idea of a punishment equal to the crime. Recorded in the Old Testament is the expression "an eye for an eye, and a tooth for a tooth." That is, the individual who has done wrong has committed an offense against society. To atone for this offense, society must get even. Only inflicting an equal injury upon him can do this. This conception of retributive justice is reflected in many parts of the legal codes and procedures of modern times. It is illustrated when we demand the death penalty for a person who has committed murder.

The German idealist, Hegel, supported this philosophy of punishment. He believed that society owed it to the criminal to administer a punishment equal to the crime committed. The criminal has by his own actions denied his true self, and it is necessary to do something to restore the self that has been denied. To the murderer, nothing less than giving up his own life will pay his debt. The exaction of the death penalty is a right the state owes the criminal, and it should not deny him his due.

Modern jurists have tried to replace retributive justice with the notion of corrective justice. The aim of the latter is not to abandon the concept of equality but to find a more adequate way to express it. It tries to preserve the ideal of equal opportunity for each individual to realize the best that is in him. The criminal is regarded as being socially ill and in need of treatment that will enable him to become a normal member of society. Before treatment can be administered, the causes that led to antisocial behavior must be found. If the causes can be removed, provisions must be made to have this done.

Only those criminals who are incurable should be permanently separated from the rest of society. This does not mean that criminals will escape punishment or be quickly returned to take up careers of crime. It means that justice is to heal the individual, not simply to get even with him. If severe punishment is the only adequate means for accomplishing this, it should be administered. However, the individual should be given every opportunity to assume a normal place in society. His conviction of crime must not deprive him of the opportunity to make his way in the society of which he is a part.

11. The best title for this selection is:

A. Fitting Punishment to the Crime.
B. Approaches to Just Punishment.
C. Improvement in Legal Justice.
D. Attaining Justice in the Courts.

12. Hegel would view the death sentence for murder as:

F. inadequate justice.
G. the best way for society to get revenge.
H. the most efficient method of removing a known danger.
J. an inalienable right of the murderer.

13. The passage implies that the basic difference between retributive justice and corrective justice is:

A. the type of crime that was committed.
B. the severity of the punishment.
C. the reason for the sentence.
D. the outcome of the trial.

14. The punishment that would be most inconsistent with the views of corrective justice is:

F. forced brain surgery.
G. solitary confinement.
H. life imprisonment.
J. the electric chair.

GO ON TO THE NEXT PAGE.

15. The Biblical expression "an eye for an eye, and a tooth for a tooth" was presented in order to:

A. justify the need for punishment as a part of law.
B. give moral backing to retributive justice.
C. show that humanity has long been interested in justice as a form of equality.
D. indicate the lack of social development during Biblical times.

16. The concept of retributive justice still reflected in many modern legal codes is:

F. giving the accused a fair trial.
G. rehabilitating the criminal.
H. separating incurable criminals from the rest of society.
J. inflicting equal injury on the criminal.

17. A major goal of modern jurists is to:

A. ensure that criminals do not escape punishment.
B. preserve the notion of equality.
C. restore states' rights.
D. select an appropriate punishment for a crime.

18. Under the notion of corrective justice, assuming "a normal place in society" (line 46) most likely means:

F. acting in one's best interests.
G. denying one's true self.
H. curing antisocial behavior.
J. accepting punishment.

19. The author's tone in the passage is best described as:

A. argumentative.
B. sympathetic.
C. explanatory.
D. conciliatory.

20. According to the author, criminals cannot be treated until:

F. they have been punished properly for their crime.
G. they have received a fair trial.
H. a legal code for treatment has been established.
J. the causes of antisocial behavior have been found.

GO ON TO THE NEXT PAGE.

Passage III

HUMANITIES: This passage describes events leading to and the effects of World War I.

The event that touched off World War I occurred in Sarajevo, the capital of the Austro-Hungarian province of Bosnia, on June 28, 1914. There the Archduke Francis Ferdinand, the Hapsburg heir to the throne of the Austro-Hungarian Empire, was shot and killed by a young Serbian nationalist seeking revenge against the Austrians for their annexation of Bosnia. Austria issued an ultimatum to Serbia. The Serbians acquiesced, in an attempt to stave off war. Austria, however, was intent on exacting retribution and in July of that year declared war on Serbia.

For almost a century, since the Congress of Vienna in 1815, European diplomats had prevented any real threat to the delicate balance of power achieved by the Congress. This time, though, they seemed powerless to stop the movement toward war. The assassination provoked a fateful series of failed diplomatic attempts that led suspicious Russia to mobilize its armed forces as Serbia's ally. Austria sought and received the mobilization aid of its ally Germany. The other members of the Triple Entente, France and Great Britain, soon joined their ally Russia against Austria. In 1917, the United States was drawn into the battle as an ally of France and Great Britain.

World War I was unlike any other war fought before or since. The profound shock it generated dramatically affected the progression of life in Europe and America and changed the course of world politics. Moreover, the war shocked millions of people throughout Europe into confronting the terrible losses and the grim and brutal realities of modern war. The few wars that had been fought since 1815 were distant colonial wars. Europeans had always been victorious, and the battles seemed nothing more than skirmishes that offered chances to experience adventure and to demonstrate bravery and heroism. The trenches and battlefields of Europe introduced millions of young men and women to a world of pain and death that they had never imagined.

The war altered the collective social sensibility of the people of Europe. It destroyed the spirit of optimism that had prevailed in the nineteenth century. Civilized, polite behavior now seemed archaic and utterly hypocritical. Moreover, the impression that there appeared to be no sane way to end the carnage only added to the sense of futility. The war changed relationships between members of the same social class. Before the war, the upper classes of Europe felt a common bond that united them across national borders. After the war, national boundaries defined social consciousness in a way that destroyed the solidarity of class.

World War I produced several dramatic changes in the political landscape of Europe. The breakup of the Austro-Hungarian, Russian, and German empires led to the reemergence of the state of Poland and the formation of other independent nation states in Europe. The war acted as a catalyst for European revolutionaries. The Russian Revolution of 1917 set the stage for the Bolshevik seizure of power, the exercise of total power by the Communist party; and the rise of Stalin as the absolute dictator of the Russian state (renamed the Union of Soviet Socialist Republics). World War I bore bitter fruit in Central and Southern Europe as well. The rise of Nazism in Germany and fascism in Italy led many historians to conclude that World War II, which was begun by Nazi Germany in 1939, was in actuality the continuation of the Great War that destroyed the social fabric of Europe in 1914.

21. The precipitating cause of World War I was:

A. an assassination.
B. a coronation.
C. a rebellion.
D. a plebiscite.

22. The event occurred in the city of:

F. Sarajevo in Bosnia.
G. Vienna in Austria.
H. Trieste in Italy.
J. Budapest in Hungary.

23. Before World War I, a balance of power had existed for:

A. nearly 15 years.
B. almost a quarter century.
C. almost 100 years.
D. nearly 10 years.

GO ON TO THE NEXT PAGE.

24. The chief reason European countries other than Austria and Serbia were drawn into the conflict was that they:

F. were members of the two alliance systems to which the combatants belonged.
G. feared the Hapsburgs.
H. wanted to ensure freedom of the seas.
J. wanted the land of neighboring countries.

25. Mobilization for war resulted swiftly when:

A. the United States declared war.
B. attempts at diplomacy failed.
C. Russia refused to help Serbia.
D. Italy joined the conflict.

26. The way in which class relationships changed as a result of the outbreak of World War I suggests that:

F. nationalism might have weakened had the war never occurred.
G. the middle classes had no real love of country.
H. the upper classes had eagerly anticipated war.
J. everyone sanctioned the war.

27. The forces of militant nationalism that were unleashed during World War I culminated in the breakup of the Russian Empire and the German Empire. The political regimes that came to power in Germany and the Soviet Union before World War II were:

A. democracies that isolated themselves from world politics.
B. ruthless dictatorships dedicated to world conquest.
C. weak states allied with the United States.
D. members of a Europe-wide common market.

28. The sense of futility felt throughout Europe during and after World War I would be evident in a study of:

F. American investment policies.
G. statistics concerning foreign language study in America.
H. the number of transatlantic voyages between 1920 and 1930.
J. European literature of the 1920s, 1930s, and 1940s.

29. World War I and its aftermath suggest the idea that:

A. nationalism has little to do with world conflict.
B. war feeds on nationalist sympathies.
C. the cause of peace is best aided by reinvigorating the spirit of nationalism.
D. diplomacy never works.

30. Archduke Francis Ferdinand, as the heir to the Austro-Hungarian Empire, was a member of the:

F. Hohenzollern family.
G. Hanover family.
H. Hapsburg family.
J. Stuart family.

GO ON TO THE NEXT PAGE.

Passage IV

NATURAL SCIENCE: This selection discusses the information gathered about the planet Uranus by the Voyager 2 spacecraft.

When the Voyager 2 spacecraft flew past Uranus and its moons in 1986, it gathered startling new information about these extraordinary celestial objects. Uranus had long been known to be different from all the other planets in one important respect: It lies tipped over on its side and instead of spinning like a top, it rolls like a ball along the path of its orbit. Its geographic poles, instead of being on the top and bottom of the planet as Earth's are, are located on either side, one facing the Sun and one facing away—as if they were the ends of a gigantic axle. Voyager found another oddity: Uranus' magnetic poles, instead of lying close to the geographic poles as Earth's do, are located not far from the planet's equator, 60° away from the geographic poles. Still another discovery is that the clouds in the Uranian atmosphere move in the same direction as the planet rotates; that is, from top to bottom and back to top, rather than horizontally, as Earth's clouds move.

The Uranian moons proved to have equally striking features. Miranda, the moon nearest the planet, bears tremendous markings where terrains of completely different types appear to have been wedged together. On Ariel, the next moon out, the landscape has been stretched apart, creating huge faults where the ground has broken apart and sunk inward. However, there is no evidence of any geological activity. Umbriel, the third moon, seems to be "painted" with some dark substance. On one side of Umbriel is a large, round bright marking called the "donut." It is presumably some type of impact crater. Each of Uranus' other seven moons is equally odd and unique in its own way. Furthermore, between the orbit of Miranda and Uranus' surface are up to one hundred charcoal-colored rings, ringlets, and bands of dust, and between some of these rings are still more tiny moonlets.

The moons and rings of Uranus are odd in still another way. Like the clouds in the planet's atmosphere, they circle Uranus in the same direction as the planet rotates. That is, they orbit over the top and bottom of the planet rather than around the sides, as Earth's moon does.

31. Because of the odd way in which Uranus rotates, one geographic pole:

A. alternates between daylight and darkness.
B. receives only indirect sunlight.
C. varies between heat from the Sun and cold.
D. is always in darkness.

32. The warmest spot on Uranus would most likely be located at:

F. one of the magnetic poles.
G. the equator.
H. one of the geographic poles.
J. a spot midway between a geographic pole and the equator.

33. On Uranus, a surface location that receives sunlight:

A. will alternate between daylight and darkness.
B. will always be in daylight.
C. will occasionally be in darkness.
D. must be near one of the magnetic poles.

34. The Uranian equator extends:

F. around the planet horizontally, as Earth's does.
G. around the planet through the geographic poles.
H. around the planet from top to bottom.
J. around the planet through the magnetic poles.

35. An observer at the Uranian equator would most likely experience:

A. a regular succession of days and nights.
B. constant, indirect sunlight.
C. a regular succession of warmth and cold.
D. only darkness.

GO ON TO THE NEXT PAGE.

36. Auroras are sky phenomena that generally appear near a planet's magnetic poles. On Earth, auroras can be seen at extreme north or south latitudes. On Uranus, auroras would most likely:

F. be visible near the planet's geographic poles.
G. never be visible.
H. be visible not far from the planet's equator.
J. be visible from everywhere on the planet's surface.

37. On Earth, atmospheric circulation patterns are largely controlled by the varying amounts of sunlight received at different latitudes. On Uranus:

A. atmospheric circulation functions in an identical way.
B. there is no atmospheric circulation.
C. the atmosphere circulates from one geographic pole to the other.
D. some other factor besides sunlight controls atmospheric circulation.

38. It has been suggested that the moon Miranda was shattered into pieces by a collision with some other object. Gravity then caused the pieces to reassemble; however, great "seam" marks most likely remained because:

F. the gravitational forces involved were weak.
G. the lack of atmosphere meant that no erosion ever took place.
H. the second object remained nearby, exerting gravitational pull.
J. the force of the collision was so great.

39. The great faults observed on the moon Ariel could have been caused by:

A. moonquakes.
B. continental drift.
C. the gravitational pull of other nearby moons.
D. volcanic activity.

40. Uranus has how many moons?

F. 3
G. 7
H. 10
J. 12

END OF TEST 3
STOP! DO NOT TURN THE PAGE UNTIL TOLD TO DO SO.
DO NOT RETURN TO THE PREVIOUS TEST.

SCIENCE TEST

35 Minutes—40 Items

DIRECTIONS: Each passage below is followed by several items. After reading a passage, choose the best answer for each item. Fill in the corresponding oval on your bubble sheet. You may refer to the passage as often as necessary. You are NOT permitted the use of a calculator on this test. Answers are on page 673.

Passage I

The table below shows selected elements from the periodic table, together with atomic radii in angstrom units (Å) and electronegativities (second number). When two atoms form a covalent bond, the approximate bond length may be calculated by adding together the two atomic radii.

H 0.37 Å 2.20						
Li 1.35 Å 0.98	Be 0.90 Å 1.57	B 0.80 Å 2.04	C 0.77 Å 2.55	N 0.70 Å 3.04	O 0.66 Å 3.44	F 0.64 Å 3.98
Na 1.54 Å 0.93	Mg 1.30 Å 1.31	Al 1.25 Å 1.61	Si 1.17 Å 1.90	P 1.10 Å 2.19	S 1.04 Å 2.58	Cl 0.99 Å 3.16
K 1.96 Å 0.82						Br 1.14 Å 2.96
Rb 2.11 Å 0.82						I 1.33 Å 2.66

The electronegativity has important chemical significance. If two atoms form a bond, the difference in the two electronegativities indicates the degree to which the bond is covalent (indicated by a small difference) or ionic (indicated by a large difference).

1. What occurs when moving down the table's columns?

A. Radii decrease; electronegativities decrease.
B. Radii increase; electronegativities increase.
C. Radii decrease; electronegativities increase.
D. Radii increase; electronegativities decrease.

2. The greatest electronegativity in the table is:

F. fluorine (F).
G. chlorine (Cl).
H. rubidium (Rb).
J. hydrogen (H).

GO ON TO THE NEXT PAGE.

3. The bond length in the P-Cl bond is:

A. 0.11 angstroms.
B. 0.97 angstroms.
C. 2.09 angstroms.
D. 5.35 angstroms.

4. The bond between which of the following is likely to have the most covalent character?

F. Sodium (Na) and iodine (I)
G. Magnesium (Mg) and oxygen (O)
H. Sulfur (S) and oxygen (O)
J. Carbon (C) and nitrogen (N).

5. The table indicates that bonds of greatest ionic character generally occur:

A. between elements by each other in a row.
B. between elements that are near each other in a column but far apart along a row.
C. between elements that are far apart along a column but close in a row.
D. between elements far apart along a column and far apart in a row.

6. The element cesium (Cs) lies directly below rubidium (Rb) in the Periodic Table. The electronegativity difference in CsF is likely to be:

F. greater than 3.16.
G. less than 3.16.
H. equal to 3.16.
J. Cannot be determined from the given information

GO ON TO THE NEXT PAGE.

Passage II

A set of experiments was carried out to investigate the relative sizes of the planets of our solar system and the relative distances from the Sun. Table 1 was given to all students performing the experiments.

Experiment 1

Using a compass, ruler, and paper (11 inches by 14 inches), students were asked to compare the sizes of the planets. Calling the size of Earth 1.00 (Earth diameter = 5 inches), a circle was made by inserting the point of the compass in the center of the paper. The circle had a radius of 2.5 inches to produce a circle with a diameter of 5 inches representing the Earth. All other planets were drawn to scale based on the size of their diameters relative to one Earth diameter (Table 1).

Table 1

Planet	Approximate Diameter (in Earth diameters)	Approximate Distance from the Sun (A.U.)
Mercury	0.38	0.40
Venus	0.95	0.70
Earth	1.00	1.00
Mars	0.54	1.50
Jupiter	11.20	5.20
Saturn	9.50	9.50
Uranus	3.70	19.20
Neptune	3.50	30.00
Pluto	0.47	40.00

Experiment 2

Using the equipment from Experiment 1, students were also asked to compare planetary distances from the Sun. The Earth is 93 million miles from the Sun. This distance is called 1.00 Astronomical Unit (1 A.U. = 0.5 inches), and it was used as a reference distance when the other planets were drawn at their proper distances (Table 1) from the Sun (a planet twice as far as the Earth is from the Sun would be drawn 2 A.U., or 1.0 inches, from the Sun).

7. In Experiment 1, the two planets represented by circles most similar in size on the paper are:

A. Earth and Venus.
B. Mars and Pluto.
C. Uranus and Neptune.
D. Mercury and Pluto.

8. In Experiment 2, if the paper were held the "long way" and the left-hand paper edge represented the Sun, which planet(s) would not fit on the paper?

F. Uranus, Neptune, and Pluto
G. Neptune and Pluto
H. Pluto only
J. All planets would fit on the paper.

9. Which of the following statements is supported by the data in Table 1?

A. The larger the planet, the greater is its distance from the Sun.
B. The smaller the planet, the greater is its distance from the Sun.
C. Only planets larger than the Earth are farther away from the Sun.
D. There is no consistent pattern between a planet's size and its distance from the Sun.

10. A planet's "year" is how long it takes to orbit the Sun and it is related to the distance of that planet from the Sun. If asteroids are found 2.8 A.U. from the Sun, an "asteroid year" should be:

F. longer than an "Earth year" but shorter than a "Mars year."
G. longer than a "Jupiter year" but shorter than a "Mars year."
H. longer than a "Mars year" but shorter than a "Jupiter year."
J. longer than a "Neptune year" but shorter than a "Pluto year."

GO ON TO THE NEXT PAGE.

11. In Experiment 1, how large would a circle representing the Sun be if its diameter is approximately 110 times greater than that of the Earth?

A. It would have a radius of approximately 550 inches.
B. It would have a diameter of approximately 550 inches.
C. It would have a radius of approximately 55 inches.
D. It would have a diameter of approximately 55 inches.

12. A third experiment was conducted in which the mass of each planet was described relative to the mass of the Earth (Jupiter had the greatest mass, Saturn had the next largest mass, Mercury and Pluto had the smallest masses). If the planets were placed in an order based on how they compared to Earth for the variables measured in all three experiments, which two orders would be expected to be most similar?

F. Diameter and distance from the Sun
G. Mass and distance from the Sun
H. Diameter and mass
J. All three orders would be similar.

GO ON TO THE NEXT PAGE.

Passage III

It is known that during photosynthesis, leaf pigments absorb light energy that eventually results in the production of glucose and other carbohydrates to be used by the green plant. Oxygen gas (O_2) is also produced during the process. Various factors affecting the rate of photosynthesis were investigated by counting the number of oxygen bubbles produced under the conditions described in the following three experiments.

Experiment 1

A sample of leaf extract (a mixture of pigments previously separated from other leaf components) from the pond plant *Elodea* was placed in a beaker containing water and a standard concentration of carbon dioxide (CO_2) (both are necessary ingredients for photosynthesis). Light of varying intensity was used to illuminate the beaker, and the number of oxygen bubbles emitted by the plant each minute was recorded. The results are illustrated in Figure 1.

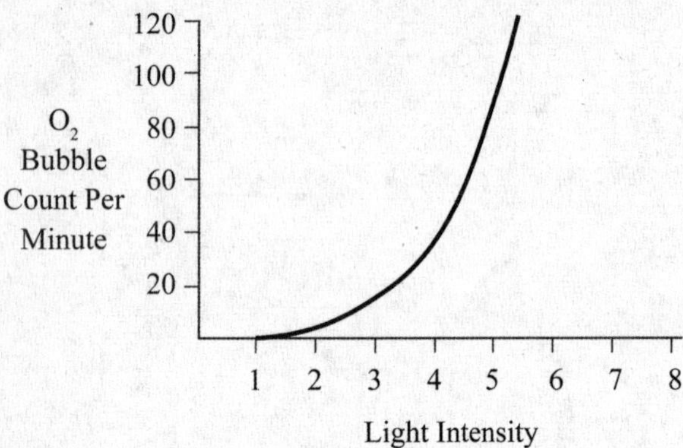

Figure 1

Experiment 2

An identical experiment was conducted in which the concentration of leaf extract was reduced four-fold (the mixture was one-fourth as concentrated as in Experiment 1). The results are shown in Figure 2.

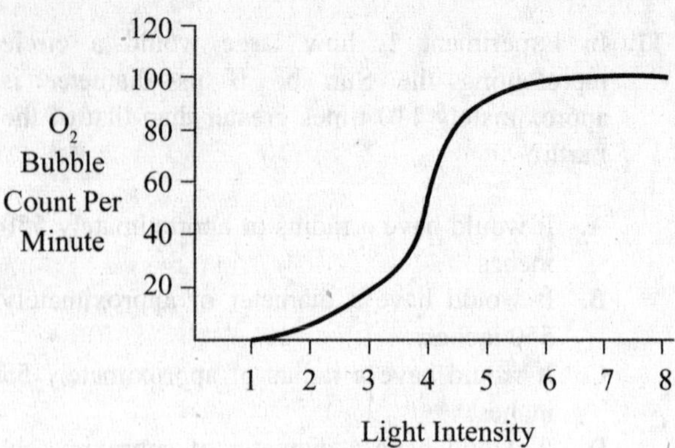

Figure 2

Experiment 3

Visible light consists of many different colors, or light wavelengths. Only those wavelengths that are absorbed by leaf pigments can provide the energy to maintain photosynthesis in the leaf. Different light wavelengths were used separately to illuminate two samples of leaf extract, each containing a different *Elodea* leaf pigment. Oxygen (O_2) bubbles were counted again as a measure of the rate of photosynthesis. Figure 3 summarizes the results.

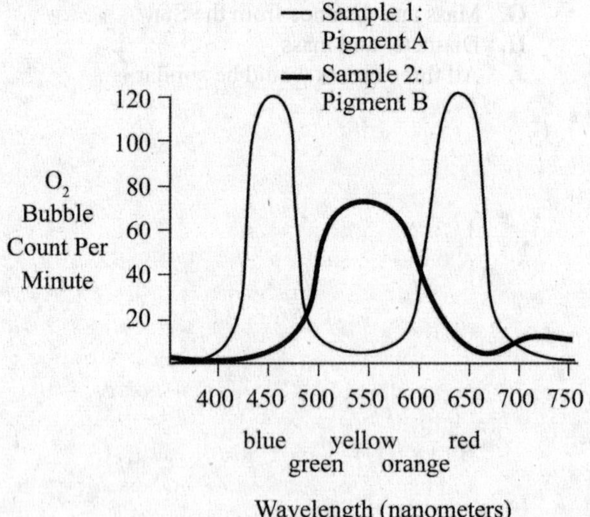

Figure 3

GO ON TO THE NEXT PAGE.

13. When running Experiment 1, which of the following changes in CO_2 should be made in order to determine its effect on the rate of photosynthesis?

A. Repeat the experiment using the same concentration of CO_2 in the beaker of water, but with different species of green plants.
B. Repeat the experiment using first no CO_2 and then varying concentrations of carbon dioxide in the beaker of water.
C. Repeat the experiment using different levels of water in the beaker containing a standard concentration of CO_2.
D. Repeat the experiment using additional light intensities.

14. The results in Experiments 1 and 2 demonstrate that in order to maintain a continued increase in the photosynthesis rate:

F. adequate amounts of light are needed.
G. adequate amounts of carbon dioxide are needed.
H. adequate amounts of oxygen are needed.
J. adequate amounts of leaf pigments are needed.

15. Based on the information in Figure 3, which of the following statements is correct?

A. Pigment A primarily absorbs light at 450 and 650 nanometers, while Pigment B absorbs light at 500–575 nanometers.
B. Pigment B primarily absorbs light at 450 and 650 nanometers, while Pigment A primarily absorbs light at 500–575 nanometers.
C. Pigment A can influence the rate of photosynthesis, while Pigment B cannot.
D. Pigment B can influence the rate of photosynthesis, while Pigment A cannot.

16. If the concentration of *Elodea* leaf extract was increased in Experiment 2, which of the following results could be expected?

F. A decrease in the number of oxygen bubbles
G. An increase in the number of oxygen bubbles
H. No change in the number of oxygen bubbles
J. A gradual dimming of light intensity

17. In Experiments 1 and 2, approximately how many oxygen bubbles/minute were produced at a light intensity level of 4?

A. 0–10
B. 20–30
C. 30–40
D. 40–50

18. According to the information in Figure 3, if an additional experiment were conducted, which condition would be LEAST effective in maintaining photosynthetic rate in *Elodea*?

F. Using blue light only
G. Using red light only
H. Using yellow light only
J. Using orange light only

GO ON TO THE NEXT PAGE.

Passage IV

The accompanying figure shows how the world records for various footraces have improved during a portion of this century. Speeds are given in both meters/minute and minutes/mile.

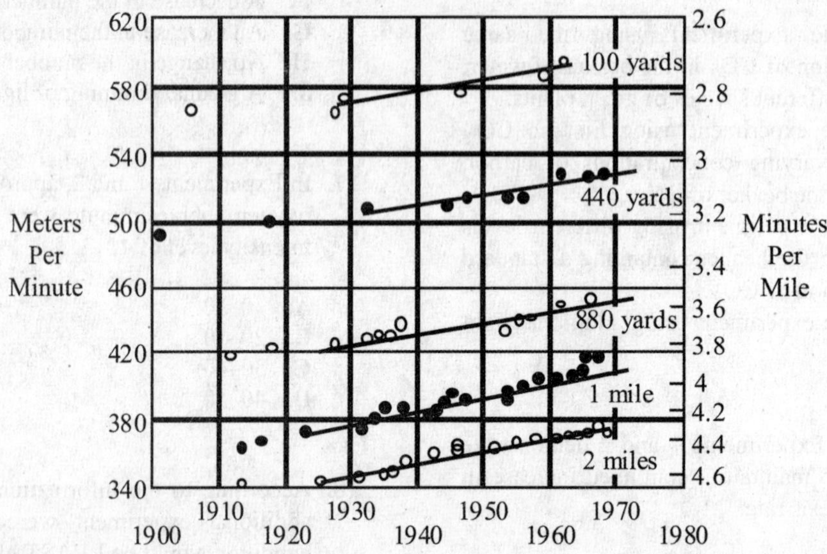

Modified from H.W. Ryder, H.J. Carr, and P. Herget, "Future performance in footracing," *Sci. Amer.* 234 (6): 109–114, 1976.

19. In what race and in what year was the greatest speed in meters/minute achieved?

A. The 440-yard dash in 1900
B. The 100-yard dash in 1930
C. The 100-yard dash in 1962
D. The 1-mile run in 1947

20. The trend in the graphs of meters/minute for the various distances shows:

F. roughly a linear increase.
G. roughly a linear decrease.
H. a linear increase for short distances and a linear decrease for long distances.
J. no systematic pattern.

21. For 1960, the ratio of minutes/mile values for the 1-mile run to that for the 440-yard dash is roughly:

A. 3/4
B. 4/5
C. 5/4
D. 4/3

22. The increase in speed, in meters/minute, for the 2-mile run from 1925 to 1967 is roughly:

F. 0.3
G. 10
H. 30
J. 100

23. If the trends shown can be expected to hold for later years, then the value of minutes per mile for the 880-yard run in 1980 is expected to be:

A. 3.5
B. 3.8
C. 420
D. 460

GO ON TO THE NEXT PAGE.

Passage V

Two experiments were performed in which constant amounts of heat were added continuously to samples over a defined period of time. The temperatures of the samples were monitored while the heat was added. The results from the two experiments are shown below.

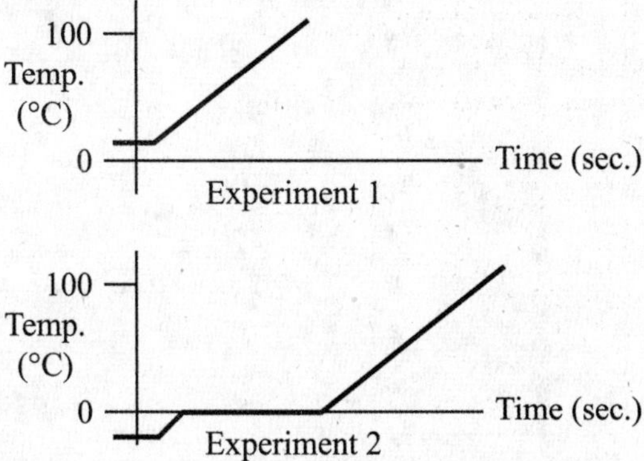

24. The results of Experiment 1 may be interpreted to show that:

F. it takes longer to heat a hot sample than a cold one.
G. the temperature of the sample rises proportionately with time as heat is applied.
H. temperature is not related to heat.
J. temperature and time measure the same thing.

25. Experiment 2 differs from Experiment 1 in that:

A. only the starting temperature is different in the two experiments.
B. the graph in Experiment 2 is not a straight line; there must have been experimental error.
C. Experiment 2 has a lower starting temperature and a time period when the temperature does not rise.
D. in Experiment 2, the heat went off for a while in the middle of the experiment.

26. The experimenter wants to explain the flat part of the graph from Experiment 2. It could represent:

F. a period when the clock was turned off.
G. a period when the heat was turned off.
H. a period when heat was added but some process that did not occur in the first experiment (such as absorption of heat), caused the temperature to remain constant.
J. a period when less heat was added.

27. The "phase" of the sample changes (an example of a phase change is the melting of a solid, or the boiling of a liquid) in conjunction with the flat part of the graph in Experiment 2. From the temperature data given, the phase change might be:

A. the melting of ice.
B. the boiling of water.
C. the melting of iron.
D. the boiling of iron.

28. The results of these experiments demonstrate that:

F. heat and temperature are basically the same.
G. heat and temperature are not the same.
H. a pause in heating can lead to a pause in temperature change.
J. constant heating leads to constant change.

GO ON TO THE NEXT PAGE.

29. If the experimenter extends Experiment 2 to higher temperatures, using water as a sample, which graph best illustrates the expected results?

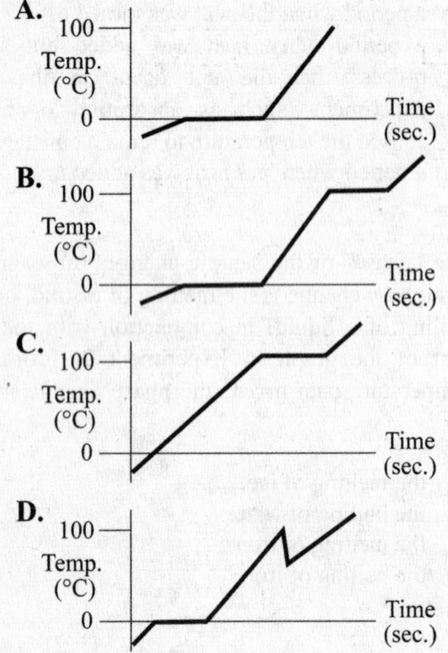

GO ON TO THE NEXT PAGE.

Passage VI

The following chart shows the generalized sequence of early developmental stages (terms in boxes) observed in most vertebrates.

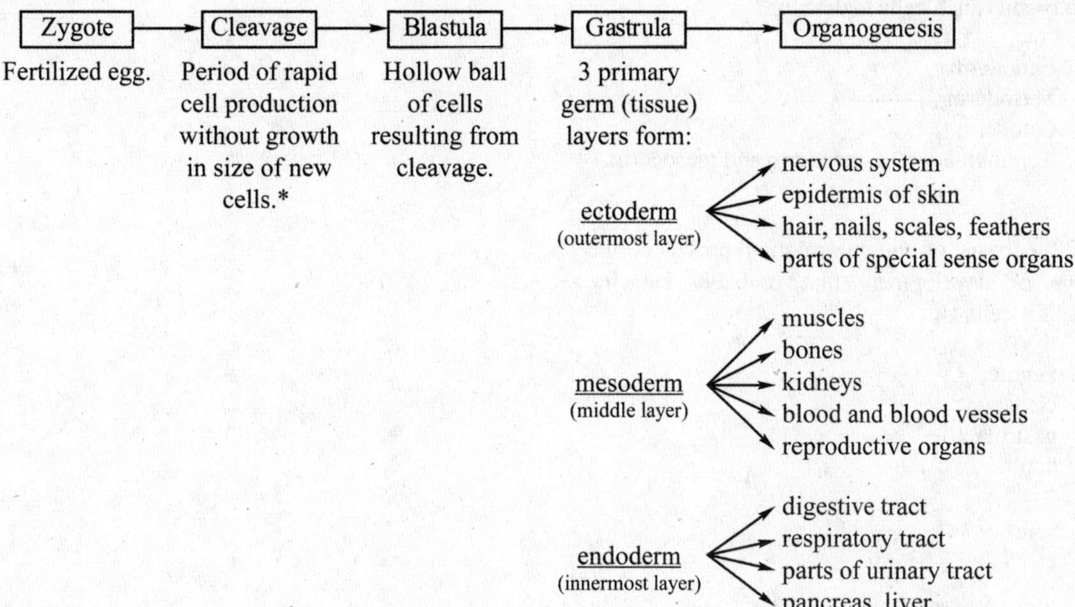

*New cells form as the zygote and its subsequent daughter cells divide and re-divide.

30. According to the chart, the stage of development when the three primary tissue layers form is:

F. cleavage.
G. blastula.
H. gastrula.
J. organogenesis.

31. Differentiation refers to a period of cell maturation during which time cells become specialized in structure and function. At which stage of development would most differentiation be expected to occur?

A. Cleavage
B. Blastula
C. Gastrula
D. Organogenesis

32. Based on the information in the diagram, which conclusion is NOT correct?

F. Most bones develop from the innermost primary germ layer.
G. Vertebrates develop three primary germ layers.
H. Diverse structures such as scales, feathers, and hair always develop from the same primary germ layer.
J. Before an organism can form different primary tissue layers, it must go through a stage in which it is in the form of a hollow ball of cells.

GO ON TO THE NEXT PAGE.

33. If a species of monkey were found to have extraordinary vision due to special receptor cells that were highly sensitive to different colors of light, from which primary germ layer(s) would you predict such cells to develop?

A. Endoderm
B. Mesoderm
C. Ectoderm
D. A combination of endoderm and mesoderm

34. On the basis of the information provided, the stage of development that probably has the smallest cells is:

F. zygote.
G. cleavage.
H. gastrula.
J. adult.

GO ON TO THE NEXT PAGE.

Passage VII

The following are two theories regarding the proportions of chemicals that will react to form products.

Theory 1

Although a chemical reaction is more than simple mixing, the two are similar in that any amounts of reactants may be brought together to form chemical products that contain the same elements as the reactants. For example, in the chemical reaction "hydrogen + oxygen ⇒ water," we may use 1 mole of hydrogen and 1 mole of oxygen, or 2 to 1, or 1 to 2, etc. The reaction will adjust to the proportions given.

Theory 2

Only certain proportions of reactants will combine chemically. For example, when hydrogen and oxygen are reacted, the amounts that will combine will be *exactly* 2 grams of hydrogen for every 32 grams of oxygen. We can show, using molecular weights, that these weights of reactants (which correspond to 2 moles of hydrogen and 1 mole of oxygen), imply the following reaction:

$$2H_2 + O_2 \Rightarrow 2H_2O$$

From this statement about the proportions of hydrogens and oxygens that react with each other, we can conclude that two hydrogen molecules must react with a single oxygen molecule to form two molecules of water.

35. Theory 1 does NOT predict which of the following?

A. 2 moles of zinc may react completely with 2 moles of sulfur.
B. 2 moles of zinc may react completely with 3 moles of sulfur.
C. 7 moles of zinc may react completely with 4 moles of sulfur.
D. If 3 moles of zinc were mixed with 4 moles of sulfur, 1 mole of sulfur would be left unreacted.

36. According to Theory 1, how many moles of water would be produced by the reaction of 2 moles of hydrogen and 1 mole of oxygen?

F. 1
G. 2
H. 4
J. Cannot be determined from the given information

37. An experimenter finds that when 170 grams of $AgNO_3$ is reacted with 58.5 grams of NaCl to form products, none of the original reactants remain in appreciable amounts. When the original amount of $AgNO_3$ is increased to 175 grams, then all of the NaCl is used up, but 5 grams of $AgNO_3$ remains. This result is:

A. consistent with Theory 1.
B. consistent with Theory 2.
C. consistent with both Theory 1 and Theory 2.
D. not consistent with either theory.

38. According to Theory 2, how might the remaining 5 grams of $AgNO_3$ be used up?

F. Add more of the reactant NaCl.
G. Remove some of the reactant NaCl.
H. Add even more of the reactant $AgNO_3$.
J. There is no mechanism for using the 5 grams of $AgNO_3$.

39. An experimenter wishes to determine which theory better fits her data for an experiment in which iron (Fe) is chemically combined with oxygen (O). She finds that 2 moles of Fe will react completely with 2 moles of O; she also finds that 2 moles of Fe will react completely with 3 moles of O. At this point she is confident that Theory 1, which is in opposition to the idea of "definite proportions," is correct. What further experiment might she do to test the success of Theory 1 over Theory 2?

A. Add 1 mole of Fe to 1 mole of O.
B. Add 2 moles of Fe to 4 moles of O.
C. Add 3 moles of Fe to 4.5 moles of O.
D. Add 4 moles of Fe to 4 moles of O.

GO ON TO THE NEXT PAGE.

40. According to Theory 1, the product of the reaction of hydrogen and oxygen:

F. is H_2O .
G. could be anything.
H. must contain hydrogen and oxygen, but lacks a specific formula.
J. has a definite proportion of hydrogen to oxygen.

END OF TEST 4
STOP! DO NOT TURN THE PAGE UNTIL TOLD TO DO SO.
DO NOT RETURN TO THE PREVIOUS TEST.

NO TEST MATERIAL ON THIS PAGE

5 5 5 5 5 5 5 5 5 5 5 5

WRITING TEST (OPTIONAL)

30 Minutes—1 Essay Prompt

DIRECTIONS: You have 30 minutes to plan and write an essay. Read the prompt carefully and make sure you understand the instructions. A successful essay will have the following features: it will take a position on the issue presented in the writing prompt; it will maintain a consistent focus on the topic; it will use logical reasoning and provide supporting ideas; it will present ideas in an organized manner; and, finally, it will include clear and effective language in accordance with the conventions of standard written English. Sample essay responses begin on page 695.

Writing Test Prompt

The founders of this country viewed public education as a way to instill civic virtues such as patriotism, honesty, hard work, and personal responsibility. Some people think that schools today do not place enough emphasis on these virtues and say that schools should require a course in civics as part of each year of the high school curriculum. Only by producing a population, they say, that knows the value of these virtues will it be possible to maintain a secure and prosperous nation. Other people think that the purpose of public schools is purely educational and that the schools should not attempt to teach civic virtues. They note that while people tend to agree that patriotism, honesty, hard work, and responsibility are virtuous, people disagree on what these ideas mean in specific circumstances. They point out, for example, that many people think it is unpatriotic to protest when the country is at war while others think that it is patriotic to oppose an unjust or unwise war. Consequently, this group says that teaching about these virtues should be left to family, religion, and other civic organizations. Do you think that schools should teach civic virtues such as patriotism, honesty, hard work, and personal responsibility?

In your essay, take a position on this issue. You can write about either point of view presented here, or you can present a different point of view on this topic. Support your position with relevant reasons and/or examples from your own experience, observations, or reading.

END OF TEST 5
STOP! DO NOT RETURN TO ANY OTHER TEST.

Timed Practice Test III*

*The bubble and essay response sheets for Timed Practice Test III are located in Appendix B.

DIRECTIONS

Timed Practice Test III includes five subject tests: English, Mathematics, Reading, Science, and Writing. Calculator use is permitted on the Mathematics Test only.

The items in each multiple-choice test are numbered and the answer choices are lettered. The bubble sheet provided in Appendix B (p. 743) has numbered rows that correspond to the items on the test. Each row contains lettered ovals to match the answer choices for each item on the test. Each numbered row on the bubble sheet has a corresponding item on the test.

For each item, first decide on the best answer choice. Then, locate the row number that corresponds to the item. Next, find the oval in that row that matches the letter of the chosen answer. Then, use a soft lead pencil to fill in the oval. DO NOT use a ballpoint pen.

Mark only one answer for each item. If you change your mind about an answer choice, thoroughly erase your first mark before marking your new answer.

Note that only responses marked on your bubble sheet will be scored. Your score on each test will be based only on the number of items that are correctly answered during the time allowed for that test. Guessing is not penalized. Therefore, it is to your best advantage to answer every item on the test, even if you must guess.

On the Writing Test, use the essay response sheets provided in Appendix B (pp. 745–748) to write your response to the prompt. (Note that the Writing Test is optional.)

You may work on each test only during the time allowed for that test. If you finish a test before time is called, use the time to review your answer choices or work on items about which you are uncertain. You may not return to a test on which time has already been called and you may not preview another test. You must lay down your pencil immediately when time is called at the end of each test. You may not for any reason fill in or alter ovals for a test after time has expired for that test. Violation of these rules will result in immediate disqualification from the exam.

GO ON TO THE NEXT PAGE.

1 1 1 1 1 1 1 1 1 1 1 1

ENGLISH TEST

45 Minutes—75 Items

DIRECTIONS: In the passages below, certain parts of the sentences have been underlined and numbered. In the right-hand column, you will find different ways of writing each underlined part; the original version is indicated by the "NO CHANGE" option. For each item, select the choice that best expresses the intended idea, is most acceptable in standard written English, or is most consistent with the overall tone and style of the passage.

There are also items that ask about a section of the passage or the passage as a whole. These items do not refer to an underlined portion of the passage; these items are preceded by statements that are enclosed in boxes.

Read the passage through once before you begin to answer the accompanying items. Finding the answers to certain items may depend on looking at material that appears several sentences beyond the item. So, be sure that you have read far enough ahead before you select your answer choice. Answers are on page 698.

PASSAGE I

Trade in the Northwest Territory

[1]

In 1849, San Francisco became the first official port of entry on the Pacific Coast. In 1851, on account of [1] the rapid growth of lumbering activity and a corresponding expansion of population in the Northwest Territory, the government established the Puget Sound District of the Bureau of Customs. Nonetheless, [2] smuggling grew rapidly, fostered by the tempting proximity of British havens and the natural cover afforded by vast forested areas and by the coves and inlets of countless heavy [3] timbered islands.

1. A. NO CHANGE
   B. since
   C. because of
   D. for

2. F. NO CHANGE
   G. Therefore,
   H. Consequently,
   J. On the contrary,

3. A. NO CHANGE
   B. countless, heavy
   C. countless, heavily
   D. countlessly heavy

GO ON TO THE NEXT PAGE.

[2]

Such fears were <u>well foundationed</u>. In 1851, U.S. customs officers <u>seize</u> the Hudson Bay Company's steamer *Beaver* <u>for a technical violation of the revenue laws</u>. This incident signaled an end to the era of unrestricted trade in the Pacific Northwest and drove some traders on both sides of the international border into illicit commercial arrangements. British wool, blankets, and liquor <u>were the principle articles</u> of this trade. <u>In fact,</u> so much British wool was smuggled into the San Juan Islands <u>selling</u> as domestic wool by American <u>sheepmen one</u> naive textbook writer credited San Juan sheep with a world's record annual production of 150 pounds of wool per animal.

4. **F.** NO CHANGE
G. well founded
H. founded well
J. well found

5. **A.** NO CHANGE
B. seized
C. were seizing
D. have seized

6. **F.** NO CHANGE
G. on account of violating the revenue laws
H. for technically being in violation of the revenue laws
J. in that they were in technical violation of the revenue laws

7. **A.** NO CHANGE
B. was the principle article
C. were the principal articles
D. was the principal article

8. **F.** NO CHANGE
G. Furthermore,
H. Moreover,
J. On the contrary,

9. **A.** NO CHANGE
B. to sell
C. and sold
D. and would be sold

10. **F.** NO CHANGE
G. sheepmen, one
H. sheepmen that one
J. sheepmen, and a

GO ON TO THE NEXT PAGE.

[3]

Although[11] American settlers in the Northwest Territory welcomed[12] the assertion of national control to the forty-ninth parallel, they were less amenable to restrictions on the trade with Vancouver Island. They wanted the duty-free rum and woolens offered by the British but were fearing[13] that the imposition and enforcement of permanent tariffs on goods from British North America might be resulting in the losing[14] of British markets for American products.

11. **A.** NO CHANGE
    B. Since
    C. Therefore
    D. Thus

12. **F.** NO CHANGE
    G. welcoming
    H. would welcome
    J. were welcomed by

13. **A.** NO CHANGE
    B. and were fearing
    C. and was fearful
    D. but feared

14. **F.** NO CHANGE
    G. might result in the losing
    H. might result in the loss
    J. results in the loss

Items #15–16 ask about the preceding passage as a whole.

15. Which of the following represents the most logical order of the three paragraphs?

    A. 1, 2, 3
    B. 1, 3, 2
    C. 2, 3, 1
    D. 3, 1, 2

16. Which of the following does NOT represent a technique used in the development of the essay?

    F. Narrative
    G. Example
    H. Statistics
    J. Quotations

GO ON TO THE NEXT PAGE.

PASSAGE II

Mapping the Cosmos

One of the beauties of astronomy is that one does not have to be an expert to enjoy it. [17] Anyone can step outside on a clear, moonless night, gaze at thousands of stars shining across the vast interstellar spaces, and then one can become [18] intoxicated by a heady mix of grandeur and existential chill. The same questions come to mind time and again, how [19] far away are the stars? How many are there? Are they strewn endlessly through space, or are we a part of an island universe of suns ending [20] abruptly somewhere out there in the black ocean of space?

It has been the sometimes heroic and often frustrating task of astronomers since the dawn of science to chart [21] our position in the cosmic ocean. In the twentieth century, significant progress had been made [22] in constructing an accurate map of the cosmos. We know, for example, that our solar system is part of a much larger system of hundreds of billions of stars.

17. **A.** NO CHANGE
B. is the not having to be an expert to enjoy it
C. is that the enjoying of it does not have to be done by an expert
D. is that one doesn't necessarily have to be an expert in order to derive some enjoyment from it

18. **F.** NO CHANGE
G. spaces—and became
H. spaces, and become
J. spaces and becomes

19. **A.** NO CHANGE
B. again and how
C. again how
D. again. How

20. **F.** NO CHANGE
G. that end
H. that ends
J. ended

21. **A.** NO CHANGE
B. charting
C. having charted
D. who charted

22. **F.** NO CHANGE
G. was made
H. is made
J. will be made

GO ON TO THE NEXT PAGE.

As such, this [23] system is the Milky Way Galaxy, a huge disk of stars and gas. We also know that ours is not the only galaxy in the universe. As far as the largest telescopes in the world can see, there are galaxies in every direction. The [24] nearest galaxies to our own are the Magellanic Clouds; the "crown jewels" [25] of the southern skies.

Since they are so near, they offer a laboratory in which astronomers can study the evolution of stars and galaxies. The nearest large galaxy to the Milky Way is the Andromeda Galaxy, which is about two million light years away. It is a giant spiral galaxy, much like [26] our own in size, shape, and number and type of stars. This nearby sister galaxy provides to us [27] an opportunity to get a bird's eye view of a galaxy much like our own—in effect, to see ourselves as others do. [28]

23. **A.** NO CHANGE
B. Obviously, this
C. Doubtless, this
D. This

24. **F.** NO CHANGE
G. These
H. (Begin a new paragraph here rather than after "skies") The
J. (Begin a new paragraph here rather than after "skies") As the

25. **A.** NO CHANGE
B. Clouds, the crown jewels
C. Clouds which is the "crown jewels"
D. Clouds, the "crown jewels"

26. **F.** NO CHANGE
G. much as
H. like much
J. much the same like

27. **A.** NO CHANGE
B. provides us
C. provide us
D. providing to us

28. **F.** NO CHANGE
G. to see ourselves the way other people tend to see us
H. so that we would be seeing ourselves the way other people would be seeing us
J. so that in this way we would see ourselves as others do

GO ON TO THE NEXT PAGE.

Item #29 asks about the preceding passage as a whole.

29. Which of the following is NOT one of the reasons the author poses a series of questions in the first paragraph?

A. To give the reader a sense of the "grandeur and existential chill"
B. To stimulate the reader's interest in astronomy
C. To give specific examples of questions about the cosmos that are still unanswered
D. To alert the reader that answers to these questions will follow later in the passage

---

PASSAGE III

A Brief History of the Mercury Space Program

The first astronauts entered the Mercury program in April 1959. They were volunteer, military pilots, graduated [30] of test pilot schools. Each were required having [31] a bachelor's degree in engineering (or its equivalent) and at least 1,500 hours of jet time. Of the first group of sixty candidates called to Washington to hear about the program, more than 80 percent volunteered. Only seven got [32] chosen. (Officials assumed that no more than seven men would have the

30. **F.** NO CHANGE
G. pilots graduates
H. pilots; graduates
J. pilots, graduates

31. **A.** NO CHANGE
B. was required to have
C. required having
D. had been required to have

32. **F.** NO CHANGE
G. were
H. had been
J. has been

GO ON TO THE NEXT PAGE.

opportunity to fly.) [33] These men were true

33. Is the second use of parentheses in the first paragraph appropriate?

A. Yes, because the information contained in the parentheses is irrelevant to the passage.
B. Yes, because the information explains something the author said but is not vital to the understanding of the passage.
C. No, because the material is vital to the understanding of the author's main argument.
D. No, because an entire sentence should never be placed in parentheses.

<u>pioneers, they</u>[34] volunteered at a time when the plans for space travel were only on paper and no one knew what the chance of success was.

34. F. NO CHANGE
G. pioneers but
H. pioneers yet
J. pioneers. They

<u>Scientists</u>[35] were able to learn from each failure.

35. Which of the following phrases would best replace the word *scientists* to provide a transition from the first to the second paragraph?

A. It was lucky that the men volunteered because scientists
B. There were failures as well as successes in the Mercury program, but scientists
C. Since the chances for success were unknown, scientists
D. Since the volunteers were also engineers, scientists

<u>Fortunately they had these failures</u>[36] early in the program. The astronauts and the animal passengers as well were flown without mishap when <u>their time came for them</u>[37].

36. F. NO CHANGE
G. Fortunately, they had these failures occurring
H. These failures occurred fortunately
J. Fortunately, these failures occurred

37. A. NO CHANGE
B. the time for them finally came
C. their time finally came for them
D. their time came

GO ON TO THE NEXT PAGE.

[3]

The most spectacular failure in the Mercury program came to be known as the "tower flight." [38] The escape tower, the parachutes, and the peroxide fuel were all deployed on the launching pad in front of the domestic and international press. A <u>relatively simple</u> (39) ground-circuit defect in the Redstone launch vehicle caused the main rocket engine to ignite <u>and then shutting</u> (40) down immediately after liftoff from the launching pad. The "flight" lasted only a second and covered a distance of inside only two inches. [41]

<u>One of the requirements</u> (42) of the Mercury program

38. Is the use of the word *spectacular* in the first sentence of the third paragraph appropriate?

F. Yes, because the author obviously disapproves of the Mercury program.
G. Yes, because the author is using the word in an ironic sense.
H. No, because the reader might be misled about goals of the Mercury program.
J. No, because the failure cited was caused by a simple defect.

39. A. NO CHANGE
B. relative and simple
C. relative simple
D. simple relatively

40. F. NO CHANGE
G. and then will shut
H. and then they shut
J. and then to shut

41. The author put the word *flight* in quotation marks because:

A. the author believes a flight must last for many miles.
B. there was no real flight at all.
C. the word is a technical term used by astronauts.
D. the word is often repeated in the passage.

42. F. NO CHANGE
G. (Do NOT begin a new paragraph) One of the requirements
H. (Do NOT begin a new paragraph) One requirement
J. (Do NOT begin a new paragraph) A requirement

GO ON TO THE NEXT PAGE.

was that an animal <u>had to precede man into space</u> [43]. The flight of Ham, the chimpanzee, was a major milestone in the program. Again, there were some problems. The pickup of the spacecraft was delayed, and <u>water had leaked into</u> [44] the capsule. Ham, however, was eventually rescued <u>unharmed</u> [45].

Sending a man into zero gravity was among the greatest medical experiments of all time. Fortunately, all astronauts found the weightlessness to be no problem. All <u>returning</u> [46] to Earth with no medical difficulties whatsoever. In this area, the only question left unanswered by the Mercury program was how long man <u>will tolerate</u> [47] weightlessness. It <u>seemed like,</u> [48] however, that longer flights would require only that

43. **A.** NO CHANGE
B. had to be the one to precede man in space
C. was going to have to go into space before man
D. needed to be the one to go into space before man did

44. **F.** NO CHANGE
G. water leaked into
H. water leaks in
J. leaking water into

45. The best placement for the underlined portion would be:

A. where it is now.
B. before the word *was.*
C. before the word *eventually*.
D. before the word *rescued.*

46. **F.** NO CHANGE
G. return
H. returned
J. will return

47. **A.** NO CHANGE
B. will be able to tolerate
C. was able to tolerate
D. could tolerate

48. **F.** NO CHANGE
G. seemed,
H. seemed as,
J. seemed to be,

GO ON TO THE NEXT PAGE.

astronauts <u>to have</u> [49] suitable methods of exercise and nutrition. [50]

49. A. NO CHANGE
B. have
C. had had
D. are sure to have

50. Which of the following might be an appropriate concluding sentence for the essay?

F. Although the Mercury program had some failures, it was on the whole a successful part of the space program.
G. Although the Mercury program had some successes, it was on the whole a failure.
H. Many people have objected that it is immoral to use animals in testing programs.
J. Science fiction writers have often written about space travel.

PASSAGE IV

Advances in Modern Medicine

It was not until the nineteenth century that medicine was able, in any broad and real <u>way, to help</u> [51] the suffering individual. During this century, technical advances aided the diagnostician <u>and also</u> [52] the surgeon, and the beginnings of an understanding of the fundamental mechanisms of disease <u>had been emerging</u> [53]. All aspects of medicine—from the research laboratory to the operating table—<u>was enjoying</u> [54] the benefits of the rigorous application of the scientific method.

51. A. NO CHANGE
B. way of help
C. way to help
D. way, of helping

52. F. NO CHANGE
G. as well as
H. with
J. as opposed to

53. A. NO CHANGE
B. was emerging
C. were emerging
D. emerged

54. F. NO CHANGE
G. were enjoying
H. is enjoying
J. enjoys

By the end of the nineteenth century, a person's chances were fairly good that a doctor could not only give a name to his medical complaint <u>yet probably had</u> [55] an elementary understanding of what it was and how it progressed. With somewhat more luck, the doctor could select the proper treatment <u>and he could also mitigate</u> [56] the symptoms if not cure the disease altogether.

55. A. NO CHANGE
B. but probably had
C. consequently probably has
D. but, probably would have

56. F. NO CHANGE
G. but could mitigate
H. and mitigate
J. and can mitigate

This transition to modern medicine depended on three important advances. First, it required an understanding of the true nature and origin of disease. Second, it required that an organized body of standard medical practice <u>be available to</u> [57] guide physicians in diagnosis and treatment of disease. Last, <u>it presupposes</u> [58] a degree of medical technology never before available.

57. A. NO CHANGE
B. was available to
C. is available for
D. be available as

58. F. NO CHANGE
G. it is presupposed
H. it presupposed
J. they presuppose

<u>Among the more dramatic</u> [59] nineteenth-century medical advances were those in the field of human

59. A. NO CHANGE
B. (Do NOT begin a new paragraph) Among the more dramatic
C. Since
D. (Do NOT begin a new paragraph) Since

GO ON TO THE NEXT PAGE.

physiology. [60] In 1822, an obscure American army camp surgeon practicing medicine <u>near where the Canadian frontier is</u> (61) was transformed almost overnight into a specialist on the mechanism of human digestion. The physician, William Beaumont, was called to treat a young trapper, accidentally shot in the stomach. <u>Beaumont's operating skill</u> (62) saved the boy's life but the patient was left with an abnormal opening leading to the stomach. To Beaumont's credit, he recognized this unique opportunity to study the human digestive <u>process, but</u> (63) for the next 10 years he conducted hundreds of experiments with the reluctant cooperation of his not-so-willing patient.

From his experiments, Beaumont was able to describe the physiology of digestion, demonstrating

60. Which of the following correctly describes the function of the first sentence of this paragraph?

F. It introduces a topic that has nothing to do with the material discussed in the first three paragraphs.
G. It introduces material that will contradict what was discussed in the first three paragraphs.
H. It provides a transition that sets up a contrast to the material that came before.
J. It provides a transition that moves from a general discussion to a more specific, but related topic.

61. **A.** NO CHANGE
B. near where the Canadian frontier is,
C. near where the Canadian frontier was
D. near the Canadian frontier

62. **F.** NO CHANGE
G. (Begin a new paragraph) Beaumont's operating skill
H. The skill of Beaumont at operating
J. (Begin a new paragraph) The skill of Beaumont at operating

63. **A.** NO CHANGE
B. process, and
C. process,
D. process. But

GO ON TO THE NEXT PAGE.

the characteristics of gastric motility <u>and describe</u> [64] the properties of gastric juice. He determined that the stomach contained hydrochloric acid and that it broke down food by a chemical process and not by maceration or putrefaction. Beaumont's pioneering work made him a famous man. The young trapper did not fare as well; he was forced to tour medical schools as "the man with the window in his stomach."

64. F. NO CHANGE
G. to describe
H. that describe
J. and describing

PASSAGE V

All About Babies

Newborn babies are not the passive creatures most people assume <u>him to be</u> [65]. Recent research shows that the newborn comes well-endowed <u>of</u> [66] charm and full potential for social graces. His eyes are equipped with surprisingly good vision. Shortly after birth, he begins to watch his mother's face, which he soon comes to recognize. He also learns to know her voice and will turn toward her when he hears <u>it. This</u> [67] is about the time when affection begins. The infant's cry alerts the mother and causes a biological <u>including</u> [68] an emotional reaction. The infant's ability to cling and

65. A. NO CHANGE
B. he was
C. them to be
D. it is

66. F. NO CHANGE
G. for
H. with
J. by

67. A. NO CHANGE
B. it, this
C. it this
D. it

68. F. NO CHANGE
G. and
H. with
J. but

GO ON TO THE NEXT PAGE.

cuddle communicates a pleasurable warmth to the mother, and the infant's odor is pleasant and uniquely its own. The newborn also smiles. The human infant, unfortunately, [69] is in possession of [70] attributes that are guaranteeing [71] its attractiveness.

69. A. NO CHANGE
B. on the other hand
C. nevertheless
D. in fact

70. F. NO CHANGE
G. possessed
H. possesses
J. are in possession of

71. A. NO CHANGE
B. guaranteed
C. guarantee
D. guarantees

Although there is some argument about whether the child sparks the development of love or whether or not [72] a special physiological state of the mother prompts her to interact with the new infant. But most [73] researchers agree that the newborn does mold or trigger adult behavior. The neonate organizes the mother's behavior by crying and by eye-to-eye contact. The newborn is not a passive creature at all.

72. F. NO CHANGE
G. or whether
H. and whether if
J. or whether if

73. A. NO CHANGE
B. infant: but most
C. infant. Most
D. infant, most

GO ON TO THE NEXT PAGE.

Items #74–75 ask about the preceding passage as a whole.

74. Which of the following best describes the function of the last sentence of the essay?

F. It introduces a new topic for the reader to investigate.
G. It contradicts everything that was said before.
H. It reiterates the main theme of the passage.
J. It establishes the author as an authority.

75. Which of the following best describes the overall development of the essay?

A. A comparison and contrast using anecdotes
B. A narrative using examples
C. A description using statistics
D. An argument using examples

END OF TEST 1
STOP! DO NOT TURN THE PAGE UNTIL TOLD TO DO SO.

NO TEST MATERIAL ON THIS PAGE

2 2 2 2 2 2 2 2 2 2 2 2

MATHEMATICS TEST

60 Minutes—60 Items

DIRECTIONS: Solve each item and choose the correct answer choice. Then, fill in the corresponding oval on the bubble sheet.

Allocate time wisely. Try to solve as many items as possible, returning to skipped items if time permits.

Calculator use is permitted on this test; however, some items are best solved without the use of a calculator.

Note: All of the following should be assumed, unless otherwise stated.

1. Illustrative figures are NOT necessarily drawn to scale.
2. The word *average* indicates arithmetic mean.
3. The word *line* indicates a straight line.
4. Geometric figures lie in a plane.

Answers are on page 698.

1. A barrel contained 5.75 liters of water and 4.5 liters evaporated. How many liters of water remain in the barrel?

A. 0.75
B. 1.25
C. 1.75
D. 2.25
E. 13.25

2. Which of the following expressions correctly describes the mathematical relationship below?

3 less than the product of 4 times x

F. $4x-3$
G. $3x-4$
H. $4(x-3)$
J. $3(4x)$
K. $\frac{4x}{3}$

DO YOUR FIGURING HERE.

GO ON TO THE NEXT PAGE.

DO YOUR FIGURING HERE.

3. If $\frac{3}{4}$ of x is 36, then $\frac{1}{3}$ of $x = ?$

A. 9
B. 12
C. 16
D. 24
E. 42

4. In the figure below, what is the value of $x + y$?

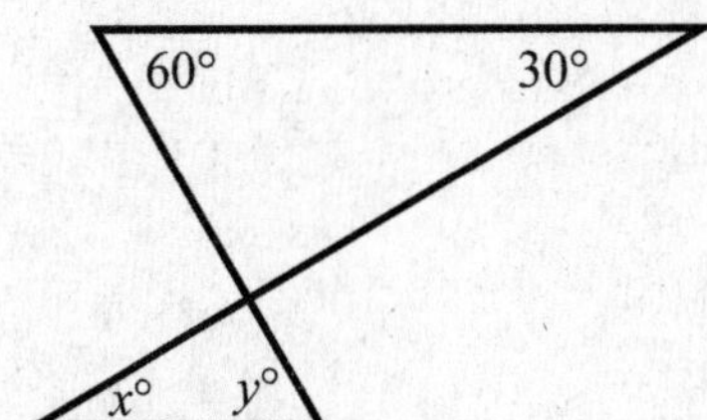

F. 45
G. 60
H. 75
J. 90
K. 120

5. If n is a multiple of 3, which of the following expressions is also a multiple of 3?

A. $2+n$
B. $2-n$
C. $2n-1$
D. $2n+1$
E. $2n+3$

6. Which of the following is NOT equal to the ratio of 2 whole numbers?

F. $\left(\frac{1}{5}\right)^2$
G. 5%
H. $\frac{\sqrt{5}}{1}$
J. 0.25
K. $\frac{1}{5}$

GO ON TO THE NEXT PAGE.

7. If the area of a square is 16 square inches, what is the perimeter, in inches?

A. 2
B. 4
C. 8
D. 16
E. 32

DO YOUR FIGURING HERE.

8. If $12 + x = 36 - y$, then $x + y =$?

F. –48
G. –24
H. 3
J. 24
K. 48

9. What is the greatest factor of the expression $3x^2y^3z + 6x^3yz^3 + 2xy^2z^2$?

A. $3x^2y^2z^2$
B. $2x^2y^2z^2$
C. $x^3y^3z^3$
D. xyz
E. xz

10. Depending on the value of k, the expression $3k + 4k + 5k + 6k + 7k$ may or may not be divisible by 7. Which of the terms, when eliminated from the expression, guarantees that the resulting expression is divisible by 7 for every positive integer k?

F. $3k$
G. $4k$
H. $5k$
J. $6k$
K. $7k$

GO ON TO THE NEXT PAGE.

11. If $\frac{1}{3} < x < \frac{3}{8}$, which of the following is a possible value of x?

A. $\frac{3}{16}$
B. $\frac{17}{48}$
C. $\frac{9}{24}$
D. $\frac{5}{12}$
E. $\frac{1}{2}$

DO YOUR FIGURING HERE.

12. If $x^2 - y^2 = 3$ and $x - y = 3$, then $x + y = ?$

F. 0
G. 1
H. 2
J. 3
K. 9

13. If n is a positive integer, which of the following *must* be an even integer?

A. $n+1$
B. $3n+1$
C. $3n+2$
D. n^2+1
E. n^2+n

14. If the area of a square inscribed in a circle is 16 square centimeters, what is the area of the circle, in square centimeters?

F. 2π
G. 4π
H. 8π
J. 16π
K. 32π

GO ON TO THE NEXT PAGE.

DO YOUR FIGURING HERE.

15. Ellen bought a CD player on sale for 25% off the usual price of $120. If the store also collected an 8% sales tax on the sale price of the CD player, how much did Ellen pay for the CD player, including sales tax?

A. $106.30
B. $101.40
C. $97.20
D. $95.10
E. $88.44

16. A certain mixture of gravel and sand consists of 2.5 kilograms of gravel and 12.5 kilograms of sand. What percent of the mixture, by weight, is gravel?

F. 10%
G. $16\frac{2}{3}\%$
H. 20%
J. 25%
K. $33\frac{1}{3}\%$

17. The figure below is the top-view of a folding room divider, hinged at *P* and *Q*. If sections *PR* and *QS* are moved as shown until *R* and *S* meet, what will be the enclosed area, in square feet? (Ignore the thickness of the hinges and the screen's sections.)

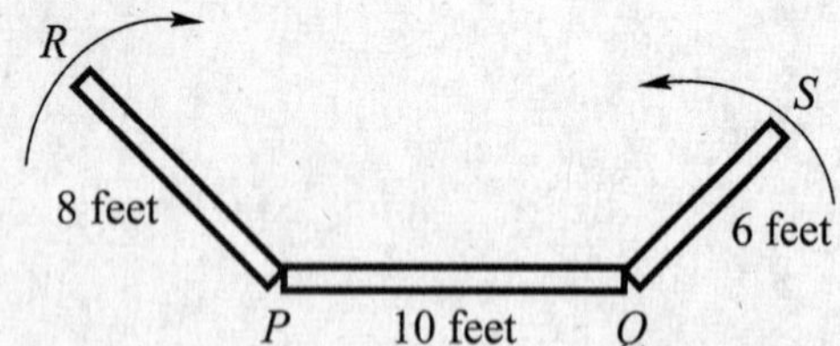

A. 6
B. 12
C. 6π
D. 24
E. 12π

GO ON TO THE NEXT PAGE.

18. Motorcycle A averages 40 kilometers per liter of gasoline while Motorcycle B averages 50 kilometers per liter. If the cost of gasoline is \$2 per liter, what will be the difference in the cost of operating the 2 motorcycles for 300 kilometers?

F. \$3
G. \$6
H. \$12
J. \$15
K. \$20

DO YOUR FIGURING HERE.

19. If $f(x) = x^2 - 2x + 1$, then what is $f(f(3))$?

A. 3
B. 9
C. 14
D. 27
E. 39

20. For a positive integer k, which of the following equals $6k + 3$?

F. $\frac{1}{2}(k+1)$
G. $\frac{1}{k}+4$
H. $2k+1$
J. $3(k+1)$
K. $3(2k+1)$

21. Mailing a letter costs x cents for the first ounce and y cents for every additional ounce or fraction of an ounce. What is the cost, in cents, to mail a letter weighing a whole number of ounces, w?

A. $w(x+y)$
B. $x(w-y)$
C. $x(x-1)+y(w-1)$
D. $x+wy$
E. $x+y(w-1)$

GO ON TO THE NEXT PAGE.

DO YOUR FIGURING HERE.

22. $|-3| \cdot |2| \cdot \left|-\frac{1}{2}\right| + (-4) = ?$

F. -1
G. 0
H. 1
J. $\frac{3}{2}$
K. 4

23. In the figure below, the area of the square *OPQR* is 2 square inches, what is the area of the circle with center *O* (in square inches)?

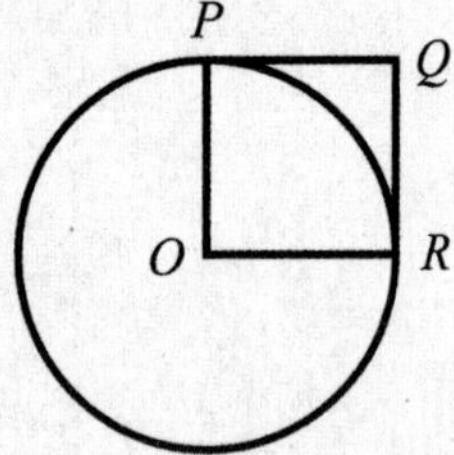

A. $\frac{\pi}{4}$
B. $\pi\sqrt{2}$
C. 2π
D. $2\sqrt{2}\pi$
E. 4π

24. Which of the following *must* be an odd number?

I. The product of a prime number and a prime number
II. The sum of a prime number and a prime number
III. The product of an odd number and another odd number

F. I only
G. III only
H. I and II only
J. II and III only
K. I, II, and III

GO ON TO THE NEXT PAGE.

25. What is the area of the shaded portion of the figure below, expressed in terms of a and b?

DO YOUR FIGURING HERE.

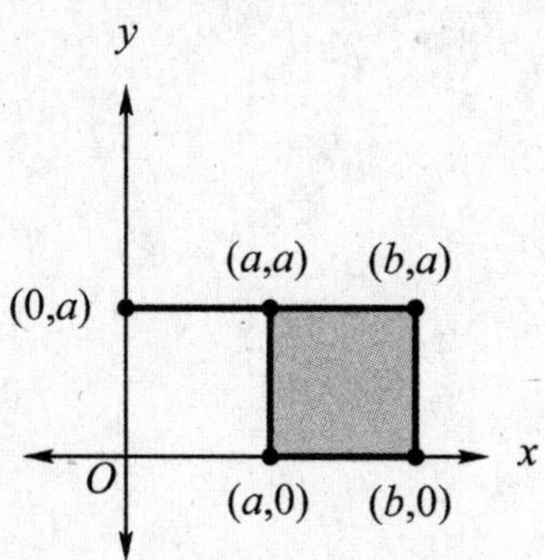

A. $a(b-a)$
B. $a(a-b)$
C. $b(a-b)$
D. $b(b-a)$
E. ab

26. $\sqrt{(43-7)(29+7)} = ?$

F. $3\sqrt{3}$
G. 6
H. 36
J. 42
K. 1,296

27. A concrete mixture contains 4 cubic yards of cement for every 20 cubic yards of grit. If a mason orders 50 cubic yards of cement, how much grit (in cubic yards) should he order if he is to use all of the cement?

A. 250
B. 200
C. 100
D. 80
E. 10

GO ON TO THE NEXT PAGE.

28. In the figure below, $\overline{QT} = \overline{QR}$. If $x = 150$, then $y = ?$

DO YOUR FIGURING HERE.

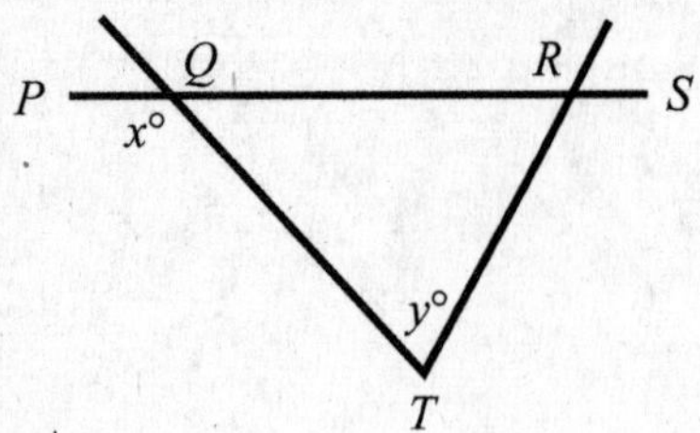

F. 30
G. 60
H. 75
J. 90
K. 120

29. If $\frac{x}{y} = -1$, then $x + y = ?$

A. 2
B. 1
C. 0
D. –1
E. –2

30. According to the table below, which fabric costs the LEAST per yard?

Fabric	Cost
F	3 yards for $8
G	2 yards for $6
H	4 yards for $9
J	5 yards for $7
K	8 yards for $10

F. F
G. G
H. H
J. J
K. K

GO ON TO THE NEXT PAGE.

31. In ΔPQR below, if $\overline{PQ} \parallel \overline{ST}$, then $y = ?$

DO YOUR FIGURING HERE.

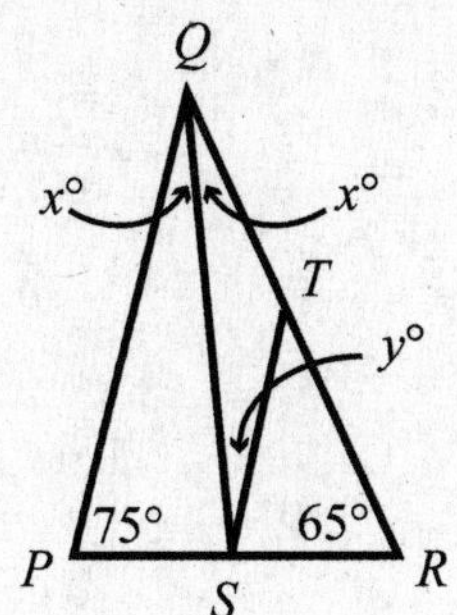

A. 20
B. 40
C. 45
D. 50
E. 55

32. $\frac{10^3\left(10^5 + 10^5\right)}{10^4} = ?$

F. 10^4
G. 10^6
H. $2\left(10^2\right)$
J. $2\left(10^4\right)$
K. $2\left(10^9\right)$

33. What is the solution set for the following equation: $x^2 - 5x + 4 = 0$?

A. $\{-4, -1\}$
B. $\{-3, -1\}$
C. $\{-1, 3\}$
D. $\{1, 4\}$
E. $\{2, 3\}$

GO ON TO THE NEXT PAGE.

DO YOUR FIGURING HERE.

34. The average of seven different positive integers is 12. What is the greatest that any one integer could be?

F. 19
G. 31
H. 47
J. 54
K. 63

35. If $x = b + 4$ and $y = b - 3$, then in terms of x and y, $b =$?

A. $x + y - 1$
B. $x + y + 1$
C. $x - y - 1$
D. $\frac{x + y + 1}{2}$
E. $\frac{x + y - 1}{2}$

36. If $5x = 3y = z$, and x, y, and z are positive integers, all of the following must be an integer EXCEPT:

F. $\frac{z}{xy}$
G. $\frac{z}{5}$
H. $\frac{z}{3}$
J. $\frac{z}{15}$
K. $\frac{x}{3}$

37. What is the width of a rectangle with an area of $48x^2$ and a length of $24x$?

A. 2
B. $2x$
C. $24x$
D. $2x^2$
E. $3x^2$

GO ON TO THE NEXT PAGE.

DO YOUR FIGURING HERE.

38. If $x = \frac{1}{y+1}$ and $y \neq -1$, then $y =$?

F. $x+1$
G. x
H. $\frac{x+1}{x}$
J. $\frac{x-1}{x}$
K. $\frac{1-x}{x}$

39. In the figure below, if the area of the triangle is 54, then $x =$?

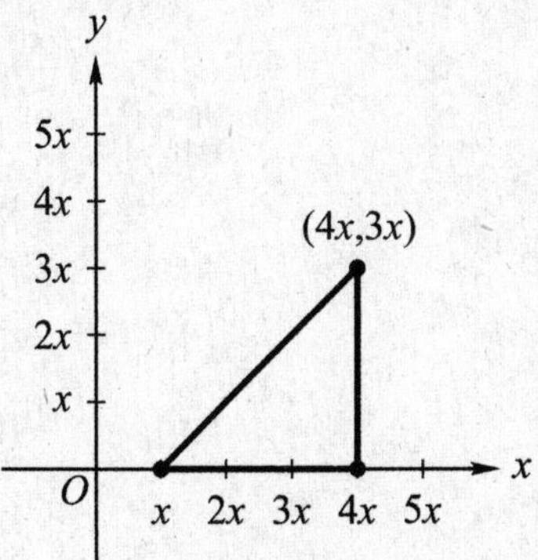

A. $3\sqrt{3}$
B. $2\sqrt{3}$
C. 3
D. 2
E. $\sqrt{2}$

40. A drawer contains 4 green socks, 6 blue socks, and 10 white socks. If socks are pulled out of the drawer at random and not replaced, what is the minimum number of socks that must be pulled out of the drawer to *guarantee* that 2 of every color have been pulled out of the drawer?

F. 6
G. 7
H. 11
J. 12
K. 18

GO ON TO THE NEXT PAGE.

41. In the figure below, the circle with center O has a radius that is 4 units long. If the area of the shaded region is 14π square-units, what is the value of x?

DO YOUR FIGURING HERE.

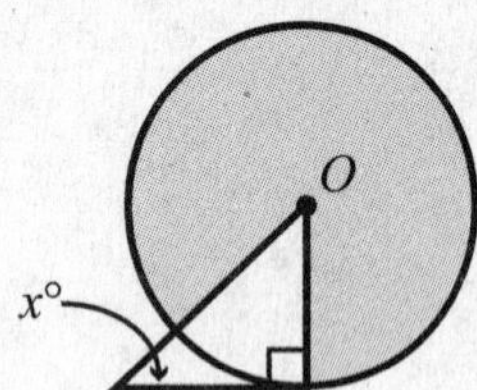

A. 55
B. 50
C. 45
D. 40
E. 35

42. In the figure below, a circle is inscribed in a square that is in turn inscribed in a larger circle. What is the ratio of the area of the larger circle to that of the smaller circle?

F. 8:1
G. 4:1
H. $2\sqrt{2}:1$
J. 2:1
K. $\sqrt{2}:1$

43. $2^0 + 2^3 - 2^{-2} = ?$

A. 4
B. $6\frac{1}{4}$
C. 7
D. $8\frac{3}{4}$
E. $9\frac{3}{4}$

GO ON TO THE NEXT PAGE.

DO YOUR FIGURING HERE.

44. The graph of $y = x^2 - 3$ is a parabola with the axis of symmetry given by the equation $x = 0$. Which of the following are the (x, y) coordinates of the point on the parabola that is symmetric, with respect to the axis of symmetry, to the point with coordinates $(-1, -2)$?

F. $(-2, -1)$
G. $(-1, 2)$
H. $(0, -3)$
J. $(1, -2)$
K. $(1, 2)$

45. If 2 lines with equations $y = m_1x + b_1$ and $y = m_2x + b_2$ are perpendicular, which of the following *must* be true?

A. $m_1 = m_2$
B. $m_1m_2 = 1$
C. $m_1m_2 = -1$
D. $b_1 = b_2$
E. $b_1b_2 = -1$

46. The figure below has lengths as marked, in units. What is the area, in square units, of the figure?

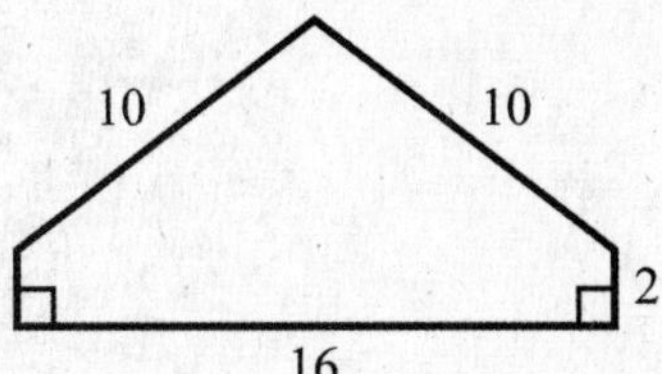

F. 36
G. 48
H. 56
J. 64
K. 80

GO ON TO THE NEXT PAGE.

DO YOUR FIGURING HERE.

47. For all $x > 0$ and $y > 0$, the radical expression $\frac{\sqrt{x}}{2\sqrt{x} - \sqrt{y}}$ is equivalent to:

A. $\frac{2x + \sqrt{xy}}{4x - y}$

B. $\frac{4x + \sqrt{xy}}{4x - y}$

C. $\frac{2\sqrt{x} + \sqrt{y}}{4xy}$

D. $\frac{2\sqrt{x} + \sqrt{xy}}{2x - y}$

E. $\frac{2\sqrt{x} - \sqrt{y}}{2}$

48. In the figure below, if $l_1 \parallel l_2$, then $x = ?$

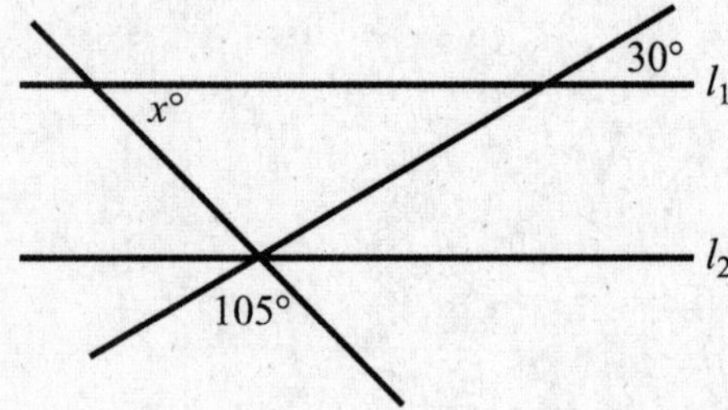

F. 20
G. 30
H. 45
J. 65
K. 130

49. The graph of $y = 2\cos(2x) + 2$ intersects the y-axis where $y = ?$

A. 0
B. 2
C. 3
D. 4
E. 5

GO ON TO THE NEXT PAGE.

50. In the figure below, *PQRS* is a square, and each of the 4 circles has a radius of *r*. What fractional part of the area of the square is shaded?

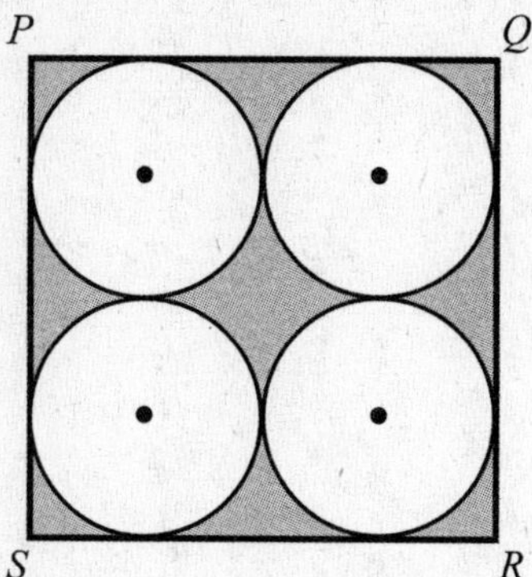

F. $\frac{\pi - 4}{2}$
G. $\frac{4 - \pi}{4}$
H. $\frac{\pi}{4}$
J. $\frac{4}{\pi}$
K. π

51. If $0° < \theta < 90°$, $\frac{\sin^2\theta + \cos^2\theta}{\sin\theta}$ is equivalent to:

A. $\sin\theta$
B. $\cos\theta$
C. $\csc\theta$
D. $\tan\theta$
E. $\cot\theta$

DO YOUR FIGURING HERE.

GO ON TO THE NEXT PAGE.

52. In the figure below, ABC is a right triangle. If $\sin 35° \approx 0.57$ and $\tan 55° \approx 1.4$, which of the following is the best approximation of the length of $\overline{AC}$?

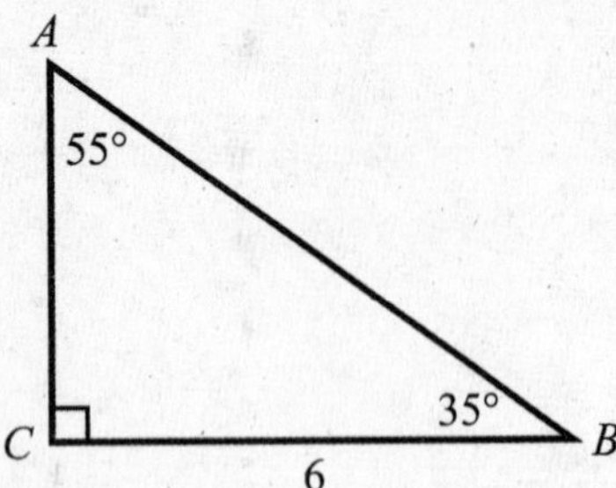

F. 3.42
G. 4.28
H. 8.57
J. 10.50
K. 12.25

53. What are the values for which $\frac{x(x+3)}{(x-1)(x+2)}$ is undefined?

A. −3 only
B. −2 only
C. 1 only
D. −2 and 1 only
E. −3, −2, and 1

54. What is the maximum value of $3y$ for x and y satisfying the system of inequalities below?

$$x \geq 0$$
$$y \geq 0$$
$$x + y \leq 6$$

F. −3
G. 0
H. 6
J. 12
K. 18

DO YOUR FIGURING HERE.

GO ON TO THE NEXT PAGE.

DO YOUR FIGURING HERE.

55. Which of the following graphs in the standard (x, y) coordinate plane correctly shows the points on the graph of $y = |x^2 - 3|$ for $x = -1, 0,$ and 1?

A.

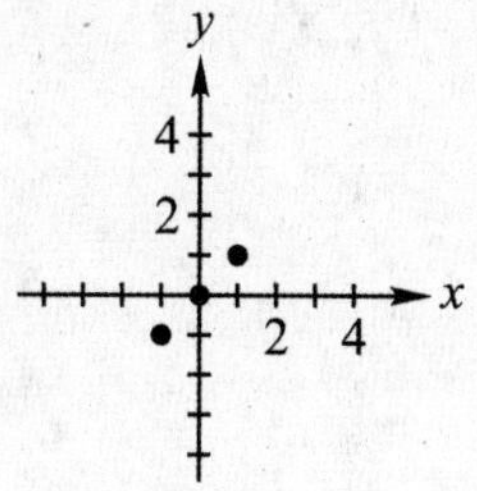

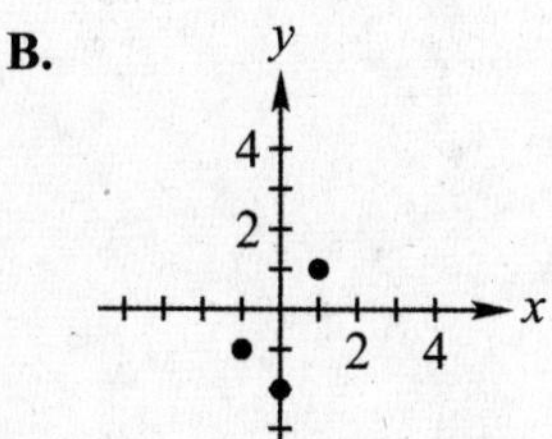

B.

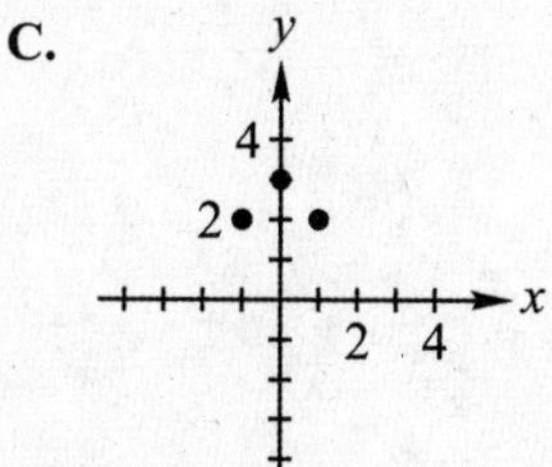

C.

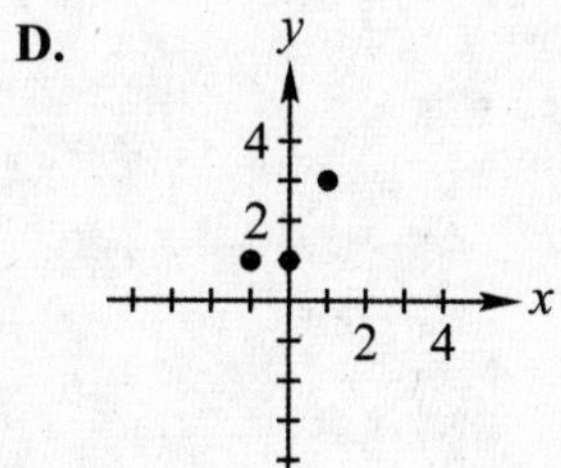

D.

E.

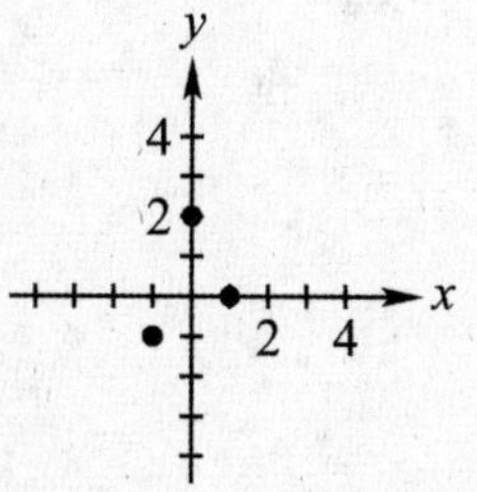

GO ON TO THE NEXT PAGE.

DO YOUR FIGURING HERE.

56. The figure below is a graph of which of the following equations?

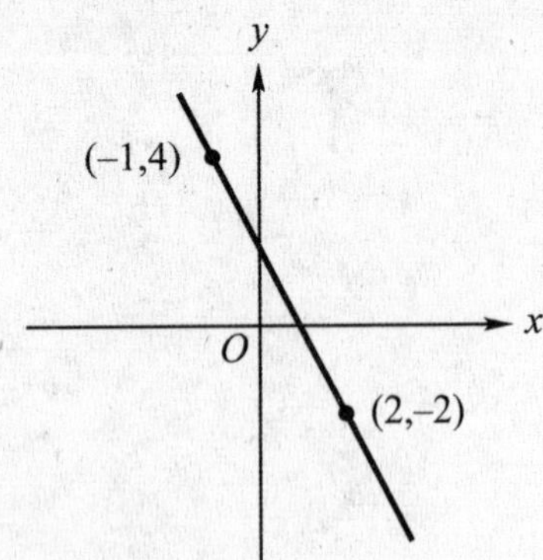

F. $y = -3x + 5$
G. $y = -2x + 2$
H. $y = -\frac{3}{2}x - 2$
J. $y = \frac{2}{3}x + 3$
K. $y = x + 2$

57. The roots of equation $ax^2 + bx + c = 0$ are $\frac{-3+\sqrt{5}}{2}$ and $\frac{-3-\sqrt{5}}{2}$. Which of the following could be the equation?

A. $x^2 + 3x + 1 = 0$
B. $x^2 - 3x + 1 = 0$
C. $x^2 + 3x - 1 = 0$
D. $x^2 - 3x - 1 = 0$
E. $-x^2 + 3x + 1 = 0$

58. The relation defined by the set of ordered pairs {(0,3), (2,1), (3,0), (−1,2), (0,5), (−2,5)} is NOT a function. Deleting which of the ordered pairs will make the resulting set a function?

F. (0,3)
G. (2,1)
H. (3,0)
J. (−1,2)
K. (−2,5)

GO ON TO THE NEXT PAGE.

59. Trapezoid $ABCD$ has lengths, in units, and angle measures as marked in the figure below. What is the area of the trapezoid $ABCD$?

DO YOUR FIGURING HERE.

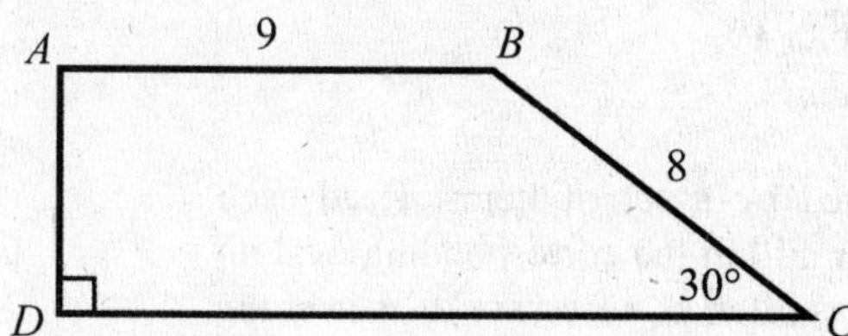

A. $18+8\sqrt{2}$
B. $18+8\sqrt{3}$
C. $36+8\sqrt{2}$
D. $36+8\sqrt{3}$
E. 42

60. What is $\tan\theta$ if $\sin\theta=\frac{3}{5}$ and $\cot\theta=\frac{4}{3}$?

F. $\frac{3}{4}$
G. $\frac{4}{5}$
H. $\frac{7}{8}$
J. $\frac{5}{3}$
K. $\frac{20}{9}$

END OF TEST 2
STOP! DO NOT TURN THE PAGE UNTIL TOLD TO DO SO.
DO NOT RETURN TO THE PREVIOUS TEST.

3 3 3 3 3 3 3 3 3 3 3 3

READING TEST

35 Minutes—40 Items

DIRECTIONS: Each passage below is followed by a set of items. Read each passage and choose the best answer for each item. Fill in the corresponding oval on your bubble sheet. You may refer to the passage as often as necessary to answer the items. Answers are on page 699.

Passage I

PROSE FICTION: In this passage, the character Miss Mix experiences an exciting robbery and learns a great deal about her employer, Mr. Rawjester.

My pupil was a bright little girl, who spoke French with a perfect accent. She said to me: "Miss Mix, did you ever have the *grande passion*? Did you ever feel a fluttering here?" and she placed her hand upon her small chest. "There is to be company here tomorrow," she added, rattling on with childish naiveté, "and papa's sweetheart—Blanche Marabout—is to be here. You know they say she is to be my mamma."

What thrill was this shot through me? But I rose calmly, and administering a slight correction to the child, left the apartment.

Blunderbore House, for the next week, was the scene of gaiety and merriment. That portion of the mansion closed with a grating was walled up, and the midnight shrieks no longer troubled me.

But I felt more keenly the degradation of my situation. I was obliged to help Lady Blanche at her toilette and help her to look beautiful. For what? To captivate him? Oh-no, no—but why this sudden thrill and faintness? Did he really love her? I had seen him pinch and swear at her. But I reflected that he had thrown a candlestick at my head, and my foolish heart was reassured.

It was a night of festivity, when a sudden message obliged Mr. Rawjester to leave his guests for a few hours. "Make yourselves merry, idiots," he said, under his breath, as he passed me. The door closed and he was gone.

A half-hour passed. In the midst of the dancing a shriek was heard, and out of the swaying crowd of fainting women and excited men, a wild figure strode into the room. One glance showed it to be a highwayman, heavily armed, holding a pistol in each hand.

"Let no one pass out of this room!" he said, in a voice of thunder. "The house is surrounded and you cannot escape. The first one who crosses yonder threshold will be shot like a dog. Gentlemen, I'll trouble you to approach in single file, and hand me your purses and watches."

Finding resistance useless, the order was ungraciously obeyed.

"Now, ladies, please to pass up your jewelry and trinkets."

This order was still more ungraciously complied with. As Blanche handed to the bandit captain her bracelet, she endeavored to conceal a diamond necklace, the gift of Mr. Rawjester, in her bosom. But, with a demoniac grin, the powerful brute tore it from its concealment.

It was now my turn. With a beating heart, I made my way to the robber chieftain and sank at his feet. "Oh, sir, I am nothing but a poor governess, pray let me go."

GO ON TO THE NEXT PAGE.

"Oh, ho! A governess? Give me your last month's wages, then. Give me what you have stolen from your master!" and he laughed fiendishly.

I gazed at him quietly, and said, in a low voice, "I have stolen nothing from you, Mr. Rawjester!"

"Ah, discovered! Hush! Listen, girl!" he hissed in a fiercer whisper, "utter a syllable to frustrate my plans and you die—aid me, and—" but he was gone.

In a few moments the party, with the exception of myself, were gagged and locked in the cellar. The next moment, torches were applied to the rich hangings, and the house was in flames. I felt a strong hand seize me, and bear me out in the open air and place me upon the hillside, where I could overlook the burning mansion. It was Mr. Rawjester.

"Burn!" he said, as he shook his fist at the flames. Then sinking on his knees before me, he said hurriedly:

"Mary Jane, I love you; the obstacles to our union are or will be soon removed. In yonder mansion were confined my three crazy wives. One of them, as you know, attempted to kill me! Ha! This is vengeance! But will you be mine?"

I fell, without a word, upon his neck.

1. The name of the narrator is:

A. Blanche Blunderbore.
B. Blanche Mix.
C. Mary Jane Mix.
D. Mary Jane Rawjester.

2. Mr. Rawjester leaves the party in order to:

F. obtain more refreshments for his guests.
G. attend to an urgent business matter.
H. disguise himself and return to the party as a robber.
J. check on the whereabouts of his daughter.

3. The degradation the narrator describes in the fourth paragraph (lines 17–19) comes from:

A. having to help the fiancée of the man she loves.
B. having to tutor a small child who speaks French.
C. her inability to earn more money.
D. her inability to sleep through the night without being disturbed.

4. What is the narrator's position at Blunderbore house?

F. The master's wife
G. The master's mistress
H. The child's governess
J. Blanche Marabout's sister

5. Mr. Rawjester's attitude towards his guests is one of:

A. warmth.
B. revulsion.
C. indifference.
D. admiration.

6. The child believes that:

F. Blanche Marabout is her natural mother.
G. Blanche Marabout is to marry her father.
H. the narrator is her natural mother.
J. her father dislikes the narrator.

7. It can be inferred that the narrator:

A. denounces Mr. Rawjester to his guests.
B. cooperates with Mr. Rawjester.
C. defends herself against Mr. Rawjester's attack.
D. gives the highwayman her month's wages.

GO ON TO THE NEXT PAGE.

8. The purpose of the visit of the highwayman is to:

F. obtain valuable jewelry.
G. kidnap the narrator.
H. kill the child.
J. deflect suspicion from Mr. Rawjester.

9. Blanche was unable to hide the diamond necklace because:

A. the highwayman had given it to her and knew she had it.
B. the narrator told the highwayman where it was hidden.
C. some of the other guests insisted that she give it up.
D. the child whispered its location to the highwayman.

10. The exchange between the narrator and the highwayman that takes place in the house was heard:

F. only by those two persons.
G. by the child.
H. by Blanche.
J. by every guest in the room.

GO ON TO THE NEXT PAGE.

Passage II

SOCIAL SCIENCE: This passage discusses legislation for the regulation of corporate takeovers.

American financial markets are regulated by the federal government through the Securities and Exchange Commission and by various state agencies. In recent years, there has been considerable discussion of the need for more regulation because of the increased number of corporate takeovers. Many observers of the economic scene argue that much of this activity has had harmful effects not only on stockholders but also on the economy as a whole.

Many corporate takeovers are hostile; that is, an outside group or company tries to seize control of an existing company whose management opposes the takeover. Most hostile takeovers begin with a tender offer in which the outside raiders offer to buy a sufficient amount of the company's outstanding stock at a stated price—usually well above the current market price. Another takeover strategy is to orchestrate a proxy battle in which a vote of shareholders of record on a specific date is taken to approve or reject a new slate of directors put forth by the raiders. The raiders generally argue that the new directors will make the company more profitable and thereby enhance the value of the stock for the existing stockholders.

Regardless of the takeover strategy employed, most raiders must purchase a significant portion of the company's stock at a price above its current market value. Outsiders usually finance such large purchases of stock through the sale of bonds that pay a very high rate of interest. The raiders argue that the debt to be incurred can easily be paid off by selling parts of the targeted company or by drawing on the additional profits that the new management insists it can make.

In 1986 and 1987, charges emerged that individuals within Wall Street firms specializing in raising capital for corporate takeovers were, in fact, selling inside information about future takeover attempts. Some of the individuals involved have already been sentenced to jail terms. In addition, such scandals have added to pressure on Congress and the Securities and Exchange Commission to provide more effective regulation of the financial aspects of attempted corporate takeovers.

Critics of hostile corporate takeovers believe that the managers of the company to be taken over usually engage in short-term activities that have very negative long-term effects. In order to avoid hostile takeovers, managers of companies generally take measures to make the takeovers less desirable. For instance, they may insert a *golden parachute clause* in employment contracts. This clause requires a company to pay very large bonuses to any management members who are fired after a takeover. Another tactic, the *poison pill,* restructures the financial base of the corporation so that an attempted takeover would make the company less profitable. Yet another anti-raid tactic is to pay *greenmail* to the raiders; that is, the target of the takeover pays the raiders, who have acquired a significant percentage of the stock at a premium, to sell those shares back to the targeted company at a much higher price. This prevents the takeover, but it usually adds a substantial sum to the company's debt.

Supporters of corporate raiders counter-argue that, in fact, it is the threat of a takeover that makes managers more efficient. For instance, it may cause managers to sell parts of the corporation that they are not managing well in order to raise the money to fend off the takeover. In addition, those who believe that takeovers are good argue that the existing shareholders always do better in a hostile takeover since they invariably get a higher price for each share of stock than the current market value.

11. Which statement expresses the main idea of this passage?

A. The government is regulating the financial aspects of corporate takeovers adequately.
B. There has been recent debate over the need for additional government regulation of corporate takeovers.
C. Hostile corporate takeovers are beneficial to the targeted corporation.
D. Trading insider secrets has become a common problem in hostile corporate takeovers.

GO ON TO THE NEXT PAGE.

12. A corporation's board of directors votes to approve a new company policy. According to the plan, each member of the board and of upper management would receive severance of two to five years' pay if the new owner fired the member after a corporate takeover. This action would be considered:

F. a poison pill.
G. a golden parachute.
H. greenmail.
J. a hostile takeover.

13. What is the most important difference between a hostile and a non-hostile takeover?

A. In a hostile takeover, stockholders must pay greenmail to the existing directors.
B. In a non-hostile takeover, raiders sell bonds with high interest rates.
C. In a hostile takeover, the existing management is opposed to the takeover.
D. In a non-hostile takeover, existing management uses golden parachutes.

14. According to the passage, which of the following parties in a hostile takeover will likely incur new debt?

F. The raiders, because they need money to buy large blocks of stock
G. The Securities and Exchange Commission, because it must oversee the transactions more closely
H. The stockholders, because they must furnish additional funds
J. The critics of hostile takeovers, because they make less money in the stock market

15. According to the passage, a poison pill strategy involves:

A. paying the raiders high prices to buy back the company's stock from them.
B. paying high bonuses to the members of the old management who are fired by the new management.
C. more regulation by the Securities and Exchange Commission.
D. restructuring the financial base of the company so that it will be less profitable or valuable to the raiders.

16. According to the passage, supporters of corporate takeovers believe that:

F. the shareholders always lose money because a takeover profits only the raiders.
G. fear of being targeted for a takeover makes managers more efficient.
H. insider trading should be made legal.
J. a proxy fight is the best way to win control.

17. According to the passage, in a proxy fight:

A. the raiders sell bonds to buy the targeted company's stock.
B. the raiders offer to buy stock at a higher-than-market price.
C. insider information is traded illegally.
D. the shareholders vote for approval or rejection of a new board of directors put forth by the raiders.

GO ON TO THE NEXT PAGE.

18. The management of a business recently targeted for takeover decides to sell two of its unprofitable subsidiaries to raise cash and cut expenses. Supporters of corporate takeovers would say that this action:

    F. is an example of how the greenmail strategy works.
    G. is an example of how a golden parachute strategy works.
    H. is an example of how the fear of a takeover makes managers more efficient.
    J. is an example of how the poison pill strategy works.

19. The Securities and Exchange Commission is a:

    A. state regulatory agency that polices financial markets.
    B. federal regulatory agency that polices financial markets.
    C. source of funding for hostile takeovers.
    D. board of business executives who promote fair business practices.

20. Some individuals working on Wall Street have been sentenced to jail terms for:

    F. attempting to greenmail other companies.
    G. forcing companies to swallow a poison pill.
    H. selling inside information about takeover attempts.
    J. agreeing to pay greenmail to corporate raiders.

GO ON TO THE NEXT PAGE.

Passage III

HUMANITIES: This passage explores the contributions of Josquin des Prez to Western music.

Until Josquin des Prez (1440–1521), Western music was liturgical, designed as an accompaniment to worship. Like the intricately carved gargoyles perched atop medieval cathedrals beyond sight of any human, music was composed to please God before anybody else; its dominant theme was reverence. Emotion was there, but it was the grief of Mary standing at the foot of the Cross, the joy of the faithful hailing Christ's resurrection. Even the secular music of the Middle Ages was tied to predetermined patterns that sometimes seemed to stand in the way of individual expression.

While keeping one foot firmly planted in the divine world, Josquin stepped with the other into the human world. He scored magnificent masses, but also newly expressive motets such as the lament of David over his son Absalom or the "Deploration d'Ockeghem," a dirge on the death of Ockeghem, the greatest master before Josquin, a motet written all in black notes, and one of the most profoundly moving scores of the Renaissance. Josquin was the first composer to set psalms to music. But alongside *Benedicite omnia opera Domini Domino* ("Bless the Lord, all ye works of the Lord") he put *El Grillo* ("The cricket is a good singer who manages long poems") and *Allegez moy* ("Solace me, sweet pleasant brunette"). Martin Luther praised Josquin, for his music blends respect for tradition with a rebel's willingness to risk the horizon. What Galileo was to science, Josquin was to music. While preserving their allegiance to God, both asserted a new importance for man.

Why then should Josquin languish in relative obscurity? The answer has to do with the separation of concept from performance in music. In fine art, concept and performance are one; both the art lover and the art historian have thousands of years of paintings, drawings, and sculptures to study and enjoy. Similarly with literature: Poetry, fiction, drama, and criticism survive on the printed page or in manuscript for judgment and admiration by succeeding generations. But musical notation on a page is not art, no matter how lofty or excellent the composer's conception; it is, crudely put, a set of directions for producing art.

Being highly symbolic, musical notation requires training before it can even be read, let alone performed. Moreover, because the musical conventions of other days are not ours, translation of a Renaissance score into modern notation brings difficulties of its own. For example, the Renaissance notation of Josquin's day did not designate the tempo at which the music should be played or sung. It did not indicate all flats or sharps; these were sounded in accordance with musician rules, which were capable of transforming major to minor, minor to major, diatonic to chromatic sound, and thus affect melody, harmony, and musical expression. A Renaissance composition might include several parts—but it did not indicate which were to be sung or played, or whether instruments were to be used at all.

Thus, Renaissance notation permits several interpretations and an imaginative musician may give an interpretation that is a revelation. But no matter how imaginative, few modern musicians can offer any interpretation of Renaissance music. The public for it is small, limiting the number of musicians who can afford to learn, rehearse, and perform it. Most of those who attempt it at all are students organized in *collegia musica* whose memberships have a distressing habit of changing every semester, thus preventing directors from maintaining the year-in, year-out continuity required to achieve excellence of performance. Finally, the instruments used in Renaissance times—krummhorns, recorders, rausch-pfeifen, shawms, sackbuts, organettos—must be specially procured.

21. The primary purpose of the passage is to:

A. introduce the reader to Josquin and account for his relative obscurity.
B. describe the main features of medieval music and show how Josquin changed them.
C. place Josquin's music in an historical context and show its influence on later composers.
D. enumerate the features of Josquin's music and supply critical commentary.

GO ON TO THE NEXT PAGE.

22. The passage contains information that would help answer all of the following items EXCEPT:

F. What are the titles of some of Josquin's secular compositions?
G. What are the names of some Renaissance musical instruments?
H. Who was the greatest composer before Josquin?
J. What are the names of some of Josquin's most famous students?

23. It can be inferred from the passage that modern musical notation has which of the following characteristics?

I. The tempo at which a composition is to be played is indicated in the notation.
II. Whether a note is sharp or a flat is indicated in the notation.
III. The notation indicates which parts of the music are to be played by which instruments.

A. I only
B. II only
C. I and III only
D. I, II, and III

24. The author would most likely agree with which of the following statements?

F. Music is a better art form than painting or sculpture.
G. Music can be said to exist only when it is being performed.
H. Josquin was the greatest composer of the Middle Ages.
J. Renaissance music is superior to music produced in modern times.

25. The passage leads most logically to a proposal to:

A. establish more *collegia musica.*
B. study Josquin's compositional techniques in greater detail.
C. include Renaissance music in college studies.
D. provide funds for musicians to study and play Josquin.

26. The author cites all of the following as reasons for Josquin's relative obscurity EXCEPT:

F. the difficulty one encounters in attempting to read his musical notation.
G. the inability of modern musicians to play instruments of the Renaissance.
H. the difficulty of procuring unusual instruments needed to play the music.
J. the lack of public interest in Renaissance music.

27. The author's attitude toward Galileo can best be described as:

A. admiring.
B. critical.
C. accepting.
D. analytical.

28. Which of the following statements about liturgical music is consistent with the selection?

F. It is lacking in any emotion.
G. It is written to entertain people.
H. It is intended to be reverential.
J. It treats primarily nonreligious themes.

29. Which of the following is NOT an example of fine art as that term is used in the passage?

A. A ballet
B. A novel
C. A poem
D. A mural

GO ON TO THE NEXT PAGE.

30. Josquin des Prez is important in the history of music because he:

F. wrote motets using only black notes.
G. wrote only nonliturgical music.
H. wrote both liturgical and nonliturgical music.
J. invented new musical instruments for his music.

GO ON TO THE NEXT PAGE.

Passage IV

NATURAL SCIENCE: This passage discusses supernova explosions and their effects.

About twice every century, the light reaches us from one of the massive stars in our galaxy that blew apart millions of years ago in a supernova explosion that sends massive quantities of radiation and matter into space and generates shock waves that sweep through the arms of the galaxy. The shock waves heat the interstellar gas, evaporate small clouds, and compress larger ones to the point at which they collapse under their own gravity to form new stars. The general picture that has been developed for the supernova explosion and its aftermath goes something like this. Throughout its evolution, a star is much like a leaky balloon; it keeps its equilibrium figure through a balance of internal pressure against the tendency to collapse under its own weight. The pressure is generated by nuclear reactions in the core of the star that must continually supply energy to balance the energy that leaks out in the form of radiation. Eventually, the nuclear fuel is exhausted, and the pressure drops in the core. With nothing to hold it up, the matter in the center of the star collapses inward, creating higher and higher densities and temperatures, until the nuclei and electrons are fused into a super-dense lump of matter known as a neutron star.

As the overlying layers rain down on the surface of the neutron star, the temperature rises until, with a blinding flash of radiation, the collapse is reversed. A thermonuclear shock wave runs through the now expanding stellar envelope, fusing lighter elements into heavier ones and producing a brilliant visual outburst that can be as intense as the light of 10 billion suns. The shell of matter thrown off by the explosion plows through the surrounding gas, producing an expanding bubble of hot gas, with gas temperatures in the millions of degrees. This gas will emit most of its energy at X-ray wavelengths, so it is not surprising that X-ray observatories have provided some of the most useful insights into the nature of the supernova phenomenon. More than twenty supernova remnants have now been detected in X-ray studies.

Recent discoveries of meteorites with anomalous concentrations of certain isotopes indicate that a supernova might have precipitated the birth of our solar system more than four and a half billion years ago. Although the cloud that collapsed to form the Sun and the planets was composed primarily of hydrogen and helium, it also contained carbon, nitrogen, and oxygen, elements essential for life as we know it. Elements heavier than helium are manufactured deep in the interior of stars and would, for the most part, remain there if it were not for the cataclysmic supernova explosions that blow giant stars apart. Additionally, supernovas produce clouds of high-energy particles called cosmic rays. These high-energy particles continually bombard the Earth and are responsible for many of the genetic mutations that are the driving force of the evolution of species.

31. According to the passage, we can expect to observe a supernova in our galaxy about:

A. twice each year.
B. 100 times each century.
C. once every 50 years.
D. once every other century.

32. According to the passage, all of the following are true of supernovas EXCEPT:

F. they are extremely bright.
G. they are an explosion of some sort.
H. they are emitters of large quantities of X-rays.
J. they are caused by the collision of large galaxies.

33. The author employs which of the following to develop the first paragraph?

A. Analogy
B. Deduction
C. Generalization
D. Example

GO ON TO THE NEXT PAGE.

34. It can be inferred from the passage that the meteorites mentioned by the author (line 41):

F. contain dangerous concentrations of radioactive materials.
G. give off large quantities of X-rays.
H. include material not created in the normal development of our solar system.
J. are larger than the meteors normally found in a solar system like ours.

35. The author implies that:

A. it is sometimes easier to detect supernovas by observation of the X-ray spectrum than by observation of visible wavelengths of light.
B. life on Earth is endangered by its constant exposure to radiation forces that are released by a supernova.
C. recently discovered meteorites indicate that the Earth and other planets of our solar system survived the explosion of a supernova several billion years ago.
D. lighter elements are formed from heavier elements during a supernova as the heavier elements are torn apart.

36. According to the passage, what is the first event in the sequence that leads to the occurrence of a supernova?

F. An ordinary star begins to emit tremendous quantities of X-rays.
G. A superheated cloud of gas envelops a neutron star.
H. An imbalance between light and heavy elements causes an ordinary star to collapse.
J. An ordinary star exhausts its supply of nuclear fuel and begins to collapse.

37. According to the passage, a neutron star is:

A. a gaseous cloud containing heavy elements.
B. an intermediate stage between an ordinary star and a supernova.
C. the residue that is left by a supernova.
D. the core of an ordinary star that houses the thermonuclear reactions.

38. The author is primarily concerned with:

F. speculating about the origins of our solar system.
G. presenting evidence proving the existence of supernovas.
H. discussing the nuclear reaction that occurs in the core of a star.
J. describing a theory about the causes of supernovas.

39. How long ago was our galaxy formed?

A. 100 million years
B. 1 billion years
C. 2 billion years
D. Over 4.5 billion years

40. What is the connection between supernovas and the evolution of species on Earth?

F. There is no connection.
G. Cosmic radiation from supernovas retards evolution.
H. Cosmic radiation from supernovas drives evolution.
J. Evolution makes possible future supernovas.

END OF TEST 3
STOP! DO NOT TURN THE PAGE UNTIL TOLD TO DO SO.
DO NOT RETURN TO THE PREVIOUS TEST.

NO TEST MATERIAL ON THIS PAGE

4 4 4 4 4 4 4 4 4 4 4 4

SCIENCE TEST

35 Minutes—40 Items

DIRECTIONS: Each passage below is followed by several items. After reading a passage, choose the best answer for each item. Fill in the corresponding oval on your bubble sheet. You may refer to the passage as often as necessary. You are NOT permitted the use of a calculator on this test. Answers are on page 699.

Passage I

Before making their historic first powered flight, the Wright Brothers made extensive lift tests in 1901 using a glider. Their data differed from that obtained twelve years earlier by the German, Otto Lilienthal.

Results of both tests (Wright: thin line; Lilienthal: thick line) are shown below. "Lift" is the force that pulls the wing away from the Earth, in a direction perpendicular to the flight path, and the "angle of incidence" is the angle that the flight path makes with the horizon.

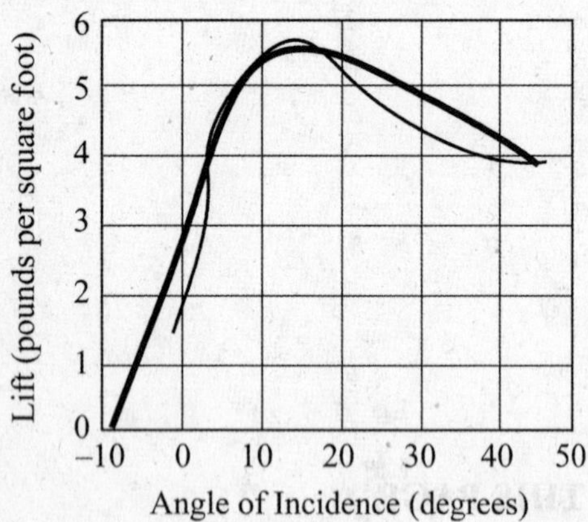

Modified from Culick, F.E.C, "The Wright 'Flyer' was the outcome of an intensive program of research." *Sci. Amer. 241* (1): 86–100, 1979.

1. The two curves differ chiefly in that:

A. the Wright's data were more accurate.
B. lift was generally greater in Lilienthal's experiments.
C. lift was generally greater in the Wright's experiments.
D. the peak value for lift was greater in Lilienthal's experiments.

2. In the Wright's experiments, the greatest lift occurred at an angle of incidence of about:

F. –5.5 degrees.
G. 0 degrees.
H. 16 degrees.
J. 46 degrees.

3. At an angle of incidence of 50 degrees, by how much would you expect the two experiments to show a difference in lift?

A. 0–1 pounds/sq. ft.
B. 1–2 pounds/sq. ft.
C. 2–3 pounds/sq. ft.
D. 3–4 pounds/sq. ft.

4. The two sets of experiments differed most in lift at which of the following angles?

F. 10 degrees
G. 15 degrees
H. 30 degrees
J. 40 degrees

GO ON TO THE NEXT PAGE.

5. The widest range of angles, in degrees, over which the Lilienthal values for lift continuously exceeded the Wright's values was:

   A. 43.
   B. 25.
   C. 19.
   D. 10.

GO ON TO THE NEXT PAGE.

Passage II

Two experiments were performed to determine the effects of temperature on the rate of cellular respiration* in germinating peas.

*Summary Equation:

$$\underset{\text{(glucose)}}{C_6H_{12}O_6} + \underset{\text{(oxygen)}}{6O_2} \Rightarrow \underset{\text{(carbon dioxide)}}{6CO_2} + \underset{\text{(water)}}{6H_2O}$$

Experiment 1

A simple respirometer was used, primarily consisting of a large test tube partially filled with germinating peas. The peas were covered with a layer of cotton and a small amount of potassium hydroxide (KOH), a substance that can absorb and remove carbon dioxide from the tube. The remainder of the tube, with its starting volume of air sealed inside (200 ml.), was closed to the outside with a rubber stopper. Attached was a meter designed to detect and measure any changes in gas volume in the tube during the experiment. The experiment was conducted at room temperature (22°C), and the respirator was monitored for 15 minutes. At the end of 15 minutes, the volume of gas inside the tube had *decreased* to 120 ml.

Experiment 2

An identical experiment was conducted at 30°C. At this temperature, the volume of gas inside the tube after 15 minutes had decreased from 200 ml (starting volume) to 60 ml.

6. Separate control experiments were performed alongside Experiments 1 and 2. The control contained plastic beads (the same size as peas) instead of germinating peas. All other conditions were identical. Any decrease in gas volume inside the control tube would suggest that:

F. plastic beads utilize oxygen at approximately the same rate as germinating peas.
G. plastic beads produce carbon dioxide at about the same rate as germinating peas.
H. plastic beads carry out all aspects of cellular respiration at approximately the same rate as germinating peas.
J. factors having nothing to do with cellular respiration must be responsible.

7. In both experiments, the decrease in volume in the tube was mainly due to a change in the volume of what specific gas?

A. Oxygen
B. Carbon dioxide
C. Potassium hydroxide
D. All of the above

8. If potassium hydroxide (KOH) were not included in the tubes, what would happen to the volume of gas during each experiment?

F. Final volumes would approximately be the same as starting volumes.
G. Final volumes would be higher than starting volumes.
H. Final volumes would decrease faster than what was observed in Experiments 1 and 2.
J. Results would not be different from what was observed in Experiments 1 and 2.

9. Experiment 2 showed a greater decrease in gas volume in the tube because:

A. at higher temperatures, peas use oxygen slower.
B. at higher temperatures, peas produce carbon dioxide faster.
C. at higher temperatures, peas use oxygen faster.
D. at lower temperatures, peas use oxygen slower than they produce carbon dioxide.

GO ON TO THE NEXT PAGE.

10. An additional set of experiments with germinating peas is conducted in the dark at 22°C and 30°C. All other conditions are identical to those in Experiments 1 and 2. After 15 minutes, if the final gas volume inside the tube at 22°C is 120 ml, and the final gas volume inside the tube at 30°C is 60 ml, which hypothesis best explains the results?

F. Darkness affects cellular respiration in germinating peas the same way that a rise in temperature affects cellular respiration in germinating peas.
G. Light/dark conditions have little or no effect on cellular respiration in germinating peas.
H. Cellular respiration in germinating peas occurs faster in the light than in the dark.
J. Cellular respiration in germinating peas occurs faster in the dark than in the light.

11. The summary equation in the passage shows that during cellular respiration, germinating peas must consume glucose. In Experiments 1 and 2, glucose molecules:

A. were in the peas.
B. were not available.
C. were consumed at equal rates.
D. were available but not consumed at all.

Passage III

Two different views of the Earth's past are presented below.

Scientist 1

The history of our planet has been marked by sudden spectacular events that have no counterpart in the natural processes observed today (Catastrophism). Today's valleys formed during periods of downward slippage by fragments of the Earth's crust. Mountains rose due to gigantic upheavals of land during the Earth's beginnings. The three major types of rock formed when one worldwide ocean precipitated out great masses of different materials during three sudden and separate events. Substances such as granite were precipitated first (today's igneous rocks), while materials in the flat upper layers precipitated last (today's sedimentary rocks). This was followed by the disappearance of much of this great ocean's water (perhaps by evaporation during years of intensive heat). Distinct assemblages of animal and plant fossils, found in successive rock layers of a region, can be explained by local catastrophic events, such as massive fires or floods. Old forms were wiped out, and eventually new forms replaced them as foreign species immigrated from other geographic areas.

Scientist 2

Processes now in operation are adequate to account for changes in the Earth's past (Principle of Uniform Change). Although today's processes seem to have negligible effects on the landscape, great changes can result from ongoing processes, if given long enough periods of time. Valleys form as flowing water cuts through the sides and bottom of the land and rock they pass across. Rocks and mountains can be formed, destroyed and reformed by processes still going on today such as volcanic activity, heat and pressure under the Earth's surfaces, erosion, weathering, and even shifts and movements that can lift massive areas below the land and ocean surfaces to high elevations. Different fossil types in successive layers of rocks represent the changes in form that can take place among related organisms as a result of evolutionary processes over vast periods of time.

12. One major difference between the views of Scientist 1 and Scientist 2 relates to:

F. where fossils are found.
G. when the processes that shape the Earth take place.
H. the size of mountain ranges.
J. whether water played a role in forming any of the Earth's characteristics.

13. Which of the following provides the strongest evidence against Scientist 1's point about mountain formation?

A. The beginnings of the Earth are not well documented.
B. Floods and fires have never been massive enough to eliminate fossils from all mountain areas.
C. Volcanic activity, weathering, and erosion are believed to be less common today than in years past.
D. Fossils of recent sea creatures can be found in rocks on mountain peaks.

GO ON TO THE NEXT PAGE.

14. Which of the following best characterizes the main difference between Catastrophism and the Principle of Uniform Change?

F. Catastrophism maintains that violent changes in the relatively recent past shaped the Earth's landscape while the Principle of Uniform Change holds that gradual changes over an enormous span are responsible.
G. Catastrophism predicts that sudden, violent events will soon reshape the Earth's landscape while the Principle of Uniform Change expects the landscape to remain mostly unchanged.
H. Catastrophism theorizes that the landscape was largely shaped by cataclysmic events in the distant past while the Principle of Uniform Change holds that the landscape is the result of a steady transformation over a long time.
J. Catastrophism holds that relatively recent events of enormous magnitude created the landscape while the Principle of Uniform Change holds that the landscape has remained relatively unchanged since the Earth's formation.

15. According to Scientist 1, which of the major types of rocks should be found at the lowest levels?

A. Igneous (granite)
B. Metamorphic (marble)
C. Sedimentary (limestone)
D. Cannot be determined from the given information

16. According to the views of Scientist 1, the number of major rock types will most likely:

F. remain unchanged.
G. decrease.
H. increase.
J. Cannot be determined from the given information

17. To refute Scientist 2's point of view about strictly uniform processes of change, Scientist 1 could argue that:

A. the streams of today are not measurably effective in cutting through the sides and bottoms of rock they pass across.
B. fossils are not found everywhere today.
C. at some early point in time, the actual formation of the Earth had to involve very different processes from those now in evidence.
D. no mountain ranges have formed in our lifetime.

18. Which argument does NOT support the views of Scientist 2?

F. There are many regions of lava where no volcanoes are present today.
G. There are three major types of rock that exist today.
H. Many rivers today are flowing far below their former channels.
J. Distinctive fossils in upper layers of rock show similarities to those in lower layers, yet they are never found in any other geographic areas.

GO ON TO THE NEXT PAGE.

Passage IV

Cold-blooded animals (poikilotherms) cannot regulate their body temperatures internally. Their body temperature varies as the environmental temperature varies. Consequently, the rates of many bodily processes also vary as outside temperatures change (as environmental temperatures increase, body temperature as well as the rates of bodily processes also may increase). Warm-blooded animals (homeotherms), on the other hand, can maintain their body temperatures internally. Therefore, the rates of their bodily processes can remain relatively stable when environmental temperatures change.

Experiments were set up to determine how the bodily process heart rate may be affected by different temperatures in two species of live laboratory animals.

Experiment 1

In this experiment, 10 individuals from Species A and 10 individuals from Species B were kept in 20 separate containers at room temperature (22°C) for 30 minutes. Their heart rates (heart beats/minute) were recorded every 10 minutes. Average heart rates for the entire experiment were then calculated for each species. Results were as follows: Species A had an average heart rate of 150 beats/minute, while Species B averaged 100 beats/minute.

Experiment 2

Identical procedures were used to repeat the original experiment except that the containers holding the individuals of each species were placed in an incubator set at 35°C. At the end of 30 minutes, the average heart rate for both species was 148 beats/minute.

19. How many values were used to calculate the average heart beats for each species in each of these experiments?

A. 1
B. 10
C. 20
D. 30

20. Which of the following hypotheses is supported by the results of both experiments?

F. Species A is most likely poikilothermic.
G. Species B is most likely poikilothermic.
H. Both species are most likely poikilothermic.
J. Neither species is poikilothermic.

21. Which of the following statements best explains why 10 individuals of each species were used in the experiments?

A. In case a few died, there would still be others available for testing.
B. If only one individual was used, it would be lonely.
C. An average value for 10 individuals reduces the chance of getting an extreme value for any one individual.
D. If only one individual was chosen from each species, it would be difficult to show differences.

22. If a third experiment were conducted at 6°C, which set of results for average heart rates (in beats/minute) is closest to what might be expected?

F. Species A = 146; Species B = 146
G. Species A = 50; Species B = 146
H. Species A = 50; Species B = 50
J. Species A = 146; Species B = 50

23. Which statement is accurate concerning Species A and Species B?

A. At 22°C, Species A has a higher average heart rate than Species B.
B. Species A has a larger average size than Species B.
C. As environmental temperature increases, average heart rate increases more for Species A than Species B.
D. As environmental temperature decreases, average heart rate increases more for Species A than Species B.

GO ON TO THE NEXT PAGE.

24. If the average body temperature for 10 individuals of each species were recorded during Experiments 1 and 2, which results would be expected?

    F. Species A: Temperature stays the same in both experiments. Species B: Temperature increases in Experiment 2.
    G. Species A: Temperature increases in Experiment 2. Species B: Temperature stays the same in both experiments.
    H. Both Species: Temperature increases in Experiment 2.
    J. Both Species: Temperature stays the same in both experiments.

GO ON TO THE NEXT PAGE.

Passage V

The chart below shows a set of "energy levels" that an electron in molecule X can occupy. The value of the energy in each level is shown to the right.

Energy Levels

E_5 ------2.07

E_4 ------1.75

E_3 ------1.52

E_2 ------1.20

E_1 ------0.60

An electron can move from one level to the next (transition) in two ways:

(1) The molecule can absorb a particle of light, called a "photon," of just the right energy to lift the electron to a higher level. For example, an electron in level 4 can be raised to level 5 if the molecule absorbs a photon whose energy is 0.32.

(2) The molecule can emit, or give off, a photon of just the right energy necessary to lower an electron to another level. For example, an electron in level 4 can move to level 3 if the molecule emits a photon whose energy is 0.23.

25. A sample containing many X molecules absorbs light, each photon of which carries 0.60 units of energy. As the light is absorbed:

A. an electron moves from level 1 to level 2.
B. an electron moves from level 2 to level 4.
C. an electron moves from level 2 to level 1.
D. an electron moves from level 4 to level 2.

26. A sample of molecule X emits light, each photon of which carries 0.32 units of energy. Which of the following statements best explains this observation?

F. An electron moved from level 3 to level 2.
G. An electron moved from level 2 to level 3.
H. An electron moved from level 5 to level 4.
J. An electron moved from level 3 to level 2 or from level 5 to level 4.

27. A sample of molecule X emits light whose photons each carry 0.92 units of energy. As the light is emitted:

A. an electron moves from level 5 to level 2.
B. an electron moves from level 1 to level 5.
C. an electron moves from level 1 to level 3.
D. an electron moves from level 3 to level 1.

28. Suppose that in a sample of molecule X, all of the electrons are in level 1. Based on the information in the chart, photons of how many different energies could be absorbed by the sample?

F. 1
G. 2
H. 3
J. 4

29. Assume that each of the molecules in a sample of molecule X has only 1 electron, whose level is not known. Light is passed through the sample, and photons, each of energy 0.23, are absorbed. A very short time later, photons of the same energy are emitted. It is likely that:

A. electrons are being promoted from level 1 to level 2.
B. electrons are moving from level 4 to level 3, and then back again to level 4.
C. electrons are moving from level 3 to level 4, then back again to level 3.
D. electrons are moving from level 5 to level 4.

30. If photons whose individual energies are each 2.07 encounter a sample of molecule X, then:

F. electrons will be promoted from level 1 to level 5.
G. electrons will be promoted from all levels to level 5.
H. electrons will drop from level 5 to level 1.
J. no electron transitions will occur.

GO ON TO THE NEXT PAGE.

Passage VI

A student performs a set of three experiments in which a light beam passes through water and air. The "refraction angles" are the angles that the light beam makes with a vertical line. In the water, this angle is called θ_1. When the beam leaves the water and passes into air, a second angle, θ_2, can be measured. Figure 1 illustrates θ_1 and θ_2.

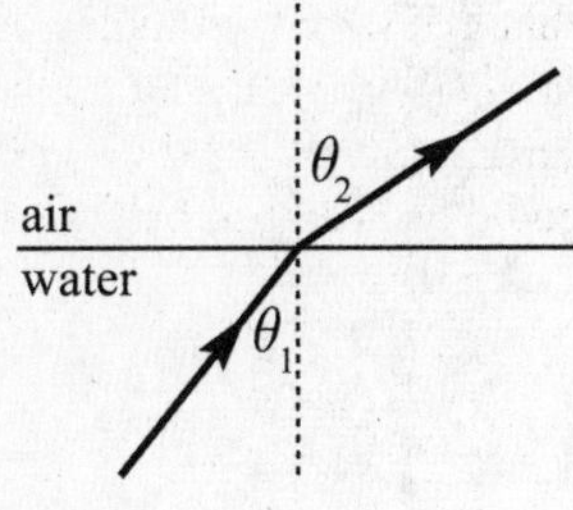

Figure 1

Experiment 1

The entry angle, θ_1, and the exit angle, θ_2, are both equal to zero.

Experiment 2

The angles observed are shown in Figure 2.

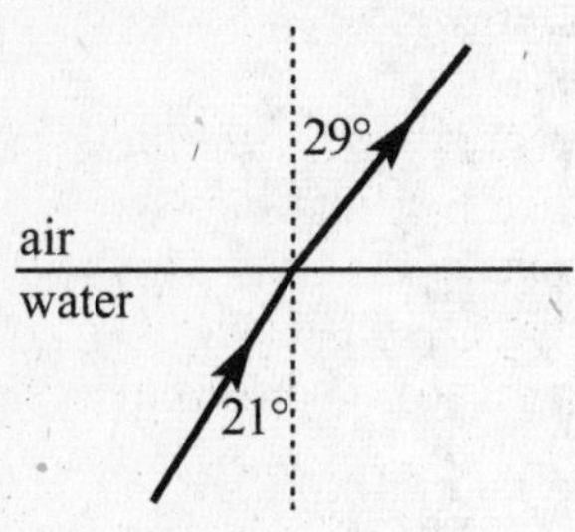

Figure 2

Experiment 3

The angles observed are shown in Figure 3.

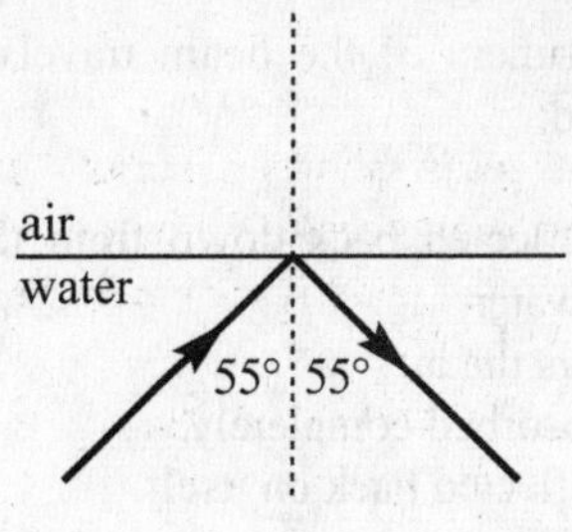

Figure 3

31. Which of the following diagrams could represent the observations of Experiment 1?

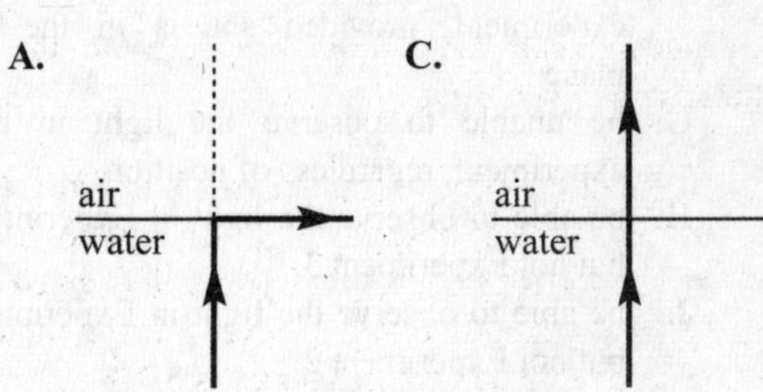

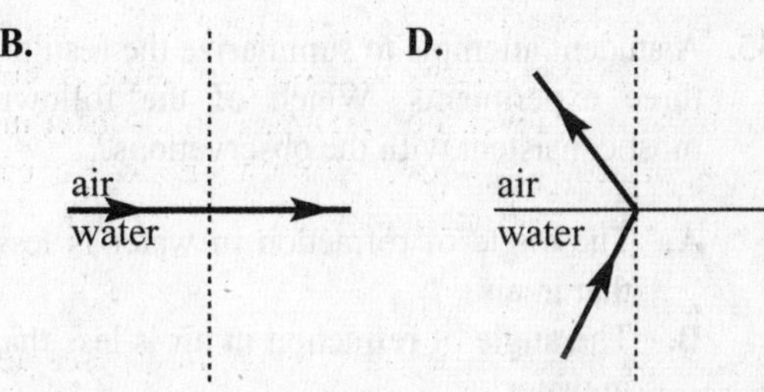

32. The student attempts to draw a conclusion from Experiments 1 and 2 that may apply to all other measurements as well. Which of the following is justified by the data?

F. Refraction angles in water are greater than those in air.
G. Refraction angles in water are less than those in air.
H. Refraction angles are equal in air and in water.
J. Refraction angles in water are equal to or less than those in air.

GO ON TO THE NEXT PAGE.

33. In Experiment 3, the beam travels through the water and:

A. is reflected back down from the surface of the water.
B. enters the air.
C. is absorbed completely.
D. is reflected back on itself.

34. An observer in the air attempts to see the beam of light in Experiments 2 and 3. She will:

F. be able to observe the light in each experiment, provided she is in the right place.
G. be unable to observe the light in either experiment, regardless of position.
H. be able to observe the light in Experiment 2 but not Experiment 3.
J. be able to observe the light in Experiment 3 but not Experiment 2.

35. A student attempts to summarize the results of all three experiments. Which of the following is most consistent with the observations?

A. The angle of refraction in water is less than that in air.
B. The angle of refraction in air is less than that in water.
C. The angle of refraction in water is less than or equal to that in air, but at high angles in the water, the light is reflected back into the water.
D. The angle of refraction in water is less than or equal to that in air.

GO ON TO THE NEXT PAGE.

Passage VII

The table below presents the results of a study in which butterflies of different size and color were captured in flight for marking with a chemical, and then recaptured in flight a few weeks later.

Size	White		Tan		Dark Brown	
	# marked	Recaptured	# marked	Recaptured	# marked	Recaptured
Small (less than 20 mm)	35	30	40	10	20	10
Medium (20–40 mm)	30	15	40	20	20	10
Large (greater than 40 mm)	50	25	60	30	30	10

36. For all sizes of butterflies, the color that seems most difficult to capture for marking is:

F. white.
G. tan.
H. dark brown.
J. Both tan and dark brown are almost equally difficult

37. The specific type of butterfly that is easiest to recapture after being marked is:

A. between 10–20 mm and tan.
B. greater than 40 mm and tan.
C. greater than 40 mm and dark brown.
D. less than 20 mm and white.

38. Based on the information in the table, which statement best represents the relationship between a butterfly's size and its tendency to be captured for marking?

F. The larger the butterfly, the harder it is to be captured for marking.
G. The larger the butterfly, the easier it is to be captured for marking.
H. Medium-sized butterflies are consistently the easiest to capture for marking.
J. The smaller the butterfly, the easier it is to be captured for marking.

39. The chemical used to mark all the butterflies was found to be poisonous to one specific type because it was being absorbed through the wings. Based on the data in the table, which type of butterfly appears most likely to have suffered from the effects of the marking chemical?

A. Greater than 40 mm and white
B. Less than 20 mm and tan
C. Greater than 40 mm and dark brown
D. Less than 20 mm and white

40. Which conclusion is correct concerning the information in the table?

F. For tan butterflies, the proportion of individuals that are recaptured always stays the same.
G. For medium-sized butterflies, the proportion of individuals that are recaptured always stays the same.
H. For small-sized butterflies, the proportion of individuals recaptured always stays the same.
J. For all sizes of butterflies, the darker the color the easier it is to recapture an individual.

END OF TEST 4
STOP! DO NOT TURN THE PAGE UNTIL TOLD TO DO SO.
DO NOT RETURN TO THE PREVIOUS TEST.

5 5 5 5 5 5 5 5 5 5 5 5

WRITING TEST (OPTIONAL)

30 Minutes—1 Essay Prompt

DIRECTIONS: You have 30 minutes to plan and write an essay. Read the prompt carefully and make sure you understand the instructions. A successful essay will have the following features: it will take a position on the issue presented in the writing prompt; it will maintain a consistent focus on the topic; it will use logical reasoning and provide supporting ideas; it will present ideas in an organized manner; and, finally, it will include clear and effective language in accordance with the conventions of standard written English. Sample essay responses begin on page 727.

Writing Test Prompt

Doctors and government leaders have become increasingly concerned about what is called the "obesity epidemic" in America. Many people are overweight, and researchers now believe that childhood eating habits have a major effect on whether an adult will be overweight. Some people now argue that schools should eliminate all "junk food" from the cafeteria offerings, remove all vending machines that sell soda pop and sugary snacks, and prohibit students from bringing into the school cafeteria from outside foods that are considered unhealthy. Other people oppose this idea. They say that the choice of what to eat should be left to individuals and families. Those parents who do not want their children eating "junk food" can take steps to regulate their diet; also, parents can determine how often their children may eat such food and how much of it. Do you think that schools should take steps to ensure that only healthful foods are served and consumed on school premises?

In your essay, take a position on this issue. You can write about either point of view presented here, or you can present a different point of view on this topic. Support your position with relevant reasons and/or examples from your own experience, observations, or reading.

END OF TEST 5
STOP! DO NOT RETURN TO ANY OTHER TEST.

Post-Assessment

Objectives:

See how far you have come and measure your improvement with this second, official test.

Practice working through the test quickly without losing accuracy.

Put into action all of the content knowledge you have learned.

Analyze your assessment scores and course performance to anticipate your adjusted plan of action.

Snapshot of Post-Assessment:

It's time to measure your progress. You will put into action everything that you've learned during this second "dress rehearsal." After taking this final exam, you will be able to compare your pre- and post-assessment scores and see how much you have improved. You will have a chance to identify any remaining areas of weakness so that you know where to focus your studies as you continue to improve your skills and prepare for the ACT®, PLAN®, and EXPLORE® tests.

POST-ASSESSMENT ADMINISTRATION

At the end of the course, you will take a post-assessment. This post-assessment consists of an official, retired ACT, PLAN, or EXPLORE test. Perforated essay response and bubble sheets for the post-assessment are located in Appendix B of this book for programs not utilizing the Cambridge Assessment Service. When you take the post-assessment, you should bring the following items to the classroom, in addition to anything else your teacher instructs you to bring:

1. Sharpened, soft-lead No. 2 pencils

2. A calculator that is approved for use on the test. This includes any four-function, scientific, or graphing calculator, except for those with the following features:

    - Built-in computer algebra systems
    - Pocket organizers or PDAs
    - Handheld or laptop computers
    - Electronic writing pad or pen-input devices
    - Calculators built into any electronic communication device, such as a cell phone
    - Models with a QWERTY (typewriter) keypad (Calculators with letters on the keys are permitted as long as the keys are not arranged in a QWERTY keypad.)

    You may use the following types of calculators if you make appropriate modifications:

    - Models with paper tape: the paper must be removed.
    - Models that make noise: the sound feature must be turned off.
    - Models that have an infrared data port: the port must be covered with duct tape, electrician's tape, or another heavy, opaque material.
    - Models that have a power cord: the power cord must be removed.

    (For more detailed information on calculator usage, go to www.actstudent.org/faq/answers/calculator.html.)

3. A watch (to pace yourself as you work through each test section)

As you take the test, remember the following points about marking the bubble sheet:

- The bubble for each answer choice must be completely darkened. If the letter within the bubble can be read through the pencil mark, then it is not dark enough. Mechanical pencils, even with No. 2 pencil lead, often fail to leave a dark mark.
- Stay within the lines.
- When erasing pencil marks, be sure to erase the marks completely. Do not leave any stray marks.

- Circle the answer choices in the test booklet. Towards the end of the section, or after each completed group of items, transfer the selected answers as a group to the answer form. Not only does this minimize erasing on the answer form, but it also saves time and minimizes transcription errors.

- When changing an answer, over-darken the final answer choice after completely erasing the original mark. This extra density tends to offset the residue left over from the original answer choice.

If your program has ordered post-assessment Student Summary reports, you will receive one of these reports with your post-assessment results. This report will help you determine the areas in which you need continued study. You can then utilize your study time to prepare in those areas so that when you take the real test, you are ready to do your best. Refer to the "How to Use the Pre-Assessment Report" section in volume 1 of the student text (p. 5) to learn more about how to read and use the Student Summary report.

HOW TO USE THE POST-ASSESSMENT REPORT

In the transition from Post-Assessment to Personal Action Plan, you and your teacher will use the results of your post-assessment to recognize your individual strengths and weaknesses. Additionally, be sure at this point in the course that you have not only reviewed the "Setting a Test Score Target," "Overcoming Test Anxiety," and "Overall Test Management" sections in the Pre-Assessment/Course Planning part of volume 1 of the student text, but that you have also followed through on your schedule for the course.

You will receive the results of your official post-assessment in the form of a Student Summary report approximately 10 days after taking the test. This report provides details about your performance and will help you to determine where to focus your efforts from now until your official test date by strategically targeting those skills, concepts, and strategies that will help you to improve in your areas of weakness. Just as you did with the pre-assessment, review the details of the sample Student Summary report on pages 6–7 of volume 1 of the student text so that you are familiar with its contents.

Once you have received your post-assessment Student Summary report, you can make connections between the report and the specific skills, concepts, and strategies that you need to study. Just as with the pre-assessment, you will be given a checklist for your post-assessment. Referring to your Student Summary report, put an "X" beside those items that you answered incorrectly and a "?" by those that you do not fully understand. The descriptions on the checklist tell you where you can look in the Item Index at the back of this book to find the appropriate items. Then, once you have your checklist of items to study, make a "to do" list using the following pages.

Topic	*Start Date*	*Date to Be Completed*	*Date Completed*

Topic	*Start Date*	*Date to Be Completed*	*Date Completed*

Personal Action Plan

Objectives:

With the post-assessment data, create a focused action plan with the help of your instructor so you know what to review.

Don't waste time on areas you've already mastered; target any remaining areas of weakness.

Learn valuable information on preparing your college applications and writing college admissions essays.

Snapshot of Personal Action Plan:

Based on the results of the post-assessment, you will collaborate with your instructor to develop a personalized action plan. You may be asked to return to items you've already reviewed but have not yet mastered. If there are any items you have not yet completed, this is the time to return to those areas. You may need to review specific test-taking strategies; to focus on pacing, timing, and guessing; or to focus on other weaknesses. In addition to developing a plan to deliver your best ACT®, PLAN®, or EXPLORE® test performance, you will also begin to learn the nuts and bolts of the college application process.

Personal Action Plan

[illegible]

Snapshot of Personal Action Plan

[illegible]

PLANNING FOR FURTHER STUDY

You have received the results of your post-assessment. You have finished the Cambridge ACT • PLAN • EXPLORE program. Now what?

In most cases you will have some spare time before the test day, so planning a study schedule between the post-assessment and the real test is critical to reinforce and maintain the skills, concepts, and strategies that you have learned throughout the course. Below are three steps that will help you make the most of your time.

Take the Timed Practice Tests

Most students grasp knowledge of the subjects, but many struggle with time management. If you have not yet done so, take Timed Practice Tests I–III included in the Practice Test Reinforcement part of this book. These practice tests:

1. reinforce skills and strategies,
2. simulate the experience of the real test by using time restrictions to emphasize time management, and
3. are an excellent guide to targeting your study plan.

Create a Written Study Plan

Use the results of your post-assessment and the timed practice tests to determine a day-by-day schedule that will create a clear and dependable guide for study. Create this plan based on the amount of time you have before the test day.

Several weeks before test day:

- Plan to review all material equally.
- As the test date approaches, devote your time to any particular areas of weakness.

Remember: picking a few subjects to focus on each week will help you manage your time between now and the test.

A few days before test day:

- Focus on core subjects that are giving you difficulty, or areas in which you would like to improve.
- Divide your time proportionally among these subjects based on your assessment of their difficulty.

Determine the topics you will study each day and allot the proper amount of time to study those sections of the book and complete relevant exercises.

Stick to the Plan

Once you have determined your rubric for study, stick to it without fail. Such discipline will surely reward you on the day of the test. Follow these helpful hints:

- Ask your teacher for insight. He or she can help you set goals for each core subject and may be able to suggest further strategies or a re-allotment of your time.
- Do not study too much. An hour or two of studying each day will be more productive than a severe study schedule.
- Practice every day.

APPLICATION PREPARATION

The title of this section echoes our analysis of the admission process in "Setting a Test Score Target" in volume 1 of the student text. To maximize your chances of success, you must create an admission application that satisfies the needs of the school to which you are applying. This does not mean that you create an application that is fictitious, but it does mean that you organize and present your experiences in a way that depicts you in the most favorable light.

Highlight Your Unique Qualities within the Application

You must create an application that satisfies the needs of the school to which you are applying in order to maximize your chances of admissions success. Many times, this means that you should have a certain GPA and ACT test score, while at the same time exhibiting unique characteristics that differentiate you from other students. You should never create a deceptive, fictitious, or over-embellished application, but you should strive to present yourself as well as possible.

Most of the application questions that you will be asked require only short answers. For example:

- Did you work while you were in school?
- What clubs did you join?
- What honors or awards did you receive?

When answering such questions, you do not have much room to maneuver, but you should try to communicate as much information as possible in your short answers. Compare the following pairs of descriptions:

- *Member of Orchestra*
- *Second Violinist of the Orchestra*

- *Played Intra-Mural Volleyball*
- *Co-captain of the Volleyball Team*

- *Member of the AD's CSL*
- *One of three members on the Associate Dean's Committee on Student Life*

- *Worked at Billy's Burger Barn*
- *Weekend Shift Leader at Billy's Burger Barn (12 hours per week)*

In addition to the short-answer questions, some college applications invite or even require you to answer in writing one or more college admissions essay questions. (Note: The next section, "Six Ways to Jumpstart Your College Admissions Essays," covers in more detail how to write successful admissions essays.) The admissions essay—also called an application essay, personal statement, personal essay, essay question, or admissions question—is a written composition from a student, generally submitted to a college at the same time as the application documents. Some college admissions essay questions ask for only a limited degree of additional information. For example:

- In a paragraph, explain to us one reason why you want to attend this college.

Other essay questions are open-ended and require providing more information:

- Tell us additional information about yourself that you think would assist us in the selection process.

Still others are more thought provoking and require a reasoned and clearly articulated answer to the specific question:

- Describe a character in fiction, a historical figure, or a creative work (as in art, music, science, etc.) that has had an influence on you, and explain that influence.

The point of the admissions essay questions is for you to give the admissions decision-makers helpful information that might not be available from your test scores, GPA, and short-answer questions.

You should consider the admissions essay to be a highly significant part of your application for two reasons. First, answers to the essay questions will be your argument to the admissions personnel for your acceptance. The answers will give them additional reasons why they should accept you. Second, the admissions essay is one aspect of the application over which you can exercise real control. Your work experience is established, your GPA is already settled, and your ACT test has been scored. Those aspects of the application cannot easily be manipulated. The writing of the admissions essay, however, is completely under your present control.

What information should be included in an open-ended admissions essay (one that asks generally for more information about yourself)? You should devise arguments that interpret your academic, employment, and personal histories in such a way as to indicate that you have the ability to complete college and that you are committed to studying and later to pursuing a career in a chosen area of study. Clearly, you should stress your strengths. Your essay answer must not be a simple restatement of facts that are already in the application. Imagine, for example, a submitted essay that reads as follows:

> *I went to high school where I got a 3.5 GPA. I was a member of the Associate Dean's Committee on Student Life, and I worked as the assistant manager on the night shift at Billy's Burger Barn. Then, I took the ACT test and got a 25. I know that I will make a really good B.A. candidate and will enjoy my job.*

This essay is not very interesting. Furthermore, all of that information is redundant because it is already included in the answers to the standard questions on the application.

Instead, describe the facts of your life in such a way that they will be interpreted as good reasons for accepting you. Let's start with your GPA. If your GPA is lower than you would like, try to highlight certain academic facts that would suggest that your abilities exceed and are therefore not reflective of your overall GPA. Did you have a particularly challenging academic schedule that included honors or advanced placement classes? Did you have one especially bad semester (during which you took physics, calculus, and Latin) that pulled your average down? Did you participate in any unusual courses that required special activities, such as field research or independent study? Also, try to emphasize any non-academic facts that would legitimately be considered "important distractions" from your studies. Was there a death in the family or some other difficult set of circumstances that interfered with your studies? How many hours did you work in an average week? What extracurricular or family commitments took time away from your studies?

These points are significant and may have an impact on the admissions committee. For example:

> *The committee will see that my final GPA is 3.5. I should point out that the average would have been higher had I not needed to work 20 hours each week to save for my college education. Additionally, my grades in the first semester of my junior year were disappointing because my grandmother, who lived with my family and with whom I was very close, died. Finally, in order to fulfill the requirements for the honors program, I wrote a 20-page honors thesis on the Dutch fishing industry of*

the eighteenth century. I have included a copy of the introduction to my thesis with this application.

You should take the same approach to your work experience. For example:

During my junior and senior years in high school, I worked an average of 12 hours per week at Billy's Burger Barn as the shift leader on the weekends. I would report to work at 10 a.m. and get off at 4 p.m. As weekend shift leader, I supervised two other employees and was responsible for making emergency repairs on kitchen equipment. For example, once I was able to keep the deep fryer in operation by using a length of telephone cable to repair a faulty thermostat. The weekend shift leader was also responsible for maintaining order. It's no easy job to convince students who become too rowdy to leave without calling the police.

Of course, if you have considerable work experience (e.g., if you graduated from high school several years ago rather than just recently), you will want to describe that experience in more detail.

Can you say anything about your test score? Probably not much—the ACT test score is fairly simple and not usually open to interpretation. However, one exception that may be taken into consideration to explain a disappointing test score is illness. For example:

The committee will see that I have two ACT test scores, 22 and 25. During the first test, I had the flu and a fever and simply could not concentrate.

Finally, you must also persuade the admissions committee that you are serious about obtaining your college degree. You must be able to give an example of something in your background that explains why you want to go to college. Also, it will help your case if you can suggest what you might do with a college degree. For example:

As a prospective environmental science major, I interned with the Student Environmental Association. Working with private company executives who had themselves satisfied E.P.A. emissions standards, we convinced the University to stop polluting the Ten-Mile Run Creek. From this experience, I learned how business helps to protect our environment. I plan to make environmental resources my area of study, and I hope to work for the government or a private agency to protect the environment.

A word of warning is in order regarding your career objectives: they must be believable. It will not be sufficient to write, "I plan to solve the environmental problems of American industry." Such a statement is much too abstract. College admissions officers are also not interested in a general discourse on the advantages of democracy or the hardship of poverty. If you write, "I want to eliminate damage to the planet and to help private industries help themselves environmentally," then there had better be something in your experience that makes this statement believable.

Thus far, we have discussed the issues of ability and motivation. You may also wish to include information in a general essay answer that demonstrates to the school how you would help create a diverse student body with interesting talents, abilities, and perspectives. This additional information can be something dramatic:

One morning, a patron choked on a burger and lost consciousness. I used the Heimlich maneuver to dislodge the food and performed CPR until a team of paramedics arrived. The patron recovered fully, in large part, according to her doctors, because of my first aid.

Or, the information may not be dramatic:

My parents are Armenian immigrants, so I am fluent in Armenian as well as English. I would enjoy meeting others who share an interest in the politics, legal developments, and culture of that part of the world.

However, do not overestimate the value of this kind of information. It is, so to speak, the icing on the cake. These details about your life make you a more interesting individual and might tip the scale in your favor when all other things are equal. Keep in mind, though, that it will not get you accepted into a school for which you would not otherwise be competitive in terms of ACT test score and GPA.

Now, we turn our attention to matters of style. Your arguments for acceptance need to be presented in an organized fashion. There is no single preferred format, but you might start with the following outline:

I. I have the ability to succeed in college.
A. My high school studies are good.
1. I had one bad semester due to an illness in the family.
2. I was in the accelerated program.
3. I wrote a comprehensive term paper.
B. My work experience is good.
1. I worked during three years of high school.
2. I was promoted to shift leader at my job.
II. I have the desire to earn a college degree.
A. During my internship, I worked with Ph.D. recipients on the pollution problem.
B. I want to become a specialist in environmental chemistry.
III. I have unique characteristics.

The prose that you use should display your own natural style of writing. Do not write something that appears contrived. Admissions officers do not want to read essays that are written as manuscripts, with footnoted "documentary evidence." You should create your outline using as many arguments as possible. Then, you must begin to edit. For most people, the final document should not be more than a page to a page and a half in length—typed, of course! During the editing process, you should strive for an economy of language so that you can convey as much information as possible. Additionally, you will be forced to make considered judgments about the relative importance of various points. You will be forced to delete those ideas that are not really very compelling. In order to compose a really good essay, it may be necessary to reduce five or six pages to a single page, and the process may require more than 20 drafts. Make sure that you have at least one other person look at your essay—a teacher, counselor, or parent would be a good resource.

Because a number of colleges elevate the importance of the college admissions essay, more thorough recommendations are presented in the next section, "Six Ways to Jumpstart Your College Admissions Essays" (p. 618).

Solicit Effective Letters of Recommendation

Perhaps the best advice that we can give you about so-called "letters of recommendation" is that you should think of them as evaluations rather than recommendations. Indeed, many admissions officers refer to letter-writers as evaluators. These letters can be very important factors in an application, so who should actually write them?

First of all, some schools require a letter from the dean of students (or some similar functionary) at your high school. Essentially, this requirement serves as an inquiry into your behavior. However, colleges do not really expect that this person will have much to say about your application since in many cases students do not become acquainted with their deans. This letter is merely intended to evoke any information about disciplinary problems that might not otherwise surface. So, the best response from a dean, and the one that most people tend to receive, is just a statement to the effect that there is nothing much to say regarding your behavior. In addition to the dean's letter, most schools require, or at least permit, you to submit two or three letters of evaluation from other sources. Who should write these letters?

Remember that a letter of evaluation does not necessarily have to come from a well-known person. How effective is the following letter?

Francis Scott
Chairperson of the Board

To the Admissions Committee:

I am recommending Susan Roberts for college. Her mother is a member of our board of directors. Susan's mother earned her doctorate at the University of Chicago and she regularly makes significant contributions to our corporate meetings. Susan, following in her mother's footsteps, will make a fine college candidate.

Sincerely,
Francis Scott

The letterhead holds great promise, but the body of the letter is worthless. It is obvious that Francis Scott does not really have any basis for his conclusion that Susan Roberts "will make a fine college candidate."

Find people who know you very well to write the very best letters of recommendation (e.g., a teacher with whom you took several courses, your intern supervisor, or an associate with whom you have worked closely). A good evaluation will incorporate personal knowledge into the letter and will make references to specific events and activities. For example:

White, Weiss, and Blanche

To the Admissions Committee:

White, Weiss, and Blanche is a consulting firm that advises corporations on environmental concerns. Susan Roberts has worked for us as an intern for the past two summers. Her work is outstanding, and she is an intelligent and genial person.

Last summer, as my assistant, Susan edited a five-page report that outlined a way of altering a client's exhaust stack to reduce sulfur emissions. In addition to ensuring that the report was free of spelling and grammar errors, she noticed an important omission in the data table, which we were able to correct before submitting the report. Additionally, Susan assisted with a live presentation during a meeting with the client's board of directors and engineers. She was confident and even answered some questions about the procedures followed in testing the new system.

Finally, Susan made an important contribution to our company softball team. The team finished in last place, but Susan played in every game. Her batting average wasn't anything to brag about, but her enthusiasm more than made up for it.

Sincerely,
Mary Weiss

This letter demonstrates that the writer knows the applicant very well. The writer is able to address several aspects of the applicant's character, personality, and work ethic from a position of familiarity. A letter like this one makes for a very meaningful contribution to any college application, so you should strive to receive this type of recommendation as part of your application portfolio.

SIX WAYS TO JUMPSTART YOUR COLLEGE ADMISSIONS ESSAYS

An admissions director sits behind a well-lit desk in a paper-strewn office. Her window overlooks a large, rolling college campus. At mid-morning, students freckle the walkways, ambling to and from the surrounding lecture halls. Of current concern for this college admissions director are not the students already enrolled but the hundreds or even thousands of students who are seeking admission for the fall semester. Near the edge of her desk rises an already teetering stack of college applications, representing the academic hopes and dreams of soon-to-be high school graduates. Students from a wide range of high schools—big, small, public, private, home-based, rural, suburban, urban—have submitted their vital statistics: test score(s); high school transcripts with summaries of classes; GPAs; class rank; extracurricular activities; and references from teachers, coaches, club advisors, and counselors. These application papers assist her in differentiating one level of student from another (e.g., students with "As" and "Bs" versus students with "Bs" and "Cs"). She pulls out two applications with very similar test scores and GPAs and considers which of these two students will receive the coveted stamp of "admitted" on his or her file. Following this task, she will move on to the even more challenging task of mining through applications to find the small percentage of students who are "diamonds in the rough"; these students did not fully flourish in high school for various reasons, but they have the potential to succeed in a college environment.

As a high school student, your goals and aspirations are tightly interwoven with your ability to obtain admission to the college of your choice. Thus, as a student applying to various colleges, it is important for you to understand the selection or admissions process that these institutions of higher education use to narrow the pool of applicants. You should ask a number of probing questions about the process: What criteria do colleges use to admit students? How does the college admissions director decide between the merits of students who hold similar test scores and grades? How does a college discover those rare, under-qualified students who have not fully demonstrated their potential in high school through grades or test scores?

Of course, college admissions directors assess potential students using tools such as GPA, test score(s), teacher references, and extracurricular participation records. But colleges also use an evaluation instrument known as the admissions essay as a significant component in determining which students will or will not receive acceptance letters.

The admissions essay—also referred to as an application essay, a personal statement, or a personal essay—is a written composition from a student, generally submitted to a college at the same time as the application documents. The written essay—typically from 100 to 500 words in length—may answer a directed content question (e.g., an opinion on some current event), or it may respond to a simple "tell us about yourself" question.

The essay prompts listed below reflect actual examples of those delivered alongside recent college admissions applications.

- Write an essay in which you tell us about someone who has made an impact on your life, and explain how and why this person is important to you.

- Choose an issue of importance to you—the issue could be personal, school related, local, political, or international in scope—and write an essay in which you explain the significance of that issue to yourself, your family, your community, or your generation.

- Evaluate a significant experience or achievement, risk you have taken, or ethical dilemma you have faced and its impact on you.

- Discuss some issue of personal, local, national, or international concern and its importance to you.
- Describe a character of fiction, a historical figure, or a creative work (as in art, music, science, etc.) that has had an influence on you, and explain that influence.
- Make a rational argument for a position that you do not personally support.
- Share an experience through which you have gained respect for intellectual, social, or cultural differences. Comment on how your personal experiences and achievements would contribute to the diversity of our college.
- As you prepare to pursue a career in music, theatre, or dance, describe your thoughts on the relationship between the arts and today's society. How relevant has your art been to your community and to you?
- What outrages you?
- If you were given a grant to research a scientific or medical issue that you deem important to the world, what would it be, why would you choose it, and what kind of research do you think would have the greatest chance of being productive?
- What have you read recently that you found enlightening?
- Consider the books, essays, poems, or journal articles that you have read over the last year or two, either for school or leisure. Discuss the way in which one of these writings has changed your understanding of the world, of other people, or of yourself.

The admissions essay provides you with an opportunity to "sell" yourself and hopefully elevate your status from a potential student to a future student in the eyes of a college. In submitting this essay, it is important to view the process as a chance to catapult yourself beyond the other candidates. Confidently articulate why a particular college needs you as a student by emphasizing your unique goals, values, aptitudes, and abilities.

What follows are six strategies to help you jumpstart the writing of a college admissions essay. While these strategies can tell you neither exactly what types of questions will be asked (since some colleges ask questions that are quite broad while others ask questions that are very targeted and specific) nor what assessment criteria specific colleges use for evaluating the admissions essay (since each institution tightly guards this type of assessment information), they should provide valuable insights to consider as you begin the essay writing process.

Present Yourself as Unique, Exceptional, or Talented

Because college admissions directors read thousands of essays, you must write in a way that distinguishes you from the crowd of applying students. A large number of college applicants submit adequate to excellent GPAs along with solid test scores. Many have been involved in extracurricular activities, such as athletics, honors clubs, music, or drama. Others have participated in a wide range of leadership or volunteer roles. Given this large pool of truly qualified students, you must leave an impression that makes you positively memorable as a candidate for admission by seizing the opportunity to compose a well-crafted essay that highlights your best characteristics and your achievements.

In preparation for writing the essay, think clearly and creatively about what makes you unique, exceptional, or talented as a potential college student. What unique experiences have you had? Do you have abilities or aptitudes that set you apart from other students? In what special events or activities have you participated? What unique cultural experiences have you encountered? Is there anything special about how or where you grew up? Have you met famous or unique people who have influenced you? Are you exceptionally talented in a particular area, such as music, art, or drama?

What motivates you to succeed beyond other students? Do you have atypical work or employment experiences? How have you overcome an individual setback, struggle, or limitation? Have you participated in significant and/or memorable athletic events? Can you identify a unique hobby in which you participate? Have you volunteered or served in your community and made a significant contribution? Do you have a one-of-a-kind talent? Have you received any special awards or commendations? Have you distinguished yourself as a leader in clubs or organizations?

The following are examples of opening essay sentences that include the positive characteristics upon which a student might desire to focus in an essay. Consider how these statements might serve as springboards for powerful admissions essays:

- *Because my grandmother moved into my family's home when I was just ten days old, I have vicariously experienced a distinct and dissimilar culture from my own. I flood my days with friends and activities found in the high-tech, suburban, media-driven, adolescent-controlled culture of Tri-City High School. During the evening hours, however, I wander in a completely different culture immersed in the foods, songs, stories, and language of the "Old World" where my grandmother lived for more than fifty years.*

- *I personally do not know of any other high school student at South High School who has willingly dined on goat intestines, but while traveling over the summer with an international student exchange program, I embraced the opportunity to feast on this unique delicacy.*

- *Senator-elect Jamison shook my hand vigorously and commented to all those within earshot that he was sure my efforts had played a significant role in contributing to his recent election.*

- *Not every seventeen-year-old might jump at the opportunity to witness a three-hour long cardiac surgery from the operating room window of a teaching hospital. But I certainly did! Dr. Rose provided me with just such a privilege in celebration of my fourth year of serving as a volunteer hospital aid at New City Hospital.*

- *Performing with a choir at the governor's mansion may seem like less than a life-changing experience. But after speaking personally with the governor following the performance and asking her one simple question, my perspective regarding the world of women in politics radically changed.*

- *Losing every single game as a senior football player at Old Lake High School may not have taught me much about celebrating victories, but I did learn valuable lessons about perseverance, dedication, and humility.*

- *I never thought I'd write a computer program that other people would regularly use. But after a friend introduced me to the world of open-source coding, I fervently dove into writing new code and improving existing code on a variety of programs that some major companies utilize every day.*

- *Working weekends at Billy B's Barbeque during high school not only allowed me to earn money for college, but it also brought me face to face with a host of truly fascinating "regulars" whose life stories I will never forget.*

- *For years, because of my love for reading, each and every librarian at the Key City public library knew me by name. But now, because of my love for writing, everyone who reads the Key City Times newspaper also knows me by name.*

- *I was shocked and honored when my name was called as the regional swimmer of the year, especially considering that my pediatrician had warned me that childhood asthma would forever hinder my ability to compete in athletics.*

Remember that the main goal in writing an admissions essay is to distinguish yourself from the other applicants. Note how this next example of a college essay response to the prompt "What has influenced your desire to study history at New College University?" shines light on a unique relationship that led to exceptional experiences.

At first blush, I look like a typical all-American girl. But I truly live a double identity. From the very day that my grandmother moved into my family's home when I was just ten days old, I have vicariously experienced a distinct and dissimilar culture from my own. I flood my days with friends and activities found in the high-tech, suburban, media-driven, adolescent-controlled culture of Tri-City High School. During the evening hours, however, I wander in a completely different culture immersed in the foods, songs, stories, and language of the "Old World" where my grandmother lived for more than fifty years.

Seeded by the nightly songs and stories of my grandmother, I had for years envisioned scenes of the Italian countryside with narrow streets and quiet villas. In an almost mystical manner, I could smell chickens roasting on open-air fireplaces, feel the breezes off the sea of the Sicilian coast, see the workers harvesting grapes in the hillside vineyards, and hear the after-dinner songs rising from family gatherings. But as a junior at Tri-City High School, those far-away images became reality after I traveled to Italy to spend the summer of my junior year in Sicily as a participant in an International Student Exchange Unlimited program. I was amazed at how my grandmother's stories took tangible shape and substance over twelve memorable and life-transforming weeks.

I knew I would learn valuable lessons traveling the Italian countryside, visiting historical sites, and meeting a rich variety of local characters, but I did not anticipate that this adventure would change my perspective on the world and redirect my future. In my final weeks of the student exchange program, I joined a group digging for archaeological relics just outside the town of Salina. Through listening to the archaeology lectures from local university professors, I discovered that civilizations had for thousands of years settled and resettled the Sicilian shores and hillsides. As I participated in the archaeological dig, I touched shards of pottery left by some of the very earliest inhabitants of the island and helped uncover the burial grounds of ancient people. I read research and became acquainted with civilizations that I never knew had even existed.

This experience, spawned by my grandmother's influence in my life, launched in me a desire to study ancient civilizations and cultures. So, now I'm applying to New College University in order to study history and archaeology. I'm convinced that as a student at New College University I will continue to live a double identity, wonderfully captured between the pull of contemporary and ancient cultures.

Tell an Engaging Story

"The universe is made of stories, not atoms." Muriel Rukeyser

To effectively communicate how you are a unique candidate, tell an engaging story—or stories if word limits permit—of experiences that highlight those personal characteristics that distinguish you from other students.

Think about the last journalistic photograph in a newspaper, magazine, or website that captured your attention. The best photographs tell a story. As you look at a great journalistic picture, you gain an emerging sense of the event, the context, the emotion, the tension, the thrill, or the struggle embedded in the image. In the same manner, the best admissions essays also portray a story that imprints a lasting mark on the reader. When the essay prompts allow, you should consider organizing your essay around meaningful and moving stories that communicate how your hopes and dreams draw you to this particular college and a specific area of study.

Bear in mind this word of warning. As you write your essay, reemphasizing your GPA, ACT test score, or class rank in a bland format does little to draw attention to yourself. Remember that the pages of your college application and high school transcript already list these figures. Yes, these numbers do provide important information to the college. (That, in fact, is why the college requires you to provide them in the first place.) However, these numbers are not central to the purpose of an admissions essay. The core function of this essay is to determine whether you can clearly and concisely articulate, in written fashion, who you are and why you make a great candidate for entrance into a particular college. If your scores are exceptional and you can communicate them in a creative manner, include them in the essay.

Review the following examples of essay paragraphs, and note how telling significant information in a story or narrative form creates a more engaging and readable essay paragraph.

Essay Paragraph 1: Poor Example

As a student at Newbury High School, I was involved in four years of Student Council, Art Club, and the Yearbook. My GPA was a 3.9. I graduated in the top 5% of students in my class. I enjoy photography. I want to be an Art teacher.

Essay Paragraph 1: Better Example

The janitor laughed loudly as he saw my sweeping red hair catapult over the empty wastebaskets strewn in the hall after school. Again, I was literally running (down the school corridor) from my responsibilities as the Student Council representative for the Senior Class to join in assisting the Yearbook production team in hitting another important deadline. As one of two student photographers for Newbury High School, I had worked late into the night selecting the last three pictures to appear on the Yearbook cover and was now excited to hear the reaction of Mrs. Jensen, the Yearbook advisor, and the rest of the production team. During lunch, I had shown the photographs to other members of the Art Club, and they all gave them two huge "thumbs up." I was really hoping to please Mrs. Jensen with these pictures, since over my four years of high school, she had mentored and encouraged me, pushing me to achieve to the highest degree not only with my academics—I have a 3.9 GPA and will graduate in the top 5% of my class—but also with my many extracurricular activities. Because of Mrs. Jensen's example, I too want to be an Art teacher who pushes students to take new challenges and to succeed in both academic and extracurricular endeavors.

Essay Paragraph 2: Poor Example

I was selected as the #1 golfer in our state my senior year in high school. In my junior year, I was ranked in the top ten. I think my test scores and my GPA are high enough for you to consider me for a scholarship. I also play in the Jazz Band.

Essay Paragraph 2: Better Example

Innovation. For me, there is a deep sense of satisfaction in finding a unique or creative solution to a problem. In last spring's state high school golf tournament, I was leading the field by a single stroke walking toward the final green. An errant tee shot on my part had landed my ball behind a stand of bushes, and my coaches had groaned when they saw the precarious position of my lie. Thinking quickly—and innovatively—I grabbed my two iron and shot the ball not over the bushes as all would have expected, but under a gap below the bushes, rolling the ball cleanly toward the middle of the green. I sunk a remaining seven-foot putt and won not only the state high school golf tournament but also the #1 ranking that accompanied the win. Throughout my four years of high school varsity golf, I over and over again discovered innovative ways to succeed. It is this deep desire to innovate, to create new avenues to answers, and to find solutions to challenges that drives my love for problem-solving in the areas of mathematics and science. As a member of the Blackstone High School Jazz Band, innovation, too, is what drives my love for creative musical expression. And this love for innovation is what drives me to apply to the honors program at Lake City University, which is known nationally for its unique approach to educating students.

Telling an engaging story about some life experience is a powerful tool in distinguishing yourself from other students. Note that not every essay prompt can be addressed through the use of a story. Some call for a more logical or deductive approach. Nevertheless, when the opportunity to tell a story presents itself within the context of a specific essay prompt, you should seize upon that opportunity to tell why you are a great potential student.

Narrow Your Essay to a Specific Theme

A college admissions essay is typically limited to a certain number of words. As you can imagine, an admissions director does not have the time to read a multiple page treatise covering your entire life story from birth to high school graduation. As you organize your essay, focus your essay on one or two major ideas or themes that express your experiences, abilities, goals, attitudes, ideas, talents, or thoughts. Do not ramble aimlessly or muse recklessly without any focus or overarching structure. Instead, narrow the thrust of your essay to a specific and manageable theme.

Read the following winning essay submitted for a college scholarship contest. Note how the student tells how just one experience in her life—being cast in a play—caused her perspectives on life to mature and grow. Consider how she narrows her theme.

My heart was pounding out of my chest in an unfamiliar rhythm. I longed for water but knew there was not time. In the crowded area, pushed up against others, I could feel their breathing, as rapid and tense as my own. The anticipation was killing me as I swallowed hard and closed my eyes. Overcome with emotion, I cracked my knuckles three times—a habit I perform during extreme nervousness. My mind was flooded with last minute worries, and I tried with difficulty to push them away. I sensed a comforting hand on my shoulder and felt a rush of momentary calmness. "Everything is going to be O.K.," someone said reassuringly.

As the show was about to begin, my anticipation was replaced by excitement. As I looked out tentatively at the audience, I felt strangely secure rather than vulnerable on the stage. Suddenly, as if by magic, my worries were gone. I was no longer Malinda Spry, a seventeen-year-old-girl concerned about monologues, dance routines, and solos; I was someone else. I was Eve, and as the heart-wrenching words to "Children of Eve" escaped my mouth, the scene of expulsion from the beautiful Garden of Eden became my reality.

When I was cast in "Children of Eve," a musical chronicling the events of the New Testament, I was overwhelmed with giving voice to Eve. I was extremely grateful to be given this unique opportunity to represent such a complex character. As the woman held accountable for the presence of sin in the world, Eve is viewed as the villain in the creation story. However, before long, I saw the other side of Eve, the intelligent, curious, gifted side; the one responsible for humanity's successes in the world rather than its defeat. Although Eve carried the burden of original sin, she was amazingly strong and blessed with an innate desire to learn. I knew that it was my responsibility to portray the story of creation through her eyes. My portrayal of Eve included her passionate response to life in and out of paradise. Inspired, I recognized a parallel between Eve and myself.

I was exhilarated to bring Eve to life. She was never content with paradise, perfection, or the Garden, as Adam was. Instead, Eve asked the difficult questions and refused to accept life the way it was presented to her. She ardently claimed that it was God's will for humanity to be expelled from Eden in order to discover free will. Although Eve defied God, she found that He never abandoned her, a fact that strengthened my own faith in life.

During the closing moments of the performance, Eve implores God and the rest of creation—her children—for forgiveness. "We were just humans, to error prone," she says, looking around. The song brought tears to my eyes as I realized Eve's influence in all of creation and her profound lesson of forgiveness, not of betrayal, of love, not of hate. As I glanced around the audience, whose faces were filled with sympathy, I knew that they too understood the creation story from Eve's perspective—as it was meant to be told.

Start with an Engaging Hook and End with a Powerful Punch

An effective essay begins with an enticing start. In your essay, write an introduction that hooks the admissions director, compelling him or her to finish reading your composition. Craft your first two or three lines in such a way that they creatively engage the reader. These first sentences are so important that you may need to work and rework them until you find a great combination of words, setting a compelling hook and subsequent direction for your essay.

Here are some tips for creating engaging hooks (not all of them will be used at once, of course):

- Use active verbs (avoid passive verbs).
- Give a sense of feeling or emotion.
- Use a moving literary, historical, or provocative quotation.
- Provide a surprise, logical twist, or emotional shock.
- Use hyperbole.
- Present a definition.
- Interject a puzzle or riddle.
- Introduce an anecdote.
- Draw an example from a current event.
- Create suspense or drama.
- Convey humor (ONLY if you can do it naturally and tastefully).
- Avoid dull facts and figures.
- Ask a question that cannot be answered.

Remember that your introductory sentences must flow naturally into the entire theme of your essay. The introduction directs the reader toward your remaining thoughts or arguments.

As you develop a powerful hook, do not forget that your essay must answer the question that is asked. Make sure your introductory sentences help you to focus clearly and intentionally on the answer to the essay prompt. No matter how powerful your essay is, if you fail to directly address the prompt that is presented, you fail the essay.

Here are three examples of essay introductions that hook the reader into an engaging story.

Essay Introduction: Example 1

> *My feet clamped to the floor, immovable, after Mr. Smith called my name as Washington High School's "Student of the Year" at the annual award ceremony. As my shock faded and I coerced my limbs to stand and walk to the stage, I thought of all the people who had helped me achieve this award. There was Mr. Paulsen, my varsity basketball coach, Mrs. Simpson, my orchestra director, and Mr. Smith, the Honor Society advisor who had nominated me for the award.*

Essay Introduction: Example 2

"Diplomacy is the art of saying 'Nice doggie' until you can find a rock," quipped Will Rogers, the U.S. humorist and showman. The danger in practicing this particular philosophy of political diplomacy is that on occasion the dog wakes from its passivity, growls ferociously, and bites aggressively, all before the rock is found and exploited as a defense. Current research in the field of political science provides effective alternatives to this overused passive/aggressive approach to diplomacy that Will Rogers humorously presented.

Essay Introduction: Example 3

Why do I always smell barbequed pork ribs, deep-fried hushpuppies, and large mugs of black coffee in my mind when I think of my love for history? Working weekends at Billy B's Barbeque during high school not only allowed me to save money for college, but it also brought me face to face with a host of truly fascinating "regulars" whose life stories I will never forget. In Mr. Brown's World History class I had studied the causes and results of the Korean War. But it was not until I met Mr. Jacob Abbot—"Jake" to his friends—that I came face to face with the real history of that military conflict.

Here is an example of an entire essay that was submitted for a scholarship contest. Observe how this student creatively hooks the reader into the history of her deep desire to become a broadcast journalist.

"Where are my spoons," my mother would ask, commenting on the ever-dwindling supply as she washed dishes. By the time I was seven, my mother discovered that her missing spoons served as microphones, enabling me to host a "live" news show with my younger siblings. With the assistance of my "guests," we performed daily newscasts from our kitchen and living room. As the clock approached our bedtime, I would usher a "breaking news" segment.

Eventually, I learned that the profession of journalism involves more than "breaking news" or playing dress-up for a make-believe camera. As I became a devout viewer of Ted Koppel and "60 Minutes," several things became apparent. Journalism required remaining abreast of both historical and contemporary events, as well as a firm belief that public issues be viewed through the lens of people's everyday experiences.

As a junior in high school, I applied to and was accepted as a student intern at the local television station. This allowed me to move even further from the world of playing broadcast journalism to truly living and breathing it. The weekend news crew took me under their wings and allowed me to try almost every facet of creating the evening news.

While many years have passed since my broadcast days from my living room, I cannot disassociate myself from that little girl and her microphone. Indeed, that girl's dream has not dimmed, nor has the insatiable desire to transform it into reality. As an aspiring broadcast journalist, I hope to ultimately inform and advance larger discourses that affect the social, political, and economic welfare of our society. If admitted to Lincoln University, I want to hone my skills in order to one day tell stories of people at their best and their worst, narratives that speak of our curiosities, our hopes, and our struggles.

You must write your introduction to capture the imagination of the reader. Remember, however, that you must also construct a meaningful ending or conclusion. In the conclusion, attempt to answer the "why," "what next," or "so what" questions of your essay in a meaningful final sentence. Although the conclusion is a summary, do not merely summarize or reword your arguments or thoughts. Give the reader an understanding of the final step or next steps following your essay. Having told a moving story or made a powerful argument, now tell the reader what you want them to remember or do with your essay.

Consider these examples of conclusions:

- *If admitted to Lincoln University, I want to hone my skills in order to one day tell stories of people at their best and their worst, narratives that speak of our curiosities, our hopes, and our struggles.*
- *Now, having held a newborn baby in my hands, I strongly desire to invest my life in preparing to become a caring and skilled pediatrician.*
- *How did meeting Senator Smithson influence my desire to study at Big Valley College? Inspiration, inspiration, inspiration! I, and other women, can indeed succeed in the world of politics.*
- *Yes, my body was still shaking with frustration, anger, and even outrage from the experience. Those memories, to this day, still motivate me to pursue study in the field of clinical psychology.*

Organize the Essay Tightly and Arrange It Meaningfully

Because most essay prompts allow for 500 words or fewer, the organization of your essay answer must be concise and clear. Your introduction should flow smoothly into your first paragraph. Each paragraph must meaningfully follow the previous one. Between the paragraphs there should exist a natural parallelism in the alignment of thoughts, arguments, or ideas.

Prepare for writing your essay by developing a formal outline of your presentation. The elements of the outline must thoughtfully connect. Here are some ways that an essay might be organized.

- Comparison and Contrast
- Point and Counterpoint
- Before and After
- Chronological Sequence
- Cause and Effect
- Logical Progression
- Increasingly Effective Arguments
- Differing Scenes or Locations
- Conflict and Resolution

Read the following example paragraph written in a "before and after" format. Notice how the paragraph is tightly wound around a single theme but moves smoothly from the "before" to the "after."

> *I failed English class—twice! After the second failure, I sobbed intensely even as my guidance counselor comforted me by explaining this was quite forgivable given that I knew absolutely no English when I had arrived in the United States just two years before. Even in the midst of great compassion, I fretted over my inability to understand a noun from a pronoun, a verb from an adverb, or an infinitive from a gerund. My high school life, so I thought, was doomed, like a never-ending hell, to repeating freshman English over and over and over again. But then Mrs. Butler arrived. Like some rare powered superhero, this gifted teacher*

had the strength to bend my mind to understand not only the basics of the English language but also the complexities of story, poetry, and verse. With her help, I passed not only freshman English, sophomore Composition, and junior Literature, but I also passed the English Advanced Placement exam with high scores. So now, even as I apply to become an English major at Jefferson State College, I'm determined to return to the high school classroom, and like Mrs. Butler, rescue those who desire not to fail anymore.

Use Proper English

This might sound like overly simplistic advice, but college admissions directors use the essay to determine whether you can write on a college-appropriate level. To impress a college, you must write in a style that follows all the rules of formal English.

As you edit your essay, check for (among other things):

- Proper grammar
- Correct punctuation
- Appropriate word usage
- Normal capitalization
- Proper spelling
- Appropriate abbreviations
- Correct notation of sources (if used)
- Normal pagination and spacing

Find someone to help proofread your essay before you submit it to the college. Consult an English instructor at your high school for direct help in proofreading your essay or for references to someone else who might be available to help.

Bonus Tips

Here are some additional tips to consider as you compose college admissions essays.

- Do not over embellish, lie about, or fabricate your experiences.
- Research and double-check any facts, dates, or numbers that you use.
- Do not overuse words from a thesaurus that you do not normally use.
- Never plagiarize an essay or portions of an essay.
- Do not tell someone else's story or experience as your own.
- Be yourself; find your own voice; be natural.
- Write about something you are passionate about.

- Do not drop names (especially if you do not have a real relationship with the person).
- Avoid clichés and slang.
- Do not try to be overly cute or trite.
- Use specific details, not just generalizations.
- Start the writing process early.
- Write, rewrite, and rewrite again.
- Ask a teacher or advisor to read your essay and provide feedback.
- Do not beg. ("I really, really, really want to attend your college.")
- Avoid odd fonts or unusual paper that might distract from the content of your essay.
- Proofread, proofread, and proofread!

Conclusion

"A finished person is a boring person." Anna Quindlen

For the vast majority of college admissions essays there exist no right or perfect answers. Instead, the college provides you blank space to fill with a well-composed and creative statement reflecting your uniqueness as a person. The questions asked will vary. But always remember that the answers you provide should point to yourself as a future college student who has untapped potential, talent, and ability. Good luck!

Appendix A:

Answers and Explanations

ENGLISH

LESSON (p. 16)

1. A
2. G
3. B
4. H
5. D
6. G
7. C
8. H
9. B
10. F
11. A
12. K
13. E
14. F
15. D
16. G
17. D
18. H
19. C
20. J
21. C
22. F
23. E
24. H
25. E
26. J
27. A
28. G
29. A
30. J
31. B
32. J
33. A
34. J
35. D
36. G
37. D
38. J
39. B
40. F
41. B
42. G
43. A
44. K
45. D
46. H
47. C
48. H
49. D
50. H
51. A
52. F
53. D
54. F
55. A
56. G
57. C
58. G
59. C
60. H
61. B
62. K
63. B
64. K
65. A
66. H
67. B
68. H
69. E
70. J
71. B
72. G
73. D
74. H
75. A
76. H
77. C
78. K
79. B
80. H
81. B
82. K
83. E
84. K
85. A
86. K
87. B
88. H
89. A
90. H
91. B
92. H
93. E
94. K
95. B
96. H
97. D
98. K
99. D
100. G
101. A
102. F
103. B
104. J
105. C
106. G
107. B
108. J
109. B
110. J
111. A
112. H
113. A
114. K
115. –
116. D
117. J
118. D
119. G
120. B
121. F
122. B
123. J
124. A
125. F
126. B
127. G
128. C
129. G
130. E
131. J
132. B
133. J
134. B
135. F
136. B
137. F
138. D
139. H
140. A
141. F
142. B
143. J
144. D
145. H

QUIZZES (p. 35)

QUIZ I

1. B	**17.** B
2. F	**18.** H
3. B	**19.** C
4. F	**20.** J
5. C	**21.** C
6. F	**22.** F
7. D	**23.** A
8. J	**24.** G
9. A	**25.** B
10. J	**26.** H
11. C	**27.** D
12. J	**28.** G
13. B	**29.** C
14. H	**30.** G
15. A	**31.** B
16. J	**32.** H

QUIZ II

1. D	**17.** D
2. F	**18.** F
3. D	**19.** C
4. J	**20.** G
5. C	**21.** A
6. F	**22.** J
7. B	**23.** B
8. G	**24.** H
9. A	**25.** D
10. F	**26.** H
11. B	**27.** D
12. F	**28.** F
13. B	**29.** B
14. G	
15. D	
16. F	

QUIZ III

1. B	**17.** C
2. H	**18.** J
3. B	**19.** C
4. F	**20.** F
5. C	**21.** A
6. F	**22.** G
7. C	**23.** A
8. H	**24.** G
9. D	**25.** A
10. J	**26.** H
11. C	**27.** C
12. G	**28.** J
13. A	**29.** A
14. F	**30.** G
15. C	**31.** B
16. J	

REVIEW (p. 53)

1. A	**8.** F	**15.** A	**22.** G	**29.** B	**36.** G	**43.** C
2. J	**9.** D	**16.** G	**23.** B	**30.** H	**37.** C	**44.** H
3. B	**10.** H	**17.** B	**24.** J	**31.** B	**38.** G	**45.** A
4. H	**11.** A	**18.** G	**25.** A	**32.** H	**39.** A	**46.** F
5. A	**12.** F	**19.** D	**26.** H	**33.** A	**40.** F	**47.** B
6. F	**13.** A	**20.** G	**27.** A	**34.** G	**41.** A	**48.** H
7. A	**14.** J	**21.** D	**28.** F	**35.** D	**42.** H	

MATHEMATICS

CALCULATOR EXERCISE (p. 81)

1. D; 1
2. K; 2
3. B; 2
4. F; 3
5. A; 1
6. H; 2
7. D; 3
8. F; 3
9. E; 3
10. H; 3

LESSON (p. 83)

1. C
2. H
3. D
4. J
5. C
6. F
7. E
8. G
9. C
10. J
11. B
12. J
13. D
14. J
15. E
16. J
17. C
18. K
19. C
20. G
21. D
22. H
23. B
24. H
25. D
26. K
27. E
28. H
29. D
30. H
31. C
32. F
33. C
34. G
35. C
36. J
37. A
38. K
39. A
40. J
41. D
42. H
43. D
44. G
45. D
46. K
47. E
48. J
49. C
50. J
51. B
52. K
53. D
54. H
55. C
56. F
57. A
58. J
59. D
60. H
61. A
62. K
63. C
64. K
65. B
66. K
67. C
68. H
69. A
70. F
71. C
72. K
73. B
74. J
75. B
76. G
77. D
78. F
79. C
80. J
81. D
82. J
83. E
84. J
85. C
86. H
87. D
88. K
89. B
90. J
91. D
92. F
93. D
94. K
95. D
96. J
97. D
98. H
99. B
100. K
101. C
102. H
103. D
104. K
105. C
106. F
107. A
108. K
109. D
110. F
111. C
112. F
113. A
114. K
115. A
116. F
117. B
118. J
119. C
120. J
121. D
122. H
123. B
124. H
125. B
126. H
127. A
128. K
129. B
130. F
131. D
132. G
133. C
134. G
135. D
136. K
137. C
138. K
139. C
140. K
141. B
142. G
143. B
144. F
145. B
146. K
147. A
148. K
149. D
150. H
151. C
152. G
153. C
154. G
155. C
156. F
157. D
158. K
159. C
160. J
161. D
162. G
163. C
164. H
165. C
166. K
167. B
168. J
169. B
170. H
171. E
172. K
173. B
174. K
175. A
176. F
177. A
178. H
179. D
180. H
181. D
182. K
183. C
184. J
185. E
186. K
187. C
188. H
189. C
190. H
191. A
192. G
193. C
194. H
195. A
196. H

197. E	**204.** K	**211.** D	**218.** J	**225.** E	**232.** H	**239.** A
198. J	**205.** C	**212.** J	**219.** E	**226.** F	**233.** E	**240.** G
199. E	**206.** H	**213.** B	**220.** F	**227.** D	**234.** G	**241.** B
200. H	**207.** D	**214.** G	**221.** D	**228.** K	**235.** E	**242.** G
201. E	**208.** H	**215.** C	**222.** H	**229.** A	**236.** J	**243.** D
202. K	**209.** D	**216.** H	**223.** D	**230.** G	**237.** B	**244.** J
203. A	**210.** H	**217.** E	**224.** F	**231.** C	**238.** G	

QUIZZES (p. 126)

QUIZ I		**QUIZ II**		**QUIZ III**	
1. A	**11.** D	**1.** C	**11.** D	**1.** C	**11.** D
2. K	**12.** J	**2.** F	**12.** J	**2.** H	**12.** F
3. D	**13.** D	**3.** C	**13.** D	**3.** E	**13.** A
4. H	**14.** F	**4.** G	**14.** K	**4.** G	**14.** F
5. D	**15.** A	**5.** C	**15.** E	**5.** D	**15.** C
6. J	**16.** G	**6.** H	**16.** H	**6.** G	**16.** G
7. E	**17.** E	**7.** B	**17.** B	**7.** B	**17.** C
8. J	**18.** J	**8.** J	**18.** H	**8.** F	**18.** G
9. B	**19.** C	**9.** A	**19.** E	**9.** D	**19.** E
10. H	**20.** J	**10.** H	**20.** J	**10.** J	**20.** H

REVIEW (p. 139)

1. B	**6.** J	**11.** A	**16.** K	**21.** B	**26.** F	**31.** E
2. H	**7.** B	**12.** J	**17.** B	**22.** G	**27.** E	**32.** K
3. C	**8.** J	**13.** C	**18.** G	**23.** A	**28.** J	
4. K	**9.** C	**14.** K	**19.** C	**24.** G	**29.** D	
5. D	**10.** J	**15.** B	**20.** H	**25.** B	**30.** H	

READING

LESSON (p. 163)

1. C
2. F
3. A
4. J
5. B
6. J
7. C
8. H
9. D
10. J
11. A
12. J
13. A
14. H
15. C
16. G
17. D
18. F
19. D
20. H
21. B
22. G
23. A
24. G
25. A
26. F
27. A
28. H
29. C
30. F
31. A
32. G
33. D
34. G
35. D
36. J
37. C
38. J
39. A
40. H
41. A
42. H
43. D
44. G
45. A
46. J
47. C
48. F
49. D
50. J
51. C
52. G
53. D
54. F
55. B
56. H
57. A
58. J
59. C
60. J
61. D
62. F
63. D
64. H
65. A
66. H
67. C
68. G
69. B
70. G
71. B
72. F
73. D
74. J
75. C
76. G
77. D
78. F
79. B
80. J
81. B
82. F
83. D
84. G
85. A
86. F
87. B
88. J
89. B
90. J
91. C
92. H
93. C
94. G
95. C
96. H
97. B
98. J
99. B
100. J
101. D
102. H
103. D
104. H
105. B
106. J
107. C
108. H
109. B
110. J
111. C
112. F
113. D
114. H
115. B
116. H
117. D
118. F
119. A
120. J
121. A
122. J
123. C
124. G
125. B
126. G
127. D
128. G
129. C
130. H

QUIZZES (p. 194)

QUIZ I

1. A
2. H
3. A
4. G
5. A
6. H
7. D
8. J
9. B
10. J
11. D
12. F
13. D
14. H
15. D
16. H
17. C
18. G

QUIZ II

1. B
2. G
3. B
4. F
5. D
6. H
7. A
8. F
9. C
10. G
11. D
12. G
13. B
14. H
15. A
16. J
17. C

QUIZ III

1. C
2. G
3. D
4. F
5. B
6. G
7. C
8. F
9. D
10. J
11. D
12. H
13. D
14. H
15. A
16. G
17. B
18. G

REVIEW (p. 206)

1. D	**10.** J	**19.** D	**28.** J	**37.** D	**46.** F	**55.** A
2. G	**11.** B	**20.** F	**29.** C	**38.** G	**47.** B	**56.** F
3. C	**12.** F	**21.** D	**30.** J	**39.** B	**48.** G	**57.** D
4. J	**13.** C	**22.** J	**31.** A	**40.** F	**49.** A	**58.** F
5. A	**14.** F	**23.** C	**32.** J	**41.** B	**50.** H	**59.** D
6. F	**15.** B	**24.** G	**33.** D	**42.** H	**51.** D	**60.** H
7. C	**16.** F	**25.** C	**34.** F	**43.** D	**52.** G	**61.** C
8. J	**17.** C	**26.** J	**35.** D	**44.** H	**53.** A	**62.** G
9. B	**18.** G	**27.** A	**36.** H	**45.** D	**54.** H	

SCIENCE

LESSON (p. 241)

1. B	**9.** C	**17.** B	**25.** A	**33.** D	**41.** B	**49.** D
2. F	**10.** H	**18.** H	**26.** H	**34.** J	**42.** H	**50.** G
3. C	**11.** A	**19.** C	**27.** A	**35.** C	**43.** C	**51.** C
4. G	**12.** H	**20.** H	**28.** J	**36.** J	**44.** J	**52.** F
5. C	**13.** D	**21.** A	**29.** B	**37.** A	**45.** A	**53.** D
6. H	**14.** F	**22.** J	**30.** G	**38.** G	**46.** H	**54.** F
7. D	**15.** D	**23.** D	**31.** B	**39.** D	**47.** B	
8. H	**16.** F	**24.** G	**32.** F	**40.** G	**48.** H	

QUIZZES (p. 258)

QUIZ I		**QUIZ II**		**QUIZ III**		
1. D	**6.** J	**1.** A	**6.** H	**1.** C	**6.** F	**11.** C
2. J	**7.** B	**2.** F	**7.** D	**2.** G	**7.** A	
3. D	**8.** H	**3.** A	**8.** F	**3.** C	**8.** H	
4. F	**9.** A	**4.** J	**9.** C	**4.** H	**9.** B	
5. C	**10.** G	**5.** C	**10.** G	**5.** A	**10.** G	

REVIEW (p. 270)

1. D	**12.** G	**23.** A	**34.** H	**45.** B	**56.** F	**67.** A
2. F	**13.** D	**24.** G	**35.** C	**46.** H	**57.** D	**68.** G
3. B	**14.** H	**25.** C	**36.** J	**47.** C	**58.** F	**69.** B
4. G	**15.** A	**26.** H	**37.** B	**48.** F	**59.** C	**70.** H
5. C	**16.** G	**27.** D	**38.** G	**49.** D	**60.** G	**71.** C
6. G	**17.** C	**28.** H	**39.** D	**50.** G	**61.** A	**72.** J
7. C	**18.** J	**29.** B	**40.** G	**51.** C	**62.** F	
8. G	**19.** A	**30.** G	**41.** B	**52.** H	**63.** C	
9. B	**20.** G	**31.** C	**42.** H	**53.** B	**64.** J	
10. J	**21.** B	**32.** H	**43.** C	**54.** G	**65.** A	
11. A	**22.** H	**33.** C	**44.** J	**55.** B	**66.** G	

WRITING

LESSON (p. 302)

Sample Essay Outline

I. Introduction
   A. Thesis: Rural life offers the best quality of life.

II. Urban life is stressful.
   A. "Street people" (who may need intervention)
   B. Traffic (delays during travel from one place to another)
   C. Lack of community

III. In rural areas, each person can have more of an impact within the community.
   A. Shared problems and solutions within a small community lead to personal responsibility.
   B. Because the community is small, there is more chance of recognition.

IV. In rural areas, there are fewer demands on personal time
   A. Less commuting
   B. Less traffic
   C. Fewer lines

V. Conclusion
   A. Restatement of Thesis: Rural life provides the best quality of life because it is less stressful; it provides a good sense of community; and, finally, it allows for better usage of time.

Sample Essay—Above Average Response

At some point, every adult must make a decision about whether he or she prefers rural life or city life. During the twentieth century, United States citizens "voted with their feet" and flocked to cities in large numbers. In more recent years, though, there has been a movement involving people who choose to move back to rural areas and the "simple life" it represents. For myself, I feel that rural life offers a superior quality of life. My opinion is rooted in issues related to emotional health, community involvement and opportunity, and how I can best make use of my time.

My first reason for preferring rural life relates to the issue of emotional health. City life is very stressful and difficult. Noise and traffic are annoyances 24 hours a day in a city. Cities also have large numbers of "street people," who may need intervention and assistance. Finally, cities are so overcrowded that any commute (whether in a car or via public transportation) is difficult and lengthy. In contrast, rural areas have none of these drawbacks. In a rural area, there is barely any noise or traffic. Rural areas also do not have "street people." Finally, rural areas are less densely populated so that it easy to travel from place to place.

My second reason for preferring rural life relates to the issue of community involvement. In a city, it is not always easy to become an active and involved member of the community. Cities have enormous numbers of people in them, and sometimes one can simply get lost and become a "face in the crowd." In addition, the scope of issues or problems in a city is sometimes so serious (i.e. widespread poverty, or endemic violence) that people can sometimes feel that one individual cannot make much of a difference. In contrast, it is comparatively easy to become involved in a rural community. In a rural area, there are simply not as many people; as a result, it is harder to "shrug off" one's responsibility to the community. In addition, although there are still problems in rural communities, it is frequently the case that the scope of these problems is more manageable; as a result, people in rural communities feel that they can, as individuals, make a difference and help solve problems.

My final reason for preferring rural life relates to the issue of how I can best make use of my time. In a city, there are countless ways in which your time is not your own. For example, there is always traffic that takes time to get through. Or there are always lines that must be waited in, whether it is at a grocery store or at a train station. In contrast, life in a rural community does not "steal" an individual's time in the same way. In a rural community, there is less traffic, less commuting, and no lines. As a result of having so much extra time, I would have more time to pursue my own interests.

In conclusion, I genuinely believe that the above reasons present a compelling case for preferring rural life over city life. In the past, there were very genuine benefits offered by city life. For example, it used to be the case that modern communications and healthcare were only available in cities. However, those benefits are now available all across the country, both in metropolitan as well as rural areas. The advantages discussed in this essay, though, are still only available in rural areas; so, in the end, I would definitely choose to live in a rural area.

Sample Essay—Below Average Response

Residents of rural areas insist that their life is better. People living in urban city areas prefer the lively life that they lead. Each has a viewpoint, but I feel that the city life is much better. Urban areas have good streets and roads and many things to do.

A city is closer together. Everything can be reached pretty quickly by car, bus, or even bicycle. The streets are maintained by the city in winter and summer. My Aunt in the mountains is snowed in each winter for days at a time. Sometimes traffic is a problem in urban areas, but that's the price you pay.

The urban areas have so many activities to do. Lots of movies, concerts, and sports events are always going on. Because the urban areas have more people and money, more famous artists visit there.

Some really important things in cities include good hospitals and healthcare. With lots of people there is a need for specialist doctors and great hospitals, even for children. I feel that I can find people in the city that share my interests whatever I decide on.

In conclusion, urban areas are the best places to live. Americans, and people around the world are moving from rural areas more each day to get to the excitement and opportunity of urban areas.

QUIZZES (p. 306)

QUIZ I

Sample Essay—Above Average Response

Study hall is beneficial to many students and should therefore not be eliminated from school. It provides the extra time needed to complete homework, review for a test, or even prepare ahead for future assignments. Since students are given the opportunity to take elective classes throughout the school day, study hall should be integrated into their schedule so that they may better manage their studies. Study hall especially helps students in the areas of time management, outside activities, and improved performance in subject areas.

Students under the strains of time management may require study hall just to keep up with their studies. Extracurricular activities, athletics, and after-school jobs can be very time-consuming and can distract students from their studies. In order to accommodate these activities, many students deprive themselves of sleep due to late hours of study at home. To a student who works after school to earn some extra spending money, or to help support his or her family, study hall may be the only chance to complete course work.

By allowing for some free time, study hall enables a student to broaden his or her skills and grow as a well-rounded person. Extracurricular activities and after-school jobs provide the necessary outlet for students to relax and socialize with their peers. Many students are even able to apply to their studies new skills learned in other environments.

Study hall is an elective that actually supports the required curriculum. Although many electives may be fun and interesting, students who take study hall can actually devote more time to math, science, and English. Study hall also provides a supportive educational environment that may not be available in every home due to the living arrangements.

In summary, study hall has many more benefits compared to those of having just another subject class. Students under oppressive time pressures can catch up with studies, expand their horizons with reading, and keep up in the face of outside activity demands with the help of study hall.

Sample Essay—Below Average Response

The study hall time I have each day is very important to me. Some schools have cut it out to add another subject to school. We only have so much time in the evening, and without study hall, students might never get their homework done. Study hall really helps students who need to work harder and students with part-time jobs, lots of chores, or athletics.

Students that have to put in a lot of extra work in subjects, really welcome study hall. They may have a poor environment for class work at home. Sometime help is available in study hall for problem subjects. Study hall has reference books not always available in the home. If you have study hall, you at least don't get more homework at that time. Some students just rest in study hall, and don't work on school. That is their choice if they want to waste time.

If you have a part-time job you really need study hall to do at least some of your homework. This also applies to athletes. They have hours of practice each evening and may be too tired afterwards to study well. Study hall provides a good break in the hard day at school, and lets students keep up better in the classroom subjects.

QUIZ II

Sample Essay—Above Average Response

At first, universal compulsory service might seem to be a good requirement because it is successful in other countries. But the real question for us is whether it would be a good idea here in America. I don't think so. America is unique in many very important ways. First, our way of life makes the idea of universal compulsory service unnecessary. Second, there are already many opportunities for volunteer work for those who want such an experience. Third, our fundamental notion of freedom means that service (such as the draft) can be required only in times of national emergency.

First, requiring universal compulsory service is not needed. When young people graduate or leave high school, they usually find jobs. Even those who go on to college will eventually get jobs when they graduate again. People that work, and that means young people too, pay taxes, and taxes are used to pay for government programs like roads, water and sewage, and aid to people in need. So, in a sense, everyone who is no longer in school and is working is already performing a compulsory service by paying taxes. There is no need to make those individuals do the actual work themselves.

Secondly, I believe there are already many opportunities for young people to volunteer for service. There is the Peace Corps for young people who might want to volunteer to help people in other countries. There is Habitat for Humanity for young people who like to work with their hands. There is the National Guard for young people who want military training. There is Big Brother/Sister for young people who want to work with children. Given these numerous opportunities to volunteer for service, there is simply no need to make service compulsory. Anyone who wants the experience of service can already get it voluntarily.

Last, but certainly not least, America is built on the idea freedom. Although this country is not perfect, most people believe it is wrong to force other people to do something they do not want to do. We do not tell people what church to go to, when to get up, when to go to bed, where they have to live and work, or who they should marry. The very notion of compulsory universal service is based on compulsion. In short, requiring people to do work they don't want to do contradicts our very notion of freedom.

There are some times when compulsory service is needed, as in a time of war. And hopefully, during such times, young people will gladly serve their country. But drafting young people into the military should be the exception and not the rule. In fact, the whole purpose of having a military is to defend our basic freedoms. It seems upside-down to sacrifice those freedoms in order to protect them.

In conclusion, I am strongly opposed to compulsory universal service. We don't need it in the first place because we pay taxes. Other kinds of service are already available for those who want to serve. And, most importantly, compulsory service is contradictory with our notion of freedom.

Sample Essay—Below Average Response

Its my opinion that high school graduates and young people leaving high school should not have to have universal compulsory service because it disrupts plans and interferes with freedoms. I'm not talking about the draft when there is a big war or something, because it is necessary. But having service when there isn't a war or anything is disruptive and interferes with freedoms.

One of our basic rights is freedom. The government isn't supposed to tell us where or when we can go that we want. But universal compulsory service will tell everyone when they graduate or leave high school when and where they have to go for two years. That's not freedom.

Also, people graduate and leave high school with important plans. Some young people want to go on to college. Some young people are going to get jobs and make decent livings. Some young people will go in the military because that's what they plan to do. When the government tells people it can't do these things, they interfere with the important plans of people as individual persons.

During World War II there was a draft and everyone had to go in the military. But remember that the U.S. was facing terrible enemies, even though Germany and Japan are our allies now. To keep them from taking over the world and the U.S. we had to have a military. That is not now the case. The military is volunteering.

Universal compulsory service would interfere with plans and violate freedom. For these reasons, it should not be done.

QUIZ III

Sample Essay—Above Average Response

The idea of an honor code is not new. West Point (the Military Academy) is famous for its honor code. It requires cadets to refrain from cheating and says that they must tell their superiors when they know about any instance of cheating at the academy. Would this model be a good idea for other schools? I doubt it. In the first place, the honor codes at military academies don't always work. Secondly, requiring students to "inform" on other students would break down the morale of the school. Lastly, even though an honor code might be appropriate in a military setting, it is not necessary in a regular school environment.

First, even though the leaders of military academies might think that an honor code is a good idea, the codes don't always work as they are supposed to work. Over the years, there have been scandals at the military academies. Sometimes these involve cheating, but sometimes they involve other kinds of unacceptable behavior such as sexual harassment. (Although sexual harassment is not the same thing as cheating, the idea of a "code" could apply here too.) These scandals don't occur all the time, but one thing is clear. When they do, they often involve many students. An entire class of math students might get caught cheating on the final exam. In other words, a lot of people are cheating. And with so many students cheating, a lot more must have known it and not said anything. That means that even in military schools honor codes don't work perfectly.

In the second place, an honor code would require students to "tell" on their classmates, and no one likes a tattletell. A student who "informs" will be ostrichsized by his/her classmates, even those who aren't cheating. Sometimes it may not be possible to know for sure when someone is cheating. Maybe you suspect someone of cheating but don't have any real proof. For example, you think they copied a paper from the web, but you google it and can't find it. Should you go to a teacher or the principle? What if you're wrong? But if you don't, then you're violating the honor code. An honor code would create a lot of problems like these.

Finally, there is a big difference between military school and regular school. A military school is built on discipline because that's the way the military operates. They are training soldiers, or pilots, or officers. In these jobs, people are expected to behave more honorably. In civilian life, people are not supposed to cheat, but they don't have to tell on other people who do. They have the option of just not being friends with them.

It seems that sometimes when there is a problem a drastic solution is needed. So if there is cheating, we need an honor code. We already have rules against cheating. If we obey those rules, we don't have a problem. If some people violate those rules, then the authorities should enforce them. In this way, the existing rules can do everything that we need to do.

Sample Essay—Below Average Response

I must agree with the teachers and administrators who say that honor code is a good idea. Honor code stands for honor and tells students what they are supposed to do. Students who know what they are supposed to do will behave different from students who don't know what they are supposed to do. If you don't know that there is cheating going on, then you can learn about them and report them.

Honor code can also make a regular school more like a military academy. When a regular school has the honor code, then it will have students that behave like military students. Everyone will trust everyone because they will know that no one is trying to get ahead with an unfair advantage such as cheating.

All students do not support the honor code. And I'm not just talking about the cheaters. Some students wont like the idea of having to report their friends who are cheating. That's tough. When someone is cheating, they are going against honor codes so they should be reported.

For the reasons that honor codes make schools more military and tell students not to cheat they would be a good idea. Thus, I am in favor of those teachers and administrators who like them.

TIMED PRACTICE TEST I

MULTIPLE-CHOICE ANSWER KEYS

DIRECTIONS: For the correct answer, check the corresponding unshaded box. Then, total the number of checkmarks for each of the content areas, and add these totals in order to determine the raw score for that test.

TEST 1: ENGLISH (p. 420)

	UM	RH		UM	RH		UM	RH		UM	RH		UM	RH
1. B	■		**16.** H	■		**31.** B	■		**46.** F	■		**61.** C		■
2. J		■	**17.** D		■	**32.** H	■		**47.** D		■	**62.** H		■
3. D	■		**18.** G		■	**33.** A	■		**48.** J		■	**63.** D	■	
4. G		■	**19.** A	■		**34.** J		■	**49.** C		■	**64.** G		■
5. A	■		**20.** F		■	**35.** A	■		**50.** F	■		**65.** D		■
6. H		■	**21.** C		■	**36.** F		■	**51.** B		■	**66.** F		■
7. A		■	**22.** H		■	**37.** B		■	**52.** F	■		**67.** A		■
8. G	■		**23.** A		■	**38.** H		■	**53.** B	■		**68.** F	■	
9. A		■	**24.** G		■	**39.** B		■	**54.** J	■		**69.** C		■
10. G		■	**25.** C		■	**40.** H		■	**55.** D	■		**70.** J	■	
11. C		■	**26.** J		■	**41.** D		■	**56.** G		■	**71.** A	■	
12. J	■		**27.** D		■	**42.** H		■	**57.** D	■		**72.** G	■	
13. B	■		**28.** G		■	**43.** A	■		**58.** H		■	**73.** B	■	
14. H		■	**29.** C		■	**44.** F		■	**59.** A	■		**74.** J	■	
15. A	■		**30.** G		■	**45.** C	■		**60.** J		■	**75.** B	■	

Usage and Mechanics (UM): _______ /44   Rhetorical Skills (RH): _______ /31   Raw Score (UM + RH): _______ /75

TEST 2: MATHEMATICS (p. 434)

	EA	AG	GT		EA	AG	GT		EA	AG	GT		EA	AG	GT
1. A		■	■	**16.** H		■	■	**31.** A		■	■	**46.** J	■	■	
2. K		■	■	**17.** B		■	■	**32.** H	■	■		**47.** A	■	■	
3. C		■	■	**18.** K	■	■		**33.** A	■		■	**48.** F	■	■	
4. K		■	■	**19.** A		■	■	**34.** K	■	■		**49.** C		■	■
5. E		■	■	**20.** F	■		■	**35.** D		■	■	**50.** K		■	■
6. H		■	■	**21.** D	■		■	**36.** J		■	■	**51.** C		■	■
7. D	■		■	**22.** G		■	■	**37.** C	■		■	**52.** J	■		■
8. H	■		■	**23.** C	■		■	**38.** G		■	■	**53.** A	■		■
9. D	■	■		**24.** F	■	■		**39.** C	■	■		**54.** F	■		■
10. G		■	■	**25.** E	■	■		**40.** G		■	■	**55.** D	■		■
11. B		■	■	**26.** G	■		■	**41.** D		■	■	**56.** H	■	■	
12. F		■	■	**27.** C		■	■	**42.** K		■	■	**57.** B	■		■
13. C		■	■	**28.** J	■	■		**43.** A		■	■	**58.** K	■	■	
14. G		■	■	**29.** E		■	■	**44.** G		■	■	**59.** A	■	■	
15. D	■	■		**30.** H		■	■	**45.** B	■	■		**60.** J	■	■	

Pre-Algebra/Elementary Algebra (EA): _______ /30   Plane Geometry/Trigonometry (GT): _______ /17

Int. Algebra/Coordinate Geometry (AG): _______ /13   Raw Score (EA + AG + GT): _______ /60

TEST 3: READING (p. 454)

	SS	AL		SS	AL		SS	AL		SS	AL
1. D			**11.** B			**21.** A			**31.** B		
2. J			**12.** F			**22.** J			**32.** H		
3. B			**13.** D			**23.** B			**33.** A		
4. J			**14.** J			**24.** H			**34.** J		
5. A			**15.** C			**25.** A			**35.** C		
6. G			**16.** F			**26.** H			**36.** F		
7. A			**17.** C			**27.** C			**37.** A		
8. F			**18.** H			**28.** J			**38.** G		
9. B			**19.** D			**29.** A			**39.** B		
10. F			**20.** G			**30.** H			**40.** H		

Social Studies/Sciences (SS): ______ /20 Arts/Literature (AL): ______ /20 Raw Score (SS + AL): ______ /40

TEST 4: SCIENCE (p. 464)

	B	C	P	ES
1. A				
2. F				
3. B				
4. H				
5. C				
6. J				
7. B				
8. H				
9. D				
10. F				
11. C				
12. H				
13. D				
14. G				
15. C				
16. J				

	B	C	P	ES
17. B				
18. J				
19. D				
20. F				
21. C				
22. F				

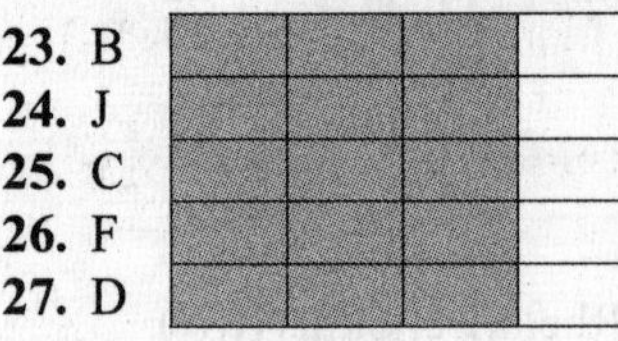

	B	C	P	ES
23. B				
24. J				
25. C				
26. F				
27. D				

	B	C	P	ES
28. G				
29. C				
30. G				
31. D				
32. F				
33. A				
34. H				
35. B				
36. J				
37. C				
38. G				
39. D				
40. F				

Biology (B): ______ /17 Physics (P): ______ /6 Raw Score (B + C + P + ES): ______ /40

Chemistry (C): ______ /12 Earth/Space Sciences (ES): ______ /5

MULTIPLE-CHOICE EXPLANATIONS

TEST 1: ENGLISH

1. **(B)** (p. 420) ***English/Rhetorical Skills/Style/Conciseness.*** The original sentence is needlessly repetitious: to begin means to start. (B) eliminates the unnecessary repetition.

2. **(J)** (p. 420) ***English/Usage and Mechanics/Grammar and Usage/Diction.*** The original sentence contains an error of diction. The correct word for making the comparison intended by the original is "from," not "than." ("Than" is a conjunction, and conjunctions are used to introduce clauses. What follows the underlined part of the sentence is a noun phrase, not a clause.) (G) fails to make the needed correction. (H) makes the needed correction but introduces a new error. In general, a modifier should be placed as close as possible to what it modifies. Here, "fundamentally" must modify "are different," but the placement of "fundamentally" after "from" suggests that it is intended to modify "weapons." Thus, (H) would result in an ambiguous sentence.

3. **(D)** (p. 420) ***English/Rhetorical Skills/Style/Conciseness.*** The underlined material is needlessly repetitious. A weapon of "mass destruction" is one "that could do a lot of harm." Eliminate the surplus material.

4. **(G)** (p. 421) ***English/Usage and Mechanics/Sentence Structure/Run-On Sentences.*** The original sentence is a run-on sentence. (G) solves the problem by starting a new sentence at an appropriate point. Neither (H) nor (J) solve the problem of the run-on sentence.

5. **(A)** (p. 421) ***English/Rhetorical Skills/No Change.*** The original sentence is correct. (B) destroys the logic of the sentence. (C) ambiguously implies that injuries are unavailable. (D) is needlessly wordy.

6. **(H)** (p. 421) ***English/Usage and Mechanics/Grammar and Usage/Diction.*** The original sentence is not idiomatic. (H) is idiomatic with "resulting from." (G) and (J) are not idiomatic.

7. **(A)** (p. 421) ***English/Usage and Mechanics/No Change.*** The original sentence is correct as written. The use of the subjunctive "would" correctly suggests that a nuclear war might or might not occur. (B) and (C) are both wrong because the indicative mood ("is" and "are") does not have this meaning. Additionally, (B) must be wrong because the subject of the sentence is the compound subject "number of deaths…and economic damage," and a compound subject requires a plural verb. (C) is also wrong because "as" makes the answer unidiomatic. In (D), although "might" preserves the element of contingency suggested by the subjunctive "would," the phrasing "more devastating even as" is not idiomatic.

8. **(G)** (p. 421) ***English/Rhetorical Skills/Strategy/Effective Concluding Sentence.*** In the second paragraph, the author is arguing that nuclear weapons are fundamentally different from conventional weapons because of their massive destructive power on multiple levels. (G) correctly summarizes this point.

9. **(A)** (p. 421) ***English/Usage and Mechanics/No Change.*** The original sentence is correct. The other choices introduce errors in modification.

10. **(G)** (p. 421) ***English/Usage and Mechanics/Sentence Structure/Run-On Sentences*** and ***Grammar and Usage/Pronoun Usage.*** The original sentence has two mistakes. It is a run-on sentence. Also, "it" is singular but refers to "weapons," which is plural. (G) makes both the needed corrections.

11. **(C)** (p. 422) ***English/Usage and Mechanics/Grammar and Usage/Diction.*** The original sentence is not idiomatic as written. The correct idiom is "neither…nor," not "neither…but."

12. **(J)** (p. 422) ***English/Rhetorical Skills/Organization/Paragraph-Level Structure.*** The original sentence is incorrect because a new paragraph should begin here. In the opening paragraph, the author announces that he or she will make three points. The second paragraph is devoted to the first point—the other two points should be presented in separate paragraphs.

13. **(B)** (p. 422) ***English/Rhetorical Skills/Style/Conciseness.*** The original sentence is awkward. (B) is more concise and reads better than the original sentence. (C) is incorrect because the subject of the sentence is the singular verb "step." (D) has the errors of the original sentence and inappropriately includes a plural verb.

14. **(H)** (p. 422) ***English/Usage and Mechanics/Grammar and Usage/Pronoun Usage.*** The ubiquitous "they" makes the original sentence ambiguous. Who are they? The other choices eliminate the ambiguous pronoun, but (H) is the most direct and concise.

15. **(A)** (p. 422) ***English/Rhetorical Skills/Organization/Passage-Level Structure.*** In the initial paragraph, the author announces that three considerations should guide our formulation of a defense policy. The author then proceeds to address each consideration.

16. **(H)** (p. 422) ***English/Rhetorical Skills/Strategy/Main Idea.*** Again, the author argues that three principles should guide our defense policy.

17. **(D)** (p. 423) ***English/Usage and Mechanics/Sentence Structure/Fragments.*** The original sentence lacks a main verb. (C) and (D) supply the verb, but (B) does not. ("Having viewed" is a participle form and cannot be a main verb.) In (C), "its" is intended to refer to "founders," but "founders" is plural.

18. **(G)** (p. 423) ***English/Usage and Mechanics/Grammar and Usage/Diction.*** The original sentence is not idiomatic. The correct idiom is "rather than," not "rather as." Both (H) and (J) are wrong because they too are not idiomatic.

19. **(A)** (p. 423) ***English/Rhetorical Skills/Strategy/Effective Transitional Sentence.*** This question tests understanding of the relationship between ideas in the passage. The idea discussed in the second sentence of the passage is the result or effect of the idea discussed in the first sentence.

20. **(F)** (p. 423) ***English/Usage and Mechanics/No Change.*** The original sentence is correct as written. (G) is needlessly wordy, so the original sentence is preferable. (H) destroys the logical structure of the sentence. The resulting construction would read: "Therefore, they viewed the kind of education needed for the new Republic largely in political terms instead of to academic excellence or individual self-fulfillment." (J) changes the intended meaning of the sentence by implying that the founders could have chosen to view education "as" academic excellence, rather than "as a means to" academic excellence.

21. **(C)** (p. 423) ***English/Usage and Mechanics/Sentence Structure/Fragments.*** The problem with the sentence as originally written is that it lacks a conjugated or main verb. "Talking" is a participle and cannot function as a main verb. Only (C) supplies a conjugated verb form.

22. **(H)** (p. 423) ***English/Usage and Mechanics/Punctuation/Commas.*** The original sentence is not punctuated correctly. "Goals" is an appositive that refers to "liberty," etc. The correct punctuation is a comma preceding the appositive. (G) is wrong because the period completely isolates the appositive from the sentence that supports it and turns everything following the comma into a sentence fragment. (J) is also incorrectly punctuated. The semicolon is too powerful—it signals that an independent clause will follow. An appositive, however, is dependent for its existence on the nouns that come before it, so a comma provides enough separation from the main body of the sentence without being too powerful.

23. **(A)** (p. 423) ***English/Usage and Mechanics/No Change.*** The original sentence is correct as written. To "take precedence over" is an English idiom meaning to be more important than something else. (B) distorts the intended

meaning of the original sentence. To "precede" means to come before in time, so the resulting sentence would make no sense. (C) and (D) are simply not idiomatic.

24. **(G)** (p. 423) ***English/Usage and Mechanics/Punctuation/Commas*** and ***Grammar and Usage/Subject-Verb Agreement*** and ***Pronoun Usage.*** The original sentence contains three errors. First, a comma, not a dash, must close the parenthetical expression signaled by the comma following "generation." (Dashes or commas may be used to set off such remarks, but not a mixture of both.) Second, the subject of the sentence is "generation," which is singular. So, the plural noun "assert" is wrong. Third, "their" refers to "generation" and so fails to agree in number with its referent. (G) makes all three changes. (H) makes two of the changes, but the semicolon is a mistake. The semicolon would be used to separate two clauses, but what follows the semicolon used in (H) is not a clause. Finally, (J) fails to correct the third error mentioned above and is incorrectly punctuated (a second comma is needed). Additionally, (J) uses the present tense verb "asserts," which is inconsistent with the other verbs in the selection.

25. **(C)** (p. 424) ***English/Usage and Mechanics/Grammar and Usage/Subject-Verb Agreement.*** The verb "was" is singular and fails to agree with its plural subject, "ingredients." (C) corrects this problem. (B) eliminates the problem of agreement. "Being" is a participle and does not show number. Unfortunately, since "being" is a participle, the resulting construction lacks a main verb, and the sentence becomes a sentence fragment. Finally, (D) distorts the intended meaning of the original sentence. The author does not mean to say that the principal ingredients of a civic education were "similar" to literacy and inculcation of patriotic and moral virtues.

26. **(J)** (p. 424) ***English/Usage and Mechanics/Sentence Structure/Run-On Sentences.*** The original sentence is a run-on sentence, with two clauses that run together without any punctuation or conjunction. (J) is one way of solving the problem: use a semicolon to separate the two clauses. (A comma and a coordinate conjunction such as "and" could also be used.) The dash cannot be used to separate two clauses, so (G) is wrong. As for (H), a comma by itself is just not strong enough to do the job.

27. **(D)** (p. 424) ***English/Usage and Mechanics/Sentence Structure/Problems of Coordination and Subordination.*** The original sentence contains an error of illogical subordination, compounded by a punctuation mistake. The two ideas joined at the underlined part have equal importance. One should not be subordinated to the other, but "since" always signals a subordinate idea. Additionally, a semicolon cannot be used to join a subordinate clause to an independent or main clause. (B) solves the subordination problem, but "and" signals a continuation of a thought. The second idea here contrasts with the first and should be signaled by a word like "but." (C) eliminates the punctuation mistake but creates a sentence fragment in the second half of the sentence. "Since" introduces a subordinate clause that must be joined to an independent or main clause.

28. **(G)** (p. 424) ***English/Usage and Mechanics/Grammar and Usage/Diction.*** The original sentence is not idiomatic. The correct idiom requires the use of the infinitive "to be" rather than the gerund "being." (H) and (J) both correct this error, but they also eliminate the only conjugated verb in the clause. The result is a fragment rather than a complete sentence. (G) correctly uses "to be" without introducing another error.

29. **(C)** (p. 424) ***English/Usage and Mechanics/Grammar and Usage/Diction.*** The placement of "almost" is not idiomatic. Given its proximity to "agreed," "almost" seems to modify "agreed" rather than "universally." The intended meaning of the sentence is that "almost" modifies "universally." (C) provides the correct and idiomatic placement of "almost." (B) is also not idiomatic. As for (D), although the words are in the correct order, the comma between "universally," an adverb, and the word it modifies, "agreed," disrupts the logical flow of the sentence.

30. **(G)** (p. 424) ***English/Usage and Mechanics/Sentence Structure/Faulty Parallelism.*** The underlined part is incorrect because it destroys the parallelism of the sentence. The sentence has a series of three elements: "emphasized," "put," and "attempt." However, the third element is a noun rather than a verb. (G) restores the parallelism of the sentence by supplying a verb. (H) fails to provide a verb. Finally, although (J) includes a verb, it also includes a subject. The result is a clause that is not parallel to the verb forms.

31. **(B)** (p. 425) ***English/Rhetorical Skills/Organization/Paragraph-Level Structure.*** The final paragraph contains a new thought that extends the logical development of the essay.

32. **(H)** (p. 425) ***English/Rhetorical Skills/Strategy/Audience.*** The passage is a discussion of old textbooks. Surely educators would be most interested in old textbooks.

33. **(A)** (p. 425) ***English/Rhetorical Skills/No Change.*** The original sentence is correct. (B) destroys the logic of the sentence. (C) and (D) are illogical because the sentence intends to refer generally to "the contribution of women" as a whole—not to the contribution of any particular individual.

34. **(J)** (p. 425) ***English/Usage and Mechanics/Grammar and Usage/Diction.*** The original sentence is non-idiomatic. (J) provides the correct idiom: "range…from…to." (G) and (H) fail to correct the problem, though (H) does change the noun "operation" to the verb "operating," creating parallelism with "knitting."

35. **(A)** (p. 425) ***English/Rhetorical Skills/No Change.*** The original sentence is correct as written. It is idiomatic, and the past tense verb "marked" is consistent with the other past tense verbs in the selection. (B) is wrong because the present perfect "has marked" implies an action that began in the past but continues into the present. (C) is wordy and awkward. As for (D), the use of the passive voice completely destroys the logic of the sentence.

36. **(F)** (p. 426) ***English/Usage and Mechanics/No Change.*** The original sentence is correct as written: "effort was made…to utilize." (G) and (H) are not idiomatic—"effort was made…being able to utilize" and "effort was made…utilizing." Finally, (J) destroys the logical structure of the sentence: "effort was made…and utilize."

37. **(B)** (p. 426) ***English/Usage and Mechanics/Grammar and Usage/Sequence and Verb Tense.*** The original sentence uses an incorrect verb tense. The present tense "falls" conflicts with the other past tense verbs of the selection. (B) and (D) both make the needed correction, but (D) is not idiomatic. The correct idiom is "falls within" a category. Although "falls in" is idiomatic, it has a meaning that is not appropriate here. (C) is grammatically incorrect because it eliminates the only conjugated verb in the clause introduced by "while."

38. **(H)** (p. 426) ***English/Usage and Mechanics/Grammar and Usage/Diction.*** The original sentence is not idiomatic. The correct idiom is "reserved for," not "reserved by." "Reserved by" has a meaning that is not appropriate here. (G) is needlessly wordy and ambiguous because it is not clear what the phrase is intended to modify. It seems to modify "women," but the intent of the sentence is for the phrase to modify "work." (J) is also wordy and awkward.

39. **(B)** (p. 426) ***English/Usage and Mechanics/Sentence Structure/Unintended Meanings.*** The original sentence uses an illogical transition word. "However" is used to signal a contrast, but the sentence that is introduced by "however" is actually a continuation of the thought contained in the previous sentence. (B) is correct; since there is no transition word, the reader will naturally assume that the next sentence will continue the train of thought. (C) is wrong because the use of "but" tells the reader to expect a contrasting thought. Finally, (D) is a fragment rather than a complete sentence.

40. **(H)** (p. 426) ***English/Usage and Mechanics/Punctuation/Colons.*** The original sentence is incorrectly punctuated. Since there is no punctuation between "activity" and "knitting," a reader will not pause after "activity." Consequently, "knitting" seems to be a participle that somehow modifies "activity." The author intends for "knitting" to be a gerund in the series including "knitting," "canning," and "planting." The correct punctuation in this series is the colon.

41. **(D)** (p. 426) ***English/Usage and Mechanics/Grammar and Usage/Pronoun Usage.*** The original sentence contains an error of pronoun usage. The pronoun "their" refers to "homemaker"—the singular "her" should be used. (B) eliminates the problem by using no pronoun at all. The resulting structure is a bit awkward ("could be demonstrating patriotism") but not incorrect. The verb in (B) is not acceptable. "Could be demonstrating" is inconsistent with the other verbs in the paragraph. (C) is incorrect—the verb "could have demonstrated" implies

that a woman might or might not have demonstrated her patriotism, but this is not the intended meaning. The author means to assert definitely that women did demonstrate their patriotism. (C) is also wrong because it fails to correct the pronoun problem.

42. (H) (p. 426) ***English/Usage and Mechanics/Punctuation/Commas.*** The original sentence is incorrectly punctuated. The colon seems to signal a clarification of the idea of hostessing at canteens. Instead, hostessing is one of a group of activities women volunteered to do. The correct punctuation is a comma.

43. (A) (p. 427) ***English/Rhetorical Skills/No Change.*** The material between the commas is an adjective phrase: "Army, dressed…and armed…with the Musket, was dispatched." The other choices destroy this logic.

44. (F) (p. 427) ***English/Usage and Mechanics/No Change.*** The original sentence is correct as written. The other choices disrupt the parallelism of the sentence. Since the two verbs "performed" and "laid" have a similar function in the sentence, they should both have similar forms. (G) and (H) use the passive voice and are not parallel to the active voice "performed." (J) is the participle and is not parallel to "performed," a conjugated verb.

45. (C) (p. 427) ***English/Rhetorical Skills/Organization/Passage-Level Structure.*** A way to fix the order of the paragraphs is to recognize that neither [2] nor [3] can be the first paragraph. "This" in the first sentence of [2] clearly refers to something that has come before.

Similarly, the phrase "much of the work" in the first sentence of [3] also refers to something that has come before. [1] appears to be the best choice for the first paragraph because [4] seems to be a summary or conclusion. Only (C) has [4] as the conclusion, so it is the correct answer.

As for [2] and [3], [2] must follow [3] because [2] is intended to contrast with [3]: most of the work was traditional but some was not. A reader cannot understand the importance of the contrast suggested by [2] without the information provided by [3].

46. (F) (p. 427) ***English/Rhetorical Skills/Strategy/Appropriate Supporting Material.*** Examples are often helpful, as they enable readers to understand a general point in a more concrete fashion.

47. (D) (p. 427) ***English/Usage and Mechanics/Sentence Structure/Fragments.*** "Undertaken" is the past participle of the verb "to undertake." A past participle is not itself a complete verb. (D) solves this problem by creating a sentence that uses the passive voice: "changes were undertaken."

48. (J) (p. 428) ***English/Usage and Mechanics/Grammar and Usage/Diction.*** The original sentence is not idiomatic. The sentence means to say that some people embraced the new values, and that is the sense of (J). (G) introduces an error in diction, substituting "excepted" for the intended word choice "accepted," as well as using the wrong preposition for "excepted." (H) is wrong for the same first reason that (G) is wrong.

49. (C) (p. 428) ***English/Usage and Mechanics/Sentence Structure/Problems of Coordination and Subordination.*** The two ideas joined at the underlined part contrast with each other: these did something; the others did not. To signal this contrast, something other than "and" must be used. "But" is an acceptable choice, so (C) is correct. (B) and (D) are incorrect because "since" and "consequently" signal a relationship in which one idea follows from or is the consequence of another.

50. (F) (p. 428) ***English/Rhetorical Skills/No Change.*** The original sentence is correct. By comparison, the other choices are needlessly wordy and awkward.

51. (B) (p. 428) ***English/Usage and Mechanics/Sentence Structure/Fragments.*** The comma and the conjunction "and" signal that the last half of the sentence is a clause. Yet, the original contains no main verb. (B) supplies a main verb in the right tense that also agrees in number with its subject, "notions."

52. **(F)** (p. 428) ***English/Rhetorical Skills/No Change.*** The original sentence is correct. This is the proper place at which to begin a new paragraph since the author is shifting from talking about the past to a discussion of the present. Since a new paragraph is needed here, (G) and (J) are wrong. (J) is wrong for two additional reasons: "Today, owing to the fact that...political life" is an incomplete sentence; and the use of "owing to the fact that" makes "democratic processes" the new subject which will no longer agree with the verb "is." "Triumph" is the necessary subject. Finally, (H) illogically isolates the subject of the sentence from its verb.

53. **(B)** (p. 428) ***English/Rhetorical Skills/Style/Conciseness.*** In the original sentence, "clear" is intended to modify "evident." However, that is a job that can be done only by the adverb "clearly." In any event, "clear" and "evident" are synonyms, so both are not needed. (B) is the best choice because it eliminates the redundant term "clear."

54. **(J)** (p. 428) ***English/Rhetorical Skills/Strategy/Effective Transitional Sentence.*** The transitional word must signal a contrast between two ideas. The best choice is "yet."

55. **(D)** (p. 429) ***English/Rhetorical Skills/Style/Conciseness.*** "Being" is a participle that can function as an adjective. However, there is no noun that can logically be modified by "being." What the sentence means to assert is that the lack of a stable value system is due to the influence of Western ideas. The word "since" in (D) is sufficient by itself to give the reason for the preceding part of the sentence. Both (B) and (C) are wrong because they are awkward.

56. **(G)** (p. 429) ***English/Usage and Mechanics/Sentence Structure/Unintended Meanings.*** "And so" distorts the logical structure of the sentence. It seems to introduce another clause, but what follows lacks a main verb. By eliminating "and so," (G) allows "emphasizing," a participle, to function as an adjective modifying "principles." (For purposes of such proximity, "emphasizing" could very well modify "democratic principles.") (H) results in a sentence that is distorted because "and" seems to join another verb to the first verb, "expound." However, "emphasis" is a noun, so the sentence reads: "textbooks expound...and the emphasis." In (J), "that" seems to introduce a relative clause, but no verb follows.

57. **(D)** (p. 429) ***English/Rhetorical Skills/Style/Conciseness.*** "Often sometimes" is not a possible phrase because the words have contradictory meanings. One of the words must be eliminated. All of the choices make this correction. (B), however, uses a verb tense that is inconsistent with the other tenses in the paragraph. In (C), "misinterpreted" and "distorted" are past participles and cannot stand alone. They require another verb such as "are."

58. **(H)** (p. 429) ***English/Usage and Mechanics/Grammar and Usage/Sequence and Verb Tense*** and ***Pronoun Usage.*** The original sentence contains two errors. The past tense "translated" is inconsistent with the present tense verbs in the rest of the paragraph. Also, "who" should replace "that" since the author is referring to people. Only (H) makes both corrections.

59. **(A)** (p. 429) ***English/Rhetorical Skills/Strategy/Appropriate Supporting Material.*** At the end, the author introduces the topic of Japanese youth; it would be appropriate for the discussion to continue along these lines.

60. **(J)** (p. 429) ***English/Usage and Mechanics/Grammar and Usage/Diction.*** The original sentence does not contain a grievous error, but it is not as idiomatic as (J). The placement of "always" directly before the main element of the verb, instead of before "has," is preferable to the original. (G) is wrong because "have" does not agree with the singular "humankind." (H) is wrong as the present tense is inconsistent with the introductory phrase "from the beginning."

61. **(C)** (p. 430) ***English/Usage and Mechanics/Grammar and Usage/Faulty or Illogical Comparisons.*** In English, if an adjective has more than one syllable, the comparative is formed by using "more" rather than by adding "-er."

62. **(H)** (p. 430) ***English/Usage and Mechanics/Punctuation/Commas.*** The comma following "agriculture" has no logical function in the sentence. (H) solves this problem by allowing it to mark the close of a parenthetical expression introduced by the first comma in front of "along." (G) attempts the correction but is wrong because the resulting phrase has no clear logical connection with the rest of the sentence. (H) does not have this problem. In (H), the noun "discovery" is the object of a preposition, and the prepositional phrase is connected to the rest of the sentence as a modifier of "domestication." (J) destroys the logical structure of the sentence by isolating the subject from the verb. The semicolon is too strong.

63. (D) (p. 430) ***English/Rhetorical Skills/Style/Conciseness.*** The underlined material is repetitious and therefore should be omitted.

64. (G) (p. 430) ***English/Usage and Mechanics/Sentence Structure/Faulty Parallelism*** and ***Grammar and Usage/Pronoun Usage.*** The original sentence contains two errors. First, it lacks parallelism. As written, it reads: "between regarding…and to consider." Second, the pronoun "them" does not agree in number with its antecedent "animal." Only (G) corrects both of these problems. (H) solves the problem of parallelism but fails to eliminate the wrong pronoun. (J) does not correct either mistake.

65. (D) (p. 430) ***English/Usage and Mechanics/Sentence Structure/Misplaced Modifiers*** and ***Grammar and Usage/Sequence and Verb Tense.*** The original sentence contains two errors. First, the placement of "seemingly" is incorrect. It is intended to modify "every," which in turn modifies "subject." However, its placement in front of the verb seems to suggest that Aristotle "seemingly" wrote. Second, the present tense "writes" is inconsistent with the other verbs in the paragraph (e.g., "seemed" and "took"). (Note: The present tense verbs are used to describe our attitudes today. Although Aristotle wrote in the past, we currently have certain attitudes about those writings.) (B) corrects the second problem but not the first. Simply putting "seemingly" into parentheses does not clarify what the word is supposed to modify. As for (C), while it eliminates the problem of verb tense by reducing the verb to a participle modifying "Aristotle," there is still the ambiguity created by "seemingly."

66. (F) (p. 430) ***English/Usage and Mechanics/No Change.*** The original sentence is correct as written. The comma following "subject" marks the end of the introductory dependent clause. Since punctuation is needed at that point, (H) is wrong. The correct punctuation is a comma. The semicolon and the colon are both too powerful, so (G) and (J) are wrong as well.

67. (A) (p. 430) ***English/Usage and Mechanics/Sentence Structure/Problems of Coordination and Subordination.*** The transition word here must connect the two ideas: Aristotle was interested in all life; he was particularly interested in marine life. "And" correctly coordinates these two ideas. Had the passage gone on to discuss marine life in particular, then the contrast set up by "but" in (C) would make it the better choice.

68. (F) (p. 430) ***English/Rhetorical Skills/No Change.*** The original sentence is correct as written. "Wedding" is a participle that modifies "observer." (G) distorts the intended meaning by suggesting that Aristotle was himself joined to something. The sentence means to say that Aristotle joined two ideas. (H) is needlessly wordy and awkward. Finally, (J) creates a prepositional phrase that does not clearly modify any other element in the sentence.

69. (C) (p. 431) ***English/Usage and Mechanics/Punctuation/Quotation Marks.*** The original sentence is incorrectly punctuated. Quotation marks must be used to indicate the start of the quotation. (B) fails to make this correction and makes another error of punctuation. A dash cannot be used instead of a period. (D) is wrong because the adverb "simply" cannot be used as a predicate complement; that is, "simply" cannot modify the subject of the sentence.

70. (J) (p. 431) ***English/Rhetorical Skills/Style/Conciseness.*** The underlined material is repetitious and therefore should be omitted.

71. (A) (p. 431) ***English/Rhetorical Skills/No Change.*** The original sentence is correct. By comparison, the other choices are needlessly wordy and awkward.

72. (G) (p. 431) ***English/Rhetorical Skills/Strategy/Appropriate Supporting Material.*** The author's use of Aristotle's own words is particularly forceful. It lets Aristotle make the point for himself.

73. (B) (p. 431) ***English/Rhetorical Skills/Strategy/Audience.*** The passage is expository but not overly technical, so (A) and (D) are wrong. Since the main topic is Aristotle, (B) is the best choice.

74. (J) (p. 432) ***English/Rhetorical Skills/Strategy/Main Idea.*** As stated in the first sentence of the second paragraph of the passage, the essay intends to show how the animal world became a source of serious study because of Aristotle.

75. (B) (p. 432) ***English/Rhetorical Skills/Organization/Paragraph-Level Structure.*** The function of the first paragraph is to place Aristotle in a certain context.

TEST 2: MATHEMATICS

1. (A) (p. 434) ***Mathematics/Algebra/Solving Algebraic Equations or Inequalities with One Variable/Equations Involving Rational Expressions.*** Solve for x: $\frac{1}{x}+\frac{1}{x}=8 \Rightarrow \frac{2}{x}=8 \Rightarrow x=\frac{1}{4}$. Also, one can reason that $\frac{1}{x}$ and $\frac{1}{x}$ are equal, and since their sum is 8, $\frac{1}{x}$ equals 4. Thus, $x=\frac{1}{4}$.

2. (K) (p. 434) ***Mathematics/Algebra/Expressing and Evaluating Algebraic Functions/Function Notation.*** $3x-4y=3(2)-4(-1)=6+4=10$.

3. (C) (p. 435) ***Mathematics/Arithmetic/Common Arithmetic Items/Percents.*** 20% of 600 boys equals $0.20(600)=120$ boys on the honor roll. 30% of 400 girls equals $0.30(400)=120$ girls on the honor roll. Therefore, there are 120 boys + 120 girls = 240 students on honor roll.

4. (K) (p. 435) ***Mathematics/Arithmetic/Common Arithmetic Items/Properties of Numbers.*** Since an even number times any other whole number yields an even number, the correct answer is (K). Since the variable t is outside the brackets and parentheses, it must be multiplied by everything within the brackets and parentheses. Therefore, t must be even. None of the other letters guarantees an even result.

Alternatively, for each letter, assume that that letter only is even and that all other numbers are odd. Only t generates an even result under those circumstances.

5. (E) (p. 435) ***Mathematics/Statistics and Probability/Data Representation/Tables (Matrices).*** The trick of this question is to see that the number of flies in each successive week is four times the number of the previous week. The final count should be $4 \bullet 192 = 768$.

6. (H) (p. 436) ***Mathematics/Arithmetic/Simple Manipulations*** and ***Statistics and Probability.*** Use the formula for finding the number of permutations: $3! = 3 \bullet 2 \bullet 1 = 6$.

Alternatively, simply count the number of possibilities: *ABC, ACB, BAC, BCA, CAB, CBA*.

7. (D) (p. 436) ***Mathematics/Coordinate Geometry/The Coordinate System.*** Since the x-coordinate of both points is 2, the line runs parallel to the y-axis. The x-coordinate of the midpoint will also be 2. As for the y-coordinate, the midpoint is halfway between 2 and −2: 0.

8. (H) (p. 436) ***Mathematics/Algebra/Solving Algebraic Equations or Inequalities with One Variable/Equations Involving Absolute Value.*** Since the absolute value of xy is positive, xy itself must be positive (since $|xy| = xy$).

Therefore, both x and y have the same sign. They might both be positive, or they might both be negative. (F), (G), (J), and (K) can all be true; x and y cannot, however, have different signs because a positive times a negative yields a negative result.

Alternatively, substitute some numbers. If $x > 0 > y$, then x could be 1 and y could be -1, and $(1)(-1) = -1$.

9. (D) (p. 437) ***Mathematics/Geometry/Rectangles and Squares.*** Convert the dimensions shown to real dimensions. Since 1 centimeter is equal to 4 meters, the width of the room is 4 meters, and the length is 4.8. Thus, the area of the room is $4 \cdot 4.8 = 19.2$.

10. (G) (p. 437) ***Mathematics/Algebra/Manipulating Algebraic Expressions/Basic Algebraic Manipulations.*** This question tests power rules. $30,000 \times 20 = 600,000 = 6 \times 10^5$. (One power of 10 for each zero.)

11. (B) (p. 437) ***Mathematics/Arithmetic/Solving Complicated Arithmetic Application Items*** and ***Algebra/Solving Simultaneous Equations.*** Use simultaneous equations to solve this problem. If x is the quantity of chocolates and y is the quantity of caramels, then: $x + y = 4$ and $3x + 2y = 10 \Rightarrow y = 4 - x \Rightarrow 3x + 2(4 - x) = 10 \Rightarrow 3x + 8 - 2x = 10 \Rightarrow x = 10 - 8 = 2$.

Alternatively, test the answer choices, starting with (C). If Karen buys 2.5 pounds of chocolates, she bought $4 - 2.5 = 1.5$ pounds of caramels and the total cost is $(2.5 \cdot 3) + (1.5 \cdot 2) = 7.50 + 3 = \$10.50$. This is too much money. Since chocolates are more expensive than caramels, Karen bought less than 2.5 pounds of chocolates. Try (B): 2 pounds of chocolates and 2 pounds of caramels cost $(2 \cdot 3) + (2 \cdot 2) = 6 + 4 = 10$.

12. (F) (p. 437) ***Mathematics/Statistics and Probability/Averages.*** All three numbers total $3 \cdot 80 = 240$. The total of the two given numbers is $2 \cdot 77 = 154$. The missing number is $240 - 154 = 86$.

13. (C) (p. 438) ***Mathematics/Arithmetic/Common Arithmetic Items/Ratios.*** The total number of ratio parts in the ratio $5:2$ is 7, and 10 is not evenly divisible by 7. As for (A), (C), (D), and (E), these are incorrect because 10 is evenly divisible by the total number of ratio parts.

14. (G) (p. 438) ***Mathematics/Algebra/Solving Algebraic Equations or Inequalities with One Variable/Simple Equations.*** Treat the equation as a proportion: $\frac{4}{5} = \frac{x}{4} \Rightarrow 4(4) = 5x \Rightarrow x = \frac{16}{5}$.

15. (D) (p. 438) ***Mathematics/Geometry/Lines and Angles*** and ***Triangles/Working with Triangles.*** Label the unlabeled angles:

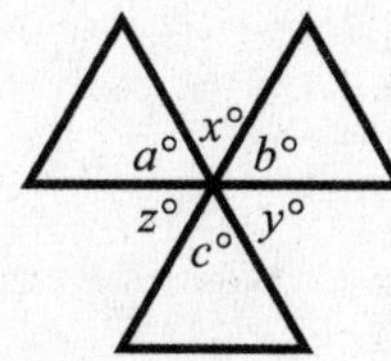

Since the measure of the degrees in a circle is 360, the sum of x, y, and z plus the sum of a, b, and c is 360. What is the value of the angles inside the triangles? Since they are equilateral triangles, each angle is 60°: $3(60) + x + y + z = 360 \Rightarrow x + y + z = 180$.

Alternatively, since you can determine from the given figure that x, y, and z each measure 60 and therefore total 180, you can use alternate interior angles to solve this item. After labeling the unlabeled angles, as done above, simply recognize that $a° = y°$, $b° = z°$, and $c° = x°$. So, $x + y + z = a + b + c = 180$.

16. (H) (p. 439) ***Mathematics/Arithmetic/Solving Complicated Arithmetic Application Items.*** If Peter spent $\frac{1}{4}$ of his allowance on Monday, he had $\frac{3}{4}$ of his allowance left. Then, he spent $\frac{1}{3}$ of that $\frac{3}{4}$ on Tuesday: $\frac{1}{3}\cdot\frac{3}{4}=\frac{1}{4}$. After spending the additional $\frac{1}{4}$, he was left with $\frac{3}{4}-\frac{1}{4}=\frac{1}{2}$ of the original allowance. Substitution of numbers would also work, but the arithmetic would be the same.

17. (B) (p. 439) ***Mathematics/Arithmetic/Common Arithmetic Items/Proportions and Direct-Inverse Variation.*** There are three ways to solve the problem. The simplest and most direct is to reason that if 100 bricks weigh p pounds, 20 bricks, which is $\frac{1}{5}$ of 100, must weigh $\frac{1}{5}$ of p. This same reasoning can be expressed using a direct proportion. The fewer the bricks, the lesser the weight, so: $\frac{x}{p}=\frac{20}{100}\Rightarrow 100x=20p\Rightarrow x=\frac{20p}{100}\Rightarrow x=\frac{p}{5}$.

Alternatively, substitute some numbers. Assume that 100 bricks weigh 100 pounds, which is 1 pound each. 20 bricks weigh 20 pounds. On the assumption that $p=100$, the correct formula will generate the number 20.

18. (K) (p. 440) ***Mathematics/Geometry/Circles*** and ***Triangles/Working with Triangles.*** The following drawings show that (I), (II), and (III) are possible.

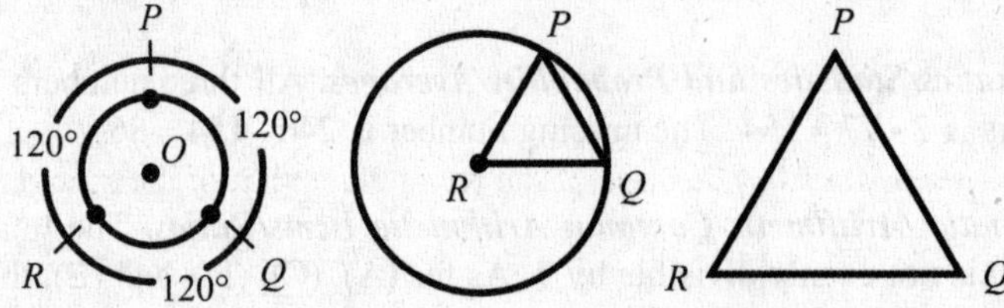

19. (A) (p. 440) ***Mathematics/Statistics and Probability/Data Representation/Tables (Matrices)*** and ***Arithmetic/Common Arithmetic Items/Percents.*** This problem can be solved with the "change-over" principle, but that would require five different calculations. It is always easier and faster to find the greatest ratio of the increased value to the original value. Therefore, look at the successive ratios. The price doubles during the first 5-year period. However, it less than doubles during each of the other periods. Thus, the answer is (A).

20. (F) (p. 440) ***Mathematics/Algebra/Manipulating Algebraic Expressions/Factoring Expressions.*** The easiest approach is just to perform the multiplication for the answer choices:

F. $(x-2)(x+6)=x^2+4x-12$ ✓

G. $(x-4)(x+3)=x^2-x-12$ ✗

H. $(x-6)(x+2)=x^2-4x-12$ ✗

J. $(x+2)(x+6)=x^2+8x+12$ ✗

K. $(x+3)(x+4)=x^2+7x+12$ ✗

21. (D) (p. 441) ***Mathematics/Algebra/Solving Algebraic Equations or Inequalities with One Variable/Simple Equations.*** Since the average of $3x-2$ and $2x-3$ is 10, the sum is 20: $3x-2+2x-3=20\Rightarrow 5x-5=20\Rightarrow 5x=25\Rightarrow x=5$. One package weighs $3(5)-2=13$ pounds and the other package weighs $2(5)-3=7$ pounds. The weight difference is $13-7=6$ pounds.

22. (G) (p. 441) ***Mathematics/Statistics and Probability/Averages.*** This question is a variation on the theme of an average with missing elements. Since 10 students have scores of 75 or more, the total of their scores is at

minimum $10 \bullet 75 = 750$. Then, even assuming the other 5 students each scored zero, the average for the 15 would be at least $750 \div 15 = 50$.

23. (C) (p. 441) ***Mathematics/Algebra/Manipulating Algebraic Expressions/Manipulating Expressions Involving Exponents.*** Since $16 = 4^2$, $16^x = \left(4^2\right)^x = 4^{2x}$. This problem is also solvable by assuming a value for x. If $x = 1$, $16^x = 16^1 = 16$. The correct answer choice will yield the value 16 when 1 is substituted for x:

A. $1^{16} = 1$ ✗
B. $2^{3(1)} = 2^3 = 8$ ✗
C. $4^{2(1)} = 4^2 = 16$ ✓
D. $8^{2(1)} = 8^2 = 64$ ✗
E. $8^{4(1)} = 8^4 = 4{,}096$ ✗

24. (F) (p. 441) ***Mathematics/Geometry/Rectangles and Squares.*** The figure is a square, so the two sides are equal: $2x + 1 = x + 4 \Rightarrow x = 3$. One side is $x + 4 = 3 + 4 = 7$. Since all four sides are equal, the perimeter is $4 \bullet 7 = 28$.

25. (E) (p. 442) ***Mathematics/Geometry/Rectangles and Squares*** and ***Triangles/45°-45°-90° Triangles*** and ***Working with Triangles.*** If w is the width of the rectangle, the length is $2w$ and the rectangle has an area of $w \bullet 2w = 2w^2$. Then, w is also the length of the hypotenuse of a 45°-45°-90° triangle. Each of the other two sides forming the right angle (altitude and base) is $\frac{1}{2} \bullet w \bullet \sqrt{2} = \frac{\sqrt{2}w}{2}$. The area of the triangle is $\frac{1}{2} \bullet \text{altitude} \bullet \text{base} = \frac{1}{2} \bullet \frac{\sqrt{2}w}{2} \bullet \frac{\sqrt{2}w}{2} = \frac{1}{2} \bullet \frac{w^2}{4}$. The ratio of the area of the rectangle to that of the triangle is $\frac{2w^2}{\frac{w^2}{4}} = \frac{2}{\frac{1}{4}} = \frac{8}{1}$.

The above explanation is difficult to follow without a diagram, so draw one:

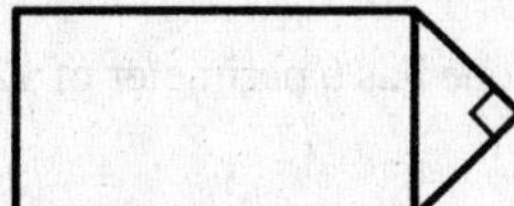

The explanation will not only be easier to follow, but it can be dispensed with altogether. The rectangle is obviously bigger than the triangle, so eliminate (A), (B), and (C). Adding to the figure shows that the area of the triangle is less than $\frac{1}{4}$ of the area of the rectangle. Approximate all of the triangles:

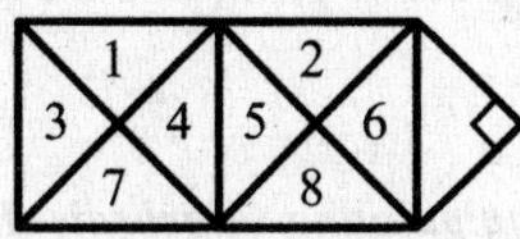

By process of elimination, (E) is correct.

26. (G) (p. 442) ***Mathematics/Coordinate Geometry/The Coordinate System.*** No diagram is provided, so sketch one:

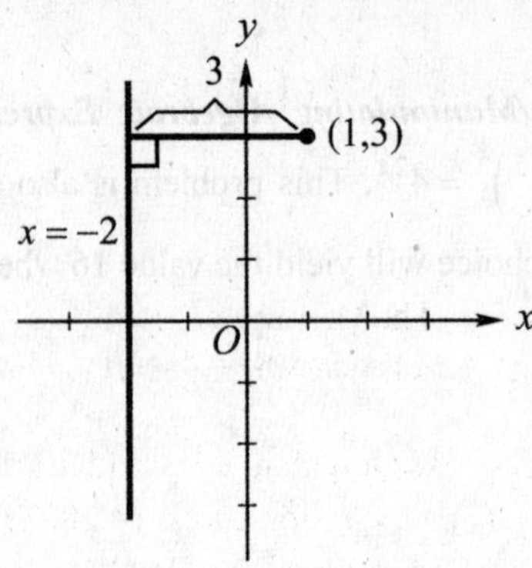

27. (C) (p. 442) ***Mathematics/Arithmetic/Common Arithmetic Items/Proportions and Direct-Inverse Variation.*** Determine how much coffee costs per pound: $\frac{\$12}{5 \text{ pounds}} = \$2.40$ per pound. Therefore, \$30 buys $\frac{\$30}{\$2.40/\text{pound}} = 12.5$ pounds.

Alternatively, the process can be represented in a single direct proportion: $\frac{\text{Cost } X}{\text{Cost } Y} = \frac{\text{Pounds } X}{\text{Pounds } Y} \Rightarrow \frac{\$30}{\$12} = \frac{x}{5} \Rightarrow$ $12x = 150 \Rightarrow x = \frac{150}{12} = 12.5$.

28. (J) (p. 443) ***Mathematics/Geometry/Triangles/Working with Triangles.*** Since the triangles are equilateral, the ratio of their perimeters is the same as the ratio of their sides. Thus, the ratio of their perimeters is also $\frac{3}{12}$, or $\frac{1}{4}$.

Alternatively, find the perimeter of each triangle. Since the triangles are equilateral, the smaller one has a perimeter of $3+3+3=9$, and the larger one has a perimeter of $12+12+12=36$. Therefore, the ratio is: $\frac{9}{36}=\frac{1}{4}$.

29. (E) (p. 443) ***Mathematics/Algebra/Expressing and Evaluating Algebraic Functions/Function Notation.*** Simply substitute −2 for x into the given function: $f(-2) = -3(-2)^3 + 3(-2)^2 - 4(-2) + 8 = -3(-8) + 3(4) - (-8) + 8 = 24 + 12 + 8 + 8 = 52$.

30. (H) (p. 443) ***Mathematics/Arithmetic/Common Arithmetic Items/Percents.*** Add 30 percent to the \$120 wholesale price: $\$120 + (0.30 \bullet \$120) = \$120 + \$36 = \$156$. Then, find the sale price: $\$156 - (0.40 \bullet \$156) = \$156 - \$62.40 = \$93.60$.

31. (A) (p. 444) ***Mathematics/Algebra/Manipulating Algebraic Expressions/Evaluating Expressions.*** $\frac{1}{3}$ of the number equals $\frac{1}{5}$ of the number plus 2: $\frac{1}{3}x = \frac{1}{5}x + 2 \Rightarrow \frac{1}{3}x - \frac{1}{5}x = 2$.

32. (H) (p. 444) ***Mathematics/Geometry/Complex Figures*** and ***Triangles/Working with Triangles*** and ***Rectangles and Squares.*** This is a composite figure. One side of the equilateral triangle is also a side of the square. The triangle has a perimeter of 12, so each side is 4. If the square has a side of 4, then the perimeter is $4+4+4+4=16$.

33. **(A)** (p. 444) ***Mathematics/Algebra/Manipulating Algebraic Expressions/Evaluating Expressions.*** Substitute $\frac{2}{3}$ for x in the expression and solve for k: $12\left(\frac{2}{3}\right)^2+k\left(\frac{2}{3}\right)=6\Rightarrow 12\left(\frac{4}{9}\right)+k\left(\frac{2}{3}\right)=6\Rightarrow 4\left(\frac{4}{3}\right)+k\left(\frac{2}{3}\right)=6\Rightarrow \frac{16}{3}+k\left(\frac{2}{3}\right)=6\Rightarrow k\left(\frac{2}{3}\right)=\frac{18}{3}-\frac{16}{3}=\frac{2}{3}\Rightarrow k=1.$

34. **(K)** (p. 445) ***Mathematics/Geometry.*** The perimeter is equal to the sum of the lengths of the sides: $2(x-2y)+4(2x+y)=(2x-4y)+(8x+4y)=2x+8x-4y+4y=10x$.

Alternatively, substitute some numbers. Assume that $x=3$ and $y=1$. The two short sides are each $3-2(1)=1$, for a total of 2. The four long sides are $2(3)+1=7$, for a total of 28. The perimeter is $28+2=30$. Thus, if $x=3$ and $y=1$, the correct formula will generate the number 30. Only (K) produces the correct value.

35. **(D)** (p. 445) ***Mathematics/Arithmetic/Solving Complicated Arithmetic Application Items.*** Let x be the number of packages in the van before the first delivery: $\left(x-\frac{2}{5}x\right)-3=\frac{1}{2}x\Rightarrow\frac{3}{5}x-3=\frac{1}{2}x\Rightarrow\frac{3}{5}x-\frac{1}{2}x=3\Rightarrow\frac{1}{10}x=3\Rightarrow x=30$.

36. **(J)** (p. 445) ***Mathematics/Algebra/Manipulating Algebraic Expressions/Evaluating Expressions.*** Perform the indicated operations in the answer choices to determine which one is equal to the expression in the stem $\left(12x^3y^2-8x^2y^3\right)$:

F. $2x^2y^2(4x-y)=8x^3y^2-2x^2y^3$ ✗

G. $4x^2y^2(2xy)=8x^3y^3$ ✗

H. $4x^2y^2(3xy)=12x^3y^3$ ✗

J. $4x^2y^2(3x-2y)=12x^3y^2-8x^2y^3$ ✓

K. $x^3y^3(12xy-8xy)=12x^4y^4-8x^4y^4$ ✗

37. **(C)** (p. 446) ***Mathematics/Algebra/Manipulating Algebraic Expressions/Basic Algebraic Manipulations.*** The fastest way to solve this problem is to simply rewrite the expression: $\frac{1}{1+\frac{1}{x}}=\frac{1}{\frac{x+1}{x}}=1\left(\frac{x}{x+1}\right)=\frac{x}{x+1}$.

Alternatively, substitute numbers into the expression. If $x=1$, then: $\frac{1}{1+\frac{1}{x}}=\frac{1}{1+\frac{1}{1}}=\frac{1}{1+1}=\frac{1}{2}$. If $x=1$, both (B) and (C) generate $\frac{1}{2}$. Therefore, try another number. If $x=2$, the correct answer should generate the value $\frac{2}{3}$; (B) is eliminated and (C) must be correct.

38. **(G)** (p. 446) ***Mathematics/Arithmetic/Common Arithmetic Items/Percents.*** Use S and T as unknowns. Since S is 150 percent of T, S equals $1.5T$. Substitute $1.5T$ for S: $\frac{T}{1.5T+T}=\frac{T}{2.5T}=\frac{1}{2.5}=40$ percent.

Alternatively, substitute real numbers. Let S be 15 and T be 10; then, $\frac{T}{S+T}=\frac{10}{10+15}=\frac{10}{25}=40\%$.

39. (C) (p. 446) ***Mathematics/Geometry/Lines and Angles.*** No figure is provided, so sketch one:

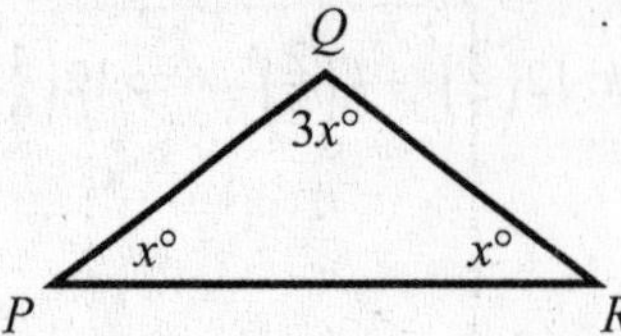

$x° + x° + 3x° = 180° \Rightarrow 5x° = 180° \Rightarrow x = 36$.

40. (G) (p. 447) ***Mathematics/Arithmetic/Common Arithmetic Items/Proportions and Direct-Inverse Variation.*** Use a direct proportion: $\frac{C}{x} = \frac{d}{b} \Rightarrow Cb = dx \Rightarrow C = \frac{dx}{b}$.

41. (D) (p. 447) ***Mathematics/Arithmetic/Common Arithmetic Items/Percents.*** First, find the reduced price: $\$64 - (25\% \text{ of } \$64) = \$64 - (0.25 \bullet \$64) = \$64 - \$16 = \$48$. Next, calculate the sales tax on \$48: $5\% \text{ of } \$48 = 0.05 \bullet \$48 = \$2.40$. Now, find the total cost: $\$48.00 + \$2.40 = \$50.40$.

42. (K) (p. 447) ***Mathematics/Algebra/Solving Simultaneous Equations.*** Use the method for solving simultaneous equations: $\frac{y}{z} = k - 1 \Rightarrow k = \frac{y}{z} + 1$. Since $\frac{x}{z} = k$: $\frac{x}{z} = \frac{y}{z} + 1 \Rightarrow x = z\left(\frac{y}{z} + 1\right) = y + z$.

43. (A) (p. 447) ***Mathematics/Algebra/Solving Algebraic Equations with Two Variables.*** If $x = 0.25y$, then $y = \frac{x}{0.25} = 4x$. Thus, *y* is 400 percent of *x*.

44. (G) (p. 448) ***Mathematics/Arithmetic/Common Arithmetic Items/Properties of Numbers.*** Since 3 is a factor of 9 and 5 is a factor of 5, any multiple of both 9 and 5 will be a multiple of $3(5) = 15$; (II) belongs in the correct choice. (I), however, is not correct. *x* could be any multiple of 45, e.g., 90, which also proves that (III) does not belong in the correct choice.

45. (B) (p. 448) ***Mathematics/Geometry/Complex Figures*** and ***Triangles/Pythagorean Theorem.*** The neat thing about a cube is that if given any one feature (e.g., volume, edge, diagonal of a face, diagonal of the cube, surface area), every other feature can be calculated. This is why cubes are often the focus of test problems. The edge has a length of 2, so use the Pythagorean theorem to find the length of the diagonal of a face:

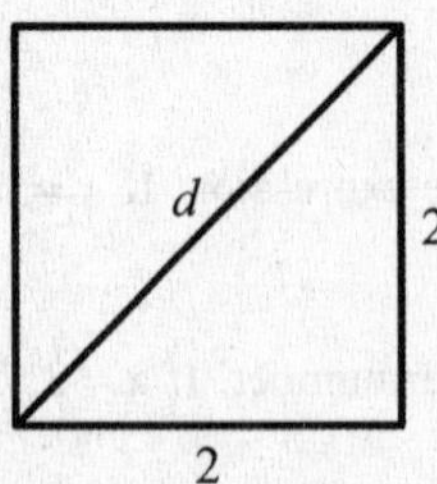

$d^2 = 2^2 + 2^2 = 4 + 4 = 8 \Rightarrow d = 2\sqrt{2}$. Now, find the length of the diagonal of the cube:

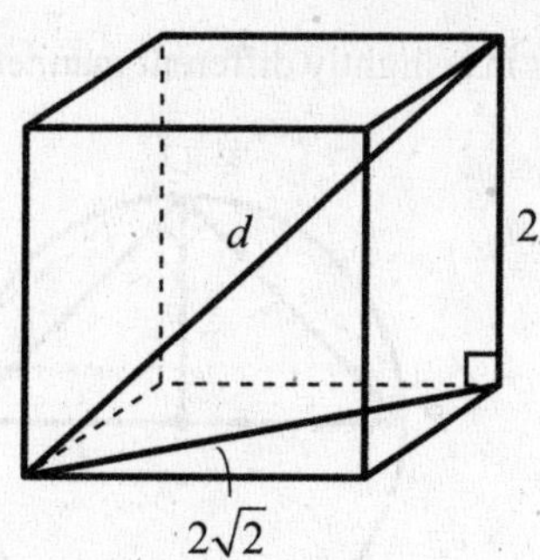

$d^2 = 2^2 + (2\sqrt{2})^2 = 4 + 8 = 12 \Rightarrow d = 2\sqrt{3}$. That is the length of the entire diagonal of the cube. The point that is the center of the cube is the midpoint of the diagonal of the cube and is $\sqrt{3}$ units of length from each vertex.

46. **(J)** (p. 448) ***Mathematics/Geometry.*** $\text{Volume}_{\text{cylinder}} = \pi r^2 h$. Redefine the dimensions of the smaller cylinder in terms of r and h: $r = kr'$ so $r' = \frac{r}{k}$ and $h = kh'$ so $h' = \frac{h}{k}$. $\text{Volume}_{\text{smaller cylinder}} = \pi\left(\frac{r}{k}\right)^2\left(\frac{h}{k}\right) = \frac{\pi r^2 h}{k^3}$. The ratio is $\frac{\frac{\pi r^2 h}{k^3}}{\pi r^2 h} = \frac{1}{k^3}$. Therefore, the correct answer is (J), $1:k^3$.

Alternatively, assume some numbers. Let the radius and height of the larger cylinder be 4 and 4, and those of the smaller cylinder be 2 and 2. Since $r = kr'$ and $h = kh'$, k must be 2. $\text{Volume}_{\text{larger cylinder}} = \pi(4)^2(4) = 64\pi$. $\text{Volume}_{\text{smaller cylinder}} = \pi(2)^2(2) = 8\pi$. The ratio 8π to 64π is 1 to 8 or $\frac{1}{8}$. Use $k = 2$ to find the answer that has a value of $\frac{1}{8}$:

F. $1:\pi = \frac{1}{\pi}$ ✗

G. $\pi:1 = \frac{\pi}{1} = \pi$ ✗

H. $k\pi:1 = \frac{k\pi}{1} = 2\pi$ ✗

J. $1:k^3 = \frac{1}{k^3} = \frac{1}{2^3} = \frac{1}{8}$ ✓

K. $k^3:1 = \frac{k^3}{1} = \frac{2^3}{1} = \frac{8}{1} = 8$ ✗

47. **(A)** (p. 449) ***Mathematics/Geometry/Complex Figures*** and ***Triangles/Pythagorean Theorem*** and ***Circles.*** This is a right triangle, so $\angle PQR$ intercepts an arc of 180°. (The inscribed angle $\angle PQR$ is equal to half its intercepted arc.) Because the arc is 180°, the hypotenuse of the triangle, $\overline{PR}$, is also the diameter of the circle. From any bit of information about a right isosceles triangle (e.g., either side lengths, the hypotenuse, or the area), the other information can be found. Using the two adjacent sides as the altitude and the base, we have: $\text{area}_{\text{triangle}} = \frac{1}{2}(s)(s) \Rightarrow 1 = \frac{1}{2}s^2 \Rightarrow s^2 = 2$. Now, use the Pythagorean theorem to solve for $\overline{PR}$: $s^2 + s^2 = \overline{PR}^2 \Rightarrow 2 + 2 = \overline{PR}^2 \Rightarrow 4 = \overline{PR}^2 \Rightarrow \overline{PR} = 2$. Since $\overline{PR} = 2$, the radius of the circle is 1, and $\text{area}_{\text{circle}} = \pi(1)^2 = \pi$.

The same conclusion can be arrived at in a slightly different manner:

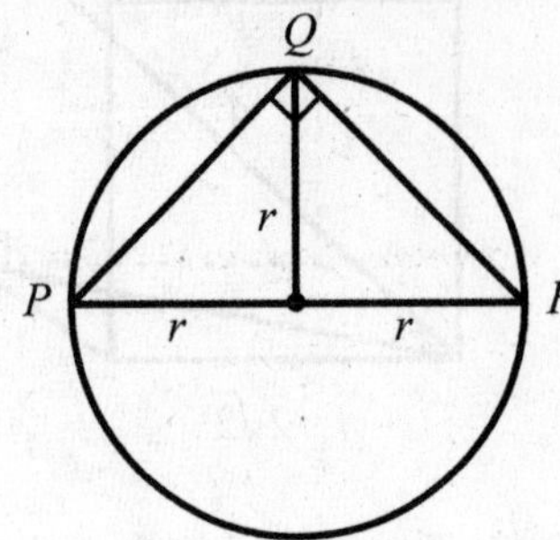

Based on the figure, r is the length of the altitude of the triangle and $2r$ is the length of the base, so $\text{area}_{\text{triangle}} = \frac{1}{2}(2r)(r) = r^2$ and $r^2 = 1 \Rightarrow r = 1$. Thus, $\text{area}_{\text{circle}} = \pi r^2 = \pi(1)^2 = \pi$.

Finally, a little common sense can solve this problem without any math. The triangle, which has an area of 1, takes up slightly less than half the circle:

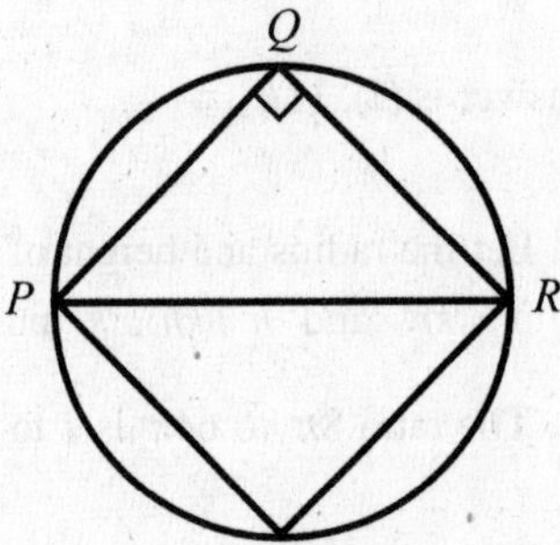

The correct answer must be a bit larger than 2, and only one choice qualifies: (A) is π and π is slightly larger than 3. Therefore, (A) is reasonable. All of the other choices are more than 6 and so are too large to be reasonable.

48. (F) (p. 449) ***Mathematics/Geometry/Complex Figures*** and ***Circles.*** This is a good exercise in organized problem-solving. Look at the figure and ask what is known: the radius of the circle and the perimeter of the shaded area consists of two arcs. There must be some way to use the information about the radius to find the length of the arcs. Arcs can be measured in terms of length or in terms of degrees.

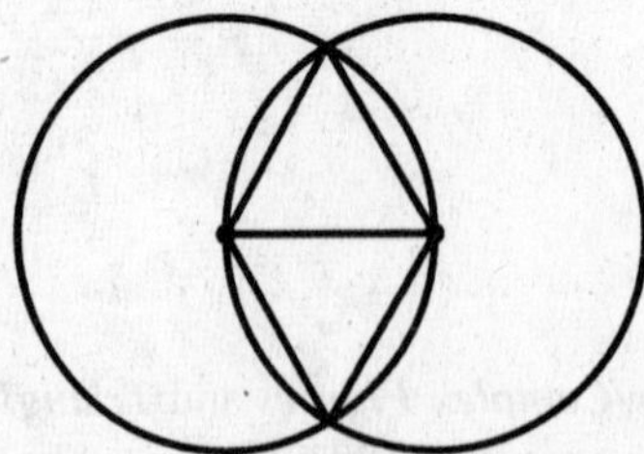

Since the sides of the triangles are all radii, the triangles must be equilateral, and the degree measure of each arc is 120. The circles have radii of 1, so they have circumferences of $2\pi(1) = 2\pi$. Each arc is a third of that length: $\frac{2\pi}{3}$. Since there are two such arcs, the perimeter of the shaded area is $2 \cdot \frac{2\pi}{3} = \frac{4\pi}{3}$.

49. (C) (p. 450) ***Mathematics/Statistics and Probability/Averages.*** For the first six tests, the student has a total point count of $6 \cdot 83 = 498$. If the student scores a 0 on each of the remaining four tests, the total point count will remain

498 and the average will be $\frac{498}{10} = 49.8$. If the student scores 100 on each of the four remaining tests, the total point count will be 898 and the average will be $\frac{898}{10} = 89.8$.

50. (K) (p. 450) ***Mathematics/Arithmetic/Common Arithmetic Items/Complex Numbers.*** Let x be the multiplicative inverse of $2-i$: $x(2-i)=1 \Rightarrow x=\frac{1}{2-i} \Rightarrow x=\frac{1}{2-i} \bullet \frac{2+i}{2+i}=\frac{2+i}{4-i^2}$. $i=\sqrt{-1}$, so $i^2=-1$. Thus, $x=\frac{2+i}{4-(-1)}=\frac{2+i}{5}$.

51. (C) (p. 450) ***Mathematics/Arithmetic/Simple Manipulations.*** From the exponential concept of logarithms, if $a^x=b$, then the equation can be written in logarithmic form as $\log_a b = x$. Let $\log_3 \sqrt{3} = x$; then $3^x=\sqrt{3} \Rightarrow 3^x = 3^{\left(\frac{1}{2}\right)}$. Thus, $x=\frac{1}{2}$.

52. (J) (p. 450) ***Mathematics/Algebra/Expressing and Evaluating Algebraic Functions/Function Notation.*** Study the structure of *f*. When will the function be at its minimum value? This is like asking for the minimum value of $(x-1)^2$. Squaring any positive number yields a positive number; squaring any negative number yields a positive number; and squaring zero yields zero. Since zero is less than any positive number, we want $x-1$ to equal zero, and this occurs when $x=1$. Now, plug in 1 for x in the given function and solve to find the minimum value of the function: $f(1)=(x-1)^2+2=(1-1)^2+2=2$.

Alternatively, test the answer choices. Plug each answer choice into the given function; the correct choice will be the lowest value:

F. $(-3-1)^2+2=(-4)^2+2=16+2=18$ ✗
G. $(-2-1)^2+2=(-3)^2+2=9+2=11$ ✗
H. $(0-1)^2+2=(-1)^2+2=1+2=3$ ✗
J. $(1-1)^2+2=(0)^2+2=0+2=2$ ✓
K. $(2-1)^2+2=(1)^2+2=1+2=3$ ✗

53. (A) (p. 451) ***Mathematics/Algebra/Manipulating Algebraic Expressions/Manipulating Expressions Involving Exponents.*** Simply use the rules for working with exponents to solve the given equation for x: $2^n+2^n+2^n+2^n=x(2^{n+1}) \Rightarrow (4)(2^n)=x\left(2^{n+1}\right) \Rightarrow (2)\left(2^1\right)\left(2^n\right)=x\left(2^{n+1}\right) \Rightarrow 2\left(2^{n+1}\right)=x\left(2^{n+1}\right) \Rightarrow 2=x$.

54. (F) (p. 451) ***Mathematics/Algebra/Expressing and Evaluating Algebraic Functions/Function Notation.*** $f(k)$ will equal $f(-k)$ when $(k)^2+2(k)+1=(-k)^2-2k+1 \Rightarrow k^2+2k+1=k^2-2k+1 \Rightarrow 2k=-2k \Rightarrow 4k=0 \Rightarrow k=0$.

Another approach is to work backwards from the answer choices. First, use the value 0: $(0)^2+2(0)+1=(-0)^2-2(0)+1 \Rightarrow 1=1$. Thus, 0 is part of the solution set; eliminate (G), (H), and (J). The only question that remains is whether the correct answer is (K). Take another value, say 1: $(1)^2+2(1)+1=(-1)^2-2(-1)^2+1=(-1)^2-2(1)+1 \Rightarrow 4 \neq 0$. This proves that the answer is (F).

55. (D) (p. 451) ***Mathematics/Algebra/Manipulating Algebraic Expressions/Factoring Expressions.*** Factor the expression: $\frac{x^2-1}{x-1}=\frac{(x+1)(x-1)}{x-1}=x+1$. Therefore, as x approaches 1, $x+1$ approaches 2.

56. (H) (p. 451) ***Mathematics/Trigonometry/Determining Trigonometric Values.*** Given the restrictions on x and since $\cos x=-1$, x must equal π and $\cos\frac{\pi}{2}=0$.

Alternatively, visualize the graph of the cosine function (or graph it on a calculator):

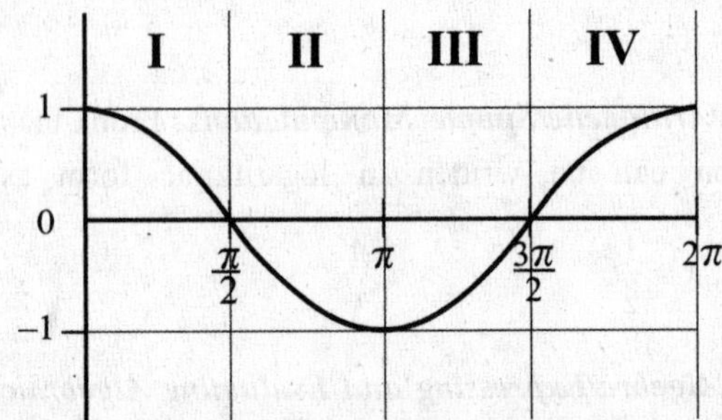

57. (B) (p. 452) ***Mathematics/Algebra/Expressing and Evaluating Algebraic Functions/Concepts of Domain and Range.*** The domain of a function is the set of all possible x values; the range of a function is the set of all possible y values. Sketch a graph of the function (or use a graphing calculator):

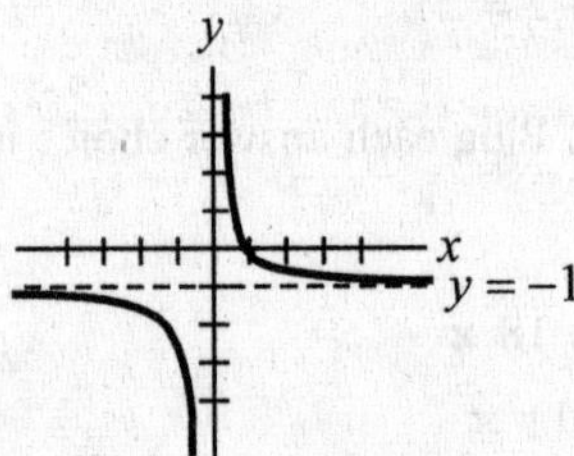

From the graph, it is obvious that the y-values both approach, but never actually reach, -1. Therefore, the range is defined by all real numbers except -1.

Alternatively, this item can be solved algebraically by solving for x. Since $f(x)=\frac{1-x}{x}$, $x[f(x)]=1-x\Rightarrow x[f(x)]+x=1\Rightarrow x[f(x)+1]=1\Rightarrow x=\frac{1}{f(x)+1}$. The range of the function is the set of all possible values for $f(x)$. Since division by zero is undefined, $f(x)+1\neq 0\Rightarrow f(x)\neq -1$. Thus, $f(x)$ can be any value except -1.

58. (K) (p. 452) ***Mathematics/Trigonometry/Trigonometric Relationships.*** $x=3(\sin\theta)$ and $y=2(\cos\theta)$; thus, $\sin\theta=\frac{x}{3}$ and $\cos\theta=\frac{y}{2}$. $\sin^2\theta+\cos^2\theta=1$; thus, $\left(\frac{x}{3}\right)^2+\left(\frac{y}{2}\right)^2=1\Rightarrow\frac{x^2}{9}+\frac{y^2}{4}=1$ is the equation of an ellipse with center (0,0) that passes through the points (3,0) and (0,2).

Alternatively, plug in values for θ. For $\theta=0$, $x=3[\sin(0)]=3(0)=0$. For $\theta=\frac{\pi}{2}$, $x=3\left(\sin\frac{\pi}{2}\right)=3(1)=3$ and $y=2\left(\cos\frac{\pi}{2}\right)=2(0)=0$. Therefore, the graph must include the points (3,0) and (0,2). The only graph given that contains both of these points is (K).

59. (A) (p. 452) ***Mathematics/Trigonometry/Definitions of the Six Trigonometric Functions.*** Sine and cosecant are reciprocal functions, so the product of the sine of any angle and the cosecant of that angle is 1. This fact can quickly be derived from the definitions of sine and cosecant. Given a triangle with sides a and b and hypotenuse c, let θ be opposite side b. $\sin\theta = \frac{b}{c}$ and $\csc\theta = \frac{c}{b}$. Therefore, $\sin\theta \bullet \csc\theta = 1$.

60. (J) (p. 453) ***Mathematics/Trigonometry/Trigonometry as an Alternative Method of Solution.*** There are several different ways of expressing the length of $\overline{BC}$: as a number, as a function of $\angle ACB$, and as a function of $\angle CAB$. "Testing-the-test" is the easiest option, and some exam wisdom will help. First, do not fall for (F) or (G). Test-takers are not expected to know values of trigonometric functions at particular angles. Since 40° and 50° are not easily remembered values, the answer is not going to be 4 or 5. The answer will be expressed using a trigonometric function. (J) is correct: $\tan A = \frac{\overline{BC}}{\overline{AB}} \Rightarrow \overline{BC} = \overline{AB}(\tan A) = 3(\tan 50°)$.

TEST 3: READING

1. **(D)** (p. 455) ***Reading/Prose Fiction/Implied Idea.*** In the final paragraph, the young man, Robin, is trying to explain to himself why the barbers laughed at him. Thus, he is talking to himself.

2. **(J)** (p. 455) ***Reading/Prose Fiction/Explicit Detail.*** The five shillings was not enough to satisfy the ferryman for having to make a special trip. The young man was forced to pay an additional three pence, bringing the total fare to five shillings and three pence.

3. **(B)** (p. 455) ***Reading/Prose Fiction/Implied Idea.*** Just after the young man gets off the ferryboat, he finds himself in a neighborhood of hovels and old houses that, he concludes, could not belong to his relative. Therefore, the young man must think his relative is well-to-do.

4. **(J)** (p. 455) ***Reading/Prose Fiction/Implied Idea.*** The scene is at night: the boat crosses at nine o'clock in the evening, the lights are on in the barber shop, and the stranger in the coat threatens to have the young man put in the stocks by morning.

5. **(A)** (p. 455) ***Reading/Prose Fiction/Implied Idea.*** In the first paragraph, the narrator remarks that the young man sets off on foot with a light step—as though he had not already traveled more than 30 miles. Thus, 30 miles is a long way to travel in a day.

6. **(G)** (p. 455) ***Reading/Prose Fiction/Explicit Detail.*** The young man finally concludes that the barbers laugh at him for approaching the stranger in the coat because it should have been obvious to him that the stranger in the coat would not know the Major.

7. **(A)** (p. 455) ***Reading/Prose Fiction/Implied Idea.*** The currency used to pay the ferryman and the length of a day's journey is suggestive. The reference to a "New England colony" clearly places the action some time before the end of the eighteenth century.

8. **(F)** (p. 455) ***Reading/Prose Fiction/Implied Idea.*** The young man bows to the stranger and addresses him as "honored sir" in order to show respect.

9. **(B)** (p. 455) ***Reading/Prose Fiction/Implied Idea.*** The passage states that nine o'clock in the evening was an "unusual hour." Such language implies that nine o'clock was an unusual time for anyone to be using the ferryboat. This is why the young man was its only passenger. Eliminate (A) because the ferry trip was not a private charter.

10. **(F)** (p. 455) ***Reading/Prose Fiction/Implied Idea.*** The phrase "small and mean wooden buildings" characterizes the neighborhood near the ferry landing. The next paragraph also mentions a hovel and an old house.

11. **(B)** (p. 456) ***Reading/Social Science/Explicit Detail.*** As stated in the last paragraph of the passage, Turner's essay challenged the traditional approach of Eastern historians. That reference refers to the views of other American historians of his time.

12. **(F)** (p. 456) ***Reading/Social Science/Explicit Detail.*** The final paragraph shows that (F) is the correct answer. Turner was the first historian to use the techniques of the social sciences to formulate and investigate historical questions. He studied the effects of economic, geographical, and sociological factors on the settlement of the American West. In addition, Turner redirected the focus of historical inquiry away from politics and political leaders, centering it instead on the lives of people in a national setting. In doing so, Turner identified what he considered to be the attributes of the American character.

13. **(D)** (p. 456) ***Reading/Social Science/Explicit Detail.*** As noted in the third paragraph of the passage, Turner's evidence for the disappearance of the American frontier drew on the census of 1880.

14. **(J)** (p. 457) ***Reading/Social Science/Explicit Detail.*** As stated in the first paragraph of the passage, Turner's essay affected the subsequent direction and methodology of inquiry in American history.

15. **(C)** (p. 457) ***Reading/Social Science/Application.*** The fact that much of the land in the West and Midwest was bought by wealthy land speculators from the East cast doubt on Turner's view that the West was settled by individuals looking to escape from the pressure of city life in the East.

16. **(F)** (p. 457) ***Reading/Social Science/Application.*** Turner's theory was that the West served as a safety-valve by providing a means for the dissipation of social dissatisfaction stemming from the frustration of city life. However, if demographic data showed that more people actually left the farms for the cities than left the cities for the frontier, this theory would no longer be valid.

17. **(C)** (p. 457) ***Reading/Social Science/Vocabulary.*** A theory can be defined as a hypothesis that contains an assumed explanation of a large number of isolated facts. It can be tested and thus can be proved or disproved.

18. **(H)** (p. 457) ***Reading/Social Science/Explicit Detail.*** The frontier line of America moved from the East, where the first English colonies were founded, to the West, where the last settlements were established.

19. **(D)** (p. 457) ***Reading/Social Science/Explicit Detail.*** In the fourth paragraph, Turner claimed that "settlers no longer depended on England for goods but had become self-sufficient." "Self-sufficient" indicates that needed goods were bought in America.

20. **(G)** (p. 457) ***Reading/Social Science/Application.*** As stated in the last paragraph of the passage, before Turner turned his attention to studying the people and the settlements of the American frontier, American historians had restricted the boundaries of American history to the history of politics and the roles played by past American political leaders.

21. **(A)** (p. 458) ***Reading/Humanities/Development.*** At the end of the first paragraph, the author raises a question, which he then proceeds to answer. (A) describes this development. (B) is incorrect because the author does not present a theory as such. A theory is a hypothetical explanation of phenomena; the author instead presents his viewpoint about what is important in life. Also, while the author offers many opinions, none "prove" his viewpoint. As for (C), the author does not contrast his own views with other views. As for (D), the author does not define a term.

22. **(J)** (p. 458) ***Reading/Humanities/Vocabulary.*** In the final paragraph, the author explains that life is much too short. The author introduces the discussion by stating that experience is the end or goal of life—to get the most out of life, one must pack it with "as many pulsations as possible." One can infer that the author means experiences.

23. (B) (p. 458) ***Reading/Humanities/Explicit Detail.*** The discussion of art is found in the closing sentences of the passage. Having said that the best life is one packed with experiences (pulsations), the author goes on to say how one can have these intense experiences. This is one function of art, he says—to do nothing but provoke feelings—not to depict reality, (A); not to encourage reform, (C); not as a means of expression, (D).

24. (H) (p. 458) ***Reading/Humanities/Application.*** Experience is everything according to the author, so he would probably agree with (H). It is the feeling of the moment that is important, not the memory of the feeling. Once the feeling is past, you should be looking for new feelings, not thinking about past ones.

25. (A) (p. 458) ***Reading/Humanities/Voice.*** The writing is highly impassioned. The intensity of the writing is evident in every sentence. The issues are those of life and death. The author uses phrases such as "passionate attitude," "tragic dividing," "awful brevity," and "splendor of our experience."

26. (H) (p. 459) ***Reading/Humanities/Implied Idea.*** In the second paragraph, the author argues that the best life is one filled with experiences of every sort. Not to seek after a variety of experiences is, in the author's words, "on this short day of the frost and sun, to sleep before evening." The phrase "to sleep before evening" must mean to stop living even before death. Thus, the "short day of the frost and sun" refers to a person's life.

27. (C) (p. 459) ***Reading/Humanities/Implied Idea.*** The author emphasizes the importance of living life to the fullest. In line 26, "awful brevity" refers to the shortness of life.

28. (J) (p. 459) ***Reading/Humanities/Explicit Detail.*** In the final paragraph, the author contrasts those who are listless with those who are the children of the world. The children of the world are high in passion, wise, and in love with art and song.

29. (A) (p. 459) ***Reading/Humanities/Implied Idea.*** Lines 36–42 say that the desire for beauty has the most power to quicken our sense of life.

30. (H) (p. 459) ***Reading/Humanities/Implied Idea.*** The author says that we are all under a sentence of death with an indefinite reprieve, meaning that we are all mortal. We have an "interval," meaning our life; and then "our place knows us no more," meaning we are gone from the earth; that is, we are dead.

31. (B) (p. 461) ***Reading/Natural Science/Explicit Detail.*** Line 3 reads, in part: "energy, which is the capacity for doing work."

32. (H) (p. 461) ***Reading/Natural Science/Explicit Detail.*** The second paragraph states that the result of the process is a mix of sugar and oxygen. O_2 names oxygen, and H_2O names water, so $C_6H_{12}O_6$ names a sugar.

33. (A) (p. 461) ***Reading/Natural Science/Explicit Detail.*** Lines 17–21 define both terms. Reduction is the addition of electrons, and oxidation is the removal of electrons.

34. (J) (p. 461) ***Reading/Natural Science/Explicit Detail.*** Lines 17–19 state that photosynthesis involves the addition of electrons, making (I) correct. Lines 23–26 state that photosynthesis involves action on hydrogen, meaning that (II) is also correct. Lines 20–21 state that "reduction stores energy, while oxidation releases it," and line 17 states that "photosynthesis is a reduction reaction." So, (III) cannot be correct. Since (I) and (II) are correct, the answer is (J).

35. (C) (p. 461) ***Reading/Natural Science/Main Idea.*** The paragraph gives a systematic analysis of the process defined in preceding paragraphs.

36. (F) (p. 461) ***Reading/Natural Science/Explicit Detail.*** (G) is supported by lines 51–52, (H) is supported by lines 64–67, (J) is stated in lines 50–51. (F) states the reverse of the truth; it is ADP that is mixed with phosphate to form ATP (see lines 51–52).

37. **(A)** (p. 461) ***Reading/Natural Science/Implied Idea.*** A careful reading of lines 64–71 can lead to no other conclusion. A five-carbon sugar (RuDP) is combined with carbon dioxide (CO_2), ultimately resulting in the formation of a three-carbon sugar (PGAL).

38. **(G)** (p. 462) ***Reading/Natural Science/Implied Idea.*** Growing periods, (J), are never discussed. Higher temperatures, (H), as indicated in the final paragraph, can lead to disagreeable conditions. Lines 72–78 state that the photorespiration, with its seemingly wasteful result, occurs when CO_2 levels are low, suggesting that a higher level of CO_2 would be a more agreeable condition. Also, more agreeable conditions facilitate carboxyilation. This process involves combining CO_2. Therefore, more CO_2 means an increase in carboxyilation.

39. **(B)** (p. 462) ***Reading/Natural Science/Explicit Detail.*** As stated in line 17, photosynthesis is a reduction reaction, which makes (III) an incorrect choice. Lines 67–69 and lines 72–75 indicate that RuDP is used in carboxyilation and photorespiration, making (I) correct. Another difference, as stated in lines 75–76, is that no ATP is created via photorespiration, (II).

40. **(H)** (p. 462) ***Reading/Natural Science/Main Idea.*** The angiosperm plants discussed in the final paragraph *do* photosynthesize—(J)—but they do it in an unusual way, using their specialized leaf structure.

TEST 4: SCIENCE

1. **(A)** (p. 464) ***Science/Data Representation/Analysis.*** All three of the tabulated properties generally increase with the number of carbons.

2. **(F)** (p. 464) ***Science/Data Representation/Comprehension.*** The changes in boiling point are as follows:

   methane ⇒ ethane: +73°C
   propane ⇒ butane: +42°C
   butane ⇒ pentane: +36°C
   nonane ⇒ decane: +25°C

   Therefore, the change in boiling point is the greatest from methane to ethane.

3. **(B)** (p. 464) ***Science/Data Representation/Analysis.*** This property can be seen by looking at propane (3 carbons: −188°C) to butane (4 carbons: −138°C), pentane (5 carbons: −130°C) to hexane (6 carbons: −95°C), etc.

4. **(H)** (p. 465) ***Science/Data Representation/Analysis.*** Only boiling points and number of carbons increase without exception.

5. **(C)** (p. 465) ***Science/Data Representation/Comprehension.*** Solve for the percentage increases using the "change-over-original" formula:

   ethane ⇒ propane: $\frac{0.07}{0.57} = 12\%$

   propane ⇒ butane: $\frac{0.08}{0.50} = 16\%$

   pentane ⇒ hexane: $\frac{0.10}{0.56} = 18\%$

   hexane ⇒ heptane: $\frac{0.02}{0.66} = 3\%$

   Therefore, the greatest percentage increase in density occurs from pentane to hexane.

6. **(J)** (p. 466) ***Science/Research Summary/Comprehension.*** Momentum equals mass multiplied by velocity. Therefore, the momentum is $2 \text{ kg} \bullet 4 \text{ m/sec} = 8 \text{ kg} \bullet \text{m/sec}$.

7. **(B)** (p. 466) ***Science/Research Summary/Comprehension.*** The momentums of the two masses are initially $2(4) = 8 \text{ kg} \bullet \text{m/sec}$ and $5(0) = 0 \text{ kg} \bullet \text{m/sec}$; afterward, the momentum of the combined mass is $2(1.14) + 5(1.14) = 7.98 \text{ kg} \bullet \text{m/sec}$.

8. **(H)** (p. 466) ***Science/Research Summary/Comprehension.*** Notice the negative sign on the final velocity for Object 1 and also the note in the text about the meaning of negative velocity.

9. **(D)** (p. 466) ***Science/Research Summary/Analysis.*** Since no actual value is given in the phrase "far more massive," it is unlikely that an explicit calculation is needed. To be successful, a reader needs to visualize a collision of a very light object with a massive one; the large one will not budge.

10. **(F)** (p. 466) ***Science/Research Summary/Analysis.*** The lighter object would recoil even faster than the observed −1.71 m/sec.

11. **(C)** (p. 467) ***Science/Research Summary/Application.*** Using the formula given, initial kinetic energy is found to be 16.0; the final kinetic energy has decreased to about 4.5. The problem is easily misread as referring to Experiment 2, where the kinetic energy remains the same.

12. **(H)** (p. 468) ***Science/Data Representation/Comprehension.*** An increase in temperature influences flowering, while a decrease in temperature is one factor that causes leaf drop-off.

13. **(D)** (p. 468) ***Science/Data Representation/Comprehension.*** The table shows that plant growth occurs when Hormones 1 and 3 increase. Yet, even if these two hormones increase, a similar increase in either H_4 or H_5 will lead to no plant growth—H_4 and H_5 inhibit growth.

14. **(G)** (p. 468) ***Science/Data Representation/Analysis.*** Based on the chart, it is clear that (F), (H), and (J) are incorrect. (G) is correct since seed germination is influenced by only one factor (H_3), while flowering is influenced by four different factors (H_3, H_5, day length, and temperature).

15. **(C)** (p. 468) ***Science/Data Representation/Analysis.*** Changing a houseplant's growing conditions from 12 hours of light per 12 hours of dark to constant light is an example of altering day length, which only affects flowering.

16. **(J)** (p. 469) ***Science/Data Representation/Analysis.*** H_2 only affects flower drop-off, fruit drop-off, and leaf drop-off. For each of these activities, H_1 must also play a role (as H_2 increases, H_1 decreases).

17. **(B)** (p. 470) ***Science/Research Summary/Comprehension.*** The only way the bag can gain weight between weighings is if additional fluid has moved inside. In this case, water moved inside (by osmosis) faster than it moved out.

18. **(J)** (p. 470) ***Science/Research Summary/Analysis.*** The fluid compartment (bag or beaker) that initially has only water (no red dye) never gets red. This indicates that the red dye is not free to pass across the bag's "membrane."

19. **(D)** (p. 470) ***Science/Research Summary/Analysis.*** In Experiment 2, the bag has gained 10 grams after only 10 minutes (water has entered the bag faster than in Experiment 1). By 20 minutes, more water will have entered and the bag should be even heavier.

20. **(F)** (p. 470) ***Science/Research Summary/Analysis.*** The experiments show that water will flow toward the compartment containing red dye. The more concentrated the red dye, the faster the flow of water.

21. (C) (p. 470) ***Science/Research Summary/Analysis.*** Water is free to flow into or out of the bag. Since there is no dye in the bag or the beaker, water will flow at an equal rate in both directions and the bag's weight should remain the same.

22. (F) (p. 471) ***Science/Research Summary/Application.*** Since salts are not able to enter or leave the cell, only water will move—in a direction that tends towards balanced concentrations. The water will flow toward the greater concentration of salt (from red blood cell to sea water), causing shrinkage of the cells.

23. (B) (p. 472) ***Science/Data Representation/Comprehension.*** Magnesium is a positively charged mineral (Mg^{+2}). The soil that has the worst relative ability to hold such minerals is coarse sand.

24. (J) (p. 472) ***Science/Data Representation/Analysis.*** As particles get larger (from less than 2 micrometers to 200–2,000 micrometers), their relative ability to retain water decreases (from 1 to 4).

25. (C) (p. 472) ***Science/Data Representation/Comprehension.*** Soils that are neither best nor worst at any ability cannot be ranked 1 or 4. The only soils that are never ranked 1 or 4 are silt (2–20 micrometers) and sand (20–200 micrometers). The total size range, therefore, is between 2 and 200 micrometers.

26. (F) (p. 473) ***Science/Data Representation/Application.*** Since loam is mostly clay, it primarily has small particles that hold minerals and water well. The larger silt and sand particles in loam are adequate at maintaining air spaces containing oxygen. None of the other predictions fit the data in the chart.

27. (D) (p. 473) ***Science/Data Representation/Analysis.*** Clay is best (relative ability: l) at both holding positively charged minerals and retaining water.

28. (G) (p. 474) ***Science/Conflicting Viewpoints/Comprehension.*** Concentrations of reactants, not products, determine rate in both theories.

29. (C) (p. 474) ***Science/Conflicting Viewpoints/Comprehension.*** This question tests critical comprehension of the passage, and it requires an understanding of the relationship between the two theories. According to the passage, Theory 2 explains that Theory 1 is based upon an incomplete understanding of the details of chemical reactions, assuming that all reactions operate by a single-step mechanism. Therefore, one can conclude that a proponent of Theory 2 believes that Theory 1 can be used for single step reactions, but should not be used for more complex reactions.

30. (G) (p. 474) ***Science/Conflicting Viewpoints/Comprehension.*** This question tests understanding of the relation of numbers of reactants in the overall equation to exponents in the rate law. For the reaction $2NO + O_2 \Rightarrow 2NO_2$, Theory 1 states that $\text{rate} = k[NO]^2[O_2]^1$,where k is the rate constant and the exponents are the coefficients in front of the reactants in the reaction. Using this formula, the rate equation for $3M + 2N \Rightarrow 4P$ must be $k[M]^3[N]^2$.

31. (D) (p. 474) ***Science/Conflicting Viewpoints/Analysis.*** The coefficients of the reactants determine their exponents in the rate law.

32. (F) (p. 474) ***Science/Conflicting Viewpoints/Analysis.*** This question tests understanding of the differences between the theories. Theory 2 disagrees with Theory 1 on the grounds that chemical reactions do not all occur in one stage. Therefore, Theory 2 may be best supported by evidence that proves that reactions occur in more than one stage.

33. (A) (p. 475) ***Science/Conflicting Viewpoints/Comprehension.*** If the first stage is very slow and the second stage is much quicker, the overall rate is essentially that of the first stage.

34. (H) (p. 475) ***Science/Conflicting Viewpoints/Analysis.*** If the sum of the rates of each stage always equaled the rate of the reaction taken as a whole, there would be no need to analyze each sub-reaction.

35. (B) (p. 476) ***Science/Research Summary/Comprehension.*** Temperature range for a life function is the high temperature minus the low temperature. For both species and both humidity conditions, oviposition always has the narrowest range.

36. (J) (p. 476) ***Science/Research Summary/Comprehension.*** For each life function, Species M achieved 90% success at the same low temperatures in moist or dry air. At high temperatures, however, dry air was detrimental. (Under dry conditions, 90% success was not achieved at the same high temperatures as when conditions were moist!)

37. (C) (p. 476) ***Science/Research Summary/Analysis.*** Since dry conditions had no effect on Species D for mating, oviposition, or pupation, it is likely that dry conditions will have little effect on caterpillar survival in Species D as well. The temperature range would, therefore, be the same as observed at 100% relative humidity.

38. (G) (p. 476) ***Science/Research Summary/Analysis.*** Mating success in the light and in the dark should be compared at the same temperature. It should be a temperature at which both species can successfully mate. Otherwise, additional variables confuse the issue. (20°C is an optimum temperature for both species under all conditions presented.)

39. (D) (p. 477) ***Science/Research Summary/Analysis.*** Species M and Species D are both equally successful at low temperatures for pupation.

40. (F) (p. 477) ***Science/Research Summary/Analysis.*** (G) and (H) are not relevant to the question. (J) only refers to light conditions. (F) is a hypothesis supported by the results.

SAMPLE ESSAY RESPONSES AND ANALYSES

TEST 5: WRITING (p. 478)

Above Average Response

I believe that it would be beneficial for schools to adopt a twelve-month school year. Although some might insist that a twelve-month school year would create problems for families and students, I don't agree. Family vacations and part-time jobs are nowhere near as important as getting a top notch education. A vacation or a summer job lasts only a few weeks, but an education will last a lifetime. A twelve-month school year would not only allow teachers to go over more material in greater detail, but it would eliminate the need to do so much review at the beginning of the year.

Perhaps the most important benefit of adopting a twelve-month school year would be improving the quality of the education in our schools. Right now, most students go to school for only 9 months or so every year. (Except for those who have to go to summer school because they failed.) But 9 months is not enough time in a year to get the best possible education. Often times, teachers find they are running out of time at the end of the year. A history book, for example, may be 400 pages long, which covers everything from the ancient Greeks and Romans all the way up to the present world situation. If a teacher runs out of time at the end of the year, there may not be enough days left to really cover the modern world. Students get a wrong view of history because they think that the longer ago something happened, the more important it is.

Another benefit of having a twelve-month school year is that teachers wouldn't have to waste time every year going over material from the year before. In math, for example, we spend the first few weeks reviewing things we've done the previous year. If you took Algebra I last year and finished up with solving quadratic equations, then you start off again solving quadratic equations, something you already knew how to do. You don't really get to the new material like graphing equations until later in the year.

Finally, I think that having schools open all year would mean that the buildings wouldn't be sitting empty part of the year. In other words, something would always be going on at the school, so the school would not have to be closed down for part of the year. Also, sports teams could benefit from the idea because it would give coaches the opportunity to schedule more practices.

In conclusion, there are many good benefits for having schools open all year. Students would get a better education, which is important, because teachers would have more time to go over the material. Also, teachers wouldn't waste time reviewing material. And finally, there would be other benefits.

Position on issue: It begins, as it should, by announcing the writer's position on the topic, and it immediately acknowledges a possible counter-argument to the position.

Topic development and essay organization: Then, it develops three reasons in support of the conclusion, using examples; and the writer adds a conclusion to pull together the various points.

One of the strong points of this essay is its use of the two examples taken from history and math. These help to make the writer's point concrete and persuasive. Without the examples, the reader would be left with just the writer's assertions.

The writer also offers an interesting observation about sports practice in the next-to-the-last paragraph. However, in that paragraph, the point about having school buildings remain open year-round doesn't seem terribly persuasive: yes, so they are open, but what does that accomplish? The point might have been strengthened by some further development, e.g., "Every year, at the close of school, the custodial staff starts putting in storage all of the computers and other electronic equipment. This is not only expensive, but it means that the equipment is not available for student use. Then, in the fall, they need another few weeks to get everything set up again." The same observation can be made about sports practice. It's an interesting point, but it is one that could have been strengthened by giving an example: "For instance, coaches could design summer conditioning programs for accomplished athletes and drills in basic skills for new team members."

Language usage, sentence structure, and punctuation: The language used in the essay is not as tight or as imaginative as it might have been. For example, in the sentence in the final paragraph that reads "students would get a better education, which is important, ...", the phrase "which is important" doesn't really serve any function. It almost seems as though it's thrown in just to add to the word count.

Summary and conclusions: This essay can be described as "adequate" to the task, so it would probably get a score of "4," though some readers might think it deserves a "5." Overall, this is not a bad essay, but it could be greatly improved.

Below Average Response

I agree with educators and parents who say that school should go twelve months every years and not just nine. Education is the most important thing that students are doing in school, and it needs to be better.

Going to school all the time would help students get an education. They would be going to school all the year and would therefore be in the classroom every day (excepts weekends and holidays). This would improve the education.

Some people might think that family vacations and summers jobs are more important than getting a good education, but I don't. A family vacation is not really all that much fun unless you go somewhere where there are kids your own age. And a summer job is the time we need to work to make some pocket money to buy things for the next school year. Without it, it wouldn't be the same.

These is only some of the important reasons for going to school 9 months and to have summer vacation. Summer vacation is a tradition, and you don't want to upset tradition.

Position on issue: A position is identified in the first sentence of the essay: "school should go twelve months every years and not just nine." However, the essay author takes the exact opposite position on the issue in the third paragraph: "And a summer job is the time we need to work...." Then, in the summary paragraph, the author supports this contrary position with the statement "These is only some of the important reasons forgoing to school 9 months and to have summer vacation." A strong essay must take only one position and support it throughout the entire essay.

Topic development and essay organization: This essay is characterized by an almost complete lack of development, in addition to contradicting its position at the conclusion of the essay. It does make an attempt to address the issue and offers a fairly basic structure, but the point seems unpersuasive because it is basically a restatement of sentences found in the prompt. These criticisms are perhaps best illustrated by comparing this response with the other sample for this topic.

Language usage, sentence structure, and punctuation: The language is too informal for this style of writing and there are several grammatical mistakes found throughout the essay.

Summary and conclusions: The response falls somewhere in between a "1" and a "2," though perhaps it would get a "2" from most readers because it is not completely lacking in the features for which the readers are looking.

TIMED PRACTICE TEST II

MULTIPLE-CHOICE ANSWER KEYS

DIRECTIONS: For the correct answer, check the corresponding unshaded box. Then, total the number of checkmarks for each of the content areas, and add these totals in order to determine the raw score for that test.

TEST 1: ENGLISH (p. 482)

	UM	RH		UM	RH		UM	RH		UM	RH		UM	RH
1. B			**16.** H			**31.** B			**46.** J			**61.** A		
2. G			**17.** A			**32.** G			**47.** D			**62.** J		
3. C			**18.** H			**33.** B			**48.** G			**63.** B		
4. H			**19.** D			**34.** J			**49.** B			**64.** J		
5. B			**20.** F			**35.** D			**50.** H			**65.** C		
6. F			**21.** C			**36.** J			**51.** A			**66.** G		
7. A			**22.** F			**37.** D			**52.** H			**67.** B		
8. H			**23.** A			**38.** H			**53.** D			**68.** F		
9. C			**24.** F			**39.** A			**54.** F			**69.** A		
10. F			**25.** D			**40.** H			**55.** A			**70.** F		
11. C			**26.** J			**41.** B			**56.** F			**71.** B		
12. J			**27.** C			**42.** G			**57.** B			**72.** F		
13. B			**28.** H			**43.** A			**58.** J			**73.** B		
14. J			**29.** D			**44.** H			**59.** A			**74.** J		
15. C			**30.** J			**45.** D			**60.** F			**75.** B		

Usage and Mechanics (UM): ______ /45 Rhetorical Skills (RH): ______ /30 Raw Score (UM + RH): ______ /75

TEST 2: MATHEMATICS (p. 496)

	EA	AG	GT		EA	AG	GT		EA	AG	GT		EA	AG	GT
1. D				**16.** K				**31.** C				**46.** H			
2. K				**17.** C				**32.** G				**47.** A			
3. C				**18.** G				**33.** C				**48.** G			
4. K				**19.** B				**34.** H				**49.** C			
5. A				**20.** J				**35.** C				**50.** J			
6. F				**21.** A				**36.** H				**51.** A			
7. C				**22.** K				**37.** E				**52.** F			
8. G				**23.** D				**38.** K				**53.** E			
9. C				**24.** J				**39.** C				**54.** K			
10. F				**25.** D				**40.** J				**55.** B			
11. E				**26.** G				**41.** D				**56.** G			
12. K				**27.** B				**42.** K				**57.** D			
13. A				**28.** G				**43.** B				**58.** J			
14. G				**29.** D				**44.** G				**59.** A			
15. C				**30.** F				**45.** A				**60.** H			

Pre-Algebra/Elementary Algebra (EA): ______ /27

Plane Geometry/Trigonometry (GT): ______ /17

Int. Algebra/Coordinate Geometry (AG): ______ /16

Raw Score (EA + AG + GT): ______ /60

TEST 3: READING (p. 514)

	SS	AL		SS	AL		SS	AL		SS	AL
1. D			**11.** B			**21.** A			**31.** D		
2. F			**12.** J			**22.** F			**32.** H		
3. C			**13.** C			**23.** C			**33.** B		
4. G			**14.** J			**24.** F			**34.** H		
5. D			**15.** C			**25.** B			**35.** B		
6. G			**16.** J			**26.** F			**36.** H		
7. A			**17.** B			**27.** B			**37.** D		
8. G			**18.** F			**28.** J			**38.** G		
9. A			**19.** C			**29.** B			**39.** C		
10. H			**20.** J			**30.** H			**40.** H		

Social Studies/Sciences (SS): ______ /20   Arts/Literature (AL): ______ /20   Raw Score (SS + AL): ______ /40

TEST 4: SCIENCE (p. 522)

	B	C	P	ES
1. D				
2. F				
3. C				
4. J				
5. D				
6. F				
7. A				
8. G				
9. D				
10. H				
11. B				
12. H				
13. B				
14. J				
15. A				
16. G				
17. D				
18. J				
19. C				
20. F				
21. D				
22. H				
23. A				
24. G				
25. C				
26. H				
27. A				
28. G				
29. B				
30. H				
31. D				
32. F				
33. C				
34. G				
35. D				
36. J				
37. B				
38. F				
39. B				
40. H				

Biology (B): ______ /11   Physics (P): ______ /5   Raw Score (B + C + P + ES): ______ /40

Chemistry (C): ______ /18   Earth/Space Sciences (ES): ______ /6

MULTIPLE-CHOICE EXPLANATIONS

TEST 1: ENGLISH

1. **(B)** (p. 482) ***English/Usage and Mechanics/Grammar and Usage/Faulty or Illogical Comparisons.*** The original sentence is incorrect for two reasons. First, the phrase "more gentler" is wrong. "More" is redundant of the "-er" suffix. Second, the rest of the passage makes it clear that the author means to say that botany is the most gentle of sciences. (C) is wrong because the passage makes it clear that the author intends the superlative "most." (D) is not idiomatic.

2. **(G)** (p. 482) ***English/Usage and Mechanics/Grammar and Usage/Diction.*** The word "ostentatious" means "showy" and is not appropriate here. "Unobtrusive" is a better fit.

3. **(C)** (p. 482) ***English/Usage and Mechanics/Grammar and Usage/Pronoun Usage.*** The original sentence is incorrect because the pronoun "it" does not have a clear and unambiguous referent. Although it must refer to "botany," on first reading it seems that it might refer to "flower." (C) eliminates the potential for misreading. (B) and (D) are incorrectly punctuated.

4. **(H)** (p. 482) ***English/Rhetorical Skills/Style/Conciseness.*** The original sentence is incorrect because the phrasing is awkward and wordy. (H) provides the most direct and concise phrasing: "but the natural world." (G) and (J) are incorrect for the same reason as the original.

5. **(B)** (p. 483) ***English/Usage and Mechanics/Grammar and Usage/Diction.*** The original sentence is not idiomatic. The correct idiom is "consists of," not "consists about." (C) is wrong because it is not idiomatic. (D) is wrong because it uses a plural verb with a singular subject.

6. **(F)** (p. 483) ***English/Usage and Mechanics/No Change.*** The original sentence is correct as written. The other choices are not idiomatic and destroy the parallelism between "knowing" and "studying."

7. **(A)** (p. 483) ***English/Rhetorical Skills/No Change.*** The original sentence is the best phrasing. The phrase "in and of themselves" serves to emphasize the thought that plants are intrinsically worth studying.

8. **(H)** (p. 483) ***English/Rhetorical Skills/Strategy/Effective Transitional Sentence.*** The second paragraph sets up a contrast with the first. In the first paragraph, the author states that plants are intrinsically worthy of study. Here, the author says that we should not entirely discount their practical value.

9. **(C)** (p. 483) ***English/Usage and Mechanics/Grammar and Usage/Verb Tense*** and ***Punctuation/Semicolons.*** The original sentence contains two errors. First, the past participle "disparaged" is needed rather than the present participle following "should." Second, the dash disrupts the logical flow of the sentence. It seems to signal an aside or a clarifying remark, but what follows is actually another clause. (C) is the best choice; it uses the correct verb form, and the semicolon is a correct choice of punctuation to separate two clauses when no coordinate conjunction is used. (B) corrects the verb but not the punctuation error. (D) contains both errors.

10. **(F)** (p. 483) ***English/Rhetorical Skills/No Change.*** "Nonetheless" sets up a contrast between the idea that plants have practical value and the idea that this very fact imposes limits on the study of plants.

11. **(C)** (p. 483) ***English/Usage and Mechanics/Grammar and Usage/Sequence and Verb Tense.*** The present tense conflicts with the other verbs in the sentence. They are all in the simple past tense. Only (C) makes the required change. (B) is wrong because there is no reason to use the past perfect. ("Had been made" suggests that one past event occurred and was completed before another past event, but that is not the intended meaning of the original.) (D) is wrong because the subject is "study," a singular noun.

12. **(J)** (p. 484) ***English/Usage and Mechanics/Sentence Structure/Problems of Coordination and Subordination.*** "Or" implies that the two ideas are alternatives. However, an assumption can be basic and still unspoken. What the author intends to say is that these ideas are very basic but no one ever makes them explicit.

13. **(B)** (p. 484) ***English/Usage and Mechanics/Grammar and Usage/Sequence and Verb Tense*** and ***Pronoun Usage.*** The original sentence contains two mistakes. First, "to have understood" is inconsistent with the other verb forms in the paragraph, for it suggests something that will occur at a future time before some other action. (e.g., John hopes to have finished his homework before his mother comes home.) Additionally, "their" is a plural pronoun and cannot substitute for the singular "plant." (B) makes both of the needed corrections.

14. **(J)** (p. 484) ***English/Usage and Mechanics/Grammar and Usage/Pronoun Usage*** and ***Sentence Structure/Problems of Coordination and Subordination.*** The original sentence contains two errors. First, "they" is a plural pronoun and cannot substitute for the singular noun "flower." Second, "but" illogically suggests a contrast where none is intended. Only (J) corrects both of these problems without creating new ones. (G) fails to correct the second problem. (H) corrects both problems but is incorrectly punctuated. Without a comma ("it exists, and") the result is a run-on sentence.

15. **(C)** (p. 484) ***English/Rhetorical Skills/Strategy/Main Idea.*** The author states that one must study plants simply because they exist, and further, that simply because they exist they are worthy of study. This circularity is characteristic of a tautology.

16. **(H)** (p. 485) ***English/Rhetorical Skills/Strategy/Appropriate Supporting Material.*** The author inserts "of course" to acknowledge that the point being made is an obvious one: of course, poverty means lack of money.

17. **(A)** (p. 485) ***English/Rhetorical Skills/No Change.*** The original sentence is correct. (B) and (C) are awkward or wordy by comparison. (D) destroys the structure of the sentence.

18. **(H)** (p. 485) ***English/Usage and Mechanics/Grammar and Usage/Pronoun Usage.*** The original sentence contains an error of pronoun usage. "Their" is intended to refer to "family," which might be either plural or singular. However, there is already another pronoun in the sentence that refers to "family," and it is singular. Thus, the first "its" determines that the author will treat "family" as a singular noun. (G) is wrong because "there" is not a pronoun. Finally, (J) is the contraction for "it is" and not a pronoun at all.

19. **(D)** (p. 485) ***English/Rhetorical Skills/Strategy/Effective Transitional Sentence.*** The logic of the sentence does not support the use of the transitional word "consequently." "Consequently" is used to show that one idea follows logically from another idea or that one event follows from another event as a matter of causality. Neither of these notions is implied by the sentence. The author has not yet explained why one would find more poverty in rural America than in other regions. The best course is simply to drop the word entirely.

20. **(F)** (p. 485) ***English/Usage and Mechanics/No Change.*** The original sentence is correct as written. (G) is wrong because "lower" cannot be substituted for "less." The phrase "may earn lower than" is not idiomatic. (H) is wrong because the correct idiom for making a comparison like this is "less than," not "less as." Finally, (J) combines the errors of both (G) and (H).

21. **(C)** (p. 485) ***English/Rhetorical Skills/Organization/Paragraph-Level Structure.*** In the first paragraph, the author provides the definition of "poor."

22. **(F)** (p. 486) ***English/Rhetorical Skills/No Change.*** The original sentence is correct as written. A new paragraph is needed here because the author is taking up a new topic. Thus, (G) and (J) are wrong. As for (H), "since" destroys the logic of the sentence.

23. (A) (p. 486) ***English/Rhetorical Skills/No Change.*** The single word "parallel" nicely expresses the thought that lack of education is associated with low income. By comparison, the alternatives are wordy. Notice also that the wrong choices use phrases that would seem out of place given the formal style of the passage.

24. (F) (p. 486) ***English/Rhetorical Skills/No Change.*** The last sentence of the paragraph expresses an idea that follows from, or is the result of, the idea that precedes it. The phrase "as a consequence" signals the reader that the second idea is the result of the first.

25. (D) (p. 486) ***English/Usage and Mechanics/Grammar and Usage/Subject-Verb Agreement*** and ***Diction.*** The original sentence contains two errors. First, the plural verb "are" does not agree with its subject, "schooling." Second, the phrase "as inadequate like" is not idiomatic. (B) corrects both errors but is punctuated incorrectly. One can treat the phrase "like family income" as an aside, but the limits of the aside cannot be marked with one dash and one comma. Either two dashes or two commas must be used. (C) is guilty of illogical expression, because it seems to imply that schooling is supposed to function "as" family income. (D) is the right choice because it corrects the problems of the original and is correctly punctuated.

26. (J) (p. 486) ***English/Usage and Mechanics/Grammar and Usage/Pronoun Usage.*** "It" has no antecedent. (J) corrects this by supplying a noun. (G) and (H) make illogical statements.

27. (C) (p. 486) ***English/Rhetorical Skills/Style/Conciseness.*** The original sentence is needlessly wordy. (C) is more concise and more in keeping with the formal tone of the selection.

28. (H) (p. 486) ***English/Usage and Mechanics/Grammar and Usage/Subject-Verb Agreement.*** The original sentence is incorrect because the plural verb "have" does not agree with its singular subject, "head." (G) fails to correct this problem. (H) and (J) are both singular verbs, but "was to have" in (J) implies a condition that was never fulfilled. This suggestion of an unfulfilled condition is out of place here. (H) is the correct choice. The present perfect is acceptable because it indicates an action that occurred at some unspecified time in the past (the head of the family had some schooling). It would also be acceptable to use the present tense: "If the head…has little schooling, the children are…."

29. (D) (p. 487) ***English/Usage and Mechanics/Grammar and Usage/Diction.*** The original sentence is incorrect because the expression "as…rather than in" is not idiomatic. An idiomatically correct alternative is supplied by (D): "is as true…as." (B) fails to correct the problem of the original sentence. Although (C) is idiomatic, "they" does not agree with the demonstrative pronoun, "this," to which it refers.

30. (J) (p. 487) ***English/Rhetorical Skills/Style/Conciseness.*** The underlined phrase is redundant of "modern." Just omit it.

31. (B) (p. 487) ***English/Usage and Mechanics/Grammar and Usage/Adjectives versus Adverbs.*** The original sentence is incorrect because the adjective "poor" cannot be used to modify another adjective (educated). The adverb "poorly" is needed for that. (B) makes the correction. (C) is wrong because it changes the intended meaning of the sentence. The author is talking about poor people who are not well educated, not "educated poor people." Finally, (D) is grammatically incorrect. The noun "education" cannot modify a noun.

32. (G) (p. 487) ***English/Rhetorical Skills/Organization/Passage-Level Structure.*** The author supplies a definition and a number in the first paragraph. Throughout the selection the author offers explanations.

33. (B) (p. 487) ***English/Usage and Mechanics/Grammar and Usage/Sequence and Verb Tense.*** The original sentence is wrong because the present tense "fail" is not consistent with the other verb in the sentence. The other verb describes a past action. Additionally, "fail" is a plural verb, but the subject of the sentence is "one," a singular noun. (B) corrects the problem of tense (and the problem of agreement since there is only one form in the simple past). (C) makes the needed corrections, but the resulting phrase is not idiomatic. Finally, (D) addresses the problem of agreement, but there is still the problem of tense.

34. (J) (p. 487) ***English/Usage and Mechanics/Grammar and Usage/Pronoun Usage*** and ***Diction.*** The original sentence contains two errors. First, it uses "that" rather than "who" to refer to people. Second, it is not idiomatic. The correct idiom is "should have," not "should of." "Of" is not a verb. (G) corrects neither of these errors. (H) corrects the first but not the second. Only (J) corrects both errors.

35. (D) (p. 488) ***English/Rhetorical Skills/Style/Conciseness.*** The underlined phrase is redundant of "dropouts." It should be deleted.

36. (J) (p. 488) ***English/Usage and Mechanics/Grammar and Usage/Verb Tense*** and ***Diction.*** The original sentence is both grammatically incorrect and not idiomatic. First, "will starting" is not an English verb form at all. Second, an infinitive is used after a verb ending in "-ing" rather than the gerund. Thus, "starting to think" is more idiomatic than "starting thinking." (J) corrects both the problems of the original sentence. (G) does not solve the idiom problem, and (H) is ambiguous. The placement of "usually" suggests that it is intended to modify "thinking" rather than "starts."

37. (D) (p. 488) ***English/Usage and Mechanics/Punctuation/Commas.*** The original sentence is incorrectly punctuated; if, for clarity, the final prepositional phrase is set apart, a comma must be used. The colon is too powerful and isolates the prepositional phrase from the rest of the sentence. (B) and (C) are wrong because connecting the prepositional phrase to the rest of the sentence with a coordinate conjunction gives it an importance equal to that of the verb: "he or she ceases…and roughly at age 14."

38. (H) (p. 488) ***English/Usage and Mechanics/Grammar and Usage/Subject-Verb Agreement.*** The original sentence is incorrect because the singular verb "is" does not agree with its subject. The subject is a compound subject (a series of elements joined by "and"), which is plural. (G) fails to correct this mistake. (H) and (J) correct the error, but the use of the past tense in (J) is incorrect. The author is describing a current problem using the present tense.

39. (A) (p. 488) ***English/Usage and Mechanics/No Change.*** The original sentence is correct. Each of the wrong answer choices creates a run-on sentence. In general, when there are two independent clauses, one of three things is done: the clauses are joined together using a comma and a coordinate conjunction such as "and" or "but"; the clauses are joined together using a semicolon; or the clauses are put in separate sentences.

40. (H) (p. 488) ***English/Rhetorical Skills/Style/Conciseness.*** The two words have the same meaning. (H) eliminates the needless repetition.

41. (B) (p. 488) ***English/Usage and Mechanics/Grammar and Usage/Faulty or Illogical Comparisons.*** The original sentence contains a grammatical mistake. It uses "most" rather than "more" to compare two things. Both (B) and (D) make the needed correction. (D) is wrong, however, because the singular "one" does not agree with its verb "stay."

42. (G) (p. 489) ***English/Usage and Mechanics/Grammar and Usage/Pronoun Usage.*** The original sentence is wrong for two reasons. First, it uses the objective case pronoun "him" to modify the gerund "dropping." Instead, the possessive case "his" must be used. Second, the use of the gerund is awkward. It is much more direct to simply say "at the time he drops out." (G) corrects the original sentence and is more direct and concise as well. (J) would be correct except that it uses the past tense. The author uses present tense verbs to describe an ongoing problem, so the present tense should also be used here.

43. (A) (p. 489) ***English/Rhetorical Skills/No Change.*** The original sentence is the best rendering. The other choices are awkward and wordy.

44. (H) (p. 489) ***English/Usage and Mechanics/Sentence Structure/Fragments.*** The original sentence is incorrect because the sentence lacks a conjugated or main verb. "Increasing" is a participle and cannot function as a main verb. Each of the other choices uses a conjugated form of "to increase" and so avoids this error. (G), however, is incorrect because "so that" seems to introduce a clause, but what follows is not a clause: "so that during the eighth grade…." (J) is wordy and indirect. Additionally, the past tense in (J) is inconsistent with the other verbs in this paragraph.

45. (D) (p. 489) ***English/Usage and Mechanics/Grammar and Usage/Diction.*** In the original sentence, "none" is a pronoun. What is required, however, is an adverb to explain how the dropout participates in activities: not at all. (B) uses the correct idiom, but the "and" results in a contradictory statement. How could one participate a little and not at all? (C) is incorrect because "not much" is equivalent to "little," so the resulting statement does not create the either/or situation intended by the original sentence.

46. (J) (p. 489) ***English/Usage and Mechanics/Grammar and Usage/Subject-Verb Agreement*** and ***Diction.*** The original sentence contains two errors. First, "goes" is a singular verb and does not agree with the subject of the sentence, "reasons." Second, the phrase "goes deeper as" is not idiomatic. (J) corrects both of these problems. (G) and (H) do correct the problem of subject-verb agreement, but they are not idiomatic.

47. (D) (p. 489) ***English/Rhetorical Skills/Strategy/Appropriate Supporting Material.*** In the final sentence, the author notes that dropping out is a symptom that has other root causes. It would be appropriate for the author to continue talking about those causes.

48. (G) (p. 490) ***English/Rhetorical Skills/Strategy/Appropriate Supporting Material.*** The word "dropout" is familiar, so the passage would not be incomprehensible without the definition. However, the definition serves to tighten up the discussion.

49. (B) (p. 490) ***English/Usage and Mechanics/Grammar and Usage/Subject-Verb Agreement.*** In the original sentence, the verb "are" does not agree with its subject, "kind." Both (B) and (C) make the needed correction, but (C) makes a change that disrupts the parallelism of the sentence: "research and developing." Since "research" and "development" have similar functions in the sentence (they are both objects of the preposition "or"), the noun "development" should be used.

50. (H) (p. 490) ***English/Usage and Mechanics/Grammar and Usage/Diction.*** The original sentence is not idiomatic. The correct idiom is "look for something to do something" (to satisfy), not "look for something doing something." (G) is incorrect because the subjunctive "would have" suggests that an anticipated past event did not occur because of some other event. (John would have come to the party, but he was taken ill.) Finally, (J) is ambiguous. "With the satisfaction of" is a prepositional phrase, but it is not clear what the phrase is supposed to modify.

51. (A) (p. 491) ***English/Usage and Mechanics/No Change.*** The original sentence is correct as written. "Its" refers to "humankind." (B) is incorrect because "humankind" is singular. (C) is wrong because "it's" is the contraction of "it is" and is not a pronoun at all. Finally, "your" cannot be substituted for "humankind."

52. (H) (p. 491) ***English/Usage and Mechanics/Grammar and Usage/Diction.*** In the original sentence, the infinitive "to find" does not have a clear logical relationship to any other part of the sentence. (H) solves this problem by turning "to find" into "finding," which can then function as an appositive for "one" ("one of the problems"). (G) doesn't solve the problem of the orphaned phrase and, if anything, makes matters worse since a colon is more powerful than a comma. Finally, (J) just creates a sentence fragment of everything that follows the period.

53. (D) (p. 491) ***English/Rhetorical Skills/Style/Conciseness.*** The original sentence is wordy. (D) is more concise and more direct. (B) is very concise, but (B) destroys the sense of the sentence: what may they be? (C) is wrong because "it" is a singular pronoun and cannot refer to "machines."

54. (F) (p. 491) ***English/Rhetorical Skills/Strategy/Effective Transitional Sentence.*** The author intends here to contrast two ideas: wind is difficult to harness, but it is valuable.

55. (A) (p. 491) ***English/Usage and Mechanics/No Change.*** The original sentence is correct as written. (B) is wrong because the singular "has" does not agree with the subject "rewards." (C) is wrong for this reason and also because the author clearly intends to make a statement about the past, not the present. Finally, (D), which uses the future tense, must be wrong as well.

56. (F) (p. 491) ***English/Usage and Mechanics/No Change.*** The original sentence is correct. Notice how the next sentence parallels the structure of this sentence. (G) is wrong because it eliminates this stylistic feature and also because the resulting sentence is ambiguous. Does the author mean to say the machine was located in China, was built in China, or was simply in China one day passing through? (H) is wrong for the same reasons as (G) and also because the verb tense is illogical. Finally, (J) is wrong because "has" switches to the active voice and implies that the machine was building something.

57. (B) (p. 491) ***English/Rhetorical Skills/Style/Conciseness.*** The original sentence does not contain a grammatical mistake, but it is awkward. By comparison, (B) is more concise and more direct than any of the other choices.

58. (J) (p. 492) ***English/Rhetorical Skills/Style/Conciseness.*** The original sentence does not contain an error but is needlessly wordy. By substituting "by" for "through the means of," the thought can be rendered more concisely and directly.

59. (A) (p. 492) ***English/Rhetorical Skills/No Change.*** The original sentence is correct. (B) is wrong because the comma separates the adjective "several" from the noun it modifies, "centuries." (C) is wrong because "but" suggests a contrast that is not intended by the author. Finally, (D) is wrong because the use of "and" suggests that what follows is similar to what comes before. However, "water lift" is not like "centuries."

60. (F) (p. 492) ***English/Rhetorical Skills/No Change.*** The original sentence is correct as written. It uses the active voice and is more direct than any of the alternatives.

61. (A) (p. 492) ***English/Rhetorical Skills/No Change.*** The original sentence is correct. The author takes up a new topic at this point, so a new paragraph is appropriate and (B) is wrong. (C) is wrong because it creates a sentence fragment from what is otherwise a complete sentence. (D) is wrong because it is needlessly wordy.

62. (J) (p. 492) ***English/Usage and Mechanics/Grammar and Usage/Faulty or Illogical Comparisons.*** The original sentence is incorrect because it implies a comparison of two machines. In fact, the author means to compare one machine with all other such machines; therefore, the superlative "most" should be used. (G) does use the superlative, but "most simplest" is redundant. Use one or the other, but not both. (H) fails to correct the problem of the original sentence.

63. (B) (p. 493) ***English/Usage and Mechanics/Sentence Structure/Faulty Parallelism.*** The original sentence suffers from a lack of parallelism. The second in the series of two verbs should have the same form as the first: "flourished" and "came." Only (B) makes the needed correction.

64. (J) (p. 493) ***English/Rhetorical Skills/Style/Idiomatic Expression.*** The phrase "real iffy" is inconsistent with the formal style of the passage. (G) and (H) are needlessly wordy. "Capricious" solves both of these problems.

65. (C) (p. 493) ***English/Rhetorical Skills/Strategy/Appropriate Supporting Material.*** The phrase "rage into a gale" has an appropriate meaning for the sentence and adds a little spice to the prose.

66. (G) (p. 493) ***English/Usage and Mechanics/Grammar and Usage/Pronoun Usage.*** The original sentence contains an error of pronoun usage. It refers to both "television" and "products," so a plural pronoun is required. (J) fails to make the needed correction. Both (G) and (H) make the correction, but (H) introduces a new error. The use of the subjunctive "would be" implies that an event is contingent upon the occurrence of some other event. However, there is no such other event mentioned in the selection.

67. **(B)** (p. 493) ***English/Usage and Mechanics/Grammar and Usage/Subject-Verb Agreement.*** The original sentence contains an error of subject-verb agreement. The subject of the sentence is "industry," so the verb should be singular: "industry is." The relative clause introduced by "which" is not part of the simple subject. (C) fails to make the needed correction. (D) corrects the original sentence but is incorrectly punctuated. The relative clause should be marked with two commas, not one comma and a dash.

68. **(F)** (p. 493) ***English/Usage and Mechanics/No Change.*** The original sentence is correctly punctuated. (G) is incorrect because a comma must be used to separate the first two elements in a series of three or more elements. (H) is wrong because the comma separates an adjective from the noun that it modifies. Finally, (J) is wrong because it separates the definite article "the" from the noun that it modifies.

69. **(A)** (p. 494) ***English/Usage and Mechanics/No Change.*** The original sentence is correct. The subject of the verb is "the episodic series," a singular noun. Since three items are being compared, "most" is the correct choice.

70. **(F)** (p. 494) ***English/Rhetorical Skills/No Change.*** The original sentence is correct as written. "With the advent of" is an idiom that identifies a certain point in time. The remaining choices are simply not idiomatic.

71. **(B)** (p. 494) ***English/Usage and Mechanics/Grammar and Usage/Sequence and Verb Tense.*** The original sentence uses the wrong verb tense. The phrase "with the advent of" pegs the time as belonging to the past. Some form of the past tense is needed. Only (B) supplies a verb that refers to a past event.

72. **(F)** (p. 494) ***English/Usage and Mechanics/No Change.*** The original sentence is correct as written. The verb "have" correctly agrees with its plural subject. Also, some form of the past tense is required here since the sentence obviously refers to events that belong to the past. Thus, the other choices are incorrect.

73. **(B)** (p. 494) ***English/Usage and Mechanics/Grammar and Usage/Verb Tense.*** The past participle of "to grow" is "grown." (B) makes the needed change. (C) and (D) are incorrect because their forms are not parallel to the other verb form, "has lost."

74. **(J)** (p. 494) ***English/Usage and Mechanics/Sentence Structure/Fragments.*** In the original underlined portion, everything following the period is a sentence fragment—there is no main verb. (J) uses a colon to introduce the list. (G) is wrong because the comma incorrectly suggests that the elements of the list will be verbs. (H) is wrong because it fails to mark the transition from the main part of the sentence to the list.

75. **(B)** (p. 494) ***English/Usage and Mechanics/Grammar and Usage/Adjectives versus Adverbs.*** The original sentence is incorrect because "controversy" is intended to be an adjective that modifies "topics." However, "controversy" is a noun—not an adjective. (B) makes the needed correction.

TEST 2: MATHEMATICS

1. **(D)** (p. 496) ***Mathematics/Arithmetic/Simple Manipulations.*** Perform the indicated operations: $2\times10^4 = 20{,}000$, and $121{,}212+20{,}000=141{,}212$.

2. **(K)** (p. 496) ***Mathematics/Algebra/Manipulating Algebraic Expressions/Factoring Expressions.*** Recognize that $6x+3$ can be factored and rewrite the equation as: $3(2x+1)=21 \Rightarrow 2x+1=7$.

   Alternatively, if you failed to see the shortcut, solve the given equation for x: $6x+3=21 \Rightarrow 6x=18 \Rightarrow x=3$. Therefore, $2x+1=2(3)+1=7$.

3. **(C)** (p. 496) ***Mathematics/Arithmetic/Common Arithmetic Items/Proportions and Direct-Inverse Variation.*** Just use "supermarket" math. The cost of renting a bowling lane for 2 hours is $2\bullet\$12=\$24$. For \$24, a ping pong table can be rented for $\$24\div\$3=8$ hours.

4. **(K)** (p. 497) ***Mathematics/Arithmetic/Common Arithmetic Items/Properties of Numbers.*** (F) is incorrect since a natural number cannot equal the sum of itself and a number greater than itself. Similar reasoning applies to (G), (H), and (J). (K) is the only choice that could be true: for example, if *j* is 5 and *k* is 10, and if *l* is 15 and *m* is 20, then $5+20=10+15$.

5. **(A)** (p. 497) ***Mathematics/Arithmetic/Common Arithmetic Items/Decimal-Fraction Equivalents.*** Use $\frac{1}{2}$ as a benchmark. Reason in this way: eliminate (C)—since $\frac{7}{14}$ is $\frac{1}{2}$, $\frac{7}{15}$ is less than $\frac{1}{2}$. Continue eliminating choices until only the correct answer, (A), is left.

   Alternatively, you can use a calculator to determine which answer choice has a decimal equivalent that is greater than the decimal equivalent of $\frac{1}{2}$, or 0.5.

6. **(F)** (p. 497) ***Mathematics/Arithmetic/Common Arithmetic Items/Percents.*** Use the "is-over-of" strategy: $\frac{\text{is}}{\text{of}} = \frac{\text{students on track team}}{\text{total students}} \Rightarrow \frac{18}{360} = \frac{1}{20} = 0.05 = 5\%$.

7. **(C)** (p. 498) ***Mathematics/Geometry/Lines and Angles.*** (I) must be true because *a* and *x* are vertically opposite each other. Similarly, (II) must be true because *y* and *b* are equal and *z* and *c* are equal. (III), however, is not necessarily true. *x* and *a* are equal and *y* and *b* are equal, but there is not information on which to base a conclusion about the relationship between *x* and *y* or the relationship between *a* and *b*.

8. **(G)** (p. 498) ***Mathematics/Geometry/Lines and Angles.*** Vertical angles have equal measures. so $x+30=2x \Rightarrow x=30$.

9. **(C)** (p. 498) ***Mathematics/Arithmetic/Complicated Manipulations/Factoring.*** Eliminate choices (A), (B), and (D) since they contain numbers that are not prime. Then, calculate the remaining choices:

   C. $2 \cdot 2 \cdot 3 \cdot 5 = 60$ ✓
   E. $3 \cdot 3 \cdot 3 \cdot 5 = 135$ ✗

10. **(F)** (p. 499) ***Mathematics/Statistics and Probability/Averages.*** Use the method for finding the missing element of an average. Since the average height of all four buildings is 20, the sum of the heights of all four is $4 \cdot 20 = 80$. The three known heights total $3 \cdot 16 = 48$. Therefore, the missing value is $80-48=32$.

11. **(E)** (p. 499) ***Mathematics/Geometry/Lines and Angles.*** The angles labeled 4*y* and 5*y* form a straight line, so $5y+4y=180 \Rightarrow 9y=180 \Rightarrow y=20$. Next, the angles of a triangle total 180°, so $4y+2y+x=180 \Rightarrow 6y+x=180 \Rightarrow 6(20)+x=180 \Rightarrow 120+x=180 \Rightarrow x=60$.

12. **(K)** (p. 499) ***Mathematics/Arithmetic/Simple Manipulations.*** Each of the marks between the numbered marks is $\frac{1}{5}$ of the distance between the numbered marks. The distance between each numbered mark is 0.1, so each of the others is worth $0.1 \div 5 = 0.02$. Thus, $\overline{PQ} = 0.02+0.1+2(0.02)=0.16$.

13. **(A)** (p. 499) ***Mathematics/Geometry/Rectangles and Squares.*** The perimeter is: $2(3a-2)+2(2a-1) = 6a-4+4a-2=10a-6$.

Alternatively, assume a value for a. For example, if $a = 1$, then the length of the figure is $3(1) - 2 = 1$, and the width of the figure is $2(1) - 1 = 1$. The perimeter would be $4 \bullet 1 = 4$. Substituting 1 for a into the correct formula yields the value 4.

14. (G) (p. 500) ***Mathematics/Statistics and Probability/Averages.*** The average of the five numbers is 51, so their sum is $5 \bullet 51 = 255$. The two known values total 114. Therefore, the remaining three numbers total $255 - 114 = 141$. And $\frac{141}{3} = 47$.

15. (C) (p. 500) ***Mathematics/Algebra/Solving Algebraic Equations or Inequalities with One Variable.*** $-2 \leq 2x \leq 2 = -1 \leq x \leq 1$, so x could be -1, 0, or 1.

16. (K) (p. 500) ***Mathematics/Algebra/Manipulating Algebraic Expressions/Manipulating Expressions Involving Exponents.*** $8 = 2^3$, so $8^x = \left(2^3\right)^x = 2^{3x}$.

17. (C) (p. 500) ***Mathematics/Geometry/Rectangles and Squares.*** One square has an area of $2 \bullet 2 = 4$, the other an area of $3 \bullet 3 = 9$, and the sum of their areas is $4 + 9 = 13$.

18. (G) (p. 501) ***Mathematics/Geometry.*** Set up an equation: $x(2x)(3) = 54 \Rightarrow 2x^2 = 18 \Rightarrow x^2 = 9 \Rightarrow x = \sqrt{9} = \pm 3 = 3$. (Remember that distances are always positive.)

Alternatively, "test-the-test," trying each answer choice until one generates a volume of 54.

19. (B) (p. 501) ***Mathematics/Algebra/Solving Algebraic Equations with Two Variables.*** Since x is 80 percent of y, $x = 0.8y$, and $y = \frac{x}{0.8} = 1.25x$. So, y is 125% of x.

20. (J) (p. 501) ***Mathematics/Algebra/Manipulating Algebraic Expressions/Evaluating Expressions.*** Rewrite $m - n > 0$ by adding n to both sides: $m > n$. As for (F), this proves that $m < n$. As for (G), this proves nothing about m and n since m and n might be either negative or positive. The same is true of (H), which is the equivalent to $m > -n$. As for (K), there are neither relative values for m and n nor their signs.

21. (A) (p. 501) ***Mathematics/Algebra/Expressing and Evaluating Algebraic Functions/Function Notation.*** First, find $f(2)$: $f(2) = (2)^2 + 2 = 4 + 2 = 6$. Next, find $f(6)$: $f(6) = (6)^2 + 6 = 36 + 6 = 42$. Thus, $f(f(2)) = 42$.

22. (K) (p. 502) ***Mathematics/Geometry/Complex Figures*** and ***Lines and Angles*** and ***Circles.*** First, find the area of the circle: $\pi r^2 = \pi(2)^2 = 4\pi$. Since the shaded area is equal to 3π, it accounts for $\frac{3\pi}{4\pi} = \frac{3}{4}$ of the circle. Thus, the unshaded area is $\frac{1}{4}$ of the circle. Therefore, $\angle x$ plus the angle vertically opposite x are equal to $\frac{1}{4}(360°) = 90°$. Thus, $2x = 90$ and $x = 45$.

23. (D) (p. 502) ***Mathematics/Arithmetic/Common Arithmetic Items/Percents.*** Solve using the "is-over-of" equation: $\frac{\text{is}}{\text{of}} = \frac{\text{tin}}{\text{entire bar}} = \frac{100}{100 + 150} = \frac{100}{250} = \frac{2}{5} = 40\%$.

24. (J) (p. 502) ***Mathematics/Algebra/Manipulating Algebraic Expressions/Basic Algebraic Manipulations.*** $\frac{1}{x} + \frac{1}{y} = \frac{1}{z} \Rightarrow \frac{y + x}{xy} = \frac{1}{z} \Rightarrow z \bullet \frac{y + x}{xy} = 1 \Rightarrow z = \frac{xy}{y + x} = \frac{xy}{x + y}$.

Alternatively, assume some values. Assume that $x=1$ and $y=1$. On that assumption, $z=\frac{1}{2}$. Substitute 1 for x and 1 for y into the choices. Only (J) generates the value $\frac{1}{2}$.

25. (D) (p. 503) ***Mathematics/Arithmetic/Common Arithmetic Items/Absolute Value.*** $|-5|=5$, $|-12|=12$, and $|-2|=2$. Thus, the expression is equal to $5+12-2+(-6)=15-6=9$.

26. (G) (p. 503) ***Mathematics/Statistics and Probability/Averages.*** Add the three elements and divide by 3: $\frac{2x+2x+1+2x+2}{3}=x-1 \Rightarrow \frac{6x+3}{3}=x-1 \Rightarrow 6x+3=3(x-1)$.

27. (B) (p. 503) ***Mathematics/Arithmetic/Solving Complicated Arithmetic Application Items.*** The profit on each box of candy is $\$2-\$1=\$1$. To earn a total profit of $500, it will be necessary to sell $\$500 \bullet \$1=500$ boxes.

28. (G) (p. 503) ***Mathematics/Arithmetic/Simple Manipulations.*** $(-2)^2-(-2)^3=4-(-8)=12$.

29. (D) (p. 504) ***Mathematics/Arithmetic/Common Arithmetic Items/Properties of Numbers.*** If the product of three different integers is 0, then one of the integers must be 0. Of x and $-x$, one is positive and the other negative, so neither can be 0. The missing integer must be 0.

30. (F) (p. 504) ***Mathematics/Arithmetic/Common Arithmetic Items/Percents.*** Use the "is-over-of" strategy: $\frac{\text{is}}{\text{of}}=\frac{\text{seniors}}{\text{total}}=\frac{90}{360}=\frac{1}{4}=25\%$.

31. (C) (p. 504) ***Mathematics/Geometry/Complex Figures*** and ***Rectangles and Squares*** and ***Triangles/45°-45°-90° Triangles.*** The diagonal of a square creates an isosceles right triangle. Since this is a 45°-45°-90° right triangle, one of the sides of the square is equal to $\frac{\sqrt{2}}{\sqrt{2}}=1$. Or, represent the length of a side of the square by x. From the Pythagorean theorem, $x^2+x^2=(\sqrt{2})^2 \Rightarrow 2x^2=2 \Rightarrow x^2=1 \Rightarrow x=\pm 1=1$ (since length is positive). Therefore, the perimeter of the square is $4(1)=4$.

32. (G) (p. 505) ***Mathematics/Geometry/Lines and Angles.*** The angles labeled $3w$ and $(5w+20)$ form a straight line: $3w+(5w+20)=180 \Rightarrow 8w+20=180 \Rightarrow 8w=160 \Rightarrow w=20$. The angles labeled $3w$ and $4x$ also form a straight line: $3w+4x=180 \Rightarrow 3(20)+4x=180 \Rightarrow 60+4x=180 \Rightarrow 4x=120 \Rightarrow x=30$.

33. (C) (p. 505) ***Mathematics/Geometry/Rectangles and Squares.*** If the floor were a perfect rectangle, it would have a width of $4 \bullet 5=20$ meters, a length of $8 \bullet 5=40$ meters, and a total area of $20 \bullet 40=800$ square meters. However, the floor is not a perfect rectangle. Its actual area is smaller. Subtract the area of the missing "corner." It has dimensions of $0.8 \bullet 5=4$. Therefore, the corner's area is $4 \bullet 4=16$. $800-16=784$.

34. (H) (p. 506) ***Mathematics/Geometry/Triangles/Working with Triangles*** and ***Arithmetic/Common Arithmetic Items/Properties of Numbers.*** The sum of the lengths of any two sides of a triangle must be greater than the length of the third side. If x is the length of the third side, then $x+4>11 \Rightarrow x>7$, and the smallest integer value for x is 8. Also, $4+11>x \Rightarrow 15>x$, and the largest integer value for x is 14.

35. (C) (p. 506) ***Mathematics/Algebra/Solving Quadratic Equations.*** Put the equation in standard form, factor, and solve for x: $-x^2=3-4x \Rightarrow 0=3-4x+x^2 \Rightarrow x^2-4x+3=0 \Rightarrow (x-3)(x-1)=0$. Therefore, either $x-3=0$ and $x=3$ or $x-1=0$ and $x=1$. The solution set is $\{1, 3\}$.

36. (H) (p. 506) ***Mathematics/Arithmetic/Solving Complicated Arithmetic Application Items.*** The club spent $\frac{2}{5}$ of the budget on the first project and was left with $\frac{3}{5}$ of $\$300 = \$180$. Then, $\frac{1}{3}$ of \$180 was spent, leaving $\frac{2}{3}$ of $\$180 = \$120$.

37. (E) (p. 507) ***Mathematics/Algebra/Manipulating Algebraic Expressions/Creating Algebraic Expressions.*** Since n nails cost c cents, each nail will cost $\frac{c}{n}$ cents. Then, x nails will cost $x\left(\frac{c}{n}\right)$ or $\frac{cx}{n}$ cents. A dollar contains 100 cents, so the cost of x nails in dollars is $\frac{cx}{100n}$: $d = \frac{cx}{100n}$.

Alternatively, use the technique of assuming some values for the variables. For example, assume that nails cost 5 cents each and 20 are to be purchased. On that assumption, the cost is \$1. If $n = 1$, $c = 5$, and $x = 20$, then $d = 1$:

A. $1 = 100(5)(1)(20)$ ✗

B. $1 = \frac{100(5)(20)}{1}$ ✗

C. $1 = \frac{100(1)(20)}{5}$ ✗

D. $1 = \frac{(1)(20)}{100(5)}$ ✗

E. $1 = \frac{(5)(20)}{100(1)}$ ✓

38. (K) (p. 507) ***Mathematics/Algebra/Manipulating Algebraic Expressions/Basic Algebraic Manipulations.*** For all real numbers, a^2 is greater than 0, so b^3c must be less than 0. However, $b^3c = b^2bc$, and b^2 is greater than 0. Therefore, bc must be less than 0, and the answer is (K). (Note that either b or c is less than 0, but not both.)

39. (C) (p. 507) ***Mathematics/Geometry/Triangles/Working with Triangles.*** Since this is an equilateral triangle, the sides are equal. Set up equations: $2x + 1 = 2x + y$, so $y = 1$. Therefore, side $y + 2 = 1 + 2 = 3$. The perimeter of the triangle is $3(3) = 9$.

40. (J) (p. 507) ***Mathematics/Coordinate Geometry/Distance Formula.*** Use the distance formula or the Pythagorean theorem.

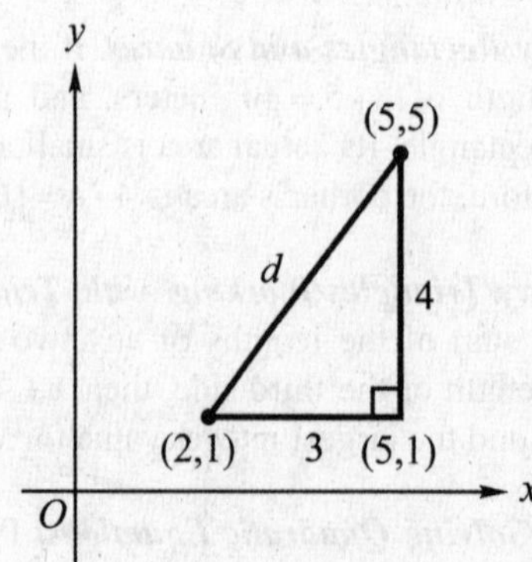

Using the distance formula, we have: $d=\sqrt{(5-2)^2+(5-1)^2}=\sqrt{3^2+4^2}=\sqrt{9+16}=\sqrt{25}=5$. Or, using the Pythagorean theorem, we have: $d^2=3^2+4^2=25 \Rightarrow d=5$.

41. (D) (p. 508) ***Mathematics/Arithmetic/Complicated Manipulations/Factoring.*** The key to combining the expressions is $\sqrt{5}$. 45 and 20 are both multiples of 5: $\sqrt{9 \cdot 5}-\sqrt{4 \cdot 5}+\sqrt{5}=3\sqrt{5}-2\sqrt{5}+\sqrt{5}=2\sqrt{5}$.

42. (K) (p. 508) ***Mathematics/Arithmetic/Simple Manipulations.*** This is a good item for testing the choices:

F. $12-3=9$ and $15-3=12$ ✗
G. $12-4=8$ and $15-4=11$ ✗
H. $12-11=1$ and $15-11=4$ ✗
J. $12-12=0$ and $15-12=3$ ✗
K. $12-13=-1$ and $15-13=2$ ✓

43. (B) (p. 508) ***Mathematics/Algebra/Solving Simultaneous Equations.*** First, substitute the values for x and y into the equations. Then, solve the simultaneous equations $3m+n=15$ and $3n+m=13$. Use the first equation to solve for n: $n=15-3m$. Substitute this expression for n in the second equation: $3(15-3m)+m=13 \Rightarrow 45-9m+m=13 \Rightarrow 8m=32 \Rightarrow m=4$. Only (B) has $m=4$. You can double-check (B) by substituting $m=4$ and $n=3$.

44. (G) (p. 508) ***Mathematics/Geometry/Rectangles and Squares.*** The total length of all 12 of the small line segments is 24. Thus, the length of each small line segment is $24 \div 12 = 2$. So, $\text{area}_{\text{square}}=2^2=4$.

Alternatively, the four large segments total 24 and each segment is 6 units long. Each large segment is divided into 3 equal parts and each part is 2 units long. The shaded area is bounded by a square with side of 2. The area of the shaded part is $2 \cdot 2 = 4$.

45. (A) (p. 509) ***Mathematics/Arithmetic/Common Arithmetic Items/Absolute Value.*** $|a-b|=-|b-a|$ only when $a-b=0$. Substituting numbers for a and b works as well: $|3-2|=-|2-3| \Rightarrow |1|=-|-1| \Rightarrow 1 \neq -1$.

46. (H) (p. 509) ***Mathematics/Trigonometry/Trigonometric Relationships.*** The easiest method is to recognize that the arccosine is the inverse function of the cosine. For all inverse functions f and f', $f'(f(x))=x$. Therefore, $\arccos\left(\cos\frac{\pi}{2}\right)=\frac{\pi}{2}$.

47. (A) (p. 509) ***Mathematics/Coordinate Geometry.*** A reflection across the line $y=-x$ maps a point P with coordinates (x,y) onto point P' with coordinates $(-y,-x)$:

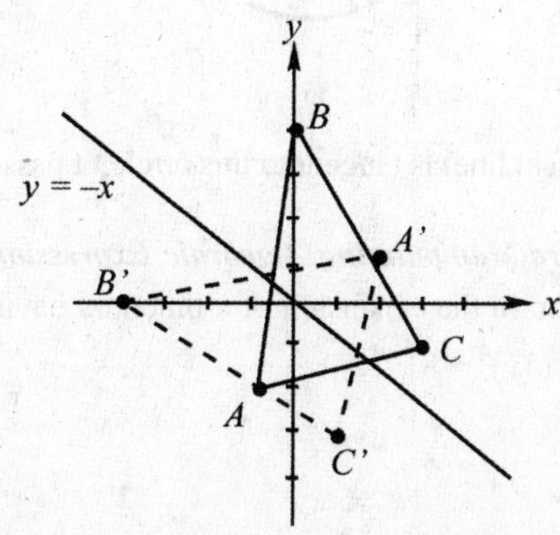

	(x,y)			$(-y,-x)$
A	$(-1,-2)$	→	A'	$(2,1)$
B	$(0,4)$	→	B'	$(-4,0)$
C	$(3,-1)$	→	C'	$(1,-3)$

48. (G) (p. 509) ***Mathematics/Trigonometry/Determining Trigonometric Values.*** Visualize the graph of the sine and cosine functions:

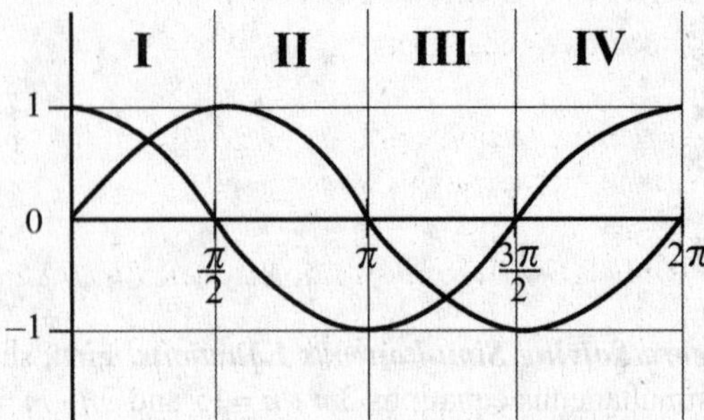

Alternatively, recall that in the first quadrant, at the coordinate $\frac{\pi}{4}$, both sine and cosine values are the same $\frac{\sqrt{2}}{2}$. Now, look at the same relative coordinates in the other quadrants. In the second quadrant, sine values are positive, but cosine values are negative. In the fourth quadrant, sine values are negative, while cosine values are positive. And in the third quadrant, both sine and cosine values are negative and they are the same at the coordinate $\frac{3\pi}{4}$. Therefore, $\sin x = \cos x$ in the first and third quadrants.

49. (C) (p. 510) ***Mathematics/Coordinate Geometry/Graphs of Quadratic Equations.*** The general form of the equation of a circle is: $(x-h)^2+(y-k)^2=r^2$, where (h,k) is the center of the circle and r its radius. The circle described in the question stem has a radius of 2 and has its center at $(2,-1)$:

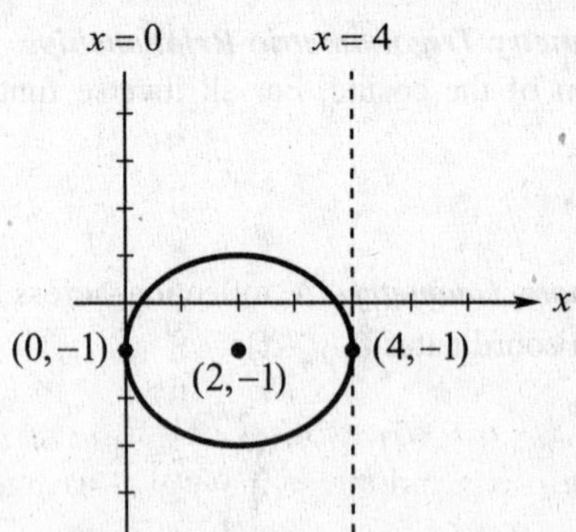

If a line of the form $x=k$ (a vertical line) is tangent to this circle, it passes through points $(0,-1)$ or $(4,-1)$.

50. (J) (p. 510) ***Mathematics/Algebra/Manipulating Algebraic Expressions/Evaluating Expressions.*** According to the binomial theorem, the last term in the expansion of a binomial having the form $(a+b)^n$ is b^n. Therefore, the last term of the expansion will be $(3y)^4=81y^4$.

51. **(A)** (p. 510) ***Mathematics/Coordinate Geometry/Graphs of Quadratic Equations.*** The quadratic formula: $x = \frac{-b \pm \sqrt{b^2 - 4ac}}{2a}$ is used to find the roots of a quadratic equation having the form $ax^2 + bx + c$. $b^2 - 4ac$ is called the discriminant because it discriminates among three possibilities:

1. When $b^2 - 4ac = 0$, the equation has one root.
2. When $b^2 - 4ac > 0$, the equation has two unequal real roots.
3. When $b^2 - 4ac < 0$, the equation has no real roots.

Therefore, for the equation given in the question stem, $ax^2 + bx + c = 0$, has only one root. The graph given in (A) is the only one that has only one point on the x-axis (where $y = 0$).

52. **(F)** (p. 511) ***Mathematics/Trigonometry/Trigonometric Relationships.*** This is a standard quotient identity: $\frac{\sin\theta}{\cos\theta} = \tan\theta$. This fact can be easily derived. Given a right triangle with sides a and b and hypotenuse c, let θ be the angle opposite side b. Since $\sin\theta = \frac{\text{side opposite } \theta}{\text{hypotenuse}} = \frac{b}{c}$ and $\cos\theta = \frac{\text{side adjacent to } \theta}{\text{hypotenuse}} = \frac{a}{c}$, $\frac{\sin\theta}{\cos\theta} = \frac{b}{c} \div \frac{a}{c} = \frac{b}{c} \bullet \frac{c}{a} = \frac{b}{a}$. For θ: $\frac{b}{a} = \frac{\text{side opposite } \theta}{\text{side adjacent to } \theta} = \tan\theta$.

53. **(E)** (p. 511) ***Mathematics/Geometry/Lines and Angles.*** Since 2π radians equals 180°, use a simple proportion, putting the unknown in the numerator: $\frac{x^\circ}{360^\circ} = \frac{\frac{3}{2}\pi}{2\pi} \Rightarrow x = \frac{\frac{3}{2}\pi}{2\pi}(360^\circ) \Rightarrow x = \frac{3}{4}(360^\circ) = 270^\circ$.

54. **(K)** (p. 511) ***Mathematics/Algebra/Solving Algebraic Equations or Inequalities with One Variable/Equations Involving Absolute Value.*** $|2x - 1| = 2x - 1$ or $|2x - 1| = -(2x - 1) = -2x + 1$ since $|n| = n$ or $|n| = -n$, whichever possibility is greater. Thus:

$$\begin{aligned} 2x - 1 &= 3 \\ 2x &= 4 \\ x &= 2 \end{aligned} \quad \text{or} \quad \begin{aligned} -(2x - 1) &= 3 \\ -2x + 1 &= 3 \\ -2x &= 2 \\ x &= -1 \end{aligned}$$

Check all absolute value equations or inequalities. Substituting the two solutions into the original equations indicates that both are actual solutions.

55. **(B)** (p. 511) ***Mathematics/Coordinate Geometry/Distance Formula.*** Since the two points have the same x-coordinate, the line is parallel to the y-axis and the midpoint will have an x-coordinate of 2. The y-coordinate of the midpoint is the average of the two y-coordinates. The midpoint formula is $(x_m, y_m) = \left(\frac{x_1 + x_2}{2}, \frac{y_1 + y_2}{2}\right)$, so $(x_m, y_m) = \left(2, \frac{5 + (-4)}{2}\right) = \left(2, \frac{1}{2}\right)$.

Alternatively, the line length is $5 - (-4) = 9$, half of which is $4\frac{1}{2}$. The y-coordinate of the midpoint is $5 - 4\frac{1}{2} = \frac{1}{2}$.

56. (G) (p. 512) ***Mathematics/Coordinate Geometry/Slope of a Line.*** To find the slope, rewrite the equation in the form $y = mx + b$, where m is the slope and b is the y-intercept: $2x + 3y - 2 = 0 \Rightarrow 3y = -2x + 2 \Rightarrow y = \frac{-2x+2}{3} = -\frac{2}{3}x + \frac{2}{3}$.

57. (D) (p. 512) ***Mathematics/Arithmetic/Complicated Manipulations/Simplifying.*** Rationalize the fraction by using the conjugate to remove the radical from the denominator: $\frac{1}{\sqrt{3}-1} \bullet \frac{\sqrt{3}+1}{\sqrt{3}+1} = \frac{\sqrt{3}+1}{3+\sqrt{3}-\sqrt{3}-1} = \frac{\sqrt{3}+1}{2}$.

58. (J) (p. 512) ***Mathematics/Arithmetic/Simple Manipulations.*** Perform the indicated operations: $(-2)^2 = -2 \bullet -2 = 4 \Rightarrow 2^{-2} = \frac{1}{2^2} = \frac{1}{4} \Rightarrow 4 - \frac{1}{4} = 3\frac{3}{4}$.

59. (A) (p. 513) ***Mathematics/Algebra/Solving Quadratic Equations.*** One way to find the roots or solutions of a quadratic equation of the form $ax^2 + bx + c = 0$ is to use the quadratic formula: $x = \frac{-b \pm \sqrt{b^2 - 4ac}}{2a}$. The root given in the question stem has the "plus" form of the "plus or minus" formula. Therefore, the other root will have a minus sign.

60. (H) (p. 513) ***Mathematics/Coordinate Geometry/Graphs of Linear Equations.*** When a graph appears to be a "V" or a rotated "V," you should suspect that the graph is an absolute value graph. One way to solve this problem is to examine each choice to determine what the graph would look like. The graph of $y = x$ is a straight line passing through the origin with a slope of +1. The graph of $y = -x$ is a straight line passing through the origin with a slope of −1. The graph of $y = |x|$ will look like the graph of $y = x$ for all $x > 0$ and will look like the graph of $y = -x$ for all $x < 0$. That is the correct answer. The graph of the equation $y = 2x$ is a straight line passing through the origin with a slope of +2. Thus, the graph of $y = x^2$ is a parabola.

Alternatively, test the values of the graphs in the equations. Only the equation $y = |x|$ will accept both values.

TEST 3: READING

1. **(D)** (p. 515) ***Reading/Prose Fiction/Implied Idea.*** The passage never specifically describes the relationship between Turkey and the narrator, but it does suggest that it is an employee/employer relationship. The narrator is judging Turkey in his professional capacity and apparently has the authority to discharge him (if necessary).

2. **(F)** (p. 515) ***Reading/Prose Fiction/Implied Idea.*** Turkey uses pen and ink and has a bad habit of spilling ink during the afternoons. That is suggestive of a copyist.

3. **(C)** (p. 515) ***Reading/Prose Fiction/Implied Idea.*** The explanation that Turkey gives to the narrator for his eccentric behavior is age, but the behavior is more than coincidental. After his lunch, Turkey's face becomes a brilliant red, he becomes careless in his work, and his behavior becomes erratic. All of these facts suggest the conclusion that Turkey's lunch is a liquid one.

4. **(G)** (p. 515) ***Reading/Prose Fiction/Implied Idea.*** In the preceding paragraph, Turkey asks the narrator to excuse his behavior on account of his age and reminds the narrator that he too is growing older. (The narrator has said that he and Turkey are the same age.) Thus, the "fellow-feeling" refers to the similarity of their ages.

5. **(D)** (p. 515) ***Reading/Prose Fiction/Explicit Detail.*** In the final paragraph, the narrator decides to continue to employ Turkey but resolves that he will deal with the narrator's "less important papers."

6. **(G)** (p. 515) ***Reading/Prose Fiction/Explicit Detail.*** In the first paragraph, the narrator says Turkey's face veritably blazes "after twelve o'clock, meridian" during his lunch hour.

7. **(A)** (p. 515) ***Reading/Prose Fiction/Implied Idea.*** The narrator compares the increased redness of Turkey's face to dropping cannel coal on anthracite. Thus, the result is a more intense fire.

8. **(G)** (p. 515) ***Reading/Prose Fiction/Implied Idea.*** The narrator says that although Turkey works well in the morning, his afternoon antics cause the narrator to feel uncomfortable.

9. **(A)** (p. 515) ***Reading/Prose Fiction/Implied Idea.*** The narrator refers to Turkey of the morning as quick and steady and a valuable asset.

10. **(H)** (p. 515) ***Reading/Prose Fiction/Explicit Detail.*** The narrator says that Turkey does not become lethargic in the afternoon. Rather, he seems to become overly active.

11. **(B)** (p. 516) ***Reading/Social Science/Main Idea.*** (B) is the best title for this selection: it discusses two different approaches to punishment—retributive and corrective. (A) is incorrect because it is basically concerned with the retributive punishment and not with corrective punishment. The answers represented by (C) and (D) are not at all appropriate to the subject of the selection.

12. **(J)** (p. 516) ***Reading/Social Science/Explicit Detail.*** The last sentence of the second paragraph clearly illustrates that the death penalty is a right of the murderer. The author's discussion of Hegel's views further substantiates this argument. (F) and (G) are in opposition to Hegel's views. (H), although a good answer and acceptable to Hegel, does not indicate the death penalty as a murderer's right and is therefore insufficient.

13. **(C)** (p. 516) ***Reading/Social Science/Implied Idea.*** (C) is the best choice for this question. The philosophy of equal injury in retributive justice differs from the philosophy in corrective justice of treating the criminal to conform with normal society. The reason for each type of justice, therefore, is quite different. (A) is wrong because both kinds of justice can be applied to any type of crime. (D) has no bearing on the question. (B) is incorrect because the severity of punishment can be the same with either form of justice.

14. **(J)** (p. 516) ***Reading/Social Science/Application.*** The philosophy behind corrective justice is one of treatment and rehabilitation, not death. (F), (G), and (H), although forms of varying degrees of punishment, do not result in death, so they would be consistent with the philosophy of corrective justice; therefore, they are wrong. (J) is the answer that should be selected, as the electric chair results in death and is therefore inconsistent with the philosophy of corrective justice.

15. **(C)** (p. 517) ***Reading/Social Science/Implied Idea.*** In line 7, the author uses the Biblical expression "an eye for an eye, and a tooth for a tooth" to show that the idea of justice as "one form of equality" (line 4) is expressed as early as in the Bible.

16. **(J)** (p. 517) ***Reading/Social Science/Explicit Detail.*** The answer to this item is clear from the sixth sentence of the first paragraph: "Only inflicting an equal injury upon him can do this." A fair trial (F), rehabilitation (G), and separation (H) are concepts associated with corrective justice rather than retributive justice.

17. **(B)** (p. 517) ***Reading/Social Science/Implied Idea.*** The key is in the third paragraph. None of the other answers are inferable from the passage.

18. **(F)** (p. 517) ***Reading/Social Science/Implied Idea.*** Denying the true self, (G), and accepting punishment, (J), are parts of the retributive justice code. Curing antisocial behavior, (H), is a means of enabling the criminal to act in his own best interests. (F) best embodies the notion of "normal" in corrective justice systems.

19. **(C)** (p. 517) ***Reading/Social Science/Voice.*** The author aims to explain the differences between ancient and modern systems of justice.

20. **(J)** (p. 517) ***Reading/Social Science/Explicit Detail.*** The fifth sentence of the third paragraph states this explicitly. A fair trial (G), and a legal code (H), do not apply to treating the criminal. Punishment (F), is a last resort of the corrective justice system. (J) is the most appropriate answer.

21. **(A)** (p. 518) ***Reading/Humanities/Explicit Detail.*** The precipitating cause of World War I was the assassination of Archduke Francis Ferdinand, the heir to the Austro-Hungarian Empire throne, by a Serbian nationalist on June 28, 1914.

22. **(F)** (p. 518) ***Reading/Humanities/Explicit Detail.*** The assassination occurred in the city of Sarajevo in Bosnia. Claimed by Serbia, Bosnia was annexed by Austria, provoking the rage of the government and the people of Bosnia and Serbia.

23. **(C)** (p. 518) ***Reading/Humanities/Explicit Detail.*** Before the outbreak of WWI, a balance of power had existed for almost 100 years. As stated in the first sentence of the second paragraph of the passage, WWI shattered the balance of power that had been established by the Congress of Vienna in 1815.

24. **(F)** (p. 519) ***Reading/Humanities/Explicit Detail.*** Russia, the protector of Serbia, and Austria were members of competing alliance systems. When war broke out between them, the member states of their alliances were drawn into the conflict. Germany intervened on the side of Austria, its alliance member, and Great Britain and France joined forces with Russia, with which both countries were allied.

25. **(B)** (p. 519) ***Reading/Humanities/Explicit Detail.*** The second paragraph describes how suspicions enkindled by the failure of diplomacy sparked the order to mobilize the Russian armed forces. German mobilization was ordered after the Russian order was issued.

26. **(F)** (p. 519) ***Reading/Humanities/Implied Idea.*** A spirit of nationalism, not class solidarity, animated the people of the individual nation states that fought against one another in World War I. No longer did the upper classes of Europe act as a unified class. Instead, they joined with their compatriots of the middle and lower classes to wage war against people in other countries with whom they had once shared values, beliefs, and a way of life.

27. **(B)** (p. 519) ***Reading/Humanities/Explicit Detail.*** The Nazi regime that came to power in Germany in 1933 and the regime of Stalin that tyrannized the Soviet people from 1927 to 1953 were ruthless dictatorships dedicated to world conquest.

28. **(J)** (p. 519) ***Reading/Humanities/Application.*** The sense of futility felt throughout Europe during and after World War I would be evident in European literature of the 1920s, 1930s, and 1940s. It is a fair assumption that the literature of a particular period mirrors as well as illuminates the spirit of the age.

29. **(B)** (p. 519) ***Reading/Humanities/Implied Idea.*** World War I and its aftermath suggest the idea that war feeds on nationalist sympathies. The sense of affront felt by the Austrian people when the heir to the throne of their empire was assassinated did not allow the Austrian leaders to adopt a moderate stance in their dealings with the government of Serbia. Similarly, the sympathies evident in the brand of nationalism that animated the rulers of Russia to undertake the protection of Serbia led the Russians to perceive the Austrians as their implacable enemies, setting in motion the chain of events that led to the outbreak of war. Moreover, the militantly nationalistic forces that came to power in Germany, Italy, and Japan in the period between the two world wars undertook conquests that precipitated World War II.

30. **(H)** (p. 519) ***Reading/Humanities/Explicit Detail.*** As noted in line 4, Archduke Francis Ferdinand, as the heir to the Austro-Hungarian Empire, was a member of the Hapsburg family.

31. **(D)** (p. 520) ***Reading/Natural Science/Explicit Detail.*** Since Uranus "rolls like a ball along the path of its orbit" with the geographic poles located like axles on either side, one pole is always in direct sunlight and the other is always in darkness.

32. **(H)** (p. 520) ***Reading/Natural Science/Implied Idea.*** The warmest location on Uranus would be the one that receives the most direct sunlight. Of the choices, the one with the most direct sunlight would be the geographic pole in the center of the planet's daylight side.

33. **(B)** (p. 520) ***Reading/Natural Science/Implied Idea.*** Because of the way Uranus rotates, one side is always in daylight and the other is always in darkness. A location on the daylight side is not necessarily near the magnetic poles, which lie in indirect sunlight near the planet's equator.

34. **(H)** (p. 520) ***Reading/Natural Science/Explicit Detail.*** A planet's equator is by definition located midway between the geographic poles. Since on Uranus these are on the sides of the planet, the equator must ring the planet from top to bottom.

35. **(B)** (p. 520) ***Reading/Natural Science/Application.*** The Uranian equator, ringing the planet from top to bottom, is located at the juncture of the planet's daylight and dark sides. An observer at the equator would most likely experience constant indirect sunlight.

36. **(H)** (p. 521) ***Reading/Natural Science/Application.*** Auroras appear near a planet's magnetic poles. On Uranus, these are near the equator and nowhere near the geographic poles, so the equator would be the most likely place to see auroras.

37. **(D)** (p. 521) ***Reading/Natural Science/Implied Idea.*** On Uranus, the daylight side receives varying amounts of sunlight at different latitudes. However, this appears to have no effect on atmospheric circulation, which instead flows along the equator around the top and bottom of the planet. Clearly, some other factor besides sunlight is in operation.

38. **(G)** (p. 521) ***Reading/Natural Science/Application.*** Lack of an atmosphere to create erosion is the only possible choice. Gravity was obviously strong enough to reassemble the planet, and in any case, gravity cannot wear away surface features. As for the possibility that the second object remained nearby, any collision strong enough to shatter Miranda most likely destroyed that object; in any case, the passage makes no mention of it.

39. **(C)** (p. 521) ***Reading/Natural Science/Application.*** (C) is the only possibility since the passage states that there is no evidence of geological activity on Ariel.

40. **(H)** (p. 521) ***Reading/Natural Science/Explicit Detail.*** The second paragraph mentions three moons by name—Miranda, Ariel, and Umbriel—and then notes that there are seven other moons.

TEST 4: SCIENCE

1. **(D)** (p. 522) ***Science/Data Representation/Analysis.*** The radii increase (0.37, 1.35, 1.54, etc.) and the electronegativities decrease (2.20, 0.98, 0.93, etc.) as one goes down each column.

2. **(F)** (p. 522) ***Science/Data Representation/Comprehension.*** It is essential to remember that the second number means electronegativity. For fluorine (F), it is 3.98.

3. **(C)** (p. 523) ***Science/Data Representation/Comprehension.*** The bond length is the sum of the radii for each of the bonded atoms $(1.10 + 0.99)$.

4. **(J)** (p. 523) ***Science/Data Representation/Comprehension.*** Carbon and nitrogen have the smallest electronegativity difference, 0.49.

5. **(D)** (p. 523) ***Science/Data Representation/Analysis.*** Electronegativities increase steadily across each row and decrease steadily along each column, so the most widely separated elements have the most ionic bonds, or greatest ionic character.

6. **(F)** (p. 523) ***Science/Data Representation/Analysis.*** Several choices include the value 3.16, which is the electronegativity difference in RbF. Since Cs is below Rb, it may be expected to have an electronegativity below the value of 0.82, which is found for Rb, a prediction that leads to an electronegativity difference for CsF that is greater than 3.16.

7. **(A)** (p. 524) ***Science/Research Summary/Comprehension.*** Venus is only 0.05 units smaller in diameter than Earth (0.95 Earth diameters).

8. **(G)** (p. 524) ***Science/Research Summary/Comprehension.*** 1 A.U. equals 0.5 inches in the scale used in Experiment 2. The paper is only 14 inches long. Neptune's distance is 30 A.U. ($30 \bullet 0.5 = 15$ inches) and would not fit on the paper (nor would Pluto's, since Pluto is even farther away).

9. **(D)** (p. 524) ***Science/Research Summary/Analysis.*** As planets get farther from the Sun (A.U. column), some are larger than the Earth (Jupiter and Saturn have larger diameters) while others are smaller than the Earth (Mars and Pluto have smaller diameters).

10. **(H)** (p. 524) ***Science/Research Summary/Application.*** If the asteroids are 2.8 A.U. away from the Sun, they would be found between Mars and Jupiter. Thus, an asteroid year is longer than that on Mars but shorter than that on Jupiter.

11. **(B)** (p. 525) ***Science/Research Summary/Analysis.*** If the Sun's diameter is 110 times greater than that of the Earth, its diameter would be $110 \bullet 5$ inches $= 550$ inches (Experiment 1 uses a scale where 1 Earth diameter = 5 inches).

12. **(H)** (p. 525) ***Science/Research Summary/Application.*** The relative mass information given in the question is very similar to the order of planets based on their relative diameters (Table 1: Earth diameters column).

13. **(B)** (p. 527) ***Science/Research Summary/Analysis.*** If carbon dioxide (CO_2) is the variable in question, all factors except carbon dioxide should remain fixed. Only then can the effects of various carbon dioxide levels be evaluated.

14. **(J)** (p. 527) ***Science/Research Summary/Analysis.*** The only difference between Experiments 1 and 2 is that the concentration of leaf extract (containing a mixture of pigments) was reduced in Experiment 2. Using the lower concentration of pigments, the rate of photosynthesis leveled off, suggesting that the amount was inadequate to maintain the previously observed increase in rate.

15. **(A)** (p. 527) ***Science/Research Summary/Analysis.*** The description of Experiment 3 states that wavelengths must be absorbed to maintain photosynthesis (which is measured by counting oxygen bubbles). The bubble counts (and therefore peak absorption) for Pigment A are at 450 and 650 nanometers. For Pigment B, peak count is between 500 and 575 nanometers.

16. **(G)** (p. 527) ***Science/Research Summary/Analysis.*** Since the reduced concentration of pigments in Experiment 2 led to a leveling off in bubble count, an increase in pigment concentration should lead to an increase in the rate of photosynthesis and an associated increase in bubbles.

17. **(D)** (p. 527) ***Science/Research Summary/Comprehension.*** In Figure 1, use a straight edge and follow the graph up from a light intensity of 4—the graph indicates an oxygen bubble count of approximately 40 bubbles per minute. Doing the same for Figure 2 at the same light intensity indicates an oxygen count of approximately 50

bubbles per minute. Therefore, the graphs in Figure 1 and 2 show that for a light intensity level of 4, 40–50 bubbles/minute are produced.

18. **(J)** (p. 527) ***Science/Research Summary/Analysis.*** Figure 3 shows that at 600 nm (orange light), both Pigments A and B show very little absorption, as measured by the low oxygen bubble count. Since light must be absorbed to provide energy for photosynthesis, orange light would be least effective.

19. **(C)** (p. 528) ***Science/Data Representation/Comprehension.*** The meters/minute scale increases from bottom to top. The highest point on the chart shows the fastest speed to be approximately 590–600 meters/minute.

20. **(F)** (p. 528) ***Science/Data Representation/Analysis.*** The lines represent the best-fitting slopes of points, which show how running speed has increased.

21. **(D)** (p. 528) ***Science/Data Representation/Comprehension.*** In 1960, the ratio is based on 4 minutes/mile (1-mile run) to approximately 3.1 minutes/mile (440-yard dash).

22. **(H)** (p. 528) ***Science/Data Representation/Comprehension.*** The speeds for the 2-mile run are all between 340 and 370 meters/minute. Since $370 - 340 = 30$, the gain in speed must be closest to the "30 meters/minute" choice.

23. **(A)** (p. 528) ***Science/Data Representation/Analysis.*** This problem, requiring the right-hand scale, asks for an extrapolation beyond the given data. The 880-yard line, when extrapolated in the graph, crosses the 1980 axis at approximately 3.5 minutes/mile.

24. **(G)** (p. 529) ***Science/Research Summary/Analysis.*** Temperature rises at an even rate during the time that the sample is heated.

25. **(C)** (p. 529) ***Science/Research Summary/Analysis.*** Experiment 1 starts above 0°C, whereas Experiment 2 starts below 0°C. In addition, the temperature in Experiment 2 stabilizes along the "x-axis" for a while.

26. **(H)** (p. 529) ***Science/Research Summary/Analysis.*** The passage states that "constant" amounts of heat were added "continuously" to samples over a "defined" period of time. Assuming that all of these given conditions remain unchanged, (F), (G), and (J) can be eliminated. Therefore, a process such as heat absorption is the best explanation for the flat part of the graph, since it is not a given condition.

27. **(A)** (p. 529) ***Science/Research Summary/Application.*** Ice melts at 0°C. This is the temperature at which the graph temporarily levels off.

28. **(G)** (p. 529) ***Science/Research Summary/Analysis.*** The experiment utilized constant heating. Yet, temperature change was not constant.

29. **(B)** (p. 530) ***Science/Research Summary/Analysis.*** At the boiling point of water (100°C), there should be another flat section corresponding to the heat absorbed by the liquid in order to convert it to vapor.

30. **(H)** (p. 531) ***Science/Data Representation/Comprehension.*** An examination of the diagram reveals that primary tissue layers and primary germ layers are names for the same developing parts. This information is part of the description of the gastrula stage.

31. **(D)** (p. 531) ***Science/Data Representation/Application.*** The diagram arrows show the changes that occur as each developmental stage follows the previous one. The greatest amount of differentiation in structure and function occurs during organogenesis as the primary germ layers in the gastrula become the many specialized systems, organs, and related structures of the organism.

32. (F) (p. 531) ***Science/Data Representation/Analysis.*** (G), (H), and (J) can be verified from the given chart. Under the organogenesis stage, arrows show that the body's bones develop from the middle primary germ layer (mesoderm), not the innermost layer (endoderm).

33. (C) (p. 532) ***Science/Data Representation/Application.*** Structures (receptor cells) that contribute to visual abilities in the monkey would develop as parts of the eye, "a special sense organ." The arrows show that parts of the special sense organs arise from the ectoderm.

34. (G) (p. 532) ***Science/Data Representation/Comprehension.*** The asterisk below the chart indicates that during the cleavage stage, the many new cells that form from the zygote and its materials do not grow. Thus, as the zygote's material is simply subdivided, the resulting cells must be extremely small.

35. (D) (p. 533) ***Science/Conflicting Viewpoints/Comprehension.*** Theory 1 states that, "The reaction will adjust to the proportions given." Therefore, all proportions of reactants will be used. (D) does not follow those guidelines.

36. (J) (p. 533) ***Science/Conflicting Viewpoints/Comprehension.*** Theory 1 simply states that any proportion of reactants may mix. It does not explain the relation of the amounts of reactants to the amounts of product produced by the reaction.

37. (B) (p. 533) ***Science/Conflicting Viewpoints/Analysis.*** Theory 2 states that a certain proportion of reactants will react; otherwise, one or another reactant will fail to react completely.

38. (F) (p. 533) ***Science/Conflicting Viewpoints/Analysis.*** Theory 2 states that both reactants must be in the appropriate proportions to be used in the process of forming more product, so adding more of the other reactant is the only way to use up the leftover reactant.

39. (B) (p. 533) ***Science/Conflicting Viewpoints/Analysis.*** This is the only response that provides a ratio of Fe to O that is different from the two ratios that proved successful in the problem.

40. (H) (p. 534) ***Science/Conflicting Viewpoints/Comprehension.*** Theory 1 only states that products contain the original elements.

SAMPLE ESSAY RESPONSES AND ANALYSES

TEST 5: WRITING (p. 536)

Above Average Response

I believe that it is a good idea for schools to do more to teach civic virtues such as patriotism, honesty, hard work, and personal responsibility. Historically, these are the virtues that have made America a great country, and to continue this standing into the future, these virtues will be necessary. Let's look first at patriotism.

First, patriotism is the most important of all civic virtues. Patriotism doesn't just mean saluting the flag or singing the national anthem. If patriotism were that easy, it wouldn't be worth very much. Instead, patriotism is a sense of national identity and an understanding that we are all in this together. Without loyalty to one's country, America would be a loose association of separate groups with different goals. Think about oil as an example. Right now, oil is a vital national concern, and we are addressing this concern as a nation. Without a sense of national identity, however, you would have people living in upstate New York whose main concern might be the price of fuel oil for heating their homes in the winter. People in Southern California might worry only about the price of gasoline for their cars. People in Alaska might be worried only about the environmental effects of drilling for oil. But who would ask the hard questions about a national policy unless there were a sense of national purpose.

This does not mean that patriotism is just about practical matters or money. Patriotism is also about ideals such as freedom and democracy, and these are national ideals. The American Revolution was fought to secure democracy and freedom from the King of England. The Civil War was fought to make sure that democracy and freedom are available to all in the country. World War I and World War II were fought to ensure that democracy and freedom are available to others.

So patriotism cannot be overstressed. And more education about how to think about patriotism as something more than just flag-waving would be a good idea. Civics classes could encourage students to ask hard questions. Is it patriotic or unpatriotic to oppose an unwise war? Is it disloyal to criticize one's country when soldiers are fighting across the sea? Do all citizens have an obligation to serve in the military? These are hard questions, and good citizens know that hard questions don't have easy answers. Additional classes devoted to discussion of these issues would help to make better citizens.

Now consider the other civic virtues mentioned. Honesty, hard work, and personal responsibility are individual virtues, as opposed to patriotism which is more a national virtue. But these other virtues are similar to patriotism in that they are more than just catchwords. No one is going to argue that honesty, for example, isn't a virtue that we should all have. Really, who would say that schools should teach stealing? But the value of honesty is how it's applied in real circumstances. Suppose that you have a close friend who you know is experimenting with an illegal drug. If someone in authority asks if you know who in your class is taking drugs, it would be dishonest to say no. But loyalty and friendship are also virtues. And it is not clear what you ought to do in this situation. Again, a civics class that explores these issues would make students better able to address the real concerns that they must face.

In conclusion, civic virtues are not easy. If we, as citizens, are truly going to attempt to live our lives in a virtuous manner, then we must have the intellectual ability to analyze the situations we will face. I doubt that students master these lessons in a one-year civics class. There are real issues that change every year, as world and domestic events unfold. An ongoing lesson in the civic virtues would certainly help students to confront these issues.

Position on issue: The position is clearly and eloquently stated in the first paragraph.

Topic development and essay organization: This is an interesting essay. One of the most striking features is that the writer goes far beyond the idea of patriotism and other virtues as parroted behavior. The writer shows a real appreciation for the complexity of the notion of "civic virtue." This distinction is developed in some detail in the discussion of patriotism. The writer dismisses the idea of patriotism as flag-waving as naïve and talks instead about patriotism as a sense of shared or national purpose. Then, the author ties this distinction back to the topic: a sense of shared purpose presents some difficult civic questions. And, the writer concludes, since hard questions have hard answers, students could benefit from further study of civics.

The writer apparently then intended to go on to talk about each of the other civic virtues mentioned but really only addresses honesty. Hard work and personal responsibility seem to get dropped along the way. This is not necessarily a weakness of the essay. After all, you can only be expected to do so much in 30 minutes, and it was probably unrealistic of the writer to think it would be possible to touch on all four virtues mentioned in the topic. It might have been better, therefore, for the writer to have said explicitly, "I am going to focus on patriotism, but a similar analysis could be applied to the others." And in a subsequent revision, the writer could do that and bring a needed balance to the essay.

Language usage, sentence structure, and punctuation: The language used in the essay is appropriate to the style of writing in a formal essay. The writer composes in such a way that the sentences flow to create a very readable and understandable essay.

Summary and conclusions: As a first draft, this is a strong response that might very well receive a "6," though some readers might find fault and give it only a "5."

Below Average Response

It is my opinion that schools should do more to teach students about important civic virtues like patriotism, honesty, hard work, and personal responsibility. In order to avoid confusion, let me say that I am not talking about religious matters. I don't mean that schools should be teaching about God or sin. Instead, I mean that virtues like those listed are ones that everyone in a democracy needs to have regardless of their religious beliefs. And the best way to teach those is in the public schools.

One of the most important civic virtues is patriotism. It stands to reason that if people don't love their country, then they won't defend it. And if we don't defend our country, then there is no guarantee that it will continue to exist. It goes without saying, that without a country, there is not reason for patriotism.

The question, therefore, is how to teach patriotism. Parents do this by teaching children about the flag and national anthem, but that is not enough. Sometimes it is necessary to go to war. During these times, citizens have to be prepared to make sacrifices. So something more than flag-waving and singing is needed. The deep love of country that we call patriotism can really only be taught in public. Why? Because patriotism makes sense only when we understand that the other people around us feel the same way that we do. Patriotism is not an individual virtue. One person along cannot be patriot. Patriotism happens when a group of people, citizens support their country and they know that everyone else is doing the same thing.

Since patriotism is a group thing, it's best taught in a group setting. In a classroom situation, the teacher can lead a discussion that will show students that their fellow classmates share their feelings about their country. When students are aware that other students share this feeling we call patriotism, then patriotism works.

Therefore, more classes in patriotism would be valuable. The same thinking can be applied to the other virtues mentioned.

Position on issue: The writer clearly states his or her position in the first paragraph.

Topic development and essay organization: This essay presents an interesting contrast with the other example. Both writers develop similar points: the distinction between patriotism as an individual and uncritical virtue such as flag-waving on appropriate occasions and patriotism as a community virtue that reflects a common purpose. Both essays concentrate on patriotism and seem to let the other virtues fall between the cracks. Again, however, this is not necessarily a bad idea because one can only do so much in the time allotted. Still, this essay would have been better if the writer had made a conscious decision at the outset to focus exclusively on patriotism, perhaps developing the point just a little more and avoiding the weak last sentence that seems intended only to make sure that the other items in the list do not go unmentioned. Further, the contrast between the two essays nicely points out the weakness in this response.

Language usage, sentence structure, and punctuation: Overall, the writer practices proper language usage in the essay. There are, however, some grammatical errors, and the style of the essay is often informal.

Summary and conclusions: Now, the fact that this essay is not as good as the first response doesn't mean that it is a bad essay. It would probably be given a "3," though a severe grader might think it deserves only a "2" and a lenient reader might go for a "4." On balance, however, this seems fairly typical of the kinds of essays that earn a "3."

TIMED PRACTICE TEST III

MULTIPLE-CHOICE ANSWER KEYS

DIRECTIONS: For the correct answer, check the corresponding unshaded box. Then, total the number of checkmarks for each of the content areas, and add these totals in order to determine the raw score for that test.

TEST 1: ENGLISH (p. 540)

	UM	RH		UM	RH		UM	RH		UM	RH		UM	RH
1. C			**16.** J			**31.** B			**46.** H			**61.** D		
2. F			**17.** A			**32.** G			**47.** D			**62.** F		
3. C			**18.** H			**33.** B			**48.** G			**63.** B		
4. G			**19.** D			**34.** J			**49.** B			**64.** J		
5. B			**20.** H			**35.** B			**50.** F			**65.** C		
6. F			**21.** A			**36.** J			**51.** A			**66.** H		
7. C			**22.** G			**37.** D			**52.** G			**67.** A		
8. F			**23.** D			**38.** G			**53.** D			**68.** G		
9. C			**24.** H			**39.** A			**54.** G			**69.** D		
10. H			**25.** D			**40.** J			**55.** B			**70.** H		
11. A			**26.** F			**41.** B			**56.** H			**71.** C		
12. F			**27.** B			**42.** F			**57.** A			**72.** G		
13. D			**28.** F			**43.** A			**58.** H			**73.** D		
14. H			**29.** D			**44.** G			**59.** A			**74.** H		
15. B			**30.** J			**45.** A			**60.** J			**75.** D		

Usage and Mechanics (UM): ______/46 Rhetorical Skills (RH): ______/29 Raw Score (UM + RH): ______/75

TEST 2: MATHEMATICS (p. 556)

	EA	AG	GT		EA	AG	GT		EA	AG	GT		EA	AG	GT
1. B				**16.** G				**31.** A				**46.** K			
2. F				**17.** D				**32.** J				**47.** A			
3. C				**18.** F				**33.** D				**48.** H			
4. J				**19.** B				**34.** K				**49.** D			
5. E				**20.** K				**35.** E				**50.** G			
6. H				**21.** E				**36.** F				**51.** C			
7. D				**22.** F				**37.** B				**52.** G			
8. J				**23.** C				**38.** K				**53.** D			
9. D				**24.** G				**39.** B				**54.** K			
10. G				**25.** A				**40.** K				**55.** C			
11. B				**26.** H				**41.** C				**56.** G			
12. G				**27.** A				**42.** J				**57.** A			
13. E				**28.** H				**43.** D				**58.** F			
14. H				**29.** C				**44.** J				**59.** D			
15. C				**30.** K				**45.** C				**60.** F			

Pre-Algebra/Elementary Algebra (EA): ______/26 Plane Geometry/Trigonometry (GT): ______/18

Int. Algebra/Coordinate Geometry (AG): ______/16 Raw Score (EA + AG + GT): ______/60

TEST 3: READING (p. 576)

Item	SS	AL
1. C		
2. H		
3. A		
4. H		
5. B		
6. G		
7. B		
8. J		
9. A		
10. F		
11. B		
12. G		
13. C		
14. F		
15. D		
16. G		
17. D		
18. H		
19. B		
20. H		
21. A		
22. J		
23. D		
24. G		
25. D		
26. G		
27. A		
28. H		
29. A		
30. H		
31. C		
32. J		
33. A		
34. H		
35. A		
36. J		
37. B		
38. J		
39. D		
40. H		

Social Studies/Sciences (SS): ______ /20 Arts/Literature (AL): ______ /20 Raw Score (SS + AL): ______ /40

TEST 4: SCIENCE (p. 588)

Item	B	C	P	ES
1. B				
2. H				
3. A				
4. H				
5. B				
6. J				
7. A				
8. F				
9. C				
10. G				
11. A				
12. G				
13. D				
14. H				
15. A				
16. F				
17. C				
18. G				
19. D				
20. G				
21. C				
22. J				
23. A				
24. F				
25. A				
26. J				
27. D				
28. J				
29. C				
30. J				
31. C				
32. J				
33. A				
34. H				
35. C				
36. H				
37. D				
38. G				
39. B				
40. G				

Biology (B): ______ /17 Physics (P): ______ /10 Raw Score (B + C + P + ES): ______ /40

Chemistry (C): ______ /6 Earth/Space Sciences (ES): ______ /7

MULTIPLE-CHOICE EXPLANATIONS

TEST 1: ENGLISH

1. **(C)** (p. 540) ***English/Usage and Mechanics/Grammar and Usage/Diction.*** The original sentence is not idiomatic. "On account of" cannot be used as a substitute for "because of." (C) is the correct answer because it makes the needed correction. As for the other answer choices, (B) is wrong because "since" is a conjunction that can only be used to introduce a dependent clause; however, the material that follows is not a clause since it does not include a verb. As for (D), "for" can be a preposition; however, its meaning is not appropriate in this context.

2. **(F)** (p. 540) ***English/Rhetorical Skills/No Change.*** The original sentence is correct. "Nonetheless" provides the meaning required in this context since it means "in spite of this." As for the other answer choices, (G) and (H) are wrong because the author means to say that smuggling grew in spite of government efforts (not because of government efforts). As for (J), "on the contrary" generally means "in opposition to what has been stated"; however, it does not provide the precise meaning ("in spite of this") that is required here.

3. **(C)** (p. 540) ***English/Usage and Mechanics/Grammar and Usage/Adjectives versus Adverbs*** and ***Punctuation/ Commas.*** The original sentence contains two errors. First, an adjective cannot modify an adjective ("heavy timbered islands"). Only an adverb can modify an adjective ("heavily timbered islands"). Second, a comma is needed after "countless" ("countless, heavily timbered islands") to make it clear that "countless" modifies "islands" (and not "heavily timbered"). (C) is the correct answer choice because it makes both of these corrections.

4. **(G)** (p. 541) ***English/Usage and Mechanics/Grammar and Usage/Diction.*** The original sentence, (H), and (J) are all incorrect because they are not idiomatic. The correct idiomatic phrase is "well founded."

5. **(B)** (p. 541) ***English/Usage and Mechanics/Grammar and Usage/Sequence and Verb Tense.*** The original sentence is incorrect because "seize" (a present tense verb) is inconsistent with the past tense verbs used throughout the rest of the paragraph. Past events are being described here, so "seized" (a past tense verb) is the correct answer choice. As for the other answer choices, (C) and (D) refer to past events; however, they provide meanings that are inappropriate in this context. First, "were seizing" (a progressive past tense verb) implies an action that occurred over and over again in the past (e.g., "during this period, customs officials were seizing tons of wool each month"). Second, "have seized" (a present perfect tense verb) implies an action that began in the past but that also continues into the present (e.g., "the British have repeatedly seized our ships and continue to do so"). Neither of these meanings is appropriate here, so both (C) and (D) are incorrect.

6. **(F)** (p. 541) ***English/Rhetorical Skills/No Change.*** The original sentence is correct. As for the other answer choices, both (G) and (J) are awkward and needlessly wordy compared to the original sentence. (H) is incorrect because it misconstrues the meaning of the original sentence. Specifically, the original states that the *Beaver* was seized because of a "technical violation"; in contrast, (H) says the *Beaver* was seized "for technically being in violation" of the law, which incorrectly suggests that the author believes the violation was minor or perhaps even non-existent.

7. **(C)** (p. 541) ***English/Usage and Mechanics/Grammar and Usage/Diction.*** The original sentence is incorrect because it includes an incorrect word choice. "Principle" is a noun which means "rule" or "belief," and it cannot modify the plural noun "articles." The word required here is the adjective "principal," which means "main" or "important." Therefore, (C) is the correct answer choice. As for the other answer choices, (B) is wrong for two reasons. First, it does not fix the original, incorrect word choice. Second, it introduces a singular verb ("was") which does not agree with the plural subject ("British wool, blankets, and liquor") of the sentence. (D) is also incorrect because it introduces a singular verb, "was," which does not agree with the plural subject of the sentence.

8. **(F)** (p. 541) ***English/Rhetorical Skills/No Change.*** The original sentence is correct. "In fact" is used to introduce a sentence that illustrates or emphasizes a point made in the previous sentence. In this paragraph, the sentence about British wool being smuggled into the San Juan Islands illustrates the point made in the previous sentence—namely, that British wool was a principal article of illicit trade. So, "in fact" is correctly used here. As for the other answer choices, (G) and (H) are wrong for the same reason. "Furthermore" and "moreover" are used to introduce a sentence that includes an idea similar to (but that is not an illustration of) an idea from the previous sentence. In this paragraph, though, the sentence about British wool being smuggled into the San Juan Islands is an illustration of an idea in the previous sentence; so, both "furthermore" and "moreover" are incorrect answer choices. Finally, (J) is incorrect because "on the contrary" is used to signal that a contrasting idea will be introduced; however, the author does not introduce a contrasting idea.

9. **(C)** (p. 541) ***English/Usage and Mechanics/Grammar and Usage/Verb Tense.*** The original sentence is incorrect because it includes an incorrect verb form. A passive past tense verb ("was smuggled") is used earlier in the sentence, and another passive past tense verb ("and sold") is needed to agree with it. So, (C) is the correct answer choice. As for the other answer choices, they are all incorrect because they do not provide the required passive past tense verb.

10. **(H)** (p. 541) ***English/Usage and Mechanics/Grammar and Usage/Diction.*** The original sentence is incorrect because it sets up an idiom ("so much...that") but does not successfully complete it. (H) is the correct answer choice because it successfully completes the idiomatic phrase ("so much British wool was smuggle...that one naïve textbook writer"). As for the other answer choices, they are all incorrect because they do not complete the idiomatic phrase.

11. **(A)** (p. 542) ***English/Rhetorical Skills/No Change.*** The original sentence is correct. In the sentence, there is a contrast between how settlers welcomed national control and how they resented the accompanying restrictions on trade. "Although" is the right word for introducing this type of contrast ("Although they welcomed...they were less amenable..."). As for the other answer choices, none of them would be appropriate for introducing the type of contrast discussed in this sentence.

12. **(F)** (p. 542) ***English/Usage and Mechanics/No Change.*** The original sentence is correct. The simple past tense verb ("welcomed") is consistent with the other verb in this sentence ("they were less amenable") as well as the other past tense verbs in the passage. As for the other answer choices, (G) is incorrect because it eliminates the only conjugated verb ("welcomed") in the clause; as a result, the sentence becomes a sentence fragment. (H) is wrong because "would welcome" is inconsistent with the past tense verbs in the paragraph. Finally, (J) is incorrect because it creates a completely illogical sentence; in short, an "assertion of national control" cannot welcome people.

13. **(D)** (p. 542) ***English/Usage and Mechanics/Grammar and Usage/Diction.*** The original sentence is incorrect because it includes an incorrect verb form. An active past tense verb ("They wanted") is used earlier in the sentence, and another active past tense verb ("but feared") is needed here to agree with it. So, (D) is the correct answer choice. As for the other answer choices, (A) and (B) are incorrect because "were fearing" is not an idiomatic expression; the correct idiomatic expression is "were fearful." (C) is incorrect because, although it uses the correct idiomatic phrase ("was fearful"), the singular verb ("was") does not agree with the plural subject ("they") of the sentence.

14. **(H)** (p. 542) ***English/Usage and Mechanics/Grammar and Usage/Sequence and Verb Tense*** and ***Diction.*** The original sentence includes two errors. First, the underlined portion includes a verb phrase ("might be resulting") that is awkward and needlessly wordy; it should be replaced by the more accurate and succinct verb phrase "might result." Second, the underlined portion includes a prepositional phrase ("in the losing of") that is non-idiomatic; the correct idiomatic phrase is "in the loss of." (H) is the correct answer choice because it makes both of these corrections. As for the other answer choices, (G) is incorrect because it only makes one of these corrections. (J) is incorrect because a present tense verb ("results") does not suggest the element of uncertainty or contingency required here. Verb phrases such as "might result" or "would result" accomplish this task. However, a present tense verb ("results") does not.

15. **(B)** (p. 542) ***English/Rhetorical Skills/Organization/Passage-Level Structure.*** In order for a passage to be in the most logical order, its paragraphs need to be in chronological order. So, (B) is the correct answer choice here. Paragraph 1 comes first because it describes the earliest event (i.e., the opening of the customs office). Paragraph 3 comes next because it describes events that followed (i.e., Americans' concerns about the new office). Paragraph 2 comes last because it describes events that occurred last (i.e., Americans' concerns turned out to be true).

16. **(J)** (p. 542) ***English/Rhetorical Skills/Organization/Passage-Level Structure.*** The author does not provide any quotations in the essay. So, (J) is the correct answer choice. As for the other answer choices, (F) is incorrect because the author describes or provides a narrative of several events. (G) is incorrect because the author gives specific examples in the essay; for example, the author cites the *Beaver* as an example of a ship that was seized. Finally, (H) is incorrect because the author provides statistics related to the production of wool.

17. **(A)** (p. 543) ***English/Rhetorical Skills/No Change.*** The original sentence is the best choice. In comparison, the other answer choices are awkward and needlessly wordy.

18. **(H)** (p. 543) ***English/Usage and Mechanics/Sentence Structure/Faulty Parallelism.*** The original sentence is incorrect due to a lack of parallelism. All three verbs in the sentence ("step," "gaze," and "become") are governed by the first instance of "can." As a result, it is unnecessary for another instance of "can" to appear in the sentence. However, the original sentence has an instance of "can" before "become." As a result, a series is created in which the elements are not parallel or do not have exactly the same form. (H) is the correct answer choice because it eliminates the problem and brings the third verb into line with the other two. As for the other answer choices, (G) is incorrect because a past tense verb ("became") destroys the parallelism needed here. (J) is incorrect because the verb ("becomes") does not agree in number with the subject ("anyone") of the sentence.

19. **(D)** (p. 543) ***English/Usage and Mechanics/Sentence Structure/Comma Splices.*** The original sentence is incorrect because it is a run-on sentence. A run-on sentence is two or more complete sentences joined together without the necessary punctuation or conjunctions. For example, the first clause in the sentence ("The same questions to come mind time and again") is a complete sentence by itself. For the sake of correctness and clarity, it would be best to put a piece of end-stop punctuation at the end of this clause and then start an entirely new sentence. (D) is the correct answer choice because it accomplishes this task. As for the other answer choices, (B) and (C) are incorrect because they also result in run-on sentences.

20. **(H)** (p. 543) ***English/Usage and Mechanics/Sentence Structure/Misplaced Modifiers.*** The original sentence is incorrect because it is too ambiguous. Specifically, "ending" seems to modify "suns"; however, the author intends for it to modify "island universe." The ambiguity is eliminated by replacing the ambiguous "ending" with the relative clause "that ends...." It is now clear that the relative clause modifies "island universe." So, (H) is the correct answer choice. As for the other answer choices, (G) creates the appropriate relative clause to modify "island universe"; however, the plural verb "end" does not agree in number with the singular noun antecedent of the relative clause ("island universe"). Finally, (J) is incorrect because it suffers from the same defect as the original; "ended" seems to modify "suns" rather than "island universe."

21. **(A)** (p. 543) ***English/Usage and Mechanics/No Change.*** The original sentence is correct. Standard written English requires the infinitive "to chart" in this context. As for the other answer choices, (B) and (C) are incorrect because standard written English does not allow for participles ("charting" or "having charted") in this context. (D) is incorrect because it creates a sentence that is illogical and impossible to understand.

22. **(G)** (p. 543) ***English/Usage and Mechanics/Grammar and Usage/Verb Tense.*** The original sentence is incorrect because it includes an incorrect verb tense. The past perfect tense ("progress had been made") implies that progress was actually made *before* the twentieth century. Of course, the author intends to say that progress was made "in the twentieth century"; so, a simple past tense verb ("was made") is needed. Therefore, (G) is the correct

answer choice. As for the other answer choices, (H) is incorrect because a present tense verb form ("is made") fails to communicate that progress has already been made during the twentieth century. (J) is incorrect because a future tense verb form ("will be made") incorrectly suggests that progress has not yet been made at all.

23. **(D)** (p. 544) ***English/Rhetorical Skills/Strategy/Effective Transitional Sentence.*** The original sentence is incorrect because it begins with a misleading introductory phrase. "As such" is a phrase which suggests that one thing happens because another thing happened before it. For example, "It was raining outside. As such, the game was canceled." So, the cancellation of the game was due to the rain. As for this particular sentence here, though, it is certainly not the case that the Milky Way was so named because our solar system was discovered to be part of it. In fact, there is not a cause-and-effect relationship between the name of the Milky Way and our solar system's relationship to it. (D) is the correct answer choice here because it eliminates any suggestion that there is any relationship of this type. As for the other answer choices, (B) and (C) are both incorrect because it is not clear why the statement made is obvious or beyond doubt.

24. **(H)** (p. 544) ***English/Rhetorical Skills/Organization/Paragraph-Level Structure.*** The original sentence is incorrect because the material in it belongs in the next paragraph. Therefore, the original sentence should actually be the first sentence of the following paragraph. It should then be immediately followed (i.e., without a break for a new paragraph) by the sentence that used to begin that paragraph ("Since they are so near…"). Both (H) and (J) make the required changes. However, (J) is incorrect because "As" would turn the sentence into a dependent clause that did not have a supporting independent clause. (H) does not introduce this error. So, (H) is the correct answer choice.

25. **(D)** (p. 544) ***English/Usage and Mechanics/Punctuation/Commas.*** The original sentence is incorrect because only a comma or a dash (and not a semicolon) should be used to separate an appositive phrase ("the 'crown jewels' of the southern skies") from the main part of the sentence. (D) is the correct answer choice because it provides the appropriate punctuation. As for the other answer choices, (B) also provides the appropriate punctuation. However, it improperly removes the quotation marks from around "crown jewels." The phrase is an example of words that are used in an uncommon, unusual, or unfamiliar way (i.e., the galaxies are not literally jewels); as a result, the phrase needs to appear inside quotation marks. (C) is incorrect because a singular verb ("is") does not agree with a plural noun ("Magellanic Clouds").

26. **(F)** (p. 544) ***English/Usage and Mechanics/No Change.*** The original sentence is correct. As for the other answer choices, they are either not idiomatic or not grammatically correct.

27. **(B)** (p. 544) ***English/Rhetorical Skills/Style/Conciseness.*** The original sentence is incorrect because the "to" in the underlined portion is unnecessary and makes the phrasing stilted. Both (B) and (C) make the needed correction. However, (C) is incorrect because a plural verb ("provide") does not agree with the singular subject ("galaxy") of the sentence.

28. **(F)** (p. 544) ***English/Rhetorical Skills/No Change.*** The original sentence is the best choice. In comparison, the other answer choices are awkward, stilted, or needlessly wordy.

29. **(D)** (p. 545) ***English/Rhetorical Skills/Organization/Paragraph-Level Structure.*** (A), (B), and (C) are incorrect because the author does pose questions for these very reasons in the essay. (D) is the correct answer choice because the author does not promise that answers will be provided later in the essay to what are, simply, many unanswerable questions (i.e., How many stars are there? Where and how does the universe end?).

30. **(J)** (p. 545) ***English/Usage and Mechanics/Grammar and Usage/Diction.*** The original sentence is incorrect because it includes an improperly formed appositive. The final phrase in the sentence ("graduated of test pilot schools") is meant to be an appositive for "volunteer, military pilots." To properly form the appositive, simply rewrite the final phrase as "graduates of test pilot schools." (J) is the correct answer choice because it makes this correction. As for the other answer choices, both (G) and (H) are wrong because an appositive can be set off only by a comma or a dash.

31. (B) (p. 545) ***English/Usage and Mechanics/Grammar and Usage/Subject-Verb Agreement*** and ***Diction.*** The original sentence is incorrect for two reasons. First, a plural verb ("were") does not agree with the singular subject ("each") of the sentence. Second, the use of a present participle ("having") here is not idiomatic. (B) is the correct answer choice because it corrects both of these errors. As for the other answer choices, (C) does not correct the second error. (D) corrects both errors, but the past perfect "had been required" is inconsistent with the past tense verbs in the rest of the paragraph.

32. (G) (p. 545) ***English/Rhetorical Skills/Style/Idiomatic Expression.*** The original sentence is incorrect because it includes low-level usage. Specifically, it is not acceptable standard written English to use "got" when forming a passive verb form. Instead, use a form of the verb "to be" (i.e., "was," "were," etc.). (G) is the correct answer choice because it makes the needed correction. As for the other answer choices, (H) is a form of the passive voice; however, the past perfect "had been chosen" is inconsistent with the past tense verbs in the rest of the paragraph. (J) is incorrect for two reasons. First, the present perfect "has been" is not consistent with the past tense verbs in the rest of the paragraph. Second, a singular verb ("has") does not agree with the plural subject ("seven") of the sentence.

33. (B) (p. 546) ***English/Rhetorical Skills/Strategy/Appropriate Supporting Material.*** The information contained in the parentheses explains why only seven astronauts were chosen. However, this information is not vital to the development of the passage. By placing the explanation in parentheses, the author signals to the reader that the information is not vital.

34. (J) (p. 546) ***English/Usage and Mechanics/Sentence Structure/Comma Splices.*** The original sentence is incorrect because it is a run-on sentence. A run-on sentence is two or more complete sentences joined together without the necessary punctuation or conjunctions. For example, the first clause in the sentence ("These men were true pioneers") is a complete sentence by itself. For the sake of correctness and clarity, it would be best to put a piece of end-stop punctuation at the end of this clause and then start an entirely new sentence. (J) is the correct answer choice because it accomplishes this task. As for the other answer choices, (G) and (H) are incorrect because they also result in run-on sentences.

35. (B) (p. 546) ***English/Rhetorical Skills/Strategy/Effective Transitional Sentence.*** The topic of the second paragraph is the failures experienced during the early days of the Mercury space program. (B) is the correct answer choice because it provides the best signal to the reader that this will be the topic of the paragraph.

36. (J) (p. 546) ***English/Usage and Mechanics/Grammar and Usage/Pronoun Usage.*** The original sentence is incorrect for two reasons. First, the subject ("they") of the original sentence is too ambiguous. Who were "they"? The scientists? The pilots? The full scientific staff? It is not clear. Second, "fortunately" should be set off from the rest of the sentence by a comma. (J) is the correct answer choice because it eliminates both of these errors. As for the other answer choices, (G) is incorrect because it does not correct the first error. (H) is incorrect because "fortunately" is improperly placed in the sentence; as a result, it almost sounds as if "fortunately" were intended to modify "early."

37. (D) (p. 546) ***English/Rhetorical Skills/Style/Conciseness.*** (A), (B), and (C) are all incorrect because they are needlessly wordy. (D) is the correct answer choice because it corrects this error.

38. (G) (p. 547) ***English/Rhetorical Skills/Strategy/Appropriate Supporting Material.*** When the author uses the word "spectacular" to describe a failure during a rocket flight, the reader is lead to expect sensational, extraordinary, and quite likely terrifying details. However, as the author quickly points out, the details of this "spectacular" failure were instead quite mundane and pathetic. In short, after all the preparation leading up to the launch, the rocket only traveled two inches due to a circuit error. This is a classic case of irony, where there is a great incongruity or difference between anticipated and actual results.

39. (A) (p. 547) ***English/Usage and Mechanics/No Change.*** The original sentence is correct. Only an adverb ("relatively") can modify an adjective ("easy"). As for the other answer choices, (B) is incorrect because "relative" is intended to modify "simple" in this context; and, as stated above, only an adverb can modify an adjective. (D) is incorrect because an adjective cannot modify an adverb.

40. (J) (p. 547) ***English/Usage and Mechanics/Sentence Structure/Faulty Parallelism.*** The original sentence is incorrect because the underlined verb ("shutting down") is not parallel with the other verb ("to ignite") in the sentence. (J) is the correct answer choice because it makes the needed correction ("to ignite and then to shut down"). As for the other answer choices, neither (G) nor (H) solves the original problem. In addition, (H) suffers from the further defect that "they" does not have a referent; in other words, it is not at all clear who or what "they" are.

41. (B) (p. 547) ***English/Usage and Mechanics/Punctuation/Quotation Marks.*** This is another example of irony. The rocket never really launched, and it never achieved true flight. In fact, as the passage tells us, the rocket only moved two inches. So, the quotation marks signal that the word "flight" is being used in a non-standard way.

42. (F) (p. 547) ***English/Rhetorical Skills/No Change.*** The original sentence is correct. A new topic is being introduced (i.e., the role of animals in the Mercury space program). So, a new paragraph should be started. As for the other answer choices, they are all incorrect because they do not introduce a change in paragraphs to signal the change in topics.

43. (A) (p. 548) ***English/Rhetorical Skills/No Change.*** The original sentence is correct. In comparison with the other answer choices, it is the most concise and least awkward.

44. (G) (p. 548) ***English/Usage and Mechanics/Grammar and Usage/Sequence and Verb Tense.*** The original sentence is incorrect because it includes a verb tense error. The "delay" in picking up the spacecraft and the "leak" of water into the capsule belong to the same time frame. So, they should be expressed in the same verb tense. The "delay" is expressed in the past tense ("The pickup...was delayed"). So, the "leak" should also be expressed in the past tense ("water leaked into the capsule"). For this reason, (G) is the correct answer choice.

45. (A) (p. 548) ***English/Usage and Mechanics/No Change.*** The original sentence is correct. As for the other answer choices, none of the other suggested positions for "unharmed" are idiomatic.

46. (H) (p. 548) ***English/Usage and Mechanics/Sentence Structure/Fragments.*** The original sentence is incorrect because "returning" is not a conjugated verb and, thus, cannot be the main verb of a sentence. (H) is the correct answer choice because it provides a conjugated verb that is consistent with the other past tense verbs in the paragraph. As for the other answer choices, (G) and (J) are incorrect because neither a present tense verb ("return") nor a future tense verb ("will return") are consistent with the past tense verbs in the paragraph.

47. (D) (p. 548) ***English/Usage and Mechanics/Grammar and Usage/Sequence and Verb Tense.*** The original sentence is incorrect because it includes a verb tense error. The question of how long an astronaut could tolerate weightlessness was unanswered at the time. So, a verb is required here which reflects that uncertainty. (D) is the correct answer choice because it provides the appropriate verb ("could tolerate"). As for the other answer choices, they are all incorrect because they do not supply a verb which suggests the degree of uncertainty required here.

48. (G) (p. 548) ***English/Usage and Mechanics/Grammar and Usage/Diction.*** The original sentence is incorrect because it includes language that is both superfluous and not idiomatic. Specifically, in the underlined portion, "like" is not grammatically required and also makes the sentence sound stilted. (G) is the correct answer choice because it eliminates this unnecessary word. As for the other answer choices, (H) and (J) are both incorrect because they introduce new language that is similarly superfluous and not idiomatic.

49. (B) (p. 549) ***English/Usage and Mechanics/Grammar and Usage/Verb Tense.*** The original sentence is incorrect because it includes a grammar error. Specifically, the underlined portion is an infinitive verb ("to have"). However, an infinitive verb cannot serve as the main verb for a clause. (B) is the correct answer choice because it supplies a main verb for the clause ("astronauts have...methods...") that is consistent with the verb tenses in the rest of the paragraph. As for the other answer choices, (C) is incorrect because the past perfect tense ("had had") suggests a sequence of events not supported by the meaning of the sentence. (D) is incorrect because the phrase "are sure to" is unnecessary before "have"; it creates a sentence that is definitely not idiomatic and that is almost grammatically incorrect.

50. (F) (p. 549) ***English/Rhetorical Skills/Strategy/Effective Concluding Sentence.*** During the course of the essay, the author emphasizes the successes of the Mercury space program and downplays its failures. (F) is the correct answer choice because it best reflects the general theme and argument of the essay.

51. (A) (p. 549) ***English/Usage and Mechanics/No Change.*** The original sentence is correct. As for the other answer choices, (B) is incorrect for two reasons. First, it omits a required comma; specifically, both the beginning and the end of an aside ("in any broad and real way") must be marked with a comma. Second, the phrase "of help" is simply not idiomatic or grammatically correct. (C) is incorrect because it too omits the required comma that is mentioned above. Finally, (D) is incorrect because the phrase "of helping" is not idiomatic or grammatically correct.

52. (G) (p. 549) ***English/Rhetorical Skills/Style/Conciseness.*** The original sentence is incorrect because it is needlessly wordy. "And" and "also" mean the same thing, so it is redundant to include both. (G) is the correct answer choice because it replaces the redundant phrase ("and also") with "as well as," a phrase which means "and." As for the other answer choices, (H) is incorrect because "with" does not provide the meaning required in this context. (J) is incorrect because "as opposed to" signals a contrast between two ideas; however, the sentence does not then include a contrast between two ideas.

53. (D) (p. 549) ***English/Usage and Mechanics/Grammar and Usage/Sequence and Verb Tense.*** The original sentence is incorrect because it includes a verb tense error. Earlier in the sentence, a simple past tense verb ("aided") is used. For the sake of consistency, another simple past tense verb ("emerged") should be used here. (D) is the correct answer choice because it is the only option that provides the appropriate required verb form.

54. (G) (p. 549) ***English/Usage and Mechanics/Grammar and Usage/Subject-Verb Agreement.*** The original sentence is incorrect because it includes an error of agreement. The plural subject of the sentence ("All aspects of medicine") requires a plural verb ("were enjoying"). (G) is the correct answer choice because it supplies the appropriate verb form. As for the other answer choices, (H) and (J) are incorrect because they do not supply plural verbs.

55. (B) (p. 550) ***English/Usage and Mechanics/Grammar and Usage/Diction.*** The original sentence is incorrect because it includes an expression that is not idiomatic. The correct idiom is "not only this but that." (B) is the correct answer choice because it provides the language needed to complete the correct idiom. As for the other answer choices, (C) is incorrect because "not only this consequently that" is not a correct idiom. (D) supplies the correct idiom ("not only this but that"), but it also includes a new error. Specifically, the comma after "but" is illogical and grammatically incorrect.

56. (H) (p. 550) ***English/Usage and Mechanics/Sentence Structure/Run-On Sentences.*** The original sentence is incorrect because it is a run-on sentence. A run-on sentence is two or more complete sentences joined together without the necessary punctuation or conjunctions. For example, the first clause ("With somewhat more luck, the doctor could select the proper treatment") is a complete sentence by itself. Similarly, the following clause ("he could also mitigate the symptoms…") is also a complete sentence by itself. Usually, there are two ways to fix a run-on sentence. First, it could be divided into two separate and correctly punctuated sentences. Second, it could be fixed by supplying the punctuation and conjunction needed between the two clauses. As neither option is offered here, though, review the answer choices for the best solution possible. (H) is the correct answer choice because it re-writes the underlined portion so there is only one subject in the sentence ("the doctor"); as a result, the sentence is no longer a run-on sentence. As for the other answer choices, (G) is incorrect because "but" signals a contrast; however, a contrast is not then introduced. (J) is incorrect because it creates a sentence where the verbs are not parallel ("the doctor could select…and can mitigate…").

57. (A) (p. 550) ***English/Usage and Mechanics/No Change.*** The original sentence is correct. The subjunctive verb form ("be available") is the appropriate verb form in this context. As for the other answer choices, (B) is incorrect because the past tense ("was available") is not required here. (C) is incorrect for two reasons. First, a present tense verb ("is available") is inconsistent with the past tense verbs in the rest of the paragraph. Second, "for" does not have the same meaning as "to"; as a result, the sentence becomes grammatically incorrect. Finally, (D) is wrong because "as" does not have the same meaning as "to"; as a result, the sentence again becomes grammatically incorrect.

58. (H) (p. 550) ***English/Usage and Mechanics/Grammar and Usage/Sequence and Verb Tense.*** The original sentence is incorrect because a present tense verb ("presupposes") is not consistent with the past tense verbs in the rest of the paragraph. (H) is the correct answer choice because it provides the past tense verb required here. As for the other answer choices, (G) is incorrect because the passive verb form ("it is presupposed") is inconsistent with the past tense verbs in the rest of the paragraph and also creates a sentence that is grammatically incorrect. (J) is incorrect for two reasons. First, a present tense verb ("presuppose") is not consistent with the past tense verbs in the rest of the paragraph. Second, a plural subject ("they") is not consistent with the singular subject ("it") used in the rest of the paragraph.

59. (A) (p. 550) ***English/Rhetorical Skills/No Change.*** The original sentence is correct. A new topic is being introduced (i.e., the physician William Beaumont and his accomplishments). So, a new paragraph should be started. As for the other answer choices, (B) and (D) are incorrect because they do not introduce a change in paragraphs to signal the change in topics. (C) is incorrect because it results in a subordinate or dependent clause ("since nineteenth century medical advances were those in the field of human physiology") that does not have a supporting independent clause.

60. (J) (p. 551) ***English/Rhetorical Skills/Organization/Sentence-Level Structure.*** The first three paragraphs are a general discussion of medical advances during the nineteenth century. The last two paragraphs are about a specific example of this progress. As for the first sentence of the fourth paragraph, it serves as a transition from the general discussion to a more detailed look at the specific example. So, (J) is the correct answer choice.

61. (D) (p. 551) ***English/Rhetorical Skills/Style/Conciseness.*** The original sentence, (B), and (C) are all awkward and needlessly wordy. (B) and (C) also introduce grammatical errors into the sentence. (D) is the correct answer choice here because it concisely and clearly conveys the idea; in addition, it also does not introduce any new errors.

62. (F) (p. 551) ***English/Rhetorical Skills/No Change.*** The original sentence is correct. The underlined portion is clear, concise, and contains no errors. As for the other answer choices, (H) is incorrect because it is awkward and needlessly wordy. (G) and (J) are both wrong because they incorrectly start a new paragraph—a new paragraph should not be started because this portion of the essay continues to be about Dr. Beaumont. (J) is also incorrect for the same reason as (H).

63. (B) (p. 551) ***English/Usage and Mechanics/Sentence Structure/Problems of Coordination and Subordination.*** The original sentence is incorrect because it includes a logical error. Specifically, "but" is used to introduce an idea that modifies or contrasts with another idea. For example, "It was sunny, but clouds were approaching." In this sentence, though, "but" introduces a clause ("for the next 10 years he conducted hundreds of experiments…") that in no way modifies or contrasts with the earlier part of the sentence. So, it is a logical error to use "but" here. (B) is the correct answer because "and" correctly signals that the following clause continues and elaborates upon information from the earlier part of the sentence. As for the other answer choices, (C) is incorrect because it creates a run-on sentence. (D) is incorrect for the same reason as (A).

64. (J) (p. 552) ***English/Usage and Mechanics/Sentence Structure/Faulty Parallelism.*** The original sentence is incorrect because it includes an example of faulty parallelism. The forms of "demonstrate" and "describe" have the same function in this sentence, and they should be expressed in the same or parallel verb forms. "Demonstrating" is a present participle. So, the present participle of "describe" must also be used. Therefore, (J) is the correct answer choice. As for the other answer choices, (G) and (H) are both wrong because they do not create the required parallelism.

65. (C) (p. 552) ***English/Usage and Mechanics/Grammar and Usage/Pronoun Usage.*** The original sentence is incorrect because it includes an error of pronoun usage. The subject of the sentence ("Newborn babies") is a plural noun. So, any pronoun used in its place must also be plural. (C) is the correct answer choice because it provides the appropriate plural pronoun. As for the other answer choices, (B) and (D) are incorrect for the same reason as the original. (B) and (D) are also incorrect because they introduce singular verbs ("was" and "is") that do not agree with the plural subject of the sentence.

66. (H) (p. 552) ***English/Usage and Mechanics/Grammar and Usage/Diction.*** The original sentence is incorrect because it is not idiomatic. The correct idiom is "endowed with." As for the other answer choices, (G) is incorrect because it is not idiomatic in any context. (J) is incorrect because, although the phrase "endowed by" is idiomatic, it is not appropriate in this context. It would be appropriate in other contexts (i.e., "…endowed by their Creator with certain inalienable rights"), but it is not correct here.

67. (A) (p. 552) ***English/Usage and Mechanics/No Change.*** The original sentence is correct. As for the other answer choices, (B) and (C) both create run-on sentences. (D) is incorrect because it removes the subject ("This") of the second clause; as a result, the reader is left with a hybrid of the two sentences which is illogical, grammatically incorrect, and nearly impossible to understand.

68. (G) (p. 552) ***English/Usage and Mechanics/Sentence Structure/Problems of Coordination and Subordination.*** The original sentence is incorrect because it includes an error related to word choice. The author intends to say that an infant's cry causes two parallel reactions—a biological reaction as well as an emotional reaction. As the sentence is currently written, though, "including" illogically implies that the emotional reaction is a part or a component of the biological reaction. (G) is the correct answer choice because "and" is a conjunction that allows the reader to understand that the author is talking about two distinct and parallel reactions. As for the other answer choices, neither (H) nor (J) accomplishes the same task.

69. (D) (p. 553) ***English/Rhetorical Skills/Strategy/Effective Transitional Sentence.*** The original sentence is incorrect because "unfortunately" has a meaning that is not appropriate here. In the last sentence of this paragraph, the author intends to make a statement that summarizes the details provided earlier in the paragraph. The word "unfortunately" is only used when introducing information that contradicts or contrasts with earlier information. For example, "He is very handsome; unfortunately, he is also unfriendly." (D) is the correct answer choice here because the phrase "in fact" can be used to introduce an idea that complements or is related to earlier ideas. As for the other answer choices, (B) and (C) are incorrect for the same reason as the original.

70. (H) (p. 553) ***English/Rhetorical Skills/Style/Conciseness.*** The original sentence is incorrect because the underlined portion is needlessly wordy. (H) is the correct answer choice because it clearly and concisely summarizes the underlined portion in one word. As for the other answer choices, (G) is incorrect because a past tense verb ("possessed") is inconsistent with the present tense verbs in the paragraph. (J) is incorrect for the same reason as the original; in addition, a plural verb ("are") does not agree with the singular subject ("the human infant") of the sentence.

71. (C) (p. 553) ***English/Usage and Mechanics/Grammar and Usage/Verb Tense.*** The original sentence is incorrect because it includes a verb tense error. A present progressive verb ("are guaranteeing") is used to describe and emphasize activity happening at this very moment. However, the author is speaking in broad terms about babies in general; the author is not talking about a specific baby and what that particular baby is doing at this very moment. (C) is the correct answer choice here because a simple present tense verb ("guarantee") is consistent with the other simple present tense verbs in the rest of the paragraph. As for the other answer choices, (B) is incorrect because a past tense verb is not consistent with the present tense verbs in the rest of the paragraph. (D) is incorrect because a singular verb ("guarantees") does not agree with its plural subject ("attributes").

72. (G) (p. 553) ***English/Usage and Mechanics/Grammar and Usage/Diction.*** The original sentence is incorrect because it is not idiomatic. The correct idiom required here is "whether *this*... or whether *that*..." The phrase "whether or not" is another English idiom, but its use here is not appropriate. As for the other answer choices, (H) and (J) are both incorrect because "whether if" is not idiomatic in any context.

73. (D) (p. 553) ***English/Usage and Mechanics/Sentence Structure/Fragments.*** The original sentence is incorrect because the period after "infant" turns the first clause into a dependent clause without a supporting independent clause; in other words, it turns the dependent clause into a sentence fragment. (D) is the correct answer choice because it connects the initial dependent clause to a supporting independent clause, combines them in one sentence, and does so without introducing any grammatical or punctuation errors. As for the other answer choices, (B) and (C) are incorrect for the same reason as the original.

74. (H) (p. 554) ***English/Rhetorical Skills/Organization/Sentence-Level Structure.*** The final sentence summarizes the author's main point in an emphatic way. So, (H) is the correct answer choice. As for the other answer choices, they are all incorrect because they are simply not true.

75. (D) (p. 554) ***English/Rhetorical Skills/Organization/Passage-Level Structure.*** The passage is an argument. The author makes a claim (i.e., newborn infants are not passive creatures) and then supports the claim with several examples of how newborn infants actively engage with their worlds and their caregivers. So, (D) is the correct answer choice. As for the other answer choices, (A) is incorrect for two reasons: first, the author does not provide contrasting information in an attempt to disprove the main argument; second, the author does not supply any anecdotes or specific stories. (B) is incorrect because this essay is not a narrative or story filled with examples or anecdotes about specific newborn infants. Finally, (C) is incorrect because the author never uses statistics.

TEST 2: MATHEMATICS

1. (B) (p. 556) ***Mathematics/Arithmetic/Simple Manipulations.*** Perform the indicated operation: $5.75-4.5=1.25$.

2. (F) (p. 556) ***Mathematics/Algebra/Manipulating Algebraic Expressions/Basic Algebraic Manipulations.*** The product of 4 times x is written as $4x$. 3 less than that would be $4x-3$.

3. (C) (p. 557) ***Mathematics/Algebra/Manipulating Algebraic Expressions/Evaluating Expressions.*** This question really just tests fractions. If $\frac{3}{4}$ of x equals 36, then: $\frac{3}{4}x=36 \Rightarrow x=36\bullet\frac{4}{3}=48$ and $\frac{1}{3}$ of 48 is 16.

4. (J) (p. 557) ***Mathematics/Geometry/Lines and Angles.*** The measure of the unlabeled angle in the top triangle is 90°. The angle vertically opposite it in the bottom triangle is also equal to 90°. Therefore: $x+y+90°=180°$ and $x+y=90°$.

5. (E) (p. 557) ***Mathematics/Arithmetic/Common Arithmetic Items/Properties of Numbers.*** There are two ways to attack this question. One is to reason as follows:

A. $2+n$ cannot be a multiple of 3. Since n is a multiple of 3, when $2+n$ is divided by 3 there will be a remainder of 2.
B. $2-n$ cannot be a multiple of 3 for the same reason that $2+n$ cannot be a multiple of 3.
C. $2n-1$ cannot be a multiple of 3. Since n is a multiple of 3, $2n$ will also be a multiple of 3, and $2n-1$ cannot be a multiple of 3.
D. $2n+1$ cannot be a multiple for the same reason that $2n-1$ cannot be a multiple of 3.
E. $2n+3$ is a multiple of 3. $2n$ is a multiple of 3; 3 is a multiple of 3; thus, $2n+3$ is a multiple of 3.

Alternatively, substitute an assumed value into the choices. Let $n = 3$:

A. $2+n=2+3=5$ ✗ (Not a multiple of 3)
B. $2-n=2-3=-1$ ✗ (Not a multiple of 3)
C. $2n-1=2(3)-1=6-1=5$ ✗ (Not a multiple of 3)
D. $2n+1=2(3)+1=6+1=7$ ✗ (Not a multiple of 3)
E. $2n+3=2(3)+3=6+3=9$ ✓ (A multiple of 3)

6. **(H)** (p. 557) ***Mathematics/Arithmetic/Common Arithmetic Items/Ratios.*** A ratio is just another way of writing a fraction. Simply inspect each of the answers. As for (F), $\left(\frac{1}{5}\right)^2$ is equal to $\frac{1}{25}$, and both 1 and 25 are whole numbers. Answer choice (G) is not the correct because 5% can be written as $\frac{5}{100}$, or $\frac{1}{20}$, which is the ratio of two whole numbers. As for (H), $\sqrt{5}$ is not a whole number, so the expression in (H) is not the ratio of two whole numbers. As for (J), 0.25 is equal to $\frac{1}{4}$, the ratio of two whole numbers. Finally, as for (K), $\frac{1}{5}$ is the ratio of 1 to 5, so (K) is a ratio of two whole numbers.

7. **(D)** (p. 558) ***Mathematics/Geometry/Rectangles and Squares.*** If the area of a square is known, the perimeter can be found, and vice versa. $\text{Area}_{\text{square}} = \text{side} \bullet \text{side} = 16 \Rightarrow s^2 = 16 \Rightarrow s = \pm 4$. Distances are always positive. Therefore, the perimeter is equal to $4s$, or $4 \bullet 4 = 16$.

8. **(J)** (p. 558) ***Mathematics/Algebra/Solving Algebraic Equations with Two Variables.*** This problem presents one equation with two variables. It is not possible to solve for x or y individually, but that is not necessary. Just rewrite the equation in the form of $x + y$: $12 + x = 36 - y \Rightarrow x + y = 36 - 12 = 24$.

9. **(D)** (p. 558) ***Mathematics/Algebra/Manipulating Algebraic Expressions/Factoring Expressions.*** The coefficients are 3, 6, and 2, and 1 is the only common factor of those numbers. The smallest term containing the variable x is simply x. Thus, the greatest factor of those terms is just x. The same is true for the terms containing y and z and the greatest common factor is xyz.

10. **(G)** (p. 558) ***Mathematics/Arithmetic/Common Arithmetic Items/Properties of Numbers.*** This item can be analyzed as follows: the sum of $3k$, $4k$, $5k$, $6k$, and $7k$ is $25k$, which is divisible by 7 if the value of k is divisible by 7. If, however, the coefficient of k were divisible by 7, then that number would be divisible by 7 regardless of the value of k. Dropping the term $4k$ from the group, the sum of the remaining terms is $21k$. Since 21 is divisible by 7, $21k$ will be divisible by 7 regardless of the value of k.

11. **(B)** (p. 559) ***Mathematics/Arithmetic/Complicated Manipulations/Decimal-Fraction Equivalents.*** Do not try to convert each of these fractions to decimals to find the value that lies between $\frac{1}{3}$ and $\frac{3}{8}$. Instead, find an escape route. Use a benchmark, approximate, or use whatever else is available. First, eliminate (E): $\frac{1}{2}$ is more than $\frac{3}{8}$. Next, eliminate (A): $\frac{3}{15}$ is equal to $\frac{1}{3}$, so $\frac{3}{16}$ is smaller than $\frac{1}{3}$. (B) is close to and slightly less than $\frac{18}{48}$, which is $\frac{3}{8}$. Therefore, (B) is the correct choice. As for (C), $\frac{9}{24}$ is equal to $\frac{3}{8}$, not less than $\frac{3}{8}$. Finally, as for (D), $\frac{5}{12}$ is equal to $\frac{10}{24}$, and $\frac{2}{8}$ is equal to $\frac{9}{24}$.

Alternatively, express each fraction in the stem and answer choices with a denominator of 48. First, $\frac{1}{3}=\frac{1 \cdot 16}{3 \cdot 16}=\frac{16}{38}$ and $\frac{3}{8}=\frac{3 \cdot 6}{8 \cdot 6}=\frac{18}{48}$. Now, compare these with the answer choices:

A. $\frac{3}{16}=\frac{3 \cdot 3}{16 \cdot 3}=\frac{9}{48}$

B. $\frac{17}{48}$

C. $\frac{9}{24}=\frac{9 \cdot 2}{24 \cdot 2}=\frac{18}{48}$

D. $\frac{5}{12}=\frac{5 \cdot 4}{12 \cdot 4}=\frac{20}{48}$

E. $\frac{1}{2}=\frac{1 \cdot 24}{2 \cdot 24}=\frac{24}{48}$

Therefore, the correct answer is (B).

12. (G) (p. 559) ***Mathematics/Algebra/Manipulating Algebraic Expressions/Factoring Expressions.*** Simply factor the expression: $x^2-y^2=(x+y)\cdot(x-y)$. Since $(x-y)=3$, then $(x+y)(3)=3 \Rightarrow x+y=1$.

13. (E) (p. 559) ***Mathematics/Arithmetic/Common Arithmetic Items/Properties of Numbers.*** As for (A), whether $n+1$ is odd or even will depend on whether n is odd or even. The same is true for (B) and (C) since whether $3n$ is odd or even will depend on whether n is odd or even. As for (D), n^2 will be odd or even depending on whether n is odd or even. However, (E) is even regardless of whether n is odd or even. n^2+n can be factored as $n(n+1)$. Since either n or $n+1$ is even, the product must be even.

14. (H) (p. 559) ***Mathematics/Geometry/Complex Figures*** and ***Rectangles and Squares*** and ***Circles.*** For any square with a side of x, the diagonal of that square is equal to $x\sqrt{2}$. Since the square has an area of 16, it has a side of 4 and a diagonal of $4\sqrt{2}$. The diagonal of the square is also the diameter of the circle. Therefore, the circle has a diameter of $4\sqrt{2}$ and a radius of $2\sqrt{2}$. Finally, a circle with a radius of length $2\sqrt{2}$ has an area of $\pi r^2=\pi\left(2\sqrt{2}\right)^2=8\pi$.

15. (C) (p. 560) ***Mathematics/Arithmetic/Common Arithmetic Items/Percents.*** First, calculate the sale price of the CD player that Ellen bought: $\$120-(25\% \text{ of } \$120)=\$120-(0.25 \cdot \$120)=\$120-\$30=\$90$. Next, calculate the sales tax: tax $=8\%$ of $\$90=0.08 \cdot \$90=\$7.20$. Therefore, the total price was $\$90+\$7.20=\$97.20$.

16. (G) (p. 560) ***Mathematics/Arithmetic/Solving Complicated Arithmetic Application Items*** and ***Common Arithmetic Items/Percents.*** Use the "is-over-of" equation. The "of," which is the denominator of the fraction, is the mixture. How much of the mixture is there? $2.5+12.5=15$. The word "is," which is the numerator of the fraction, is the 2.5 kilograms of gravel. Thus: $\frac{\text{is}}{\text{of}}=\frac{\text{gravel}}{\text{mixture}}=\frac{2.5}{15}=\frac{1}{6}$. Remember that $\frac{1}{6}=.01\overline{6}=16\frac{2}{3}\%$.

17. (D) (p. 560) ***Mathematics/Geometry/Triangles/Working with Triangles.*** The triangle has sides of 6, 8, and 10 (multiples of 3, 4, and 5). Therefore, the triangle is a right triangle. The sides of 6 and 8 form the right angle, so they can be used as altitude and base for finding the area: $\text{area}_{\text{triangle}}=\frac{1}{2}\cdot\text{altitude}\cdot\text{base}=\frac{1}{2}\cdot 6 \cdot 8=24$.

18. (F) (p. 561) ***Mathematics/Arithmetic/Common Arithmetic Items/Proportions and Direct-Inverse Variation.*** Proportions make this calculation easy. First, complete the calculation for Motorcycle A: $\frac{\text{Fuel Used } X}{\text{Fuel Used } Y} = \frac{\text{Miles Driven } X}{\text{Miles Driven } Y} \Rightarrow \frac{1}{x} = \frac{40}{300} \Rightarrow 40x = 300 \Rightarrow x = 7.5$. Thus, Motorcycle A uses 7.5 liters of fuel for the 300-mile trip. Now, do the same for Motorcycle B: $\frac{1}{x} = \frac{50}{300} \Rightarrow 50x = 300 \Rightarrow x = 6$. Therefore, Motorcycle B uses 6 liters of fuel for the trip. Since Motorcycle A uses $7.5 - 6 = 1.5$ liters more than Motorcycle B, the fuel for Motorcycle A costs $1.5 \cdot \$2 = \$3$ more.

19. (B) (p. 561) ***Mathematics/Algebra/Expressing and Evaluating Algebraic Functions/Function Notation.*** First, substitute 3 for *x*: $f(3) = 3^2 - 2(3) + 1 = 9 - 6 + 1 = 4$. Now, substitute 4 for *x*: $f(4) = 4^2 - 2(4) + 1 = 16 - 8 + 1 = 9$. Therefore, $f(f(3)) = 9$.

20. (K) (p. 561) ***Mathematics/Algebra/Manipulating Algebraic Expressions/Factoring Expressions.*** Factor $6k + 3$: $6k + 3 = 3(2k + 1)$. Substituting 1 for *k* in the answer choices also works. The correct answer choice, (K), yields the value 9: $6k + 3 = 6(1) + 3 = 6 + 3 = 9$.

21. (E) (p. 561) ***Mathematics/Algebra/Manipulating Algebraic Expressions/Creating Algebraic Expressions.*** Devise the formula as follows. The formula will be *x*, the cost for the first ounce, plus some expression to represent the additional postage for each additional ounce over the first ounce. The postage for the additional weight is *y* cents per ounce, and the additional weight is *w* minus the first ounce, or $w - 1$. Therefore, the additional postage is $y(w-1)$, and the total postage is $x + y(w-1)$.

Alternatively, assume some numbers. For ease of calculations, assume that the first ounce costs 1 cent and every additional ounce is 2 cents. If $x = 1$ and $y = 2$, then a letter, of say, 3 ounces ($w = 3$) will cost $1 + 2(2) = 5$ cents. Substitute these values for *x*, *y*, and *w* into the answer choices and the correct choice will return the value 5:

A. $w(x+y) = 3(1+2) = 3(3) = 9$ ✗
B. $x(w-y) = 1(3-2) = 1(1) = 1$ ✗
C. $x(x-1) + y(w-1) = 1(1-1) + 2(3-1) = 1(0) + 2(2) = 4$ ✗
D. $x + wy = 1 + 3(2) = 7$ ✗
E. $x + y(w-1) = 1 + 2(3-1) = 1 + 2(2) = 5$ ✓

22. (F) (p. 562) ***Mathematics/Arithmetic/Common Arithmetic Items/Absolute Value.*** $|-3| = 3$ and $\left|-\frac{1}{2}\right| = \frac{1}{2}$. Therefore: $|-3| \cdot |2| \cdot \left|-\frac{1}{2}\right| + (-4) = 3 \cdot 2 \cdot \frac{1}{2} - 4 = 3 - 4 = -1$.

23. (C) (p. 562) ***Mathematics/Geometry/Complex Figures*** and ***Rectangles and Squares*** and ***Circles.*** The side of the square is also the radius of the circle. Since the square has an area of 2, its side is: $s \cdot s = 2 \Rightarrow s^2 = 2 \Rightarrow s = \sqrt{2}$. $\sqrt{2}$ is the radius of the circle. Therefore, the area of the circle is $\pi r^2 = \pi\left(\sqrt{2}\right)^2 = 2\pi$.

24. (G) (p. 562) ***Mathematics/Arithmetic/Common Arithmetic Items/Properties of Numbers.*** Test each statement. As for statement (I), 2 is the first prime number, and the product of 2 and any other number must be even. Thus, (I) is not part of the correct answer. As for (II), the sum of two prime numbers might be odd, (e.g., $2 + 3 = 5$), but the sum of two prime numbers might also be even, (e.g., $3 + 5 = 8$). As for (III), however, the product of two odd numbers is necessarily odd.

25. **(A)** (p. 563) ***Mathematics/Coordinate Geometry/The Coordinate System.*** The coordinates establish that this figure is a rectangle. The width of the rectangle is a, and the length is $b-a$. Therefore, the area is $a(b-a)$.

Alternatively, "test-the-test," assuming that $a=2$ and $b=4$. The rectangle has a width of 2, a length of $4-2=2$, and an area of $2 \cdot 2=4$. Substitute 2 for a and 4 for b into the answer choices and the correct formula will yield 4.

26. **(H)** (p. 563) ***Mathematics/Arithmetic/Simple Manipulations.*** $\sqrt{(43-7)(29+7)}=\sqrt{(36)(36)}=36$.

27. **(A)** (p. 563) ***Mathematics/Arithmetic/Common Arithmetic Items/Proportions and Direct-Inverse Variation.*** Set up a direct proportion: $\frac{\text{Cement } X}{\text{Cement } Y}=\frac{\text{Grit } X}{\text{Grit } Y} \Rightarrow \frac{4}{50}=\frac{20}{x} \Rightarrow 4x=(20)(50) \Rightarrow x=\frac{(20)(50)}{4}=250$.

28. **(H)** (p. 564) ***Mathematics/Geometry/Lines and Angles.*** Label the other two angles in the triangle:

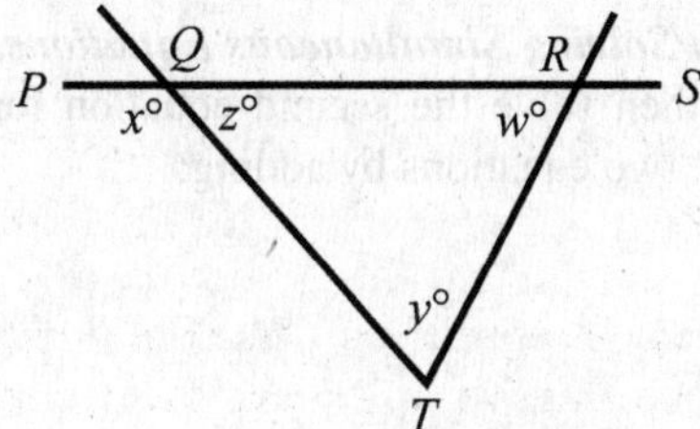

$x+z=180 \Rightarrow 150+z=180 \Rightarrow z=30$; $z+w+y=180$. Since $\overline{QT}=\overline{QR}$, $y=w$. $30+y+y=180 \Rightarrow 2y=150 \Rightarrow y=75$.

29. **(C)** (p. 564) ***Mathematics/Algebra/Solving Algebraic Equations with Two Variables.*** There is only one equation but two variables, so x and y cannot be solved for individually. Instead, look for a way to rewrite the first equation to give the information needed: $\frac{x}{y}=-1 \Rightarrow x=-y \Rightarrow x+y=0$.

30. **(K)** (p. 564) ***Mathematics/Statistics and Probability/Data Representation/Tables (Matrices)*** and ***Arithmetic/Common Arithmetic Items/Decimal-Fraction Equivalents.*** Do not do lengthy calculations. Set up the cost of each fabric as a fraction and compare the fraction directly, using a benchmark:

F. $\frac{8}{3}=2\frac{2}{3}$

G. $\frac{6}{2}=3$

H. $\frac{9}{4}=2\frac{1}{4}$

J. $\frac{7}{5}=1\frac{2}{5}$

K. $\frac{10}{8}=\frac{5}{4}=1\frac{1}{4}$

(K) is the smallest.

31. **(A)** (p. 565) ***Mathematics/Geometry/Lines and Angles.*** Since $\overline{PQ} \parallel \overline{ST}$, we know $x=y$ because the alternate interior angles of parallel lines are equal. Furthermore, since the sum of angles in ΔPRQ is 180°: $75+65+x+x=180 \Rightarrow 2x+140=180 \Rightarrow 2x=40 \Rightarrow x=20$. Therefore, $y=20$.

32. **(J)** (p. 565) ***Mathematics/Arithmetic/Complicated Manipulations/Simplifying.*** Perform the indicated operations: $\frac{10^3\left(10^5+10^5\right)}{10^4}=\frac{10\left(10^4+10^4\right)}{10}=2\left(10^4\right)$.

33. **(D)** (p. 565) ***Mathematics/Algebra/Solving Quadratic Equations.*** Factor and solve for x: $x^2-5x+4=0 \Rightarrow (x-4)(x-1)=0$. So, either $x-4=0$ and $x=4$, or $x-1=0$ and $x=1$.

    Alternatively, substitute the values in the choices back into the equation to find the set that works.

34. **(K)** (p. 566) ***Mathematics/Statistics and Probability/Averages.*** Use the method for finding the missing elements of an average. The smallest possible sum for 6 different positive integers is $1+2+3+4+5+6=21$. The sum of all 7 integers is $7 \bullet 12=84$. Therefore, the largest that the seventh number could be (with the average of the seven numbers still 12) is $84-21=63$.

35. **(E)** (p. 566) ***Mathematics/Algebra/Solving Simultaneous Equations.*** To find b in terms of x and y, solve the first equation for b in terms of x and then solve the second equation for b in terms of y: $x=b+4 \Rightarrow b=x-4$ and $y=b-3 \Rightarrow b=y+3$. Combine the two equations by adding:

$$\begin{array}{r} b=x-4 \\ +\ b=y+3 \\ \hline 2b=x+y-1 \Rightarrow b=\frac{x+y-1}{2} \end{array}$$

    Alternatively, substitute some numbers. Let $b=1$. Therefore, $x=1+4=5$, and $y=1-3=-2$. Substitute 5 for x and -2 for y into the answer choices. The correct choice will yield the value 1.

36. **(F)** (p. 566) ***Mathematics/Arithmetic/Common Arithmetic Items/Properties of Numbers.*** Since $z=5x=3y$, and x, y, and z are integers, z is a multiple of both 3 and 5, so z is evenly divisible by 5, 3, and 15. z is divisible by both x and y individually, but z is not necessarily divisible by the product of x and y. Finally, since $5x=3y$, and x and y are integers, x is a multiple of 3 (and evenly divisible by 3).

    Alternatively, substitute some numbers. The most natural assumption is to let $z=15$, so $x=3$ and $y=5$. However, on that assumption, every answer choice is an integer. Try the next multiple of 15. Let $z=30$, so $x=6$ and $y=10$. (F) is no longer an integer: $30 \div (6 \bullet 10)=\frac{1}{2}$.

37. **(B)** (p. 566) ***Mathematics/Geometry/Rectangles and Squares.*** Use the equation for the area of a rectangle: $\text{area}_{\text{rectangle}}=\text{width} \bullet \text{length} \Rightarrow 48x^2=w(24x) \Rightarrow w=\frac{48x^2}{24x}=2x$.

    Alternatively, substitute some numbers, such as $x=2$. The area of the rectangle is $48\left(2^2\right)=48(4)=192$, and the length is 48. 48 times the width is equal to 192, so the width is $192 \div 48=4$. Therefore, if $x=2$, the correct choice yields the value 4. Only (B) works.

38. **(K)** (p. 567) ***Mathematics/Algebra/Manipulating Algebraic Expressions/Basic Algebraic Manipulations.*** Rewrite the equation: $x=\frac{1}{y+1} \Rightarrow x(y+1)=1 \Rightarrow y+1=\frac{1}{x} \Rightarrow y=\frac{1}{x}-1 \Rightarrow y=\frac{1-x}{x}$.

39. **(B)** (p. 567) ***Mathematics/Coordinate Geometry/The Coordinate System.*** The length of the base of the triangle is $4x-x=3x$, and the length of the altitude is $3x-0=3x$ (the difference in the y coordinate). Use the formula for

finding the area of a triangle to determine x: $\frac{1}{2}(3x)(3x) = 54 \Rightarrow (3x)(3x) = 108 \Rightarrow 9x^2 = 108 \Rightarrow x^2 = 12 \Rightarrow x = \sqrt{12} = 2\sqrt{3}$.

40. (K) (p. 567) ***Mathematics/Statistics and Probability/Probability.*** This question is a little tricky, but it does not require advanced mathematics. If the room were completely dark, what is the worst thing that might happen? You might happen to pull all the blue and white socks first (the two colors with the largest number of socks). So you might have pulled 16 socks. Now, the only color left is the color (green) with the smallest number of socks. Then you would need to pull 2 of the only 4 socks left. On the worst assumption, $16+2=18$ picks will *guarantee* you a pair of each color.

41. (C) (p. 568) ***Mathematics/Geometry/Complex Figures*** and ***Circles*** and ***Lines and Angles.*** The question supplies the area of the shaded part of the figure, which is a portion of the circle. First, find what fraction of the circle is shaded. Then, use that value in order to determine the value of the unshaded angle at the center of the circle. The area of the entire circle is $\pi r^2 = \pi(4^2) = 16\pi$. $\frac{14\pi}{16\pi} = \frac{7}{8}$ of the circle is shaded, so $\frac{1}{8}$ of the circle is unshaded.

Therefore, the unshaded angle at the center of the circle is $\frac{1}{8}$ of $360° = 45°$. Now, find x: $x+45+90=180 \Rightarrow x+135=180 \Rightarrow x=45$.

42. (J) (p. 568) ***Mathematics/Geometry/Circles*** and ***Triangles/45°-45°-90° Triangles.*** This is a composite figure. Redefine one figure in terms of another. The diameter of the smaller circle is equal to the side of the square. The diagonal of the square is the diameter of the larger circle.

Let r be the radius of the smaller circle, so the smaller circle has an area of πr^2. The diameter of the smaller circle is $2r$, which is also the side of the square:

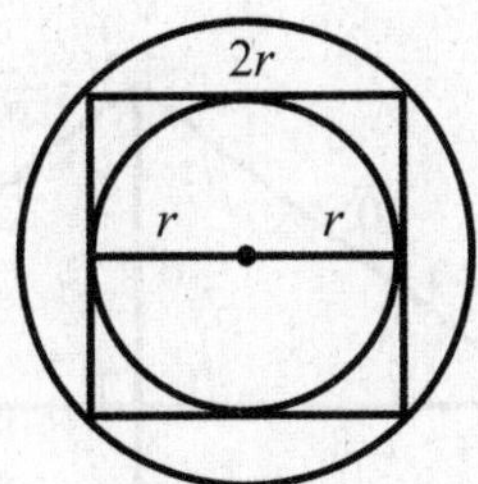

The diagonal of the square creates a 45°-45°-90° triangle with the sides. The hypotenuse of that triangle is equal to the side $s\sqrt{2}$. The diagonal of the square is equal to $2r \cdot \sqrt{2} = 2\sqrt{2}r$. This is also the diameter of the larger circle. Thus, the larger circle has a radius of $2\sqrt{2}r \div 2 = \sqrt{2}r$, and an area of $\pi\left(\sqrt{2}r\right)^2 = 2\pi r^2$. Therefore, the ratio is $2\pi r^2 : \pi r^2 = 2:1$.

43. (D) (p. 568) ***Mathematics/Arithmetic/Simple Manipulations.*** Just perform the indicated operations:

$2^0 = 1$

$2^3 = 8$

$2^{-2} = \frac{1}{2^2} = \frac{1}{4}$

$1+8-\frac{1}{4} = 8\frac{3}{4}$

44. (J) (p. 569) ***Mathematics/Coordinate Geometry/Graphs of Quadratic Equations.*** Since the axis of symmetry of the parabola is given by the equation $x = 0$, the parabola is symmetric about the y-axis. The point symmetric to the point with coordinates $(-1,-2)$ will have the same y-coordinate, and the x-coordinate of the point will be the same distance from the y-axis but in a positive direction: $(1,-2)$. It might be easier to find the solution with a sketched graph of the equation:

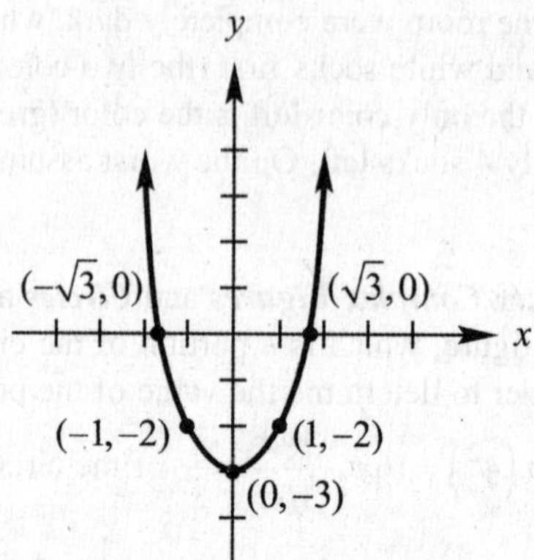

45. (C) (p. 569) ***Mathematics/Coordinate Geometry/Slope-Intercept Form of a Linear Equation.*** Each equation is written in slope-intercept form, so the slope of the first line is m_1, and the slope of the second line is m_2. If two lines in the coordinate plane are perpendicular to each other, then the product of their slopes is -1. Thus, $m_1 m_2 = -1$.

46. (K) (p. 569) ***Mathematics/Geometry/Complex Figures*** and ***Triangles/Working with Triangles*** and ***Rectangles and Squares.*** Draw some additional lines to carve the figure up into some more familiar shapes, and use the Pythagorean theorem to determine the length of the shared third side of the two small triangles: $a^2 + 8^2 = 10^2 \Rightarrow a^2 + 64 = 100 \Rightarrow a^2 = 36 \Rightarrow a = 6$.

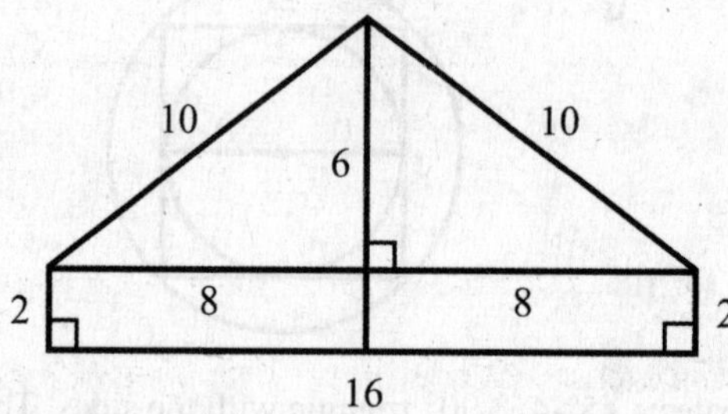

The area of the large rectangle is $16 \bullet 2 = 32$. Using 6 and 8 as the altitude and base of each triangle, respectively, determine the area of each triangle: $\frac{1}{2} \bullet 6 \bullet 8 = 24$. Therefore, the area of the composite figure is: $32 + 24(2) = 32 + 48 = 80$.

47. (A) (p. 570) ***Mathematics/Algebra/Manipulating Algebraic Expressions/Evaluating Expressions.*** Rationalize the denominator: $\frac{\sqrt{x}}{2\sqrt{x}-\sqrt{y}} \bullet \frac{2\sqrt{x}+\sqrt{y}}{2\sqrt{x}+\sqrt{y}} = \frac{2x+\sqrt{xy}}{4x+2\sqrt{xy}-2\sqrt{xy}-y} = \frac{2x+\sqrt{xy}}{4x-y}$.

Alternatively, assume some values for x and y. Since the problem involves square roots, pick a couple of perfect squares, e.g., $x = 9$ and $y = 4$. The expression in the question stem becomes: $\frac{\sqrt{9}}{2\sqrt{9}-\sqrt{4}} = \frac{3}{2(3)-2} = \frac{3}{4}$. Now, substitute 9 for x and 4 for y into the answer choices. The correct choice will generate the value $\frac{3}{4}$:

A. $\frac{2x+\sqrt{xy}}{4x-y} = \frac{2(9)+\sqrt{(9)(4)}}{4(9)-4} = \frac{18+6}{32} = \frac{24}{32} = \frac{3}{4}$ ✓

B. $\frac{4x+\sqrt{xy}}{4x-y} = \frac{4(9)+\sqrt{(9)(4)}}{4(9)-4} = \frac{36+6}{36-4} = \frac{42}{32}$ ✗

C. $\frac{2\sqrt{x}+\sqrt{y}}{4xy} = \frac{2\sqrt{9}+\sqrt{4}}{4(9)(4)} = \frac{2(3)+2}{144} = \frac{8}{144}$ ✗

D. $\frac{2\sqrt{x}+\sqrt{xy}}{2x-y} = \frac{2\sqrt{9}+\sqrt{(9)(4)}}{2(9)-4} = \frac{6+6}{14} = \frac{12}{14}$ ✗

E. $\frac{2\sqrt{x}-\sqrt{y}}{2} = \frac{2\sqrt{9}-\sqrt{4}}{2} = \frac{2(3)-2}{2} = \frac{4}{2} = 2$ ✗

48. (H) (p. 570) ***Mathematics/Geometry/Lines and Angles.*** This question requires the deduction of further conclusions based on the given information. Since vertical angles are equal, the figure becomes:

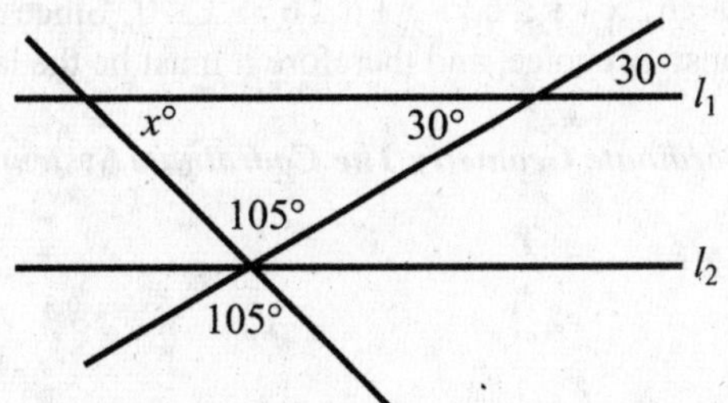

The center triangle has angles 30, 105, and x. Solve for x: $30+105+x=180 \Rightarrow x=45$.

49. (D) (p. 570) ***Mathematics/Trigonometry/Determining Trigonometric Values.*** The graph intersects the y-axis where $x=0$: $y=2\cos(2\bullet 0)+2=2\cos 0+2$. Since $\cos 0=1$: $y=2(1)+2=4$.

50. (G) (p. 571) ***Mathematics/Geometry/Complex Figures*** and ***Rectangles and Squares*** and ***Circles.*** This is a typical "shaded area" question. The shaded area will be the whole square minus the four circles: $\text{area}_{\text{shaded}} = \square - (4 \bullet \bigcirc)$. The entire solution statement is: $\frac{\text{area}_{\text{shaded}}}{\text{area}_{\text{square}}}$. On the assumption that each circle has a radius of r, the side of the square must be $4r$, and the area of the square is $4r \bullet 4r = 16r^2$. This is the denominator of the solution statement, and it is also an element in the calculation of the shaded area. To complete the calculation of the shaded area, reason that each circle with radius r has an area of πr^2. Therefore, $\text{area}_{\text{shaded}} = 16r^2 - 4\pi r^2$. Fill in the solution statement: $\frac{16r^2-4\pi r^2}{16r^2} = \frac{4r^2(4-\pi)}{16r^2} = \frac{4-\pi}{4}$.

A little common sense goes a long way when applied to the answer choices. Since π is less than 4, (F) is a negative number and is therefore impossible. Both (J) and (K) are greater than 1, asserting that the shaded area is larger than the square, an equally absurd conclusion. Now, there are only two answer choices remaining: (G) asserts that the shaded area is a little less than one-quarter of the square, and (H) asserts that the shaded area is about three-quarters of the square. After careful inspection of the figure, it is safe to assume that (G) is correct.

51. (C) (p. 571) ***Mathematics/Trigonometry/Trigonometric Relationships.*** One of the Pythagorean identities is: $\sin^2\theta+\cos^2\theta=1$. Therefore, the expression given in the question stem is equivalent to $\frac{1}{\sin\theta}$. The reciprocal identity for the sine function is the cosecant function.

52. (G) (p. 572) ***Mathematics/Trigonometry/Definitions of the Six Trigonometric Functions.*** Since $\tan\theta=\frac{\text{side opposite }\theta}{\text{side adjacent to }\theta}$, $\tan 55°=\frac{6}{AC}\Rightarrow 1.4\approx\frac{6}{AC}\Rightarrow \overline{AC}\approx\frac{6}{1.4}\approx 4.28$.

53. (D) (p. 572) ***Mathematics/Algebra/Manipulating Algebraic Expressions/Evaluating Expressions.*** We need to look for values of x that will make the value of the denominator equal to zero. When $x=1$, $x-1=0$, so the entire expression is undefined because the value of the denominator becomes zero. Similarly, when $x=-2$, $x+2=0$, and the expression is undefined. However, when $x=-3$, $x+3=0$, and the value of the numerator becomes zero. When the numerator, but not the denominator, is zero, the value of the expression is 0.

54. (K) (p. 572) ***Mathematics/Algebra/Solving Simultaneous Equations.*** Since the sum of x and y is less than or equal to 6, y will have its maximum value when x has its minimum value. The minimum value of x is 0; the maximum value of y is 6. $3(6)=18$.

Alternatively, test the answer choices. Since the question asks for the maximum value of y, start with the largest choice: 18. If $3y=18$, then $y=6$. $x+y\le 6\Rightarrow x+6\le 6\Rightarrow x\le 0$. Since x can be 0, $y=6$ satisfies the system of inequalities. 18 is the largest answer choice, and therefore it must be the largest value possible for $3y$.

55. (C) (p. 573) ***Mathematics/Coordinate Geometry/The Coordinate System.*** Find the corresponding values for y:

$$y=\left|(-1)^2-3\right|=|1-3|=|-2|=2$$
$$y=\left|(0)^2-3\right|=|-3|=3$$
$$y=\left|(1)^2-3\right|=|1-3|=|-2|=2$$

(C) is the correct plotting of the points (–1,2), (0,3), and (1,2).

56. (G) (p. 574) ***Mathematics/Coordinate Geometry/Graphs of Linear Equations.*** Calculate the slope: $m=\frac{(-2)+(-4)}{(2)-(-1)}=\frac{-6}{3}=-2$. Each answer choice is an equation of a line in slope-intercept form ($y=mx+b$), and each has a different slope. Only (G) has the correct slope: $m=-2$.

57. (A) (p. 574) ***Mathematics/Algebra/Solving Quadratic Equations.*** There are at least three different ways of attacking this problem, but one method is clearly superior. Use the roots to create the equation. If $x=a$ or $x=b$, then $x-a=0$ or $x-b=0$. The factors of the equation are $(x-a)$ and $(x-b)$, and the equation is: $(x-a)(x-b)=x^2-ax-bx+ab=0$. Given the roots of this equation, that will take a little time.

Similarly, substitute the solutions into each of the equations to find the equation that will accept both solutions. This, too, is a lot of work.

The best approach is to see that the roots are expressed in a form that is suggestive of the quadratic formula. Thus, $-b=-3$, so $b=3$. Eliminate (B) and (D). Next, $2a=2$, so $a=1$; eliminate (E). Finally, $b^2-4ac=5$. Since $b=3$ and $a=1$: $b^2-4ac=5 \Rightarrow (3)^2-4(1)(c)=5 \Rightarrow 9-4c=5 \Rightarrow 4c=4 \Rightarrow c=1$. Thus, the equation is $x^2+3x+1=0$.

58. **(F)** (p. 574) ***Mathematics/Algebra/Expressing and Evaluating Algebraic Functions/Concepts of Domain and Range.*** A function is a relationship such that each element of the domain is paired with one and only one element in the range. The domain is the set of all possibilities for the first coordinate. In the relationship given in the question stem, two pairs—(0,3) and (0,5)—have the same first coordinate. So, one element of the domain, 0, is paired with two different elements in the range: 3 and 5. We need to eliminate either (0,3) or (0,5). By dropping (0,3), the element, 0, is paired only with 5, and the set becomes a function.

59. **(D)** (p. 575) ***Mathematics/Geometry/Complex Figures*** and ***30º-60º-90º Triangles*** and ***Rectangles and Squares.*** Consider the trapezoid as a composite figure. Draw a line from point *B* perpendicular to $\overline{CD}$. The trapezoid is a combination of a right triangle and a rectangle. Since the triangle has degree measures of 30, 60, and 90, the side opposite the 30° angle has a length half that of the hypotenuse, or a length of 4. Thus, the rectangle has sides of 4 and 9 and an area of 36. Then, the side of the triangle opposite the 60° angle has a length equal to $4\sqrt{3}$. The area of the triangle is: $\frac{1}{2}(a)(b)=\frac{1}{2}(4)\left(4\sqrt{3}\right)$. The area of the triangle is $8\sqrt{3}$. So, the area of the trapezoid is $36+8\sqrt{3}$.

60. **(F)** (p. 575) ***Mathematics/Trigonometry/Trigonometric Relationships.*** There are several routes by which to reach the right conclusion. The shortest is to reason that the cotangent and tangent are reciprocal functions, so if $\cot\theta=\frac{4}{3}$, then $\tan\theta=\frac{3}{4}$.

TEST 3: READING

1. **(C)** (p. 577) ***Reading/Prose Fiction/Explicit Detail.*** (C) is the correct answer choice. In lines 2–3, the child addresses the narrator as Miss Mix. In line 73, Mr. Rawjester addresses the narrator as Mary Jane.

2. **(H)** (p. 577) ***Reading/Prose Fiction/Implied Idea.*** (H) is the correct answer choice. In line 59, the narrator reveals to the reader the true identity of the highwayman. The highwayman is Mr. Rawjester. He assumes the role of a robber as part of an elaborate plot whereby he will destroy his former home, leave his old life behind, be free of his former wives, and be able to marry his true love—namely, the narrator.

3. **(A)** (p. 577) ***Reading/Prose Fiction/Implied Idea.*** (A) is the correct answer choice. As we learn in the first paragraph, the narrator is employed as a governess. We subsequently learn she is the governess for the daughter of Mr. Rawjester, who has a sweetheart named Blanche Marabout (line 7). The narrator experiences feelings of degradation because she too loves Mr. Rawjester, but she is required by her position in the household to help Blanche make herself beautiful and attractive for Mr. Rawjester (lines 17–19).

4. **(H)** (p. 577) ***Reading/Prose Fiction/Explicit Detail.*** (H) is the correct answer choice. The first paragraph establishes that the narrator is a governess in a home; specifically, the narrator has the care of a young girl, who she describe as "my pupil." (line 1). Also, during the robbery, the narrator explicitly identifies herself as a "poor governess" (line 54).

5. **(B)** (p. 577) ***Reading/Prose Fiction/Implied Idea.*** (B) is the correct answer choice. As he leaves the party, he calls his guests "idiots" (line 27) under his breath. In addition, when he returns disguised as a robber, he forces them to experience the indignity of being robbed and roughly handled while he holds a gun trained upon them.

6. **(G)** (p. 577) ***Reading/Prose Fiction/Explicit Detail.*** (G) is the correct answer choice. In the first paragraph, the child tells the narrator that "Blanche Marabout…is to be here. You know they say she is to be my mamma" (lines 7–9).

7. **(B)** (p. 577) ***Reading/Prose Fiction/Implied Idea.*** (B) is the correct answer choice. There are at least two details that imply the narrator cooperated with Mr. Rawjester. First, after the narrator quietly reveals to Mr. Rawjester that she sees through his disguise, he says "utter a syllable to frustrate my plans and you die" (lines 62–63); the narrator survives the encounter, so we can infer that she cooperated and did not utter a syllable regarding his true identity. Second, the narrator says that Mr. Rawjester gagged and locked all the guests in the cellar "with the exception of myself" (lines 64–65); the narrator does not experience the same fate as the guests, so we can infer this is due to the narrator's continuing cooperation with Mr. Rawjester. Whether the narrator willingly cooperated (or whether she did so because she feared for her life) is another question left unanswered by the passage.

8. **(J)** (p. 578) ***Reading/Prose Fiction/Explicit Detail.*** (J) is the correct answer choice. Mr. Rawjester engages in the elaborate plot of slipping away from his party, returning disguised as a highwayman, and proceeding to rob his own guests for the sole reason that he does not want to be suspected of the crime he actually wants to commit—namely, killing his former wives. As for the other answer choices, (F) is incorrect because the theft of jewelry was not Mr. Rawjester's primary motive; it was only a detail in the plot. (G) is incorrect because, as noted above, the primary motive behind Mr. Rawjester's plot is much more sinister; also, it is never clear if the narrator is kidnapped, or if she somewhat willingly cooperates with Mr. Rawjester. Finally, (H) is incorrect for the same reason as (G); in addition, the fate of the child is also unknown at the end of the passage.

9. **(A)** (p. 578) ***Reading/Prose Fiction/Explicit Detail.*** (A) is the correct answer choice. Although it is never stated during the encounter between Blanche and Mr. Rawjester while he's disguised as the highwayman (lines 46–51), it is implied that he knows about the diamond necklace because he was the person who gave it to her at an earlier time.

10. **(F)** (p. 578) ***Reading/Prose Fiction/Implied Idea.*** (F) is the correct answer choice. The narrator reveals to Mr. Rawjester that she sees through his disguise "in a low voice" (line 59). Mr. Rawjester then responds to her in a "whisper" (line 62). So, we can assume that their conversation was only heard by them.

11. **(B)** (p. 579) ***Reading/Social Science/Main Idea.*** (B) is the correct answer choice. It accurately summarizes the main idea developed in the passage; in addition, it is the only statement general enough to cover the full range of information discussed in the passage. As for the other answer choices, (A) is incorrect because it is contradicted by the passage; as the author says, the current lack of regulation may have lead to events that have "had harmful effects not only on stockholders but also on the economy as a whole" (lines 7–9). (C) and (D) are incorrect because they are only two points or opinions presented during the passage; in other words, neither is a statement broad enough to encompass the main idea of the passage. In addition, it is hardly clear that the author shares or would endorse either of these opinions.

12. **(G)** (p. 580) ***Reading/Social Science/Application.*** (G) is the correct answer choice. In lines 48–52, the author outlines the basic details of how a "golden parachute clause" works. The description in the question stem matches what is described in lines 49–53.

13. **(C)** (p. 580) ***Reading/Social Science/Implied Idea.*** (C) is the correct answer choice. In lines 10–13, the author gives the defining characteristic of a hostile takeover; specifically, the current management is opposed to it.

14. **(F)** (p. 580) ***Reading/Social Science/Explicit Detail.*** (F) is the correct answer choice. In the third paragraph, the author explains how raiders must raise substantial capital to buy large quantities of a targeted company's stock (usually at above market price). According to the author, the raiders acquire "debt" (line 30) that they then attempt to liquidate by running the targeted company more efficiently.

15. (D) (p. 580) ***Reading/Social Science/Explicit Detail.*** (D) is the correct answer choice. In lines 53–56, the author outlines the basic details of a "poison pill" strategy. The description in (D) matches what is outlined in lines 53–56. As for the other answer choices, (A) is incorrect because it describes the "greenmail" strategy (lines 56–61). (B) is incorrect because it describes the "golden parachute" strategy (lines 49–53). Finally, (C) is incorrect because it is not supported by any material in the passage.

16. (G) (p. 580) ***Reading/Social Science/Explicit Detail.*** (G) is the correct answer choice. In the final paragraph, the author explicitly says that supporters of corporate takeovers believe "the threat of a takeover…makes managers more efficient" (lines 64–65). As for the other answer choices, they are all incorrect because there is no evidence in the passage to suggest that supporters of corporate takeovers would hold these beliefs.

17. (D) (p. 580) ***Reading/Social Science/Explicit Detail.*** (D) is the correct answer choice. A proxy fight is defined in lines 18–21. The description in (D) matches what is outlined in lines 18–21. As for the other answer choices, they are all incorrect because they are unrelated to proxy fights.

18. (H) (p. 581) ***Reading/Social Science/Application.*** (H) is the correct answer choice. In the final paragraph, the author says that supporters of corporate takeovers believe "the threat of a takeover…makes managers more efficient" (lines 64–65). Selling unprofitable subsidiaries to raise cash and cut expenses is an example of being more efficient. As for the other answer choices, see the second to last paragraph of this passage for correct definitions of these terms.

19. (B) (p. 581) ***Reading/Social Science/Explicit Detail.*** (B) is the correct answer choice. In the first sentence of the passage, the author explains that the Securities and Exchange Commission is a federal agency that regulates American financial markets.

20. (H) (p. 581) ***Reading/Social Science/Explicit Detail.*** (H) is the correct answer choice. In the fourth paragraph, the author explains that people have been sent to jail for "selling inside information about future takeover attempts" (lines 37–38).

21. (A) (p. 582) ***Reading/Humanities/Main Idea.*** Although the passage includes an abundance of detail, nearly all of these details can be grouped into two main categories: first, a general introduction to Josquin des Prez; and, second, an explanation as to why he is relatively unknown. (A) is the correct answer choice because it mentions both of these main points.

22. (J) (p. 583) ***Reading/Humanities/Explicit Detail.*** (J) is the correct answer choice because the author never mentions any of Josquin's students. As for the other answer choices, (F) is answered in the second paragraph (*El Grillo, Allegez moy*, etc.). (G) is answered in the final paragraph (sackbuts, organettos, etc.). (H) is answered in the second paragraph (Ockeghem).

23. (D) (p. 583) ***Reading/Humanities/Implied Idea.*** In the fourth paragraph, the author lists several difficulties associated with reading a musical score from the Renaissance. The author specifically mentions that no tempos are given, flats and sharps are not specified, and no instructions are provided as to which instruments are to play each part. It is logical to assume that, since these are mentioned as difficulties associated with musical scores from the Renaissance, modern musical notation must contain all of these features.

24. (G) (p. 583) ***Reading/Humanities/Implied Idea.*** In the third paragraph, the author discusses a distinction between concept and performance. The author states that music does not exist in notes printed on a page; instead, the author argues, a musical score is merely a set of instructions for producing music. Therefore, the author would agree with (G).

25. (D) (p. 583) ***Reading/Humanities/Application.*** Each answer choice provided here has a certain amount of merit. On the one hand, (A) seems like a good choice because the author mentions that members of *collegia musica* are generally the only ones who attempt to perform Renaissance music; however, the author also lists several shortcomings associated with these organizations. (B) seems like a good choice because study in general is an excellent method for producing a positive results; however, the author mentions several deficiencies associated with musical scores from the Renaissance that even a lifetime of dedicated study could never overcome. (C) might seem like a good choice for the same reason as (B) since additional study or attention normally leads to positive results; however, the essay gives no specific evidence that merely adding Renaissance music to a college curriculum would increase public appreciation of this remote and esoteric art-form. In the end, (D) is the best answer choice because it is actually supported by evidence from the essay. In lines 64–66, the author explicitly mentions that musicians cannot afford to study the type of music written by Josquin des Prez due to lack of financial support from an audience. If financial support were available from another source, though, musicians could afford to study and promote the music of Renaissance composers like Josquin des Prez.

26. **(G)** (p. 583) ***Reading/Humanities/Explicit Detail.*** (G) is the correct answer choice because, although the author says that musicians who read modern musical notation have difficulty reading Renaissance notation, the author never says that these musicians cannot play Renaissance instruments. As for the other answer choices, (F) is mentioned in the fourth paragraph. (H) and (J) are mentioned in the final paragraph.

27. **(A)** (p. 583) ***Reading/Humanities/Implied Idea.*** (A) is the correct answer choice because there are at least two reasons to believe that the author admires Galileo. First, in lines 29–31, the author says that both Josquin and Galileo "asserted a new importance for man." The author does not qualify or given any reason to doubt the goodness of this accomplishment. Second, the author has only praise and admiration for Josquin. If the author then says that Josquin and Galileo were comparable figures in their respective fields, we can assume that the author would have similar praise and admiration for Galileo.

28. **(H)** (p. 583) ***Reading/Humanities/Implied Idea.*** In line 6, the author states that the dominant theme of liturgical music "was reverence." So, (H) is the correct answer choice.

29. **(A)** (p. 583) ***Reading/Humanities/Implied Idea.*** (A) is the correct answer choice. In lines 34–35, the author says that "in fine art, concept and performance are one." Specifically, in arts such as painting and poetry, there is a permanent and physical artifact (i.e., a mural or a book of poems) that does not change. In contrast, the author says there is a "separation of concept from performance in music" (lines 33–34). Specifically, a composer writes a musical score which consists of notes on a page. However, the music itself does not exist until musicians perform it; the music then varies from performance to performance based on the quality and the interpretation of the musicians. Similarly, a choreographer creates a ballet and leaves instructions as to its performance. However, the ballet itself does not exist until dancers perform it; and, again, the ballet varies from performance to performance based on the same factors mentioned above.

30. **(H)** (p. 584) ***Reading/Humanities/Implied Idea.*** (H) is the correct answer choice. In lines 1–2, the author says Western music was only liturgical up to the time of Josquin des Prez. The author then says that, while Josquin des Prez wrote liturgical music, he also "stepped with the other [foot] into the human world" (lines 14–15). In other words, Josquin des Prez also wrote non-religious music. For example, the author cites the "Deploration d'Ockeghem," a musical piece written in tribute to a fellow composer, as well as *Allegez moy*, a musical piece about a beautiful woman.

31. **(C)** (p. 585) ***Reading/Natural Science/Explicit Detail.*** (C) is the correct answer choice. In the first sentence of the passage, the author says that a supernova occurs about "twice every century" (line 1) or about once every fifty years.

32. **(J)** (p. 585) ***Reading/Natural Science/Explicit Detail.*** (J) is the correct answer choice. The passage never mentions or implies that supernovas are caused by the collision of large galaxies. As for the other answer choices, (F) is incorrect because supernovas are described as extremely bright (lines 30–31). (G) is incorrect because supernovas are described as being similar to explosions (lines 2–4). Finally, (H) is incorrect because supernovas are said to emit large quantities of X-rays (lines 35–36).

33. **(A)** (p. 585) ***Reading/Natural Science/Development.*** (A) is the correct answer choice. Starting at line 1, the author compares a star to a leaky balloon. An analogy is a comparison.

34. **(H)** (p. 586) ***Reading/Natural Science/Implied Idea.*** (H) is the correct answer choice. The key word used to describe these meteorites is "anomalous," which means "uncharacteristic." These meteorites are uncharacteristic because they contain "certain isotopes" (line 42) not found in our solar system. If these isotopes are not found in our solar system, it can be inferred that they came from a supernova which gave birth to our solar system. As the author notes, artifacts such as these isotopes "are manufactured deep in the interior of stars and would…remain there if it were not for the cataclysmic supernova explosions that blow stars apart" (lines 49–52).

35. **(A)** (p. 586) ***Reading/Natural Science/Implied Idea.*** (A) is the correct answer choice. In the second paragraph, the author explains that the hot gas from a supernova "will emit most of its energy at X-ray wavelengths, so it is not surprising that X-ray observatories have provided some of the most useful insights into the nature of the supernova phenomenon" (lines 35–38). The author also notes that X-ray studies have detected "more than twenty supernova remnants" (line 39). In short, the author implies it is easiest to find evidence of a supernova using equipment that detects X-rays (rather than equipment that views visible light).

36. **(J)** (p. 586) ***Reading/Natural Science/Explicit Detail.*** (J) is the correct answer choice. In the first paragraph, the author describes how a star becomes a supernova. The sequence of events begins when, within the star, "the nuclear fuel is exhausted…[and] the matter in the center of the star collapses inward" (lines 19–21).

37. **(B)** (p. 586) ***Reading/Natural Science/Explicit Detail.*** (B) is the correct answer choice. In the first paragraph, the author begins the process of describing how a star becomes a supernova. According to the author, once a star completes its initial collapse, its "nuclei and electrons are fused into a super-dense lump of matter known as a neutron star" (lines 23–24). In the second paragraph, the author then explains what follows this stage—namely, a supernova. Therefore, a neutron star is an intermediate stage between an ordinary star and a supernova.

38. **(J)** (p. 586) ***Reading/Natural Science/Main Idea.*** (J) is the correct answer choice for two reasons. First, it accurately summarizes the author's main purpose, which is to describe the sequence of events that precedes and follows a supernova. Second, it is the only statement general enough to cover the full range of information discussed in the passage. As for the other answer choices, they are all incorrect because they focus on only one element of the passage; in other words, (F), (G), and (H) are all too narrow to describe fully the author's main purpose in writing this passage.

39. **(D)** (p. 586) ***Reading/Natural Science/Explicit Detail.*** (D) is the correct answer choice. In line 44, the author says our galaxy was formed "more than four and a half billion years ago."

40. **(H)** (p. 586) ***Reading/Natural Science/Implied Idea.*** (H) is the correct answer choice. In the last paragraph, the author says "supernovas produce clouds of high–energy particles…[which] are responsible for many of the genetic mutations that are the driving force of the evolution of species" (lines 53–57).

TEST 4: SCIENCE

1. **(B)** (p. 588) ***Science/Data Representation/Analysis.*** Generally, the Wright data show lower lift at a given angle than the Lilienthal data.

2. **(H)** (p. 588) ***Science/Data Representation/Comprehension.*** The highest point on the graph is at 16 degrees (approximately 5.5 pounds/sq. ft.).

3. **(A)** (p. 588) ***Science/Data Representation/Comprehension.*** By extending both lines to the 50° mark, the difference between them is clearly observed to be less than 1 pound/sq. ft.

4. **(H)** (p. 588) ***Science/Data Representation/Comprehension.*** Count the crossing points of the two curves.

5. **(B)** (p. 589) ***Science/Data Representation/Comprehension.*** The widest region is between 18° and 43°: 43 − 18 = 25 degrees.

6. **(J)** (p. 590) ***Science/Research Summary/Analysis.*** Since plastic beads are not alive, they cannot possibly carry out cellular respiration. This control is designed to detect any atmospheric changes (in the laboratory) that may cause a change in gas volume inside the tubes.

7. **(A)** (p. 590) ***Science/Research Summary/Comprehension.*** Oxygen in the air of the tube is consumed by the peas during cellular respiration (see summary equation).

8. **(F)** (p. 590) ***Science/Research Summary/Analysis.*** Without KOH to remove the carbon dioxide produced during cellular respiration, the same number of gas molecules ($6CO_2$) would always be added to the tube as gas molecules were being consumed in the tube ($6O_2$).

9. **(C)** (p. 590) ***Science/Research Summary/Analysis.*** Experiment 2 was conducted at a higher temperature than Experiment 1. The greater decrease in gas in the same time period (15 minutes) demonstrates a faster consumption of oxygen.

10. **(G)** (p. 591) ***Science/Research Summary/Analysis.*** If results are identical in light and dark (Experiments 1 and 2), then light/dark conditions are irrelevant to cellular respiration rates in the experiment; only temperature conditions are important.

11. **(A)** (p. 591) ***Science/Research Summary/Comprehension.*** Glucose must be consumed in order for cellular respiration to occur. Since cellular respiration did not occur at equal rates in Experiments 1 and 2, (A) is the only possible answer. Peas are seeds containing a supply of glucose.

12. **(G)** (p. 592) ***Science/Conflicting Viewpoints/Analysis.*** Scientist 1 believes that processes associated with sudden events in the past shaped the Earth, whereas Scientist 2 believes that the processes are continuing in the present.

13. **(D)** (p. 592) ***Science/Conflicting Viewpoints/Analysis.*** Mountains could not have formed only when land masses were raised at the beginnings of the Earth if recent fossils of sea creatures are found at mountain tops. This evidence suggests that the rocks were underwater relatively recently.

14. **(H)** (p. 593) ***Science/Conflicting Viewpoints/Analysis.*** The two scientists agree that the changes that have shaped the landscape have operated over a long time span, but they disagree as to whether those changes were sudden and violent (Catastrophism) or constant and gradual (Principle of Uniform Change).

15. **(A)** (p. 593) ***Science/Conflicting Viewpoints/Comprehension.*** If the worldwide ocean precipitated granite first, it must be the lowest layer, with other precipitated materials covering it later.

16. **(F)** (p. 593) ***Science/Conflicting Viewpoints/Comprehension.*** If the major rock types (three) formed when the worldwide ocean precipitated different materials on three occasions, no further types can be expected since this ocean no longer exists (possibly due to evaporation).

17. **(C)** (p. 593) ***Science/Conflicting Viewpoints/Analysis.*** Processes cannot be uniform from the beginning. Processes that formed the Earth at its origin must have differed from those that maintain and mold the Earth as an existing planet.

18. **(G)** (p. 593) ***Science/Conflicting Viewpoints/Analysis.*** Scientist 1 refers to three rock types forming during three separate precipitations. Regions of lava (with no present volcanoes), rivers presently continuing to cut their channels, and "related" fossils that could not have immigrated from other geographic areas are factors that support the views of Scientist 2.

19. **(D)** (p. 594) ***Science/Research Summary/Comprehension.*** Ten individuals had their heart rates recorded every 10 minutes during a 30–minute experiment (three times). Therefore, 30 values were used to calculate the average heart rate for each of the experiments.

20. **(G)** (p. 594) ***Science/Research Summary/Analysis.*** Since Species B had an increase in heart rate when environmental temperature increased, it is the likely species to be poikilothermic (Species A's heart rate stayed about the same).

21. **(C)** (p. 594) ***Science/Research Summary/Analysis.*** Just by chance alone, any one individual might have an extremely high or extremely low heart rate. The larger the sample of individuals tested, the lower the chances of getting extreme average values.

22. **(J)** (p. 594) ***Science/Research Summary/Analysis.*** Since Species B (poikilothermic) had an increase in average heart rate when environmental temperature increased, a decrease in average heart rate is likely when temperatures drop. Species A should have approximately the same average heart rate at all three temperatures.

23. **(A)** (p. 594) ***Science/Research Summary/Analysis.*** At 22°C, Species A had an average heart rate of 150 beats/minute, while Species B averaged 100 beats/minute.

24. **(F)** (p. 595) ***Science/Research Summary/Analysis.*** The poikilothermic Species B should have an increase in body temperature in Experiment 2 (35°C conditions in the incubator compared to 22°C in Experiment 1). The homeothermic Species A should have no significant change in body temperature during the experiments.

25. **(A)** (p. 596) ***Science/Data Representation/Comprehension.*** Each photon can promote an electron from level 1 to level 2 since the difference in energies is 0.60. (Note that the actual value of level 1 alone, which happens to be 0.60 also, does not determine the answer. Differences in energy are what matter.)

26. **(J)** (p. 596) ***Science/Data Representation/Comprehension.*** There is no way to distinguish between the two emissions since each releases a photon of equal energy.

27. **(D)** (p. 596) ***Science/Data Representation/Comprehension.*** Only the level 3 to level 1 emission has an energy difference of 0.92.

28. **(J)** (p. 596) ***Science/Data Representation/Comprehension.*** Each electron can go from level 1 to any of 4 other levels, with each of the four transitions requiring a photon of a different energy.

29. **(C)** (p. 596) ***Science/Data Representation/Analysis.*** Since absorption of photons occurs first, then emission, electrons must be promoted (gaining the necessary energy from the absorbed photons), then emitted. Transitions between levels 3 and 4 have the necessary energies, namely 0.23.

30. **(J)** (p. 596) ***Science/Data Representation/Comprehension.*** Although 2.07 is the absolute energy of level 5, there is no difference of energy levels anywhere on the diagram that equals 2.07; hence, the photons will not be absorbed.

31. **(C)** (p. 597) ***Science/Research Summary/Comprehension.*** Note how θ_1 and θ_2 are defined on the original drawing, then imagine how the diagram will change as the angles become smaller. (B) would be correct if the angles were defined as those between the ray and the horizontal, not vertical, axis.

32. **(J)** (p. 597) ***Science/Research Summary/Analysis.*** Only the last choice fits both experiments.

33. **(A)** (p. 598) ***Science/Research Summary/Comprehension.*** This question simply requires interpretation of the meaning of the diagram.

34. (H) (p. 598) ***Science/Research Summary/Comprehension.*** The beam of light only passes into the air for observation in Experiment 2.

35. (C) (p. 598) ***Science/Research Summary/Analysis.*** This response covers all elements of the three diagrams.

36. (H) (p. 599) ***Science/Data Representation/Comprehension.*** The number of butterflies captured for marking is found under the heading: "# marked". Reading across the table for each size group, the "dark brown" category always has the fewest butterflies marked.

37. (D) (p. 599) ***Science/Data Representation/Comprehension.*** By comparing the number of butterflies recaptured to the number marked, students can derive a proportion that represents how easy it is to recapture each type of butterfly. The proportion for small, white butterflies (30/35) is much higher than that for any of the other choices.

38. (G) (p. 599) ***Science/Data Representation/Analysis.*** An examination of the table shows that for all colors, as size increases the number of butterflies marked gets larger.

39. (B) (p. 599) ***Science/Data Representation/Application.*** A poisonous chemical will have adverse effects on the butterfly after marking (perhaps by killing or by preventing flight). The group with the lowest number (and proportion) of individuals recaptured in flight ($10/40 = 1/4$ recaptured) is the group consisting of small, tan butterflies.

40. (G) (p. 599) ***Science/Data Representation/Analysis.*** For medium–sized butterflies, the proportion of individuals recaptured in each color is as follows: white ($15/30 = 1/2$), tan ($20/40 = 1/2$), and dark brown ($10/20 = 1/2$).

SAMPLE ESSAY RESPONSES AND ANALYSES

TEST 5: WRITING (p. 600)

Above Average Response

I think that it would be a good for schools to ban all food that is not healthy for students. Although some people will argue that a total ban on unhealthy food will interfere with the freedom of students to choose what they eat, there are two points to remember. One, freedom to eat what one chooses is not like freedom of speech of freedom from policy brutality. In the big picture, being told that one cannot buy "Twinkle Cakes" from the machine in the cafeteria is not like being told that one can't criticize the government. Two, banning foods from school doesn't mean that these foods are banned altogether. One can still buy them and eat them before and after school and on weekends. All that the ban means is that you can't eat them in school when you are under the school's authority.

Banning unhealthy food from schools would have three benefits. First, during the school day, students would be getting only healthy food. This means that for at least one meal (lunch), they wouldn't be eating junk. That would mean that they would be eating food that contains important nutrients and doesn't have all of the calories and additives that are usually found in regular junk food. This alone would probably have an important impact on the health of the country. Second, students would learn about good nutrition. Many students now may not understand that they need certain vitamins and minerals and these usually come from eating foods like broccoli and fresh fruit. You just don't find a lot of vitamins in "Twinkle Cakes." Also, junk food often contains additives and preservatives that are not good for us. Someone who eats too much junk food gets too much of these bad elements. This would be especially important for younger children because their nutritional needs are more significant than older children. They would begin to learn at an earlier age the important difference between healthy food and junk food. And these lessons would stay with them.

Third, having schools set a good example might help adults as well. When parents see that their children are eating right, they could also become interested in having better diets. If everyone were eating better, then there would be less incentive to eat things that are bad, and everyone would benefit.

Banning unhealthy foods in school is not the first step to a dictatorship. Schools prohibit a lot of behavior (think of obscene T–shirts) that is allowed outside of school. So a new policy really would not hurt anyone. Plus, the new policy would have some definite benefits, so it should be accepted.

Position on issue: The writer clearly states his or her position at the very beginning of the essay. As a result, the essay is immediately easier to follow because the reader is aware of the writer's point of view.

Topic development and essay organization: The writer clearly explains three specific benefits of having a school policy that bans certain foods. The three benefits are each discussed in some detail, and the writer clearly signals when a new benefit is about to be discussed. One criticism that could be made of the essay is that the writer doesn't explicitly relate these three benefits to a larger good. For example, the writer explains how this policy would encourage kids to eat good foods (i.e., broccoli and fresh fruit) and discourage them from eating bad foods (i.e., "Twinkle Cakes," which is a humorous and clever reference to "Twinkies"), but the writer does not connect these improved habits to a larger good—namely, the promotion of long-term health or a reduction in childhood obesity. In general, though, the writer does a good job of organizing the essay and providing enough detail to support a point of view.

Language usage, sentence structure, and punctuation: In general, the writer uses correct grammar and ties ideas together logically.

Summary and conclusions: The essay makes several good points, and it is well organized. As mentioned above, it could be improved if the writer provided a tighter focus (i.e., if the three benefits were more explicitly related to a larger good). As it stands, the essay would probably get a "4." It is too well-organized to receive a "3," and it's possible some readers might even give it a "5."

Below Average Response

> *Some people will argue that a total ban on unhealthy food will interfere with the freedom of students to choose what they eat. Freedom to eat what one chooses is not like freedom of speech o freedom from policy brutality. In the big picture, being told that one cannot buy "Twinkle Cakes" from the machine in the cafeteria is not like being told that one can't criticize the government. Banning foods from school doesn't mean that these foods are banned altogether. One can still buy them and eat them before and after school and on weekends. All that the ban means is that you can't eat them in school when you are under the school's authority.*
>
> *By banning unhealthy food from schools, students would be getting only healthy food. This means that for at least one meal (lunch), they wouldn't be eating junk that would mean that they would be eating food that contains important nutrients and doesn't have all of the calories and additives that are usually found in regular junk food. This alone would probably have an important impact on the health of the country. Students would learn about good nutrition. Many students now may not understand that they need certain vitamins and minerals and these usually come from eating foods like broccoli and fresh fruit. You just don't find a lot of vitamins in "Twinkle Cakes." Junk food often contains additives and preservatives that are not good for us. Someone who eats too much junk food gets too much of these bad elements. This would be especially important for younger children because their nutritional needs are more significant than older children. They would begin to learn at an earlier age the important difference between healthy food and junk food. And these lessons would stay with them.*
>
> *Having schools set a good example might help adults as well. When parents see that their children are eating right, they could also become interested in having better diets. If everyone were eating better, then there would be less incentive to eat things that are bad, and everyone would benefit.*
>
> *Banning unhealthy foods in school is not the first step to a dictatorship. Schools prohibit a lot of behavior (think of obscene T–shirts) that is allowed outside of school. So a new policy really would hurt anyone. Plus, the new policy would have some definite benefits, so it should be accepted.*

Position on issue: The writer fails to clearly state his or her position on the issue. Instead, the writer begins the essay by saying "some people will argue that a total ban on unhealthy food will interfere with the freedom of students to choose what they eat." This statement does not establish the writer's attitude towards the issue, and it makes the writer's point of view ambiguous at best.

Topic development and essay organization: This essay is a modified version of the first essay. However, several topic sentences (i.e., the first sentence of a paragraph where the main point should be stated) have been removed; in addition, much of the organizational language (i.e., "There are three benefits…First….Second…Third") has also been removed. Due to these changes, the essay is not as well-organized and is much more difficult to follow.

Language usage, sentence structure, and punctuation: The essay includes several spelling, punctuation, and grammatical errors.

Summary and conclusions: This essay would probably receive a "2" or a "3." The writer does not clearly state a point of view, so the essay is hard to follow. The writer does not organize the essay clearly, so the essay is very confusing at times. Finally, there are several spelling and grammatical errors, which would seriously frustrate a reader. A generous reader might give the essay a "3." However, it's quite likely that the essay would receive a "2."

Appendix B:

Test Answer Sheets

TIMED PRACTICE TEST I
BUBBLE SHEET

Name ______________________ Student ID Number ______________________

Date ______________ Instructor ______________________ Course/Session Number ______________

TEST 1—ENGLISH

1 A B C D	16 F G H J	31 A B C D	46 F G H J	61 A B C D
2 F G H J	17 A B C D	32 F G H J	47 A B C D	62 F G H J
3 A B C D	18 F G H J	33 A B C D	48 F G H J	63 A B C D
4 F G H J	19 A B C D	34 F G H J	49 A B C D	64 F G H J
5 A B C D	20 F G H J	35 A B C D	50 F G H J	65 A B C D
6 F G H J	21 A B C D	36 F G H J	51 A B C D	66 F G H J
7 A B C D	22 F G H J	37 A B C D	52 F G H J	67 A B C D
8 F G H J	23 A B C D	38 F G H J	53 A B C D	68 F G H J
9 A B C D	24 F G H J	39 A B C D	54 F G H J	69 A B C D
10 F G H J	25 A B C D	40 F G H J	55 A B C D	70 F G H J
11 A B C D	26 F G H J	41 A B C D	56 F G H J	71 A B C D
12 F G H J	27 A B C D	42 F G H J	57 A B C D	72 F G H J
13 A B C D	28 F G H J	43 A B C D	58 F G H J	73 A B C D
14 F G H J	29 A B C D	44 F G H J	59 A B C D	74 F G H J
15 A B C D	30 F G H J	45 A B C D	60 F G H J	75 A B C D

TEST 2—MATHEMATICS

1 A B C D E	13 A B C D E	25 A B C D E	37 A B C D E	49 A B C D E
2 F G H J K	14 F G H J K	26 F G H J K	38 F G H J K	50 F G H J K
3 A B C D E	15 A B C D E	27 A B C D E	39 A B C D E	51 A B C D E
4 F G H J K	16 F G H J K	28 F G H J K	40 F G H J K	52 F G H J K
5 A B C D E	17 A B C D E	29 A B C D E	41 A B C D E	53 A B C D E
6 F G H J K	18 F G H J K	30 F G H J K	42 F G H J K	54 F G H J K
7 A B C D E	19 A B C D E	31 A B C D E	43 A B C D E	55 A B C D E
8 F G H J K	20 F G H J K	32 F G H J K	44 F G H J K	56 F G H J K
9 A B C D E	21 A B C D E	33 A B C D E	45 A B C D E	57 A B C D E
10 F G H J K	22 F G H J K	34 F G H J K	46 F G H J K	58 F G H J K
11 A B C D E	23 A B C D E	35 A B C D E	47 A B C D E	59 A B C D E
12 F G H J K	24 F G H J K	36 F G H J K	48 F G H J K	60 F G H J K

TEST 3—READING

1 A B C D	9 A B C D	17 A B C D	25 A B C D	33 A B C D
2 F G H J	10 F G H J	18 F G H J	26 F G H J	34 F G H J
3 A B C D	11 A B C D	19 A B C D	27 A B C D	35 A B C D
4 F G H J	12 F G H J	20 F G H J	28 F G H J	36 F G H J
5 A B C D	13 A B C D	21 A B C D	29 A B C D	37 A B C D
6 F G H J	14 F G H J	22 F G H J	30 F G H J	38 F G H J
7 A B C D	15 A B C D	23 A B C D	31 A B C D	39 A B C D
8 F G H J	16 F G H J	24 F G H J	32 F G H J	40 F G H J

TEST 4—SCIENCE

1 A B C D	9 A B C D	17 A B C D	25 A B C D	33 A B C D
2 F G H J	10 F G H J	18 F G H J	26 F G H J	34 F G H J
3 A B C D	11 A B C D	19 A B C D	27 A B C D	35 A B C D
4 F G H J	12 F G H J	20 F G H J	28 F G H J	36 F G H J
5 A B C D	13 A B C D	21 A B C D	29 A B C D	37 A B C D
6 F G H J	14 F G H J	22 F G H J	30 F G H J	38 F G H J
7 A B C D	15 A B C D	23 A B C D	31 A B C D	39 A B C D
8 F G H J	16 F G H J	24 F G H J	32 F G H J	40 F G H J

TIMED PRACTICE TEST I
ESSAY RESPONSE SHEET

Name

Student ID Number

Date

Instructor

Course/Session Number

TIMED PRACTICE TEST II BUBBLE SHEET

Name ____________________ Student ID Number ____________________

Date ____________ Instructor ____________________ Course/Session Number ____________

TEST 1—ENGLISH

1 (A) (B) (C) (D)	16 (F) (G) (H) (J)	31 (A) (B) (C) (D)	46 (F) (G) (H) (J)	61 (A) (B) (C) (D)
2 (F) (G) (H) (J)	17 (A) (B) (C) (D)	32 (F) (G) (H) (J)	47 (A) (B) (C) (D)	62 (F) (G) (H) (J)
3 (A) (B) (C) (D)	18 (F) (G) (H) (J)	33 (A) (B) (C) (D)	48 (F) (G) (H) (J)	63 (A) (B) (C) (D)
4 (F) (G) (H) (J)	19 (A) (B) (C) (D)	34 (F) (G) (H) (J)	49 (A) (B) (C) (D)	64 (F) (G) (H) (J)
5 (A) (B) (C) (D)	20 (F) (G) (H) (J)	35 (A) (B) (C) (D)	50 (F) (G) (H) (J)	65 (A) (B) (C) (D)
6 (F) (G) (H) (J)	21 (A) (B) (C) (D)	36 (F) (G) (H) (J)	51 (A) (B) (C) (D)	66 (F) (G) (H) (J)
7 (A) (B) (C) (D)	22 (F) (G) (H) (J)	37 (A) (B) (C) (D)	52 (F) (G) (H) (J)	67 (A) (B) (C) (D)
8 (F) (G) (H) (J)	23 (A) (B) (C) (D)	38 (F) (G) (H) (J)	53 (A) (B) (C) (D)	68 (F) (G) (H) (J)
9 (A) (B) (C) (D)	24 (F) (G) (H) (J)	39 (A) (B) (C) (D)	54 (F) (G) (H) (J)	69 (A) (B) (C) (D)
10 (F) (G) (H) (J)	25 (A) (B) (C) (D)	40 (F) (G) (H) (J)	55 (A) (B) (C) (D)	70 (F) (G) (H) (J)
11 (A) (B) (C) (D)	26 (F) (G) (H) (J)	41 (A) (B) (C) (D)	56 (F) (G) (H) (J)	71 (A) (B) (C) (D)
12 (F) (G) (H) (J)	27 (A) (B) (C) (D)	42 (F) (G) (H) (J)	57 (A) (B) (C) (D)	72 (F) (G) (H) (J)
13 (A) (B) (C) (D)	28 (F) (G) (H) (J)	43 (A) (B) (C) (D)	58 (F) (G) (H) (J)	73 (A) (B) (C) (D)
14 (F) (G) (H) (J)	29 (A) (B) (C) (D)	44 (F) (G) (H) (J)	59 (A) (B) (C) (D)	74 (F) (G) (H) (J)
15 (A) (B) (C) (D)	30 (F) (G) (H) (J)	45 (A) (B) (C) (D)	60 (F) (G) (H) (J)	75 (A) (B) (C) (D)

TEST 2—MATHEMATICS

1 (A) (B) (C) (D) (E)	13 (A) (B) (C) (D) (E)	25 (A) (B) (C) (D) (E)	37 (A) (B) (C) (D) (E)	49 (A) (B) (C) (D) (E)
2 (F) (G) (H) (J) (K)	14 (F) (G) (H) (J) (K)	26 (F) (G) (H) (J) (K)	38 (F) (G) (H) (J) (K)	50 (F) (G) (H) (J) (K)
3 (A) (B) (C) (D) (E)	15 (A) (B) (C) (D) (E)	27 (A) (B) (C) (D) (E)	39 (A) (B) (C) (D) (E)	51 (A) (B) (C) (D) (E)
4 (F) (G) (H) (J) (K)	16 (F) (G) (H) (J) (K)	28 (F) (G) (H) (J) (K)	40 (F) (G) (H) (J) (K)	52 (F) (G) (H) (J) (K)
5 (A) (B) (C) (D) (E)	17 (A) (B) (C) (D) (E)	29 (A) (B) (C) (D) (E)	41 (A) (B) (C) (D) (E)	53 (A) (B) (C) (D) (E)
6 (F) (G) (H) (J) (K)	18 (F) (G) (H) (J) (K)	30 (F) (G) (H) (J) (K)	42 (F) (G) (H) (J) (K)	54 (F) (G) (H) (J) (K)
7 (A) (B) (C) (D) (E)	19 (A) (B) (C) (D) (E)	31 (A) (B) (C) (D) (E)	43 (A) (B) (C) (D) (E)	55 (A) (B) (C) (D) (E)
8 (F) (G) (H) (J) (K)	20 (F) (G) (H) (J) (K)	32 (F) (G) (H) (J) (K)	44 (F) (G) (H) (J) (K)	56 (F) (G) (H) (J) (K)
9 (A) (B) (C) (D) (E)	21 (A) (B) (C) (D) (E)	33 (A) (B) (C) (D) (E)	45 (A) (B) (C) (D) (E)	57 (A) (B) (C) (D) (E)
10 (F) (G) (H) (J) (K)	22 (F) (G) (H) (J) (K)	34 (F) (G) (H) (J) (K)	46 (F) (G) (H) (J) (K)	58 (F) (G) (H) (J) (K)
11 (A) (B) (C) (D) (E)	23 (A) (B) (C) (D) (E)	35 (A) (B) (C) (D) (E)	47 (A) (B) (C) (D) (E)	59 (A) (B) (C) (D) (E)
12 (F) (G) (H) (J) (K)	24 (F) (G) (H) (J) (K)	36 (F) (G) (H) (J) (K)	48 (F) (G) (H) (J) (K)	60 (F) (G) (H) (J) (K)

TEST 3—READING

1 (A) (B) (C) (D)	9 (A) (B) (C) (D)	17 (A) (B) (C) (D)	25 (A) (B) (C) (D)	33 (A) (B) (C) (D)
2 (F) (G) (H) (J)	10 (F) (G) (H) (J)	18 (F) (G) (H) (J)	26 (F) (G) (H) (J)	34 (F) (G) (H) (J)
3 (A) (B) (C) (D)	11 (A) (B) (C) (D)	19 (A) (B) (C) (D)	27 (A) (B) (C) (D)	35 (A) (B) (C) (D)
4 (F) (G) (H) (J)	12 (F) (G) (H) (J)	20 (F) (G) (H) (J)	28 (F) (G) (H) (J)	36 (F) (G) (H) (J)
5 (A) (B) (C) (D)	13 (A) (B) (C) (D)	21 (A) (B) (C) (D)	29 (A) (B) (C) (D)	37 (A) (B) (C) (D)
6 (F) (G) (H) (J)	14 (F) (G) (H) (J)	22 (F) (G) (H) (J)	30 (F) (G) (H) (J)	38 (F) (G) (H) (J)
7 (A) (B) (C) (D)	15 (A) (B) (C) (D)	23 (A) (B) (C) (D)	31 (A) (B) (C) (D)	39 (A) (B) (C) (D)
8 (F) (G) (H) (J)	16 (F) (G) (H) (J)	24 (F) (G) (H) (J)	32 (F) (G) (H) (J)	40 (F) (G) (H) (J)

TEST 4—SCIENCE

1 (A) (B) (C) (D)	9 (A) (B) (C) (D)	17 (A) (B) (C) (D)	25 (A) (B) (C) (D)	33 (A) (B) (C) (D)
2 (F) (G) (H) (J)	10 (F) (G) (H) (J)	18 (F) (G) (H) (J)	26 (F) (G) (H) (J)	34 (F) (G) (H) (J)
3 (A) (B) (C) (D)	11 (A) (B) (C) (D)	19 (A) (B) (C) (D)	27 (A) (B) (C) (D)	35 (A) (B) (C) (D)
4 (F) (G) (H) (J)	12 (F) (G) (H) (J)	20 (F) (G) (H) (J)	28 (F) (G) (H) (J)	36 (F) (G) (H) (J)
5 (A) (B) (C) (D)	13 (A) (B) (C) (D)	21 (A) (B) (C) (D)	29 (A) (B) (C) (D)	37 (A) (B) (C) (D)
6 (F) (G) (H) (J)	14 (F) (G) (H) (J)	22 (F) (G) (H) (J)	30 (F) (G) (H) (J)	38 (F) (G) (H) (J)
7 (A) (B) (C) (D)	15 (A) (B) (C) (D)	23 (A) (B) (C) (D)	31 (A) (B) (C) (D)	39 (A) (B) (C) (D)
8 (F) (G) (H) (J)	16 (F) (G) (H) (J)	24 (F) (G) (H) (J)	32 (F) (G) (H) (J)	40 (F) (G) (H) (J)

TIMED PRACTICE TEST II ESSAY RESPONSE SHEET

Name

Student ID Number

Date

Instructor

Course/Session Number

TIMED PRACTICE TEST III BUBBLE SHEET

Name	Student ID Number

Date	Instructor	Course/Session Number

TEST 1—ENGLISH

1 A B C D	16 F G H J	31 A B C D	46 F G H J	61 A B C D
2 F G H J	17 A B C D	32 F G H J	47 A B C D	62 F G H J
3 A B C D	18 F G H J	33 A B C D	48 F G H J	63 A B C D
4 F G H J	19 A B C D	34 F G H J	49 A B C D	64 F G H J
5 A B C D	20 F G H J	35 A B C D	50 F G H J	65 A B C D
6 F G H J	21 A B C D	36 F G H J	51 A B C D	66 F G H J
7 A B C D	22 F G H J	37 A B C D	52 F G H J	67 A B C D
8 F G H J	23 A B C D	38 F G H J	53 A B C D	68 F G H J
9 A B C D	24 F G H J	39 A B C D	54 F G H J	69 A B C D
10 F G H J	25 A B C D	40 F G H J	55 A B C D	70 F G H J
11 A B C D	26 F G H J	41 A B C D	56 F G H J	71 A B C D
12 F G H J	27 A B C D	42 F G H J	57 A B C D	72 F G H J
13 A B C D	28 F G H J	43 A B C D	58 F G H J	73 A B C D
14 F G H J	29 A B C D	44 F G H J	59 A B C D	74 F G H J
15 A B C D	30 F G H J	45 A B C D	60 F G H J	75 A B C D

TEST 2—MATHEMATICS

1 A B C D E	13 A B C D E	25 A B C D E	37 A B C D E	49 A B C D E
2 F G H J K	14 F G H J K	26 F G H J K	38 F G H J K	50 F G H J K
3 A B C D E	15 A B C D E	27 A B C D E	39 A B C D E	51 A B C D E
4 F G H J K	16 F G H J K	28 F G H J K	40 F G H J K	52 F G H J K
5 A B C D E	17 A B C D E	29 A B C D E	41 A B C D E	53 A B C D E
6 F G H J K	18 F G H J K	30 F G H J K	42 F G H J K	54 F G H J K
7 A B C D E	19 A B C D E	31 A B C D E	43 A B C D E	55 A B C D E
8 F G H J K	20 F G H J K	32 F G H J K	44 F G H J K	56 F G H J K
9 A B C D E	21 A B C D E	33 A B C D E	45 A B C D E	57 A B C D E
10 F G H J K	22 F G H J K	34 F G H J K	46 F G H J K	58 F G H J K
11 A B C D E	23 A B C D E	35 A B C D E	47 A B C D E	59 A B C D E
12 F G H J K	24 F G H J K	36 F G H J K	48 F G H J K	60 F G H J K

TEST 3—READING

1 A B C D	9 A B C D	17 A B C D	25 A B C D	33 A B C D
2 F G H J	10 F G H J	18 F G H J	26 F G H J	34 F G H J
3 A B C D	11 A B C D	19 A B C D	27 A B C D	35 A B C D
4 F G H J	12 F G H J	20 F G H J	28 F G H J	36 F G H J
5 A B C D	13 A B C D	21 A B C D	29 A B C D	37 A B C D
6 F G H J	14 F G H J	22 F G H J	30 F G H J	38 F G H J
7 A B C D	15 A B C D	23 A B C D	31 A B C D	39 A B C D
8 F G H J	16 F G H J	24 F G H J	32 F G H J	40 F G H J

TEST 4—SCIENCE

1 A B C D	9 A B C D	17 A B C D	25 A B C D	33 A B C D
2 F G H J	10 F G H J	18 F G H J	26 F G H J	34 F G H J
3 A B C D	11 A B C D	19 A B C D	27 A B C D	35 A B C D
4 F G H J	12 F G H J	20 F G H J	28 F G H J	36 F G H J
5 A B C D	13 A B C D	21 A B C D	29 A B C D	37 A B C D
6 F G H J	14 F G H J	22 F G H J	30 F G H J	38 F G H J
7 A B C D	15 A B C D	23 A B C D	31 A B C D	39 A B C D
8 F G H J	16 F G H J	24 F G H J	32 F G H J	40 F G H J

TIMED PRACTICE TEST III ESSAY RESPONSE SHEET

Name

Student ID Number

Date

Instructor

Course/Session Number

POST-ASSESSMENT BUBBLE SHEET

Name ____________________ Student ID Number ____________________

Date ____________ Instructor ____________________ Course/Session Number ____________

TEST 1—ENGLISH

1 A B C D	16 F G H J	31 A B C D	46 F G H J	61 A B C D
2 F G H J	17 A B C D	32 F G H J	47 A B C D	62 F G H J
3 A B C D	18 F G H J	33 A B C D	48 F G H J	63 A B C D
4 F G H J	19 A B C D	34 F G H J	49 A B C D	64 F G H J
5 A B C D	20 F G H J	35 A B C D	50 F G H J	65 A B C D
6 F G H J	21 A B C D	36 F G H J	51 A B C D	66 F G H J
7 A B C D	22 F G H J	37 A B C D	52 F G H J	67 A B C D
8 F G H J	23 A B C D	38 F G H J	53 A B C D	68 F G H J
9 A B C D	24 F G H J	39 A B C D	54 F G H J	69 A B C D
10 F G H J	25 A B C D	40 F G H J	55 A B C D	70 F G H J
11 A B C D	26 F G H J	41 A B C D	56 F G H J	71 A B C D
12 F G H J	27 A B C D	42 F G H J	57 A B C D	72 F G H J
13 A B C D	28 F G H J	43 A B C D	58 F G H J	73 A B C D
14 F G H J	29 A B C D	44 F G H J	59 A B C D	74 F G H J
15 A B C D	30 F G H J	45 A B C D	60 F G H J	75 A B C D

TEST 2—MATHEMATICS

1 A B C D E	13 A B C D E	25 A B C D E	37 A B C D E	49 A B C D E
2 F G H J K	14 F G H J K	26 F G H J K	38 F G H J K	50 F G H J K
3 A B C D E	15 A B C D E	27 A B C D E	39 A B C D E	51 A B C D E
4 F G H J K	16 F G H J K	28 F G H J K	40 F G H J K	52 F G H J K
5 A B C D E	17 A B C D E	29 A B C D E	41 A B C D E	53 A B C D E
6 F G H J K	18 F G H J K	30 F G H J K	42 F G H J K	54 F G H J K
7 A B C D E	19 A B C D E	31 A B C D E	43 A B C D E	55 A B C D E
8 F G H J K	20 F G H J K	32 F G H J K	44 F G H J K	56 F G H J K
9 A B C D E	21 A B C D E	33 A B C D E	45 A B C D E	57 A B C D E
10 F G H J K	22 F G H J K	34 F G H J K	46 F G H J K	58 F G H J K
11 A B C D E	23 A B C D E	35 A B C D E	47 A B C D E	59 A B C D E
12 F G H J K	24 F G H J K	36 F G H J K	48 F G H J K	60 F G H J K

TEST 3—READING

1 A B C D	9 A B C D	17 A B C D	25 A B C D	33 A B C D
2 F G H J	10 F G H J	18 F G H J	26 F G H J	34 F G H J
3 A B C D	11 A B C D	19 A B C D	27 A B C D	35 A B C D
4 F G H J	12 F G H J	20 F G H J	28 F G H J	36 F G H J
5 A B C D	13 A B C D	21 A B C D	29 A B C D	37 A B C D
6 F G H J	14 F G H J	22 F G H J	30 F G H J	38 F G H J
7 A B C D	15 A B C D	23 A B C D	31 A B C D	39 A B C D
8 F G H J	16 F G H J	24 F G H J	32 F G H J	40 F G H J

TEST 4—SCIENCE

1 A B C D	9 A B C D	17 A B C D	25 A B C D	33 A B C D
2 F G H J	10 F G H J	18 F G H J	26 F G H J	34 F G H J
3 A B C D	11 A B C D	19 A B C D	27 A B C D	35 A B C D
4 F G H J	12 F G H J	20 F G H J	28 F G H J	36 F G H J
5 A B C D	13 A B C D	21 A B C D	29 A B C D	37 A B C D
6 F G H J	14 F G H J	22 F G H J	30 F G H J	38 F G H J
7 A B C D	15 A B C D	23 A B C D	31 A B C D	39 A B C D
8 F G H J	16 F G H J	24 F G H J	32 F G H J	40 F G H J

POST-ASSESSMENT ESSAY RESPONSE SHEET

Name

Student ID Number

Date

Instructor

Course/Session Number

Appendix C:
Progress Reports

TEST MECHANICS, CONCEPTS, AND STRATEGIES PROGRESS REPORTS

The progress reports on the following pages are designed to help you monitor your progress on the "Lesson," "Review," and "Quizzes" sections in each lesson of the "Test Mechanics, Concepts, and Strategies" part of this book. Complete the assigned items by the due date given by your instructor. Check your answers using the answer keys in Appendix A of this book*, and record both the number and percentage of items answered correctly on the *student copies* of the progress reports. Identify the date on which you completed each section. List the numbers of any items that you would like your instructor to review in class. Then, transfer this information to the corresponding *instructor copies* of the reports and give them to your instructor. Be sure to leave the last three columns of the *instructor copies* blank; these are for your instructor's use in evaluating your progress.

*Consult with your instructor to determine whether you will use Appendix A to complete the Test Mechanics, Concepts, and Strategies Progress Reports.

TEST MECHANICS, CONCEPTS, AND STRATEGIES

(Student Copy)

Exercise	Total # of Items			% of Items Correct	Date Completed	Item #s to Review
	Possible	Assigned	Correct			
ENGLISH						
Lesson (p. 16)	145					
Quiz I (p. 35)	32					
Quiz II (p. 41)	29					
Quiz III (p. 47)	31					
Review (p. 53)	48					
MATHEMATICS						
Lesson (p. 83)	244					
Quiz I (p. 126)	20					
Quiz II (p. 131)	20					
Quiz III (p. 135)	20					
Review (p. 139)	32					
READING						
Lesson (p. 163)	130					
Quiz I (p. 194)	18					
Quiz II (p. 198)	17					
Quiz III (p. 202)	18					
Review (p. 206)	62					

Exercise	*Total # of Items*			*% of Items Correct*	*Date Completed*	*Item #s to Review*
	Possible	*Assigned*	*Correct*			
SCIENCE						
Lesson (p. 241)	54					
Quiz I (p. 258)	10					
Quiz II (p. 262)	10					
Quiz III (p. 266)	11					
Review (p. 270)	72					
WRITING						
Lesson (p. 302)	1		N/A	N/A		N/A
Quiz I (p. 306)	1		N/A	N/A		N/A
Quiz II (p. 310)	1		N/A	N/A		N/A
Quiz III (p. 314)	1		N/A	N/A		N/A

TEST MECHANICS, CONCEPTS, AND STRATEGIES

(Instructor Copy)

Name ______________________ Student ID Number ______________________

Date ______________ Instructor ______________________ Course/Session Number ______________

Exercise	*Total # of Items*			*% of Items Correct*	*Date Completed*	*Item #s to Review*	*Instructor Skill Evaluation (Check One Per Section)*		
	Possible	*Assigned*	*Correct*				*Mastered*	*Partially Mastered*	*Not Mastered*
ENGLISH									
Lesson (p. 16)	145								
Quiz I (p. 35)	32								
Quiz II (p. 41)	29								
Quiz III (p. 47)	31								
Review (p. 53)	48								
MATHEMATICS									
Lesson (p. 83)	244								
Quiz I (p. 126)	20								
Quiz II (p. 131)	20								
Quiz III (p. 135)	20								
Review (p. 139)	32								
READING									
Lesson (p. 163)	130								
Quiz I (p. 194)	18								
Quiz II (p. 198)	17								
Quiz III (p. 202)	18								
Review (p. 206)	62								

Exercise	Total # of Items			% of Items Correct	Date Completed	Item #s to Review	Instructor Skill Evaluation (Check One Per Section)		
	Possible	Assigned	Correct				Mastered	Partially Mastered	Not Mastered
SCIENCE									
Lesson (p. 241)	54								
Quiz I (p. 258)	10								
Quiz II (p. 262)	10								
Quiz III (p. 266)	11								
Review (p. 270)	72								
WRITING									
Lesson (p. 302)	1		N/A	N/A		N/A			
Quiz I (p. 306)	1		N/A	N/A		N/A			
Quiz II (p. 310)	1		N/A	N/A		N/A			
Quiz III (p. 314)	1		N/A	N/A		N/A			

PRACTICE TEST REINFORCEMENT PROGRESS REPORTS

The progress reports on the following pages are designed to help you monitor your progress on the multiple-choice portions of the practice tests in the "Practice Test Reinforcement" part of this book. Complete the assigned items by the due date given by your instructor. The Self-Guided Practice Test should be done *without* time restrictions; the explanations are included in the presentation of the exam. Timed Practice Tests I–III should be done *with* time restrictions. Correct your answers using the answers and explanations in Appendix A of this book*, and record both the number and percentage of items answered correctly on the *student copies* of the progress reports. Identify the date on which you completed each test. List the numbers of any items that you would like your instructor to review in class. Then, transfer this information to the corresponding *instructor copies* of the reports and give them to your instructor. Be sure to leave the last three columns of the *instructor copies* blank; these are for your instructor's use in evaluating your progress. (Note: In the first column of each report, the numbering refers to the test sections and the page numbers refer to the locations of those sections in the "Practice Test Reinforcement" part of this book.)

*Consult with your instructor to determine whether you will use Appendix A to complete the Practice Test Reinforcement Progress Reports.

PRACTICE TEST REINFORCEMENT

(Student Copy)

Exercise	*Total # of Items*			*% of Items Correct*	*Date Completed*	*Item #s to Review*
	Possible	*Assigned*	*Correct*			
TIMED PRACTICE TEST I						
1. **English Test** (p. 420)	75					
2. **Mathematics Test** (p. 434)	60					
3. **Reading Test** (p. 454)	40					
4. **Science Test** (p. 464)	40					
5. **Writing Test** (p. 478)	1		N/A	N/A		
TIMED PRACTICE TEST II						
1. **English Test** (p. 482)	75					
2. **Mathematics Test** (p. 496)	60					
3. **Reading Test** (p. 514)	40					
4. **Science Test** (p. 522)	40					
5. **Writing Test** (p. 536)	1		N/A	N/A		
TIMED PRACTICE TEST III						
1. **English Test** (p. 540)	75					
2. **Mathematics Test** (p. 556)	60					
3. **Reading Test** (p. 576)	40					
4. **Science Test** (p. 588)	40					
5. **Writing Test** (p. 600)	1		N/A	N/A		

PRACTICE TEST REINFORCEMENT

(Instructor Copy)

Name ____________________ Student ID Number ____________________

Date ____________ Instructor ____________________ Course/Session Number ____________

Exercise	*Total # of Items*			*% of Items Correct*	*Date Completed*	*Item #s to Review*	*Instructor Skill Evaluation (Check One Per Section)*		
	Possible	*Assigned*	*Correct*				*Mastered*	*Partially Mastered*	*Not Mastered*
TIMED PRACTICE TEST I									
1. **English Test** (p. 420)	75								
2. **Mathematics Test** (p. 434)	60								
3. **Reading Test** (p. 454)	40								
4. **Science Test** (p. 464)	40								
5. **Writing Test** (p. 478)	1		N/A	N/A		N/A			
TIMED PRACTICE TEST II									
1. **English Test** (p. 482)	75								
2. **Mathematics Test** (p. 496)	60								
3. **Reading Test** (p. 514)	40								
4. **Science Test** (p. 522)	40								
5. **Writing Test** (p. 536)	1		N/A	N/A		N/A			
TIMED PRACTICE TEST III									
1. **English Test** (p. 540)	75								
2. **Mathematics Test** (p. 556)	60								
3. **Reading Test** (p. 576)	40								
4. **Science Test** (p. 588)	40								
5. **Writing Test** (p. 600)	1		N/A	N/A		N/A			

CAMBRIDGE ACT® • PLAN® • EXPLORE® VICTORY, 10th EDITION ERROR CORRECTION AND SUGGESTION FORM

Name/Location: ______________ Day Phone: ______________ E-mail Address: ______________

Part of Materials:
- ☐ Student Text (Volume 1), Specify Subject: ______________ Page: ______ Item: ______
- ☐ Student Text (Volume 2), Specify Subject: ______________ Page: ______ Item: ______
- ☐ Teacher's Guide, Specify Subject: ______________ Page: ______ Item: ______
- ☐ Test Explanations, Specify Year/Code: ______________ Page: ______ Item: ______

Error/Suggestion: ______________

Part of Materials:
- ☐ Student Text (Volume 1), Specify Subject: ______________ Page: ______ Item: ______
- ☐ Student Text (Volume 2), Specify Subject: ______________ Page: ______ Item: ______
- ☐ Teacher's Guide, Specify Subject: ______________ Page: ______ Item: ______
- ☐ Test Explanations, Specify Year/Code: ______________ Page: ______ Item: ______

Error/Suggestion: ______________

Part of Materials:
- ☐ Student Text (Volume 1), Specify Subject: ______________ Page: ______ Item: ______
- ☐ Student Text (Volume 2), Specify Subject: ______________ Page: ______ Item: ______
- ☐ Teacher's Guide, Specify Subject: ______________ Page: ______ Item: ______
- ☐ Test Explanations, Specify Year/Code: ______________ Page: ______ Item: ______

Error/Suggestion: ______________

Part of Materials:
- ☐ Student Text (Volume 1), Specify Subject: ______________ Page: ______ Item: ______
- ☐ Student Text (Volume 2), Specify Subject: ______________ Page: ______ Item: ______
- ☐ Teacher's Guide, Specify Subject: ______________ Page: ______ Item: ______
- ☐ Test Explanations, Specify Year/Code: ______________ Page: ______ Item: ______

Error/Suggestion: ______________

Part of Materials:
- ☐ Student Text (Volume 1), Specify Subject: ______________ Page: ______ Item: ______
- ☐ Student Text (Volume 2), Specify Subject: ______________ Page: ______ Item: ______
- ☐ Teacher's Guide, Specify Subject: ______________ Page: ______ Item: ______
- ☐ Test Explanations, Specify Year/Code: ______________ Page: ______ Item: ______

Error/Suggestion: ______________

Mail form to Cambridge Educational Services, Inc. or fax form to 1-847-299-2933. For teacher's assistance, call 1-800-444-4373 or e-mail solutions@CambridgeEd.com. Visit our Web site at www.CambridgeEd.com.

ITEM INDEX

In the following index, all of the numeric references are designed as follows: Page #/Item #. The parenthetical information beside each item category refers to the subject-area in which that item category appears.

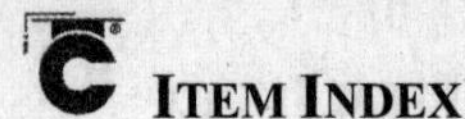